THE UNIVERSAL STANDARD ENCYCLOPEDIA

SCULPTURE. *Top, left: Cretan figurine of the Minoan mother goddess, ivory and gold. Top, right: Mexican figure, pre-Columbian period. Bottom, left: Egyptian portrait head of Queen Nefertiti, about 1370 B.C. Bottom, right: Chinese glazed-pottery figure, Ming dynasty.*

THE UNIVERSAL STANDARD ENCYCLOPEDIA

VOLUME 7

DEAFNESS—EDUCATION

An abridgment of The New Funk & Wagnalls Encyclopedia
prepared under the editorial direction of
JOSEPH LAFFAN MORSE, Sc.B., LL.B.
Editor in Chief

UNICORN PUBLISHERS, INC., NEW YORK

THE UNIVERSAL
STANDARD
ENCYCLOPEDIA

LIST OF ABBREVIATIONS USED

abbr., abbreviated
A.D., Anno Domini
alt., altitude
A.M., ante meridiem
anc., ancient
approx., approximately
Ar., Arabic
AS., Anglo-Saxon
A.S.S.R., Autonomous Soviet Socialist Republic
at.no., atomic number
at.wt., atomic weight
b., born
B.C., before Christ
b.p., boiling point
B.T.U., British Thermal Unit
Bulg., Bulgarian
C., centigrade, syn. Celsius
cent., century
Chin., Chinese
cm., centimeter
Co., County
colloq., colloquial
cu., cubic
Czech., Czechoslovakian
d., died
Dan., Danish
Du., Dutch
E., east, easterly, eastern
ed., edition
e.g., for example
Egypt., Egyptian
Eng., English
est., estimated
et seq., and following
F., Fahrenheit
fl., flourished
fr., from
Fr., French
ft., foot

Gael., Gaelic
Gen., General
Ger., German
Gr., Greek
Heb., Hebrew
Hind., Hindustani
Hon., Honorable
h.p., horsepower
hr., hour
Hung., Hungarian
I., Island
i.e., that is
in., inch
Ind., Indian
Ir., Irish
It., Italian
Jr., junior
kg., kilogram
km., kilometer
lat., latitude
Lat., Latin
lb., pound
lit., literally
long., longitude
m., mile
M., Middle
min., minute
M.L., Medieval Latin
mm., millimeter
mod., modern
m.p., melting point
M.P., Member of Parliament
m.p.h., miles per hour
Mt., Mount, Mountain
N., north, northerly, northern
N.T., New Testament
OE., Old English
OF., Old French
OHG., Old High German
ON., Old Norse

ONF., Old Norman French
O.T., Old Testament
oz., ounce
Phil., Philippine
P.M., post meridiem
Pol., Polish
pop., population
Port., Portuguese
prelim., preliminary
pron., pronounced
q.v., which see
R., River
rev., revised, revision
Rev., Reverend
Rom., Romanian
Russ., Russian
S., south, southerly, southern
sec., second
Skr., Sanskrit
Sp., Spanish
sp.gr., specific gravity
sq., square
S.S.R., Soviet Socialist Republic
Sum., Sumerian
Sw., Swedish
syn., synonym
temp., temperature
trans., translation, translated
Turk., Turkish
U.K., United Kingdom
U.N., United Nations
U.S., United States
U.S.A., United States of America
U.S.S.R., Union of Soviet Socialist Republics
var., variety
W., west, westerly, western
yd., yard

Note.—The official abbreviations for the States of the Union are used throughout. For academic degrees, see article DEGREE, ACADEMIC. Other abbreviations or contractions are self-explanatory.

DEAFNESS, complete or partial loss of the sense of hearing. It may be congenital or acquired, and may be transient or permanent. Transient deafness may be caused by an accumulation of wax in the external ear passages, or by the use of drugs such as quinine or the salicylates. It may also arise from rupture of the eardrum, from the closing of the Eustachian tubes (see EAR) by upper respiratory infections, or from sudden or continued loud noise. Permanent deafness may arise from injury or disease of the auditory centers of the brain, the acoustic nerve, or the inner ear (see SPECIAL SENSES). Inflammations of the middle ear may cause the small earbones to grow together; unable to move freely, the bones cannot transmit vibrations of sound from the ear drum to the inner ear, and a progressive deafness ensues. *Word deafness,* caused by damage to the auditory-association areas of the brain, is inability to understand the meaning of words. The patient can hear words, and can often reproduce them in speech or writing, but without comprehension. See AUDITION; DEAF-MUTE; HEARING AIDS.

DEÁK, FERENCZ (1803–76), Hungarian statesman, born at Sötjör. He was educated as a lawyer, and at the age of thirty was first elected to the Hungarian legislature. He served for three years and was again a member of the legislature in 1839–40. During the period before the Revolution of 1848 Deák became known as a leader of the group of Hungarian patriots favoring the establishment by legal means of the autonomy of Hungary within the Austrian Empire. He became minister of justice under Count Lajos de Batthyány in 1848, but took no part in Lajos Kossuth's attempt to establish an independent Hungary by force of arms. After the counterrevolution of 1849 Deák retired from public office for several years. He again sat in the legislature in 1861 and in 1866, always urging a liberal constitution for Hungary. The defeat of Austria in wars with Italy (1859) and with Prussia (1866) convinced the Austrian government that improved relations within the Empire were desirable, and Deák's moderation in refusing to exploit Austria's weakness after the defeat at Königgrätz (q.v.) encouraged the Austrian emperor to initiate negotiations for a new constitution for Hungary modeled after that of 1848. The result was the Aus-

gleich of 1867 (q.v.)., under which a dual monarchy of Austria and Hungary was established. Deák declined the premiership of the newly established kingdom of Hungary, and returned to private life.

DEAKIN, ALFRED (1856–1919), Australian statesman, born in Melbourne and educated at Melbourne University. He was elected to the legislature of the state of Victoria in 1880, and became solicitor general of the state in 1883. He devoted himself to the movement for the establishment of a federal union of Australian states, and when the Commonwealth was established (1900) Deakin became attorney general in the first federal cabinet (1901–03). He was premier of Australia three times (1903–04, 1905–08, and 1909–10), and was a supporter of the integration of Australia in a British Empire defense system. From 1910 until his retirement in 1912 Deakin was a leader of the Opposition group in the Australian legislature.

DEAN, BASHFORD (1867–1928), American zoologist and armor expert, born in New York City, and educated at the College of the City of New York and in Europe. In 1891 he joined the faculty of Columbia University, becoming professor of zoology in 1904. He also served, from 1903, as curator of herpetology and ichthyology for the American Museum of Natural History and as an expert on armor for the Metropolitan Museum of Art. Besides taking part in several zoological expeditions, he served as a major in World War I, acting in an advisory capacity for the design and production of body armor. His works include many papers on ichthyology and on arms and armor, and the books *Fishes, Living and Fossil* (1895) and *Bibliography of Fishes* (3 vols., 1916–23).

DEANE, SILAS (1737–89), American Revolutionary diplomat, born at Groton, Conn. He was elected to the colonial legislature of Connecticut in 1772, and to the Continental Congress in 1774, serving until the Congress sent him to France, in 1776, to seek aid for the American Revolutionary armies. Shortly thereafter the Congress sent Benjamin Franklin and Arthur Lee to France on a similar mission, and accredited all three as commissioners. Deane was largely responsible for the recruiting of foreign volunteers, including the Marquis de Lafayette, Baron de Kalb, and Casimir Pulaski, and for the sending of supplies which proved invaluable at the Battle of Saratoga (1777). After that battle French aid to America was formally negotiated by a treaty (1778) to which Deane was one of the signatories. Soon thereafter he returned to America to answer charges preferred by Arthur Lee that he had mishandled funds. He was permitted to return to France in 1781 to obtain evidence in his defense. A letter written by Deane in that year, in which he expressed doubt concerning the possibility of American success in the war, was published and made his immediate return to America impossible. He lived in England thereafter, but wrote in 1784 a defense of his views, *An Address to the Free and Independent Citizens of the United States of North America*. Five years later, while on shipboard en route to the United States, he died. His memory was vindicated by the U.S. Congress in 1842 through a resolution which awarded $37,000 to his heirs in payment of a claim.

DEARBORN, city of Wayne Co., Mich., adjoining southwestern Detroit. It is largely a residential suburb of Detroit, although it is important as a manufacturing center. Dearborn was the birthplace of Henry Ford, and is the site of the Ford Motor Co. River Rouge Plant. Automobiles, tools, dies, road-paving materials, and bricks are manufactured in the city. Dearborn also contains greenhouses, and coal mines are in the vicinity. The city is the site of the Henry Ford Trade School; the Edison Institute of Technology; and Greenfield Village, containing a collection of historic houses which have been collected from all parts of the United States and from England. The historic houses include the Courthouse from Lincoln, Ill., where Abraham Lincoln practiced law; Edison's Laboratory, in which the phonograph, incandescent lamp, microphone, and telephone transmitter were invented; the Edison homestead; Luther Burbank's office from Santa Rosa, Calif.; and the Cotswold cottage, built about 250 years ago in England. The population of Dearborn was 2470 in 1920. With the growth of the automobile industry the population increased rapidly, reaching 50,358 in 1930. Pop. (1950) 94,994.

DEARTH, HENRY GOLDEN (1864–1918), American landscape and figure painter, born in Bristol, R.I. He studied in Paris at the École des Beaux-Arts and with Antoine Auguste Hébert and Aimé Morot. Many of his landscapes were painted in Normandy, France; others, in Connecticut and New York State. His paintings are distinguished by rich coloring and a unique atmospheric quality. They include "Cornelia" and "Boulogne Harbor" (Metropolitan Museum of Art, New York City); "In the Gloaming" (Detroit Institute of Arts); "Black Hat" and "Sunset in Normandy" (John Herron Art Institute, Indianapolis); "Old Church at Montreuil" (National Gallery of Art, Washington, D.C.); and "Dreamland" and "Golden Sunset" (Brooklyn Museum).

DEATH, the cessation beyond possibility of resuscitation of the vital functions of plant or animal organisms or tissues. *Somatic death* is the death of the organism as a whole; it usually precedes *molecular death*, the death of the individual cells and tissues. However, the continuance of organized life is dependent upon the death and replacement of individual cells, and in certain diseases (see GANGRENE), entire tissues may die independently of the organism. The precise time of somatic death is difficult to determine because the symptoms of such transient states as coma, syncope, and trance are closely similar to the signs of death. Many signs of death have been proposed as tests, including cessation of respiration and heart action, development of rigor mortis, and onset of putrefaction. Cessation of respiration and heart action are the signs usually employed, but they may be so reduced in certain states of deep unconsciousness as to be indetectable by ordinary means. Moreover, resuscitation is sometimes possible several minutes after either or both of these processes have ceased. Rigor mortis, the rigidity of the muscles developing from postmortem accumulation of acid and coagulation of the protoplasm, is often simulated by the rigidity of certain trance states (see CATALEPSY). Moreover, in true death, rigor mortis may be slight or transient, or its onset may be considerably delayed. The onset of putrefaction is usually an infallible sign of death, but it may be inhibited by a particularly dry climate or by the action of certain poisons. Moreover, gangrenous putrefaction is not necessarily accompanied by death.

In the event of the unexplained disappearance of a person, his death is presumed at common law after an absence of seven years. In several States of the United States this period is shortened by statute to five years, and may be further shortened by establishment of conditions surrounding the disappearance indicating an earlier death. The law.

in all such cases, establishes a presumption of death, without attempting to determine the date. For relative frequency of causes of death see VITAL STATISTICS. See also MORTUARY CUSTOMS.

DEATH ADDER, a poisonous elapid snake, *Acanthophis antarcticus,* found throughout Australasia. Its short, thick body and wide head give the snake an adder-like appearance, although it is not related to the true adders. The snake is about two feet in length and carries a spine at the end of its tail. Its color varies with its habitat and may be gray, brown, pink, or reddish, crossed with darker bands. It has long fangs and secretes a large quantity of powerful neurotoxic poison. Despite its small size, its bite is more dangerous than that of any other Australian snake. Other poisonous snakes of Australia, such as the black snake and tiger snake (qq.v.) belong to the same family as the death adder but do not resemble it.

DEATH CUP, common name of the highly-poisonous fungus *Amanita phalloides.* The death cup is common in woods and fields. This fungus, which is also known as the deadly amanita, has a cup-shaped membrane surrounding the bottom of the stem or stipe, from which it takes its name. The death cup has a flat top, white to yellowish in color, supported on a slender stem about 6 in. tall. A skirtlike fringe or annulus surrounds the stem about an inch below the top.

DEATH, DANCE OF, an allegorical theme, dating from the 14th century, in which death converses with a number of persons of all degrees and eventually leads them all away to the grave in a solemn dance. It is probable that the first appearance of this allegory was in a German morality play of the 14th century, but it undoubtedly formed the theme of moralities in most Christian countries. The subject became a favorite with painters and other artists and a number of works were created with this title or its French equivalent, *La Danse Macabre.* Many paintings of the dance of death were formerly found on the walls of European churches and cemeteries, such as those at Basel in Switzerland and the cemetery of the Holy Innocents in Paris, but many of them have been destroyed. Examples remain at the Campo Santo in Pisa and the Marienkirche at Lübeck. Hans Holbein the Younger also did a series of engravings on the same subject. Literary treatments of the dance of death include

The death's-head moth

Goethe's ballad *Der Todtentanz* and W. H. Auden's *The Dance of Death* (1933). The symphonic poem *La Danse Macabre* (1874) by Camille Saint-Saëns is a musical expression of the same theme.

DEATH MASK. See MASK.

DEATH RATE. See VITAL STATISTICS.

DEATH'S-HEAD MOTH, a species of hawkmoth, *Acherontia atropos,* widely distributed over the Old World. It measures almost 5 inches from tip to tip of the extended wings. The general color is dark, and the woolly body yellow, with black markings; the thorax has markings which resemble a skull, the upper wings are mottled with brown, black, and yellow, the hind wings are dark yellow with two black bands. The large caterpillar is greenish yellow, the back is speckled with black, with transverse lines partly blue and partly white. The tail end bears an S-shaped horn. It feeds on the potato, tomato, and other plants.

DEATH VALLEY, an arid, depressed, desert region largely in Inyo Co., S.E. California. It was given its name by one of 18 survivors of a party of 30 attempting in 1849 to find a short cut to the California gold fields. Much of the region is below sea level, and in the Valley proper, at Badwater, 280 ft. below sea level, is the lowest point in North America. Less than 80 miles w., in the Sierra Nevadas, is the highest elevation in the U.S., Mount Whitney, 14,495 ft.

The Death Valley region lies N. of the Mojave Desert and extends eastward from the Sierra Nevadas into Nye Co., Nevada. The Valley proper, wholly in Inyo Co., is from 4 to 16 m. wide and about 140 m. long, and almost entirely enclosed by mountain ranges, volcanic in origin, bare and brilliantly colored. The Panamints on the w., which rise to a maximum altitude of 11,045 ft. (Telescope Peak), shut out the moist Pacific winds. On the E. are the peaks of the Funeral Range. From crest to crest of these ranges the distance is 20 to 30 m.

The summer temperatures in Death Valley, one of the hottest regions known, reach over 125 °F. in the shade and rarely fall below 70°. The U.S. Weather Bureau recorded 134° on July 10, 1913. The air is exceptionally dry, and dew never forms, the relative humidity averaging only about 23%. Average rainfall in a normal year is about 4 inches. Rainfall is heavier on the enclosing mountain ranges, the erosion of which is slowly building up the valley floor with debris brought down by freshets occurring after the rains. Sandstorms and dust whirlwinds of a few hours' duration are common.

Water is exceedingly scarce throughout the Valley. Places where drinking water can be obtained are at Saratoga Springs in the S.E., Bennett Wells in the W., and a point near the mouth of Furnace Creek at the N. end of Funeral Range; other springs are so impregnated with minerals that they are unfit for use. Several watercourses enter the Valley, among them the Amargosa R. from the S. and Furness Creek from the E., but it is only after heavy rains, which are of rare occurrence, that they contain water. The Valley is the sink of the Amargosa, which disappears in it, leaving the surface crusted with salt.

The lowest parts of the valley floor are salt flats, destitute of vegetation; higher portions contain a mixture of sand and salt grains, occasionally forming dunes. The W. side of the valley floor is bordered by stunted mesquite, and in a marsh in the northern section a growth of tall coarse grass is found; the E. and W. slopes possess a sparse vegetation of cacti and desert shrubs and grasses. Animal life is confined to a few species of desert reptiles, such as horned toads and lizards, which, however, usually migrate to more hospitable country before the summer sets in. Flocks of blackbirds have been seen there.

Gold has been found in Death Valley, and silver, copper, and lead have been taken in paying quantities. In the 1860's the famous borax deposits of Death Valley were discovered. Colemanite, first discovered in Death Valley and once the principal source of commercial borax in the U.S., was named after W. T. Coleman, one of the early discoverers. In the 1880's the first roads were built, over which the famous "twenty-mule teams" drew wagonloads of borax from the desert. The borax-mining industry in Death Valley declined, however, when richer deposits were discovered elsewhere in California. Ryan, terminus of the Death Valley Railroad, was deserted by the end of 1930, along with other mining towns. Death Valley Junction (pop., about 250), E. of the Valley, is field headquarters of the Pacific Coast Borax Company. See DEATH VALLEY NATIONAL MONUMENT.

DEATH VALLEY NATIONAL MONUMENT, a national monument in California and Nevada, established in 1933. Its area of about 1,900,000 acres embraces historic Death Valley (q.v.). Summer temperatures are extremely high on the valley floor, and the tourist season runs from early November to early May.

DEATHWATCH, a name given to any of several types of insects which live in the woodwork of houses and emit ticking noises. Deathwatches include members of the order Corrodentia commonly called book lice, and bookworms (q.v.) of the family Anobiidae. The insects produce their characteristic tick by striking their heads against the wood, probably as a mating call. The name deathwatch comes from the old superstition that the sounds made by the insects foretells a death in the house.

DEAUVILLE, town in Calvados Department, France, on the English Channel and across the Touques R. from Trouville, with which it shares the port formed by the Touques. It is a noted resort town. Pop. (1946) 5438.

DE BARY, HEINRICH ANTON (1831-88), German botanist, born at Frankfurt am Main, and educated at Heidelberg, Marburg, and Berlin. After serving as a professor at the universities of Freiburg and Halle, he was appointed rector of the University of Strassburg in 1872. De Barry was the founder of the science of mycology, and introduced the method of systematic study of the life cycles of fungi from spore to spore. His chief field of research was the parasitic fungi, but he also made studies of algae and ferns. Among his works are *Die Mycetozoen* (1859), *Vergleichende Anatomie der Vegetations Organe der Phanerogamen und Farne* (1872), and *Vorlesungen über Bakterien* (1885).

DEBORAH, prophetess and "judge" of the Old Testament, who helped to deliver the Israelites from the oppression of the Canaan-

French Embassy, Information Division
Quaint buildings along a street in Deauville, France

ites. The Song of Deborah (Judges, 5:2–31), universally attributed to her, celebrates this victory, and is one of the oldest examples of Hebrew literature.

DEBRECEN, capital of Hajdu County, Hungary, and one of the largest cities of the country, situated about 135 miles E. of Budapest. The city is an important commercial center and railway junction, servicing a rich agricultural region. The chief articles of trade are grain, cattle, and hogs. Agricultural fairs are held in the city annually. Industrial products of Debrecen include woolen fabrics, dairy products, leather goods, casks, soap, foodstuffs and tobacco products. The University of Debrecen, founded in 1912, has a student enrollment of more than 1000. One of the notable edifices of the city is the Protestant church in which, in 1848, the Hungarian patriot Lajos Kossuth (q.v.) proclaimed the deposition of the Hapsburg dynasty. The traditional center of Hungarian Protestantism, Debrecen was once popularly known as "the Calvinistic Rome". Pop. (1941) 125,936.

DE BROGLIE. See BROGLIE, LOUIS VICTOR, PRINCE DE.

DEBS, EUGENE VICTOR (1855–1926), American Socialist leader and labor organizer, born in Terre Haute, Ind. Between 1871 and 1883 he was a locomotive fireman on the Terre Haute and Indianapolis Railroad, a wholesale grocery salesman, and city clerk of Terre Haute. In 1885 he served as a member of the Indiana Legislature. He was grand secretary and treasurer of the Brotherhood of Locomotive Firemen from 1880 to 1893, when he resigned to organize and be president (1893–97) of the American Railway Union. Under his leadership the union won an important strike on the Great Northern Railway in 1894. In the same year, having espoused the cause of the poorly paid Pullman workers, the union brought about a tie-up of the Western roads. This strike was broken by the interference of the Federal courts and by action of President Cleveland, based upon the right of the Federal government to maintain the uninterrupted transmission of the mails. Debs was arrested first upon a charge of conspiracy to murder, but the charge was never pressed, although Debs insisted that his name be cleared through trial on the charge in open court. In July, 1894, Debs, with the other officers of the union, was arrested on the charge of violating an injunction, and was sentenced to six months in jail for contempt of court.

Debs' introduction to Socialism began during his imprisonment in the Woodstock jail, where he was visited by Victor Berger and given Marx's *Capital* and other Socialistic works to read. In 1897 he organized the Social Democratic Party of America, and in 1900 was its candidate for President of the United States. He received 96,116 votes. Thereafter Debs spent most of his time as lecturer and organizer in the Socialist movement. He was the candidate of the Socialist Party for President of the United States in 1904, 1908, and 1912. Debs was a pacifist and during World War I was sentenced to ten years in jail for his beliefs. His sentence was commuted in 1921. While in prison he ran again for President on the Socialist ticket and received 915,302 votes. As one of the first targets of "government by injunction", and because of his personality Debs commanded the respect of American unionists and radicals, even of those who did not accept his economic doctrines. Besides the articles he wrote as contributing editor of *Appeal to Reason*, his writings include a widely read speech, *Industrial Unionism* (1911).

DEBT, in law, a sum of money due upon a certain and expressed agreement. This obligation may be founded on simple contract, may be contained in a sealed instrument, or may be established by the judgment of a court. In this meaning a debt is a definite sum due, not merely a claim for damages. In some applications, however, the word has been much more broadly used. Thus, it has been held that a debt may be a certain sum of money promised to be paid in the future as well as a sum already actually due and payable; but if the sum be payable upon a contingency at a future time, it cannot properly be called a debt. In its more general sense debt is that due from one person to another, whether money, goods, or service. Under the United States legal-tender statutes the term embraces any obligation by contract, expressed or implied, which may be discharged by money through the voluntary action of the party bound. A bequest of "whatever debts" might be due the testator at the time of his death has been held to include money deposited with his bankers. A tax is not of the nature of a debt, not being founded on contract, but being rather an impost laid by a government.

Formerly the courts, both in the United States and England, employed the drastic process of imprisonment of the debtor to enforce the payment of debts, but this has generally been done away with by statute. The present tendency of legislation is to afford an easy and simple procedure for the enforcement of debts, so that they may be collected quickly and as summarily as is consistent with the right of defense and of appeal. Where the element of fraud, false pretenses, or concealment of property enters into the question, the courts, both in the United States and England may still restrain and under some conditions imprison the debtor. See ATTACHMENT; BANKRUPTCY; DEBTOR; GARNISHMENT; IMPRISONMENT; SEQUESTRATION; TRUSTEE PROCESS.

DEBT, NATIONAL, or **PUBLIC,** the sum total of governmental pecuniary obligations, originating in borrowing by a state from its population, from foreign governments, and from international institutions such as the United Nations International Bank for Reconstruction and Development. Excluded from the public debt are such items as unpaid salaries to government employees and balances due on contracts for work performed, supplies delivered, and services rendered. Public debts comprise large-scale credit operations and are contracted on a national scale by central governments and on a lesser scale by provincial, regional, district, and municipal administrative bodies. In the U.S., public debts are also contracted by the States. For statistical purposes, the public debts of sub-national governments are included when computing the total national public debt of a country.

National public debts are contracted chiefly through the flotation of interest-paying loans, for two main purposes: to raise money for war, and to finance public works. Public debts have also been contracted to supplement state revenue from taxation and other sources when the totals realized by these means are insufficient to meet normal fiscal expenditures. But the operation is not regarded favorably by most economists and statesmen, because they believe that it creates more difficulties than it solves. The flotation of government loans at lower interest rates than those paid by existing government securities, to raise money for the retirement, on maturity, of outstanding obligations, is also regarded by some authorities as a form of public debt; it is considered by others as comprising only a public-debt financing operation because it does not materially change the indebtedness total.

The latter operation, strictly speaking, is a form of debt redemption. Other means of redeeming public debts include the repayment of principal on maturity; amortization through periodic payment of part of the principal; and the buying up of government securities on the open market. Many governments have established sinking funds for the purpose of redeeming public debts; debts redeemed in this way are called funded debts. Most government loans fall due at fixed dates, but a number, known as perpetual loans, have no definite expiration dates, and governments floating them have the privilege of redeeming them when convenient or desirable.

Although government loans are for the most part not secured by physical assets, they are regarded in law as contracts carrying an obligation on the part of the debtor to repay. Nevertheless, governments, when hard pressed during economic crises or as a result of political upheavals, have sometimes repudiated their public debts in whole or in part. See REPUDIATION OF DEBT.

National public debts, considered historically, are of comparatively recent origin. In feudal times, debts contracted by heads of states had the legal status of personal debts; they were contracted to meet the expense of maintaining kings and courts in luxury and for the purpose of waging war. The need to raise money for war purposes has remained a constant factor in the creation of public debts, but in practically every other respect they have undergone a transformation of tremendous significance. This transformation has resulted from and accompanied the rise of representative governments and the development of large-scale industry and modern banking and credit systems, especially since the early part of the 19th century.

Today, the finances involved in contracting and redeeming the public debt of a country comprise a considerable proportion of its government budget. As the money for redemption of the public debt is raised principally through taxation, the size of the national debt is a factor in determining taxation rates.

National public debts, taken on a world scale, have almost without exception shown a tendency to increase. The estimated total public indebtedness of the world at the end of the 18th century was about 2½ billion dollars. During the 19th century, England was the only world power to reduce its national debt. In 1890 the world total of public indebtedness had risen to an estimated 27½ billion dollars, an increase in a little less than a century of more than 1000%. Thereafter the increase continued until the close of World War I, after which there was a decline. Following the onset of the world-wide economic crisis in 1929, public debts rose as governments resorted to public works to provide work for the unemployed. World War II caused national debts to soar to astronomical proportions and created indebtedness which will weigh heavily on future generations.

United States Public Debt. In 1790, when Alexander Hamilton as secretary of the treasury made his first report on the national debt of the United States, he estimated it at close to 70 million dollars. After alternately rising and falling, the debt stood at only 4 million dollars (or 21¢ per capita) in 1840. That was the lowest point ever reached by the public debt of the United States. After 1840 it rose to a peak, in the last year of the Civil War, of almost $2,678,000,000 and a per capita figure of $75.01. The debt subsequently fell and fluctuated around $1,150,000,000 for a number of years, until it began to rise again during World War I. In 1919 the total national public debt was at a record high of almost 25½ billions and the per capita figure was a little over $240. Throughout the prosperity years of the 1920's, the public debt declined. With the onset of the economic crisis in 1929–30 it began to rise again, especially as a result of the deficit spending of the Roosevelt Administration. Following the entry of the United States into World War II, in 1941, the national debt reached staggering proportions; in 1946 it was $269,422,000,000 and the per capita figure was $1905.42. In subsequent years the national public debt declined slightly. However, by June, 1954, it had risen to $271,341,000,000 and the per capita figure was approximately $1675.

DEBUSSY, (ACHILLE) CLAUDE (1862–1918), French composer, born at St. Germain-en-Laye. He received his musical education at the Paris Conservatoire, where he studied principally under Jules Massenet. In 1884 he won the Prix de Rome for his cantata *L'Enfant Prodigue.* During the residence in Italy granted him by terms of the prize, he composed the orchestral suite *Printemps* (1887); and after his return to Paris, the cantata *La Demoiselle Élue* (1887–88). These and others of his early works show the influence of the French composers Massenet, Alexis Emmanuel Chabrier, and Gabriel Fauré, and of the German composer Richard Wagner. However, Debussy soon developed a distinctly personal style, with some influence from medieval church music, and from Russian, Javanese, and Annamite music. The music of Debussy's fully matured style was the forerunner of much modern music and made him one of the

Portrait of Claude Debussy

most important of late 19th- and early 20th-century composers. Debussy's originality consists mainly in his treatment of chords; he arranged successions of chords in such a way as to avoid adherence in a composition to any specified key. This purposeful lack of fixed tonality in his music gave it a vague, dreamy character which some contemporary critics termed musical "impressionism", after the resemblance they saw between it and the type of pictorial effect achieved by the painters of the contemporary Impressionist school (see IMPRESSIONISM). Among Debussy's most important works are the opera *Pélleas et Mélisande* (composed 1892–1902); the orchestral works *L'Après-midi d'un Faune* (1892–94), *Nocturnes* (1893–99), *La Mer* (1903–05), and *Images* (1909), consisting of *Gigues, Iberia,* and *Rondes de Printemps;* the chamber music work *Premier Quatuor* (1893); the works for piano *Suite Bergamasque* (1890–1905), *Estampes* (1903), *Images* (first series 1905, second, 1907), *Children's Corner* (1906–08) and *Douze Préludes* (first book, 1910, second, 1910–13); and the song cycle *Le Promenoir des Deux Amants* (1904–10).

DEBYE, PETER JOSEPH WILHELM (1884–   ), theoretical physicist, born in Maastricht, Holland, and educated at the Technische Hochschule, Aachen, and the University of Munich, both in Germany. From 1911 to 1935 he held the post of professor of physics successively at the universities of Zurich,

Utrecht, and Göttingen, the Zurich Technical College, and the University of Leipzig. He then became director of the Kaiser Wilhelm Institute for Physics, in Berlin, and in 1940 became professor, and head of the chemistry department, at Cornell University in Ithaca, N.Y.

In 1912 Debye developed a modification of Einstein's theory of specific heat by calculating the probability of any frequency of molecular vibration up to a maximum frequency; the theory of specific heat constituted one of the earliest theoretical successes of the quantum theory. He also applied the quantum theory to explain the heat conductivity of crystals at low temperature, the variation of saturation intensity of magnetization with temperature, the theory of "space quantization" (with A. Sommerfeld), and the phenomena of scattering of X rays (with A. H. Compton). In 1923 Debye developed a theory of ionization of electrolytes (now called the Debye-Hückel theory, from E. Hückel, who improved on Debye's theory), which is of great importance in chemistry; see IONIZATION. Later, he worked on the theory of quantum mechanics, including its applications to the diffraction of electrons in gases. He received many honors, including the Nobel Prize in chemistry in 1936. Among his writings are *Quantum Theory and Chemistry* (1928), *Polar Molecules* (1929), *Molecule Structure* (1931), and *Collected Papers* (1954).

DÉCADENTS. See SYMBOLISTS.

DECALCOMANIA. See LITHOGRAPHY.

DECALOGUE or **DECALOG** (Gr. *deka,* "ten"; *logos,* "word"), designation applied to the divine law, commonly known as the Ten Commandments, which, according to the Old Testament, was given by God to Moses on Mt. Sinai. According to the Book of Exodus, the Decalogue was inscribed on two stone tablets by the "finger of God". Moses later destroyed the tablets in anger over his people's abandonment of their faith. He was then commanded by God to hew and inscribe new tablets (Ex. 34:1, 27–28). According to Deuteronomy (4:13), however, God made the new inscription. The Commandments have basic importance in the ethical codes of Christianity, Judaism, and Mohammedanism.

Slight variations in the terminology and sequence of the commandments occur in the various Scriptural texts, but all are essentially uniform with regard to substance. As listed in both Exodus and Deuteronomy, and as accepted in the Jewish faith, in the Eastern

Church, and in most Protestant denominations, the commandments are stated as follows: (1) prohibition of any worship besides that of God; (2) prohibition of graven images; (3) prohibition of the use of the name of God for vain purposes; (4) the command to keep the Sabbath holy; (5) the command to honor father and mother; (6) prohibition of murder; (7) prohibition of adultery; (8) prohibition of stealing; (9) prohibition of bearing false witness; and (10) prohibition of coveting the property or wife of one's neighbor. In the Roman Catholic and Lutheran churches, however, the first two commandments are combined into one and the last is divided into two, i.e., commandments prohibiting, respectively, the coveting of one's neighbor's wife and his property.

DECAMERON, THE, a collection of one hundred tales by Giovanni Boccaccio (q.v.), written between 1348 and 1353. The framework for the narrative is provided by a group of friends, seven women and three men, all "well-bred, of worth and discretion", who take refuge in the countryside above plague-ridden Florence, and entertain each other with a series of anecdotes, told in turn by members of the party. At the end of the hundredth tale, the friends return home.

The Decameron, more than any other of Boccaccio's works, establishes his place among the great writers of all time. In it Boccaccio gathers material from all sources—the French *fabliaux* (q.v.), the classics, current folklore, and contemporary life. *The Decameron* has been a storehouse for writers of narrative from Boccaccio's era to modern times; hundreds of writers including Chaucer and Shakespeare have drawn from it. The perfection of Boccaccio's craftsmanship, likewise, has made his work a model for storytelling.

DECAMPS, ALEXANDRE GABRIEL (1803–60), French landscape and genre painter, born in Paris. He studied with Abel de Pujol and others, but was largely self-taught. He traveled in Italy, Switzerland, Greece, and the Near East, and became known for his paintings of Oriental life and of biblical subjects, and as the leading colorist of France. His first genre paintings, exhibited in 1831, were popular. Decamps was fond of indulging in satire, and the "Monkey Connoisseurs" and his travesties of King Charles X are examples of this aspect of his work. He reached the height of his fame in 1839, in which year the Salon exhibited three of his paintings, and he was made a chevalier of the Legion of Honor. His work is well represented in both the United States

and in Europe, and includes "The Good Samaritan" and "Night Patrol at Smyrna" (Metropolitan Museum, New York City), and "The Watering Place" (Wallace Collection, London). He made about 100 lithographs and 20 etchings.

DECAPODA. 1. A large and important order of crustaceans including most of the best-known species. They are distinguished by a thorax entirely covered by a carapace, and by five pairs of thoracic legs. The first pair of legs is modified into grasping pincers, while the last four pairs are used for walking. Many hundreds of species of decapods are known, the majority of them living in the sea; some live in fresh water, and a few (see COCONUT CRAB) are terrestrial when adult. The order is divided into three suborders. Species of the suborder Macrura have a long, shell-covered abdomen and include the lobster, crayfish, shrimp (qq.v.), and prawn. The suborder Brachyura is marked by a short abdomen. Crabs (q.v.) are the typical members of this group. The hermit crab (q.v.) belongs to the third suborder, Anomura, (perhaps part of Macrura) characterized by having the abdomen permanently flexed and twisted; see CRUSTACEA. **2.** An order of cephalopod mollusks which includes the squid and the cuttlefish (qq.v.) and the fossil belemnites. The decapod mollusks have ten arms, suckers on stalks, and an internal shell. See CEPHALOPODA.

DECATUR, county seat of Macon Co., Ill., 38 miles E. of Springfield, on Lake Decatur, an artificial lake created by the damming of the Sangamon R. The surrounding area contains coal mines, but is particularly noted for the cultivation of soybeans and corn. The principal industries in the city are the manufacture of corn and soybean products. The city also contains railroad shops, packing houses, and factories producing brass plumbing fixtures, bottling machinery, lighting fixtures, structural and sheet steel, and malleable and gray iron. Decatur is the site of James Millikin University and the Millikin Conservatory of Music, a hospital for the employees of the Wabash Railroad, and the Lincoln Log Cabin Courthouse. The city, incorporated in 1836, was the first home in Illinois of Abraham Lincoln. There, on May 6, 1860, at the Illinois Republican Convention, he received his first endorsement as a presidential candidate. Post No. 1 of the Grand Army of the Republic was organized at Decatur on April 6, 1866. Pop. (1950) 66,269.

DECATUR, STEPHEN (1779–1820), American naval officer, born at Sinepuxent, Md., and educated at the University of Pennsylvania. At the age of nineteen he was appointed midshipman in the U.S. Navy, and was promoted to the rank of lieutenant a year later. During the war with Tripoli (1801–05) Decatur was one of the leading U.S. naval commanders. His destruction of the U.S. frigate *Philadelphia*, stranded on a sand bar in the harbor of Tripoli and captured by the enemy, was an unusually bold venture which won the praise of the great British admiral, Horatio Nelson, and resulted in Decatur's promotion to the rank of captain. At the outbreak of the War of 1812 Decatur was the commanding officer of the frigate *United States,* on which he had first seen service as a midshipman. As master of that ship he defeated and captured the British frigate *Macedonian* in October, 1812. The following year he became a commodore. In January, 1815, while commanding the frigate *President,* he encountered a squadron of British ships. He defeated one of them, the *Endymion,* but after losing a large part of his crew was forced to surrender to the British commander of the squadron. After the war was ended, Decatur was sent on a mission to the Barbary Coast (q.v.) of North Africa to end the depredations of the pirates infesting that region and to demand reparations of the rulers of the states of Algiers, Tunis, and Tripoli, who permitted or encouraged the piracy. He succeeded in this mission and was honored, on his return to the U.S.(1815), at a banquet, where he proposed the famous toast: "Our country! In her intercourse with foreign nations may she always be in the right; but our country, right or wrong!" Soon thereafter he was made a member of a board of three commissioners of the U.S. Navy. In the course of his duties he opposed the return to active service of Commodore James Barron, an officer who had been found guilty by a court-martial in connection with the surrender of the U.S. frigate *Chesapeake* to a British ship in 1807. Barron challenged Decatur to a duel and killed him.

DECCAN, a term sometimes applied to all of the Indian peninsula s. of the Nerbudda R., but generally restricted to that portion bounded on the N. by the Nerbudda and on the S. by the Kistna R., which at one time formed the southern border of the Mohammedan empire of Delhi. The name is applied also to the entire triangular plateau which forms the larger part of the peninsula. The former Deccan and Kolhapur States Agency included in its territory several princely states of the Deccan.

DECEDENT, in American and English law, a deceased person, the term being employed only in connection with the passing of the estate of such person, or the administration thereof. When the estate in question is disposed of by will, the decedent is properly described as testator, or devisor, and thus the term decedent has come to be commonly appropriated to a person dying intestate. As thus restricted, decedents' estates come under the operation of two sets of rules, which, although now usually embodied in statute form, still reflect the common-law doctrines in which they originated. These rules are, first, that the real estate of a decedent shall descend to his heir, and, second, that his personal property shall pass to his personal representative for purposes of administration and distribution. This personal representative may or may not be a person entitled to share in the ultimate distribution of the property, and under some circumstances the duty of administration is undertaken by the state. In the early history of the law in England it devolved upon the church, the right of administering the estate of a decedent being vested in the bishop of the diocese in which he died. This jurisdiction has now been assumed by the High Court of Justice in England. In the United States it is commonly exercised by local tribunals of the rank of county courts, known, variously, as surrogates' courts, probate courts, orphans' courts, and the like. See those titles; also DESCENT; HEIR; EXECUTOR.

DECEMBER, the last month in the Gregorian calendar. It was the tenth month (Lat. *decem,* "ten") in the Roman calendar, and the name became so well established that it was retained when the month became the twelfth in the present calendar (q.v.).

DECEMBRIST, name applied to Russian officers who in December, 1825 sought to overthrow the autocracy of the czars, and to establish political and social reforms. The plot was conceived by Russian officers who attempted to take advantage of the confusion following the death of Czar Alexander I. The uprising broke out on Dec. 14, and was quickly suppressed; the leaders were executed or exiled.

DECIDUOUS PLANTS, plants which shed their leaves annually at the approach of a season of cold or drought. The term is also applied to plants which drop leaves, fruits, or flowers at maturity, in contrast to plants with *persistent* foliage or flowers. Deciduous plants are in direct contrast to evergreens (q.v.).

DECIMAL SYSTEM, a system of positional notation for numbers, based on 10 and the powers of 10. A number written in the decimal system consists of a digit from 0 to 9, which indicates the number of units to be counted, preceded by digits indicating the number of 10's, 10^2's (100's), 10^3's (1000's), and so on, that make up the entire number. The digit indicating the number of units is followed by a period, called a *decimal point,* after which are placed further digits indicating successively the number of 1/10's, 1/100's, 1/1000's that the entire number contains. The decimal system has many advantages, particularly for rapid calculation, and has been widely adopted as the basis for currencies and measurements; see METRIC SYSTEM. The disadvantages of the decimal system are that it requires the use of ten digits (as against the two of the binary system) and that the base number ten is divisible only by two numbers, 2 and 5 (as against the four factors of 12, which is the basis of the duodecimal system). See NOTATION.

DECIMATION (Lat. *decimus,* "tenth"), the practice of executing one tenth of a group as a penalty against the entire group. Decimation was most frequently used as a punishment in the armed forces, in situations, such as mutiny, where no individual in the group to be punished was more culpable than any other individual.

DĚČIN (Ger. *Tetschen*), a city of N. Bohemia, Czechoslovakia, on the E. bank of the Elbe R., opposite the town of Podmokly (Ger. *Bodenbach*), and near the border of Saxony, Germany. In the Sudetenland, Děčín was occupied by the Germans in 1938, but was restored to Czechoslovakia after Germany's defeat in World War II. The city has varied industries, among which are the manufacture of chemicals and dyes, plaster of Paris, cellulose, cotton textiles, confectionery, flour, and beer. Pop. (1947) 30,753.

DECIUS, or in full GAIUS MESSIUS QUINTUS TRAJANUS DECIUS (201–51), Roman Emperor, born in Lower Pannonia (modern Hungary). He was in command of troops along the Danube River in 249 when his soldiers, against his will, proclaimed him emperor. The Emperor Philip led an army against Decius, but was defeated at Verona, and Philip was killed in action. Decius is best known as the instigator of the first thoroughgoing persecution of the Christians, which he accomplished by ordering all inhabitants of the Roman Empire to signify their willingness to worship the pagan gods. Among the victims of this persecution were Pope Fabian, who was martyred; Cyprian, Bishop of Carthage, who was forced into exile; and Origen, the church father, who was imprisoned and tortured. The Christian Church was long divided on the question of the proper treatment of those (called *lapsi*) who publicly accepted the orders of Decius but afterward returned to the Church. Decius was compelled to meet attacks on the borders of the Empire by the Goths, who were defeated and surrounded but refused to surrender unconditionally. In a final attack on the Goths, Decius was killed in battle.

DECLARATION, DYING, a statement as to the cause of his death, made by a person who has been physically injured at the hands of another, and who has given up all hope of recovery and who subsequently dies of such injury. Such statements are in English and American law permitted to be given in evidence as an exception to the rule excluding hearsay evidence from the consideration of the jury.

The exception is based on the assumption that statements made by a dying person in the apprehension of death are as trustworthy as those made in open court under the sanction of an oath. To be admissible, however, dying declarations must have been made by the victim of the homicide and must relate to the circumstances of the crime; they can be used only on the trial of the person charged with the death of the declarant and are equally admissible whether favorable or unfavorable to the accused.

Dying declarations made by others than the victim of a homicide are inadmissible, either in civil or in criminal cases. Thus, a confession of guilt made by a person *in articulo mortis* will not be received in favor of a person accused of the crime. This narrow scope of the rule has been much criticized, but is almost universally maintained. See EVIDENCE.

DECLARATION OF INDEPENDENCE, UNITED STATES, a document proclaiming the independence of the thirteen English colonies in America, adopted by the Continental Congress on July 4, 1776. The Declaration recounted the grievances of the colonies against the English crown and declared the colonies to be free and independent States. The proclamation of independence marked the culmination of a political process which had begun as a protest against oppressive restrictions imposed by the mother country on colonial trade, manufacturing, and political liberty, and had developed into a revolutionary struggle which resulted in the establishment of a new nation (see CONTINENTAL CONGRESS; UNITED STATES: *History*). After the United States was established, the statement of grievances in the Declaration ceased to have any but historic significance. But the political philosophy enunciated in the Declaration had a continuing influence on political developments in America and Europe for many years. It served as a source of authority for the Bill of Rights of the U.S. Constitution (see CONSTITUTION OF THE UNITED STATES). Its influence is manifest in the Declaration of the Rights of Man (q.v.), adopted by the National Assembly of France in 1789, during the French revolution. And in the 19th century, various peoples of Europe and of Latin America fighting for freedom, incorporated in their programs the principles formulated in the Declaration of Independence.

The procedure by which the Declaration of Independence came into being was as follows: On June 7, 1776, Richard Henry Lee, in the name of the Virginia delegates to the Continental Congress, moved that "these united Colonies are and of right ought to be free and independent States, that they are absolved from all allegiance to the British Crown, and that all political connection between them and the State of Great Britain is and ought to be totally dissolved". This motion was seconded by John Adams, but action thereon was deferred until July 1, and the resolution was passed on the following day. In the meantime, a committee (appointed June 11) comprising Thomas Jefferson, Benjamin Franklin, John Adams, Roger Sherman, and Robert R. Livingston was at work preparing a declaration in line with Lee's resolution. Jefferson prepared the draft, using "neither book nor pamphlet", as he later said. Adams and Franklin made a number of minor changes in Jefferson's draft before it was submitted to Congress, which, on July 4, made a number of additional small alterations, incorporated Lee's resolution, and issued the whole as the Declaration of Independence.

The Declaration was adopted by a unanimous vote of the delegates of twelve colonies, those representing New York not voting because they had not been authorized to do so. On July 9th, however, the New York Provincial Congress voted to endorse the Declaration. The document was engrossed on parchment in accordance with a resolution passed by Congress on July 19, and on August 2 was signed by the 53 members then present; the absentees signed subsequently.

The 56 signers of the Declaration were as follows: Roger Sherman, Samuel Huntington, William Williams, and Oliver Wolcott, of Connecticut; Cæsar Rodney, George Read, and Thomas McKean, of Delaware; Button Gwinnett, Lyman Hall, and George Walton, of Georgia; Samuel Chase, William Paca, Thomas Stone, and Charles Carroll of Carrollton, of Maryland; John Hancock, Samuel Adams, John Adams, Robert Treat Paine, and Elbridge Gerry, of Massachusetts; Josiah Bartlett, William Whipple, and Matthew Thornton, of New Hampshire; Richard Stockton, John Witherspoon, Francis Hopkinson, John Hart, and Abraham Clark, of New Jersey; William Floyd, Philip Livingston, Francis Lewis, and Lewis Morris, of New York; William Hooper, Joseph Hewes, and John Penn, of North Carolina; Robert Morris, Benjamin Rush, Benjamin Franklin, John Morton, George Clymer, James Smith, George Taylor, James Wilson, and George Ross, of Pennsylvania; Stephen Hopkins and William Ellery, of Rhode Island; Edward Rutledge, Thomas Heyward, Jr., Thomas Lynch, Jr., and Arthur Middleton, of South Carolina; and George Wythe, Richard Henry Lee, Thomas Jefferson, Benjamin Harrison, Thomas Nelson, Jr., Francis Lightfoot Lee, and Carter Braxton, of Virginia.

Congress directed that copies be sent "to the Assemblies, Conventions, and Committees or Councils of Safety, and to the several commanding officers of the continental troops; that it be proclaimed in each of the United States and at the head of the army".

Upon organization of the national government in 1789, the Declaration of Independence was assigned for safekeeping to the Department of State. In 1841, it was deposited in the Patent Office, then a bureau of the Department of State; in 1877 it was returned to the State Department. Owing to the rapid fading of the text and the deterioration of the parchment, the Declaration was withdrawn from exhibition in 1894. With other historic American documents, Jefferson's draft of the Declaration of Independence was exhibited to public view, in 1947–48, in a special train, called the Freedom Train, which toured the United States.

A reproduction in facsimile of the Declaration was made in 1823, by order of John Quincy Adams, then secretary of state, for the original signers and their families, and it is from a copy struck from the copperplate then made that the following text is reproduced.

In CONGRESS. July 4, 1776.

The unanimous Declaration of the thirteen united States of America,

Portions of a facsimile of the original copy of the Declaration of Independence

THE UNANIMOUS DECLARATION OF THE THIRTEEN UNITED STATES OF AMERICA

When, in the course of human events, it becomes necessary for one people to dissolve the political bands which have connected them with another, and to assume among the powers of the earth, the separate and equal station to which the laws of nature and of nature's God entitle them, a decent respect to the opinions of mankind requires that they should declare the causes which impel them to the separation.

We hold these truths to be self-evident, that all men are created equal, that they are endowed by their Creator with certain unalienable rights, that among these are life, liberty and the pursuit of happiness. That to secure these rights, governments are instituted among men, deriving their just powers from the consent of the governed, that whenever any form of government becomes destructive of these ends, it is the right of the people to alter or to abolish it, and to institute a new government, laying its foundation on such principles and organizing its powers in such form, as to them shall seem most likely to effect their safety and happiness. Prudence, indeed, will dictate that governments long established should not be changed for light and transient causes; and accord-

ingly all experience hath shown, that mankind are more disposed to suffer, while evils are sufferable, than to right themselves by abolishing the forms to which they are accustomed.

But when a long train of abuses and usurpations, pursuing invariably the same object evinces a design to reduce them under absolute despotism, it is their right, it is their duty, to throw off such government, and to provide new guards for their future security. Such has been the patient suffrance of these Colonies; and such is now the necessity which constrains them to alter their former systems of government. The history of the present King of Great Britain is a history of repeated injuries and usurpations, all having in direct object the establishment of an absolute tyranny over these States. To prove this, let facts be submitted to a candid world.

He has refused his assent to laws, the most wholesome and necessary for the public good.

He has forbidden his Governors to pass laws of immediate and pressing importance, unless suspended in their operation till his assent should be obtained; and when so suspended, he has utterly neglected to attend to them.

He has refused to pass other laws for the accommodation of large districts of people, unless those people would relinquish the right of representation in the Legislature, a right inestimable to them and formidable to tyrants only.

He has called together legislative bodies at places unusual, uncomfortable, and distant from the depository of their public records, for the sole purpose of fatiguing them into compliance with his measures.

He has dissolved Representative Houses repeatedly, for opposing with manly firmness his invasions on the rights of the people.

He has refused for a long time, after such dissolutions, to cause others to be elected; whereby the legislative powers, incapable of annihilation, have returned to the people at large for their exercise; the State remaining in the meantime exposed to all the dangers of invasion from without, and convulsions within.

He has endeavored to prevent the population of these States; for that purpose obstructing the laws for the naturalization of foreigners; refusing to pass others to encourage their migration hither, and raising the conditions of new appropriations of lands.

He has obstructed the administration of justice, by refusing his assent to laws for establishing judiciary powers.

He has made judges dependent on his will alone, for the tenure of their offices, and the amount and payment of their salaries.

He has erected a multitude of new offices, and sent hither swarms of officers to harass our people, and eat out their substance.

He has kept among us, in times of peace, standing armies without the consent of our legislatures.

He has affected to render the military independent of and superior to the civil power.

He has combined with others to subject us to a jurisdiction foreign to our constitution, and unacknowledged by our laws; giving his assent to their acts of pretended legislation:

For quartering large bodies of armed troops among us:

For protecting them, by a mock trial, from punishment for any murders which they should commit on the inhabitants of these States:

For cutting off our trade with all parts of the world:

For imposing taxes on us without our consent:

For depriving us in many cases, of the benefits of trial by jury:

For transporting us beyond seas to be tried for pretended offenses:

For abolishing the free system of English laws in a neighboring province, establishing therein an arbitrary government, and enlarging its boundaries so as to render it at once an example and fit instrument for introducing the same absolute rule into these Colonies:

For taking away our charters, abolishing our most valuable laws, and altering fundamentally, the forms of our governments:

For suspending our own legislatures, and declaring themselves invested with power to legislate for us in all cases whatsoever.

He has abdicated government here, by declaring us of out of his protection and waging war against us.

He has plundered our seas, ravaged our coasts, burnt our towns, and destroyed the lives of our people.

He is at this time transporting large armies of foreign mercenaries to complete the works of death, desolation and tyranny, already begun with circumstances of cruelty and perfidy scarcely paralleled in the most barbarous ages, and totally unworthy the head of a civilized nation.

He has constrained our fellow citizens taken captive on the high seas to bear arms against their country, to become the executioners of their friends and brethren, or to fall themselves by their hands.

He has excited domestic insurrections amongst us, and has endeavored to bring on the inhabitants of our frontiers, the merciless Indian savages, whose known rule of warfare, is an undistinguished destruction of all ages, sexes and conditions.

In every stage of these oppressions we have petitioned for redress in the most humble terms: our repeated petitions have been answered only by repeated injury. A prince, whose character is thus marked by every act which may define a tyrant, is unfit to be the ruler of a free people.

Nor have we been wanting in attention to our British brethren. We have warned them from time to time of attempts by their legislature to extend an unwarrantable jurisdiction over us. We have reminded them of the circumstances of our emigration and settlement here. We have appealed to their native justice and magnanimity, and we have conjured them by the ties of our common kindred to disavow these usurpations, which, would inevitably interrupt our connection and correspondence. They too have been deaf to the voice of justice and of consanguinity. We must, therefore, acquiesce in the necessity, which denounces our separation, and hold them, as we hold the rest of mankind, enemies in war, in peace friends.

We, therefore, the Representatives of the *United States of America,* in General Congress, assembled, appealing to the Supreme Judge of the world for the rectitude of our intentions, do, in the name, and by authority of the good people of these Colonies, solemnly publish and declare, That these United Colonies are, and of right ought to be free and independent States; that they are absolved from all allegiance to the British Crown, and that all political connection between them and the State of Great Britain, is and ought to be totally dissolved; and that as free and independent States, they have full power to levy war, conclude peace, contract alliances, establish commerce, and to do all other acts and things which independent States may of right do. And for the support of this Declaration, with a firm reliance on the protection of Divine Providence, we mutually pledge to each other our lives, our fortunes and our sacred honor.

DECLARATION OF INTENTION. See NATURALIZATION.

DECLARATION OF PARIS, an agreement establishing certain principles of international maritime law in time of war, signed by plenipotentiaries of Great Britain, Austria, France, Prussia, Russia, Sardinia, and Turkey, at Paris, April 16, 1856. The agreement declared that privateering (see PRIVATEER) was and should remain abolished; that enemy goods when on a neutral vessel, with the exception of contraband of war, were to be immune from capture by a belligerent; that neutral goods on enemy vessels, with the exception of contraband of war, were not liable to capture; and that blockades (see BLOCKADE), in order to be binding, must be effective, that is, maintained by a force sufficient to prevent access to the coast of the enemy. The United States declined to accept the Declaration on the ground that because the nation did not have a large navy, it would have to depend on privateers to operate against enemy shipping in time of war. Spain, Mexico, Uruguay, Bolivia, and Venezuela also declined to adhere to the Declaration. In the war (1898) between the United States and Spain, however, the two belligerents announced their intention of acting according to the principles of the Declaration of Paris during hostilities.

The development of large navies by the great powers in the last half of the 19th and first half of the 20th centuries made the question of privateering of little consequence and rendered the first provision of the Declaration obsolete. The actions of the various belligerents in World War I almost completely nullified the provisions concerning neutral vessels. The provision laid down by the Declaration concerning blockades is still a principle of international law.

DECLARATION OF THE RIGHTS OF MAN AND OF THE CITIZEN, a revolutionary manifesto adopted on Aug. 26, 1789, by the National Assembly of France, as the preamble of a new constitution then being drafted. The Declaration enumerated a number of rights with which all men were held to be endowed and which were described as inalienable or imprescriptable. In effect, this revolutionary pronouncement nullified the age-old basis of French government, the divine right of kings to rule.

These inalienable rights included participation, through chosen representatives, in the making of laws; equality before the law; equitable taxation; protection against loss of property through arbitrary action by the state; freedom of religion, speech, and the press; and protection against arbitrary arrest and punishment.

Historians are divided in their opinions on the political origins of the Declaration. Some see in its revolutionary pronouncements the influence of the American Declaration of Independence and of the bills of rights of a number of American State Constitutions. Others trace the ideas embodied in the Declaration to English principles of democratic rights. Still others interpret the strong emphasis on individual rights embodied in the Declaration as an expression of the Calvinistic doctrine of freedom of conscience. A large body of opinion holds that the Declaration was a product of the current of ideas known as the Enlightenment (q.v.) and expounded by Jean Jacques Rousseau in his *Contrat Social.* Marxists regard the Declaration as a statement of the basic principles of the revolutions which brought feudalism to an end and established the capitalist system of society.

The Declaration had a tremendous influence on subsequent political thought and institutions. It was a model for most of the declarations of political and civil rights adopted by European states in the 19th century, and for the bill of rights of the constitution of the so-called Weimar Republic of Germany (1919–33).

DECLARATION OF WAR, a formal announcement of hostile intentions by one country to another. Such declarations are of two types: **1.** DECLARATIONS PRECEDING HOSTILITIES. The practice of making a declaration before actually committing an act of war originated in the feudal custom of sending heralds to warn an enemy of impending hostilities. Such declarations of war were usual from feudal times until about the middle of the 18th century. Modern international law does not require a formal declaration of war preceding hostilities; nevertheless, occasionally a war is still declared in this manner. One of the best-known examples of a declaration preceding hostilities was the French declaration of war against Prussia in 1870. The declaration was made on July 19; the first overt act of the Franco-Prussian War, an attack by French troops on Prussian forces in the town of Saarbrücken, took place on August 2. **2.** DECLARATIONS OF WAR AFTER HOSTILITIES HAVE COMMENCED. Such a declaration is usually made by nations in modern times. Preceding such declarations, however, there are usually diplomatic exchanges over controversial issues. In some cases a nation presents an ultimatum stating that unless a favorable reply to its terms is received within a certain time, that nation will open war upon the other. On January 13, 1904, the Japanese government issued such an ultimatum to the Russian government, which did not meet its terms; actual hostilities in the ensuing Russo-Japanese War began on February 8, and both governments issued formal declarations of war on February 10. Sometimes a sudden attack by one nation upon another takes place without ultimatum or declaration of war. An example of this procedure was the attack by Japan on the United States naval base at Pearl Harbor (q.v.) on December 7, 1941. The declaration of war against Japan which drew the United States into World War II was declared by Congress on December 8, 1941.

In most states the power to declare war belongs to the executive or sovereign. In the United States the Constitution (Art. 1, Sec. 8, Cl. 11) vests this power in Congress.

For the declarations of war of World War I and additional declarations of war of World War II, see WORLD WAR I; WORLD WAR II.

DECLINATION, MAGNETIC. See TERRESTRIAL MAGNETISM.

DECOMPOSITION, the separation of a chemical compound into simpler compounds, or into its elements. It is usually accomplished by the application and absorption of some form of physical energy; as, for example, heat decomposes calcium carbonate into calcium oxide and carbon dioxide, or mercuric oxide into mercury and oxygen; a current of electricity decomposes water into hydrogen and oxygen, or solutions of metallic salts into metals and acids. Light causes decomposition in many cases, for example in the silver salts used in photography; and mechanical force, or percussion, initiates the decomposition of sensitive explosives such as lead azide or nitrogen iodide. However, the net result of an explosive decomposition is an emission of energy, not an absorption.

Decomposition, or decay, is an essential part of the biological cycle, changing dead organic matter into forms suitable for plant food. It is also important in geology, causing, with disintegration, the decay of rocks and the formation of soil.

DECOMPRESSION SICKNESS. See BENDS.

DECORATED STYLE, the term applied to the particular Gothic style which prevailed in England from the end of the 13th to the beginning of the 15th centuries, a period covered approximately by the reigns of Edward I, II, and III. It is the second of the three styles of Gothic architecture which flourished in England from the end of the 12th century to the middle of the 16th century (see ARCHITECTURE). In general, Decorated style was a more elaborate and ornate type of architecture than the Early English (q.v.) style which preceded it and from which it was derived. The chief characteristics of Decorated style are geometrical bar tracery (see TRACERY) and the use of floral decoration. Some art historians subdivide the style into the Early Decorated, which is characterized by the use of geometrical figures in its ornamentation; and the Curvilinear, which emphasizes the use of flowing tracery. Decorated style finally gave way to the Gothic style known as Perpendicular style (q.v.).

DECORATION DAY, properly **MEMORIAL DAY,** legal holiday observed annually on May 30 in most of the States of the United States, the District of Columbia, the Territories, the Canal Zone, the Virgin Islands, and Guam in honor of deceased war veterans and soldiers, sailors, and airmen killed in wartime. Originated in 1868 by the Grand Army of the Republic for the purpose of commemorating the Union soldiers and sailors who fell in the Civil War, the holiday is marked traditionally by parades, memorial exercises, and the decoration of graves with flowers and flags. In Virginia May 30 is observed as Confederate Memorial Day. The latter holiday is observed on April 26 in Alabama, Florida, Georgia, and Mississippi, on May 10 in North Carolina and South Carolina, and on June 3 in Kentucky, Louisiana, and Tennessee.

DECORATIVE ART, the general term applied to all the arts that are employed to ornament utilitarian structures and articles. The decorative arts are divided into two principal classes, the major decorative arts, which are those used to decorate buildings and other structures; and the industrial or minor decorative arts, which are used to embellish movable objects. Among the principal major decorative arts are those of mural painting (see MURAL DECORATION), mosaic, sculpture (when part of the structure), and stained glass (qq.v.). The minor decorative arts include furniture (q.v.) making; the designing and manufacturing of various forms of textiles, including carpets, rugs, and lace (qq.v.); and the making of jewelry, pottery (qq.v.), wallpaper, and medals (see MEDAL).

The decorative arts, because they make their primary appeal to the esthetic sense, may be classed among the fine arts (q.v.). However, they differ from the type of fine art which is produced for its esthetic value as an independent entity and not for any value as decoration for a specific structure or object. The term "free fine art", or "independent fine art", may be applied to this type of fine art, and the expression "dependent fine art" to the decorative arts. In many cases the minor decorative arts come under the classification "useful arts" (see ART). Each of the departments of the Metropolitan Museum of Art, New York City, including the Egyptian, Greek, Roman, Medieval, and Renaissance and Modern Art, contains examples of the decorative art belonging to its particular time and place. The American Wing of the museum has examples of American decorative art from the middle of the 17th century to the year 1825. See INTERIOR DECORATION.

DE COSTA, BENJAMIN FRANKLIN (1831–1904), American clergyman and historian, born at Charlestown, Mass. As a Protestant Episcopal minister he was chaplain in the Union Army during the Civil War (1861–63). He was rector of the church of St. John the Evangelist in New York City from 1863 until he joined the Catholic Church in 1899. Among his works are *The Pre-Columbia Discovery of America by the Northmen* (1869) and *Verrazano the Explorer* (1880).

DEDICATION FEAST. See HANUKKAH.

DEDUCTION, in logic, the process of reasoning from the general to the particular, usually regarded as the opposite of induction (q.v.). The most common form of deduction or deductive reasoning is the syllogism, in which a conclusion (often called a deduction) is derived from two premises. The term deduction has been given special and extended meanings by several philosophers, among them René Descartes and Immanuel Kant, but its general usage is limited to the form of reasoning described. See LOGIC.

DEE, a river in Wales and England. From its source in Lake Bala, Merionethshire, Wales, it flows generally northeastward as far as Chester, England, and then follows a N.W. course to the Irish Sea. It is navigable, by means of a dredged channel, from its estuary, which is 14 m. long and from 3 to 5½ m. wide, as far inland as Chester. About 70 m. long, the Dee drains parts of Merionethshire, Denbighshire, Shropshire, Flintshire, and Cheshire. Its drainage basin, about 813 sq.m. in area, contains some of the most picturesque country in England and Wales.

DEE, the name of two rivers in Scotland. **1.** The larger stream rises on the N. slopes of the Grampian Mountains, in Aberdeen County. Its course, generally eastward, is turbulent for distance of about 45 m., passing through a series of chasms, notably the Linn of Dee. The river has a total length of 90 m., and empties into the North Sea at Aberdeen harbor. Balmoral Castle (q.v.) is situated on the banks of the Dee. The river is noted for its salmon. **2.** The smaller Dee, 50 m. in length, rises in mountainous country in the N. of Kircudbright County, widens into a long, narrow lake, called Dee Lake, about midway in its course, and empties into Solway Firth, at Kircudbright Bay.

DEED, in law, a written instrument whereby a legal right is created or transferred. Although the term *deed* is popularly employed only in connection with instruments for the conveyance of land, it is not, in the legal sense, thus restricted, being equally applicable to a considerable variety of other legal transactions effected by the same solemn form. A contract, an appointment to office, the surrender of a right of action, and transfer of title to land or goods, all may be effected by deed.

Deeds have been employed from an early period for the transfer of certain interests in land, but their general and almost exclusive use for this purpose is quite modern. Formerly, at common law, freehold interests in land were created or conveyed by the formal ceremony known as livery of seizin, while all estates less than freehold were subject to alienation by parole, deeds being required only to convey the class of interests known as incorporeal, such as easements, profits, future interests in land, and the like.

But deeds have now, under the technical description of grants, almost entirely superseded other modes of conveyance of interests in land. In most of the United States and Great Britain, the general use of deeds for the purposes of conveyance is regulated by specific statutes, and the nature of the estates conferred thereby are specifically defined therein. In a number of U.S. States, however, the requirement for a deed to be under the seal of the grantor has been abolished. It is sufficient, in those States, that the deed be acknowledged as the act of the grantor before a notary public or a commissioner of deeds.

DEEPING, (GEORGE) WARWICK (1877–1950), British author, born in Southend, Essex, and educated at the Merchant Taylor's School and Trinity College, Cambridge. He became a doctor, but after practicing a year, turned to literature. The appealingly human qualities of his characters made his novels popular. Among his writings are *The Return of the Petticoat* (1916); *Sorrel and Son* (1925), the novel which made his reputation; *Old Pybus* (1928); *The Man Who Went Back* (1940); *The Impudence of Youth* (1946); and *Laughing House* (1947).

DEEP RIVER, a 125-mile-long river rising in Guilford Co., North Carolina, and flowing S.E., then E., to Chatham Co., where it unites with the Haw R. to form the Cape Fear R. The Deep R. drains an area of over 1300 sq.m. It is navigable to Carbonton, and furnishes water power, chiefly for Lockville.

DEEP-SEA EXPLORATION, the investigation of physical, chemical, and biological conditions at the bottom of the ocean, for scientific or commercial purposes. The depths of the sea have been investigated with precision only during comparatively recent years. Such investigations were originally undertaken because of the necessity for accurate soundings for submarine cables. Soundings were formerly made by carefully paying out weighted lines or wires until the weight struck bottom, and then measuring the length of the line. The process was slow, each sounding taking about one hour for each mile of depth. Modern sounding is ac-

complished by means of an echo-sounding apparatus, similar in principle to sonar (q.v.), which measures and records the depth within three or four seconds. Much has also been learned for scientific purposes by dredging, and by submarine exploration with the bathysphere and the bathyscaphe (qq.v.).

Our most important knowledge of deep-sea conditions has been gained since 1870. The Challenger Expedition, sent out by the British government in 1872, engaged in pelagic investigations for nearly four years. Other extensive deep-sea investigations have been conducted at various times by most of the European governments, and vessels of the U.S. Coast Survey and Fish Commission (later the Coast Guard and the Coast and Geodetic Survey) have been engaged in deep-sea investigations since 1870.

The greatest known depth in the Atlantic Ocean is the Milwaukee Deep, situated off the N.E. coast of the Dominican Republic. Discovered in 1939, it lies in the submarine depression known as the Puerto Rico Trench and has a depth of 30,346 ft. In the Pacific Ocean, the greatest known depth (35,640 ft.) was discovered in 1951 by H.M.S. *Challenger* in the Marianas Trench, a depression situated to the E. of the southern Marianas Islands. See OCEAN AND OCEANOGRAPHY; OCEAN CURRENTS.

DEER, common name of animals of the family Cervidae (see PECORA), divided into twenty genera which are found throughout Europe, Asia, and the Americas, and in N. Africa. All but one of the genera are characterized by the absence of a gall bladder; all but one species are characterized by the presence of antlers, usually only in the male. These antlers are bony outgrowths from the front of the skull and are covered with hairy skin during growth. When growth is completed, the blood supply stops and the skin dries and is sloughed off. At the close of the breeding season, the antlers are shed, and a new pair grows in the following year. The number of points or branchings of the antlers increases as the deer matures. The species of deer vary widely in size, from the moose, which may reach a shoulder height of 7 ft. to the South American pudu, which is just over a foot high at the shoulder.

The true deer of the genus *Cervus* are represented by only one species in the U.S. This is the wapiti, *C. canadensis*, of the Rocky Mountain area. This deer has massive antlers and stands about 5½ ft. high. It is frequently miscalled an elk, but the only true American elk is the moose. *Alces americanus*, with

N.Y. Zool. Soc.; U.S.D.I. Fish & Wild. Ser.; M.G.M

THE DEER FAMILY. *Top, left: The wapiti, of the Rocky Mountains of the U.S. Top, right: European red deer. Above: The white-tailed or Virginia deer. At right: Mule deer, of the western U.S. Below, right: The black-tailed deer, also of the western U.S.*

broad, flattened antlers bordered with snags.

The most common deer of the U.S. belong to the genus *Odocoileus*. The white-tailed or Virginia deer, *O. virginianus*, with tined antlers and a prominent white spot under the tail, is found in most parts of the U.S., as well as in other areas from Alaska to Bolivia. The mule deer, *O. hemonius*, and the black-tailed deer, *O. columbianus*, are confined to the western part of this country. They are both larger than the white-tailed deer but smaller than the wapiti.

The caribou, *Rangifer caribou*, of Canada

and Alaska, belongs to the same genus as the reindeer. The females of both species grow antlers. The common deer of Europe is the red deer, *Cervus elaphus,* which ranges as far east as Persia.

The musk deer of central Asia, *Moschus moschiferus,* is unique among the deer in that it has a gall bladder. The male has an abdominal musk gland which gives the species its name. It is a small, brownish deer standing only about 20 in. high.

The adult male of most deer is called a buck, although this term was originally applied only to the fallow deer of England, and is still sometimes restricted to this species. The adult female is called a doe, and the young a fawn. The corresponding terms for elk and moose are bull, cow, and calf. The term stag, often applied to any buck, is properly restricted to the red deer. The adult male and female of the red deer are also called hart and hind, respectively.

See ELK; WAPITI; CARIBOU; REINDEER; FALLOW DEER; RED DEER; MULE DEER; VIRGINIA DEER; MUSK DEER; BLACK-TAILED DEER; SAMBUR; MUNTJAK; ROE DEER.

DEERFIELD, town of Franklin Co., Mass., on the Connecticut and Deerfield rivers, 33 miles N. of Springfield. The surrounding region is agricultural, producing tobacco, onions, and cucumbers. Deerfield was settled in 1669, and was for many years a frontier post, exposed to Indian attacks, the most notable of which were the Bloody Brook massacre in 1675 and the French and Indian raid of 1704. In the latter, 49 inhabitants of Deerfield were killed and over 100 were captured. A number of captives were murdered, and the rest were taken to Canada. Some of the survivors were liberated in 1706. Deerfield is the site of Deerfield Academy, a boys' preparatory school. Memorial Hall, the academy's first building, was erected in 1799, and now contains a collection of colonial, Indian, and Civil War relics. Pop. (1950) 3086.

DEERHOUND, SCOTTISH, a breed of hound which originated in Scotland about the 16th century and was once widely used in the hunting of deer. The dog is also known as the buckhound. In the United States, because the hunting of antlered animals with dogs is prohibited, the deerhound is used to hunt other animals, including wolves and coyotes. The deerhound is large, and usually of a dark blue-gray color. It has a wiry coat; a head broad at the ears and narrowing toward the eyes; dark-brown, brown, or

hazel eyes; a deep chest; broad flat legs with broad forearms and elbows; and a long, tapering tail. The male is from 30 to 32 inches high at the shoulder and weighs from 85 to 110 pounds; the female is from 28 to 32 inches high and weighs from 75 to 95 pounds. The dog is graceful and dignified and in general appearance resembles an oversized greyhound.

DEERSLAYER, THE. See COOPER, JAMES FENIMORE.

DE FACTO, a legal phrase, signifying "actual, based on fact"; as distinguished from *de jure* meaning "by right of law, based on law, rightfully, legally". It is commonly used to characterize the occupancy of public office, or the exercise of political or other authority without legal warrant, or by one whose legal title thereto is defective. Under a government of law, a merely de facto authority may always be impeached; the proper legal remedy in England and in the United States is by the common-law writ of quo warranto, issued by a court of competent jurisdiction, to bring the offender into court and inquire by what warrant he has presumed to exercise the office or authority in question.

Used in its general sense, as opposed to a de jure, or lawful, authority, the exercise of de facto authority is always a usurpation, and it maintains this character so long as it continues, or until it is legalized by proper legislative or other authority. Thus, in administrative law, mere usurpation of an office, without the actual exercise of its functions, does not constitute the usurping officer a de facto officer. The authority claimed must be effective and actually exercised for it to be de facto.

Also, in administrative law, the term de facto is commonly used to describe the exercise of illegal authority, but with apparent right and under color of legal authority. The acts of an officer thus functioning have a degree of validity so far as the interests of the public and of third persons are concerned and cannot be questioned in any collateral proceeding.

In constitutional and international law, the term de facto is employed in the sense of a power actually exercised but without established legal basis. Thus it has been applied to a revolutionary government, such as the Continental Congress which had no legal basis, but whose effective authority was manifest in the victorious conduct of the Revolutionary War. Success in the war resulted in recognition of the independence of the thirteen colonies, and in de jure recognition of the Continental Congress by Great Britain and other countries. For various reasons, states wishing to enter into relations with governments, revolutionary or otherwise, but unwilling to accord them de jure recognition generally accord them de facto recognition. Thus, in May, 1948, the U.S. accorded de facto recognition to the new state of Israel.

DE FALLA, MANUEL. See FALLA, MANUEL DE.

DEFENSE, in criminal law, the right of forcible resistance to an attack by force on person or property. The exercise of this right may be a justification of the charge of assault or homicide. It is restricted to the employment of as much force as is reasonably necessary for the protection of one's self, his wife, children, and other members of his household, his personal property, and, where a felony is threatened, as burglary or arson, his real property. He may also resist by force a violent attempt to commit a trespass, even without felonious intent, upon the premises constituting his dwelling.

In the law of civil and criminal procedure, the defense is the answer of the defendant in a suit to the cause of action set up by the plaintiff.

DEFENSE, DEPARTMENT OF, formerly NATIONAL MILITARY ESTABLISHMENT, one of the ten departments of the executive branch of the Federal government of the United States, created by the National Security Act of 1947, and reorganized in 1953. The department is administered by the secretary of defense, a member of the Cabinet who is appointed by the President with the approval of the Senate. The Department is charged with providing a comprehensive program for the security of the United States; with setting up integrated policies and procedures for all of the departments and agencies of the Federal government whose functions relate to national security; and with the co-ordination and unified direction under civilian control of the armed services, in order to provide them with effective strategic supervision and to promote their efficient operation. The component units of the Department of Defense include the Department of the Army, the Department of the Navy, the Department of the Air Force, the Armed Forces Policy Council, and the Joint Chiefs of Staff.

The first two departments listed above enjoyed the status of separate executive departments of the Federal government prior to the passage of the National Security Act of 1947. Under that act the War Department was redesignated the Department of the Army, and with the Department of the Navy was transferred to the National Military Establishment. For an account of the history of the War Department from its inception up to the enactment of the act of 1947, see WAR DEPARTMENT; for an account of the present organization of the Department of the Army, see ARMY, DEPARTMENT OF THE. The history and present organization of the Department of the Navy are described in the article entitled NAVY, DEPARTMENT OF THE. For the history and present organization of the Department of the Air Force, see AIR FORCE, DEPARTMENT OF THE; AIR FORCE, UNITED STATES.

Operated jointly by the departments of the Army, Navy, and Air Force are the National War College, the Industrial College of the Armed Forces, and the Armed Forces Staff College.

The National Security Act of 1947 set up a number of bodies within the National Military Establishment designed to further the effective co-ordination of the armed forces. The most important of these is the Joint Chiefs of Staff, comprising the chiefs of staff of the Army, Navy, and Air Force, which performs joint strategic and logistic planning and provides United States representation on the Military Staff Committee of the United Nations. Matters of broad policy relating to the armed forces are considered by the Armed Forces Policy Council, which consists of the secretary of defense, the deputy secretary of defense, the chairman of the Joint Chiefs of Staff, and the secretaries and chiefs of staff of the three armed services.

DEFOE, DANIEL (1659?–1731), English author, born in London. Little is known of Defoe's early life, but it is certain that he volunteered in King William's army in 1688 and that he traveled in both France and Spain. In 1701 his poem *The True-Born Englishman, a Satyr* won him a reputation as a writer. He was active in the struggle of the Dissenters against the High Church party, and his pamphlet *The Shortest Way with Dissenters* (1702) brought about his arrest and sentence to imprisonment, a fine, and a period of standing in the pillory. When he was pilloried, however, a sympathetic crowd gathered and protected him. Defoe

"L'Absinthe," painting by Degas

was soon released from prison, and in 1704 began to issue the *Review*, a newspaper which he wrote virtually singlehanded, and which was published until 1713. He also acted as a secret agent of the government, and it is believed that this was a condition of his release. Defoe's greatest work, *The Life and Adventures of Robinson Crusoe*, appeared in 1719. This is a fictional tale of a shipwrecked sailor, based on the adventures of an actual seaman, Alexander Selkirk, who was marooned on the island of Juan Fernandez off the coast of Chile. Defoe's other important novels were *Memoirs of a Cavalier* (1720), *Captain Singleton* (1720), *The Fortunes and Misfortunes of Moll Flanders* (1722), and *Roxana or the Fortunate Mistress* (1724). Defoe brought his vigorous style and his gift for realistic narrative to play in a number of other works including the *Journal of the Plague Year* (1722) and a number of biographies of famous criminals. He was one of the most prolific of English authors and produced in addition a large number of minor works and political tracts.

DE FOREST, LEE (1873–   ), American inventor, born at Council Bluffs, Ia., and educated at Yale University. De Forest was a pioneer in the development of wireless telegraphy, and designed a number of the earliest high-power spark transmitters. His most important invention, however, was the three-electrode thermionic tube, or triode, which he called the audion. This tube, patented in 1907, was the first to use a control grid by means of which the fluctuations of a small electric current can be used to control the flow of a larger current. The invention of this tube made possible the amplification of sound and the transmission and reception of radio-telephone signals over long distances. In fact, the entire field of electronics, from radar to high-frequency heating, is based on the principle first applied by De Forest in his three-element audion. De Forest also patented over 300 other electrical and electronic devices, including several in the field of sound motion pictures. He received a medal and awards for his work from the Institute of France, the Franklin Institute, the Institute of Radio Engiueers, and several international expositions. Among his writings are *Television Today and Tomorrow* (1942), *Father of Radio: An Autobiography* (1950), and numerous papers for scientific publications.

DEFREGGER, FRANZ VON (1835–1921), Austrian painter, born in Dölsach, Tyrol. He studied art in Innsbruck, Munich, and Paris. He is noted for his delineations of Tyrolean everyday life and of episodes of Tyrolean history. Among his works are "The Zither Player" and "The Last Summons" (both in the Vienna Museum); "Return of the Tyrolese Riflemen in 1809" (National Gallery, Berlin); "Andreas Hofer on his Way to Execution" (Königsberg Museum): and "German Peasant Girl" (Metropolitan Museum of Art, New York City).

DEGAS, HILAIRE GERMAIN EDGAR (1834–1917), French painter, born in Paris. He studied in Paris at the École des Beaux-Arts, and also in Rome. Degas became one of the leaders of the Impressionist school of French painting (see IMPRESSIONISM). He was a painter of portraits, nudes, and studies of contemporary life, which he executed chiefly in oils or pastels. Among his characteristic genre subjects were working women, café singers, horse races, and especially the ballet, of which his pastel studies are particularly notable. Degas' work is characterized by originality of design, which often shows the influence of Japanese art; excellent drawing, particularly of the human figure; and color that is both rich and subtle. His paintings, pastels, water colors, and etchings are in many important museums and private collections. The Metropolitan Museum of Art, New York City, has many examples of his work, including the pastels "Dancers Practicing at the Bar", "The Toilet", "Woman with Chrysanthemums", and "At the Milliner's"; and the oil paintings "Portrait of James Tissot", "Collector of Prints", and "Le Foyer".

DE GAULLE, CHARLES ANDRÉ JOSEPH MARIE (1890–   ), French soldier and political leader, born in Lille, and educated at Saint-Cyr military school. He served in World War I as captain of infantry, and later was appointed aide-de-camp (1924–27) to Marshal Henri Philippe Pétain. He won prominence by his advocacy of a highly mechanized French army. Early in World War II, he attained the rank of brigadier general, and in 1940 was dispatched to England to discuss military needs. He was in London when the Pétain government sued for an armistice with

Germany, and on the night of June 18, in a radio address to the French people, inaugurated the Free French national committee. In 1942, this committee was officially recognized by the Allied governments and Resistance leaders in France as the French National Committee; it commanded the French troops, both those with the French Resistance and those fighting with Allied armies, who were collectively known as the Fighting French.

De Gaulle's volunteer forces, supported by French colonials and a considerable part of the French fleet, made an unsuccessful attack on Dakar (Sept., 1940), joined the British in the conquest of Syria (1941), and took control of Madagascar (1942). De Gaulle was copresident (June–Nov., 1943), with General Henri Honoré Giraud, and later full chairman (from Nov., 1943) of the French Committee of National Liberation, which moved from Algiers to liberated Paris in Aug., 1944, and the following month was recognized by the United States government as the de facto French government. He was president of the provisional government of France from Nov., 1945 to Jan., 1946. In 1947, he became head of the political movement *Rassemblement du Peuple Français.* Under his leadership, the R.P.F. worked for a strong central government which could, by balancing the budget, promote pri-

French Embassy, Information Division
Charles De Gaulle

vate enterprise and lift state controls over the economic life of France. Furthermore, De Gaulle's movement hoped to free labor and capital from political interference, and to stimulate their co-operation in a plan for industry in which workers might hold stock. The strength of the movement, though considerable for several years, had so declined by May, 1953, that the R.P.F. was dissolved as a party in parliament. De Gaulle wrote *At the Sword's Edge* (1932), *The Army of the Future* (1934), and *France and Its Army* (1938).

DEGREE, in trigonometry, an arc equaling 1/360 of the circumference of a circle, or the angle subtended at the center of a circle by such an arc. The degree is the chief unit of measurement for both angles and circular curves. It is divided into 60 minutes, each equal to 1/21,600 of the circumference of a circle; and each minute is divided into 60 seconds, each equal to 1/1,296,000 of the circumference of a circle. Degrees, minutes, and seconds, whether used for the measurement of circumferences or of angles, are usually abbreviated °, ′, and ″ respectively (as for example 41°18′09″).

Measurement in degrees is widely used in astronomy, navigation, and surveying, for the only means of accurately locating either a star, or a point on the face of the earth, is by its angular distance in degrees, minutes, and seconds from certain given reference points. Positions on the surface of the earth are measured in degrees of latitude north and south of the equator and degrees of longitude east and west of the prime meridian, which is usually arbitrarily taken as the meridian which passes through Greenwich in England.

Degree of Latitude. If the earth were exactly spherical, a degree of latitude would be equal to 1/360 of the circumference of a circle drawn on the surface of the earth and passing through the north and south poles. The earth, however, is flattened at the poles, so that the actual length of a degree on the surface of the earth (as determined astronomically) varies from the equator to the poles. At the equator a degree of latitude is equal to 362,756.5 ft. or about 68¾ statute miles. The length of a degree at 45° N. or s., the so-called middle degree, is equal to 364,606 ft., about 69⅛ statute miles.

Degree of Longitude. The length of a degree of longitude varies from a maximum value at the equator to zero at the north and south poles, because longitude is measured as the arc of a given parallel of latitude, and the circles forming these parallels decrease in radius as the latitude increases. At the equator a degree of longitude equals 69.65 miles, whereas at 40° N. or s. a degree equals 53.43 miles. Longitude is also measured in hours east or west of the prime meridian, with an hour equal to 15 degrees and a minute equal to 15 angular minutes. Thus the longitude of New York City can be stated as 74° or as 4 hours, 56 minutes west of Greenwich.

DEGREE, ACADEMIC, a title granted by a college or university, usually signifying completion of an established course of study. Honorary degrees are conferred as marks of distinction, not necessarily of scholarship; some, such as LITT.D. (Doctor of Letters), are generally honorary in the United States.

Institutions of higher learning have granted degrees since the 12th century. The word itself was then used for the baccalaureate and licentiate, the two intermediate steps which led to the certificates of master and doctor, requisites for teaching in a medieval university. During the same period, honorary degrees were sometimes conferred by a pope or an emperor. In England, the Archbishop of Canterbury, by an act passed during the reign of King Henry VIII, acquired the authority to grant Lambeth degrees.

During the Middle Ages, the conferring of a doctorate also gave the recipient the authority to practice the profession in which his certificate was awarded; this condition still holds true for the legal and medical professions in European countries, such as France, in which the government controls the universities. In the United States, however, the doctor's degree in medicine and law in itself is only a measure of academic attainment; the holder of the degree of M.D., for example, cannot practice his profession until he has complied with the regulations, including the passing of an examination, of the State in which he desires to practice, and has been granted a license.

In Germany and at most Continental universities, only the doctor's degree is conferred, except in theology, in which the licentiate, or master's degree, is also granted. Granting of the doctorate is contingent upon the acceptance of a dissertation and the passing of examinations. The bachelor's degree, or baccalaureate, is usually not a university degree in Europe. In France, it is acquired by passing a State examination at the completion of the course of secondary education; the only university-conferred baccalaureate is that awarded by the faculty of law.

Oxford and Cambridge universities in England grant the bachelor's degree after the satisfactory completion of a three-year course, and the master's degree in arts or science after a further period of residence and study and the payment of fees. Other English universities grant the master's degree only after a candidate has passed a series of examinations and presented an approved thesis. The various doctorates are awarded for distinguished work in a special field of scholarship or given *honoris causa* to prominent public figures.

The most commonly granted degrees in the United States are the B.A. and B.S., given, generally, after the completion of a four-year course of study and sometimes followed by a mark of excellence, such as *cum laude, magna cum laude,* or *summa cum laude.* The master's degree is granted after one or two years of postgraduate work and may require the writing of a thesis or dissertation. The doctorate requires two to five years of postgraduate work, the writing of a thesis, and the passing of oral and written examinations. In American higher education, a great number and variety of special degrees are granted by schools for specialized training. In a recent year, American institutions of higher learning granted about 375,000 bachelor's degrees, more than 6000 undergraduate degrees in medicine, and more than 2800 undergraduate degrees in dentistry. They also conferred about 65,000 master's degrees and 7300 doctor's degrees. The most familiar degrees are:

A.B. or B.A. . . . . Bachelor of Arts
A.M. or M.A. . . . . Master of Arts
B.B.S. . . . . Bachelor of Business Science
B.C.L. . . . . Bachelor of Civil Law
B.D. or S.T.B. . . . . Bachelor of Divinity
B.Lit., B.Litt., or Lit.B. . . . Bachelor of Letters
B.LL. or LL.B. . . . . Bachelor of Laws
B.S., B.Sc., or Sc.B. . . . . . Bachelor of Science
B.S.S. . . . . Bachelor of Social Science
C.E. . . . . Civil Engineer
C.M. or Ch.M. . . . . Master of Surgery
Ch.E. . . . . Chemical Engineer
D.C.L. . . . . Doctor of Civil Law
D.D. or S.T.D. . . . . Doctor of Divinity
D.D.S. . . . . Doctor of Dental Surgery
D.Litt. or Litt.D.
    Doctor of Letters (or Literature)
D.M.D. . . . . Doctor of Dental Medicine
D.S. or D.Sc. . . . . Doctor of Science
D.V.M. . . . . . Doctor of Veterinary Medicine
E.E. . . . . Electrical Engineer
J.D. . . . . Doctor of Law
J.U.D. . . . . . . Doctor of Civil and Canon Law
L.H.D. . . . . Doctor of Humanities
LL.D. Doctor of Laws

M.C.E. . . . . Master of Civil Engineering
M.D. . . . . Doctor of Medicine
M.E. . . . . Mining or Mechanical Engineer
Mus.B. . . . . Bachelor of Music
Mus.D. . . . . Doctor of Music
Ph.D. . . . . Doctor of Philosophy
Ph.G. . . . . Graduate in Pharmacy
V.S. . . . . Veterinary Surgeon
See GOWN; UNIVERSITIES.

DE HAVEN, FRANKLIN (1856–1934), American painter, born at Bluffton, Ind. He was noted for his landscapes. Examples of his work are in the National Gallery, Washington, D.C.; the Brooklyn Museum of Arts and Sciences; and the Butler Art Museum, Youngstown, Ohio.

DEHMEL, RICHARD (1863–1920), German lyric poet, born in Wendisch-Hermsdorf, Brandenburg, and educated at the University of Berlin. Many of his writings show an acute sense of form and great emotional power. Among his works are *Erlösungen* (1891), his first volume of poetry; *Zwei Menschen* (1903), a novel in lyrical form; and *Zwischen Krieg und Menschheit* (1919), a diary of World War I.

DEHRA DUN, capital of the district of the same name, Meerut Division, Uttar Pradesh State, Union of India, about 75 miles E. of Ambala. It is a commercial center. The chief point of interest in the city is a temple, dating from 1699, which is regarded as a classical example of Mohammedan architecture. Dehra Dun has several institutions of higher learning, notably a school of forestry. Pop. (1951) 144,216.

DEHYDRATION. See FOOD, PRESERVATION OF.

DEINOTHERIUM. See DINOTHERIUM.

DEISM, the belief in a personal transcendent God Who created the world but does not intervene in its affairs. According to this doctrine, the world operates and develops eternally on the basis of mechanical and unchanging laws established by God. Rejecting the belief in revelation from God, Deism holds that, by the light of reason and an understanding of nature, the individual may determine for himself religious doctrine and practice. See also THEISM.

The name *Deists* designates in particular a series of English writers of the 17th and 18th centuries. In accordance with the prevailing philosophy of rationalism (q.v.), they sought to establish Natural Religion, based on reason and experience, in place of institutionalized religion, based on faith. Among these writers were Edward Herbert (q.v.) and Matthew

Tindal. Scripture was severely criticized by this group, and miracles, the Trinity, and the atonement by Christ was denied. See also FREETHINKERS.

DE KALB, BARON. See KALB, JOHANN.

DEKAY'S SNAKE. See BROWN SNAKE.

DEKKER, EDUARD DOUWES (1820–87), Dutch civil servant and author. He entered the Dutch Colonial Civil Service in 1838, holding various posts in the Dutch East Indies, and resigned in 1857 in protest against Dutch colonial policies in Java. In 1860 he wrote *Max Havelaar,* the Dutch counterpart of *Uncle Tom's Cabin,* which revealed the oppressed condition of the natives in the Dutch colonies. In 1866 he withdrew to Germany, where he wrote *Vorstenschool,* a drama in Dutch; *La Sainte Vièrge,* a novel; and several studies in political and social economy.

DEKKER, THOMAS (about 1572–about 1632), English dramatist and pamphleteer. In collaboration with Ben Jonson he wrote plays for the English theater manager, Philip Henslowe, as early as 1598. By 1601 the two dramatists had quarreled; in that year Ben Jonson ridiculed Thomas Dekker in *The Poetaster* and was answered with *Satiromastix, or the Untrussing of the Humourous Poet* (1602). Among the more than forty plays which Dekker wrote alone or in collaboration are the comedies *The Shoemaker's Holiday* (1600), *Old Fortunatus* (1600), *The Honest Whore* (in collaboration with Thomas Middleton, 1604), *If It Be not Good the Devil Is in It* (about 1610), and *The Witch of Edmonton* (in collaboration with John Ford and William Rowley, first published in 1658). Among the pamphlets he wrote are *The Wonderful Year* (1603), a description of London during the plague; and *The Gull's Hornbook* (1609), a satirical account of the London gallants of the time.

DE KOVEN, (HENRY LOUIS) REGINALD (1859–1920), American composer, born in Middletown, Conn., and educated at St. John's College, Oxford University. He studied music in Stuttgart, Florence, Vienna, and Paris, and became noted for his operettas and songs. Among his works are the operettas *The Begum* (1887), *Robin Hood* (1890), *The Highwayman* (1897), and *The Student King* (1906); the operas *The Canterbury Pilgrims* (1917) and *Rip Van Winkle* (1920); and more than 400 songs. His best-known song is *O Promise Me,* which occurs in the most successful of his operettas, *Robin Hood.*

DE KRUIF, PAUL (1890–   ), American bacteriologist and author, born at Zeeland, Michigan, and educated at the University of Michigan. He was a research worker at the Rockefeller Institute from 1920 to 1922, and became a reporter for the Curtis Publishing Co. in 1925. He collaborated with Sinclair Lewis on the novel *Arrowsmith* and specialized in popular writing on new advances in science. His works include *Microbe Hunters* (1926), *Hunger Fighters* (1928), *Men Against Death* (1932), *Kaiser Wakes the Doctors* (1943), *The Male Hormone* (1945), and *Life among the Doctors* (with Rhea de Kruif, 1949).

DELACROIX, FERDINAND VICTOR EUGÈNE (1799–1863), French painter, born in Charenton-St. Maurice, near Paris. He studied with the French painter Baron Pierre Narcisse Guérin, and was considerably influenced by the work of the old masters Veronese and Rubens and that of the contemporary painters Jean Géricault and John Constable. Delacroix became one of the most important leaders of the romantic movement in painting, which represented a revolt against the prevailing classic school inaugurated by Jacques Louis David (q.v.). Delacroix's subject matter, usually of a strongly dramatic nature, was drawn from contemporary events from history, poetry, and legend, and from scenes and incidents with an exotic background, such as that of Spain and Morocco. He also painted portraits, genre studies, and hunting scenes. His total work comprises over 800 oil paintings and almost 1600 water colors, pastels, and etchings. His work is characterized by brilliant coloring, vivid imagination, and dramatic power; its weakest element is craftsmanship. Among his works are the paintings "Dante and Virgil", "Massacre of Chios", "Liberty Leading the People", "The Entry of the Crusaders", "Algerian Women", and "Jewish Wedding in Morocco" (all in the Louvre, Paris); and "The Abduction of Rebecca" (Metropolitan Museum of Art, New York City). Among his mural paintings, all in Paris, are those for a number of churches, including the church of St. Sulpice; for the ceiling of the Galerie d'Apollon in the Louvre; and for the Chambre des Députés, the Palais du Luxembourg, and the Hôtel de Ville.

DELAGOA BAY, an inlet of the Indian Ocean, on the E. coast of Mozambique (q.v.), Portuguese East Africa. It is about 26 m. long from N. to S. and about 26 m. wide. Protected on the S. by the peninsula of Inyak and easily accessible to deep-water vessels, it affords one of the best harbors on the E.

coast of Africa. The chief port on the bay is Lourenço Marques (q.v.). The bay receives the waters of a number of rivers, including the Esperito Santo, Lisuthu, and Funti. The Portuguese navigator Antonio de Campo discovered Delagoa Bay in 1502. Trading stations were subsequently established along its shore by the Portuguese and British. Early in the 19th century, both Great Brtain and Portugal attempted to establish sovereignty over the bay area, with Portugal finally obtaining control by the end of that century.

DE LA MARE, WALTER (JOHN) (1873–), English poet and novelist, born at Charlton, Kent, and educated at St. Paul's Cathedral Choir School. While employed in business in London, he wrote poems and stories under the name "Walter Ramal". In 1908 a royal grant of £100 a year from the government supplemented his slender literary income and enabled him to devote himself entirely to writing. Many of his works deal with an imaginary realm of fantasy. Among his writings are *Songs of Childhood* (1902), *The Listeners and Other Poems* (1912), *The Memoirs of a Midget* (1921), *Lewis Carroll* (1932), *The Burning Glass* (1945), *Rhymes and Verses* (for children, 1947), and *Collected Tales* (1950).

DELAND, MARGARETTA WADE CAMPBELL (1857–1945), American novelist, born at Allegheny, Pa. Among her works are *John Ward, Preacher* (1888), *Dr. Lavendar's People* (1904), *Old Chester Tales* (1919), *New Friends in Old Chester* (1924), *Captain Archer's Daughter* (1932), and *Golden Yesterdays* (1941).

DE LA RAMÉE, MARIE LOUISE. See RAMÉE, MARIE LOUISE DE LA.

DE LA RIVE, AUGUSTE ARTHUR. See LA RIVE, AUGUSTE ARTHUR DE.

DELAROCHE, (HIPPOLYTE) PAUL (1797–1856), French painter, born in Paris. He studied principally with Baron Antoine Gros. The work of Delaroche was characterized by its eclectic quality; his style combined the clear-cut linear composition of the Classic school of painting with the dramatic subject matter and vivid coloring of the Romantic school. Among his works are the historical paintings "The Death of Queen Elizabeth" (Louvre), "Cromwell Contemplating the Remains of Charles I" (Nîmes Museum), and "The Field of Battle" (New York Public Library). He is best known for the mural (27 meters long) covering the semicircular wall of the theater of the École des Beaux-Arts, Paris; the painting contains 75 life-size portraits of artists of various periods and nationalities.

DE LA ROCHE, MAZO (1885–), Canadian writer, born in Toronto, and educated at the Parkdale College Institute and at the University of Toronto. The novel *Jalna* (1927), for which she was awarded the *Atlantic Monthly* $10,000 prize, was the first of a series of novels concerning a rural Canadian family named Whiteoak. Among her other works are *Low Life and Other Plays* (1928), *Portrait of a Dog* (1930), *Growth of a Man* (1938), *History of the Port of Quebec* (1944), and *Boy in the House* (1952).

DELAWARE, southernmost of the Middle Atlantic States of the United States, bounded on the N. by Pennsylvania, on the E. by the estuary of the Delaware R. (which separates it from New Jersey), Delaware Bay, and the

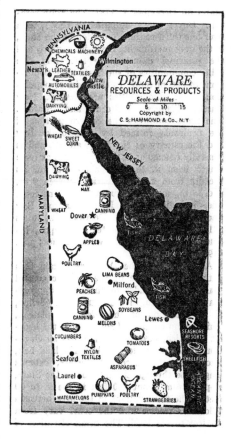

DELAWARE RESOURCES & PRODUCTS
Scale of Miles
0   5   10   15
Copyright by
C. S. HAMMOND & Co., N.Y.

Delaware State Archives

The State Capitol in Dover, Delaware

Atlantic Ocean, and on the s. and w. by Maryland. It ranks as the 47th State of the Union in area and 46th (1950) in population. It is the first of the thirteen original States, having ratified the Constitution of the United States on December 7, 1787. The State capital is Dover (q.v.). Wilmington (q.v.), with over one third of the population of the State, is the only metropolis, the chief seaport, and the principal industrial center. Only five other communities of the State have populations of 300 or more. In the order of population, these communities are Newark, New Castle, Elsmere, Milford, and Seaford. The State comprises the eastern portion of the peninsula formed by Chesapeake Bay and the estuary of the Delaware R., and is generally triangular in shape, with an extreme length from N. to s. of about 110 m. Its breadth from E. to w. varies between 9 m. and 35 m., averaging about 20 m. The coast line, including that along Delaware Bay and the estuary of the Delaware R., totals 381 m. Area of the State, 2057 sq.m., including 79 sq.m. of inland water surface; pop. (1950) 318,085.

About 95% of the Delaware terrain falls within the province of the Atlantic coastal plain; the remainder of the State, approximately 100 sq.m. in the extreme N. portion, is an extension of the Piedmont plateau. This section consists of rolling hills, the highest of which, near Centreville, has an elevation of about 440 feet. A broad upland belt, known as the Wicomico terrace, extends lengthwise through the interior of the State, sloping from about 100 feet in the N. to 60 feet in the s. Elevations in the area between Wicomico terrace and the coast vary from 40 feet to sea level. The mean elevation of

the State is 60 feet, the lowest of any State in the Union. Among other noteworthy features of the Delaware terrain are 50 fresh water lakes and extensive areas of tidal marshlands, notably Cypress Swamp (about 30,000 acres) in the extreme s. The forested areas of the State occupy about 225,000 acres. Delaware has numerous creeks and rivers, none of which is navigable by ocean-going vessels. The Christina and Brandywine rivers, the chief streams, have a common estuary, the harbor of Wilmington. The only other good harbors are those of New Castle and Lewes. A number of shallow bays or lagoons, separated from the ocean by sandy shoals, indent the coast line of the State. The largest of these are Rehoboth and Indian River bays, accessible to craft drawing less than six feet of water. Substantial portions of the coast, particularly in the vicinity of Cape Henlopen and Rehoboth Bay, afford excellent recreational opportunities, with facilities for salt-water fishing and bathing. Small game and waterfowl are abundant in southern Delaware. The State has six State forests, totaling 4318 acres, and two State parks, totaling 25 acres.

Delaware has a mild temperate climate, with a mean annual temperature of about 55 °F. Sharp seasonal variations occur, however. The average midsummer and midwinter temperatures are about 25 °F. and 85 °F., respectively. Prevailing winds are from the N.w. in winter and from the s.w. in summer. Precipitation averages between 40 and 45 inches annually, with the heaviest rainfall occurring in the coastal areas.

Of the total area of the State 67.2 percent is farmland, divided among 7748 farms (in 1950). About 80% of the cash income from farm products is derived from livestock, notably broiler chickens, the largest single source of farm income. Dairy cows, pigs, sheep, and horses are also raised in the State. The principal crops are fruits, notably apples and peaches, and corn, winter wheat, barley, oats, rye, hay, potatoes, tomatoes, yams, sweet potatoes, and soybeans. The total value of all farm products marketed in 1953 was estimated at $101,364,700.

The vast majority of the industrial establishments of Delaware are concentrated in New Castle County, in the northern portion of the State. This region, containing Wilmington and relatively near the coal and iron fields of Pennsylvania, contains a wide diversity of industries. Several of these, notably the manufacture of braided hose, are centered in the largest plants of their kind in the world. Numerous enterprises of the E. I. Du Pont de Nemours and Company, world-prominent manufacturers of diversified chemicals, are located in Wilmington and its environs, producing such products as explosives, plastics, synthetic rubber, rayon, nylon, dyestuffs, fertilizers, and paints. Of noteworthy importance among other industrial products of the State are vulcanized fiber products, iron and steel, ships, machinery, machine tools, railway equipment, hardware, paper, cotton textiles, and canned goods.

Delaware also has a flourishing fishing industry. In addition to large quantities of oysters, lobsters, clams, and other types of shellfish, taken in Delaware Bay, the catch includes such food fish as herring, shad, and striped bass. The total catch in 1951 amounted to 175,657,200 pounds. Productive mineral deposits in the State consist mainly of granite, sand, gravel, and kaolin; the total value of the mineral output in 1951 was $644,000.

The industrial region of the State is serviced by several major railways, including the Baltimore and Ohio, the Reading, and the Pennsylvania systems. Connections with other areas of Delaware are provided by the last-named line. Main-track mileage totaled 360 in 1953. The principal ports of the State are reached regularly by ocean-going vessels, particularly those in the coastwise and foreign trade en route to and from Philadelphia. The Chesapeake and Delaware Canal provides a short inland water route, navigable by deep-draft vessels, to Baltimore and other points on Chesapeake Bay. A total of 3974 miles of roads, including 3193 miles of surfaced highways, were maintained by the State in 1953. In the same year there were fifteen airfields and airports.

The name of the State of Delaware is derived from that of Lord De La Warr, captain general and governor of the colony of Virginia. He is credited with having visited, in 1611, the bay and river which also bear his name. At the time of De La Warr's visit, the region was inhabited by the Leni-Lenape (later called Delaware) Indians, one of the principal tribes of the Algonquian linguistic stock. In 1631, David Pietersen De Vries, an agent of the Dutch West India Company (q.v.), established a trading post near the site of present-day Lewes. Hostile Indians destroyed the settlement before the end of the year. The first successful attempt at colonization occurred in 1638, when a party of Swedish colonists, led by Peter Minuit (q.v.), settled on the site of what is now Wilmington. Minuit named the settlement Fort Christina, in honor of the daughter of the Swedish king Gustavus Adolphus, founder of the corporation that sponsored the colony. The surrounding territory was called New Sweden. Within the next ten years the Swedes established several additional settlements near Fort Christina. Although the Dutch regarded these activities as encroachments, they made no aggressive moves against the Swedes until 1651. In that year, Peter Stuyvesant (q.v.), governor of New Netherlands, established Fort Casimir on the site of present-day New Castle. The Swedes captured Fort Casimir in 1654. In the following year, Stuyvesant led a large expedition into New Sweden, seizing control of the entire territory. Dutch sovereignty over the region was terminated, in 1664, by the British seizure of New Netherlands. Except for the one-year period (1673–74) of renewed Dutch control, obtained by the recapture of New York, the region remained a British colonial possession until the American Revolution.

In 1682, William Penn (q.v.), founder of Pennsylvania, obtained a deed to the territory from the Duke of York (later James II), to whom the territory had been granted

Delaware State Archives

Old Immanuel Church, New Castle, built 1703

by Charles II. Termed the "Territories or Three Lower Counties on the Delaware", the region was administered for the next twenty years by the colonial authorities of Pennsylvania. The Three Counties were represented in the general assembly of Pennsylvania, but popular demands for greater local autonomy led to the establishment, in 1704, of a separate legislature. This was supplemented, six years later, by a separate executive council. However, executive control of the Three Counties was retained by the colonial governor of Pennsylvania. The Three Counties were established as "Delaware State" in 1776, following the outbreak of the American Revolution.

Nearly 5000 volunteers from Delaware fought in the war against Great Britain. The military detachments from the State were popularly known as the "Blue Hen's Chickens", a term said to be derived from the gamecocks hatched from the eggs of a famous blue hen and kept as mascots by a Delaware regiment. The American flag was officially displayed for the first time on land at Cooch's Bridge, Delaware. This event occurred on September 3, 1777, during a skirmish between British and American troops, the only Revolutionary battle fought in Delaware. By the terms of the constitution of 1792, "Delaware State" became officially known as the State of Delaware.

Considerable opposition to the War of 1812 developed in Delaware, where the Federalist Party (q.v.) was then predominant. During the controversy on the slavery issue, the Congressional delegation from Delaware, a slave State, supported the Missouri Compromise (q.v.) and other measures designed to avoid a rupture between the North and South. Pro-Southern sentiment was pronounced in the southern section of the State, but the overwhelming majority of the population was opposed to secession. When the rebellion finally began, the people of Delaware responded enthusiastically to President Lincoln's call for volunteers. Approximately 13,650 soldiers from the State served in the Union armies during the conflict. Several hundred volunteers, mainly from the southern areas, served in the Confederate armies.

The decade following the Civil War was a period of intensive industrial expansion in the northern section of the State, particularly around Wilmington. Despite this development, the economy of the State remained basically agrarian until the United States entered World War I. Industrial growth was especially rapid in New Castle County during the war, resulting in the first relative increase in the urban over the rural population of the State. By 1940 the urban population was 139,432, the rural, 127,073. The tercentenary of the founding of Fort Christina by the Swedes was celebrated at Wilmington in 1938. During World War II, a further expansion of industrial activity, notably shipbuilding, took place in the Wilmington area.

In national politics Delaware, a Democratic stronghold during most of the last half of the 19th century, has shown a marked preference for the Republican Party since 1896. Between that year and 1952 Democratic Presidential candidates carried the State in only four elections, those of 1912, 1936, 1940, and 1944. In 1952 the Republican candidate Dwight D. Eisenhower received 90,059 votes; his Democratic opponent Adlai E. Stevenson received 83,315 votes.

DELAWARE, county seat of Delaware Co., Ohio, situated on the Olentangy R., 24 miles N. of Columbus. Industries in the city are the manufacture of chairs, stoves, rubber goods, and tool and machine parts. Delaware is the birthplace of President Rutherford B. Hayes, and the site of Ohio Wesleyan University, a coeducational institution founded in 1841. Pop. (1950) 11,804.

DELAWARE AQUEDUCT, a part of the water supply system of New York City, carrying water to the city chiefly from the Delaware watershed. The aqueduct is part of the Delaware Water Supply System of the New York City Board of Water Supply.

The Delaware Water Supply System was originally planned in 1921 to supplement the various reservoirs in the Catskill Mountains and in Westchester County. It was designed to bring water from portions of the Delaware River and its tributaries lying in New York State in the vicinity of Port Jervis. The plan included the construction of reservoirs on the East Branch of the Delaware, on the Neversink River, and on Rondout Creek, a tributary of the Hudson River, and the construction of an 85-mile aqueduct connecting the Rondout Reservoir with Hillview Reservoir near New York City. Construction of the system was delayed until 1937 by lack of funds and by prolonged litigation with the States of New Jersey and Pennsylvania over the amount of water to be diverted from the Delaware River. A further delay in construction of the reservoirs and aqueduct occurred during World War II.

The aqueduct itself is a tunnel 13½ to 19

ft. in inside diameter, bored entirely through solid rock and lined with concrete. It passes beneath the Hudson River, and beneath the West Branch Reservoir and the Kensico Reservoir of the Catskill Water Supply System. The aqueduct is so planned that its flow can either bypass these reservoirs or pass through them.

Construction of the first section of the aqueduct, from Rondout Reservoir to West Branch Reservoir, was a difficult engineering feat because the route of the tunnel led almost entirely through strata of loose, water-bearing rock. For greater strength the tunnel in this section was enlarged to 24 ft. in diameter for approximately ninety percent of its length and a steel roof was set in place before the tunnel was lined with concrete. 800,000 tons of concrete were used in the tunnel lining in this section alone.

When the Delaware System has been completed, the aqueduct will carry approximately 540,000,000 gallons of water a day to New York City. Of this quantity 370,000,000 gallons will come from the Pepacton Reservoir on the East Branch of the Delaware, 70,-000,000 from the Neversink Reservoir, and 100,000,000 from the Rondout Reservoir. See AQUEDUCT.

DELAWARE BAY, an arm of the Atlantic Ocean, bounded on the N.E. by New Jersey and on the s.w. by Delaware. From its mouth, a channel about 12 m. wide between Cape May, N.J. and Cape Henlopen, Del., it extends generally northwestward to the mouth of the estuary of the Delaware R. Its length is approximately 50 m., and its width ranges from about 4 m., at the point of its confluence with the Delaware R. estuary, to about 30 m., at its central portion. The depth of the bay varies between 30 and 60 ft. In addition to the Delaware R., it receives the waters of numerous streams and creeks of New Jersey and Delaware. The bay has few natural harbors, but Delaware Breakwater, 1200 yards long, at Cape Henlopen, provides Lewes, Del., with an excellent, protected anchorage, 24 to 35 ft. deep. Delaware Bay is the natural route followed by shipping en route to and from Wilmington, Del., Philadelphia, Pa., Camden, N.J., and Baltimore, Md. The last-named port and other points on Chesapeake Bay are reached by means of the Chesapeake and Delaware Canal, a sea-level, inland waterway navigable by deep-draft vessels. The waters of Delaware Bay yield large annual catches of oysters, clams, crabs, and lobsters.

DELAWARE INDIANS, a tribe formerly inhabiting the regions surrounding the Delaware River. In their own language they were called *Leni-Lenape,* meaning "true men". They were of Algonquian stock, and were held in much esteem and respectfully addressed as "grandfather" by members of other Algonquian tribes. In 1720 they were conquered by the Iroquois, who dominated and harassed them until 1763. These attacks, combined with the increasing pressure of the settlements of the European colonists, drove them gradually westward. Today their numbers have been reduced to about 2000, most of whom reside in Oklahoma. See AMERICAN INDIAN.

DELAWARE RIVER, one of the major rivers of the eastern United States. Its sources are situated on the w. slopes of the Catskill Mountains, in Schoharie County, N.Y. There, the river consists of two branches, the chief of which, West Branch, flows in a south-westerly direction as far as Deposit, N.Y., then turns southeastward. From a point near Hale Eddy, N.Y., to Hancock, N.Y., it forms the boundary between Pennsylvania and New York. East Branch parallels the course of that portion of West Branch above Deposit. The confluence of the two branches is situated at Hancock, N.Y. From this point, the Delaware, flowing s.e., continues as the New York-Pennsylvania boundary as far as Port Jervis, N.Y., where it becomes the boundary between Pennsylvania and New Jersey, following a generally southward course to its outlet in Delaware Bay. The lower reaches of the river form part of the boundary between New Jersey and Delaware. In its descent from the Catskills, the Delaware traverses a region noted for its scenic beauty. Particularly outstanding is the Delaware Water Gap (q.v.). Among the important tributaries of the Delaware are the Neversink, Callicoon, and Mongaup rivers, in New York; the Lehigh, Schuylkill, and Lackawaxen rivers, in Pennsylvania; and the Maurice and Musconetcong rivers, in New Jersey. The Delaware has a total length of about 360 m., and drains an area of about 12,000 sq.m. It is a source of hydroelectric power and an important water highway, navigable by ocean-going vessels as far inland as Philadelphia, Pa., and by shallow-draft vessels to Trenton, N.J. A canal extends from Trenton to New Brunswick, N.J., on the Raritan R. The Chesapeake and Delaware Canal, navigable by ocean-going vessels, connects the Delaware, at a point below Wilmington, Del., with Chesapeake Bay.

DELAWARE, UNIVERSITY OF, a State institution of higher learning, with co-ordinate colleges for men and women, located in Newark, Del. It was established in 1743, and under the name of Newark Academy in 1769 received a charter from Thomas and Richard Penn, sons of William Penn and proprietary governors of the territory of Pennsylvania, which at that time included part of the present State of Delaware. The school came to be known as Newark College in 1833, but was soon renamed Delaware College and became a Land Grant college (q.v.) in 1870. Through large gifts, received from public and private sources after 1915, its facilities were expanded, and in 1921 the institution became a university. Its schools and departments include agriculture, arts, engineering, home economics, and teaching. In 1953–54 the enrollment was 4204, including 1818 full-time students; the faculty numbered 210.

DELAWARE WATER GAP, the name of two localities on the Delaware River. **1.** The gorge of the Delaware R. through the Kittatinny Range of the Appalachian Mountains, situated on the Pennsylvania-New Jersey boundary, about 3 miles E. of Stroudsburg, Pa. The gorge, about 2 miles long and 1500 feet deep, ranks among the scenic wonders of the United States, and is interesting geologically, exposing Devonian, Silurian, and Ordovician strata. **2.** A borough and summer resort of Monroe County, Pa., adjoining the Delaware Water Gap and about 108 m. by rail N. of Philadelphia. Pop. (1950) 734.

DELBRÜCK, HANS (1848–1929), German historian, born at Bergen, on the island of Rügen, and educated at the universities of Heidelberg and Bonn. In 1882 and 1883 he was a member of the Prussian diet, and from 1884 to 1890 he was a member (Conservative) of the Reichstag. He was appointed professor of modern history at the University of Berlin in 1885. His writings on history and military science had a strong nationalist tendency, and he was an important member of the school of German historians which attempted to exculpate Germany from responsibility for World War I. His works include *Geschichte der Kriegskunst im Rahmen der Politischen Geschichte* (5 parts, 1900–27) ; *Weltgeschichte* (3 vols., 1923–26) ; and *Vor und Nach dem Weltkriege* (1926).

DELCASSÉ, THÉOPHILE (1852–1923), French statesman, born at Pamiers, department of Ariège. He began his political career as a writer on politics and foreign affairs for French newspapers and periodicals. He was elected to the Chamber of Deputies in 1889, became minister of colonies in 1893, and was minister of foreign affairs from 1898 to 1905. In the last-mentioned office he exerted a profound influence on European politics. His policy was designed to bring about an alliance of France, Great Britain, and Russia to counterbalance the Triple Alliance (q.v.) already existing among Germany, Austria, and Italy. In pursuit of this aim, Delcassé was instrumental in settling peaceably (1899) a dispute between France and Great Britain which, culminating in the Fashoda incident (q.v.) in the Egyptian Sudan, had almost brought about war between the two nations. In 1904 he negotiated an agreement with Great Britain over conflicting claims in the Nile Valley and Central Africa (see FRANCE: *History*). This agreement led to a friendly understanding between the two nations, the Entente Cordiale, which in turn paved the way for the Triple Entente (qq.v.) involving France, Great Britain, and Russia (1907). Although Delcassé was largely responsible for the Triple Entente, he was forced to resign as foreign minister, in 1905, before his policy had reached its full fruition. His resignation was considered a necessary concession to Germany, which threatened war in its dispute with France over the extent of France's authority in Morocco (q.v.). In 1906 he was re-elected to the Chamber of Deputies. He served as minister of marine from 1910 to 1911, and as ambassador to Russia from 1913 to 1914. In the Ministry of National Defense formed in 1914 at the outbreak of World War I, he became minister of foreign affairs for the second time. During this term of office he played an important part in the diplomatic moves that persuaded Italy to desert the Triple Alliance and join the Allies (1915) ; but he was forced to resign in 1915 because of serious errors in policy made in regard to Balkan affairs. Despite his failures, Delcassé is generally regarded as one of the ablest of French foreign ministers of the period of the Third Republic.

DELEDDA, GRAZIA (1875–1936), Italian novelist, winner of the Nobel Prize for literature in 1926, born at Nuoro, Sardinia. Her works realistically reflect the conditions of peasant life in Sardinia; among them are *Racconti Sardi* (1893), a collection of short stories; *Il Vecchio della Montagna* (1900) ; *Il Nonno* (1909) ; *La Madre* (1920) ; *La Fuga in Egitto* (1926) ; *Annalena Bilsini* (1928).

DELEGATE, APOSTOLIC. See LEGATE.

Netherlands Information Bureau

Bridge near the east gate in the town of Delft, the Netherlands

DE LESSEPS, VICOMTE FERDINAND MARIE. See LESSEPS, VICOMTE FERDINAND MARIE DE.

DELFT, town of the Netherlands, in South Holland Province, on the Schie R., 8 miles N.W. of Rotterdam. It was famous in the 17th and 18th centuries for its pottery, called delft-ware. The principal manufactures in the present-day town are chemicals, tobacco products, carpets, cloth, soap, mathematical instruments, pottery (called new delft), and leather. In Delft is the Institute of Technology, the leading engineering school of the Netherlands. The town is intersected by canals, and contains a number of notable buildings, including the Prinsenhof, now a museum, where William I of Orange was assassinated in 1584; the Old Church, founded in the 11th century; and the New Church, dating from the 14th century, and noted for its tall Gothic tower and set of chimes. The town hall (1618) contains portraits by Michiel van Mierevelt (1567–1641). Delft was founded in the 11th century; it suffered great damage in 1536 by fire, and in 1654 by the explosion of a powder magazine. Pop. (1953 est.) 67,186.

DELGADA. See PONTA DELGADA.

DELHI, Centrally Administered Area of the Union of India. It consists of a narrow strip of territory along each bank of the Jumna R. The capital is Delhi (q.v.), or Old Delhi. Originally a part of the Punjab, the tract on the W. bank of the Jumna was created a separate province in 1912, when the seat of government of British India was transferred from Calcutta to Delhi. The tract on the E. bank was added to the province in 1915; it was formerly a part of Meerut Division, United Provinces. Area, 574 sq.m.; pop. (1951) 1,743,992.

DELHI or **OLD DELHI,** capital of the Centrally Administered Area of Delhi, Union of India, situated on the W. bank of the Jumna R., about 10 miles N. of New Delhi. The city is about 956 m. by rail N.W. of Calcutta and about 982 m. by rail N.N.E. of Bombay. Delhi occupies an elevated site, with slightly more than 2¼ m. of river frontage. It was built in 1639–48 on and near the sites of several earlier cities as the capital of Hindustan by the Mogul emperor Shah Jahan (q.v.). Delhi is enclosed by a high wall, 5½ m. long. Seven arched gateways give access to the city. Mogul architecture was at the zenith of its development when Delhi was constructed and the city contains many notable edifices, especially the Imperial Palace, now known as "the Fort". This structure, completed in 1648, consists of

British Information Services

IN OLD DELHI, INDIA

*Above: Crowds on a busy street, seen from
the steps of the Jama Masjid Mosque.
Left: Inner yard of Jama Masjid Mosque.*

a group of buildings surrounded by high walls, including river battlements. Among the most interesting of the buildings are the Hall of Public Audience, or Diwan-i-am, and the Hall of Private Audience, or Diwan-i-khas. The first, a vast chamber with a flat roof supported by 60 columns of red sandstone, served as the emperor's throne room. There was located the solid gold Peacock Throne, inlaid with precious gems. Its value was estimated at about $30,000,000. The Hall of Private Audience, constructed chiefly of white marble and considered a masterpiece of Hindu ornamentation, abounds with delicately executed inlays. An inscription in Persian characters in the hall has been translated as follows: "If there is a heaven on earth, it is this —it is this". Another imposing structure erected during the reign of Shah Jahan, the Jama Masjid, or Great Mosque, is one of the finest buildings of its kind in India. The mosque, 261 feet in length and situated on an elevated site near Chandni Chauk, the central thoroughfare of the city, is mainly of white marble and red sandstone. A minaret, 150 feet high, commands each of its two front corners, and between these are three lofty domes. Of special interest among other mosques in Delhi is the Pearl Mosque, built by Aurangzeb, son of Shah Jahan. Delhi also has several modern buildings of note, including the Protestant church of St. James, the former Vice-regal Lodge, the former Residency, and the Cambridge Mission and Hospital.

Scattered among the ruins in the environs of Delhi are a number of other interesting structures, including the tomb of Humayum, second Mogul emperor of Hindustan; the Iron Pillar, a shaft of inscribed wrought iron nearly 24 feet high and 16 feet in diameter, which dates from 400 A.D.; and the Kutb Minar, a tower 238 feet in height, of beautiful design, dating from about 1200.

Delhi is a busy commercial city, serviced by several railway systems. It has a flourishing trade in produce from the surrounding agricultural region, and in precious stones, Cashmere and Cabul shawls, horses, and local manufactures. The last-named include jewelry, a product for which the city has long been famous; cotton textiles; glazed pottery; carved ivory products; silver, brass, and copper ware; flour; and sugar. Delhi also has a modern electrolytic alkali plant which has a daily output of about 5 tons of liquid chlorine.

According to legend, Delhi was founded in the 15th century B.C. The name of the city, however, appears in history for the first time in the 1st century B.C. The city did not figure prominently in Indian history until the 11th century A.D., when a fort was established there by a warlike tribe, the Tomaras. In 1052 the chief of this tribe, Anangapala, had the Iron Pillar brought from its original site, believed to be Muttra, and erected in Delhi. Captured by Moslems in 1193, the city became the capital of the Mohammedan domain in India. Moslem control of Delhi ended with its capture and destruction toward the close of the 14th century by the Mongol conqueror Tamerlane. Although the Moslems subsequently regained the city, they were expelled, about the middle of the 15th century, by the Afghans, who established their capital at Agra. The Afghans were in turn expelled, in 1526, by Baber (q.v.), a descendant of Tamerlane and founder of the Mogul dynasty of India. His son Humayun later re-established Delhi as the Mogul capital. In 1540 the city

was seized by the Afghan king Sher Shah, who completely rebuilt it. Humayun regained Delhi in 1555, but his son and successor Akbar (q.v.) allowed it to fall into decay.

Following the reconstruction of Delhi during the reign of Shah Jahan, the city continued as the Mogul capital until 1739, when it fell to the Persian ruler Nadir Shah. He sacked it of most of its treasures, including the Peacock Throne. About 1771 the Marathas (q.v.) acquired control of the city, which remained under their overlordship until British forces captured it in September, 1803. Delhi was a center of the Indian mutiny (q.v.) of 1857. The city became the administrative center of the newly established province of the same name in 1912. It was the capital of British India from 1912 to 1929, when the seat of government was transferred to New Delhi. Pop. (1951) 914,790.

DELIAN LEAGUE, or CONFEDERATION OF DELOS, a federation of city-states of ancient Greece. The league was founded in 478 B.C. after the Persian attempt to invade Greece (see PERSIAN WARS) failed. Its main purpose at that time was to prepare against a possible renewal of aggression by Persia, and since it appeared probable that such aggression might come by sea rather than by land, Athens as the greatest sea power in Greece became the leading member of the league. The headquarters of the league were on the island of Delos, and each of the member states, which at one time numbered over two hundred, made a contribution in proportion to its capacity. As time passed, fewer of the allies in the league contributed men and ships, most of them substituting money payments which became in effect tribute to Athens. As this trend continued, and as the program of the league gradually changed from that of preparedness against Persia to that of strengthening Athens, the alliance of sovereign states was transformed into what modern scholars call the Athenian Empire.

All but three of the allies were paying their contribution in money by 449 B.C., when the Peace of Callias ended the war against Persia. Five years earlier the treasury had been moved from Delos to Athens, and the following year several city-states on the Greek mainland, having nothing to fear from Persia but much to gain by winning Athenian support, joined the league. From this period until the conclusive defeat of Athens by Sparta in the Peloponnesian War (q.v.) in 404 B.C., the members of the league were subject to Athens in foreign policy and were prevented from seceding by force of arms. After the conquest of Athens, the league disintegrated, but it was reconstituted in 377 B.C. by those states which feared Spartan power. Following the conclusion of peace with Sparta (371) the league again became a group of Athenian subject states, but Athens was no longer able to enforce its authority and the membership of the league constantly fluctuated. After Philip of Macedon defeated the Athenians at Chæronea in 338 B.C., the league ceased to exist.

Modern scholars have studied the organization of the Delian League and the changing relationships of the members with great interest, because this organization is the first example in history of a federal alliance of sovereign states maintained over a long period, and in one of its phases is the first example of what has become known as imperialism.

DELIBES, CLÉMENT PHILIBERT LÉO (1836–91), French composer, born in St.-Germain du-Val. He studied music at the Paris Conservatory, and began his career by writing operettas and comic operas for the French commercial theater (1855–1869). In 1866, while serving as second chorus-master at the Opéra, he established his reputation as a writer of ballet music by the music he contributed to the ballet *La Source,* which he composed in collaboration with the Polish composer Minkous. In 1870 Delibes composed the ballet *Coppélia,* his masterpiece; and in 1876, the mythological ballet *Sylvia.* He also composed a number of grand operas, one of which, the five-act opera *Lakmé* (1883), still holds the stage. His works also include a book of songs (1872), which contains the well-known melodies *Bonjour, Suzon* and *Les Filles de Cadiz.*

DELILAH (Heb., "delicate"), in the Bible, the Philistine paramour of Samson (q.v.), the Danite, whom she betrayed to her people when bribed by the "lords of the Philistines" (Judges 16:4–31).

DELIRIUM, a temporary condition, common in many illnesses, in which the sufferer is disoriented and incoherent and may have hallucinations and delusions. Any disease causing high fever may bring on delirium. In severe cases, the victim may be maniacal and require physical restraint. Delirium is a symptom rather than a disease, and hence is not treated by any specific measures other than those used to combat the causative disease and to reduce the patient's fever. Delirium may be due to causes other than high

fever. See, for example, DELIRIUM TREMENS.

DELIRIUM TREMENS, acute organic disorder occurring frequently as a symptom of alcoholic intoxication (q.v) and chronic alcoholism (q.v.). The seizures generally last from 3 to 6 days and are characterized by terrifying hallucinations and violent tremors. The patient is disoriented and usually incoherent in speech; the tremors are so physically exhausting that the condition, if untreated, may be fatal. Present-day treatment includes intensive sedation, nutritive therapy designed to restore normal metabolism, and the administration of ACTH (q.v.). A new sedative known as chlorpromazine (q.v.) was reported in 1954 to have very favorable results in the treatment of delirium tremens.

DELIUS, FREDERICK (1863–1934), English composer, born in Bradford, Yorkshire, of German parents. He exhibited musical talent as a child, but his parents intended him for a commercial career. Unwilling to follow their desires, Delius went to the United States and became an orange grower in Florida (1884–86), where he studied music with Thomas F. Ward, an organist of Jacksonville, and by himself. Subsequently he studied at the Leipzig Conservatory. In 1888 Edvard Grieg, the Norwegian composer, persuaded Delius' father to permit Frederick to follow a musical career; two years later Delius settled in Paris, receiving financial aid from an uncle living in that city. The music of Delius received its early appreciation in Germany, mainly through performances under the German conductor Hans Haym. Later, the efforts of Sir Thomas Beecham (q.v.), the English conductor, made the music well known in Great Britain and, mainly through phonograph records, in the United States. The music of Delius is characterized by poetic atmosphere and subtle evocation of moods, and by lyric and rich harmonic qualities rather than by contrapuntal or rhythmic values. Among his works are the operas *Koanga* (1895–97), *A Village Romeo and Juliet* (1900–01), an excerpt from which, *The Walk to the Paradise Garden,* receives frequent orchestral performances today; and *Fennimore and Gerda* (1910); the incidental music (1921) to the play *Hassan* by the English poet H. J. E. Flecker; the works for orchestra *Over the Hills and Far Away* (1895), *Paris: The Song of a Great City* (1899), *Brigg Fair* (1907), *In a Summer Garden* (1908), *On Hearing the First Cuckoo in Spring* (1912), and *Eventyr* (1917); the choral works *Appalachia* (1902) and *A Mass of Life* (1904–05); concertos, including the *Concerto for Violin and Orchestra* (1916) ; chamber music; and songs.

DELIVERY. See OBSTETRICS.

DELLA ROBBIA. See ROBBIA, LUCA DELLA.

DELOS, an island in the s: Ægean Sea, situated 2 miles w. of Mykonos Island. Delos is the smallest of the Cyclades group, having an area of about 2 sq.m. It is now uninhabited, but in ancient times was famous as a shrine of Apollo and as a trading center of the early Greeks and Romans. According to mythology, Delos was at first a floating island, but was chained by Zeus to the bottom of the sea in order that it might become a safe home for Leto during the birth of Apollo and Artemis.

The earliest historical inhabitants of the island were Ionians, who made it the site of a periodical festival in honor of Apollo. A confederation of Greek states, called the Delian League (q.v.) or Confederacy of Delos, was founded with headquarters on the island in 478 B.C. In 426 B.C., when the Athenians were in ascendancy over the Delians, the island was purified, for religious purposes, by removal from it of all tombs, and it was declared that no birth or death should occur on the sacred spot. Delos was independent from 322 to 166 B.C., when the Romans restored control of religious worship to the Athenians and also permitted the island to become the seat of extensive commerce and a large slave market. The great festival at Delos and the situation of the island on the direct route from southern Europe to the coasts of Asia combined to make it a port highly favored by merchants. Delos was sacked, however, in the Mithridatic War (87 B.C.), and never fully recovered its prestige and prosperity.

The town of Delos, which stood at the foot of Mt. Cynthus, a granite crag about 380 ft. high, is now a mass of ruins. However, the remains of the great temple of Apollo, and of the colossal statue raised in his honor, may still be traced. Extensive excavations, begun in 1877 by the French School at Athens, have revealed many of the porticos and altars of the sacred precinct; and also the wharves and the warehouses, the bazaars of the merchants, the theater, the gymnasium, and a number of private houses apparently belonging to the prosperous period of the 2nd century B.C. The island has yielded some important statues of the 6th century B.C., such as the "Nike" by Archermus of Chios and female figures similar to those found on the Acropolis of Athens. Relics of a later period in Greek art include a fighting warrior and a fine copy of the "Diadumenos" of Polyclitus. Among the excavated materials are numerous inscriptions, showing not only the long lists of treasures of the temple and the decrees and dedications common to sanctuaries, but also important financial accounts of the temple that show how a Greek shrine was administered in antiquity.

DELOS, CONFEDERACY OF. See DELIAN LEAGUE.

DELPHI, a town of ancient Greece, celebrated for its oracle of Apollo (q.v.). The site is now occupied by Delphoi (pop. in 1940, 998), in the department of Phthiotis and Phocis. Delphi was situated on the s. slope of Mt. Parnassus, in the province of Phocis, about 6 m. inland from an indentation in the N. shore of the Gulf of Corinth. The town occupied a terrace on the steep slopes of the valley of the Pleistos R. Historic landmarks in the vicinity include the fountain of Castalia and, about 7 m. to the N., the famed Corycian Cave, now called "Forty Courts". Little is known regarding the origin of Delphi. Evidence exists that an oracle of Gæa (q.v.), goddess of the earth, was located on its site in very ancient times. In Greek mythology, Apollo expelled Gæa from the sanctuary, which he shared with Dionysus (q.v.).

Delphi is always referred to in the Homeric poems as Pytho. This name is derived from Python, the monstrous serpent which Apollo slew on Parnassus. According to some accounts, the founders of Delphi were Cretans, brought to the site by Apollo and designated by him as priests. In the course of time, the latter developed an elaborate ritual, centered around a chief priestess whose title was Pythia. Her utterances, solemnly regarded as the words of Apollo, were recorded by priestly poets and transcribed into hexameter verse. The oracle was consulted by kings and public officials on matters of national policy, and by private citizens on various personal problems, such as marriage and business ventures. As the fame of the Delphic oracle increased, Delphi grew in wealth and importance. Prosperous visitors, one of whom was Crœsus (q.v.), contributed rich offerings to the town. The Sacred Way to the temple was lined with structures containing treasures given by the various cities of Greece.

At first, as the Homeric Hymn to Apollo implies, the town was a dependency of the Phocian city of Crisa (Crissa; Cirrha). Phocis subsequently became a member of the Amphictyonic League (q.v.), which assumed

Temple ruin of the ancient town of Delphi

responsibility for the protection of Delphi. As a result of the Phocian practice of levying tribute on pilgrims en route to the oracle, the League (about 595 B.C.) began the first of the Sacred Wars against Phocis, destroying Crisa. Shortly afterward, the first of the Pythian Games (q.v.) was held near Delphi. The Persians attempted a raid on the town in 480 B.C. This venture ended in failure, chiefly because of an earthquake, which was attributed to Apollo. Another of the Sacred Wars, directed again at the Phocians, who had seized Delphi, was fought between 357 and 346 B.C. The Phocians were finally defeated by Philip II of Macedon, father of Alexander the Great. Toward the end of the 4th century B.C., Delphi passed under the control of the Ætolian League (see ÆTOLIA). During the years that followed, the wealth and splendor of the town invited attack from various quarters, including a raid by Gauls in 279 B.C. After the conquest of Greece by Rome, Delphi steadily declined in importance, although the oracle continued to function. Much of the art and treasure of the town was confiscated by the Romans, notably the emperor Nero, who removed 500 bronze statues. By the end of the Roman era, Delphi had ceased to exist.

The site of the town was eventually occupied by the village of Castri. In 1891, the French government, in support of the archeological work of the French School of Athens, financed the removal of Castri to a new site. Excavation of the site of Delphi began in the following year. Among the numerous discoveries are remnants of several temples and treasury buildings, the stadium and theater (both excellently preserved), the Great Altar, the ancient wall (called Hellenico) that surrounded the town, a number of sculptures and other works of art, and more than 4000 valuable inscriptions. Data obtained from these inscriptions have contributed to modern knowledge of ancient Greece.

DELPHINIDAE. See DOLPHIN.

DELPHINIUM. See LARKSPUR.

DEL RIO, county seat of Val Verde Co., Tex., 154 miles w. of San Antonio, and about 4 m. from the Rio Grande, where an international bridge crosses to Villa Acuna, Mexico. Del Rio is a port of entry and contains offices of the U.S. customs, immigration, and border-patrol services. The city is noted as a shipping center for the largest lamb- and wool-producing county in the United States. Average annual shipments are 12,000,000 pounds of wool and 400,000 lambs. Cattle, goats, and mohair (about 3,000,000 pounds annually) also are shipped from Del Rio, and the city contains two wineries and establishments producing saddles and leather goods. Near the city limits is San Felipe Springs, producing 100,000,000 gallons of water daily and furnishing the municipal water supply as well as irrigating several thousand acres of land. Del Rio was founded in 1872. It has a commission form of government. Pop. (1950) 14,211.

DELTA, the deposit (q.v.) of soil or silt formed wherever a swift stream or river empties into a lake, ocean, or slower river, so called because its triangular shape resembles the Greek letter Δ (delta). The triangular shape and the great width at the base are due to the blocking of the river mouth by silt, with resulting continual formation of distributaries at angles to the original course. Many of the world's largest rivers have built up extensive deltas. These are usually characterized by the high fertility of their soil. The delta of the Mississippi is about 12,500 sq.m. in extent, and the combined delta of the Ganges and Brahmaputra rivers in India has an area of over 50,000 sq.m. The Nile delta in Egypt is about 200 m. wide at its base and 100 m. long.

DELUGE, in Biblical history, the flood of waters, described in Genesis, 6, 7, 8, and 9, that inundated the entire earth or a large part of it. The only survivors were the occupants of the Ark, a vessel with a beam of 87.5 feet, and a length of 525 feet, built by Noah at God's command. On the Ark, besides Noah, were his wife, his three sons and their wives, and mated pairs of every species of animal. The narrative of the Deluge, as contained in Genesis, consists of two inter-woven versions, the Yahwist and Elohimic. Except on the reason for the flood, which is attributed to God's anger at man's wicked-ness, the two versions are frequently contra-dictory or divergent. According to the Yahwist sections of the narrative, for example, the flood is caused by a rain lasting forty days. Noah sends out a raven at the end of this period, but it fails to return. He then re-leases a dove, which returns with an olive twig. Sent out again seven days later, the dove does not return. Noah disembarks after another seven-day interval, builds an altar, and offers a sacrifice. God smells the "rest-giving odor" and promises not to destroy the world again. In the Elohimic sections of this part of the narrative, the flood is accom-panied by an upsurge of subterranean waters. It increases in intensity for 150 days, or five months of a solar year, and begins to recede in the seventh month. The Ark then grounds on one of the mountains of Ararat. On the first day of the next solar year, Noah leaves the Ark and is blessed by God, who causes a rainbow to appear as a token of his cove-nant that a flood shall not occur again.

Flood stories similar to the Biblical nar-rative are found in the folklore and traditions of a number of ancient nations, notably Babylon. There are two preserved Babylonian stories, the best-known of which, the Gil-gamesh Epic, dating from about 3000 B.C., bears a remarkable resemblance to the story in Genesis. In certain important aspects the stories differ, however. Thus, the Babylonian hero Ut-napishtim has deeper concern than Noah for the preservation of civilization and loads his craft with treasure and skilled arti-sans, as well as with animals. The Biblical narrative, on the other hand, has a profounder religious and ethical content than the Gil-gamesh epic. Although a number of scholars have concluded that the Biblical narrative is derived from the Babylonian story, it is pos-sible that each was taken from a common earlier source now lost.

Events similar to those described in the Biblical story also occur in Greek mythology; see DEUCALION. Among other peoples whose folklore and legends contain accounts of a devastating deluge are the peoples of southern Asia, the aborigines of North, Central, and South America, and the natives of Polynesia. The Chinese and Japanese have stories of floods, but these do not, as a rule, destroy the entire earth. Curiously enough, flood leg-ends do not occur among the ancient inhabi-tants of the Nile valley, and are not common anywhere else in Africa, or in Europe. The opinion of most authorities is that all legend-ary accounts of a universal deluge originated in local catastrophes caused by tidal waves, cloudbursts, or prolonged rainfalls.

DEMAND AND SUPPLY. See SUPPLY AND DEMAND.

DEMARCATION, LINE OF, the boundary established by Pope Alexander VI on May 4, 1493 to define the spheres of Spanish and Portuguese possessions in the New World. It ran due north and south 100 leagues west of the Azores. All new lands discovered east of this line were to belong to Portugal; all of those to the west, to Spain. Dissatisfaction with this arrangement on the part of Portu-gal led to the Convention of Tordesillas be-tween Portugal and Spain, in which a new line of demarcation, sanctioned by Pope Julius II in 1506, was set 370 leagues west of the Cape Verde Islands. As a result of this change, Brazil became Portuguese. The line of demarcation, and all agreements based on it, were abrogated in 1750 by a treaty settling a dispute over the southwestern boundary of Brazil. The 1750 treaty was in turn abrogated in 1761, and disputes between the Portuguese and Spanish over spheres of possession were settled by a new treaty in 1779.

DEMAVEND, MOUNT, extinct volcano of Iran, 50 miles N.E. of Teheran. It extends 18,603 ft. above sea level, and is the loftiest peak of the Elburz mountain range. The sum-mit is conical and the crater still intact. At the base are many hot springs giving evi-dence of volcanic heat comparatively near the surface of the earth. Demavend was first as-cended by a European, William T. Thompson, in 1837. Sulfur and pumice are mined in the Demavend crater.

DEMENTIA. See PSYCHOLOGY, ABNORMAL.

DEMESNE. See FEUDALISM.

DEMETER, in Greek mythology, one of the major divinities, goddess of agriculture and rural life, and of marriage. She was the daugh-ter of Cronus and Rhea. By her brother Zeus she became the mother of Persephone, who, without the knowledge of Demeter, was given by Zeus to Pluto. Demeter left Olympus in search of her daughter, not to return until Persephone was restored, and wandered upon the earth bestowing blessings or punishment according to her reception. Fearing the de-struction of the human race by famine, Zeus sent Hermes into Erebus to obtain Perseph-one, who was freed only after it had been agreed that she spend part of each year with Pluto. The Romans identified Demeter with their goddess Ceres.

DE MILLE, Cecil B(lount) (1881–   ), American actor, playwright, and motion picture director and producer, a son of Henry Churchill De Mille, born at Ashfield, Mass., and educated at the Pennsylvania Military College and the American Academy of Dramatic Arts. He was an actor from 1900 to 1902, and then turned to the writing of plays, including *The Return of Peter Grimm* and *Who Laughs Last.* In 1904 he became a theatrical manager and, nine years later, entered upon his career in the film industry. He helped to organize the Jesse L. Lasky Feature Play Company, and served as its director-general. In that capacity he produced the first motion picture made in Hollywood, *The Squaw Man* (1913), which, because of its subject (the marriage of an English nobleman to an American Indian), created a furore. He established and became president of Cecil B. De Mille Productions, Inc. in 1921, and in succeeding years became known as a master of techniques involving the depiction of lavish spectacles and battle scenes. The De Mille company became a subsidiary of Paramount Pictures, Inc., in 1932. In 1950 the Academy of Motion Picture Arts and Sciences gave De Mille a special award for his thirty-seven years of service to the film industry. Among films produced by De Mille are *The Ten Commandments* (1923), *The King of Kings* (1927), *The Sign of the Cross* (1932), *Cleopatra* (1934), *The Plainsman* (1936), *The Story of Dr. Wassell* (1944), *Unconquered* (1947), *Samson and Delilah* (1949), and *The Greatest Show on Earth* (1952). In addition to his work in films, De Mille also produced, from 1936 to 1945, weekly radio plays.

DEMOCRACY (Gr. *demos,* "the people"; *kratein,* "to rule"), rule by the people, which may be embodied in a variety of governmental forms. In modern democracies supreme authority is exercised by representatives who are elected and may be supplanted in accordance with popular will, expressed by law, and are, at least in theory, directly responsible to the electorate. These representatives may include the legislators and the executive head of the government, as in a republic (q.v.), or only the legislators, as in the constitutional monarchies of the United Kingdom and Norway.

Rule by the people played an important part in the pre-Christian Era. The democracies of the city-states of classical Greece and of Rome in the early years of the Republic (see Co-

mitia), were unlike the democracies of today. They were absolute democracies in which all citizens could speak and vote in assemblies. Representative government was unknown and, because of the smallness (almost never more than 10,000 citizens) of the city-states, unnecessary. Ancient democracy did not presuppose equality of all individuals; because of the prevalence of slavery, the majority of the populace had no political rights. Athens (q.v.), greatest of the city democracies, limited its franchise to native-born citizens. Roman democracy was similar to that of the Greeks, though Rome granted citizenship to men of non-Roman descent. The Roman Stoic philosophy (q.v.), which defined man as part of a divine principle, and the Jewish and Christian religions, which emphasized the rights of the poor and underprivileged and the equality of all men before God, contributed to the development of modern democratic theory.

Although the Roman Republic ended in the despotism of the Empire, the independent cities of Italy, Germany, and Flanders had forms of democracy during the Middle Ages. Slavery ceased to be a major factor in national populations and, as feudalism ended, a rich commercial middle class arose, having the money and leisure necessary for participation in governmental affairs. One result was the rebirth of a spirit of freedom based on ancient Greek and Roman principles. The Renaissance with its concentration on Humanism (q.v.), followed by the Reformation and its fight for freedom in religious matters, added further concepts of the political and social rights of every man.

Beginning with the first popular rebellion against monarchy in England (1642), which was brought to a climax by the execution of Charles I, political and revolutionary action against autocratic governments has resulted in the establishment of modern democratic governments. Such action was largely inspired and guided by political philosophers, notably John Milton, John Locke, Thomas Paine, Thomas Jefferson, and Karl Marx. Before the end of the 19th century, every important Western European monarchy had adopted a constitution limiting the power of the crown and giving a considerable share of political power to its people. In many of them, a representative legislature modeled on the British Parliament was instituted. Indeed, British modern political history has been possibly the greatest single influence on the organization of world democracies.

The major features of modern democracy

include personal freedom, which entitles each citizen to the liberty and responsibility of shaping his own career; equality before the law; and universal suffrage and education. Such features have been expressed in the great documents of history; as, for example, the guarantees of the right to life, liberty, and the pursuit of happiness, in the Declaration of Independence, and the four freedoms expressed in the Atlantic Charter (q.v.).

By the middle of the 20th century, every independent country in the world, with minor exceptions, had a government which, in form at least, was democratic. See CONSTITUTION; COMMUNISM; GOVERNMENT; VOTE; SUFFRAGE; SOCIAL LEGISLATION; SOCIALISM.

DEMOCRATIC PARTY, one of the two major political parties in the United States. It has existed under that name since 1829, the first year of the administration of Andrew Jackson. During the 1828 political campaign, the Democratic-Republican Party, which had been founded in 1792 by Thomas Jefferson as the Republican Party, split into two factions. One faction, known as the National Republican Party, lasted only a few years after its defeat in the 1828 election; the other faction became the present Democratic Party and supported the political principles advanced by Jefferson.

Policies. These principles, which are still collectively known as Jeffersonian democracy, include the strictest possible interpretation of the Constitution of the U.S.; a broad interpretation of State rights (q.v.); a minimum of executive action by the Federal government; and advocacy of individualistic, or laissez-faire (q.v.), economic and political activity. However, since the administration of Woodrow Wilson (1913–21), to a limited extent, and particularly since the administration of Franklin D. Roosevelt (1933–45), the Democratic Party has abandoned its traditional opposition to action by the Federal government regulating the economic life of the country, and now regards such action as frequently desirable. Moreover, every President elected on the basis of the Jeffersonian principles written into the party platform has departed from strict interpretation of these principles according to the needs of the time in which he has served; for example, the transaction of the Louisiana Purchase (q.v.) by President Jefferson in 1803 was in no way authorized by the Constitution.

Others of the important planks in successive Democratic platforms include, since the platform of 1888, advocacy of a low tariff (q.v.),

essentially for revenue purposes; and, since the platform of 1920, advocacy of active participation by the U.S. in international political affairs, as in the League of Nations and the United Nations.

History. Although Jefferson's Republican Party declared itself for popular self-government, its leaders, until 1829, were men who were aristocrats by birth and breeding. After the election of Jackson, who came from a lower economic class, the people as a whole began to participate actively in party politics. Jackson built the first large American political machine and introduced a "spoils system" (q.v.), the rewarding of party service by public office. His administration followed Jeffersonian principles closely; one of Jackson's most important and successful struggles with Congress was caused by his veto of the bill to recharter the Second Bank of the United States, which he regarded as an instrument of monopoly and privilege.

After the administration of Martin Van Buren (1837–41) and the end of Jackson's leadership of the Democratic Party, Southern interests began to dominate the party. The Southerners regarded the increasingly important slavery question as the province of the individual States and not of the Federal government, and they wished to consider it settled by the Compromise Measures of 1850 (q.v.). Slavery, however, became the most pressing issue in the United States and, when the Democratic convention of 1860 refused to pass proslavery resolutions, half the Southern delegates formed their own convention with a separate ticket.

After the American Civil War, the Southern States became and, generally, remained adherents of the Democratic Party because of their opposition to the Republican administration of Abraham Lincoln (1861–65); they blamed the Lincoln administration particularly for the Thirteenth, Fourteenth, and Fifteenth Amendments to the Constitution, which abolished slavery and gave Negroes political and civil rights.

The split in 1860 and the Civil War left the party disorganized. The Democrats remained out of office until the election of Grover Cleveland in 1884, although, in 1876, Samuel J. Tilden (q.v.) had received a majority of the popular vote (see ELECTORAL COLLEGE). The Democratic campaign for Cleveland's re-election in 1888 was unsuccessful, largely because of Democratic support of a low tariff. However, the Republican administration of 1888–92 passed a high-tariff law, the McKinley Act, which caused an increase in prices and popular disapproval; and Cleveland won the election of 1892 because the Democrats favored a low tariff.

The party split again in 1896 over the issue of free coinage of silver and bimetallism (q.v.); the minority, known as National Democrats, convened separately and refused to endorse the majority candidate, William Jennings Bryan. The Democrats were defeated overwhelmingly in the 1896 election; they remained the minority party until the election of Woodrow Wilson, the Democratic Presidential candidate in 1912.

Despite the success of the Wilson administration both in domestic legislation, notably the Federal Reserve Act (q.v.), and the conduct of World War I, the Democrats lost the 1920 election mainly because of Wilson's support of the League of Nations, which became a plank in the Democratic Party platform. They were out of office until the election of Franklin D. Roosevelt in 1932. During the intervening twelve years, there was dissension within the party organization, first, because of the Prohibition (q.v.) issue; and, second, because in 1928 the controversy surrounding the nomination of Alfred E. Smith, a Roman Catholic, raised the issue of religious prejudice within the party itself.

In 1932, a platform which included measures to combat the depression and a promise to repeal the 18th, or Prohibition, Amendment to the Constitution helped to bring about the election of Franklin D. Roosevelt and a Democratic Congress by an overwhelming majority of votes. Directly after the inauguration of Roosevelt, Congress, under the leadership of the President, began to put into effect domestic recovery measures and social legislation called collectively the New Deal (q.v.). In 1936, he was returned to the Presidency with the largest plurality ever recorded in the United States.

Beginning with Roosevelt's second term, opposition to his domestic policies increased among Democratic leaders and members of Congress. However, his political skill and his popularity with the electorate enabled the President to maintain control of the party; he was nominated and elected for a third term in 1940, and for a fourth term, with Harry S. Truman as Vice-President, in 1944. (For additional details, see ROOSEVELT, FRANKLIN D.).

World War II ended shortly after Truman became President following the death of Roosevelt in 1945. The return to a peace-time economy and the domestic disorganization caused by reconversion brought new dissension between the President and the Democratic Congress, notably concerning the treatment of labor and the control of prices, in which Truman followed, generally, a New Deal policy. (See LABOR LEGISLATION; OFFICE OF PRICE ADMINISTRATION.) In 1946, Democrats in local and State offices began to be unseated by Republicans in a popular trend to the latter party; in the Congressional elections of that year, the Republicans received a majority in both houses of Congress.

In 1948 Truman approved a civil-rights program, including guarantees of social and political rights for Negroes, which alienated Southern Democratic leaders. Despite a vehement Southern protest, the Democratic national convention of that year nominated Truman for the Presidency, with Alben W. Barkley as running mate, and included the full civil-rights program in the party platform. Several Southern delegations immediately withdrew from the convention and, organizing themselves as the States' Rights Party, nominated J. Strom Thurmond for the presidency. Another rift in the party structure was caused by Henry A. Wallace (Vice-President in the third term of Franklin D. Roosevelt), who left the Democratic Party in 1947 and, a year later, helped to organize the new Progressive Party (q.v.) which chose Wallace as its Presidential candidate.

In the face of opposition from his own party, many leaders of which refused to support him, and predictions of failure from newspapers, political figures, and all the public-opinion polls, Truman waged an intense, personal campaign, stressing in particular the Democratic program for a substantial expansion of the New Deal. His victory, a plurality in 28 States with an aggregate of 303 electoral votes, shocked the public-opinion samplers, practically all of whom had predicted a Republican triumph.

Though the election gave the Democratic Party a majority in the 81st Congress, most of Truman's domestic legislative program, which became known as the "Fair Deal", was blocked by a coalition of Republicans and conservative Democrats. The Democratic foreign-aid program received bipartisan support.

In the Congressional and gubernatorial elections of 1950 the Democratic Party suffered severe setbacks, losing 30 seats in the House of Representatives, 5 in the Senate, and 6 governorships. The anti-Democratic trend, undoubtedly sustained by disclosures of corruption within Administration circles, by Republican charges of "softness" toward Communism, and by popular dissatisfaction with the high prices and taxes consequent on the Korean War, continued through 1951 into 1952. As the date for the national convention approached many prominent Democrats, especially in the South, openly opposed Truman's leadership of the party, further weakening the organization.

Following Truman's decision not to seek re-election six outstanding Democrats entered the contest for the Presidential nomination. The leading contenders, on the eve of the convention, were Senator Richard B. Russell of Georgia, Mutual Security Administrator Averell Harriman, Senator Estes Kefauver of Tennessee, who had made the most vigorous fight for the nomination, and Truman's choice, Governor Adlai E. Stevenson of Illinois, who had repeatedly expressed unwillingness to become a candidate. Stevenson was nominated on the third ballot.

The Democratic candidate waged a brilliant and energetic campaign, but the personal popularity of his Republican opponent General Dwight D. Eisenhower and effective Republican exploitation of such issues as corruption in Washington, the Korean War, and Communism foredoomed the Democrats to defeat. The Republican Party carried 39 States with an aggregate of 442 electoral votes. In the Congressional contests, however, the Democrats showed surprising strength, winning 213 seats in the House and limiting the Republicans to a one-vote majority in the Senate. See TAMMANY HALL; REPUBLICAN PARTY; FEDERALIST PARTY. For organization of the Democratic Party, see CAUCUS; CONVENTION: POLITICAL PARTIES IN THE U.S.; PRIMARY ELECTION.

DEMOCRITUS (fl. 400 B.C.), Greek philosopher, born at Abdera, in Thrace. He studied under the philosopher Leucippus, whose system he developed. His name is associated with the first exposition of the atomic theory of matter (see ATOM AND ATOMIC THEORY), according to which all matter is composed of single, indivisible atoms (Gr. *a*, "not"; *temnein*, "to divide") which are qualitatively exactly alike. This theory was a departure from that of the earlier Ionic philosophers, who held that matter is composed of particles differing qualitatively from each other, and disagreed only concerning the nature of those differences. Democritus believed that the atoms, the space within which they move, and their motion within that

space, are eternal. He wrote extensively on the nature of matter, but only fragments of his works remain. The later philosophers Epicurus and Lucretius were his disciples.

DEMOGRAPHY, branch of the science of statistics concerned with the social well-being of the people. The term was first used by Achille Guillard in his *Éléments de Statistique Humaine ou Démographie Comparée* (1855). Demographic data may include: (1) analysis of the population on the basis of age, parentage, physical condition, race, occupation, and civil position, giving the size and density of each composite division; (2) changes in the population as a result of birth, marriage, and death; (3) statistics on migrations and their effects, both individual and local, and their relation to economic conditions; (4) statistics of crime, illegitimacy, and suicide; (5) degrees of education; and (6) economic and social statistics, especially relating to insurance. See also VITAL STATISTICS.

DEMOISELLE, or DAMSELFISH, any fish of the family Pomacentridae, possessing brilliant colors and graceful form. They abound in tropical seas, feeding upon corals and other small creatures. An example is the cow pilot, *Pomacentrus saxatilis,* so called because it is believed always to accompany the cowfish.

DEMOLITION, the scientific destruction of works or property. Demolition is one of the chief weapons of defensive warfare, being used to destroy material which might benefit the enemy if captured. Examples of material often demolished in warfare are guns, railroads, bridges, ammunition and oil storage depots, communication lines, and airfields. Historically, the destruction of the Sublican bridge across the Tiber by the Romans, while Horatius held off the invading Etruscans as a delay measure, is one of the first cases of large-scale demolition in defensive warfare.

In World War II there were numerous cases of large-scale demolition. The destruction of the Palembang oil installations and rubber works in the Netherlands East Indies by the Dutch in 1942, to preclude their use by the Japanese, was one of the most expensive voluntary demolitions ever undertaken. In 1941 the Russians destroyed the Dnieper Dam when its capture by the German armies was imminent.

Frequently, when the resources available for demolition are limited, crippling, or partial demolition, may be just as effective as total destruction. The number of men and the amount of material that must be diverted by the enemy to repair the destruction may be nearly the same in both cases. Those in charge of demolition may also restrict its extent because they expect to recapture the crippled material.

The most effective weapons for demolition are explosives and fire. Among the explosives used in World War II by the United States Army for demolition were TNT, ammonium nitrate, and other, more specialized compounds which could be molded around the object to be destroyed (see MUNROE EFFECT). In the U.S. Army and the armies of most other countries, demolition work is generally a function of the Engineer Corps. Procedures for destruction of small field equipment are outlined in the field manuals of all military forces.

DEMON, in popular usage, a malevolent spirit or force, not a deity but capable of working evil, by supernatural means, upon human affairs. In the Greek conception the term (*daimon*) was used to denote an intermediary power between gods and men, capable variously of assuming a protective guardianship over man's destiny or acting as the minister of divine displeasure. The gradual differentiation between the benign and maleficent qualities of demons resulted in their division into good spirits or guardian angels, and evil spirits or devils. Christian theology, developing earlier Hebraic ideas, created out of the former category an elaborate hierarchy of angels and archangels, and of the latter a host of fallen angels, or devils, marshaled under the leadership of Satan. In English versions of the Bible the term demon is translated as "devil", and in the New Testament the demon is identified with the evil spirit. See DEVIL.

Belief in evil spirits and their power to enter into and "possess" the person of a human being, rendering him demoniac, antedates classical and Christian cultures. Primitive man did not differentiate between the human and the divine; every physical manifestation of nature had its spiritual archetype and the distinction between the two was merely the distinction between the visible and the invisible. Demons and ghosts were interchangeable, either representing the spiritual form in which the dead continued to maintain the influence they had enjoyed when living. The conception of the demon was basically that of a being with human attributes but with any number of terrible and inscrutable qualities superimposed. Savage man practiced the cult of ancestor worship and worship of the dead for practical reasons; he was enabled to attribute his good or bad fortune to the direct interference of ghosts or demons. These same spirits, it was believed, not only affected the fortune of the individual but even entered into his body, causing frenzy, epilepsy, and other diseases. A similar explanation of disease is found in the beginnings of recorded history in Egypt and Babylonia where there is evidence of a complicated demonism and system of possession, providing a spirit for every important organ of the body and every familiar illness. The belief in demonism spread from these two countries and directly or indirectly influenced all the nations of western Asia and Europe. It was a familiar conception among the ancient Hebrews and held an important place in the life of the Christian peoples until the end of the 18th century. The necessity for curing possession by expelling the demon occurred even to primitive man and created the function of exorcist (q.v.) or sorcerer. In early Christian times, *energumens,* or those demoniacally possessed, were grouped into a class under the care of a special order of clerical exorcists, and after the time of St. Augustine the rite of exorcism came to be applied to all infants before baptism. Exorcists still form one of the minor orders of the Catholic Church.

Demons exist in literature and folklore in an enormous number of forms, varying with different peoples and cultures, but the term is generally applied only to such spirits as are capable of engaging in relations with the human race. They may be human or non-human, hostile or friendly, and devoted to one or many places or functions. They include demons like those of the nightmare; the Slavonic vampires, or witch-ghosts, who suck the blood of living victims; *incubi* and *succubi,* who consort with women and men in their sleep and by whose means children may be engendered between demons and women; the Roman *genius,* or *dœmon,* a guardian spirit which accompanied man through life; the Norse *fylgia,* or guardian genius in animal form; the Hindu *rakshasa,* malignant ogres who can assume any shape at will; in Christian mythology, fallen angels like Lucifer and witches who owe allegiance to Satan; the Norse one-eyed monsters, called *Trolls;* and the Celtic and Teutonic Giants who destroy men and devour their flesh; the Drakos and Lamias of modern Greece; the Lithuanian Laume; the Russian fiery and flying snakes, and Baba Yaga, the flying hag propelled on a revolving pestle.

One of the most systematic hierarchies of demons is that elaborated by the Moslem theologians. The Jinn were created two thousand years before Adam, but sinned against God and were degraded from their original high estate. The greatest among them was Eblis; he was cast out by Allah for refusing to worship Adam who was made of earth, basing his refusal on his own origin in smokeless fire. The Sheytáns form his host; other species of subordinate fiends are the Jánn, the 'Efreets, and Márids. Eminent among the evil Jinn are the five sons of Eblis: Teer who causes calamities, losses, and injuries, El-Aawar who encourages debauchery, Sot who suggests lies, Dásim who promotes hatred between man and wife, and Zelemboor who presides over places where illicit activities are conducted. Inferior demons are the Ghoul, often in human form, who devours the bodies of the dead; the Sealáh who inhabits forests; and the Shikk, shaped like a man halved lengthwise.

Demons with specialized functions exist in all mythologies. Among them are the Japanese Oni, who bring on the winds and live at the center of the storm; the Chinese air-dragons whose battles bring on waterspouts; the demons of floods in old Egyptian and Akkadian mythology; the specters and phantoms that infest the sea, such as the nixies of northern Europe, the kelpies of Scotland who haunt pools to drown unwary travelers, and the sirens like the Lorelei of the Rhine who by their beauty or singing draw men to their ruin.

The doctrine or branch of learning devoted to demons or the investigation of the beliefs in demons is called *Demonology.*

DEMOSTHENES (385?–22 B.C.), greatest orator of ancient Greece, born in the deme of Pæania, near Athens. His father, a manufacturer of the same name, died when the boy was seven years old, leaving a fortune in trust for his son. As soon as Demosthenes became of age, he prosecuted the trustees, who had attempted to defraud him. He succeeded in retrieving only a portion of his inheritance, and turned to the profession of writing speeches for use in legal actions. According to his biographers, he was afflicted with a speech impediment and his attempts to deliver his own speeches were so unsuccessful that he resorted to unusual means to overcome his defect, including the practice of shouting against the sound of the surf and orating while holding pebbles in his mouth.

He continued his activities in private law practice throughout his lifetime, and became increasingly interested in public affairs. He devoted himself to the revival of public spirit in Athens, and to the preservation of Greek culture, at that time threatened by the aggressions of King Philip of Macedon. Most of his major orations were directed against the threat of Macedonian conquest of the Greek cities. The theme of his first speech against Philip, known as the *First Philippic* (351), was preparedness. Two years later Philip attacked Olynthus, an ally of Athens, and Demosthenes urged in three speeches, called the *Olynthiacs,* that Athens aid its ally. Olynthus was destroyed, and Demosthenes was among those sent on a mission (346) to negotiate peace between Athens and the conqueror. During the next eight years, however, he continued his warnings against Macedonian power. Among his orations of this period were the *Second Philippic*; a speech, known as *On the False Embassy,* against Æschines, a rival orator and a supporter of Philip; and the *Third Philippic,* considered the best of this group, demanding resolute action against Philip. Largely through the efforts of Demosthenes, Philip's attempt to capture Byzantium (340) was delayed. An alliance between Thebes and Athens, cities which had long been hostile to each other, was accomplished by Demosthenes, but Philip defeated the allies at Chæronea in 338. Despite the conquest of Greece by Macedon, Demosthenes continued to speak for liberation. In 336 the orator Ctesiphon proposed that Athens honor Demosthenes for his service by presenting him, according to custom, with a golden crown. This proposal was made a political issue, and in 330, on a legal technicality, Demosthenes' enemy Æschines prosecuted Ctesiphon for having offered the crown. Demosthenes defended Ctesiphon in a speech, *On the Crown,* which is considered a masterpiece of oratory. As a result of this speech, Ctesiphon was acquitted and Æschines was forced to go into exile.

In 324 Demosthenes was convicted, probably unjustly, of accepting a bribe from Harpalus, to whom Alexander the Great, Philip's successor, had entrusted huge treasures and who had absconded and found refuge in Athens. After Alexander's death in 323, Demosthenes again urged the Greeks to liberate themselves, but Alexander's successor in Macedonia, Antipater, quelled all resistance and demanded that the Athenians turn over

Jack Dempsey

the leading patriots, including Demosthenes, to him. The orator Demades proposed, and the Athenian assembly adopted, a decree condemning the patriots to death. Demosthenes escaped to a sanctuary on the island of Calauria, where he committed suicide.

DEMOTIC ALPHABET. See HIEROGLYPHICS.

DEMPSEY, JACK (1895–   ), American boxer, former world's heavyweight champion, born at Manassa, Col. His real name was William Harrison Dempsey; he was known as "the Manassa Mauler" for his birthplace and aggressive style of boxing. At seventeen he began boxing in Western mining camps and entered the professional ring two years later. He won the world's heavyweight title from Jess Willard in 1919. In this bout, his most famous, he knocked Willard down seven times in the first round. His victories over Georges Carpentier in 1921 and Luis Firpo in 1923 were highlights in his successful defense of his title. In 1926 he lost the title to Gene Tunney on a decision, and failed to regain it in a return bout the next year. He fought 69 bouts, winning 49 by knockouts. He retired from the ring in 1932 and opened a restaurant in New York City. In 1944 and 1945, during World War II, Dempsey toured Pacific war theaters as a lieutenant commander in the navy, exhibiting films of his bout with Jess Willard in 1919.

DEMPSTER, ARTHUR JEFFREY (1886–1950), American physicist, born in Toronto, Canada, and educated at the universities of Toronto, Göttingen, Munich, Würzburg, and Chicago. In 1927 he became professor of physics at the University of Chicago. He was president of the American Physical Society in 1944. Dempster helped develop the mass spectrograph (q.v.), and discovered many isotopes, including the atomic bomb isotope, U-235. He also measured the energy content of various atomic nuclei.

DENARY SCALE. See NOTATION.

DENATURED ALCOHOL. See ALCOHOL.

DENBIGHSHIRE, a county of Wales, on the Irish Sea, between the Conway and Dee rivers. In considerable part the surface is rugged and mountainous, but more than half of the land consists of cultivated fields and of pastures for cattle and sheep. The chief crops are oats and turnips. In the southeastern part of the county, near Chirk, Ruabon, and Wrexham, are important coal and lead deposits. Woolen textiles are manufactured in the towns of Llangollen and Llansantffraid (St. Bridgit's). Other products of the county are paving flags, slates, limestone, kaolin, and sandstone. The county seat is Denbigh (pop., about 8100). Area of the county, 669 sq.m.; pop. (1951 est.) 170,699.

DENBY, EDWIN (1870–1929), American politician, born at Evansville, Ind., and educated at the University of Michigan. He practiced law in Detroit until the outbreak of the Spanish-American War, in which he participated as an enlisted man in the U.S. Navy. From 1905 until 1911 he represented Michigan in the U.S. House of Representatives. He enlisted as a private in the U.S. Marines during World War I, and rose to the rank of major of the reserves. In 1921 he was appointed secretary of the navy, the first exserviceman to hold such an office. During his administration, the oil reserves at Teapot Dome and Elk Hills were transferred from the Navy Department to the Department of the Interior. The scandal arising from the fraudulent leasing of these reserves (see TEAPOT DOME) to private interests caused Denby to resign from office in 1924. During the trial of those directly involved in the scandal, the Supreme Court declared that there was no evidence of Denby's implication in the fraud.

DENDERA (anc. *Tentyra*), a village of Upper Egypt, on the w. bank of the Nile opposite Qena (Kena). It is famous for its temple dedicated to the goddess Hathor (Gr. *Aphrodite*). The temple was begun by Ptolemy XI in the 1st century B.C. and completed during the reign of the Roman emperor Augustus. It is one of the most imposing and magnificently preserved edifices of ancient Egypt. The temple is constructed of sandstone, and is almost 300 ft. long and about 135 ft. at its widest point. The enormous portico is supported by 24 columns, each 50 ft. high and more than 22 ft. in circumference. The walls and columns are covered with hieroglyphics and ornamentation belonging to the eclectic or declining period of Egyptian art. One of the most spectacular objects in the temple, a celestial zodiac which formed the ceiling of one of the upper chambers, was removed about 1820 and transported to the Bibliothèque Nationale in Paris. Pop. (1947) 16,320.

DENGUE, DANDY FEVER, or BREAKBONE FEVER, an infectious tropical disease characterized by fever, extreme pain of the joints and muscles, and a skin eruption. The causative agent of dengue is a filterable virus which is transmitted from one person to another by mosquitoes of the species *Aëdes aegypti*, the same species which transmits yellow fever. Dengue is endemic in some parts of the tropics and has occurred in epidemic form in both tropical and temperate-zone countries. More than 80,000 cases of dengue occurred among U.S. troops during World War II. The last serious epidemic among civilians took place in Greece and Egypt in 1928.

Patients become ill with dengue in from four to ten days after being bitten by a disease-bearing mosquito. The first symptoms are a high fever, headache and muscle pains, chills, and sweating. On about the third day of the attack a skin eruption appears. In a few more days there is a remission of symptoms, followed by a relapse which lasts for approximately a day and a half. During the second attack the characteristic skin eruption, like that of measles, becomes marked. The disease is seldom fatal, but convalescence is usually slow. No specific treatment for dengue is known, but mosquito control helps to prevent outbreaks of the disease.

DENHAM, SIR JOHN (1615–69), English poet, born in Dublin, Ireland, and educated at Trinity College, Oxford. At the outbreak of the Civil War he joined the Royalists and performed secret services for the imprisoned Charles I. Obliged to flee, he went to Holland and France in 1647, returning to England in 1652. He was made Knight of the Bath at the Restoration (1660) and in the same year

was appointed surveyor-general of His Majesty's buildings. Denham was one of the first English poets to use the heroic couplet. He wrote *Cooper's Hill* (1642), a descriptive poem concerning the scenery around Egham; *Sophy* (1642), a historical tragedy; and *Elegy on Cowley* (1667).

DEN HARTOG, J(ACOB) P(IETER) (1901–), American engineer, born in Java, Netherlands East Indies (now Republic of Indonesia), and educated at the University of Delft, the Netherlands, and at the University of Pittsburgh. In 1930, after completing his education, he became a naturalized citizen of the United States. He was assistant professor of mechanical engineering at Harvard University from 1932 to 1936 and associate professor from 1936 to 1941. From 1941 to 1945, during World War II, he served in the U.S. Navy. Den Hartog was appointed professor of mechanical engineering at Massachusetts Institute of Technology in 1945. His works include *Mechanical Vibrations* (1934), *Mechanics* (1948), and *Strength of Materials* (1949).

DEN HELDER. See HELDER, DEN.

DENIS, MAURICE (1870–1943), French painter, born at Granville, department of Manche. He studied at the École des Beaux-Arts, Paris. Denis is noted for his religious murals, the style of which was influenced by the work of the 15th-century Italian fresco painters and by that of the modern French painters Paul Gauguin and Georges Seurat. His murals include those in the churches of St. Paul and Le Vésinet, both in Geneva; in the chapel of the priory at Saint Germain-en-Laye; and on the ceiling of the Champs Élysées Theater, Paris. Among his writings on art are *Du Symbolisme et de Gauguin, vers un Nouvel Ordre Classique* (1912) and *Nouvelles Théories sur l'Art Moderne, sur l'Art Sacré* (1914–21).

DENIS or **DENYS,** or (Lat.) DIONYSIUS, SAINT (fl. 3d century), apostle to France and first bishop of Paris. There are various contradictory accounts of his life. He is supposed, traditionally, to have set out from Rome about 250 A.D. to preach the gospel to the Gauls, and after settling on an island near the present city of Paris to have made numerous converts. His arrest was ordered by Sisinnius Fescennius, the Roman governor of that part of Gaul, and Denis and his two companions, a priest and a deacon, were subjected to torture. They remained firm in their faith, however, and were beheaded. According to one legend, Denis arose after his execution and walked a considerable distance carrying his head in his hand; he is usually represented on medallions and paintings in this act. According to other accounts, the bodies of the three martyrs were thrown into the Seine, from which they were eventually recovered by a Christian woman called Catulla, who buried them with the proper rites. A chapel was later built over their tomb, and in 636 King Dagobert I of the Franks founded the Abbey of St. Denis on the spot. For a long time his name was the war cry of the French soldiers who charged or rallied to the words "Montjoye Saint Denis!" In the Greek Orthodox Church St. Denis is identified with Dionysius the Areopagite (q.v.). In the Roman Catholic Church his feast day is October 9th.

DENISON, city of Grayson Co., Tex., situated about 75 miles N.N.E. of Dallas and 4 miles s. of the Denison Dam on the Red R. The dam, constructed for hydroelectric power and flood control, is the largest rolled-fill earth dam in the world (length of main dam, 15,350 ft.; height, 165 ft.); it impounds Lake Texoma, the fifth-largest artificial lake in the U.S. (area, 140 sq.m.; shore line, 1250 m.). The U.S. Fish and Wildlife Service has stocked the lake with fish and has established there two migratory waterfowl refuges. The city of Denison is an important rail center and the shipping point for large quantities of peanuts, wheat, cotton, and fruit. Manufacturing industries in Denison include the processing of milk, cheese, and eggs; the production of peanut butter and oil; poultry dressing, meat packing, flour milling, and sawmilling; and the making of power saws, earth-boring machinery, farm machinery, railway freight cars, cotton textiles, mattresses, and pickles.

Denison was settled in 1872 and incorporated as a city in 1891. It was the birthplace, in 1890, of President Dwight David Eisenhower. Pop. (1950) 17,504.

DENISON UNIVERSITY, a coeducational institution of higher learning, situated in Granville, Ohio, and conducted under the auspices of the Baptist Church. Denison was founded in 1831 as a manual training school. Later a theological department was added, but in 1870 both departments were discontinued in favor of such fields as liberal arts, music, and social science. In 1900 Shephardson College for Women was merged with the university. In 1953–54 the enrollment was 1123, including 1115 full-time students; the faculty numbered 93.

DENIZLI, capital of the il of the same name, Anatolia, Turkey. The town lies about 115 miles S.E. of Izmir, and at the base of Baba Dagh (Mt. Salbacus). Numerous vineyards are in the vicinity, and nearby are the ruins of ancient Laodicea. The town is noted for its many flower gardens, and is a trade center for the livestock and agricultural produce of the surrounding area. Pop. (1950) 22,029. Area of il, 4244 sq.m.; pop. (1950) 340,010.

DENKA. See DINKA.

DENMARK (Dan. *Danmark*), a kingdom of N.W. Europe. It consists of a mainland, forming part of the continental mass of Europe, and a large number of islands. The mainland, comprising the greater part of the peninsula of Jutland (q.v.), extends northward between the North and Baltic seas for about 190 m. from Schleswig-Holstein, Germany. On the N., Jutland is separated from Norway by the Skagerrak (q.v.), an arm of the North Sea. On the E., it is separated for about half its length from Sweden, by the Kattegat (q.v.), in which are situated the Danish islands of Anholt and Læsö. South of the Kattegat, separating that arm of the North Sea from the Baltic Sea, and lying between Jutland and Sweden, are about 200 Danish islands. The largest of these islands are Falster, Fyn, Lolland, Zealand (qq.v.), Langeland, and Möen. Zealand is separated from Sweden by The Sound, only 3 m. in width at its narrowest point. About 80 m. to the E. of Zealand, in the Baltic, is the Danish island of Bornholm (q.v.). Far to the N.W. of Jutland, in the Atlantic Ocean, between the Shetland Islands and Iceland, is a group of about 20 Danish islands called the Faeroes or Faeroe Islands (q.v.). Although geographically distant from the main part of Denmark, Bornholm and the Faeroes comprise integral parts of the country. (For topography of Denmark, see articles on Jutland, the larger Baltic islands, including Bornholm, and the Faeroes). Excluding Greenland (q.v.), the total area of Denmark is 17,116 sq.m. (Jutland, 11,411 sq.m.; the Baltic Islands, including Bornholm, 5165 sq.m.; and the Faeroes, 540 sq.m.). Pop. of Denmark (1950) 4,281,275.

The capital and largest city of Denmark is Copenhagen (q.v.), on the island of Zealand. Other important Danish cities include the seaports of Aalborg and Aarhus (qq.v.), on Jutland; the seaport of Odense (q.v.), on Fyn Island; and Esbjerg (q.v.), Horsens, and Randers.

Agriculture and Industry. Denmark is primarily an agrarian country, with dairy farming as the chief source of wealth. About nine tenths of the land of Denmark is arable, and about three quarters of the land is under cultivation. Danish governmental policy favors small landholdings, and the merger of small holdings to form large estates is forbidden by law. About 98% of the approximately 208,000 farms (in 1950) of Denmark are less than 150 acres in size.

In 1953 a total of 7,684,950 acres were under cultivation; 3,335,927 acres planted to grain yielded 2,191,000 metric tons of barley, 820,000 metric tons of oats, 290,000 metric tons of wheat, 324,000 metric tons of rye, and 818,000 metric tons of mixed grain; 2,471,040 acres were planted to fodder crops and grass; 1,440,619 acres were planted to root crops, including sugar beets and potatoes; and the balance was planted to other crops, including flax, hemp, hops, tobacco, and fruit. The country's livestock, in 1953, included 3,070,000 head of cattle, of which almost one-half were milk cows; 397,000 horses; 4,336,000 swine; 40,000 sheep and lambs; and 25,115,000 chickens. The total production of dairy and poultry products, in 1953, included 5,388,000 metric tons of milk, 173,000 metric tons of butter, 87,000 metric tons of cheese, and 136,000 metric tons of eggs. In addition 478,000 metric tons of pork and bacon were produced.

A notable feature of agriculture in Denmark is the influence of the co-operative movement (q.v.). Co-operative associations dominate the production of dairy products and bacon. Members of co-operatives own almost 90% of all the cows in Denmark and approximately 75% of the pigs; they control upward of 25% of the production of eggs. A large percentage of the agricultural produce of the country is sold through marketing co-operatives. Most co-operatives are organized in national associations which are members of the Agricultural Council, the central agency for the co-operatives in dealings with the government and industry, and in foreign trade.

Fisheries are important in the economy of Denmark. Before World War II, the Danish fishing fleet comprised more than 12,000 vessels of all kinds. These craft plied the Baltic and North seas and the Skagerrak, and were used in the shallower waters of the fjords of the Baltic islands and along the east coast of Jutland. They were employed to hunt seals, to dredge oysters, and to catch haddock, cod, herring, salmon, and other fish. In 1952, the total haul was 305,361 metric tons, valued at $14,000,000. In 1950 approx-

Guard at Amelienborg Palace, the residence of the king of Denmark

imately 30,000 persons earned their livelihood from fishing. The fishermen are organized into marketing co-operatives and co-operatives for the purchase of fishing supplies. The Danish Fisherman's Association is subsidized by the government.

The forest resources of Denmark are negligible. The country's mineral resources comprise small quantities of coal, kaolin, and granite, and are insufficient for the needs of Denmark's industry. Peat, mined in the moorlands of western and northern Jutland, is an important domestic fuel in Denmark.

Danish industries produce primarily for the home market, and consist for the most part of small-scale enterprises. In 1948 there were 102,303 industrial plants which gave employment to 684,939 persons, about a fourth of whom are women. A little less than half of these plants use mechanical power; the balance are largely handicraft enterprises.

The principal industrial establishments of Denmark are food-processing plants, and factories producing metals; machinery, notably marine and railway Diesel engines; clothing; and textiles. These establishments gave employment to 147,225 persons in 1952. Other important industries include iron founding, shipbuilding, the manufacture of cement, chemicals and drugs, earthenware, and porcelain, the assembling of automobiles, the production of hand-wrought silver, the manufacture of stoves, bicycles, paper, and oleomargarine, and tanning, woodworking, sugar refining, brewing, and distilling.

Commerce. Prior to World War II, Great Britain was the leading market for Danish exports and the chief source for imports, taking more than a third of the total exports and supplying approximately half of all Danish imports. Germany ranked behind Great Britain, taking about one fourth of all Danish exports and supplying about one fifth of all Danish imports. Other outlets and sources for Danish exports and imports were Sweden, the United States, Norway, and the Netherlands. During the war years, when Denmark was under German occupation, Germany became the chief market for Danish exports and the principal source of Danish imports. After the end of hostilities, Great Britain again became Denmark's leading export and import market.

The principal articles of the export trade are agricultural products. In 1953, dairy products comprised about 27 percent of all exports; meat and meat products, about 25 percent; machinery, about 10 percent; and live meat animals, about 5 percent. Industrial products comprise a little more than a quarter of all Danish exports, the chief items being metals, machinery, and transport equipment; other items include chemicals, porcelain, and silverware. The principal imports include iron and steel, coal and coke, petroleum, machinery and vehicles, fertilizers, oilcake for fodder, glassware, textiles, paper, coffee, and fruit.

Communications. Denmark is a maritime nation. Before World War II, the country's merchant marine, the fourth largest in the world on a per capita basis, comprised about 2700 vessels totaling approximately 1,200,000 registered tons gross. Losses during the war reduced these totals considerably; in 1952, the Danish merchant marine comprised 1046 vessels totaling 1,387,129 tons. Because of the country's discontinuous terrain, ferries are important in Denmark's transportation system. They link Jutland with the Baltic islands, the Baltic islands with one another, and both Jutland and the Baltic islands with Germany, Sweden, and Norway. Of Denmark's total (1952) of 2971 m. of railways, approximately half are state property; the rest of the rail system is nominally private property, but the shares are owned by the government and the larger towns. The main rail route leads southward through Jutland to Hamburg, Germany. Auto transport in Denmark is facilitated by 5146 m. of roads (1953). Air transport is important; in 1950 Danish commercial airlines became part of the Scandinavian Airlines System, which flew more than 17,400,000 m. in 1952, and carried 583,457 passengers. The telephone and tele-

Swedish Travel Info. Bureau

Kronborg Castle, scene of Shakespeare's "Hamlet," at Elsinore, Zealand Island, Denmark

Danish Information Office

Above: A section of a Danish village in the north of Zealand Island. Right: Women and children dressed for a festival, in village of Dragör, on small island east of Zealand.

graph system of the country is partly owned by the state; in 1952 the number of telephones totaled 599,000.

Religion and Education. Almost all Danes are Lutherans, and the Evangelical Lutheran Church is the established church of Denmark. About 100,000 persons profess other faiths, the majority of these being Roman Catholics.

The entire adult population of Denmark is literate. Education is compulsory for all from the age of seven to fourteen, and, for the most part, free. In 1952 there were 3592 elementary schools and 483 secondary schools, with a combined enrollment of 555,334 pupils. Higher education is provided by a high school of commerce, approximately 210 other commercial schools, 27 agricultural schools, 55 high schools for adults, the University of Copenhagen (see COPENHAGEN, UNIVERSITY OF), the University of Aarhus (opened in 1933), a royal academy of arts (founded in 1754), a polytechnic institution, and a number of other colleges and schools, including a veterinary and agricultural college, a college of pharmacy, a school of dentistry, 340 technical schools, and 21 training colleges for teachers.

Language and Literature. See DANISH LANGUAGE; DANISH LITERATURE.

Government. Denmark is a constitutional and hereditary monarchy. It is governed under a constitution adopted in 1953.

Executive power is vested in the king, who must be a member of the Evangelical Lutheran Church. The king appoints the premier and the ministers who comprise his cabinet. Legislative power is vested jointly in the king and in a unicameral legislature, called the *Folketing* or Diet. The concurrence of king and Folketing are necessary for the enactment of legislation, a declaration of war, and the signing of a peace treaty. The legislative term is four years, but the king may dissolve the Folketing before the end of the term. There are 179 members, who are popularly elected for four-year terms. Elections are conducted chiefly on the basis of proportional representation. All Danes, of both sexes, over 23 years of age, who are permanent residents, are eligible to vote and to stand for election to the Folketing. Measures passed by the legislature may be submitted to a referendum with the consent of one-third of the members; if at least 30 percent of the eligible voters disapprove the measure, it is defeated. The government may co-operate with international organizations, but if Danish sovereignty is involved must secure approval of five-sixths of the Folketing, or popular consent through a plebiscite. Judicial power is vested in 94 lower courts, presided over by individual judges; two superior courts, one situated in Copenhagen, the other in Viborg; and a supreme court, sitting in Copenhagen.

For administrative purposes, Denmark is divided into 25 counties, the city of Copenhagen and the borough of Frederiksberg. County councils administer the 1300 rural municipalities of Denmark. The 88 urban municipalities are administered by mayors and town councils. Copenhagen is administered by a town council, which makes municipal policy, and an executive council, which is a purely administrative body. The five mayors and mayor-in-chief of Copenhagen are members of the executive council; an official with the title of Lord Lieutenant represents the national government in the executive council. Rural and municipal administrative bodies are elected on the basis of proportional representation.

History. Numerous remains discovered by archeologists attest the existence of prehistoric man in Denmark. Knowledge of the early ages of Danish civilization derives largely from myths and sagas (see SCANDINAVIAN MYTHOLOGY). Some historians believe that Danes, who had inhabited the south part of the Scandinavian peninsula in the first centuries after Christ, migrated in the 5th and 6th centuries to the peninsula of Jutland and the adjacent islands in the Baltic Sea. In the following centuries they expanded westward; within a century after their first raid (787) on the British Isles, the Danes became masters of part of England (see DANELAW). Under King Harold Bluetooth, who reigned from 940 to 985, the Danes became a united people and the Christianization of their realm was begun. Harold's son, Sweyn Forkbeard, king of the Danes from about 985 to 1014, conquered England in 1013. The Danes ruled England until 1035. Sweyn's son, Canute, king of England (1016–35) and of Denmark (1018–35), completed the Christianization of Denmark. (See NORTHMEN.)

In the latter part of the 12th and the early part of the 13th centuries, the Danes expanded to the east. They conquered the greater part of the northern and southern littorals of the Baltic Sea, establishing a powerful and prosperous realm about twice the size of modern Denmark. This era of expansion was also the epoch in which feudalism in Denmark attained its zenith: the monarchy became powerful and wealthier than it had ever been; the nobility, comprising principally large landowners, prospered; and the clergy were rich and politically influential. Large masses of the once-free peasantry of the country were reduced to serfdom. Marked economic progress was made in this era, principally in the development of the herring-fishing industry and of stock raising, and constituted the basis for the rise of a middle class and of a number of guilds.

Efforts on the part of the monarchy, in the second half of the 13th century, to tax the church, precipitated a protracted struggle for supremacy in Denmark between the kings of Denmark and the popes. Growing discord between the Danish crown and nobility also led to a struggle, in which the nobility, in 1282, compelled King Eric V to sign a charter, called the Danish Magna Carta. By the terms of this charter, the Danish crown was made subordinate to law and the Danehof, or national assembly, was made an integral part of the country's administrative institutions. In the first part of the 14th century, the nobility, in alliance with the clergy, compelled King Christopher II to issue a charter which still further limited the crown's prerogatives, in-

Swedish Travel Info. Bureau

Above: Danish women in a typical home of the Faeroe Islands, to the west of Jutland. Right: Drying herring on Bornholm Island, one of the most eastern of Danish islands.

creased their own privileges, and decreased taxation.

A temporary decline in Danish power, which followed the death of Christopher II in 1332, was followed, in the reign of Waldemar IV (1340–75), by the re-establishment of Denmark as the leading power on the Baltic Sea. In 1381 and 1386 Denmark acquired Iceland (q.v.) and the Faeroes. Waldemar's daughter Margaret (1353–1412), widow of King Haakon VI of Norway, and regent for her son Olaf of both Norway and Denmark, seized the crowns of both kingdoms, following Olaf's death in 1387. Two years later she began the struggle, completed successfully in 1397, to obtain the crown of Sweden. Later in the same year she succeeded in forming the Union of Kalmar, a political union of the three countries. Denmark was the dominant national power in the Union. The Kalmar Union lasted until 1523, when Sweden won its independence (see SWEDEN: *History*). In 1443 the national capital of Denmark was moved from Roskilde to Copenhagen.

In the reign of Christopher III (1534–59), the Reformation triumphed in Denmark and the Lutheran Church was established as the state church. Denmark's intervention in the religious struggle in Germany on behalf of the

Protestant cause there and against the pope, led to its participation, in the 17th century, in the Thirty Years' War. Commercial rivalry with Sweden for domination of the Baltic Sea led to the indecisive War of Kalmar (1611–13) between Sweden and Denmark; and to the Swedish Wars of 1643–45 and 1657–60, in which Denmark was badly defeated. As a result, Denmark lost a number of its Baltic islands and part of its territory on the Scandinavian peninsula.

Economic reverses resulting from the above defeats had far-reaching consequences in Denmark. The growing bourgeoisie, hard hit by the loss of foreign markets and trade, joined with the church and the monarchy to curtail the power and privileges of the nobility. In 1660 the monarchy, theretofore largely dependent for its political power on the nobility, was made hereditary; in the following years it became absolute. The tax exemption privileges of the nobility were ended, and nobles were displaced by burghers in the administrative apparatus of the country. Needed administrative reforms also were made.

In the 18th century Denmark began the colonization of Greenland, Danish trade in the Far East expanded, and trading companies were established in the West Indies, where Denmark acquired a number of islands. Serfdom was abolished in 1788 after a long struggle with the nobility.

During the Napoleonic Wars, efforts by England to blockade the European continent led to naval clashes with Denmark; Copenhagen was twice bombarded by British fleets (1801 and 1807), and the Danish navy was destroyed. As a result, Denmark sided with Napoleon. By decision of the Congress of Vienna (1815), following the defeat of Napoleon, Norway was taken from Denmark and given to Sweden, Lauenberg was given to Denmark in exchange, and Swedish Pomerania was given to Prussia.

A growing demand for constitutional government in Denmark led to the proclamation of the charter, or *grundlov*, of 1849. By the terms of this charter, Denmark became a constitutional monarchy, civil liberties were juridically guaranteed, and a bicameral legislature which was to share legislative power with the crown was established. In 1864, Prussia and Austria went to war with Denmark to prevent the latter from incorporating into its territory and constitutional structure the duchies of Schleswig and Holstein (see SCHLESWIG-HOLSTEIN), long the objects of dispute between Danish kings and German monarchs. As a result of its defeat in that war, Denmark lost possession of the two duchies and of other territory. In 1866, the constitution of Denmark was revised, making the upper chamber, or Landsting, more powerful than the lower house, or Folketing. During the last decades of the 19th century, commerce, industry, and finance flourished, and dairy farming and the co-operative movement were greatly expanded. The working class grew in numbers. After 1880 the then newly organized Social Democratic movement played a prominent role in the Danish labor movement and in the struggle for a democratic constitution.

Denmark was neutral during World War I. In 1914, Denmark sold the Virgin Islands, its possession in the West Indies, to the United States. Constitutional reforms, enacted in 1915, established many of the basic features of the present governmental system. Universal suffrage went into effect in 1918. In the same year, Denmark recognized the independence of Iceland, but continued to exercise control of the foreign policy of the new state, and the king of Denmark continued as the nominal head of the Icelandic government. In 1920, the northern part of Schleswig, called North Schleswig, was incorporated into Denmark as a result of a plebiscite carried out in accordance with the terms of the Treaty of Versailles terminating World War I; the southern part of Schleswig, called South Schleswig, had voted to remain in Germany. In May, 1939, Denmark signed a 10-year non-aggression pact with the Hitler government of Germany. In 1940, during World War II, Germany occupied Denmark, and England occupied Iceland and the Faeroes. Iceland was occupied later in 1941 by American troops, pursuant to an agreement between the United States and Denmark. The American and Danish governments also agreed in 1941, on the establishment of a temporary American protectorate over Greenland. During the war, the U.S. established various weather stations, and air bases on Greenland and Iceland (qq.v.). In 1944, as a result of a referendum conducted in Iceland, that country severed all ties with Denmark and became an independent republic. Following the defeat of Germany in 1945, a movement developed in Denmark for the annexation of South Schleswig, which lay in the British zone of occupation of Germany. Danish reluctance to become a buffer in the postwar rivalry between the U.S. and the U.S.S.R., coupled with reports that Greenland contained large deposits of uranium, led the Danish press to demand the termination of the United States protectorate over Greenland. In May, 1947, the Danish government requested that the United States end the 1941 agreement. The U.S. reply stressed the importance of Greenland "in the defensive system of the United States and of the Western Hemisphere" and asked for a "new agreement in keeping with the letter and spirit of the Charter of the United Nations . . .". Protracted negotiations ensued, and meanwhile (April, 1949) Denmark became a signatory of the North Atlantic Treaty (q.v.). In April, 1951, Denmark and the United States concluded a twenty-year agreement permitting the U.S. to station troops in Greenland and giving Denmark control of naval and air bases there.

Economic conditions deteriorated in Denmark during 1951 as a result of the disparity between the high prices paid for imports and the low prices received for exports. In an effort to contain the consequent inflationary pressures the government subjected consumers' buying power to severe restrictions, among them a forced-savings program. The inflationary threat diminished during 1952.

Denmark began actively to participate in the defense planning of the North Atlantic Treaty Organization in September, 1952.

On May 28, 1953, the Danish electorate ratified a new constitution. The document includes provisions for succession of the monarch's eldest daughter to the throne, in the absence of a male heir, and for transforming Greenland from a colony into an integral part of the realm. The improved economic situation was marked by the termination (June 30) of U.S. aid under the European Recovery Program; the aid had totaled $300 million in grants and loans. Denmark continued to build up her defenses; in October, the government indicated, despite rumors to the contrary, that it was not prepared to grant bases on the Danish mainland to N.A.T.O. forces.

In 1954 Denmark participated in the Geneva Conference on Far Eastern Affairs (April 26–July 21), which negotiated a cease-fire agreement in Indochina.

DENSITY, the ratio of the mass of a body to its volume, usually expressed as its *specific gravity*. The specific gravity is the ratio of the density of a body to the density of water, the latter density being taken as unity. In the metric system a cubic centimeter of water at 4° C. weighs one gram; therefore the weight-to-volume ratio of any substance measured in metric units will be its specific gravity. A cubic ft. of water weighs 62.4 lbs.; hence density in English measurements equals 62.4 times specific gravity.

Specific gravity can be determined in a number of ways. Solid bodies which have a higher specific gravity than water can be weighed separately in air and then in water. The specific gravity is obtained by dividing the weight in air by the loss of weight when the bodies are immersed in water. For measuring the specific gravity of liquids, a hydrometer (q.v.) is commonly used. For more accurate measurements, the weight of a known volume of liquid is determined, under controlled temperature conditions. The usual method of obtaining the specific gravity of gases is similar.

Osmium, with a specific gravity of 22.5, is the densest substance existing on the earth.

Liquid hydrogen, by contrast, has a specific gravity of only .07. The highest density known is that of the so-called white dwarf stars, such as the star Sirius$_2$, which have a specific gravity of approximately 50,000. A cubic inch of this stellar material has a mass of almost a ton.

DENTALIUM. See SCAPHOPODA.

DENTALS. See PHONETICS.

DENTIFRICE, any compound used for routine cleansing of teeth. The most common forms of dentifrices are pastes and powders, but liquid dentifrices and dentifrices in cake form are also manufactured.

In general *tooth pastes* contain five different ingredients: an insoluble polishing agent, a detergent, a binder, flavoring, and a liquid to give plasticity. The polishing agent most commonly used is calcium carbonate, but phosphates such as dicalcium phosphate and tricalcium phosphate are increasingly employed by manufacturers. Castile soap and neutral soaps are frequently used as detergents in tooth paste, but in recent years synthetic detergents have begun to supplant the soaps; see DETERGENT. These synthetics have the advantage of cleaning equally well in hard and soft water, and can also be utilized in a comparatively small quantity to give a detergent effect equal to that of a larger quantity of soap. Soap also sometimes serves as a binding agent in tooth pastes, but gum tragacanth and, recently, seaweed derivatives or cellulose derivatives are employed as binders. A wide variety of flavoring oils is used to give products a distinctive and pleasant taste, and in most pastes saccharin is added for sweetening. For liquid almost all tooth pastes employ either glycerin or water.

Tooth powders are essentially identical with tooth paste except that they contain no liquid. The binder is sometimes also omitted.

Liquid dentifrices differ from tooth pastes in that they contain more liquid and generally do not contain polishing agents.

Compounds used by dentists for removing stains from the teeth are not suitable for routine tooth hygiene and are not classed as dentifrices. See DENTISTRY: *Prophylaxis*.

DENTISTRY, the branch of medical science which deals with diseases and lesions of the teeth, gums, and adjacent parts of the mouth, the care and preservation of the teeth, and the application of contrivances for the correction of malposition, injury, or loss of the teeth. The practitioners of this science are called dentists or dental surgeons. To qualify as such a practitioner, a person must generally attend a special four-year dental school for which the usual prerequisite is a four-year college course. Such dental schools confer the degree of D.D.S. (Doctor of Dental Surgery) or D.M.D. (Doctor of Dental Medicine).

Classification. The principal branches of dentistry are oral surgery, operative dentistry, periodontia, prosthodontia or dental prosthesis, and orthodontia. *Oral surgery,* which comprises such surgical operations as tooth extractions, removal of abcesses, cysts, and tumors, and treatment of jaw fractures, is on the borderline between dentistry and medical surgery. Although a dentist may perform any of these operations, particularly in an emergency, in routine practice many dentists turn over most such cases other than simple extractions to a specialist called an oral surgeon.

The care and repair of natural teeth, and particularly the repair of damage caused by the common disease of dental decay or caries (see CARIES, DENTAL) are included in *operative dentistry.* The most frequently applicable technique is the removal, by drilling, of all of the decayed and infected portions of the tooth, followed by the filling of the cavity with a suitable material. The treatment of such diseases as pyorrhea and trench mouth (qq.v.) is the subject of *periodontia,* the treatment and cure of diseases of the soft tissues surrounding the teeth. *Orthodontia* comprises the correction of dental and oral anomalies and particularly the straightening of maloccluded teeth, i.e., teeth which do not meet properly at the masticatory (biting or chewing) surfaces. *Prosthodontia* is the art of replacing lost natural teeth by artificial ones. The artificial tooth is usually a close imitation of the natural *crown,* the part of the tooth extending beyond the gum, and is itself sometimes called a crown. The term "crown" is also applied to a porcelain cap which is fitted over a tooth. The artificial tooth is also called a bridge tooth or pontic. When a large number of teeth are replaced, they are attached to a *denture,* a plate or frame which fits in the mouth, or to a *bridge,* a metal framework attached to neighboring teeth.

Among dental specialists are the orthodontist, periodontist, and oral surgeon, and the pedodontist, who specializes in dentistry for children.

History. Prior to about 1800, dentistry was not a specialized profession. It was customary for doctors to perform operative dentistry,

barbers to perform oral surgery, blacksmiths to perform extractions, and silversmiths or jewelers to perform prosthodontia. These individual dental operations, however, had been practiced almost from the beginning of civilization. Specimens of dental work in the shape of natural teeth bound together with gold, or artificial teeth of ivory, bone, wood, or stone, attached to the natural ones by means of cord or of gold or silver bands or ligatures, have been found in the jaws of mummies entombed at least as early as the 6th century B.C. Some authorities maintain that the ancient Egyptians practiced the filling of teeth with gold, but probably any gold observed in the mouth of mummies came from the gold bands placed around the teeth for support, or through gilding of the surface of the teeth for decorative purposes.

References to dental operations are found in the writings of Herodotus and Hippocrates in the 5th century B.C., and of Aristotle in the 4th century B.C. False teeth must have been common in Rome about the beginning of the Christian Era, for they are mentioned in the writings of Horace, Ovid, and Cicero, and their use was frequently ridiculed by Martial, one of whose couplets runs:

> "False teeth and hair flaunts Lælia
> shamelessly,
> But not false eyes, for these she can-
> not buy."

Galen, an anatomist of the 2nd century A.D. wrote extensively on the subject of the teeth.

The oldest known book on dentistry is the *Artzney Buchlein,* written in German anonymously in 1532 and printed in Leipzig by Peter Jordan. It consists principally of quotations from such ancient authorities as Pliny, Galen, Mesua, and Avicenna. Quoting from a book written by Mesua (physician to Harun al-Rashid) in 857, the author advises treatment of tooth decay by scratching and cleaning with a chisel, knife, or file, and then filling the cavity with gold leaf. If this quotation is authentic, drilling and filling teeth in essentially the modern fashion was known in the 9th century, and it was certainly known by the 16th century.

Among the 16th-century writers on dentistry were Eustachio, Fallopio, and Paré (qq.v.). John Hunter (q.v.) wrote on anatomical dentistry in the 18th century. The first dental practitioner in America was probably Robert Woofendale, who came to this country from England in 1766. His *Practical Observations on the Human Teeth* was published in London in 1783.

The 19th century was notable for the rise of dentistry as both a science and a profession. Virtually all the methods and instruments of modern dentistry have been developed within the past 100 years. The first dental college was the Baltimore College of Dental Surgery, which was chartered and opened in 1840. In the same year the American Society of Dental Surgeons was organized in New York. American dental schools and practitioners have since risen to a position of world pre-eminence.

Diagnosis. The hard part of a tooth, composed of dentine and enamel (q.v.), surrounds a soft, central portion called the pulp, consisting of living tissue; see TEETH. Many authorities believe that infection of this central portion may be transmitted to other portions of the body, causing localized symptoms or general septicemia. More frequently, infection or decay in the teeth is indicated by localized pain in the form of a toothache, which may either be continuous, or appear only when sweet, cold, or hot substances in the mouth touch the tooth. Still more frequently decay starts without any symptoms whatsoever, and pain arises only when injury to the tooth has progressed considerably. For this reason, dentists advocate an examination of the teeth at least twice each year.

In the absence of any pain, looseness, or deformity of the teeth, the dentist examines the teeth and supporting structures to determine their general health, and looks primarily for cavities. He probes for any softness or opening on all exposed surfaces of the teeth, and usually X-rays the teeth (see X RAYS). By these means he determines not only the presence, but also the exact position and size of all cavities, and is able to take steps to prevent the decay from progressing. X rays are also valuable particularly for investigating conditions below the surface of the gum, such as unerupted teeth, impacted teeth, and growths in the jaw.

Caries. The first step in the treatment of a cavity is to remove all of the decayed matter, and as much additional undecayed matter as is necessary to have a cavity of desirable shape for filling. This material was originally removed by hand with small chisels and knives. Drills driven by foot were subsequently used until the introduction of the dental engine, essentially an electric motor supplying power, through a series of pulleys mounted on articulated rods, to a drill chuck which can be placed at any angle in any position in the patient's mouth. The drill chuck can

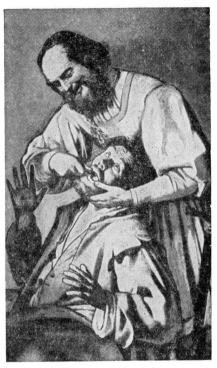

Dentistry as practiced in the 16th century (from painting by Gerard van Honthorst)

hold any one of a variety of tools, and the dentist chooses a drill or burr suitable to the position, size, and hardness of the material which he is cutting.

The development of a type of tooth drill employing ultrasonic sound waves was announced in 1954 by U.S. Navy scientists. Still in the experimental stage, the ultrasonic drill is reported to eliminate the discomfort caused by the heat, vibration, noise, and pressure associated with burr drilling.

If the decay is so extensive that the dentist must expose the pulp, there is danger of infection, and formerly such infection was the rule rather than the exception. By working under aseptic conditions, with a rubber dam (cofferdam) to isolate the tooth from the rest of the mouth, it is now possible to avoid such infection. The living pulp is treated with antiseptic and sedative substances, is usually capped with a thin layer of metal (often platinum), and is finally covered with a layer of cement, preparatory to filling the cavity above the pulp. It is also possible to kill the entire pulp, remove all organic remains of this tissue from the tooth and its roots, and then fill the space with inert materials. In this way pulpless (and therefore dead) teeth may be preserved for many years, and even pulpless roots from which the natural crown has been entirely removed may be preserved as a valuable foundation for an artificial replacement.

Fillings. A filling serves two principal purposes: to protect the tooth against further decay, and to provide a substitute for the missing portion of the natural crown so that the tooth will again be able to perform its masticatory function. In addition, if the filling is on a visible surface, it should, for esthetic reasons, be made similar in color and texture to the nearby surfaces of the teeth.

The material of the filling must be soft enough to be shaped to the cavity and readily inserted, yet hard enough to withstand the grinding action of mastication. Materials of intermediate hardness such as gold and lead were the first materials used for fillings. More desirable is a substance which is soft when placed in the cavity, but soon hardens; cements and amalgams supply this property to a greater or lesser degree. A third method of achieving this compromise is by building up a filling of thin, pliable layers of a hard, cohesive material. It was found in 1855 that annealed gold foil possessed these properties. A fourth method is to use an *inlay,* a hard filling which is shaped outside the mouth and then cemented into the tooth cavity. Gold and other metals have been used for inlays, and so has porcelain, which has the additional advantage of being virtually indistinguishable from natural teeth.

A metal for use in fillings should be a poor conductor of heat; in consequence, silver, an excellent conductor, is rarely used, and base fillings of cement, an insulator, are used under gold, a good conductor. The filling material must be noncorrosive; thus iron and certain other metals cannot be used. Moreover, if two different metals are placed in the mouth they may act like the two plates of a battery, not only setting up painful electric currents in the mouth but also rapidly corroding the more electropositive of the two metals, and forming acids which may cause caries. Highly inert metals, such as gold and platinum, are therefore desirable for use in fillings, and dentists avoid using different metals for filling adjacent or opposing teeth.

The filling must fit snugly in the natural crown, to prevent reinfection of the cavity by infiltrating fluids. If a plastic substance is used, it must be one which does not contract on setting.

During the last half of the 19th century, annealed gold foil was the commonest filling material. This was inserted bit by bit, and welded by compacting with a mallet. The mallet was first operated by hand, but an electric mallet was developed in 1887 which automatically struck repeated blows. The presence of saliva interferes with cohesion of the gold, but this difficulty was obviated by the invention of the rubber dam in 1864, which isolates the tooth from the fluids of the mouth.

The most popular modern materials for temporary fillings and for base fillings in deep cavities are gutta-percha; and cements made either of zinc ozide mixed with eugenol or with oil of cloves, or of zinc oxyphosphate mixed with phosphoric acid. Amalgams, first used for fillings in 1826, and silicate cements are now generally employed for exposed, permanent fillings. Porcelain and gold are commonly used for inlays.

Prosthesis. The considerations in constructing and inserting false teeth are similar to those for fillings, except that appearance and comfort are more important, and that the false teeth must support remaining natural teeth. The materials used have been the same as those used for fillings; wood, bone, animal teeth, and ivory were also formerly employed. Porcelain, attached to a base plate by gold or platinum, has long been used for replacements. The base plate was originally made of metal, but plastics have been generally used for this purpose since the first hard-rubber plate was made in 1855, and methyl methacrylate resins are now employed. One-piece acrylic dentures, including acrylic teeth, are sometimes used. Individual porcelain teeth are attached to adjacent teeth by bridgework or partial dentures, or to living roots by metallic pins called *pivots.* Bridges may be either fixed or removable.

In shaping a filling it is possible to mold the filling to the cavity and then to polish the exposed surface. In prosthesis, shaping in the mouth is not possible, and the plates and crowns must be accurately shaped before they are inserted in the mouth. To obtain the correct shape, an impression of the mouth and gums is taken; wax, gutta-percha, plaster of Paris, or various modeling compounds were formerly used to take the impression, but colloidal materials called alginates are now preferred. From this impression, which is a negative, a plaster-of-Paris positive model is made, which is an exact replica of the jaw of the patient. On this replica the dentist then builds up in wax or some other suitable plastic a denture, and tries it by fitting it in the patient's mouth. If the wax denture is satisfactory, it is returned to the plaster cast of the jaw, and fresh plaster is built up around it. The wax is then melted out of this solid cast, which is used for casting the final denture. Generally this method is used only for making the plate, and the individual teeth are made separately and attached to the plate by metal. The teeth are made of porcelain, and glazed and fired by the usual ceramic techniques (see CERAMICS).

When any teeth remain in the jaw, false teeth are fastened to them by bridgework. When all the teeth of a jaw are replaced, some other method must be used for holding the denture in place. Springs were formerly used for this purpose, to the great discomfort of the wearer. In 1800 it was discovered that if the plate were snugly fitted to the floor and roof of the mouth it would be kept in place by atmospheric pressure. Later it was discovered that if a space were left between the upper plate and the roof of the mouth, the wearer, by sucking the air out of this space, could greatly increase the stability of the plate.

Dental prosthetics includes numerous miscellaneous techniques, such as correction of defects of the palate, construction of splints for jaw fractures, and even the construction of orthodontic devices and the restoration of facial features deformed through improper occlusion (meeting) or other malformations of the teeth.

Anesthesia. Although the origin of anesthesia is clouded in controversy, it is certain that many of the earliest experiments with anesthesia, performed during the 1840's, were made by dentists; see ANESTHESIA. The high degree of pain associated with most operative dentistry is not only unnecessary, but tends to make the patient recoil, thus interfering with the dentist's work. Many dentists now use anesthesia as regular procedure in all but the simplest dental operations. General anesthesia, using ether, chloroform, or nitrous oxide (laughing gas), was originally employed, but is difficult and now considered unnecessary; in addition, general anesthesia prevents the patient from co-operating with the dentist by opening or closing the mouth or making other movements as directed. Analgesia is sometimes used, the commonest procedure being to give the patient a general anesthetic such as nitrous oxide, in quantity sufficient to make him insensible to pain, but insufficient to produce complete unconsciousness. The most general procedure, particularly for routine drilling and filling of cavities, is to use such local anesthetics as novocaine, which are injected by needle in such a way as to block off the nerves in a localized area of the jaw. Since about 1946 a few dentists have used a high-pressure syringe for injecting the anesthetic directly into the gum, thus avoiding the pain even of the needle. Pain may also be greatly lessened by careful and skillful drilling, or by removing, with a minute stream of water, the heat generated by the burr.

Prophylaxis and Oral Hygiene. The exact cause of the most important dental disease, caries, is unknown, and therefore some uncertainty exists as to the true value of many prophylactic measures. Diet and general nutrition apparently play an important role. Calcium is necessary to the building and maintenance of the teeth; an inadequate supply of calcium, or of the vitamin (D) or hormone (parathyroid) which together control its metabolism, causes tooth decay, particularly in children or pregnant women.

A small amount of fluorine (about one part per million) in drinking water apparently inhibits caries, and some communities regularly add fluorine to their water supply for this reason. Larger amounts of fluorine are undesirable, since they cause mottling of the teeth. Application of fluorine compounds directly to the teeth has also been found beneficial.

Certain acids apparently accelerate the processes of dental decay. Particles of food which lodge between the teeth and ferment or putrefy often give rise to such acids; the removal of such particles is one of the principal objects of cleaning the teeth (see DENTIFRICE). Sugar, or certain kinds of sugars, may also have deleterious effects on the teeth.

Even when the teeth are cleaned twice each day, a hard, bonelike deposit, called tartar, slowly forms on them. This deposit may cause recession of the gums, or other injurious effects, and should be periodically removed. A dentist usually cleans the teeth of his patients about twice each year with instruments which remove the tartar and with a hard abrasive which removes stains from the surfaces of the teeth. Such an abrasive, however, if used daily, would destroy the enamel of the teeth in a short time.

DENTITION. See TEETH; TEETHING.

D'ENTRECASTEAUX ISLANDS, an island group in the Pacific Ocean, about 10 miles off the s.e. coast of New Guinea, forming a part of the Australian Papua Territory. The group consists of the main islands of Ferguson, Goodenough, and Normanby, and a number of islets. The islands are mountainous (some peaks rising 7000 feet above sea level) and contain extinct volcanoes and hot springs. This group was named after the French admiral and explorer, Bruni D'Entrecasteaux, who discovered it in 1792. The inhabitants of the islands are Papuans. Total area, about 1200 sq.m. Pop. (1950 est.) 33,800.

DENVER, capital of the State of Colorado, and county seat of Denver Co., situated in the foothills of the Rocky Mountains, 1 m. above sea level, at the junction of the South Platte R. and Cherry Creek. The Front Range of the Rockies, 12 m. to the w., is visible for 150 m., from Pikes Peak on the s. to Longs Peak on the n. To the e. of Denver stretch great plains. The city's area, coextensive with that of Denver Co., totals 58.75 sq.m.

Denver is served by major air lines, and is located on direct transcontinental railway routes. The State Capital, costing about $3,-000,000 upon its completion in 1896, is built of Colorado granite and is topped by a dome covered with gold leaf; part of the interior decorations are of Colorado onyx. It is located in an area, extending ½ m. through the center of the city, which includes also the State office building and the State historical museum. Nearby is the Civic Center, containing the public library and also the city and county building, which was completed in 1932 at a cost of $5,000,000. Besides a park area of 1563 acres within the city limits, Denver has a system of mountain parks covering nearly 25,000 acres and linked by 100 m. of highway. Educational institutions in the city include the University of Denver (see Denver, University of), Westminster Law School, Colorado Woman's College (Junior), the Iliff School of Theology (Methodist), and Regis and Loretto Heights colleges (Catholic).

Because of its railroad facilities and its proximity to rich mining and agricultural areas, Denver is the leading commercial, financial, and manufacturing city of the Rocky Mountain region. It is the largest sheep market in the world, one of the most important cattle markets w. of the Mississippi R., and the wholesale-distribution point for communities in fourteen States besides Colorado. The city ranks fourth in the United States as an insurance center. Nearly 150 offices of the Federal government are situated in the city, which is sometimes characterized as the western capital of the nation. Denver is also the site of one of the three coinage mints of the United States government. The chief industries include slaughtering and meat packing, canning, automobile assembling, and the manufacture of mining equipment, candy, flour, rubber products, luggage, sugar-mill equipment, and railroad cars. Because of its dry, bracing climate, the city is an important health resort, equipped with modern sanitoriums, hospitals, and other facilities chiefly for people suffering from pulmonary disorders.

Denver was first settled by gold prospectors in 1857, and received a charter as a city of Colorado Territory in 1861. Despite a fire in 1863 and a flood in 1864, the city grew rapidly. It became the Territorial seat of government in 1867. The population increased from 4759 in 1870 to 106,713 in 1890. Pop. (1950) 415,786.

DENVER, UNIVERSITY OF, a coeducational, nonsectarian institution of higher learning, owned by the Methodist Church, and situated in Denver, Colo. The school was founded in 1864 as the Colorado Seminary, but was reorganized in 1880 as the University of Denver. Among its colleges and departments are liberal arts, science and engineering, law, commerce, graduate, social work, and library science. In 1953–54 the enrollment was 5580, including 3446 full-time students; the faculty numbered 230.

DEODAR. See Cedar.

DE PAUW UNIVERSITY, a coeducational institution of higher learning, conducted under the ausipces of the Methodist Church, and located in Greencastle, Ind. It was founded in 1837 as the Indiana Asbury University, and received its present name in 1884. At various times the institution has conducted schools of law, divinity, art, music, teaching, and medicine, but in recent years it has had only a college of liberal arts and a school of music. In 1953–54 the enrollment was 1626, including 1602 full-time students; the faculty numbered 130.

DEPENDENT CHILDREN. See Maternal and Child Welfare.

DEPEW, Chauncey Mitchell (1834–1928), American politician and corporation lawyer, born at Peekskill, N.Y., and educated at Yale College. He was admitted to the bar in 1858 and from 1861 to 1862 served in the

New York State Assembly. He was elected secretary of state of New York in 1863 and three years later was retained as counsel for the railroad interests of Cornelius and William H. Vanderbilt, becoming general counsel in 1875. From 1885 to 1898 he was president of the New York Central and Hudson River Railroad, and in 1898 became chairman of the board of the Vanderbilt-owned railroad lines. In 1899 he was elected U.S. Senator from New York State, and served until 1911. In 1888 he was nominated for the Presidency but withdrew in favor of Benjamin Harrison. From that year until 1925, he was a leader at Republican National Conventions, where he frequently made nominating speeches. He was renowned as an orator and after-dinner speaker. His reminiscences were published as *Memories of Eighty Years* (1922).

DEPORTATION, the enforced removal of an alien from a country in which he is a resident to the country of his origin. Technically, deportation is distinguished from exclusion which is a denial of entry into a country; in common speech, however, the latter term is sometimes included in the meaning of the former expression. Deportation is also distinguished from banishment and exile, two forms of punishment for crimes by citizens, usually imposed on political offenders and entailing an enforced absence from a city, place, or country; and transportation (q.v.), a penalty imposed on criminals and involving imprisonment or other forms of loss of liberty, in a distant place, usually outside the country.

Prior to modern times deportation was used as an occasional means of ridding a community of undesirable aliens, the grounds for removal being mostly political. Of this character were a number of statutes, enacted from 1793 to 1826 by the British Parliament, to remove and exclude from England alien supporters of the French Revolution. Also partly similar in character were the Alien and Sedition Acts (q.v.), enacted by the U.S. Congress in 1798, which empowered the President to arrest and deport any alien he considered dangerous.

In later times, in the United States, as in the rest of the world generally, deportation became an instrument of national policy, closely associated with immigration policies, and varying with political events and economic developments. Congress, in 1882, enacted the Chinese Exclusion Act designed to exclude Chinese immigrants from the United States, and to provide for the deportation of those adjudged illegally resident in the country.

Current United States policy, however, may be said to have begun with a Congressional enactment in 1891. That legislation provided for a time limit to deportation of one year after an alien's entry into the United States, and for the deportation within that time of aliens who for certain causes became public charges; established administrative procedure as the means effecting deportation; greatly restricted judicial review of deportation proceedings; and created the Bureau of Immigration and Naturalization as a branch of the Treasury Department (now of the Justice Department) to administer the deportation laws.

Later, as the need in the United States for immigrant workers began to decline, legislation reflected a growing antipathy toward aliens who came to be regarded as a cause of unemployment of American workers. The categories of deportable aliens were increased to include convicts, persons likely to become public charges, contract laborers, illiterates, feeble-minded persons, diseased persons, epileptics, procurers, prostitutes, persons entering the country illegally in excess of the immigration quotas, anarchists, and persons professing a belief in, or membership in an organization advocating the overthrow of the U.S. government by force and violence. The time limit after entry, during which the government may resort to deportation, was extended; according to the cause it was made three to five years, and, in the case of criminals and anarchists, the limit was removed.

Until World War I, deportation for anarchist beliefs, made a cause for expulsion from the country in 1903, occurred occasionally. Following the Bolshevik revolution in Russia in 1917, new legislation, enacted by Congress between 1917 and 1920 in an effort to combat the introduction of Communist beliefs and tactics, extended the political basis for exclusion and deportation to include many radical beliefs. Subsequently thousands of aliens were arrested, and deported.

Deportations for all causes reached a peak during the four-year depression period (1930–34), when the number was approximately 83,000. Thereafter the number fell. In 1948, the deportation laws were invoked by the Immigration and Naturalization Service in an effort to deport from the United States a number of union leaders and others, alleged to be Communist Party members and to have entered the country illegally.

DEPOSIT, in geology, any natural accumulation of mineral material formed by gradual deposition by water, glaciers, or the wind. *Alluvial deposits* are those formed by rivers and streams. Running water carries sand, silt, or clay in suspension and these substances gradually settle to the bottom or at the sides of the stream, particularly at places where the stream widens and the current slows. The deltas of rivers are typical alluvial deposits. Where swift mountain streams reach the floor of a flat valley, the sudden change in grade, and consequent slowing of the stream, often results in the deposition of an *alluvial fan,* another form of alluvial deposit. The action of running water tends to sort out the different sizes and weights of particles which are carried in suspension. Thus gravel and pebbles will be deposited farther upstream than the lighter sand, and fine silt will be carried farther downstream than sand. *Sedimentary deposits* are formed on the floor of the ocean or of lakes by the settling of sand or silt. Sedimentary rocks (q.v.) are formed by the petrification of such deposits. Alluvial deposits are caused by the mechanical action of gravity, but chemical precipitation from water is also a factor in the production of such rocks as limestone. *Stalactites* and *stalagmites* (see CAVE) are typical of precipitation deposits. Mineral salts contained in hot underground water are often precipitated in rock fissures, leaving *veins* of mineral ore. Subsurface water containing dissolved mineral salts sometimes dissolves organic matter which is present underground and precipitates mineral matter in its place. This type of deposition is called *replacement,* and is typified by the formation of petrified wood in which precipitated silica replaces the organic matter of buried trees.

The glaciers of the great ice ages, as well as modern glaciers, are responsible for several kinds of deposits. *Glacial till* consists of the rock debris carried along by the glacier and deposited usually at its foot. The debris consists of rock fragments of all sizes from boulders to clay. When till is directly deposited by the glacier, it is not assorted according to size, but when the melting water of the glacier or other streams has acted on a till deposit, the material is graded as in the case of other alluvial deposits. *Eskers,* which are long winding ridges of sand and gravel, are a special form of glacial deposit. They mark the position of ice tunnels or streams flowing beneath a glacier. See GLACIER.

The commonest wind-formed deposit is the sand dune, found in deserts and on the shores of oceans and lakes. Dunes are formed by sand accumulating around any object that serves as an obstacle to the wind. As wind-blown sand is deposited in the lee of such an obstacle, the wind is slowed still more, and the dune continues to grow. In some localities dunes reach a height of 500 ft. and dunes of 100 ft. are common in many parts of the world. When materials finer than sand are carried by the wind and finally dropped to earth, the deposit that results is known as *loess.* Thick layers of loess are found in Europe and the Americas, and, loess deposits of Asia reach a thickness of several hundred feet. They are the basis for some of the world's richest agricultural soils.

DEPOSITION, in law, the testimony of a witness made in the presence of a judge, commissioner, or other competent party, and put into writing for use at a trial. In courts of equity the whole evidence is usually submitted in the form of depositions, but in courts of common law these are allowed only when the witness is unable to give the testimony orally in open court. The Sixth Amendment to the United States Constitution provides that in criminal cases the accused shall enjoy the right of being confronted with the witnesses against him. Accordingly, the prosecutor cannot use depositions without the prisoner's consent. In civil cases, each State has its own regulations on the matter.

DEPRECIATION, in accounting, the decrease in the value of capital assets invested in a business, resulting from such causes as: physical wear and tear in ordinary use, as in the case of machinery; deterioration primarily by action of the elements, as in the case of a building or the erosion of farmlands; or obsolescence due to technological changes and the introduction of new and better machinery and methods of production.

The primary aim of the accountant in recording and reporting depreciation is to present a true and undistorted picture of net income and the value of the capital assets owned by a business. The provision of a means for replacing capital assets as they wear out may be looked upon as an additional function of depreciation accounting.

Several methods are used by accountants in calculating periodic depreciation, or apportioning the value of a capital asset over its expected useful life. The most widely used is the "straight-line method", in which the rate of depreciation is constant for the entire working life of the capital assets. Thus, if a machine

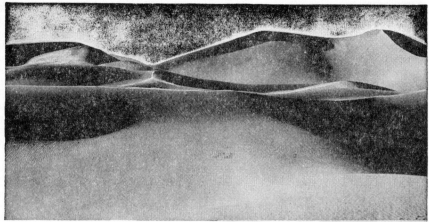

South African Govt. Info. Office

DEPOSITS BY WIND AND PRECIPITATION

Above: Sand dunes, commonest type of wind-formed deposit, in Death Valley, California. Right: Stalactites deposited by precipitation in Cango Caves, Oudtshoorn, S. Africa.

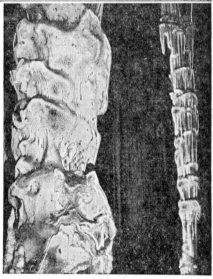

cost $1100 and is assumed to have a ten-year use-life and a scrap value of $100 at the end of ten years, the amount of annual depreciation would be $100 and the annual depreciation rate ten percent (annual depreciation divided by cost minus scrap value). When the decrease in value of a capital asset is not constant over a period of time, a second method called the "service-unit method" or "unit of production method" is utilized. Here the scrap value is deducted from the cost of the asset and the remainder divided by the number of units (for example, miles or loads in the case of a truck, or number of units of output in the case of a machine) the asset is expected to yield. The result is depreciation expressed in units produced or units of service performed. A truck costing $2100 with a salvage value of $100 and estimated to run 200,000 miles during its use-life would thus have a depreciation rate of one cent a mile ($2000 divided by 200,000). A third method, using a constant percentage of the remaining value (depreciated value) each year, gives effect to the substantial loss in value incurred immediately after the asset is acquired, as well as the relatively minor cost of upkeep at this time. During the latter years, however, the annual depreciation diminishes, but the cost of maintenance tends to increase. As a result, an approximately uniform charge is made against business income each year for the use of the

asset as reflected in depreciation and maintenance.

The accumulated reduction in value resulting from use and obsolescence is shown as a depreciation reserve. Therefore, an asset which cost $2100 and which has depreciated $500 has a value of $1600. The accounting presentation calls for the listing of the asset at cost, or $2100, and the showing of the accumulated loss in value as a reserve for depreciation of $500. The existence of the reserve for depreciation does not imply, however, that because an enterprise has consistently made profits and therefore recouped the cost of the depreciated value of its capital assets, it will be sure to have the funds available for replacing worn-out assets. The management of funds can be looked upon as an independent problem. But the establishment of a specific fund of cash or its equivalent in amounts more or less equal to the accumulated loss in value of an asset will assure an enterprise of its ability to replace worn-out and obsolete capital assets.

For depreciation, in the sense of a depreciated currency, i.e., a currency which has declined in value, see MONEY.

DEPRESSION, ECONOMIC, an extended decline in business activity, usually following an economic crisis (see BUSINESS CYCLE) and involving curtailment of production, falling prices and profits, and general unemployment. The term "depression" used in this sense refers specifically to widespread economic stagnation, as part of the economic cycle, and does not apply to periods of subnormal activity in one or a small group of industries. Acute depressions have occurred in the United States during the years 1825, 1836, 1847, 1857, 1866, 1873, 1882, 1890, 1900, 1907, 1914, 1920, and 1930. See BANK AND BANKING; FINANCE; UNEMPLOYMENT.

DEPTFORD, a metropolitan borough of London, England, on the Thames R., 3 miles S.E. of London Bridge. It contains large wharves for timber imports, and factories for making furniture, casks, packing cases, and soap. Among its other industrial establishments are marine-engineering plants, oil refineries, and plants processing cacao and coffee. On the river front is the Royal Victoria Victualing Yard, which supplies the British navy with provisions. From 1547 to 1869, Deptford was the site of the Admiralty shipbuilding yards, where Peter I (Peter the Great) of Russia served as an apprentice in order to learn shipbuilding. Pop. (1951 est.) 75,694.

DEPTH CHARGE, or DEPTH BOMB, an explosive charge designed to explode at a given depth under water by means of a hydrostatic detonator, and used as a weapon against submarines. It is not necessary to make a direct hit with depth charges, since their concussion is effective at some distance under water. Depth charges first came into use in World War I. The early forms of the weapon consisted of large cylinders containing TNT, which were rolled or catapulted, usually two at a time, from the stern of a ship. In World War II many improvements were made both in depth charges themselves and in machinery for launching them. By the use of a new and more powerful explosive called Torpex, a mixture of RDX, TNT, and aluminum, the size of depth charges was materially reduced. The casings were also streamlined so that they would sink faster. Two types of multiple launching mortars were also developed. One, nicknamed Hedgehog, threw charges in a circular pattern far ahead of the ship that launched it; a lighter launcher with less recoil, nicknamed Mousetrap, threw a pattern of charges in a straight line ahead of the launching vessel and at right angles to its path.

DE QUINCEY, THOMAS (1785–1859), English author, born in Manchester, and educated at Bath and Manchester. At the age of seventeen he ran away from school to Wales, and from there to London where he spent a year in poverty. Later, however, he was sent to Oxford University for five years. In 1809 he settled in Grasmere, and began his career as a writer, joining the literary circle of Coleridge, Wordsworth and Southey. For a year and a half he edited the *Westmoreland Gazette,* a weekly paper. Returning to London in 1820, he wrote his *Confessions of an English Opium Eater* (first published in the *London Magazine,* 1821), a vivid description of his own experiences as an opium addict. He spent twelve years (1828–40) in Edinburgh, and thereafter took up a roving existence. In addition to many contributions in *Blackwood's, Tait's Magazine,* and *Hogg's Instructor,* De Quincey's writings include *Murder Considered as One of the Fine Arts* (1821), *Suspiria De Profundis* (1845), *Joan of Arc* (1847), and *The English Mailcoach* (1849).

DERAIN, ANDRÉ (1880–1954), French painter, born in Chatou, department of Seine-et-Oise. He studied at the Académie Julien, Paris, and with Eugène Carriére. Derain's work was influenced by that of Paul Cezanne and by the principles of the group of painters known as the Fauves (q.v.), who revolted against Impressionism at the beginning of the 20th century. Later Derain was influenced by Cubism (q.v.), and subsequently by other forms of abstract art. His work is characterized by simple and clearly articulated design, the objects of which are often heavily outlined; and by subdued coloring, variety in which is obtained by the use of shadings of a single color rather than by the use of many colors. Among his works are "Les Baigneuses" (1908), "La Route d'Albano" (1921), and "Landscape" (1926).

DERA ISMAIL KHAN, capital of the district of the same name in the North-West

Official U.S. Navy Photos

DEPTH CHARGE. *Top: Loading the charge. Bottom: Left, firing the charge (in upper left corner); right, powerful blast under water sends spray billowing above the surface.*

Frontier Province, Pakistan. The city, situated near the w. bank of the Indus R., about 120 miles N.W. of Multan, is a busy commercial center, with an extensive trade with Afghanistan. Much of the terrain of the district is hilly, barren country, inhabited by nomadic tribes. Among the chief of these are the Sherani and Ustarana, both of Pathan stock. Area of district, 4216 sq.m.; pop. (1951 prelim.) 283,000. Pop. of city (1941) 49,238.

DERBY, county, municipal, and parliamentary borough and county town of Derbyshire, England, situated on the Derwent R., 60 m. by rail S.E. of Manchester. Derby is noted as a rail center and for the manufacture of porcelain (dating from about 1750) and silk (dating from 1717, when John Lombe, introducing the manufacture of silk from Piedmont, Italy, to England, built the first silk mill at Derby). Among other industries are the manufacture of aircraft, automobiles (including the Rolls-Royce), electrical apparatus, hosiery, elastic webbing, paints, and varnishes. In addition, the town contains chemical plants, sawmills, and tanneries. Derby was a royal borough in the time of Edward the Confessor (1002?–1066), and received its first charter in 1026. Among its ecclesiastical buildings are the 14th-century chapel of St. Mary-on-the-Bridge and All Saints' Church, which contains a 16th-century Gothic tower. The city is the site of a technical college, an agricultural institute, schools of science and art, and the Liverage almshouses. Derby grammar school dates from 1159. Pop. of borough (1951 est.) 141,264.

DERBY, the name of an English earldom. It is one of the three surviving titles of that rank antedating the 17th century, the other two being the earldoms of Huntingdon and Shrewsbury. The title was created in 1485 for Thomas Stanley, 2nd Baron Stanley, and has been held since by members of the Stanley (q.v.) family.

DERBYSHIRE, a county of England, in the N. Midland district. It is level and fertile in the s., but hilly in the N., with poor soil, harsh climate, and heavy rainfall. The Derby Highlands are noted for their scenery; in the Peak District is Kinder Scout, 2088 ft. above sea level. The towns of Matlock and Buxton, lying among the hills, are health resorts with warm mineral springs. The county's largest river is the Trent, which forms part of the southern boundary. The Derwent rises in the Peak District and flows southward, almost bisecting the county. In the north, sheep are raised; wheat and oats are the principal crops of the fertile south. A large part of the valley of the Trent is given over to cattle and dairy farming. Mining and manufacturing, however, are the principal industries of Derbyshire. The county contains coal, iron, and lead mines, and limestone and marble quarries. Among the industrial products are iron, automobiles, silk and cotton goods, woolens, hosiery, lace, braids, porcelain and china, chemicals, paper, malts, and ales. The county's chief industrial towns are Derby, the county borough, and Belper, Chesterfield, Glossop, Ilkeston, and Alfreton. Derbyshire has prehistoric, Celtic, and Roman remains, and many ruins of medieval abbeys, monasteries, and feudal castles. Area, 993 sq.m. Pop. (1951 est.) 826,336.

DERBYSHIRE NECK. See GOITER.

DERBYSHIRE SPAR. See FLUORITE.

DERMATITIS, inflammation of the true skin, or derma. The term is often used interchangeably with eczema (q.v.), which refers more specifically to certain noncontagious diseases of the skin. The inflammation may be caused by parasites or by physical and chemical irritants. *Streptococcus* or *Staphylococcus* infections of the skin are examples of bacterial dermatitis (see BACTERIA). The yeastlike *Blastomyces dermatitis* causes a skin infection. Tuberculosis, coccidioides, syphilis, and other systemic diseases often result in dermatitis in the form of ulcerous conditions of the skin.

Sunburn is a common example of dermatitis resulting from the action of the actinic rays of the sun on the skin. The sun's actinic rays may also cause diseases such as *Hydroa aestivale* and the more serious *Xeroderma pigmentosum.* The former is a chronic inflammation of the face and hands, affecting light-sensitive people. The latter is characterized by a freckled condition and horny thickenings of the skin. It is closely akin to chronic burns from X rays (q.v.) and may lead to malignant growths. Other causes of dermatitis are burns, frostbite, circulatory disturbances, the action of certain drugs taken internally, wounds, caustic chemicals, and contact with certain plants such as poison ivy. See SKIN.

DERMATOLOGY, the science of the structure, functions, and diseases of the skin (q.v.).

DERMATOPHYTES, parasitic fungi which grow on the skin of man and animals. They are the causative agents of certain diseases, such as favus and ringworm, especially prevalent in the tropics, where the high humidity and temperature favor the growth of the parasites. See ATHLETE'S FOOT; HAIR DISEASES; RINGWORM.

DERMESTIDAE, a family of small beetles of the superfamily Cleroidea. The adult beetles are generally dark in color and have bodies covered with fine short hairs. The bodies are oval and are shorter than ½ inch in all species. The antennae of all species are clubbed and blunt. The larvae of many feed on dried animal matter and cause much destruction of leather, woolens, feathers, dried meats, horn, cheese, and hair goods. Among the common species are the carpet beetle (q.v.), and the bacon beetle or larder beetle, *Dermestes lardarius,* the larva of which is brown, hairy, and about half an inch long. The bacon beetle is one of the most destructive dermestids. The larvae of dermestids of the genus *Anthrenus* are pests in museums, for they devour the dried insects in entomological collections. These larvae are often called buffalo bugs, probably from the fact that they were known to attack buffalo-skin robes.

DERRY. See LONDONDERRY.

DE RUYTER. See RUYTER.

DERVISH (Turk., from Per. *darvish,* "beggar"), one of a class of Mohammedan devotees, similar in some ways to Christian monks. Brotherhoods of dervishes are numerous, each having its own rule, garb, rites, and method of novitiation and initiation. Not all orders conform strictly to the Mohammedan ceremonial and ritual law, and the occupations required by the different brotherhoods vary. Some dervishes are wanderers, depending on alms; others are settled in convents, called Takyas or Khânkâs, where they observe special rites or devote themselves to meditation and penance. Others are ordinary tradesmen and laborers, performing the ceremonies of their order only on specific occasions. Some form a class of religious entertainers, who are hired to chant their dirge or *Zikr* at public and private festivals. Frequently the devotees work themselves into a frenzy and become capable of remarkable acts of strength, eventually falling into a state of convulsion.

Although Mohammed was an advocate of poverty, it was after his time, when Islamic thought came into contact with other religions, such as Persian and Hindu, that the dervish orders developed. Tradition ascribes the founding of these orders to the caliphs Abu Bekr and Ali in the 7th century A.D.

Among the best known and perhaps the earliest of the dervishes are the Kâdiris, founded in 1165 A.D. and known in Europe as the "howling dervishes" on account of their peculiar chant. Also well known are the Rifâ'is (1182), famous for their feats of eating glass and live coals and of swallowing swords; the Mevlevis (1273), or "dancing" dervishes; and the Kalenderis, the "calenders" of the *Arabian Nights,* who must vow to travel perpetually.

DERWENT, JAMES RADCLIFFE (or RADCLYFFE), EARL OF. See RADCLIFFE, SIR JAMES.

DESCARTES, RENÉ, or (Lat.) RENATUS CARTESIUS (1596-1650), French philosopher and mathematician, born at La Haye, Touraine. He was the son of a minor nobleman and belonged to a family that had produced a number of men of learning. At the age of eight Descartes was enrolled at the Jesuit school of La Flèche in Anjou, where he remained for eight years. Here, besides the usual classical studies, he received instruction in mathematics and in scholastic philosophy. Catholicism exerted a strong influence on Descartes throughout his life. Upon graduation from school, he studied law at the University of Poitiers, graduating in 1616. Descartes, however, never practiced law; in 1618 he entered the service of Prince Maurice of Nassau at Breda in Holland, with the intention of following a military career. In succeeding years he served in other armies, but his attention had already been attracted to the problems of mathematics and philosophy to which he was to devote the rest of his life. He made a pilgrimage to Italy in 1623-24, and spent the years from 1624 to 1628 in France. While in France, he devoted himself to the study of philosophy and also experimented in optics. In 1628, having sold his properties in France, he moved to Holland, where he spent most of the rest of his life. He lived for varying periods in a number of different cities, including Amsterdam, Deventer, Utrecht, and Leyden.

It was probably during the first years of his residence in Holland that Descartes wrote his first major work. This was *Essais Philosophiques,* published in 1637, which contained four parts: an essay on geometry, another on optics, a third on meteors, and *Discourse on the Method of Rightly Conducting the Reason,* which described his philosophical speculations. This was followed by other philosophical works, among them *Meditations on First Philosophy* (1641) and *The Principles of Philosophy* (1644). The latter volume was dedicated to Princess Elizabeth of Bohemia, who lived in Holland and with whom Descartes had formed a deep friendship. In 1649 Descartes was invited to the court of Queen Christina of Sweden at Stockholm to give the queen instruction in philosophy. The rigors of the northern winter brought on the illness which caused his death.

Philosophy. Descartes has often been called the father of modern philosophy, and the appellation is justified in that he attempted to apply the rational inductive methods of science, and particularly of mathematics, to philosophy. Prior to his time, philosophy had been dominated by the method of scholasticism, which was entirely based on comparing and contrasting the views of recognized authorities. Rejecting this method, Descartes stated, "In our search for the direct road to truth, we should busy ourselves with no object about which we cannot attain a certitude equal to that of the demonstrations of arithmetic and geometry." He therefore determined to hold nothing true until he had established grounds for believing it true. The single sure fact from which his investigations began was expressed by him in the famous words, *Cogito, ergo sum,* "I think, therefore I am." From this postulate that a clear consciousness of his thinking proved his own

French Embassy, Information Division
René Descartes (from portrait by Frans Hals)

existence he argued the existence of God. God, according to Descartes' philosophy, created two classes of substance which make up the whole of reality: thinking substances or minds, and extended substances or bodies.

Science. Descartes' philosophy, sometimes called Cartesianism, carried him into elaborate and erroneous explanations of a number of physical phenomena, which, however, had value, because he substituted a system of mechanical interpretations of physical phenomena for the vague spiritual concepts of most earlier writers. Although he had at first been inclined to accept the Copernican theory of the universe with its concept of a system of spinning planets revolving around the sun, he abandoned this theory when it was pronounced heretical by the Catholic Church. In its place he devised a theory of vortices in which space was entirely filled with matter, in various states, whirling about the sun.

In the field of physiology, Descartes held that part of the blood was a subtle fluid which he called animal spirits. The animal spirits, he believed, came into contact with thinking substances in the brain and flowed out along the channels of the nerves to animate the muscles and other parts of the body.

Descartes' study of optics led him to the independent discovery of the fundamental law of reflection: that the angle of incidence is equal to the angle of reflection. His essay on optics was the first published statement of this law. His treatment of light as a type of pressure in a solid medium paved the way for the undulatory theory of light.

Mathematics. The most notable contribution that Descartes made to the science of mathematics was the systematization of analytical geometry; see GEOMETRY. He was the first mathematician to attempt to classify curves according to the types of equations which produce them. He also made contributions to the theory of equations, and succeeded in proving the impossibility of trisecting the angle and doubling the cube. Descartes was the first to use the last letters of the alphabet to designate unknown quantities and the first letters to designate known ones. He also invented the method of indices (as in x^2) to express the powers of numbers. Descartes likewise expressed the rule known as Descartes' rule of signs for finding the number of positive and negative roots for any algebraic equation.

DESCENT, the transmission of real property by operation of law to the heir or heirs of one who dies intestate. It is a principle common to most if not all legal systems that the property of a decedent, if not otherwise disposed of by him, shall pass in a fixed line of descent to those related to him by ties of blood. Under some systems, as that of Rome, no distinction was made between the two classes of property now distinguished as real and personal, the whole passing, along with the liabilities of the owner, to a personal representative, and this has been the nature of descent generally, both in ancient and in modern nations. In the common-law system of England and the United States, however, a different principle has prevailed, only the personal property passing to the representatives of the deceased, the real property devolving upon a descendant, who became known as the heir. The personal representative was not necessarily a descendant, nor even related by any ties of consanguinity to the decedent, and the use of the term "descent" was therefore confined to the devolution of the real property—the terms "administration" and "distribution" being employed to describe the corresponding disposition made of the personal property after the owner's death.

DESCHAMPS, EUSTACHE (1340?-1407?), French poet, born at Vertus, Champagne. He received many honors from his patron, King Charles V of France. In addition to ballades and rondeaus, he wrote *Le Miroir de Mariage,* a 13,000-line satire on women, and *De l'Art de Dictier.* His complete works were published posthumously (11 vols., 1878-1902).

DESCHANEL, PAUL EUGÈNE LOUIS (1856–1922), French statesman and author, born in Brussels. He studied law and began his political career as secretary to the politicians Deshayes de Marcères (1876) and Jules Simon (1876–77). He was elected to the Chamber of Deputies in 1885, and became known as one of the greatest orators in the progressive wing of the Republican Party. He was vice-president of the chamber in 1896 and president from 1898 until 1902 and from 1912 to 1920. He was elected to the French Academy in 1899. As a progressive leader, in 1904–05 he supported legislation calling for separation of the Church and state. He headed the commission of foreign and colonial affairs (1905–09) and became the tenth president of the Republic in 1920. Ill-health forced him to resign from the presidency in the same year. Among his most famous works are *Les Intérêts Français dans l'Océan Pacifique* (1887), *Orateurs et Hommes d'État* (1888), *Figures de Femmes* (1889), *La Décentralization* (1895), *La Question Sociale* (1898), and *Gambetta* (1920).

DESCHUTES RIVER, a river of Oregon, rising in the Cascade Range in Klamath County and flowing N.E. through Crook and Wasco counties, emptying into the Columbia R. For about 140 m. of its 320-mile course the river cuts into the great northwestern lava bed, forming a canyon with steep walls, 1000–2500 ft. in depth. The Deschutes is known to fishermen as an excellent trout stream.

DESCRIPTIVE GEOMETRY, the science of making accurate, two-dimensional drawings (or representations) of three-dimensional geometrical forms, and of solving graphically problems relating to the size and position in space of such forms. Descriptive geometry is the basis of all engineering and architectural drafting (q.v.).

The usual technique of representing lines, surfaces, or solids in plane drawings is by means of *orthographic projection.* In this type of projection, the object to be represented is referred to one or more imaginary planes which are at right angles to one another. A point in space is represented by the point in the reference plane touched by a ray perpendicular to the plane and passing through that point. A line in space is represented by a line in the projection plane which joins the projections of the two end points of the line.

In the system of representation devised by Gaspard Monge (q.v.), which is now in universal use, two perpendicular projection planes are normally employed. For compli-

cated figures, a third plane is sometimes added. From the two or three orthographic projections produced on these planes it is possible to calculate all dimensions of the object and to express the spatial relations of its parts. An important use of the Monge method is in finding the two-dimensional form of certain curved surfaces. These surfaces, which can be formed by bending a plane surface without deforming it, are known as *developable surfaces.* They include all forms of cylinders and cones, but do not include spherical surfaces. See PERSPECTIVE.

DESERET, STATE OF, name given by the Mormons in 1849 to their settlement in the present State of Utah, *deseret* being a word taken from the Book of Mormon and meaning "land of the honeybee". In September, 1850, Congress created the Territory of Utah, and the old name fell into disuse. See UTAH; MORMONS.

DESERT, a name properly applied to regions of scanty rainfall which are unsuitable for human habitation, but also applied more broadly to any region which is not suited to the support of human life, such as the great ice waste of Greenland and the arctic tundra.

The arid deserts of the world can be divided into two groups, those of the tropics and those of the temperate zones. The former are sometimes called "hot deserts", and the latter "cold deserts", but these terms are misleading, for one of the most important characteristics of any desert climate is extreme variation in temperature. Because of the lack of moisture in the ground and in the atmosphere, the days in desert regions are extremely hot, rising to as much as 130 °F. in the shade, while nighttime temperatures may fall below freezing. Such a temperature range is typical of the Sahara desert of Africa, and even more extreme ranges are found in the deserts of central Asia. The hot deserts of the world include the Sahara, Libyan, and Nubian deserts of N. Africa, and the Arabian, Persian, and Indian deserts of Asia. Cold deserts, which usually are more elevated than the deserts of the tropics, include the Turkestan and Gobi deserts of Central Asia, the great Australian desert, the Great Basin of North America, and the coastal deserts of Peru, Chile, and Argentina in South America.

Desert landscapes range from flat, sandy plains to mountainous plateaus. The rocks of deserts are typically eroded into fantastic shapes by the action of wind-driven sand, and so-called desert pavements composed of masses of pebbles are frequently formed from

Joseph Miller; Canad. Pacific Ry.;
New Mexico State Tourist Bureau

*Above: Arizona desert, cactus
plants silhouetted against sky.
Left: Well of Moses, in small
desert oasis near Suez, Egypt.
Below: White Sands Monument, a
desert in southern New Mexico.*

the harder portions of wind-eroded rocks and boulders. In sandy deserts, such as the Sahara and portions of the Great Basin desert in Colorado, sand dunes are a typical feature. These wind-built mounds of sand may reach a height of 500 ft. In deserts which have a strong prevailing wind, such as the coastal desert of southern Peru, sand dunes assume an extremely regular crescent shape and move continually across the desert floor. Another feature of arid deserts is the occurrence of salt lakes or playas. These are depressions which are filled with water during the infrequent desert rains. As the water evaporates after the rain, the salts dissolved from the earth become concentrated, and eventually, when the lake is completely dry, a salt pan or surface deposit which is almost entirely a mixture of salts is left behind. Salt lakes, such as the Great Salt Lake of Utah, where evaporation is never complete, but is still enough to concentrate the salts in the lake water, are also a common feature of deserts.

Arid deserts support little vegetable or animal life in their natural state. Vegetation is usually confined to specially adapted plants, such as those of the Cactus family, which transpire little moisture. Because of the dearth of vegetation, the animal population is necessarily limited as well. Much desert land, however, is extremely fertile when water is made available by irrigation either from rivers or wells. Thousands of acres in Peru have been successfully irrigated by water from mountain streams for many centuries, and there is always lush growth in the oases that surround desert wells. In the w. United States, N. Africa, and parts of Australia much valuable desert land has been reclaimed by sinking artesian wells and damming rivers for irrigation.

Tundra. A greater part of northern Siberia, Canada, and Alaska is given over to low-lying, flat plains known as tundras (q.v.), which, because they are badly fitted to support human life, are sometimes called deserts.

Ice Wastes. The entire central portion of Greenland is covered by an ice-cap, as are some of the other islands of the arctic. The Greenland ice-cap, approximately 6000 ft. thick in the center of the island, behaves like a gigantic glacier (q.v.), moving slowly outward to the shore and breaking off into icebergs which are carried southward by the currents.

DESERTION, the offense of abandoning military service, by one in such service. The term is also used to describe the actions of those who leave a post to avoid hazardous duty, or to shirk assignments of an important nature.

In time of peace, desertion is punishable by imprisonment or such other penalty as a court-martial may adjudge, except death. In time of war, punishment for desertion, in the military services of almost all countries, may be death. However, courts-martial of the U.S. Army during World War II often abated desertion charges and punished the offenders for absence without official leave, even after an absence of as long as eight months.

In the merchant marine service, absence without leave for 48 hours is regarded as conclusive evidence of desertion, and is punishable by discharge. When desertion occurs on government-owned merchant ships in time of war, the offenders are liable to fine or imprisonment.

DESERTION, in the law of domestic relations, the abandonment or renunciation of marital relations and obligations by either spouse, with intent not to resume them, and without the consent or wrongful conduct of the other. In most of the States of the United States, willful desertion is a legal cause for divorce; the period of time following desertion, necessary before proceedings can be instituted, varies, however, from one to five years. In some States, a husband's continued financial support of the wife whom he has willfully abandoned is no bar to an action for divorce on her part.

In maritime law, desertion is the unauthorized absence of a seaman from a ship on which he had signed for a voyage, before expiration of his term of service, and with the intention of not completing the term. It is the intention not to complete the voyage which, in law, distinguishes desertion from other unauthorized absences from a vessel. See DIVORCE; FAMILY; HUSBAND AND WIFE.

DESERT, MOUNT. See MOUNT DESERT.

DESIDERIO DA SETTIGNANO (1428–64), Florentine sculptor, born at Settignano, near Florence. He was a pupil of Donatello (q.v.), whom he reputedly helped with the work on the pedestal of his famous statue "David", and was also probably an assistant to the Italian sculptor Mino da Fiesole (see FIESOLE, MINO DA). Desiderio's style was characterized by delicacy and refinement. Among his works are the tomb of Carlo Marsuppini, secretary of state of the Florentine republic (church of San Croce, Florence); the tabernacle of the Annunciation (church of San Lorenzo, Florence) ; and busts in the Museo Nazionale, Florence, the Louvre, Paris, the Berlin Museum, and in private collections.

DESMID, common name for single-celled, fresh-water algae of the family Desmidiaceae. The cell is divided into two symmetrical halves, held together by an isthmus which contains the nucleus. Each half of the cell contains a single chloroplast, a plastid with chlorophyll. Desmids sometimes grow in colonies which remain attached after cell division. Many species are capable of self-locomotion and these species are phototropic, i.e., the direction of their movement is determined by their sensitivitiy to light.

Desmids reproduce both sexually and asexually. Asexually, the desmids reproduce by a simple division of the one cell into two across the isthmus. Each new part develops into a complete desmid. In sexual reproduction, the desmids come together in pairs and their vital cell contents fuse. From this fused body come two new desmids. Although sexual reproduction is not a method of multiplication, it strengthens the species for further asexual reproduction.

Desmids of the common genus *Closterium* are crescent-shaped, and have a small vacuole at each end of the cell. These vacuoles contain minute crystals of gypsum, which are in constant movement.

DES MOINES, capital and largest city of the State of Iowa, and the county seat of Polk Co., situated on the Des Moines R. near its confluence with the Raccoon R., about 125 miles N.E. of Omaha, Nebr. The site of the city, generally high ground covering 55.9 sq.m., is traversed in a N. and S. direction by the Des Moines R. Eighteen bridges, including six railway bridges, link the eastern and western divisions of the city. Des Moines is the commercial and financial center of a rich corn-producing and coal-mining region. The city is serviced by seven trunkline railroad systems, by motorbus and trucking carriers, and by major air lines. More than 45 insurance companies maintain their home offices in Des Moines, and the city is one of the chief publishing centers of farm periodicals in the Midwest. The industries of the city and vicinity include the mining of bituminous coal, meat packing, food processing, and the manufacture of clothing, agricultural implements, cosmetics, cement, lumber, and leather products. The city has a number of educational institutions, including Drake University (q.v.), the Cumming School of Art, a Roman Cath-

olic and a Lutheran junior college, and the Still College of Osteopathy. Outstanding among the public buildings of Des Moines is the State Capitol (constructed 1871–96), situated on a hill and surrounded by a park of 85 acres. Other buildings include the Historical, Memorial and Art Building, the State Library, and the structures comprising the Civic Center. Among this group, which extends along the river front, are the City Hall, the Municipal Courthouse, and the Federal Building. The park system of the city occupies more than 1400 acres. By the terms of the city charter, adopted in 1907, legislative and administrative authority is vested in a commission of five members, one of whom has the title of mayor. The commission is elected at large biennially.

The original settlement developed around Fort Des Moines, established by the U.S. government in 1843. In 1851 the settlement was incorporated as the town of Fort Des Moines, and in 1857 as the city of Des Moines. In January, 1858, it became the State capital. Fort Des Moines, re-established as a cavalry post of the U.S. Army in 1900, served, during World War II, as the headquarters and one of the training centers of the Women's Army Corps (WAC). Pop. (1950) 177,965.

DES MOINES RIVER, a river rising in S.W. Minnesota, and flowing S.S.E. through Iowa to the city of Des Moines, and then S.E., emptying into the Mississippi R. below Keokuk. It is about 500 m. long, and flows through a coal, timber, and agricultural area. The Des Moines is navigable in its upper course; in its lower course it falls rapidly, furnishing water power for manufacturing. Among the tributaries of the river are the Raccoon, Boone, North, Middle, and South rivers.

DE SOTO, HERNANDO or FERNANDO (1500?–1542), Spanish adventurer and explorer in America, born in Barcarrota, Spain. From 1519 to 1532 he was an explorer and military leader in Central America and Peru, where he served under Francisco Pizarro. After the conquest of Peru in 1532, De Soto returned to Spain with a fortune. In 1537, with the permission of Charles V of Spain, De Soto organized an expedition at his own expense to bring under control the Spanish-owned region of Florida. His company of nearly one thousand landed on the west coast of Florida in 1539 and prepared to search for a rich empire, like that of the Incas of Peru, which was believed to exist somewhere in the wilderness before them. The search for the nonexistent empire lasted three years, during which De Soto and his band ranged over present-day Florida, South and North Carolina, Alabama, and Mississippi; discovered the Mississippi River (1541); and then crossed it and explored territory now part of Arkansas, Oklahoma, and northern Texas. Finding no gold or treasure, in the spring of 1542 they at length turned back. De Soto died of fever after they had regained the Mississippi River. His men buried his body in the river to keep the Indians from learning of his death and desecrating the body. Only a few members of the expedition survived, reaching the Spanish settlements on the Gulf of Mexico by way of the Mississippi.

DESPENSER, LE, the name of a powerful English family, the most important members of which were: **1.** HUGH (d. 1265), one of the barons participating in the Mad Parliament which formulated the Provisions of Oxford in 1258. During the period of truce (1258–63) between the barons and King Henry III, Despenser became chief justiciar of England (1260), but upon the outbreak of the Barons' War (q.v.) against the king, he sided with the barons' leader, Simon de Montfort, serving as Simon's justiciar in 1264. He was killed at the Battle of Evesham, in which Prince Edward (later King Edward I) defeated the barons. **2.** HUGH (1262–1326), son of the justiciar, and supporter of the king against the barons. He fought under King Edward I, and secured papal release for that monarch from an oath to refrain from excessive taxation. When the barons forced Edward II to banish Piers Gaveston, the king's foster-brother and favorite, Despenser supported Gaveston and succeeded him as royal favorite in 1312. Edward made him Earl of Winchester in 1322, and Despenser, together with his son (also named Hugh), acquired vast wealth and became the virtual ruler of England. In 1326 Edward's wife, Queen Isabella, formed an alliance with the barons against King Edward and the Despensers, and both father and son were captured and hanged.

DESPIAU, CHARLES (1874–1946), French sculptor, born in Mont-de-Marsan. He studied at the École des Arts Decoratifs and the École des Beaux-Arts in Paris, and was for some time assistant to Auguste Rodin. Despiau first exhibited with the Artistes Français in 1899. He is known for his portrait busts and his sculpture studies in bronze. Among his most famous works are "Bacchante Assise" (1909), "Monument aux Morts" (1920), and "Ève" (1925). Sculpture by Despiau is in museums in various cities of France, and in Algiers, Prague, Zurich, and Stockholm. In the

U.S., several of his works are in the Buffalo Fine Arts Academy and the Detroit Institute of Arts.

DES PLAINES, city of Cook Co., Ill., on the Des Plaines R., 16 miles N.W. of Chicago. Its products are electrical supplies and greenhouse specialties. Pop. (1950) 14,994.

DESPOT, an absolute ruler, unrestricted by any legal or constitutional process. In modern usage the word carries connotations of cruel and oppressive policies, but in the original Greek usage it meant the master of a household, therefore the ruler of slaves, and denoted merely the possessor of unlimited power. In the Byzantine, or Eastern Roman, Empire, the term "despot" was used as a title of honor and was applied to the emperor and later to his immediate male relatives; subsequently it was applied to the governors of Asiatic provinces and towns. After the Turkish conquest of the Empire the title was retained by the rulers of Serbia and other Near Eastern countries. Bishops and patriarchs of the Greek Church were also called despots.

DESSALINES, JEAN JACQUES (1758–1806), Negro leader in Haiti and emperor from 1804 to 1806. He was born a slave at Grande Rivière, Haiti, and adopted the name of his master. In 1790 he joined the revolutionary forces against the French, and from 1797 served under the Haitian liberator Toussaint L'Ouverture, becoming his lieutenant general. He surrendered to the French general Charles Victory Emmanuel Leclerc (q.v.) in 1802. After the British had helped to drive the French out of Haiti in 1803, and after a republic had been set up, the British appointed Dessalines governor-general for life. In October, 1804, he proclaimed himself Emperor Jean Jacques I. He made enemies among his own followers, two of whom, Henri Christophe (q.v.) and Alexandre Sabès Pétion, assassinated him in an ambuscade near Port au Prince.

DESSAU, city of former Saxony-Anhalt State, East Germany, and former capital of Anhalt State, situated on the Mulde R., 35 m. N. of Leipzig. Dessau is an important rail center. Its manufactures include sugar, chemicals, textiles, and iron products, and it has a considerable trade in grain and garden produce. Dessau became commercially important at the end of the 17th century, after religious freedom had been granted (1686) to the Jews and later (1697) to the Lutherans. During World War II, the city was the site of the Junkers aircraft plant and was subjected to heavy Allied bombings. After the war Dessau was included in the Soviet zone of occupation. Pop. (1946) 88,139.

DESTERRO. See FLORIANOPOLIS.

DESTINN, EMMY (1878–1930), Bohemian operatic soprano, born in Prague. Her real name was Ema Kittl. She made her operatic debut in Berlin in 1898 in the role of Santuzza in *Cavalleria Rusticana.* She became one of the leading operatic sopranos of her time, with over 80 roles in her repertoire. In 1905 she sang the leading role of Giacomo Puccini's opera *Madame Butterfly* at its first performance in London; and in 1907 she created the leading role of Richard Strauss's *Salome* in Paris and Berlin. From 1908 to 1916 she was a member of the Metropolitan Opera Company, New York City. She retired in 1921.

DESTINY, STONE OF. See CHAIR.

DESTROYERS. See VESSELS, NAVAL.

DESTRUCTOR, REFUSE. See GARBAGE.

DETAILLE, (JEAN BAPTISTE) ÉDOUARD (1848–1912), French painter, born in Paris. He was noted for his paintings of battle scenes and of soldiers. Among his works are the paintings "Defense of Champigny" (Metropolitan Museum of Art, New York City), "The Passing Regiment" (Corcoran Gallery, Washington, D.C.), and "The Surrender of Huningue" (Luxembourg Museum); and the water color "Napoleon I and his Generals at Austerlitz" (New York Public Library).

DETECTION, in radio, the process of separating the modulating signal from the carrier wave in amplitude-modulated or continuous-wave radio reception; see RADIO. The original signal as picked up and amplified by a radio receiver consists of a carrier wave oscillating at an extremely high frequency, plus the modulation in the form of a rising and falling voltage which represents the dots and dashes of International Morse code or the vibrations of such sounds as voice or music. In order to make this signal intelligible in a loud-speaker, the high-frequency carrier must be removed. Removal of the carrier is accomplished by transformation of alternating current into pulsating direct current, a process called rectification, by means of any of several types of vacuum-tube circuits. For detection at extremely high frequencies, such as those used in radar (q.v.), crystal rectifiers or detectors are used. The term detection is also applied to the action of various circuits used in frequency-modulation receivers. A common detector for frequency modulation, called a discriminator, consists of a pair of rectifying tubes or crystal rectifiers so arranged that their output increases as the frequency of the signal deviates from the center or carrier frequency.

DETECTIVE. See POLICE.

DETECTIVE STORY, a popular type of fiction in which the action is provided by the logical solution of a crime in the course of an investigation of motives, methods, and guilt. The crime, usually a murder, is generally presented first, as a *fait accompli,* and the narrative structure of the novel follows an inversion of the sequence of events leading up to the crime, during the course of which clues are revealed and suspicion is cast upon various characters; the solution is finally provided by the detective-hero in a climax of explanation in which the identity and motives of the criminal are exposed and proven. The element of suspense for the reader is in competing with the detective in arriving at the correct solution, and sometimes in following the continued danger to the remaining characters from the criminal still at large.

The art of the detective story was developed almost at the same time in Europe and the United States, and in either case may be traced to the same event, the publication in France in 1829 of the *Mémoires* of the famous criminal-detective François Eugène Vidocq. This autobiography served Edgar Allan Poe and then Émile Gaboriau with a source and inspiration for their pioneer work in the fiction of "deductive reasoning". Poe's *Murders in the Rue Morgue* is considered the first modern detective story, and his *The Mystery of Marie Rogêt* is the first detective story based on an actual police case. Gaboriau, in *L'Affaire Lerouge* (1866) and *Monsieur Lecoq* (1869), wrote the first detective novels, and although these differ in many respects from modern detective fiction, their historical importance to the *genre* is unquestionable. The first artistically mature detective novels in English were those of Wilkie Collins, notably *The Woman in White* (1860) and *The Moonstone* (1868), which rivaled the so-called "serious" novel in complexity of plot and characterization and influenced the later works of Charles Dickens, such as *The Mystery of Edwin Drood* (1870). The next innovation in the detective story was the detective-hero of unique personality and a talent for scientific deductions, introduced by Sir Arthur Conan Doyle in the form of Sherlock Holmes (1889). Since Doyle's time, and with the continual growth in popularity of the detective story as reading matter, the medium has been subjected to a variety of minor changes and improvements. Some of the best-known detective-story writers are

Margery Allingham, Eric Ambler, H. C. Bailey, E. C. Bentley, Nicholas Blake (pseudonym of Cecil Day Lewis), John Dickson Carr (Carter Dickson), Raymond Chandler, Leslie Charteris, G. K. Chesterton, Agatha Christie, George Harmon Coxe, Freeman Wills Crofts, Mignon G. Eberhart, J. S. Fletcher, Leslie Ford, R. Austin Freeman, Erle Stanley Gardner, Anna Katharine Green, Dashiell Hammett, H. F. Heard, E. W. Hornung, Richard Hull, Francis Iles, Michael Innes, Gaston Leroux, Frances and Richard Lockridge, Mrs. Belloc Lowndes, Philip MacDonald, J. P. Marquand, Ngaio Marsh, A. E. W. Mason, Van Wyck Mason, E. Phillips Oppenheim, Eden Phillpotts, Raymond Postgate, Ellery Queen, Craig Rice, Mary Roberts Rinehart, Dorothy Sayers, Mabel Seeley, Joseph Shearing, Mickey Spillane, Georges Simenon, Rex Stout, Phoebe Atwood Taylor, Josephine Tey, S.S. Van Dine, Edgar Wallace, R. A. J. Walling, Carolyn Wells, Patricia Wentworth, Percival Wilde, and Cornell Woolrich (William Irish).

DETERGENTS, term originally applied to any substances having a cleansing action, but now generally used to denote soaps and other substances which have the property of lowering the surface tension of a liquid. A large number of synthetic detergents, popularly known as "soapless soaps", have been developed in recent years. Chemically, many of these compounds are the sodium salts of sulfates of the higher alcohols; others are organic quaternary ammonium compounds. Such detergents make suds freely in hard or salt water without causing insoluble scum such as that formed by soap under similar conditions. Synthetic detergents are widely used as household cleansers and shampoos, but their most important uses are in industry, particularly in the processing of textiles.

DETERMINANT, a mathematical notation which leads to a simple method of solution of simultaneous, linear, algebraic equations. Determinants were first investigated by Gottfried Leibnitz (q.v.) about 1693. This method of notation is used in almost every branch of higher mathematics.

The symbol $\begin{vmatrix} A_1 & A_2 \\ B_1 & B_2 \end{vmatrix}$ is a determinant of the second order for it has two columns and two rows of elements. This determinant has, by definition, a value equal to the expression $A_1 B_2 - B_1 A_2$. In general, a determinant of the nth order has n rows and n columns of elements, where n may be any integer. Such a determinant is of the form:

$$\begin{vmatrix} A_1 & A_2 & A_3 & . & . & . & A_n \\ B_1 & B_2 & B_3 & . & . & . & B_n \\ C_1 & C_2 & C_3 & . & . & . & C_n \\ . & & & & & & \\ . & & & & & & \\ . & & & & & & \\ K_1 & K_2 & K_3 & . & . & . & K_n \end{vmatrix}$$

The nth order determinant has, by definition, a value equal to the algebraic sum:

$$A_1 B_2 C_3 \ldots + A_2 B_3 C_4 \ldots + \ldots$$
$$- A_2 B_1 C_n \ldots - A_3 B_2 C_1 \ldots - \ldots$$

For example, three simultaneous, linear equations, such as,

$$ax + by + cz = j$$
$$dx + ey + fz = k$$
$$gx + hy + iz = l$$

where x, y, and z, are unknown variables and the other letters are constants, may be solved by determinants. The theory of determinants gives as a solution for x the quotient:

$$\frac{\begin{vmatrix} j & b & c \\ k & e & f \\ l & h & i \end{vmatrix}}{\begin{vmatrix} a & b & c \\ d & e & f \\ g & h & i \end{vmatrix}}$$

For y or z, the denominator is the same, and the numerator differs from it in the second or third column instead of the first. This method may be extended to equations with any number of unknowns, if an equal number of simultaneous equations containing them can be found.

DETERMINATE PROBLEM. See INDETERMINATE EQUATION.

DETERMINISM, the doctrine that every event, mental as well as physical, has a cause, and that, the cause being given, the event follows invariably (see CAUSALITY). This theory denies the element of chance or contingency. It is opposed to indifferentism, or indeterminism, which maintains that, in the phenomena of the human will, preceding events do not definitely determine the event. Because determinism is generally assumed to be true of all events except volition, the doctrine is of greatest importance in its application to ethics (q.v.). See also FREE WILL; WILL.

DETONATION, an extremely rapid, explosive chemical reaction. In common speech the terms "combustion", "explosion", and "detonation" are often used interchangeably. Technically, however, combustion is an inclusive term for any chemical reaction which produces heat and light; explosion is a loose term for any combustion which proceeds rapidly and violently with liberation of considerable energy; and detonation is a term for an explosion which takes place with unusual rapidity. Many explosive reactions, such as the decomposition of TNT or the burning of gasoline vapor, can take place in either of two ways: a comparatively rapid reaction, often called burning; and a very rapid reaction, properly called detonation. The end products produced and the total energy released are essentially the same in both burning and detonation, but the mechanism of the reaction is different in the two cases.

Detonation of Explosives. When a wax candle is lit, the combustion of the first portion of wax heats the next portion to its kindling point, and the reaction thus progresses through the candle at a speed of several inches per hour. The burning of an explosive such as TNT or ballistite is analogous, except that the reaction progresses through the mass at a speed of several inches (or several feet) per second. A mass of ballistite, used to propel a shell through the barrel of a cannon, takes several hundredths of a second to explode, gradually exerting its full force on the shell, but at one time creating pressure great enough to burst the cannon.

On the other hand, if the ballistite is confined so that the explosion products cannot expand, the increase in temperature and pressure may initiate an entirely different type of reaction: detonation. This reaction progresses through the medium at a rate of from one to six miles per second. The extremely high pressure which results is valuable when the explosive is to be used for blasting, destruction, or shattering effect. Detonation may also be initiated directly by using a detonator (q.v.).

Detonation of nuclear and thermonuclear weapons is described in the articles ATOMIC ENERGY AND ATOMIC BOMB: *Construction of an Atomic Bomb,* and HYDROGEN BOMB. See also FUZE.

Detonation in Gasoline Engines. The power of an ordinary automobile or airplane engine is produced by the explosion of a gasoline-air mixture. After ignition, the reaction progresses through the mixture at a speed of some hundreds of feet per second, delivering power smoothly and comparatively slowly. As the reaction progresses, however, the unburned portion of the mixture is compressed by the expanding gases and warmed by radiation. When the pressure and temperature in the unburned portion pass a critical point, detonation commences and progresses at a rate of

some miles per second. The chemical energy is thus released suddenly, and much of it is converted to heat (instead of mechanical energy) which is both wasteful and destructive. Damaging pressure waves are also produced. Severe detonation in a high-performance engine, such as a powerful airplane engine, may completely destroy it within a few minutes. Such severe detonation does not occur in the comparatively low-performance engines of automobiles, but even mild detonation causes damage as well as loss of power. The vibration caused by the detonation pressure wave creates a peculiar sound, easily audible, which is commonly called "knock" or "ping".

If the normal burning of the fuel mixture proceeds swiftly, little time is available for detonation to commence in the unburned portion. Therefore any factor (such as increased turbulence) which increases normal burning rate will tend to suppress detonation. Conversely, detonation is most likely to appear when the engine is turning slowly (causing little turbulence), but exerting maximum power (creating high pressure in the engine).

Detonation in gasoline engines has been the subject of intensive research for many years, but the exact mechanisms of both the normal reaction and the detonation reaction are extraordinarily complex and are not fully understood. The temperature and pressure in the engine can be reduced by several methods (such as using a lower compression ratio or retarding the spark), but all such methods reduce the power of the engine as well as inhibiting detonation. The presence of water vapor in the fuel mixture inhibits detonation efficiently in the cylinder. The most practical method of reducing detonation is altering the chemical nature of the gasoline. Certain chemical compounds which are or can be constituents of gasoline are highly susceptible to detonation, while others are highly resistant to it. Straight-chain hydrocarbons, such as *n*-heptane, are the most susceptible; branched-chain hydrocarbons, such as *i*-octane, are among the most resistant. The detonation resistance of any actual gasoline is measured by comparison with mixtures of these two standard compounds. Pure *i*-octane is said to have an "antiknock rating" or "octane number" of 100; pure *n*-heptane is said to have an octane number of 0; a mixture of 70% *i*-octane and 30% *n*-heptane is said to have an octane number of 70. If a particular gasoline, when tested in a standard engine, has the same detonation resistance as this mixture, it also is said to have an octane number of 70.

Fuels of higher octane number make possible the use of more powerful and efficient engines. Great strides have been taken in production of high-octane gasoline, both by chemical treatment of the petroleum from which the gasoline is derived, and by the addition of certain "antiknock compounds". The most efficient of these additives is ethyl fluid. At the time of World War I, 60-octane fuel was considered excellent. Today automobiles regularly use 80-octane fuel, and aircraft use fuels of 100-octane and even higher ratings. For fuels more detonation-resistant than pure i-octane, the usual standard is i-octane plus a certain amount of ethyl fluid, but the rating depends somewhat on the manner in which the test is administered, and no standard has yet been universally accepted.

Detonation in Diesel Engines. The problem of detonation in Diesel engines is essentially different from that in gasoline engines, and substances such as ethyl fluid aggravate rather than inhibit detonation. The compound in Diesel fuels analogous to i-octane in gasoline is cetane.

DETONATOR, any device or chemical used to initiate high explosive action. Detonation is distinguished from deflagration by the rapidity of the decomposition of the detonating substance (see EXPLOSIVES). The term detonator is usually restricted to highly sensitive explosives which can be easily set off and will in turn detonate a large mass of such explosives as dynamite or TNT. The latter explosives, although powerful, are comparatively stable under mechanical shock. A typical detonator used to detonate dynamite charges is a small tube partly filled with fulminate of mercury. The detonator is fastened to the dynamite and ignited by a burning fuze or an electric spark. Such detonators are often called blasting caps or exploders. The term detonator is sometimes applied to primers or, incorrectly, to fuses (q.v.). See also FUZE.

DETROIT, county seat of Wayne Co., Mich., port of entry, the largest city of the State, and, in 1950, the fifth-largest city in the United States. It is situated on the Detroit and Rouge rivers, opposite Windsor, Ontario, and about 18 miles N. of Lake Erie. The city is 791 miles N.W. of New York City, 283 miles N.E. of Chicago, and 251 miles W. of Buffalo, N.Y. Detroit is the foremost automobile-manufacturing center in the world, and a leading industrial center of the United States. The city occupies 142 sq.m. (including about 4 sq.m. of water area), and is polygonal in shape, with one side consisting of river frontage. More than 100 sq.m. of the city area have been acquired since World War I, largely through annexation of contiguous communities. As a result of this process, the city limits entirely surround Hamtramck and Highland Park (qq.v.), cities which retained local autonomy. Downtown Detroit, comprising the main business section of the city, centers about Grand Circus, a semicircular park of 5½ acres situated about a mile inland from the Detroit R. Most of the major traffic arteries of the city converge on this section from the outlying areas. Notable among these radial highways, superimposed on a street layout which conforms generally to the checkerboard, or gridiron, pattern, are Fort Street, and Michigan, Grand River, Gratiot, and Woodward avenues. The last-named avenue is the principal business thoroughfare of the city. Grand Boulevard, which formerly encompassed the heart of the city, is a semicircular avenue, beginning and ending on the Detroit R. It has a radius of nearly 4 m. from Campus Martius, a broad open square, situated midway between Grand Circus and the Detroit R. Cadillac Square, occupying the site of the old City Hall, is another famed square in the downtown section of Detroit. Local transportation facilities consist of a motorbus and trolley-car system, which is municipally owned. Chiefly because of the general inadequacy of these facilities, the ratio of privately-owned automobiles in Detroit ranks among the highest in the United States. Vehicular traffic between the city and Windsor is accommodated by Ambassador Bridge, a suspension bridge, nearly 2 m. long, which was opened in 1929; and by the Detroit and Windsor Fleetway Tunnel, 1 m. long, completed in 1930. This is the only existing vehicular tunnel between two countries.

The location of the city on the Detroit R. (q.v.), linking Lake Erie with Lake Saint Clair, the Saint Clair R., and Lake Huron, makes Detroit one of the chief inland ports of the United States. More than 13 m. of the 24 m. of river frontage available to the port are developed, containing numerous piers, warehouses, and other cargo-handling facilities. The port is serviced by freight and passenger steamship lines operating on regular schedules to major points on the Great Lakes. In a recent year, approximately 16,000,000 tons of cargo were handled at the port. Detroit is also served by 10 major railway systems, including the New York Central,

Detroit Convention & Tourist Bureau

Tall buildings frame the City Hall, on Cadillac Square in downtown Detroit, Michigan

Pennsylvania, Baltimore and Ohio, Michigan Central, and Canadian Pacific. Connections with major Canadian points are provided by the two last-named systems by means of a railroad tunnel under the Detroit R. The city has, in addition, extensive networks of motor-truck, motorbus, and air lines.

Detroit has been one of the leading industrial centers of the United States since the American Civil War. However, its present status as the third-ranking manufacturing city of the nation dates from the decade following World War I, a period of vast expansion in the industrial production of the city, particularly of motor vehicles. The automotive industry, introduced in Detroit between 1899 and 1903 by such pioneers as Ransom Eli Olds and Henry Ford (qq.v.), developed into one of the major industries of the nation between World Wars I and II. Following World War II, more than 4,500,000 motor vehicles were being manufactured annually in Detroit and nearby cities. The output of Detroit automotive plants, retooled for the manufacture of tanks, airplanes, amphibious

vehicles, and other military equipment, was a decisive factor in the victory of the United Nations over the Axis Powers in World War II. Additional important industries in the city include shipbuilding, steel and iron making, meat packing, and the manufacture of tires and tubes, machine tools, foundry products, nonferrous metal alloys, stoves, paints, varnishes, lacquers, pharmaceuticals and other chemical products, bakery products, vacuum cleaners, refrigerators, marine engines, aircraft parts, and television equipment.

Detroit has many points of interest. Outstanding among these are its automobile-manufacturing plants, notably those producing the Cadillac, Lincoln, Packard, Hudson, Chrysler, Plymouth, and Kaiser-Frazer cars. Noteworthy buildings include the Greater Penobscot, the Union Guardian, the Book Tower; the Detroit City Hall, a structure in the French Renaissance style; the General Motors Building, one of the largest office buildings in the country; the Public Library, an imposing edifice of white marble, designed in the early Italian Renaissance style by the architect Cass Gilbert; and the Masonic Temple, the auditorium of which has a seating capacity of 5000. Prominent among the numerous churches of Detroit are Blessed Sacrament Cathedral, seat of the Archdiocese of Detroit; Temple Beth El, the place of worship of the oldest Jewish congregation (founded in 1850) in Michigan; Fort Street Presbyterian Church, built in 1855; and Ste. Anne's Shrine, housing a Roman Catholic congregation, dating from 1701. Among other points of interest in the city are Fort Wayne, a federal military reservation established in 1851; Briggs Stadium (seating capacity, 60,000), home grounds of the "Tigers", Detroit American League professional baseball club; and Olympia Stadium, one of the largest sports arenas in the world.

The educational and cultural facilities of Detroit compare favorably with those of other large cities. In addition to a modern public-school system, more than 100 parochial schools, and numerous privately operated technical and art institutes, the city has a number of schools of higher learning. These include Wayne University (q.v.); the University of Detroit (see DETROIT, UNIVERSITY OF); Marygrove College, the oldest Roman Catholic college for women in Michigan; the Detroit Institute of Technology; and the Detroit College of Law. Other important cultural and educational institutions of the city are the Detroit Public Library, which has about 18 branches and nearly a million volumes; the Detroit Institute of Arts, a municipal museum with exhibits representing the development of art in human society, more than 1000 paintings, a valuable collection of sculptures, and other art objects; Russel A. Alger House, a branch of the Institute, noted for its collection of Italian Renaissance art and decoration; and the Children's Museum, containing biological and Indian-lore displays, and other exhibits. Detroit is also the home of the Detroit Symphony Orchestra (q.v.). Daily newspapers published in the city include the Detroit *News,* the Detroit *Times,* and the Detroit *Free Press.*

The Detroit park system comprises nearly 4000 acres. One of the outstanding units of the system is Belle Island Park, about 1000 acres in area, situated on Belle Island, in the Detroit R. This park, connected to the city by a bridge, has extensive recreational facilities, including bathing beaches, a golf course, and a yacht basin. Additional features of Belle Island Park are a botanical conservatory, an aquarium, and a zoological garden. Other units of the Detroit park system are River Rouge Park, a tract of 1204 acres along the River Rouge; Water Works Park (70 acres), which contains a number of artificial lakes and the municipal water-purification plant, the largest in the world; and Palmer Park (287 acres). The Detroit Zoological Park, covering an area of 121 acres, is situated in Royal Oak, about 10 miles N. of the city.

The name of the city is the anglicized version of *d'étroit* (Fr., "of the strait"), from *Pontchartrain d'Étroit,* the name of the original settlement. This was established in 1701 by Sieur Antoine de la Mothe Cadillac (q.v.), the French military commander in the region. The settlement remained under French control until 1760, when it was captured by the British in the course of the French and Indian War. During the American Revolution, the headquarters of the British army of the Northwest was in Detroit, a strategic point in the organization of Indian warfare against the Americans. The British evacuated Detroit in 1796, under the provisions of the Jay Treaty (q.v.). The settlement was incorporated as a town by the legislature of the Northwest Territory in 1802. With the establishment of Michigan Territory and Wayne County, in 1805, the town became the territorial and county administrative center. A disastrous fire virtually destroyed Detroit in the same year, but the town was quickly reconstructed. On August 16, 1812, during the War of 1812, Detroit was occupied by the British, who held it until September 29, 1813. In 1824 it was incorporated as a city, the population then being less than 2000. The opening of the Erie Canal in the following year initiated a period of growth and commercial activity in Detroit. On the admission of Michigan to the Union, in 1837, Detroit became the State capital. It retained this status until 1847, when the seat of government was transferred to Lansing. Between 1850 and 1870, the population of Detroit increased from about 21,000 to 79,577. Industrial development was particularly marked in the post-Civil War period, notably in such fields as carriage making, shipbuilding, and the manufacture of railway equipment and marine engines. These industries subsequently provided the skilled workmen who figured decisively in the establishment of the automobile industry in Detroit. The development of this industry transformed Detroit into a metropolis within the span of three decades. Between 1900 and 1930, the population of the city increased from 285,704 to 1,568,662. The city was the scene of considerable labor strife in 1937 and 1938, when hundreds of thousands of automobile workers, led by the United Automobile Workers of America (q.v.), struck for union recognition, better working conditions, and higher pay. Additional strikes, chiefly for higher pay, occurred in the post-World War II period.

The Golden Jubilee of the Automobile Industry, marking the manufacture of more than 90,000,000 motor vehicles in the United States during the preceding fifty years, was celebrated in Detroit between May 29 and June 11, 1946. Pop. (1950) 1,849,568.

DETROIT RIVER, a river, about 25 m. long and from ½ to 3 m. wide, extending from Lake Saint Clair to Lake Erie, and forming part of the international boundary between Canada and the United States. It is sometimes called "the Dardanelles of America", and is one of the most important inland waterways of the North American continent, comprising with Lake Saint Clair and the Saint Clair R. the natural shipping route between Lake Erie and the other Great Lakes. It contains a number of islands, notably Grosse Isle and Belle Island. The river follows a southwesterly course to a point slightly beyond Detroit, and then flows generally southward. Important cities along its banks, besides Detroit, are Windsor, in Ontario, and River Rouge, Michigan.

DETROIT SYMPHONY ORCHESTRA, a musical society founded in Detroit, Michigan, in 1914 by Weston Gales, with Otto Kirchner as its president. Gales served as its conductor from 1914 to 1918. Ossip Gabrilówitsch joined the orchestra as guest conductor in 1918, and at the close of the season became the society's permanent conductor, a post which he held until his death in 1936. Victor Kolar succeeded Gabrilówitsch and shared the direction of the symphony with various guest conductors, including Bernardino Molinari, Fritz Reiner, José Iturbi, Georges Enesco, and Vladimir Golschmann. From 1943 to 1949 Karl Krueger was the orchestra's permanent conductor. In 1951 he was succeeded by Paul Paray.

DETROIT, UNIVERSITY OF, a coeducational institution of higher learning, conducted under the auspices of the Roman Catholic Church, and located in Detroit, Mich. It was founded in 1877 as Detroit College, and attained university status in 1911. It maintains a liberal arts college, and schools of architecture, arts, business, dentistry, engineering, and law. In 1953–54 the enrollment was 6661, including 4794 full-time students, and the faculty numbered 485.

DEUCALION, in Greek mythology, the son of Prometheus, and husband of Pyrrha. When Zeus resolved to destroy the race of men by a flood, Deucalion built an ark or ship, in which he and his wife floated during the nine days' flood which drowned all the other inhabitants of the world. After the subsidence of the waters the ark rested on Mt. Parnassus. To repeople the world Deucalion and Pyrrha were told by the goddess Themis to throw behind them the bones of their mother. They therefore cast behind them the stones of the earth; and from those thrown by Deucalion sprang up men, and from those of Pyrrha, women.

DEURNE, a city in the province of Antwerp, Belgium, about 5 miles E. of the city of Antwerp. Pop. (1952 est.) 59,202.

DEUS RAMOS, João de (1830–96), Portuguese poet, born at San Bartholomeu des Messines, and educated at the University of Coimbra. In 1862 he became editor of the newspaper *O Bejense,* and four years later of *Folha do Sul.* He was elected deputy to the Cortes in 1869, and turned his attention mainly to educational problems. Deus Ramos was considered the most important Portuguese poet of his time, and was particularly known for his love poems. His works include *Ramos de Flores* (1875) and *Folhas Soltas* (1876).

DEUTERIUM, an isotope of hydrogen having an atomic weight of 2.01363. It is commonly called heavy hydrogen, because its atomic weight is approximately double that of ordinary hydrogen, but it has identical chemical properties. Hydrogen as it occurs in nature contains approximately .02 percent of deuterium. The boiling point of deuterium is 3.5° C. (6.3° F.) higher than that of hydrogen. Heavy water (deuterium oxide, D_2O) boils at 101.42° C. as compared to 100° C., the boiling point of ordinary water. It freezes at 3.802° C. as compared to 0° C. for ordinary water. Its density at room temperature is 10.79 percent greater than that of ordinary water.

Deuterium, which was discovered by H. C. Urey and his associates in 1932, was the first isotope to be separated in a pure form. Several methods have been used to separate the isotope from natural hydrogen. The two processes which have been most successful have been fractional distillation of water and a catalytic exchange process between hydrogen and water. In the latter system, when water and hydrogen are brought together in the presence of a suitable catalyst, about three times as much deuterium appears in the water as in the hydrogen. Deuterium has also been concentrated by electrolysis, by centrifuging, and by fractional distillation of liquid hydrogen.

The nuclei of deuterium atoms, called deuterons, are much used in research in physics because they can be readily accelerated by cyclotrons and similar machines and used as "atomic bullets" to transmute elements; see ATOM AND ATOMIC THEORY. Deuterium also has important uses in biological research as a tracer element for studying problems of metabolism.

The use of heavy water as a moderator in atomic piles was suggested during World War II, but in the first U.S. piles, graphite was employed instead; see ATOMIC ENERGY AND ATOMIC BOMB. Deuterium and the other heavy hydrogen isotope tritium (q.v.) probably were used in the first hydrogen device, exploded (1952) by the U.S. near Eniwetok Atoll in the Pacific Ocean. See HYDROGEN BOMB.

DEUTEROCANONICAL BOOKS, a designation applied to a number of disputed Biblical books and passages. Those in the Old Testament are found only in the Septuagint (q.v.) and not in the Hebrew versions of the Bible (q.v.); they are Esther 10:4–16, and 14; 1 and 2 Maccabees; Baruch; Daniel 3:24–90; Judith; Tobit; Ecclesiasticus; and Wisdom of Solomon. In the New Testament, they are Mark 16:9–20; Luke 22:43–44; John 7:53 and 8:11; Hebrews; James 2; 2 Peter; 2 and 3 John; Jude; and Revelation.

By determination of the ecumenical Council of Trent (see COUNCIL; TRENT, COUNCIL OF), on April 8, 1546, all these books and passages were included in the Canon of the Holy Scriptures; see CANON. With certain exceptions they are accepted by Christian churches of the Eastern Rite. The Old Testament books and passages, listed above, are rejected as apocryphal by Protestants, who, however, accept as genuine and inspired by Holy Scripture the New Testament passages listed above, with the exception of John 7:53 and 8:11, which are separated by brackets in the Revised Version of the Bible.

DEUTERONOMY (Gr. *deuteros,* "second"; *nomos,* "law"), name of the fifth book of the Pentateuch (q.v.) in the Old Testament. Deuteronomy contains the last injunctions of Moses to his people, delivered in the land of Moab and expanding the Decalogue (q.v.), which was originally given 38 years earlier on Mt. Sinai. With the exception of chapters 27, 28, and 34, and a few verses elsewhere, the book is in the form of an address. The introductory part of the book (1 to 4:43) is mainly a discourse on past events. The section from 4:44 to 6 repeats the Decalogue and urges observance of the Law. A code of religious and civil laws is contained in chapters 7 to

28, and a farewell address in chapters 29 to 31. There are two poems in the work, the "Song of Moses" and the "Blessing of Moses", which are probably non-Mosaic writings composed after the 8th century B.C. The conclusion (34) describes the death of Moses.

Passed down by oral tradition, the doctrines contained in Deuteronomy were preached by Isaiah in the 8th century B.C. and recorded by his followers in the 7th century B.C. It is likely that this work is the book reported, in 2 Kings 22, 23, to have been found in the temple during the reign of King Josiah, who promulgated the contents of the document as law in 621 B.C.

DEUTZIA, a genus of deciduous shrubs of the Hydrangea family, natives of Asia. They produce an abundance of white or pinkish-tinted flowers. Numerous varieties of *D. scabra* and *D. gracilis* are popular ornamental shrubs in the United States.

DEUX-SÈVRES, an inland department of western France. The capital is Niort. Other important towns are Thouars (pop., about 9800), Parthenay (6700), St. Maixent (5850), Bressuire (5700), and Melle (2500). The principal rivers are the Sèvre of Niort and the Sèvre of Nantes. Deux-Sèvres contains three regions of varying arability. In the N. is the Gâtine, the thin, sour soil of which is made productive by the use of lime. The Plaine in the s. is naturally fertile; the Marais in the s.w. contains drained bottom land. The leading industry of the department is agriculture. Cereal grains, grapes, root crops, flax, hemp, rape, apples, and walnuts are grown; and cattle (Parthenay breed), horses (Poitou breed), and mules are raised. Among other important industries are coal mining, the production of lime, flour milling, wine making, and the production of vegetable oil. Shoes, hats, leather goods, and gloves are manufactured at Niort. Area, 2338 sq.m.; pop. (1953 est.) 320,000.

DE VALERA, EAMON (1882–   ), Irish republican leader and first premier of Eire, born in New York City, and educated at Royal University, Dublin. During his early life he was a student and teacher of mathematics in Ireland, but he soon became well known for his activities in behalf of Irish independence. He commanded a group of Sinn Fein (q.v.) rebels during the uprising of Easter Week, 1916, and was sentenced to life imprisonment when the British put down the revolt. He was released in the general amnesty of 1917, and in the latter part of that year, when the Sinn Fein members of the British Parliament withdrew from that body to form their own government, he was elected president.

Irish Press

Eamon de Valera

He was rearrested by the British in May of the following year on the charge of suspicion of rebellion, but escaped with the help of a group of Sinn Feiners in 1919. De Valera then went to the United States, where he succeeded in raising a fund of more than $5,000,000 to support the revolutionary movement. In 1922, when the Dail (Irish parliament) ratified a treaty with Great Britain which he had denounced as a humiliating compromise, he resigned the presidency. Because of his opposition, the Irish Free State government, which had been officially recognized by this same treaty, imprisoned him in 1923, releasing him after eleven months. Thereupon he again became head of the Sinn Fein party, which followed a policy of nonparticipation in the Dail until 1927. In that year a dissident faction of Sinn Fein, the Fianna Fail, re-entered the Dail under de Valera's leadership.

He was president of the executive council of the Irish Free State from 1932 to 1937, and then elected premier of Eire under the new constitution of 1937. In 1933, and again from 1938 to 1939, he served as president of the League of Nations Assembly. His policies were consistently characterized by nationalism and isolationism, both political and economic. In 1938 he approved the policy of Prime Minister Neville Chamberlain of England, who was then attempting to appease the Hitler government of Germany, and during World War II he successfully advocated a policy of strict neutrality for Ireland. He lost the premiership in 1948, but regained it in 1951. He was defeated for re-election in 1954.

DEVALUATION, in economics, a method of lowering the legal value of currency, instituted by legislative enactment or executive decree. It consists, essentially, in the establishment of a new legal value of the monetary unit of a currency. The legal value may be reduced in several ways, such as the substitution for a depreciated unit of currency of a new unit, containing a lesser weight of gold or silver, or the retention of the existing unit and reduction of its bullion content, sometimes called *de jure* stabilization. Notable examples of the first form of devaluation occurred during the disturbed economic conditions following World War I, in Germany, Austria, and Poland in 1924, in Hungary in 1925, and in Belgium in 1926, and since World War II, in Hungary and China, where the old monetary units became virtually valueless. An important devaluation of the second type took place in the United States in 1934, when the gold content of the dollar was reduced; see below.

Bearing in mind that economists are not agreed on an authoritative view of devaluation, the following points may be regarded as essential to an understanding of the subject: (1) the monetary unit of a currency is usually defined by law as consisting of a stipulated weight of precious metal—gold or silver; (2) the monetary unit has two principal values, as money and as bullion; (3) its value as money is expressed by its purchasing power, i.e., the quantity and quality of the commodities it commands; (4) its value as bullion is expressed by the price paid on the open market for the amount of precious metal contained in the monetary unit; (5) when these values are equal or approximately equal, i.e., when the monetary unit is worth as much in terms of commodities as is its metallic content, the currency is in a stable condition; (6) a condition is sometimes reached, however, chiefly as a result of the depreciation or disorganization of a currency, in which the value of the monetary unit as money is less than its value as bullion; (7) an important result of this condition is a general loss of confidence in the stability of the currency, manifested by such developments as a withdrawal of coins containing precious metal from circulation, and runs on banks; and (8) to establish approximate equality, or parity, between the value of the monetary unit as money and its value as bullion, and to restore confidence in the stability of the currency, a government may resort to devaluation.

In devaluing a currency, a government may elect to fix the metallic content of the monetary unit in terms of parity with its purchasing power domestically, or in terms of parity with its value in foreign exchange. Among important effects of the first method, some economists hold, are a general rise in domestic prices and an expansion of credit. They postulate a definite relationship between prices of commodities and the gold content of the currency, and hold therefore that devaluation of the currency causes a corresponding rise in prices. The second method is used today, when the international gold standard has virtually ceased to exist and currencies are not freely convertible into gold or silver. Among important effects of the second method is an increase in exports, since it becomes easier for foreigners to buy the nation's goods. Because rising prices, expanding credit, and an increase in exports tend to stimulate production, some economists see in devaluation an important contributory means of overcoming unfavorable economic conditions resulting from a depression. These as well as other considerations motivated a number of European and other governments to resort to devaluation during the world-wide economic depressions of the 1930's.

In the United States, the metallic content of the gold dollar remained essentially unchanged for almost 100 years, following Congressional coinage enactments in 1837; see DOLLAR: *United States Dollar*. In 1933, during the depression which followed the economic crisis of 1929–30, widespread runs on banks took place in the United States and led to a temporary closing of all banks (March 6–13) by Presidential proclamation. Among the means adopted by the Federal government to cope with the economic situation, after the banks were reopened, was the prohibition by law of hoarding by citizens of gold coins and bullion; all gold, other than that used for industrial, medical, and other nonmonetary purposes, subsequently became Federal property in exchange for other forms of money. In October, 1933, the Reconstruction Finance Corporation of the Federal government began to purchase domestically-mined gold at progressively higher prices above the former mint price of $20.67 an ounce, thus effecting a *de facto* devaluation of the dollar in terms of gold. Subsequently, the RFC extended its purchases to foreign markets as well.

This experiment with a fluctuating dollar was soon abandoned, and in January, 1934, Congress passed the Gold Reserve Act, empowering the President to devalue the currency of the United States, and authorizing him to fix the weight of the gold dollar at not more than 60% and not less than 50% of its then existing weight (23.22 grains of pure gold). By official proclamation on January 31, 1934, President Franklin D. Roosevelt fixed the weight of the gold dollar at 13.714 grains of pure gold, or 59.06% of its former weight. The Treasury thereupon began paying $35 an ounce for gold. The purposes behind this Act were to raise the domestic price level and to stimulate exports, thus causing increased business activity and greater employment. Many economists believe that devaluation in itself does not raise the price level, which, they hold, is determined by the supply of and demand for commodities, the purchasing power of the people, and other factors. In the disturbed economic conditions following World War II, a number of countries, notably Italy in 1947, France in 1948 and 1949, and Great Britain and Canada in 1949, devalued their currencies. The establishment of the International Monetary fund after World War II was motivated by the desire of the participating nations to stimulate world trade and production by promoting currency stabilization and discouraging competitive devaluation of currencies. See GOLD STANDARD; FOREIGN EXCHANGE; INFLATION; MINT; MONEY.

DEVELOPER. See PHOTOGRAPHY.

DEVENTER, town of Overijssel Province, the Netherlands, situated at the junction of the Ysel and Schipbeek rivers, 10 m. by rail N. of Zutphen. Deventer contains two old churches, the Groote Kerk dating from 1334, and the Romanesque Bergkerk dating from 1206. The school and the town hall date from the 16th and 17th centuries, respectively. Three 8th-century gospels are preserved in the Roman Catholic Broederkerk and the town library contains a 13th-century copy of the fable, *Reynard the Fox*. Deventer is of interest to scholars as the locale of the 14th-century religious movement connected with the name of Gerhard Groote (q.v.), and as the scene of the boyhood of Erasmus, the great humanist of the Renaissance. The town is noted for the manufacture of honey cakes known as "Deventer koek", Smyrna carpets, and textiles. Pop. (1953 est.) 49,443.

DE VERE, AUBREY THOMAS (1814–1902), Irish poet and critic, born at Curragh Chase,

Limerick, and educated at Trinity College, Dublin. His first published work was *The Waldenses and Other Poems* (1842). It was followed by many, volumes of verse, literary criticism, and political opinion. After joining the Roman Catholic Church in 1851, de Vere wrote many hymns and devotional poems, some of which were collected and published under the title of *St. Peter's Chains* (1888). His other writings include the volumes of poetry *May Carols* (1857), *The Sisters* (1867), and *Legends of the Saxon Saints* (1879); the prose works *English Misrule and Irish Misdeeds* (1848) and *Ireland's Church Property and the Right Use of It* (1867); and *Essays, Chiefly on Poetry* (1887).

DEVEREUX, ROBERT, 2nd EARL OF ESSEX (1566–1601), English court favorite and statesman, born at Netherwood, Hereford-shire, and educated at Trinity College, Cambridge. In 1584 his guardian, Lord Burghley (see CECIL, WILLIAM), introduced him at court, where he became a favorite of Queen Elizabeth. Accompanying his stepfather, the Earl of Leicester, on an expedition to aid the Low Countries in their revolt against Spain, he distinguished himself at the battle of Zut-phen. After the death of Leicester, Essex continued to rise in the favor of Elizabeth. However, he angered the queen by joining Sir Francis Drake's expedition against the Spanish Armada in 1589 without Elizabeth's permission and by marrying the widow of Sir Philip Sidney in 1590. In 1592, after commanding the forces sent to assist Henry IV of France against the Spaniards, Essex returned to a position of influence at court. In 1596 he was appointed one of the commanders of the victorious expedition against Cadiz. In 1598, in command of the Azores expedition against the Spanish fleets, he failed to accomplish his mission and was reproached by the queen. In that same year, he was made earl marshal of England, but he did not consider that title a worthy reward for his services at Cadiz in 1596. At the outbreak of the Irish Rebellion in 1599, he went to Ireland as lieutenant and governor general. After defeat at Arklow, he was forced to make a truce with the rebels. Contrary to the queen's commands, he returned to London to vindicate himself. The queen received him kindly, but, in June, 1600, he was brought to trial before a special court, consisting of the principal judges and officers of state, on charges of contempt and disobedience. The court sentenced him to dismissal from all offices of state and to imprisonment in his own house. Through the intercession of Francis Bacon, one of the queen's counsel, his liberty was restored. However, when he tried to incite an insurrection in London to compel Elizabeth to remove his enemies from her council, he was imprisoned and condemned to death. The signing of the warrant for his execution was postponed many times by Elizabeth, but ultimately Essex was beheaded on February 25, 1601.

DEVI (Skr., "goddess"), in Hinduism, the mother goddess worshipped as the supreme power in the universe. The term is also applied to any female divinity, especially to the consort of Siva (q.v.), who was the daughter of Himavat (the Himalayas) and who represented the *Shakti,* or female energy of Siva. The word *Devi* is also used after the personal name of any married woman and may be translated *Mrs., Madam,* or *Lady.*

DEVIATION, MAGNETIC. See MAGNET-ISM, TERRESTRIAL.

DEVIL, in later Hebrew and in Christian belief, the supreme spirit of evil who for immeasurable time has ruled over a kingdom of evil spirits and is in constant opposition to God. The belief in such a spirit developed very gradually in Hebrew theology and was affected by extranational influences. There is no indication in the Scriptures that the Hebrews who lived in the period before the Babylonian captivity had any concept of evil spirits as beings separated from God, evil in essence and act. *Moral* evil was regarded as, properly, the act of man; *physical* evil or misfortune, on the other hand, was interpreted as of divine origin, a punishment for sin inflicted by a just and holy God who logically became the source of all calamity. The angels of scripture or tradition, who foretold and executed God's will, were considered the instruments of physical, never of *moral* evil. The concept of an angel capable of moral evil first occurs after the Hebrew contact with Babylonian demonism, when there appears for the first time an angel called Satan, who, however, still figures as a minister of God and, along with the other angels, appears in heaven before the throne of Jehovah, but with the function assigned to him of accuser and seducer. In the Apocrypha, which reveals both Chaldaico-Persian and Ægypto-Alexandrian influences, the older Hebrew doctrine of misfortune coming from the angel of Jehovah disappears, and demons or evil spirits are for the first time mentioned as the authors of calamities. According to these writings, the evil spirits dwell in waste places and sometimes band together for the injury or destruction of men, enter into them as tormentors, and can be expelled only by magical or mysterious means. The heathen deities were relegated to this class of beings. The first mention of the Devil proper as a force opposed to life occurs in the Old Testament Book of Wisdom (2:24) in relation to the seduction of Eve, where it is said that through the Devil the necessity of death has come into the world.

During the period immediately preceding the appearance of Jesus, the Hebrew concept of angels as well as of demons and the Devil was modified and influenced by Persian Zoroastrianism. The idea of spiritual hierarchies and orders, and the names of specific spirits and demons, such as Asmodeus (Heb. *Ashmadai*) in the Book of Tobias, are drawn from the Persian system. According to Zoroastrian belief, the evil power was supposed to have existed from the beginning of the world but to be destined to eventual defeat. Later Hebrew belief represented the Devil and his demons as having been originally angels who had fallen from their "high estate", had been punished by God, and had therefore assumed a position of hostility, without, however, being able materially to frustrate the divine purposes. This theory was rejected by the Sadducee, or priestly, sect of the Hebrew religion and prevented the Jews from developing their concept of the Devil and his demons into an established and dogmatic system.

Nevertheless, the Hebrew demonology was widely disseminated and the New Testament contains distinct recognition of its prevalence in popular belief, particularly in the attributing of diseases to the agency of evil spirits; see DEMON. The chief demonic power bears a variety of names, as Satan (Matt. 4:10 et seq.), the Devil (Heb. 2:14), the Adversary (1 Tim. 5:14), the Accuser of the Brethren (Rev. 12:10), the Old Serpent (Rev. 20:2), the Great Dragon (Rev. 12:9), frequently Beelzebub (Matt. 10:25 et seq.), and once Belial (2 Cor. 6:15). He is generally characterized as the "evil one" and the "tempter" who opposes Jesus and seeks to draw the disciples as well as their Saviour into sin. Jesus nowhere concretely defines the function of the Devil; among the few positive statements he makes about the Devil are that "he was murderer from the beginning, and stood not in the truth" and that "he is a liar" (John 8:44). The primitive Church assumed the existence of the Devil as an unquestionable fact. Holding firmly to the belief of a satanic kingdom

Satan cast out of heaven (illustration by Gustave Doré for Milton's "Paradise Lost")

of darkness opposed to Christ's kingdom of light, the majority of the early Christians ascribed all evil, physical as well as moral, to the Devil and his demons: failures of crop, sterility, pestilence, heresies, individual vices, and the whole body of heathenism with its mythology and religious worship. The heathen gods were believed to have been conquered by the work of Christ but not rendered wholly powerless; they were degraded into demons, and so a part of their mythology passed into the doctrine of the Devil. The doctrine of the lordship of the Devil over the human race, insofar as man was unregenerate, gave rise to the custom of exorcising, not only those in whom special signs of demoniacal possession appeared (see EXORCISM), but all candidates for baptism, whether infants or adults. But while the power of the Devil over all not guarded by the Christian faith and rites was supreme, over those who were so protected it was utterly weak. No Christian, even the weakest, could be forced to do evil; the sign of the cross was sufficient to rout Satan. During the Middle Ages theologians speculated as to the reason for the fall of Satan. Some held that he was originally the highest of all angels; others that he was a prince in one of the lower orders. Pride was usually assigned as the reason for the revolt which led to his fall. The general theological speculations on the subject form the basis of the theme and narrative of John Milton's *Paradise Lost*.

DEVILFISH. 1. Any of several large rays of the genus *Manta* and allied genera, inhabiting warm seas; see RAY. **2.** Any large cephalopod, such as the octopus, squid, and cuttlefish (qq.v.). **3.** The gray whale (q.v.).

4. Any of various fish of the order Pediculati, such as the angler and batfish (qq.v.).

DEVIL'S ADVOCATE. See ADVOCATUS DIABOLI.

DEVIL'S APRON. See KELP.

DEVIL'S BIBLE, THE, name given to a manuscript Bible written on three hundred asses' skins and taken to Stockholm after the Thirty Years' War. According to legend, it was done by a monk who was condemned to die unless he could copy the entire Bible on asses' skins in a single night. With the aid of the devil, to whom he sold his soul, the monk, was able to accomplish his lifesaving task in the allotted time.

DEVIL'S-BIT. See SCABIOSA.

DEVIL'S-DARNING-NEEDLE. See DRAGONFLY.

DEVIL'S ISLAND, a small rock formation, 16 sq.m. in area, situated 7 m. off the coast of French Guiana, South America, opposite the mouth of the Maroni R. The island is one of three, including Royal Island and Saint-Joseph Island, which were formerly known as the Îles du Diable ("Devil's Islands"), but are now called the Îles du Salut or the Safety Islands. They are part of a penal settlement established in French Guiana in 1852 by the French government. The name Devil's Island is frequently applied to the entire penal settlement, especially since the widely publicized imprisonment on the island of the French army captain, Alfred Dreyfus (q.v.), in 1895-99. The penal settlement, officially centered about the port of Saint-Laurent (20 m. inland on the Maroni R.) and called the Commune of Maroni, was maintained entirely separate from the life of the colony of French Guiana. The Îles du Salut were places of confinement for those convicts classed as desperate; the majority of prisoners were held in camps of the mainland settlement. The convicts were classed as follows: 1. *Relégués,* or criminals under sentence of deportation and also habitual offenders who were transferred to Guiana after serving out their prison term in Europe. 2. *Déportés,* either political prisoners sentenced simply to deportation, or men condemned to imprisonment but permitted to have limited liberty of movement. 3. *Transportés,* or felons sentenced to penal servitude with hard labor. If their sentences were for less than eight years, they were obliged, by a system called *doublage,* to remain in French Guiana for an equivalent term. If their sentences were for more than eight years, they were forced to

stay in the Guiana colony for the remainder of their lives. The liberated convicts were called *libérés,* and those who were not required to remain in Guiana had to earn their passage home by working in the colony.

From 1852 to 1867, the penal settlement received about 18,000 convicts. During the 20 years after 1867, most of the déportés were sent to a penal center in New Caledonia (q.v.). In 1885 the French Guiana penal settlement was made a place of confinement only for criminals with sentences of more than eight years.

Early in its existence the penal settlement, situated in the torrid zone, proved extremely unhealthful. So many convicts contracted tropical diseases and died that the penal area became known as a place from which there was no return. During the existence of the settlement a total of about 70,000 convicts and *libérés* died in French Guiana. Escape was considered almost impossible, but a few convicts managed to make their way to the outside world.

In 1928, Major Charles Péan of the Salvation Army of France visited the penal settlement of French Guiana, and after a prolonged investigation made the following report. Of the 1000 or more convicts sent to the settlement each year, less than 100 lived as long as five years. Most convicts contracted fever and dysentery. At night, 60 or 70 convicts, according to Major Péan, might be confined to one stifling compartment, where fights and killings were common. In the disciplinary barracks for incorrigibles, brutal prison measures prevailed; in cell blocks were men who had become insane after years of solitary confinement. In Camp Saint-Jean du Maroni, the "dead end of the settlement", Major Péan found men chained together or kept in cells and blockhouses near tubercular, cancerous, and leprous inmates.

Measures in relief of conditions in the penal settlement were undertaken by the French Salvation Army, backed by the French government, in the early 1930's; and in 1938 the government abolished penal servitude in French Guiana. By Nov., 1947, more than 1800 French convicts and *libérés* had been repatriated. Only 800 men remained at Saint-Laurent du Maroni, and of these 600 to 700 were returned to France during the summer of 1948. A number of the *libérés* did not wish to return to France, among them those who had married native women of French Guiana and had settled in the colony, and others who were too old or too ill to travel and take up a new life. The Salvation Army was officially authorized to look after the remaining *libérés.*

It was generally agreed, in France and elsewhere, that the penal settlement of French Guiana had failed in its purpose; it had neither effectively deterred criminals nor offered them any true means of moral reformation, nor had it helped colonize and develop French Guiana as had been originally planned. French Guiana had long been the least-developed European colony in the Americas, and one of the deterrents to its economic advancement had been the presence of the penal settlement.

DEVILS POSTPILE NATIONAL MONUMENT, a national monument in Madera Co., California, established in 1911. It consists of an 800-acre tract in the eastern part of the Sierra Nevada range, the chief feature of which is a mass of hexagonal blue-gray basaltic columns rising, like a pile of posts, as high as 60 feet. The formation, a remnant of a basaltic lava flow, is said to rank with the Giant's Causeway (q.v.) in Ireland.

DEVIL'S RIDING HORSE. See KISSING BUG; MANTIS.

DEVILS TOWER NATIONAL MONUMENT, the first of the U.S. national monuments, established in Sept., 1906, in Crook Co., N.E. Wyoming. Its area of 1153 acres contains Devils Tower, a natural rock formation of volcanic origin, resembling a colossal, petrified, tree stump. It rises about 800 feet from sedimentary rocks, which in turn rise nearly 500 feet above the Belle Fourche R. The top of Devils Tower covers an area of about one and one-half acres; the base is approximately a third of a mile in diameter.

DEVIL, TASMANIAN. See DASYURE.

DEVINE, EDWARD THOMAS (1867–1948), American economist, sociologist, and social worker, born in Union, Iowa, and educated at Cornell College, Iowa, and the University of Pennsylvania. He was special representative for the Red Cross in San Francisco in 1906, after the earthquake and fire of that year, and at Dayton, Ohio, in 1913, in charge of storm and flood relief. During World War I, he was chief of the Red Cross Bureau of Refugees and Relief in France. He was general secretary of the Charity Organization Society from 1896 to 1917, director of the New York School of Philanthropy from 1904 to 1907 and 1912 to 1917, professor of social economy at Columbia University from 1905 to 1919, and at American University, Washington, D.C., from

1926 to 1928, and editor of the social-service periodical *Survey* from 1897 to 1912. Among his writings are *Economics* (1898), *Social Forces* (1909), *Misery and Its Causes* (1909), *The Normal Life* (1915), *and Progressive Social Action* (1933).

DE VINNE, THEODORE LOW (1828–1914), American printer, born at Stamford, Conn. He served his apprenticeship on the Newburgh (N.Y.) *Gazette,* and in 1850 entered the printing shop of Francis Hart in New York City. He became a partner in 1858 and took over the business as Theo. L. De Vinne & Co. when Hart died in 1877. After 1908 it was known as the De Vinne Press, and was regarded as the finest printing house in the United States. De Vinne wrote extensively on the history of printing, and was one of the founders of the Grolier Club and of the International Typothetæ Society. He was noted for his typography in limited editions but showed, in his production of the *Century Dictionary* (1889–91), that fine printing could be done on a mass scale. In a period of overelaborate printing style, his type designs, now known by his name, were characterized by simplicity and severity.

This is De Vinne Type.

DEVOLUTION, WAR OF THE, one of the wars of conquest waged by King Louis XIV of France. It was also called the Queen's War, and was waged for the two years 1667–68. The pretext for the war was Louis' claim against Spain for the unpaid dowry of his wife, Marie Thérèse, daughter of King Philip IV of Spain. Although Marie Thérèse, before marrying the French king, had renounced her rights to any part of the Spanish dominions, Louis demanded the Spanish Netherlands in lieu of the claimed dowry. He based his claim on a law of Brabant which provided for the devolution (or transfer) of property to children born of the first marriage of the deceased; if applied in the case of the dominions of Philip IV, Marie Thérèse would inherit in place of her half brother Charles II. French armies under the Vicomte de Turenne invaded the Spanish Netherlands in 1667 and occupied Franche-Comté early in 1668. The Spaniards made no effort to resist the French, but the United Provinces (the independent states of the Netherlands), Great Britain, and Sweden formed an alliance with which Louis concluded a peace. By the treaty of Aix-la-Chapelle of May, 1668, Franche-Comté and a number of Netherlands cities were restored to Spain, part of the former Spanish Netherlands was ceded to France, and the question of the devolution was undecided.

DEVONIAN SYSTEM, a geological grouping of rocks dating from the middle of the Paleozoic era, lying above the Silurian system and below the Carboniferous. The Devonian period began approximately 330 million years ago and lasted for about 50 million years. The system takes its name from the English county of Devon where formations of this period were first studied about 1840. The Devonian period is sometimes popularly called the Age of Fishes.

At the beginning of the Devonian period, the North American continent had roughly the same shape that it has today. An arm of the sea, however, covered much of Vermont, New York, Pennsylvania, West Virginia, Kentucky, Tennessee, Mississippi, Alabama, Oklahoma, and Missouri. Parts of the southeastern States, together with what is now the adjacent bed of the Atlantic Ocean, were above water and formed a large island or subcontinent sometimes known as Appalachia. In the middle of the period the inland sea spread westward and northward, covering most of the Middle West as well as much of N.W. Canada and Alaska. An arm of the middle Devonian sea swept southward to cut off an area now covered by the western coastal States. At the end of the period the island of Appalachia was again joined to the mainland, but a similar island called Cascadia had been formed, comprising a coastal strip from central California northward to Alaska. Much of the area of Wisconsin, Minnesota, the Dakotas, Nebraska, and Montana formed another late Devonian island.

Structures. As is typical of a system formed by cycles of subsidence and emergence of large areas of land, the structures of the Devonian are largely water-deposited. In the U.S. they include beds of red and brown shales and sandstones found exposed from the Appalachian Mountains of Pennsylvania westward to Nebraska and Kansas. These beds sometimes reach a thickness of 8000 ft. or more. Sandstones and shales are also typical of the Devonian system in Europe, South America, and Africa. The Devonian "Old Red Sandstone" of England is 37,000 ft. thick in some places.

Devonian Life. The Devonian period marks the first emergence of terrestrial life in the form of fernlike seed-bearing trees which were the ancestors of the plants of the subsequent Coal Age. The lungfishes, the first vertebrates, also appeared in this period. The chief animal forms of the period, however, were marine invertebrates, including corals, echinoderms, trilobites, and brachiopods. See GEOLOGY.

DEVONSHIRE or **DEVON,** county of s.w. England, between the Bristol and the English channels. The surface of the county is generally hilly. The N. coast, 60 m. long, is steep and rocky, with a deep indentation at Bideford Bay, which receives the River Taw, and another at Barnstable Bay, which receives the Torridge. The s. coast, 100 m. long, is also fronted by cliffs, which are penetrated in the E. by the River Exe, and in the w. by the Tamar. A distinguishing feature of Devon is the granite tableland of Dartmoor (q.v.). The climate of the county as a whole is comparatively humid. On the s. coast frost is little known and the equable temperature there has given rise to various resort towns. The chief agricultural products of Devonshire are oats, wheat, barley, and root crops. Large numbers of sheep and cattle, especially the famous Devon breed of cattle are raised. Considerable acreage is given to apple orchards, where the fruit is grown for the manufacture of cider. Important fisheries are operated out of Plymouth (q.v.), the largest city in Devon. The county's principal industries are centered about the naval and military establishments at Plymouth and Devonport. However, at Tiverton (q.v.) are lace factories and at Buckfastleigh (pop., about 2600) are woolen mills. Potteries and terra-cotta plants are located at Bovey Tracy and Watcombe. The county furnishes some tin, copper, iron, zinc, and other minerals, but in diminishing quantities because of the increasing cost of raising the ores from deeply worked deposits. Granite is quarried in the Dartmoor area. Other building stones, including marble and slate, are taken from various points in the county.

The native Welsh of Devon were conquered by the Saxons some time before the 8th century. In the 11th century the area came under Norman control. The coast of Devon was frequently under attack by the French during the 14th and 15th centuries. Devon has been represented in the British Parliament since 1920. The seat of the county government is at Exeter (q.v.). Area, including county boroughs, 2612 sq.m.; pop. (1951 est.) 798,283.

DEVONSHIRE, the name of an English earldom and dukedom. The title of Earl of Devonshire was first created for Charles Blount in 1603. He died three years later, and the title became extinct. It was revived for William Cavendish, second son of Sir William Cavendish, in 1618. A great-grandson of

Sir William Cavendish, also named William, became the first Duke of Devonshire and Marquis of Huntington in 1694, and the title has been held since that time by members of the Cavendish (q.v.) family.

DE VOTO, BERNARD AUGUSTINE (1897–), American writer, born in Ogden, Utah, and educated at Harvard University. He taught English at Harvard from 1929 to 1936. In 1935 he became editor of "The Easy Chair" in *Harper's Magazine*, and from 1936 to 1938 he edited the *Saturday Review of Literature*. In addition to his writings on historical and literary subjects, he also wrote popular fiction under the pseudonym JOHN AUGUST. In 1948, he was awarded the Pulitzer Prize in history for *Across the Wide Missouri* (1947). He also wrote *The Crooked Mile* (1924), *Mark Twain's America* (1932), *We Accept with Pleasure* (1934), *Forays and Rebuttals* (1936), *Minority Report* (1940), *The Year of Decision—1846* (1943), *The Literary Fallacy* (1944), *World of Fiction* (1950), and *The Course of Empire* (1952). He edited *The Journals of Lewis and Clark* (1953).

DE VRIES, HUGO (1848–1935), Dutch botanist, born at Haarlem, and educated at the universities of Leyden, Heidelberg, and Würzburg. He was a professor at the University of Amsterdam from 1878 to 1917. De Vries was one of the first botanists to recognize the value of the work of Gregor Mendel (q.v.), whose writings he republished. He introduced the experimental method of studying evolution, through the breeding of many generations of plants. His observations of the evening primrose, *Oenothera,* led to his greatest discovery, the phenomenon of evolution through mutation (q.v.). In his experiments, some of which took many years, De Vries produced a number of new forms of plants. Among his works are *Intracellular Pangenesis* (1889), *Die Mutationstheorie* (1900–03), and *Plant Breeding* (1907).

DEW, water which condenses on cool objects from the water vapor in warm air, particularly the condensate formed during cool nights in warm seasons of the year. Air at a given temperature can contain only a definite amount of water vapor. This amount is larger as the temperature rises and smaller as the temperature decreases. When air which is nearly saturated with vapor cools in the evening after a warm day, it passes the temperature at which it is fully saturated. On cooling further, the excess water vapor condenses on any surface such as a leaf of grass or a window pane. The temperature at which

dew begins to form from air containing a given amount of water vapor is known as the *dew point.* If the dew point is below the freezing temperature of water, hoarfrost is formed. See HUMIDITY; HYGROMETER.

DEWAR, SIR JAMES (1842–1923), British chemist, born in Kincardine-on-Forth, Scotland, and educated at Edinburgh University. He became professor of experimental natural philosophy at Cambridge University in 1875, and professor of chemistry at the Royal Institution in 1877. In 1897 he was elected president of the Chemical Society, and in 1902 of the British Association. He was knighted in 1904. The Copley Medal of the Royal Society was awarded to him in 1916, and the Franklin Medal of the Franklin Institute of Philadelphia in 1919. With Sir Frederick Abel he invented cordite, a smokeless gunpowder. He introduced vacuum flasks (commonly known as thermos flasks) for keeping substances cold or hot for long periods of time; see CRYOGENICS. By evaporating liquid hydrogen under a reduced atmospheric pressure, he obtained the lowest temperature reached up to that time, 13°C. above absolute zero. He wrote, with G. D. Liveing, *Collected Papers in Spectroscopy* (1915).

DEWBERRY, popular name for any of several trailing varieties and species of blackberries, as *Rubus flagellaris, R. trivialis,* and *R. hispidus.* Dewberries differ from other types of blackberry (q.v.), to which their fruits are similar, chiefly in having long, slender stems that trail along the ground. *R. flagellaris* is often grown in gardens, where its fruits ripen as much as two weeks earlier than those of other blackberry species. The western dewberries, *R. ursinus* and *R. macropetalus,* are also trailing, and by hybridization the Logan, Young, and Boysen horticultural varieties have been derived from them.

DE WET, CHRISTIAAN RUDOLPH (1854–1922), Boer soldier and statesman, born in Leeuwkop, Orange Free State. He served in the Transvaal-British War of 1880–81, and the Boer War of 1899–1902, becoming commander in chief of the Orange Free State forces in 1900. In 1907 he became a member of the first legislative body of the Orange River Colony, and Minister of Agriculture. He later joined General James Barry Munik Hertzog (q.v.) in furthering the separatist policy and in organizing the Nationalist Party (1913). At the outbreak of World War I he rebelled against the South African government, and was tried for treason. He was

Official U.S. Navy Photo

Admiral George Dewey

sentenced to six years imprisonment, but the penalty was removed on condition that he refrain from political agitation. He wrote *Three Years' War* (1902), an account of his military campaigns.

DEWEY, CHARLES MELVILLE (1849–1937), American painter, born at Lowville, New York. He studied in Paris, with Carolus Duran. Dewey's landscapes in oil and water color are in many public galleries and private collections in the United States. Among his paintings are "The Sun Shower" (Metropolitan Museum of Art, New York City), "The Edge of the Forest" (Corcoran Gallery, Washington, D.C.), "The Harvest Moon" and "The Close of Day" (National Gallery, Washington, D.C.), and "The Gray Robe of Twilight" (Albright Art Gallery, Buffalo, N.Y.).

DEWEY, GEORGE (1837–1917), American naval officer, born in Montpelier, Vt., and educated at the United States Naval Academy, from which he was graduated in 1858. On the outbreak of the Civil War, he was commissioned a lieutenant in the Union Navy. Under Admiral David Farragut in 1862, in command of the sloop *Mississippi,* Dewey took part in Farragut's successful efforts to force a passage up the Mississippi River. Dewey also fought in other naval battles in the Civil War; in 1865 he was made a lieutenant commander.

After the war, he was promoted to the rank of commander in 1875, captain in 1884, and commodore in 1896. At the beginning of 1898,

he was given command of the Asiatic Squadron of the U.S. Navy.

The outbreak of the Spanish-American War, later in 1898, found Dewey's squadron in China. On receipt of orders to "capture or destroy the Spanish squadron", then believed to be based on Manila in the Philippines, Dewey set sail at once. On May 1, Dewey engaged the Spanish fleet in Manila Bay. He forcefully defeated an attempt by German naval vessels in the bay to interfere with his operations, and completely destroyed the Spanish fleet without the loss of a single American and with only nine casualties. Six days later Dewey was made a rear admiral. On August 18, Dewey aided General Wesley Merritt in capturing Manila. In further recognition of his services, he was promoted to the rank of admiral in 1899, and the passage of a special act by Congress enabled him to continue in active service past the legal retirement age for naval officers. He also served as president of the General Board of the Navy from 1901 until his death.

DEWEY, JOHN (1859–1952), American philosopher, psychologist, and educator, born at Burlington, Vt., and educated at the University of Vermont and at Johns Hopkins University. He was professor of philosophy at the universities of Minnesota (1888–89), Michigan (1889–94), and Chicago, where he was also director of the School of Education (1894–1904). In 1904 he was appointed professor of philosophy at Columbia University, becoming professor emeritus there in 1931. After World War I, he lectured for two years at the University of Peking; in 1924 he prepared a plan for the reorganization of the national schools for the Turkish government, and in 1929 he delivered the Gifford Lectures at the University of Edinburgh.

Dewey became actively interested in the reform of educational theory and practice while at the University of Chicago, and put his educational principles to the test in a series of pedagogical experiments at the University High School. These principles, which had a profound influence on educational practice in America, emphasized learning through experimentation, and opposed authoritarian methods as the offshoot of an outmoded aristocratic society which offered contemporary man no realistic preparation for life in a democratic society. As a philosopher, too, he emphasized the practical; the process of thinking, in his philosophy, is a means of realizing human desire, removing the obstacles between what is given and what is wanted; in the same sense, truth is not absolute but merely an idea or hypothesis that has worked. Dewey ranks with William James as one of the two great leaders of the pragmatic movement from which Dewey's own philosophy, *instrumentalism* stems. (See PRAGMATISM; INSTRUMENTALISM.) His writings include *Leibnitz* (1888), *School and Society* (1899), *How We Think* (1909), *Democracy and Education* (1916), *Reconstruction in Philosophy* (1920), *The Quest for Certainty* (1929), *Liberalism and Social Action* (1935), *Logic: The Theory of Inquiry* (1938), and *Knowing and the Known* (with Arthur Bentley, 1949).

DEWEY, MELVIL (1851–1931), American librarian and educator, born in Adams Center, N.Y. and educated at Amherst College. While still a senior at college, he devised a decimal system for classifying and cataloging books, which is now used in libraries throughout the world. From 1883 to 1888, he was head librarian at Columbia University where, in 1887, he established and was appointed director of the School for Library Economy, the first institution to train librarians. He was the founder of the *Library Journal* and *Library Notes,* and one of the founders of the American Library Association. Dewey contributed probably more than any other single person to the development of library science in the U.S. See LIBRARY ASSOCIATION, AMERICAN; DEWEY DECIMAL SYSTEM.

DEWEY, THOMAS EDMUND (1902–), American politician and leader of the U.S. Republican Party, born in Owosso, Mich., and educated at the University of Michigan and Columbia University. In 1933 Dewey became U.S. Attorney for the southern district of New York, and he served as a special assistant to U.S. Attorney General Homer S. Cummings in 1934–35. In the latter year Dewey was appointed by Governor Herbert H. Lehman of New York as special prosecutor in connection with an investigation of vice and racketeering in New York City. Dewey secured seventy-two convictions in connection with that investigation and gained national prominence as a crusading prosecutor.

At the New York State Republican Convention in 1938, Dewey was nominated for governor; in the election which followed, he was defeated by Lehman, the Democratic nominee. Wendell L. Willkie defeated Dewey for the Republican Presidential nomination in 1940. Two years later Dewey was elected governor of New York State, and he was subsequently re-elected in 1946 and 1950. In 1944 he was the unanimous choice of the Republican National Convention for the party's Presidential nomination. In the national election which followed in that year, Dewey was defeated by President Franklin D. Roosevelt. In 1948 he was again the unanimous choice of the Republican National Convention, and was defeated by President Harry S. Truman in the election which followed. Dewey was a leading supporter of General Dwight D. Eisenhower for the Republican Presidential nomination in 1952, and played a prominent role in the campaign which preceded Eisenhower's election. He is the author of *Journey to the Far Pacific* (1952), a report of his travels in southeastern Asia in 1951.

DEWEY DECIMAL SYSTEM, in library science, a method of classifying the fields of knowledge for cataloguing books. Under this system all knowledge is divided into ten main classes, each of which is designated by a three-digit number, as 000, 200, 300. The main classes are divided into subclasses, as 900, 910, 920, which are in turn divided, as 910, 911, 912. More specialized subdivisions are designated by numbers after a decimal point which follows the third digit. Thus, 800 is the main class of literature, 810 is American literature, 813 is American fiction, 813.4 is American fiction from 1861 to 1900, and 813.46 is a work by or about Henry James; 813.5 is contemporary American fiction. Every subject is classified and indexed in the *Decimal Classification and Relativ Index* by Melvil Dewey (q.v.). See LIBRARY ASSOCIATION, AMERICAN; LIBRARY OF CONGRESS.

DEWI, SAINT. See DAVID, SAINT.

Thomas E. Dewey

DEWING, THOMAS WILMER (1851–1938), American portrait and figure painter, born in Boston. Among his works are "Tobit and the Angel" (Metropolitan Museum of Art, New York City), "Lady in Gold" (Brooklyn Museum), "The Lady in Green and Gray" (Chicago Art Institute), and 20 paintings in the Freer Collection of the National Gallery, Washington, D.C.

DE WITT, name of two Dutch statesmen, CORNELIS (1623–72) and JAN or JOHN (1625–72), brothers, born in Dort, and educated at Leiden. They were sons of Jacob De Witt, burgomaster of Dort and the town's representative in the most powerful Dutch provincial assembly, called the States. The brothers made distinguished contributions to their country's history.

Cornelis and Jan supported their father in his struggle to establish the supremacy of the States over the princely House of Orange. In 1650 the De Witt brothers achieved political prominence; Cornelis became burgomaster of Dort and a member of the States of Holland; Jan was appointed the leading functionary of the town of Dort with the title of Pensionary (q.v.) and the leader of the town's deputation in the States of Holland. Three years later, during the First Anglo-Dutch War (1652–54), in which Cornelis fought as a naval commander, Jan became the Grand Pensionary of the province of Holland and, thereby, the leader of the province's deputation in the States-General of the Republic of the United Provinces, as the Netherlands was then called. Jan served in that capacity until shortly before his death.

Jan De Witt is accounted one of the outstanding statesmen of his age; his tenure of office was marked by remarkable achievements in which he was ably supported by his brother. Following the conclusion of the Treaty of Westminster (1654), terminating the First Anglo-Dutch War, De Witt negotiated with Oliver Cromwell, then Protector of England, a secret treaty, called the Seclusion Act. The Act provided that the office of stadholder of Holland be left vacant; members of the House of Orange were thus barred from that office. In 1660, following the restoration of the Stuarts in England, the Act of Seclusion was abrogated. Jan De Witt nevertheless adamantly opposed the appointment of the Prince of Orange as stadholder. The resulting friction between the Dutch and English, and a sharpening commercial and colonial rivalry between them, led to the outbreak of the Second Anglo-Dutch War (1665–67).

Cornelis and Jan fought in this war as naval commanders and Jan negotiated the Treaty of Breda, terminating the war. (See DUTCH WARS.)

In 1668 Jan De Witt negotiated an alliance of Holland, England, and Sweden, against France, but in 1672, after France had succeeded in isolating Holland diplomatically, France and England made war on Holland. The Dutch turned for leadership to William III, Prince of Orange; the De Witt brothers were repudiated, and Cornelis, after fighting against the British and French at sea, was arrested on a charge of conspiracy and sentenced to banishment. Just before his release from prison, he was visited by his brother. A mob broke into the jail and lynched both men.

DEWSBURY, town in the West Riding of Yorkshire, England, on the Calder R., 8 miles s.s.w. of Leeds. Its chief manufactures are blankets, carpets and rugs, and worsted yarns, but it also has important iron foundries and machinery factories. At Dewsbury, in 627, the Roman missionary Paulinus first preached Christianity to the Northumbrians. In nearby Kirklees park are the remains of the Cistercian convent, where, according to tradition, Robin Hood died and was buried. Pop. (1951 est.) 53,476.

DEXTRAN. See TRANSFUSION OF BLOOD: *Plasma.*

DEXTRIN, also called *British gum* or *starch gum,* an amorphous, soluble carbohydrate with the formula $(C_6H_{10}O_5)_n$, produced by the action of acids, heat, or enzymes (such as diastase) on starch paste. The first product formed in this reaction is soluble starch, which in turn hydrolyzes to form dextrin. Dextrin is prepared commercially by moistening potato starch with weak nitric acid, and then drying and heating the mass at 110° C. (230° F.). Dextrin is used in the manufacture of beer, and as a substitute for gum arabic in calico printing. Because it is less brittle than gum when dry, it is used as an adhesive on the back of postage stamps. See CARBOHYDRATE.

DEXTROSE. See GLUCOSE.

DEZHNEV, CAPE. See CAPE DEZHNEV.

DHABB. See DAB.

DHARWAR, capital of the district of the same name, Bombay State, Union of India, situated in the s. part of the State, about 290 miles s.s.e. of Bombay and 50 miles s.e. of Belgaum. It is a railroad and cotton-trading center. Its principal manufacture is cotton textiles. Dharwar contains a number of educational institutions, including three schools of higher learning. Agriculture is the leading industry of the district, and cotton, pulse, and millet are the chief crops. The district also contains valuable stands of timber. Area of district, 5261 sq.m.; pop. (1951) 1,575,386. Pop. of town (1941) 47,992.

DHAULAGIRI, one of the highest peaks of the Himalayas, rising to a height of 26,795 ft. above sea level, in N. Nepal.

DHOLE, wild dog of India. See DOG.

DHYAL BIRD. See DIAL BIRD.

DHYANI BUDDHA, name given to any of the five (according to some Buddhist sources, six or ten) Buddhas subordinate to the primordial Adi Buddha and capable, through meditation (*dhyāna*), of causing the emanations from which more Buddhas or Bodhisattvas might develop. These noncorporate eternal Buddhas and their female counterparts, the Taras or Shaktis, may be considered the nearest approximation to gods and goddesses in Buddhism, which is essentially atheistic. In art the Dhyāni Buddhas are distinguished from other Buddhas by varieties of ornamentation on their lotus seats, by the position of their hands, and sometimes by different colors of paint.

DIABASE. See GABBRO.

DIABETES INSIPIDUS, a rare disease caused by deficiency of pitressin, one of the hormones of the posterior pituitary gland which controls water storage in the body. Its symptoms are marked thirst and passing of large quantities of urine: as much as 3C to 40 pints a day. This urine has a low specific gravity, contains no sugar. Blood sugar is, however, normal. In many cases either injection of pitressin or application of this hormone to the mucous membranes of the nose will control the symptoms of the disease.

DIABETES MELLITUS, a metabolic disease arising from an insufficient supply of insulin (q.v.) in the body. The latter is necessary for the utilization of carbohydrates by the body, and in its absence the metabolism of carbohydrates, and to some extent of proteins and fats, is incomplete.

The disease is caused by degeneration of insulin-manufacturing islets of Langerhans in the pancreas. Inhibitory effects by the pituitary, adrenal, or thyroid glands probably play an important role in some cases. The usual symptoms are: an excessive flow of sugary urine, hunger, thirst, loss of weight, weakness and itchy skin. A high content of sugar in the blood (hyperglycemia) is the decisive sign. The sugar-tolerance test is employed in doubtful cases. After ingesting sugar both normal and diabetic individuals show an increased percentage of sugar but the percentage stays high in the diabetics. In severe and untreated diabetes the intermediate products of fat metabolism tend to accumulate (ketosis) and may cause coma and death. The uncontrolled diabetic is predisposed to infections, arteriosclerosis, neuritis, and development of cataract. In mild cases, constituting the majority of all cases, dietary treatment is usually all that is necessary. The diet should be well-balanced, with a measured amount of carbohydrate- or sugar-forming foods and a decrease in the usual amount of food. If diet alone fails to control the disease, insulin is necessary by prescription of a physician. Overdoses may produce a drop in the blood sugar (hypoglycemia), symptoms of which are headache, nervousness, sweating, and rapid heartbeat; infrequently, with persistence of a severe degree of hypoglycemia, convulsions may occur and then death. Diabetes is more common in the obese and among certain racial groups. It is more commonly a disease of middle life, although it may occur at any time. Women frequently develop it at menopause. Insulin and diet carefully followed can control but not cure diabetes. A well-controlled diabetic is a perfectly normal individual. His activities need not be limited or the span of life decreased.

In recent years there has been an annual rise in the number of cases of diabetes, probably due to (1) the increasing age of the population, as diabetes is chiefly a disease of middle and later life; (2) improved diagnostic facilities and more frequent urine examinations; and (3) probably also the hereditary predisposition to diabetes. Approximately 2,000,000 sufferers from diabetes are in the United States alone.

DIACRITICAL MARK, or DIACRITIC, in written language, a mark or sign used to indicate a special sound or value for the character to which it is attached. Such marks may be used to distinguish one character from another similar character, as the Scandinavian *å* and a; or they may be invented or chosen for a special purpose, as to indicate the accented syllables or the pronunciation of words in reference works.

Some diacritical marks were developed when books were copied by hand; in frequently occurring combinations of vowels, the second was written above the first, as a means of convenience or to save space. Thus, the German *ae, oe,* and *ue* were written as $\overset{e}{a}$, $\overset{e}{o}$, and $\overset{e}{u}$; and the superior *e* eventually became two dots (see

UMLAUT). The Swedish *ao* was written *å*, and the superior *o* was later made into a small circle. The cedilla (ç) used in French and Portuguese was once a *z*. The dot over the *i* was originally a diacritical mark, a stroke (') which distinguished the letter from the shaft of an *n* or *m*; it is still used in that form over the Roman numerals in prescriptions written by physicians.

The English language usually employs only the diæresis, or dieresis (¨), the cedilla, the acute accent ('), the grave accent (`), and the tilde (˜). The diæresis is placed over one of two adjacent vowels to separate them into two distinct syllables, as in *Chloë*. The cedilla, used in words taken from the French and Portuguese, gives the *s* sound to a *c* which would otherwise be pronounced as *k*, as in *façade*. The acute accent is sometimes used to indicate the pronunciation of a final *e*, as in *Bronté*. The grave accent indicates that a final *-ed* is to be made a distinct syllable, as in *blessèd*. The tilde occurs in words taken from Spanish and indicates that the *n* below it is to be palatalized, i.e., followed by the sound of the consonant *y*, as in *cañon*; originally, the tilde in Spanish meant that the character over which it stood was followed by an *n*, as in *año*, instead of *anno*.

The diacritical marks used in simple phonetic systems, as in many dictionaries, have acquired generally fixed meanings through long usage. The signs ˉ and ˘ are placed over vowels to denote long and short sounds respectively, as in *ōver* and *ŏdd*. The sign ^, sometimes called the circumflex accent, usually denotes a broad sound or the combination of a rising and falling sound, as in *câre*. These marks, however, are used only in elementary systems which try to give an approximation of the pronunciation of a word; in scientific phonetics (q.v.), the marks have different meanings from those explained above.

DIÆRESIS. See DIACRITICAL MARK.

DIAGHILEV, SERGEI PAVLOVICH (1872–1929), Russian ballet producer and art critic, born in Novgorod. He graduated from the St. Petersburg Conservatory of Music in 1892, and in 1899 joined the staff of the Imperial Russian Theater in Moscow; in the latter year he also founded a journal of art. In 1908 he produced Moussorgsky's opera *Boris Godunoff* in Paris with Feodor Chaliapin heading the cast. The following year he organized his Ballet Russe in Paris with the collaboration of the choreographer Michel Fokine, the dancer Waslaw Nijinsky, and the painters Aleksandr Benois and Léon Bakst. This co-ordination of dancing, stage décor, costuming, music, and lighting produced entertainment on a highly artistic level. Diaghilev continued to introduce, in Paris, new ballets adapted to such orchestral works as Rimski-Korsakov's *Schéhérazade* and Debussy's *L'Après-midi d'un Faune;* he also commissioned original music for his ballets from Maurice Ravel, Igor Stravinsky, Manuel de Falla, Serge Prokofieff, Darius Milhaud, Francis Poulenc and other composers. From 1911 his company also performed in London, and in 1916 toured America. After 1921 Diaghilev made Monte Carlo his headquarters, and his ballets were presented chiefly in Paris and London.

DIAGNOSIS, the determination of the nature of a disease by a comprehensive examination of the patient. Accurate diagnosis is the foundation of medical practice, for proper treatment is possible only when the cause of illness is known.

Diagnosis begins with the taking of an exhaustive history of the patient's heredity, past health, and habits, followed by a thorough physical examination of the patient, and often by the application of a number of tests. Specific tests may include chemical and physical tests of body excreta and blood, and skin testing for immune and nonimmune reactions. Superficial physical examination of the patient may be supplemented by X-rays and by examinations with special instruments such as the stethoscope, bronchoscope, electrocardiograph, sphygmomanometer, and devices for testing basal metabolism. Tissue specimens may be examined microscopically, and specimens of tissue, blood, or excreta cultured to discover the presence of microorganisms. From the data assembled in these ways and from his own knowledge of the syndromes (groups of symptoms) characteristic of particular diseases, the skilled diagnostician is usually able to determine with accuracy the disease from which the patient is suffering.

DIAGRAM. See DRAFTING; GRAPHIC METHODS; MAP.

DIAL. See SUNDIAL.

DIAL BIRD, DAYAL BIRD, or **DYHAL BIRD,** common name for several species of Asiatic thrushes, particularly *Copsychus saularis*. This bird, also called magpie robin, is common from China to Ceylon, and is frequently kept as a cage bird because of its pleasing song. The plumage of the male is black and white, and that of the female is brownish. The name "dial bird" is also given to the Indian robin, *Thamnobia fulicata,* which resembles and is related to the European robin.

DIALECT, a version of a language differing in accent, grammar, pronunciation, and vocabulary from other forms of the language, particularly from the standard or written language, and restricted in usage to a particular tribe, class, locale, or trade. The designation of dialect as a spoken language which exists apart from the literary or standard language is, however, entirely relative, for the literary language is frequently the development and result of a written dialect. Thus the Tuscan dialect, employed with such literary genius by Dante and Petrarch, dominated all other Italian dialects and became the written language of Italy; the High German dialect into which Martin Luther translated the Bible became the standard language of Germany; and Chaucer's East Midland dialect became the basis of the English language. The English frequently refer to the Americans as speaking the "American dialect", and Americans loosely divide their speech into such regional dialects as New England, Western, and Southern. Eccentric and isolated examples of American dialects may be found among the inhabitants of the Appalachian Mountains in the States of Kentucky, Tennessee, Virginia, North Carolina and Georgia, and among the Gullah Negroes of South Carolina.

DIALECTIC or DIALECTICS, in logic, the science of investigating the nature of truth by critical analysis of concepts and hypotheses. Plato's *Dialogues,* wherein he sought to study truth by means of discussion in the form of questions and answers, is one of the earliest examples of the dialectical method. Aristotle thought of dialectic as the search for the philosophic basis of science, and frequently used the term as a synonym for logic. To Immanuel Kant, dialectic meant the study of ultimate realities as distinguished from objective phenomena. Georg Wilhelm Friedrich Hegel applied the term to his own philosophic system, based on the idealistic concept of a universal mind which, through evolution, seeks to arrive at the highest level of self-awareness and freedom. The "dialectical materialism" of Karl Marx, frequently considered to be a revision of the Hegelian system, asserts that the material or objective universe exists independently of mind, which is essentially a reflection of material reality.

The term dialectic is also used in a derogatory sense to signify futile, impractical, or destructive disputation.

DIALLAGE. See DIOPSIDE.

DIALYSIS. See COLLOIDAL DISPERSIONS; DIFFUSION; OSMOSIS.

DIAMAGNETISM, the property of being repelled by a magnet. Certain substances such as copper, silver, bismuth, and antimony have a negative magnetic susceptibility and a magnetic permeability of less than 1, and are therefore slightly repelled by a magnetic field. Such diamagnetic substances also have the property of being weakly magnetized in an electric field, but the magnetism they show is opposite in polarity to the magnetism of such paramagnetic substances as platinum and such ferromagnetic substances as nickel and iron. See MAGNETISM.

DIAMOND, a mineral form of carbon, valued as a precious stone and also used for various industrial purposes. Diamonds occur in various forms, including the diamond proper (a crystalline gem stone), *bort, ballas,* and *carbonado.* Bort is an imperfectly crystallized type of diamond, sometimes fibrous in structure, and dark in color. The term bort is also sometimes applied to imperfect crystals and fragments of gem diamonds: Ballas is a compact, spherical mass of tiny diamond crystals of great hardness and toughness. Carbonado, sometimes called black diamond or carbon, is an opaque grayish or black form of diamond with no cleavage. Carbonado, ballas, and bort are all used industrially in lapidary work and for the cutting edges of drills and other cutting tools.

Diamond is the hardest substance known, and is given a value of 10 in the Mohs' hardness scale. Diamonds from different localities show some variation in hardness, and there are also slight differences in the hardness of individual stones from the same areas. In general the diamonds found in Borneo and Australia are the hardest, followed by Indian, Brazilian, and South African stones in descending order of hardness. Diamonds from the beds of streams are in general harder than those from mines. In addition, the hardness of the crystals is greater on the exterior than on the interior, and is greater on certain crystal faces than on others, and in certain directions along a single face.

The crystallization of the diamond is in the isometric system. Octahedrons and rhombic dodecahedrons are the crystal forms most commonly found, but cubic and other forms also occur. Rounded, distorted, and twinned crystals are also not uncommon. Crystalline diamonds always cleave cleanly along planes

De Beers Consolidated Mines

Above: Natives in an African diamond mine, shoveling "blue ground," the diamond ore, into a car. Left: Famous diamonds. Top, left, Koh-i-noor; top, right, Nassak. Bottom, left, Polar Star; bottom, right, Pitt.

parallel to the faces of an octahedron. In specific gravity, diamonds range between 3.15 and 3.53, but the value for pure crystals is almost always 3.52.

Diamonds exhibit a wide range of transparency and color. All good gem diamonds are transparent, and colorless or blue-white stones are usually considered the most valuable. A yellowish or brownish tinge often occurs and is regarded as an imperfection, although the valuable Tiffany diamond (see below) is deep yellow. Red diamonds are not uncommon. Green and blue diamonds are rarities and, if of good quality otherwise, are highly prized. Color in diamonds is believed to be caused by

the inclusion of minute amounts of oxides of various metals.

Two important characteristics of the diamond when used as a gem are its brilliancy and fire. Both the index of refraction and the dispersion (the physical properties which determine luster and fire, respectively) are higher for diamond than for any other natural, transparent, colorless stone. Uncut diamonds have a greasy luster and are not brilliant, but the same stones when cut exhibit a high luster, characterized technically as adamantine. The effect of the high dispersion is to separate the colored components of white light in a marked fashion so that the stone, when properly cut, sparkles with spectral colors.

Other characteristics of the diamond add nothing to its appearance but are frequently useful in identifying the stone and in differentiating between true diamonds and imitations. Because diamonds are excellent conductors of heat, they are cold to the touch. Diamonds are not good electrical conductors, and become charged with positive electricity when rubbed. Genuine diamonds are transparent to

X rays, whereas imitation diamonds, usually made of lead-containing glass, are not. Individual stones may show the phenomena of fluorescence and phosphorescence (qq.v.) when exposed to radium, ultraviolet light, or X rays. Colorless stones sometimes exhibit a light-blue glow when exposed to sunlight or other ultraviolet source, although not all stones react in this way.

Another important physical characteristic of the diamond is its resistance to attack by acids or alkalies; however, the stone becomes oxidized if heated in a mixture of potassium bichromate and sulfuric acid. Diamonds burn in air or oxygen at temperatures above 850° C. (1562° F.), forming carbon dioxide.

History. The name diamond is derived from the Greek word *adamas,* meaning invincible, which was probably applied by the Greeks to any hard stone, such as corundum. The first distinct and undoubted reference to diamonds occurs in Roman literature of the 1st century A.D. The diamonds known to the Romans undoubtedly came from India. Until the 18th century, India was the only known source of the stones, and they were believed to be found only in the fabled mines of Golconda. Golconda was in fact the market city of the diamond trade, and gems sold there came from a number of mines. In 1728, diamonds were discovered in Brazil, and in 1867 in South Africa. The latter area is now the chief source of diamonds.

Formation and Occurrence. The exact mechanism of the production of diamonds is still a matter of debate among geologists, but it is certain that both tremendous heat and tremendous pressure are required for the crystallization of carbon into this form. Hence diamonds were probably produced in molten rock or magma, in which these conditions prevail, far below the surface of the earth, and were carried to the surface by the magma, which later hardened. The parent rock is apparently peridotite (q.v.), but diamonds are seldom, if ever, found in their original rock matrix. Most diamonds are recovered either from weathered and decomposed deposits of various types of peridotite or from alluvial deposits at a distance from their point of origin. In some instances the stones are found also in sandstones, conglomerates, or other sedimentary rocks, which presumably represent alluvial deposits of earlier geologic eras.

Indian diamond deposits are entirely in the form of sedimentary rocks, and gravels derived from such rocks. Although India was for centuries the only source of diamonds, its dia-

mond workings have now been abandoned.

Diamonds are found in two widely separated localities in Brazil, one near the city of Diamantina in Minas Geraes, and the other in the province of Bahia. In both fields the gems occur in clays and conglomerates. Diamonds have been mined in Minas Geraes since about 1740 and in the Bahia district since 1844. The Brazilian diamond workings have been overshadowed as a source of gem stones since the discovery of diamonds in South Africa, but remain important in the production of bort and ballas, and are virtually the only source of carbonado.

A "pebble" picked up by a child on the banks of the Orange River in South Africa, and identified in 1867 as a 21-carat diamond, was the first step in opening the diamond fields of that region, which have become the greatest in the world. A diamond rush to the Orange and the Vaal rivers took place in 1870 and 1871 following the discovery of "dry diggings", particularly in the Kimberley district. These diggings were roughly circular patches of yellow clay in which diamonds were found. As the miners dug deeper in the clay, often called the "yellow ground", they found below it a hard bluish rock which also proved to be productive. This "blue ground", scientifically identified as kimberlite (a form of peridotite), is the parent material from which yellow ground is formed by weathering. Further mining disclosed that the circular areas of yellow and blue ground are the tops of funnel-shaped "pipes" of kimberlite which continue downward for an undetermined distance. Similar pipes, not all of which contain diamonds, have been found at various other locations in South Africa. Pipes are believed to be of volcanic origin.

Diamonds have been found in alluvial deposits in various other parts of the world, including Australia, Borneo, the Congo region of Africa, the Ural Mountains, Siberia, and British Guiana. In the United States, stones have been recovered from such deposits in Virginia, the Carolinas, Georgia, Tennessee, Kentucky, Ohio, Indiana, Michigan, Wisconsin, Arkansas, California, and Oregon.

Mining. The processes used for mining diamonds in India and later in Brazil were extremely primitive, consisting chiefly of manual washing of alluvial clays and gravels, and breaking up of the conglomerate and other diamantiferous rocks. Similar methods were employed at first in the South African diamond diggings, but since 1889, when the mines were consolidated under the control of a single company, modern mining practices have been introduced.

The original mine workings at Kimberley and the other pipes were open pits, first in the yellow ground and later in the deeper blue ground. As these pits progressed, it became more difficult and expensive to remove the mined material. The mine workings became craters hundreds of feet deep, constantly menaced by rock slides and falls from the nearly vertical sides and from the walls and pillars of barren rock which were left standing between individual pits. Because of these difficulties the open-pit method of mining was completely abandoned and a system of underground mining was instituted. Vertical shafts were sunk parallel to the pipe, and horizontal drifts were dug from the shaft into the diamond-bearing ground. When working of the upper drifts and their associated transverse galleries was complete, the mine galleries were abandoned and work was continued at a lower level. The Kimberley mine, the deepest of the South African mines, has been worked to a depth of more than 3600 ft.

The blue ground, as brought to the surface, is a hard rock. The earliest method of processing used was to break it up by hand with hammers. The miners then discovered that if the rock were allowed to weather in the open air for from three months to a year it would disintegrate. The mined material was therefore spread out over many acres of level *depositing floors* for weathering. This system of breaking up the blue ground has been supplanted by the use of crushing machinery which, although entailing the risk of crushing some diamonds, is a swift, efficient method of treatment.

After the rock is crushed, it is washed in circular tanks. In these tanks a stream of water and constant shaking separate the lighter material from the heavier. The light material is washed away, while the heavier concentrates sink to the bottom of the tank. The efficiency of the washing process is such that only one percent of the original material remains after washing. Further elimination of unwanted material is accomplished by means of machines called *jigs*, which further separate the materials according to their specific gravity. The jig is a box with a screen bottom through which a pulsating stream of water is passed. Light material is kept in suspension and flows off through an opening near the top of the jig. The heavier mineral materials, including the diamonds, sink and pass through the screen at the bottom of the jig.

At one time diamonds were picked by hand from the concentrates produced by the jigging process, but hand sorting has been supplanted by an automatic machine called a *greaser.* This device depends for its operation on the fact that diamonds will stick to a greasy surface much more readily than will the other mineral materials in the concentrates. The greaser is an inclined vibrating table coated with petroleum grease. As the concentrates are fed in at the top of the table, the diamonds are held by the grease, and the other minerals are shaken down to the foot of the table and discarded after removal of such semiprecious stones as garnets ("Cape rubies") and zircons. The action of the greaser is almost 100-percent efficient. The elaborate system of concentration used in the recovery of diamonds is necessary, because diamonds comprise only about one part in 15,000,000 of the blue ground. By contrast, the upper limit for the economical recovery of gold from ore is one part in 300,000.

Diamond Cutting. To bring out the beauty of a gem diamond, a number of additional processes are necessary. These processes, which include *cleaving, sawing, cutting,* and *polishing,* are usually known collectively as diamond cutting and are the most exacting and difficult techniques of lapidary art; see GEM CUTTING. The primary object of diamond cutting is to bring out the fire and brilliance of the stone; equally important, however, is the cutting of the stone according to a plan that will eliminate imperfections such as cracks, flaws, and cloudiness, and will produce a gem of the greatest size, best appearance, and hence maximum value. For many years the cities of Holland and Belgium had a virtual monopoly of the diamond-cutting trade. During World War II, however, many of the skilled artisans left those countries to come to the U.S., and New York City has become the foremost diamond-cutting center of the world.

The first step in cutting a diamond is the careful examination of the stone. During the course of this examination the expert cutter determines the cleavage planes of the diamond and decides how the stone can best be divided by cleaving and sawing. The rough diamond is then marked with lines of India ink as a guide for the later operations. For cleaving, the stone is firmly cemented into a wooden holder, and a notch is cut with a diamond fragment on the surface, along one of the previously-decided cleavage lines. The cutter then mounts the stone and its holder firmly in a vise, and holds a cleaving iron, an instrument like a heavy,

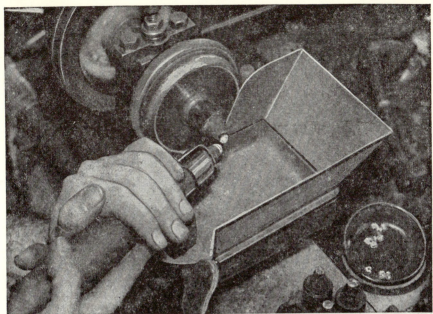

Above: Rough diamonds are cut to shape by lathe-bruting. Two gems, one in lathe and one on end of stick, serve to shape each other simultaneously.
Right: Grinding the facets on the diamonds, mounted in lead dops, with abrasive wheel.

blunt knife, in the notch and parallel to the cleavage plane of the diamond. He then cleaves the stone by striking the iron with a light blow of a hammer. The tools used for cleaving are of great simplicity, but expert skill is needed in their use, because too hard a blow applied in the wrong direction may ruin the stone.

After cleaving, the stone is often cut into still smaller pieces by sawing, and in some instances rough diamonds are sawed rather than cleaved. The saw employed is a thin disk of phosphor bronze, the edge of which is charged with a mixture of diamond dust and oil. The stone, cemented firmly in a holder, is held against the edge of the disk, which revolves at between 2500 and 4000 revolutions per minute. It takes about eight hours to saw a one-carat diamond, and up to several days for larger gems.

The actual cutting of the stone to remove imperfections and bring it to its rough final shape was formerly accomplished by *bruting*, i.e., rubbing two mounted diamonds together

by hand. Most diamond cutters today mount the stone to be cut in a chuck which revolves horizontally and turn it to shape with another diamond operated like a lathe-turning tool. Great care is taken to salvage all the fragments removed during the cutting for later use as an abrasive in the sawing and polishing of other diamonds.

The final step in the cutting of a diamond, called polishing, consists of forming the facets of the finished stone. For the polishing process the gem is held firmly in a mount called a *dop*. The older forms of dops were hemispherical cups in which the stone was mounted in a matrix of solder. Mechanical dops in which the stone is held by prongs and screw clamps are now largely employed. Most diamonds today are cut in the form of brilliants with a total of fifty-eight facets. The preliminary stage of polishing is to cut the eighteen primary facets, a process known as *lapping*. The final stage is *brillianteering*, the cutting of the remaining forty facets. Both lapping and brillianteering are accomplished on a flat, horizontally revolving wheel of cast iron called a *skeif*. The wheel is charged with a mixture of diamond dust and oil, and the stone in its dop is held against the surface until the facet is formed. In the course of lapping and brillianteering the stone is moved many times in its dop to present new surfaces to be polished. Formerly, all diamond polishing was done by hand, but in recent years polishing machines have been developed which automatically regulate the angle and depth of the cutting of facets. Use of polishing machines does not require outstanding technical skill on the part of the operator and permits him to polish a number of diamonds at once on several machines.

Weight and Quality. The unit of weight usually employed for diamonds and other gems is the metric carat, which is equal to one fifth of a gram or about .007 ounces. Another unit used to express the weight of diamonds is the point, a weight equal to a hundredth of a carat. A stone of 82 points would therefore weigh .82 carats.

In judging the value per carat of a cut diamond, four factors must be taken into account. The first is the color. The best way to determine the color of a diamond is to look at a sheet of white paper through the thickest portion of the stone. The shaping and proportion of the cut stone is another important criterion in evaluating diamonds. In a perfect stone the facets are perfectly symmetrical, and the heights of the crown or upper portion of the stone and the pavilion or lower portion are in proper proportion with the diameter of the stone. The presence or absence of internal blemishes and flaws and of external chips is the third factor in determining the value of a diamond. The diamond's weight is the final factor; a stone of five carats is worth more than five one-carat stones.

Imitation Diamonds. Because of their great value, diamonds are frequently imitated. The most common imitations are those made of a form of lead glass known as *paste* or *strass*. The better glass imitations are cut and polished

like true stones, but cheaper counterfeits are molded in the form of brilliants, and in consequence have rounded edges. Any glass imitation can easily be identified. It will not scratch ordinary glass, it will feel warm to the touch, it will often contain air bubbles which can be seen with a magnifying glass, and it will generally be opaque to X rays. Rock crystal, a transparent crystalline form of quartz, is properly known as rhinestone (q.v.) when cut as a brilliant, but is also sometimes sold under misleading names such as Herkimer diamond, Lake George diamond, Mexican diamond, or Alaska diamond. Such stones can easily be scratched by a real diamond. Semiprecious zircons, which have a strong dispersion of light, can be made almost colorless by heat treatment. They resemble true diamonds and are sometimes sold under the name of matura diamonds. Zircons also can be scratched by real diamonds. Another form of imitation stone, known in the gem trade as a doublet, is composed of two pieces cemented together. Diamond doublets are sometimes composed of two actual diamonds joined to form a single stone, in which case they are known as true doublets. False doublets, which are more common, consist of a diamond crown cemented to a base or pavilion of a less valuable gem material or of glass. Many attempts have been made to synthesize diamonds in the laboratory; see ARTIFICIAL GEMS.

Famous Diamonds. A number of individual diamods have become historic, chiefly because of their size. The largest of all known diamonds is the *Cullinan*, which was discovered in the Premier mine in South Africa in 1905 and was presented to Edward VII of England by the government of the Transvaal. The Cullinan weighed 3106 carats (more than a pound) before cutting, and was pronounced by crystallographers to be a cleavage fragment of a considerably larger stone. When the stone was cut, a total of 105 gems were produced, weighing 1063 carats in all. The largest of these was a drop-shaped stone called the *Star of Africa*, 530.2 carats, the largest cut diamond in existence. The *Vargas* diamond, found in Brazil in 1938, weighed 726.6 carats in its uncut state. When cut in 1945, it yielded 29 stones with a total weight of 411 carats. In 1934 a diamond of almost precisely the same weight, the *Jonker* diamond, was discovered in an alluvial deposit near the Premier mine which yielded the Cullinan. The Jonker is the finest large diamond ever found. It was cut into 12 gems ranging from 142.9 to 5.3 carats in weight, giving a total of 370.87 carats of gems. The weight of the stones cut from the Jonker amounted to 51 percent of the weight of the uncut diamond, and those cut from the Vargas to 56.6 percent, very high ratios of yield.

The *Great Mogul* diamond, reputed to have weighed 240 carats when cut, has disappeared since it was described by the French traveler J. B. Tavernier in India in 1665. Some authorities believe that the *Koh-i-noor* diamond, which now weighs 106.1 carats and is one of the British crown jewels, is a part of the Great Mogul. The *Pitt* or *Regent* diamond, an Indian stone of 136.9 carats, was originally the property of William Pitt, governor of Madras. He sold it in 1717 to Philippe, Duke of Orléans, at that time regent of France. This diamond was stolen during the French Revolution but later returned. A nameless blue Indian brilliant of 67.1 carats stolen at the same time was never recovered, and some experts believe that the *Hope* diamond, 44.5 carats, which has the same color, is part of the stolen gem. The *Orloff* diamond, 194.8 carats, was supposedly stolen from the eye of an idol in an Indian temple. It was formerly mounted in the imperial Russian sceptre. Other noteworthy diamonds include the *Jubilee*, 245.3 carats, the *Florentine*, 133.2; the *Tiffany*, 128.5; the *Star of the South*, 125.5; the *Stewart*, 120; and the *Dresden Green*, 40. The *Braganza* "diamond", weighing 1680 carats, which is part of the crown jewels of Portugal, is believed to be a topaz.

For further industrial use of diamonds, see WELL SINKING.

DIAMONDBACK. See RATTLESNAKE; TERRAPIN.

DIAMOND BIRD. See DICAEIDAE.

DIAMOND, CAPE. See CAPE DIAMOND.

DIAMOND DRILL. See WELL SINKING.

DIAMOND NECKLACE, THE AFFAIR OF THE, a sensational scandal and theft of 1784-86, involving several persons prominent at the court of Louis XVI, King of France. The central figures of the affair were Cardinal de Rohan, grand almoner of France and archbishop of Strasbourg; his mistress, an adventuress known as the Countess de La Motte; Queen Marie Antoinette; and Boehmer and Bassenge, a firm of Parisian jewelers. The last-named were owners of the necklace, a magnificent collar of diamonds valued at 1,600,000 livres (today, about $300,-000). It had been ordered by Louis XV for his mistress, Madame du Barry, but the king died before its completion. According to evidence produced at the subsequent trial of the culprits, Rohan, in disfavor at the French court since 1774, was duped by the Countess into believing that, through her influence, he could secure the patronage of the Queen. A correspondence ensued, in which Rohan's hopes were encouraged by letters purportedly written by Marie Antoinette, but in reality written by the Countess. Rohan shortly became convinced that the Queen desired him as her paramour. This deception was supplemented by a more astounding hoax. In July, 1784, the Cardinal received word that the Queen would grant him a private audience. The Countess then proceeded to arrange a secret midnight tryst between Rohan and a Mademoiselle Olivia, who closely resembled Marie Antoinette. Convinced of the authentic character of this meeting, which took place in the garden of Versailles Palace, the Cardinal was easily victimized by the Countess's next move. She persuaded him that the Queen wanted the diamond necklace and would buy it if he would provide the surety. The jewelers, believing Rohan and the Countess to be the Queen's agents, completed the transaction on February 1, 1785, delivering the necklace to the Cardinal on the basis of his agreement to pay 1,600,000 livres in four installments. Rohan then took the necklace to the Countess's home, where he surrendered it to a man disguised as a valet of the Queen. The necklace, along with the husband of the Countess, was never seen again.

On August 1, 1785, Rohan failed to make his payment to the jewelers. They in turn complained to the police. He and the Countess were arrested about two weeks later. Although Louis XVI undoubtedly prevented an impartial investigation because of the Queen's involvement, the Cardinal and the Countess were finally brought to trial. The Cardinal was acquitted, on May 31, 1786, and the Countess was sentenced to be scourged, branded, and imprisoned for life. Her husband was sentenced, in absentia, to the galleys. She later escaped from prison and fled to England. Popular revulsion at the scandalous revelations of the trial contributed to the political ferment that culminated in the French Revolution.

DIAMOND RATTLESNAKE. See RATTLESNAKE.

DIAMOND SNAKE. 1. Common name of a large constricting snake, *Python spilotes,* found in Australia and New Guinea, also known as the diamond python. The snake is extremely variable in color. Some individuals have diamond-shaped markings of yellow and black on their backs and abdomens, while others, usually called carpet snakes, have irregular greenish markings. Specimens of the diamond snake up to 14 ft. in length have been found, but the average length is about 8 ft. **2.** Common name given in Tasmania to the Australian copperhead snake, *Denisonia superba*. This elapid snake is 5 ft. or more in length and is extremely poisonous. **3.** A name sometimes used for the diamondback rattlesnake (q.v.).

DIANA, a Roman nature goddess, in later times identified with the Greek goddess Artemis (q.v.). In earlier times Diana was believed to aid women in childbirth and to protect the forests. After the identification of Diana with Artemis, her characteristics were similar to those of her Greek prototype, and she was best known as goddess of the moon and of the chase. Her festival was celebrated on August 13th. Each successive priest of Diana was traditionally a runaway slave who had plucked a certain bough in the woods and then subdued his predecessor in combat. The worship of Diana centered from early times in a grove (Lat. *nemus*) near Aricia, the *Nemus Dianæ*. The shrine was moved to the Aventine hill in Rome, according to tradition in the 7th century B.C. by Servius Tullius.

DIANA, TEMPLE OF, a structure built in the 4th century B.C. at Ephesus, in Syria, by the Greek architect Dinocrates, and regarded as one of the seven wonders of the world. From the 8th century B.C. the site was the seat of the worship of the Asiatic nature goddess, whom the Greeks identified with Artemis (q.v.). Legend told of many temples which were burned before Ephesians, at the close of the 7th or the beginning of the 6th century B.C., began the erection of a series of famous temples to Artemis. In the time of Crœsus, King of Lydia (d. 546 B.C.), a large temple was begun which apparently had two rows of eight columns across the front and the rear, and two rows of twenty columns on each side (in this statement the corner columns have been counted twice). According to the Roman historian Pliny, 120 years elapsed before it was completed, but this statement has been challenged on the ground that the sculptured bases of the columns and the frieze and cornice all belong to the period of King Crœsus, who contributed largely to the building. This temple was burned in 356 B.C. by Herostratus. The fire seems to have destroyed only a part of the temple, and its reconstruction was at once begun, under the direction of Dinocrates.

This structure came to be regarded as one of the wonders of the world; its columns of great diameter, were over 60 feet high. This temple, sacred to Artemis (identified by the Romans with Diana), seems to have been plundered and perhaps burned by the Goths in 262 A.D. The temple was, however, restored, and lasted till the emperor Theodosius by an edict closed the pagan temples. Its stones were then used in the building of a great cathedral of St. John on a hill near by. Of these structures, some remains were found by the English archeologist J. T. Wood, who conducted excavations at Ephesus from 1863 to 1874, though not till December, 1869, was the true site determined. In 1904–05 D. G. Hogarth, under commission from the British Museum, re-examined the site. Beneath Wood's earliest temple he found remains of three earlier shrines and a rich array of offerings belonging to the earliest sanctuary; these offerings, which included many fine objects of Hellenic workmanship, among them the earliest-known coins of electrum, prove that there was a sanctuary on this site long before the time of Crœsus. Sculptures and fragments of the architecture of the various temples are now in the British Museum; so too is part of the treasure found by Hogarth.

In the temple were many fine works of art, e.g., statues of Amazons by Phidias, Polyclitus, Cresilas, and Phradmon, and a painting by Apelles which represented Alexander the Great as holding a thunderbolt.

DIANTHUS. See CARNATION; PINK.

DIAPHRAGM, the thin muscular partition which separates the thoracic (chest) cavity from the abdominal cavity. It occurs in all mammals, and is a major characteristic of this class, although some birds have a rudimentary diaphragm. In man, the diaphragm is attached to the lumbar vertebrae, the lower ribs, and the sternum (breastbone). Through three large openings in the diaphragm pass the esophagus and the major artery and vein supplying the lower portion of the body with blood.

The diaphragm is roughly elliptical in man, with its longest diameter from side to side. It slants upward, being higher in front than in the rear, and is dome-shaped, being convex above. Breathing is accomplished by contraction and expansion of the diaphragm. During inspiration the diaphragm contracts, becoming flattened and increasing the capacity of the thorax. Air rushes into the lungs to fill the partial vacuum thus formed. Air is exhaled when the diaphragm is relaxed and returns to its former position. When the diaphragm contracts, in addition to causing suction in the thorax it exerts pressure on the abdomen. It therefore plays an important part in defecation and childbirth, and a small part in peristalsis and other digestive functions and in the circulation of blood and other body fluids. A hiccup (q.v.) is caused by a spasmodic contraction of the diaphragm.

DIAS. See DIAZ.

DIAS or **DIAZ,** BARTHOLOMEU (1450?–1500), Portuguese navigator and discoverer of the Cape of Good Hope, Africa. Nothing is known of his early life. In 1481 he commanded a vessel in a flotilla sent by King John II of Portugal to the Gold Coast of Africa. Five years later, the king placed Dias in command of an expedition to continue the exploration of the western coast of Africa, begun in 1482 by the navigator Diogo or Cão, who had conducted it as far as 22° south of the equator. Dias set sail from Lisbon in 1487, and in February, 1488, rounded the southern extremity of the African continent as far as the estuary of what was later named the Great Fish River, from which, he observed, the coast fell away to the northeast. Dias thus opened a sea route from Europe to the Far East, which European merchants and statesmen held to be essential to the prosperity of Europe.

On his return voyage, Dias stopped at the tablelands at the southeastern extremity of Africa, which, historians believe, he named Cabo Tormentoso ("Cape of Storms"). King John later gave it the name of Cabo da Bôa Esperança, which has survived in its English form, Cape of Good Hope. Dias explored a total of about 1260 m. of previously unknown African coast. He returned to Lisbon in Dec., 1488. In 1500 he sailed in an expedition under the navigator Pedro Cabral and participated in the discovery of Brazil, but subsequently perished in a storm off the Cape of Good Hope.

DIASPORA (Gr., "a scattering"), a collective term applied originally to the Jews dispersed throughout Europe, Asia, and Africa after the Babylonian captivity (6th century B.C.). Diaspora later came to include the early Christians, and by extension all Christians living in isolation among peoples of other faiths. See JEWS.

DIASPORE, a hydrated aluminum oxide, intermediate in composition between bauxite and corundum. It has the formula AlO_2H, and has hardness 7 and sp. gr. 3.4. It is transparent to translucent, usually white or gray in color, but sometimes yellowish or brownish. It is frequently a decomposition product of corundum, and is sufficiently common to be classified as a minor ore of aluminum. It is found in the Ural Mts., in Hungary, in Sweden, and in Asia Minor. In the U.S. it occurs at Chester, Mass., and Franklin, Macon Co., N.C.

DIATOMACEOUS EARTH, or KIESELGUHR, a powdery natural material formed almost entirely from the skeletons of diatoms (q.v.), deposited in most cases during the Cenozoic era. It is usually extremely fine in texture and gray or white in color. Diatomaceous earth, when pure, is composed almost entirely of silicon dioxide or silica, but it is often found mixed with clay or organic matter. The material is extensively used as an abrasive, as a filtering material, as an inert ingredient of explosives, and as an insulating material for boilers and steam pipes. When diatomaceous earth is compacted into a chalky solid rock it is known as *diatomite* or *tripoli*. It was once believed that diatomaceous earth was formed from the fossils of infusoria, and the material is sometimes incorrectly called *infusorial earth*. Deposits of diatomaceous earth are found in many parts of the world. The thickest known deposit, about 3000 ft. in depth, is in California.

DIATOMS, popular name of a group or class of microscopic algae, the Bacillarieae, characterized by having a siliceous wall or shell. Diatoms are common in both fresh and salt water, and about 6000 species are known. In the ocean, diatoms form an important component of plankton (q.v.). Some species of

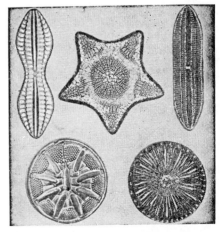

Various living diatoms (greatly enlarged)

diatoms are solitary while others form chalk-like or branching colonies. The cell walls of diatoms consist of two halves fitting together like a box and its lid. The walls assume a variety of forms in different species and are marked with regular patterns of lines. The shells also have rows of small holes through which the cell body or protoplast thrusts out the processes with which it swims.

Diatoms reproduce both sexually and asexually. The asexual form of reproduction is more common. In this method the cell body grows, opening the halves of the cell wall, and then divides, each half occupying one valve of the shell. Each of the daughter organisms then forms another valve to make the complete shell. Sexual reproduction of diatoms is accomplished by the fusion of two organisms or of gametes or germ cells formed by two separate organisms.

The fossil remains of diatoms are the chief ingredient of diatomaceous earth (q.v.).

DÍAZ, ARMANDO (1861–1928), Italian soldier, born in Naples. He fought in the war with Ethiopia (1895–96) and in the Italo-Turkish War (1911–12); in 1914 he was made a major general. During World War I, he was appointed a lieutenant general in 1916, and after the disastrous defeat sustained by the Italians in 1917 in the Battle of Caporetto (q.v.), Díaz replaced Luigi Cadorna as chief of the general staff. Under Díaz' command, the Italians, in the fall of 1918, won the campaign which, in November, led to the capitulation of Austria. Later, Díaz was appointed inspector general of the army and, in 1921, was created Duca della Vittoria ("Duke of Victory"). After Mussolini came to power in Italy in 1922, he appointed Díaz minister of war, and, in 1924, elevated Díaz to the newly created rank of marshal.

DÍAZ, BARTHOLOMEU. See DIAS, BARTHOLOMEU.

DÍAZ, PORFIRIO (1830–1915), in full JOSÉ DE LA CRUZ PORFIRIO DÍAZ, Mexican soldier and statesman, born in Oaxaca. He entered the army and served with distinction in three wars: the war with the United States (1846–48); the civil war (1857–60) between liberals and conservatives, known as the War of the Reform, in which he supported the liberal cause led by Benito Juárez (q.v.); and the patriotic war (1863–67) against the attempt of Emperor Napoleon III of France to make Mexico a French dependency. Díaz was the outstanding Mexican general in the last-named war.

He was an unsuccessful candidate for the presidency of Mexico in 1867 and 1871; after each defeat he led an unsuccessful military uprising, ostensibly to terminate the power and influence of foreign capitalists in Mexico, but in reality to further his personal ambition for power. He overthrew the government of President Sebastián Lerdo de Tejada in 1876 and was installed as president the following year. Because, under the Mexican constitution, he could not serve two consecutive terms, Díaz relinquished the presidency in 1880. He was re-elected in 1884, secured passage of an amendment to the constitution permitting a succession of presidential terms, and remained in power until 1911.

His regime was marked by notable achievements, but also by a brutal tyranny which has led many historians to characterize him as a dictator. Under Díaz, Mexico's finances were stabilized and the country experienced an unprecedented economic development. Foreign capital, especially American, was invested in the exploitation of the country's mineral resources; the mining, textile, and other industries were expanded; railroad and telegraph lines were constructed; and foreign trade increased about 300%.

On the other hand, foreign investors drained a great part of the country's wealth; large numbers of Indians were deprived of their ancient communal lands, called ejidos, and these lands were concentrated in the hands of a relatively small number of landowners, known as hacendados; and poverty and illiteracy were widespread. Manifestations of the resulting social discontent were suppressed by Díaz with an iron hand. Accumulated dissatisfaction, however, burst forth in the revolution of 1911, led, among others, by Francisco Madero (q.v.). Díaz was compelled to resign and leave the country. He died in exile in Paris. See MEXICO: *History*.

DÍAZ DE LA PEÑA, NARCISSE VIRGILE (1807?–76), French painter, born in Bordeaux. He was a member of the Barbizon school (q.v.). His vividly colored landscapes, peopled with nymphs, satyrs, and cupids, brought him fame and wealth. His works are to be found in the chief galleries of Europe and the United States. Among his best-known paintings are "Venus and Adonis", "Foolish Girls", "Descent of the Gypsies", "Sous Bois", and "Forest of Fontainebleau".

DÍAZ DEL CASTILLO, BERNAL (1492?–1581?), Spanish conquistador and historian, born in Medina del Campo. He went to the New World in 1514 and achieved distinction as a soldier under Hernando Cortes, fighting in more than 100 battles in 1517–19, during the conquest of Mexico. In 1523–24 he fought under Pedro de Alvarado, who conquered the territory now known as El Salvador and Guatemala. Later, Díaz was made governor of the Guatemalan town of Almolonga, subsequently renamed Santiago de los Caballeros. His history of the conquest of Mexico, finished in 1568 and published in 1632, in 3 vols., under the title *Historia Verdadera de la Conquista de la Nueva España,* is distinguished for its objectivity.

DIAZ MIRON, SALVADOR (1853–1928), Mexican poet, orator, and journalist, born at Vera Cruz. He was a deputy to the Mexican Congress and was nationally renowned as an orator. He was considered the national poet of Mexico. His works include *A Lord Byron, El Czar de Todas las Rusias, ¿Qué es Poesía?,* and *Lo Eterno.*

DIAZO COMPOUNDS, organic chemical compounds which contain a group of two nitrogen atoms attached to each other; see Azo. The name is most commonly applied to three closely related groups of compounds, only one of which is technically called diazo, the other two being called azo and diazonium, respectively. In each of these three groups, the two nitrogen atoms are attached to each other by a double or triple bond, and at least one of the nitrogen atoms is attached to an aromatic nucleus (see AROMATIC COMPOUNDS). All three of these groups were discovered about 1860 by the English chemist Peter Griess.

All of these groups of compounds are derived from primary aromatic amines by treatment with nitrous acid, the reaction being called *diazotization.*

Diazonium compounds, when pure and dry, are usually unstable, and have even been used as explosives. They decompose rapidly on exposure to light, and have been used in photographic processes similar to blueprinting. In the absence of strong light they are stable in solution if kept at a temperature near the freezing point of water. They readily undergo a wide variety of reactions, and are therefore of great importance in organic syntheses. Their most important reaction is *coupling.* When a solution of a diazonium compound is mixed with a solution of almost any aromatic amine or phenol, the two molecules couple together, forming a large molecule in which the two aromatic nuclei are linked by a diazo group, $-N{=}N-$. The new compound thus formed is called an azo compound or azo dye. It is remarkably stable and is invariably colored. See DYE.

DIBRANCHIATA. See CEPHALOPODA.

DIBSTONE. See JACKSTONE.

DICAEIDAE, a family of Oriental and Australasian oscine birds, resembling the sunbirds (q.v.), to which they are closely related. They are sometimes called honeypeckers or flowerpeckers. All are small, brilliantly colored, insect-eating birds, with melodious voices. Most of them build nests of soft materials suspended from bushes. The swallow dicaeum, *Dicaeum herundinaceum,* is colored red or purple. A replated species, *D. erythrorrynchus,* is the smallest bird of the Old World, a fully grown adult averaging only $\frac{1}{4}$ ounce in weight.

The diamond birds, of the genera *Pardalotus* and *Nesopardalotus,* are usually included in this family, although they may be more closely related to the honey eaters (q.v.). The commonest species is *P. affinis,* a small insectivorous bird with beautiful plumage. Its general color is ashy gray and white, spotted with red, yellow, orange, and black. It is a migratory bird, and frequents the gum forests of southern Australia during the summer.

DICARBOXYLIC ACIDS, organic acids containing two acid or carboxyl ($-$COOH) groups. They can be conveniently divided into the aliphatic and aromatic acids. Aliphatic dicarboxylic acids are open-chained hydrocarbon derivatives. Except for oxalic acid, the simplest member of the series, the carboxyl groups are separated by a chain of carbon atoms. In oxalic acid, two carboxyl groups are joined to each other by their carbon atoms. In malonic acid, the carboxyl groups are separated by one methylene radical ($-CH_2-$), and in succinic acid by two methylene radicals. The acids become weaker as the carbon chain separating the carboxyl group becomes longer. Thus, oxalic acid is the strongest of the series.

These aliphatic acids are well distributed in the plant and animal world. Oxalic acid is found in sorrel and rhubarb; and is used in dyeing, in removing ink and iron stains from clothing, and in the manufacture of ink. Malonic acid, which is found in beet roots, is used in the synthesis of veronal, a barbiturate. Succinic acid is used in medicine, and in the dye and perfume industries. Adipic acid is used in the manufacture of nylon.

Aromatic dicarboxylic acids are closed-chain or cyclic hydrocarbons containing two substituted carboxyl groups. The most important of these are the three benzenedicarboxylic acids known as the phthalic acids. Derivatives of *o*-phthalic acid are used in the production of lacquers and synthetic resins.

Aliphatic Dicarboxylic Acids

Name	Formula	Melting Point °C
Oxalic acid	$(COOH)_2$	186–7 dec.
Malonic acid	$CH_2(COOH)_2$	130–5 dec.
Succinic acid	$(CH_2)_2(COOH)_2$	189–90
Glutaric acid	$(CH_2)_3(COOH)_2$	97.5
Adipic acid	$(CH_2)_4(COOH)_2$	151–3
Sebacic acid	$(CH_2)_8(COOH)_2$	134.5

DICE, small cubes, usually made of bone or plastic, with variously marked faces, used as implements in a number of games of chance. The commonest form of marking for dice is to number the faces with dots from one to six. The six faces of poker dice are marked like cards with the ace, king, queen, jack, ten, and nine. Dice have been used from remote antiquity and probably originated in Asia. Dice marked with dots have been recovered from Egyptian tombs, and Greek and Roman literature contains many references to dice playing.

In play, dice are thrown from the hand or from a dice cup, and the total number of dots showing on the top of the dice at rest determines the value of the throw. The commonest dice game in the U.S. is craps, a form of the old English game of hazard. It is played with two dice. In craps the thrower makes a money bet, covered by one or more of his opponents. If he throws 7 or 11 on the first throw he wins, but if he throws 2, 3, or 12 he loses. In any of these cases he bets and throws again. If he throws 4, 5, 6, 8, 9, or 10, that number becomes his point, and he continues to throw until he either makes the same point again or throws a 7. If he makes his point he wins, but if he throws a 7 he loses both his bet and the right to throw again. The aim of the game of poker dice, which is played with five dice, is to build up a winning poker hand in three or fewer throws; see POKER. A number of varieties of the game of poker dice are also played, including liar dice. In this game the player does not show his throw to his opponents but announces either its true value, or another value, in an attempt to *bluff* as in poker, before the throws are disclosed. Dice are also used as an adjunct in the play of other games such as backgammon (q.v.) and parchesi.

DICENTRA, formerly incorrectly known as *Dielytra,* a genus of North American and Asiatic herbs of the family Fumariaceae. They are hardy perennial plants with attractive yellow, white, or rose-colored blossoms. Their deeply incised leaves are fernlike. *D. specta-*

bilis, the popular bleeding heart, bears bright-pink, heart-shaped blossoms in drooping clusters. *D. chrysantha,* known as golden eardrops, bears panicles of erect, golden flowers. Other species commonly grown in gardens are *D. cucullaria* (Dutchman's-breeches), *D. canadensis* (squirrel corn), and *D. eximia* (the wild bleeding heart).

DICE SNAKE, a harmless water snake, *Natrix tessellatus,* belonging to the subfamily Colubrinae. It is native to Switzerland, the valleys of the Rhine and Moselle Rivers, Italy, S.E. Europe, N. Africa, and W. Asia. The snake is named for the pattern of its markings, which consist of small, square, dark spots arranged in checkerboard fashion on a yellow, gray, or greenish body. It is a small snake, one to two feet long.

DICHROITE. See IOLITE.

DICHROMATISM, in zoology, the possession, by different individuals of the same species, of two entirely different colors or color combinations. Dichromatism is particularly frequent in birds. This kind of difference in color is due neither to the age or sex of the bird, nor to the geographical locality in which it occurs, and thus far no satisfactory explanation has been advanced.

A common example of dichromatism occurs in the screech owl, *Otus asio,* some of which are predominantly red-brown, while others are gray. The dichromatism in the screech owl is of the form called erythrism, in which one of the phases (color varieties) is reddish. Other forms are albinism (see ALBINO), in which one phase is white, and melanism (q.v.) in which one phase is black.

It was believed at one time that the little blue heron, *Florida caerulea,* exhibited albinism, but the white phase of that bird is now regarded as its immature stage. True albinism occurs in the reddish egret, *Dichromanassa rufescens.* An example of melanism is found in the American rough-legged hawk, *Buteo lagopus sancti-johannis,* in which one phase is grayish-brown and white, and the other is all black.

DICK, GEORGE FREDERICK (1881–   ), American physician and bacteriologist, born in Fort Wayne, Indiana, and educated at Rush Medical College. With his wife, Gladys Henry Dick (1881–   ), he isolated the germ of scarlet fever, and produced a serum to combat the disease. They also devised a test for determining susceptibility to scarlet fever (Dick test). In 1933, after teaching medicine at Rush Medical College, he became professor and chairman of the department of medicine at the University of Chicago medical school.

DICKCISSEL, a black-throated bunting, *Spiza americana,* inhabiting the central regions of the U.S. It is a loud and persistent singer, about 6 inches in length. The color of the back of the male is black, chestnut, and grayish. It has a white chin, a conspicuous black throat, and a yellow breast, changing to white toward the tail. The female lacks the chestnut colors and black throat patch. The dickcissel winters in Central America and the northern part of South America. It builds its nest on the ground or in a low bush.

DICKENS, CHARLES (JOHN HUFFAM) (1812–70), English novelist, born at Portsmouth. He was brought up in poverty; at the age of eleven he was obliged to support himself by working in a dye warehouse, while his father spent more than a year in debtors' jail. However, an unexpected legacy restored the elder Dickens to liberty, and for a brief period (about 1824–26) the boy attended school. He then entered, a solicitor's office as a clerk, and worked there for about two years while learning shorthand with the intention of becoming a newspaper reporter. At twenty, he began covering debates in the House of Commons for *The True Sun,* and for the next sixteen years continued his newspaper career on *The Mirror of Parliament* and *The Morning Chronicle.* During this period he also contributed sketches to several periodicals, his first piece, *A Dinner at Poplar Walk,* appearing in *The Old Monthly Magazine,* December, 1833. In August, 1834, he began to sign these sketches with the pen name *Boz,* and for the next two years continued to contribute them to *The Old Monthly Magazine* as well as to *The Morning Chronicle.* The success of these sketches attracted the attention of the publishers Chapman and Hall, who employed Dickens to write the literary commentary for a series of humorous drawings by the then popular artist Robert Seymour. Dickens' role in this collaboration was intended to be secondary, but it resulted in the *Posthumous Papers of the Pickwick Club* (1837) and won international fame for its author. Thereafter, Dickens maintained his popularity at a prodigious rate of literary productivity. In addition to writing, he lectured in America (1842) on the international copyright and against slavery, managed a touring theatrical company (1847–52), edited the weekly magazines *Household Words* (1849) and *All the Year Round* (1859), and gave public readings of his works (beginning in 1858 and including a tour of America, 1867–68).

Charles Dickens

Dickens' writings have been variously estimated. His humor, his perception of human frailty, and his instinct for the drama inherent in human relations are universally admitted. But to some his humor verges on the burlesque, his pathos is exaggerated, and his style is careless and loose. His creative power was prodigious, encompassing thousands of characters, and as many situations. The essence of his art was caricature based, however, on a profound sense of social justice, so that the more satirical was his writing, the more clearly it delineated the necessity for reform. His chief writings are *Sketches by Boz* (1836), *Oliver Twist* (1837–39), *Nicholas Nickleby* (1838–39), *Old Curiosity Shop* (1840–41), *Barnaby Rudge* (1841), *Martin Chuzzlewit* (1843–44), *A Christmas Carol* (1843), *The Chimes* (1844), *Dombey and Son* (1846–48), *David Copperfield* (1849–50), *Bleak House* (1852–53), *Hard Times* (1854), *Little Dorrit* (1855–57), *A Tale of Two Cities* (1859), *Great Expectations* (1860–61), *Our Mutual Friend* (1864–65), and *Mystery of Edwin Drood* (incomplete, 1870).

DICKINSON, EMILY (ELIZABETH) (1830–86), American poet, born at Amherst, Mass., and educated at Amherst Academy and (briefly) at Mount Holyoke Female Seminary. At the age of 23, she suffered a romantic disappointment, whereupon she retired to her family home at Amherst and lived there, almost a recluse, and nearly unknown during her lifetime. She wrote a large number of poems, simple in form, but conveying a penetrating mystical insight. Only two of her poems were .

printed during her lifetime, both of them without her permission. In 1890, her lifelong friend, Thomas Wentworth Higginson (q.v.) edited *Poems*, the first selection of her poems to be published. It enjoyed great popular and critical success. Her other works were published in the volumes *Poems: Second Series* (1891), *Poems: Third Series* (1896), *The Single Hound* (1914), *Further Poems* (1929), and *Unpublished Poems* (1936).

DICKINSON, G(OLDSWORTHY) LOWES (1862–1932), English writer. He was educated at Charterhouse and King's College, Cambridge, where he became fellow and lecturer. Later, he lectured at the London School of Economics and Political Science. The pacifist temper of his writing on current events made him a controversial figure during and after World War I. His works include *The Greek View of Life, Letters from a Chinese Official* (1903), *An Essay on the Civilization of India, China and Japan* (1914), *The European Anarchy* (1916), *The Choice Before Us* (1917), *The Magic Flute* (1920), *War: Its Nature Cause, and Cure* (1923), *The International Anarchy, 1904–14* (1926), and *Goethe and Faust* (1928).

DICKINSON, JOHN (1732–1808), American statesman, born in Talbot County, Md. He was admitted to the bar in 1757 and practiced law in Philadelphia. As a member of the Continental Congress (1774–76) he favored appeasing England, opposed any violent uprising, and voted against the Declaration of Independence. After the Revolutionary War, he represented Delaware at the convention which framed the Constitution (1787), and in a series of letters signed "Fabius" effectively urged the adoption of that instrument of government. It was chiefly due to his influence that Delaware and Pennsylvania were the first two States to ratify the Constitution. He helped establish Dickinson College (named in his honor) at Carlisle, Pa., in 1783, and served as the first president of its board of trustees. He was a prolific political writer and pamphleteer. His works include *Letters from a Farmer in Pennsylvania* (1767); *The Late Regulations Respecting the American Colonies, Essay on the Constitutional Power of Great Britain over the American Colonies* (1774); and the first draft of the *Articles of Confederation and Perpetual Union* (1776).

DICKSON, CARR or CARTER. See CARR, JOHN DICKSON.

DICOTYLEDONS, popular name for plants belonging to the subclass Dicotyledones of the Angiospermae class of the phylum Spermatophyta; see BOTANY. Dicotyledons differ from monocotyledons in having two embryo leaves in their seeds rather than one. The class contains over 100,000 species, both annuals and perennials, ranging from plants less than an inch tall to towering forest trees. Most plants of economic importance, as well as those used for decorative purposes, are dicotyledons, with the exception of grasses, palms, and conifers.

DICTATOR, the title of a magistrate in ancient Rome, appointed in times of emergency by the Senate, and ratified by the *comitia curiata*. The first such appointment, according to Roman historians, was made in 501 B.C.; the last responsible dictator was appointed during the Second Punic War, in 216 B.C. The dictator held office usually for six months, and during his term was the chief magistrate of the state, with power of life and death. The civil jurisdiction was retained by the regular magistrates, who were subordinate to him, and his military jurisdiction was limited to Italian territory. According to Cicero, the office was originally created to cope with civil disturbances. In the last years of the Republic, Roman politicians occasionally assumed the office of dictator with extralegal powers; notable among these were Lucius Cornelius Sulla, whose dictatorship lasted from 82 to 79 B.C., and Gaius Julius Cæsar, who became dictator for life in 45 B.C. In modern times men who have assumed power over the state have been called dictators; notable among these have been Porfirio Díaz of Mexico, Miguel Primo de Rivera and Francisco Franco of Spain, Kemal Atatürk of Turkey, Józef Pilsudski of Poland, Antonio de Oliveira Salazar of Portugal, Benito Mussolini of Italy, Adolf Hitler of Germany, and Joseph Stalin of the Soviet Union. See FASCISM; TOTALITARIANISM.

DICTIONARY, an alphabetical compilation of the words of a language, or part of a language, giving their meanings, spellings, derivation, pronunciation, and syllabication; in a more general sense, the term "dictionary" is also applied to any alphabetically arranged compendium in which special terms or subjects are defined. Thus in recent times there have been dictionaries devoted to science, biography, geography, mathematics, history, philosophy, slang, and other topics and terminology. The earliest-known dictionaries were found in the library of the Assyrian king Ashurbanipal (reigned 669–626 B.C.) at Nineveh. These consisted of clay tablets inscribed in columns of cuneiform, and remain the chief key of knowledge of Mesopotamian culture.

Sanskrit dictionaries appeared as early as the 5th century B.C. and were for the most part collections of rare words and meanings. These dictionaries, most of them written after the 5th century A.D., are invariably in verse and are divisible into two general classes, lexicons of synonyms and of homonyms. Sanskrit works also include special dictionaries on botany, medicine, and astronomy, as well as Buddhistic glossaries in Pali, and polyglot lexicons in Sanskrit, Tibetan, Mongolian, and Chinese. The first attempt to gather the entire Arabic vocabulary into one work was made probably by Khalil ibn Ahmed of Oman (died 791), who adopted an arrangement not alphabetical but based on certain phonetic and physiological principles. The compilation of Hebrew dictionaries began about the 10th century (although some scholars place the beginnings of Hebrew lexicography between the 6th and 8th centuries), originating from, and being stimulated by, the study of Arabic.

Dictionaries of language, however, as they exist in contemporary times, are relatively modern in origin. They are an outgrowth of the importance of Greek and Latin literature to the scholars of the Middle Ages, and may be traced to the medieval custom of inserting marginal glosses or explanatory words in texts of classical authors. The Greeks and Romans did not conceive of a work containing all the words of their own or a foreign language, and their early dictionaries were merely glossaries of unusual words or phrases. According to the Greek lexicographer Suidas, the first Greek lexicon, *Homeric Words,* was written by Apollonius, a Sophist of the days of Augustus. This is the most ancient dictionary extant, and was last published in Berlin in 1883. One of the earliest works in Latin lexicography, by Verrius Flaccus (fl. 1st century A.D.), is *De Verborum Significatu,* which survives as part of the compilation of Pompeius Festus entitled *De Significatione Verborum;* this work, in which the words are arranged alphabetically, has been of great service in giving information on antiquities and grammar. The earliest polyglot dictionary was the work of an Augustine monk, Calepino, dated 1502. At first it was a Latin-Greek lexicon, then came to be extended to include Italian, French, and Spanish, and finally in the 1590 Basel edition included eleven languages.

The first English dictionary is *Promptorium Parvulorum,* compiled in 1440 by the Dominican monk Galfridus Grammaticus in Norfolk, England, and printed in 1499; this work contained English words defined in Latin. It was followed by Sir Thomas Elyot's *Bibliotheca* (1538), another English-Latin dictionary, and by the *Dictionary in Englyshe and Welshe* (1547) compiled by William Salesbury (about 1520–1600). Robert Cawdrey (fl. 1604), in *The Table Alphabetical of Hard Words* (1604), produced the first dictionary giving definitions in English of English words, and in 1656 Thomas Blount (1618–79) issued his *Glossographia,* also entirely in English with ". . . hard words together with Divinity Terms, Law, Physick, Mathematicks and other Arts and Sciences explicated". These early works characteristically confined themselves to "hard words" and phrases not generally understood, because the daily vocabulary of the language was not expected to require elucidation. The first attempt at a comprehensive inventory of the English language, the *Dictionarium Brittannicum: A More Compleat Universal Etymological Dictionary Than any Extant* (1730), was the work of Nathan Bailey (d. 1742). This work served Samuel Johnson as the basis for his famous two-volume lexicon, *A Dictionary of the English Language* (1755). Dr. Johnson's dictionary, which introduced the practice of employing quotations from established literary works to confirm and supplement definitions, remained the model of English lexicography for over a century. In 1780 Thomas Sheridan, an actor and the grandfather of the playwright Richard Brinsley Sheridan, compiled a *General Dictionary of the English Language* with the object of establishing a simple and permanent standard of pronunciation, a consideration neglected in previous works.

The first historically important contribution to American lexicography was the volume *A New and Accurate Standard of Pronunciation* (1783), popularly known as *Webster's Spelling Book.* This work was issued by Noah Webster (q.v.) as the first part of his *Grammatical Institute of the English Language* (1783–85). Although not a dictionary in the strict sense of the term, the *Spelling Book,* because of its American origin and emphasis and its simplification of English, became a household reference wordbook throughout the country. Its success led Webster to compile his first American lexicon, *A Compendious Dictionary of the English Language* (1806), which also contained supplementary encyclopedic material on American life. Webster's major contribution to lexicography, *An American Dictionary of the English Language,* begun in 1807 and published in 1828, included typically American usage as distinguished from the British idiom, as well as 12,000 more words and 40,000 more definitions than had ever appeared in any dictionary of the English language. Webster brought out a revised edition of this work in 1841, shortly before his death; the *American Dictionary* has since undergone various revisions and editions, including the contemporary *Webster's New International Dictionary of the English Language,* for which it provided the basis. In 1860 Joseph Emerson Worcester (q.v.) published *A Dictionary of the English Language* with the intention of displacing Webster's *American Dictionary,* which he considered frequently vulgar in vocabulary and pronunciation, but his work enjoyed little success. In 1891 *The Century Dictionary,* an American dictionary containing encyclopedic information, was first published in six volumes; it was a notable example in English of the French tradition of the combined dictionary-encyclopedia, established by Pierre Larousse (q.v.) in his *Grand Dictionnaire Universel du XIX Siècle* (1866–76). The *Standard Dictionary of the English Language,* published in one volume in 1895, rivaled Webster's *American Dictionary* in popularity for a time. Both the *Century* and the *Standard* have been frequently revised, editions of the former appearing in a two-volume abridgment called *New Century Dictionary* and the latter as the Funk and Wagnalls *New Standard Dictionary of the English Language.*

The most comprehensive lexicographic work in the English language, popularly known as the *Oxford English Dictionary,* was begun under the auspices of the *English Philological Society* in 1857 and completed in seventy years with the collaboration of numerous specialists and their assistants after the editorship of the work had been undertaken by Sir James A. H. Murray in 1879. The dictionary, entitled *A New English Dictionary on Historical Principles; founded mainly on the materials collected by the Philological Society,* issued its first section in 1884; the tenth and closing volume was brought out in 1928, and a supplement, containing an introduction and bibliography, was added in 1933. The *Shorter Oxford Dictionary,* a two-volume abridgment of this work with some revisions in pronunciation, was published in 1933. In 1936 Sir William A. Craigie, who collaborated on the editing of the *Oxford English Dictionary,* began a companion work, *A Dictionary of American Eng-*lish *on Historical Principles,* which was completed with the publication of its fourth volume in 1944.

A by-product of these scholarly works should be mentioned to complete this survey, namely the one-volume dictionary which is frequently an anonymous abridgment of the larger works and ranges from pocket-size to about 1500 pages. Dictionaries of this sort, although they reflect many of the disadvantages of condensation, are handier and less expensive; they have in recent years, and particularly in America, enjoyed a popularity of sale equaled only by the Bible.

DICTYOTALES, an order of marine algae that reproduce both sexually, by sperms and eggs, and asexually, by nonmotile tetraspores. They have a brown pigment characteristic of the brown algae, tetraspores characteristic of the red algae, and sperms peculiar to themselves. They are usually regarded as an aberrant group of red algae.

DICUMAROL, an anticlotting chemical which causes a hemorrhagic disease in cattle. The chemical was discovered in improperly cured sweet clover (see MELILOT) in 1939 by the American biochemist Karl Paul Link, at the University of Wisconsin. It is a derivative of coumarin, which gives sweet clover its characteristic odor. Dicumarol is now being successfully used to combat clotting of blood, particularly to prevent postoperative embolus and coronary thrombosis (see THROMBOSIS). It has a more persistent effect than does heparin.

DIDACHE, or TEACHING OF THE TWELVE APOSTLES, ancient Christian document written in Greek and dealing with the organization, belief, and worship in the early Church. It probably originated in Egypt or Syria between 120 and 150 A.D. It was found in 1873 by Bryennios, Archbishop of Nicomedia, in an 11th-century manuscript in the Monastery of the Holy Sepulchre in Istanbul.

The *Didache* is composed of two parts. The first contains a description of the Two Ways, one of life, the other of death, in the form of rules for Christian conduct. This first part was used in catechetical instruction to prepare converts for baptism. The second portion deals with the rites of baptism and the Lord's Supper, and defines the office and duties of the Christian leaders. It forms the basis of the seventh book of the *Apostolic Constitutions* (q.v.).

DIDELPHIA. See MAMMALS; MARSUPIALS.

DIDELPHIS. See OPOSSUM.

DIDEROT, DENIS (1713–84), French encyclopedist, philosopher, and dramatist, born at Langres, and educated in Jesuit schools. He went to Paris in 1734, and spent ten years as an ill-paid tutor and hack writer. His reputation, which grew throughout the period of The Enlightenment (q.v.), began with the publication in 1746 of his *Pensées Philosophiques*. In the same year he was invited to edit a French translation of the English *Cyclopedia* of Ephraim Chambers. Diderot secured the collaboration of the mathematician Jean Le Rond d'Alembert (q.v.), and converted the project into a vast, new, and controversial work. Aided by the most celebrated French writers of the day, including Voltaire and Montesquieu (qq.v.), Diderot used the *Encyclopédie* as a massive propaganda weapon against ecclesiastical authority and the semifeudal intellectual and social forms of French society. All the editors and contributors of the *Encyclopédie*, Diderot especially, became the object of clerical and royalist antagonism. The Parliament of Paris ordered his *Pensées* burned in 1746. Three years later, he was briefly imprisoned when publication of another work, his *Lettre sur les Aveugles*, angered the clerical party. Such opposition delayed publication of the *Encyclopédie*. Twice, in 1752 and in 1757, Diderot's opponents succeeded in revoking the royal decree granting permission for the work to proceed. In 1759, the *Conseil du Roi* formally suppressed the first ten volumes of the *Encyclopédie* published from 1751 onward and forbade further publication. Nevertheless, Diderot continued preparation of the remaining ten volumes and had them secretly printed. The work finally appeared in 1765, and miscellaneous supplements continued to be published until 1780. Its full title was *Encyclopédie ou Dictionnaire Raisonné des Sciences, des Arts et des Métiers* (34 vols. incl. supps., 1751–80). Diderot's old age was free of worry and persecution. When in need of money for his daughter's dowry, he was aided by Catherine II of Russia, who bought his library, but allowed him to keep the books and paid him to look after them.

His voluminous writings include the stories *Jacques le Fataliste* (1796) and *La Religieuse*, the latter an attack on conventual life. He wrote two plays, *Le Fils Naturel* (1757) and *Le Père de Famille* (1758), but they were never performed. He was a pioneer in aesthetic criticism; he founded *Les Salons*, a journal for which from 1759 to 1779 he wrote criticisms of the annual exhibitions of paintings in Paris. His correspondence was excelled by few in an age of famous letter writers, and he is the author of numerous essays. Among his philosophical works are *La Promenade du Sceptique* (1747) and *Lettres sur les Sourds et Muets*.

DIDO, legendary founder and queen of the city of Carthage, in North Africa. She was also known by the Greek name of Elissa, and was worshiped by the Carthaginians as Tanit. She was said to have been a Tyrian princess who fled from her homeland after her husband was killed by her brother, Pygmalion. Arriving in Africa, she purchased the site of Carthage from a native chief, Iarbas. When Iarbas attempted to force her to marry him, Dido killed herself. The Roman poet Vergil introduced Dido into the story in the *Æneid*. According to Vergil, Æneas stopped in Africa on his journey from Troy and won the love of the Carthaginian queen. Intent on continuing his journey, he left Carthage, whereupon Dido killed herself in grief.

DIDYMIUM, a rare metal, discovered in the mineral cerite by the Swedish chemist Carl Gustav Mosander (1797–1858) in 1842. Although it was originally believed to be an element, subsequent investigation has showed it to be a mixture of the elements neodymium and praseodymium (qq.v.).

DIE, any of several types of tools used for the shaping of materials, especially those employed in the pressworking of cold metals.

In presswork, dies are used in pairs. The smaller die, or *punch,* fits inside the larger die, called the *matrix* or simply the *die.* The metal to be formed, usually a sheet or precut *blank,* is placed over the matrix, which is mounted on the bed of the press. The punch is mounted on the ram of the press and is forced down by hydraulic or mechanical pressure. A number of different forms of dies are employed for different operations. The simplest are *piercing dies,* used for punching holes in the blank. *Blanking dies* are employed to stamp out special shapes of metal sheet for later operations. *Bending* and *folding dies* are designed to make single or compound bends in the blank. Hollow cupped shapes are formed by *drawing dies;* if the hollow is deep, *redrawing dies* are often employed in a second operation after the hollow shape has been partially formed. To produce a reduced section on a hollow part, such as the neck of a rifle cartridge, special *reducing dies* are used. When the finished part must have a bulge at the bottom or in the middle, *hy-*

Simplex Tool & Die Corp.

Pair of dies for casting six parts of a toy knight in armor (shown at bottom, between the dies).
In operation molten metal is forced into the closed dies under pressure.

draulic dies are usually employed, in which the punch is replaced by a ram which forces oil or water into the part under pressure to force the metal outward against the matrix. *Curling dies* form a curved edge or flange on a hollow part, and a special form of curling die called a *wiring die* is used to form a wired edge in which the outside edges of the metal are tightly wound around a wire inserted for strength.

In manufacturing, it is common practice to combine several dies in one *combination die* or *progressive die*. A combination die is designed to perform more than one of the above operations at one stroke of the press; a progressive die permits successive forming operations with the same die.

In *coining*, metal is forced to flow into two matching dies, each of which bears a reverse or intaglio of the relief pattern to be formed on the finished coin or part.

Wire-Drawing Dies. In the manufacture of wire, a drawplate is usually employed. This tool is a metal plate containing a number of tapered or bellshaped openings, successively finer in diameter. The openings are known as wire dies. In use, a piece of metal is pulled through the largest die to make a coarse wire. This wire is then drawn through the next smaller opening, and then through the next, until the wire is reduced to the desired measurement. Wire-drawing dies are subject to extreme wear, and are commonly made from

very hard materials, such as tungsten carbide or diamonds. See Wire.

Thread-Cutting Dies. For cutting threads on bolts or on the outside of pipe, a special form of die is used. A thread-cutting die is usually made of hardened steel in the form of a round plate with a hole in the center. The hole is threaded in the appropriate form and pitch, and the threads are cut away for part of their circumference, leaving longitudinal grooves in the die. These grooves give clearance for the chips of metal which are formed when a thread is being cut. To cut a thread, the die is simply screwed onto an unthreaded bolt or piece of pipe in the same way in which a nut is screwed onto a bolt. The corresponding tool for cutting a female thread, as inside a nut, is called a tap. See Die Casting; Forging.

DIE CASTING, a method of producing castings of nonferrous metals in which the molten metal is forced into a steel mold or die under pressure. The advantage of die casting over the older method of casting with sand molds (see Founding) is that castings can be produced quickly and economically on automatic machines. By the use of multiple dies a number of similar parts can be cast in one operation. Die castings can be produced with finer finish and detail than ordinary sand castings and hence are often used for precision parts. Because of the high temperatures required for melting iron and steel, ferrous metals are not suitable for the die casting process, as they would soften or melt the mold.

DIELECTRIC, a substance which is a non-conductor of electricity and which will sustain the force of an electric field passing through it. No conducting substances exhibit this property. Two oppositely charged bodies placed on either side of a piece of glass (a dielectric) will attract each other, but if a sheet of copper is interposed between the two bodies, there will be no attraction.

In most instances the properties of a dielectric are due to the polarization of the substance. When the dielectric is placed in an electrical field, the electrons and protons of its constituent atoms reorient themselves, and in some cases molecules become similarly polarized. As a result of this polarization, the dielectric is under stress, and energy is stored in it which becomes available when the electric field is removed. The polarization of a dielectric resembles the polarization which takes place when a piece of iron is magnetized, and, as in the case of a magnet, a certain amount of it remains when the polarizing force is removed. A dielectric composed of a wax disk which has hardened while under electric stress will retain its polarization for years. Such semipermanently polarized dielectrics are known as *electrets*.

The effectiveness of dielectrics is measured by their relative ability to store energy compared to a vacuum, and is expressed in terms of a *dielectric constant,* with the value for a vacuum taken as unity. The values of this constant for usable dielectrics varies from slightly more than one for air up to a hundred or more for certain ceramics containing titanium oxide. Glass, mica, porcelain, and mineral oils, often used as dielectrics, have dielectric constants ranging from about two to nine. The ability of a dielectric to withstand electrical fields without losing its insulating properties is known as its *dielectric strength*. A good dielectric must return a large percentage of the energy stored in it when the field is reversed. The fraction lost through electrical "friction" is called the *power factor* of the dielectric. Dielectrics, particularly those with high dielectric constants, find extensive use in all branches of electrical engineering, where they are used to increase the electrical capacity of condensers. See ELECTRICITY.

DIELS, OTTO (1876–1954), German chemist, born in Hamburg, and educated at the Royal Joachimsthalsches Gymnasium and at the University of Berlin. He joined the staff of the Chemical Institute of the University of Berlin in 1899, rose to the rank of titular professor in 1906, and became extraordinary professor in 1915. He was professor of chemistry and director of the Chemical Institute at the University of Kiel from 1916 to 1945, when he became professor emeritus. In 1950 Diels and the German chemist Kurt Alder, a former pupil, were awarded the Nobel Prize in chemistry for their joint development of diene synthesis, the chemical process by which complex organic compounds are synthesized. Diene synthesis, known also as the Diels-Alder reaction, has important applications in present-day technology, especially in the manufacture of plastics. Among Diel's writings are *Einfuhrung in die organische Chemie* (1907) and numerous scientific papers on organic chemistry.

DIEPPE, a commune and seaport of the department of Seine-Inférieure, France, on the English Channel, about 33 miles N. of Rouen. Dieppe lies on the w. shore of the mouth of the Arques R., at the foot of the steep slopes of a range of chalk hills. The harbor consists of an outer harbor, protected by jetties, and an inner harbor equipped with several tidal basins which are accessible at flood tide to vessels drawing up to 20 feet of water. Regular steamboat service is maintained with Newhaven, in Sussex, England. Dieppe also has railway connections with the interior of France. Leading imports are iron, coal, cement, timber, textiles, and machinery. The exports consist chiefly of wines, brandies, potatoes, fruits, and local manufactures. Among the principal manufactures are rope, lace, porcelain, tobacco products, lumber, briquettes, and horn, bone, and ivory products. In addition, Dieppe has shipyards, sugar refineries, oil refineries, distilleries, and fisheries. The last-named industry is centered in Le Pollet, a small suburb on the opposite side of the Arques. The commune is one of the most popular summer resorts in France. Among outstanding points of interest are a beach promenade, the 13th-century church of St. Jacques, a castle dating from 1435, and the 16th-century church of Notre-Dame de Bon Secours.

Dieppe has figured prominently in the maritime history of France since the 12th century. It was sacked in 1339 by the English. The English occupied it from 1420 to 1435, and laid unsuccessful siege to it in 1442. During the 16th century, Dieppe was a prosperous commercial center, frequented by merchants and pirates, and a center of the Reformation. Severe reprisals against the town were exacted

British Information Services

The British royal arms, showing the motto, "Dieu et mon droit"

by the Catholics, following the revocation in 1685 of the Edict of Nantes. In 1694, Dieppe was virtually destroyed by the English and Dutch. Many of its inhabitants emigrated to Canada in the 17th and 18th centuries. The Germans occupied the town during the Franco-Prussian War and again, in June, 1940, during World War II. On August 19, 1942, the port, transformed by the Germans into one of the most strongly fortified points on the English Channel, was raided by an Allied force of commandos. Executed by about 5000 Canadians, 2000 British, and small detachments of American Rangers and Fighting French, the raid was an experimental venture, launched for the purpose of obtaining data for the subsequent invasion of Europe. The raiders penetrated a number of German defenses, inflicting considerable damage. Casualties were severe, however, especially among the Canadians. The German occupation force was expelled from Dieppe in September, 1944. Pop. (1946) 20,877.

DIERESIS. See DIACRITICAL MARK.

DIESEL, RUDOLF (1858–1913), German inventor, born in Paris. After studying in England, he attended the Polytechnic school in Munich, where he settled in 1893. In 1892 he patented an internal-combustion engine employing autoignition of fuel. Additional research led him to the construction of the first

successful Diesel engine, an engine utilizing low-cost fuel, which he built while associated with the Krupp firm in Essen. In 1913, while on a trip to England, he was drowned in the English Channel. He wrote *Theorie und Konstruktion eines Rationellen Wärmemotors* (1893), and *Die Entstehung des Dieselmotors* (1913). See INTERNAL COMBUSTION ENGINES.

DIES NON JURIDICUS, often simply DIES NON, in law, a day on which the administration of justice cannot lawfully be carried on; the courts are closed and no legal process may be issued or served. A legal holiday may or may not be a nonjuridical day. In the United States, Sunday and Christmas Day generally, and a small number of other legal holidays in various States are nonjuridical days; most legal holidays are juridical days. In the interest of public policy and the prevention of irremediable wrong, provision has been made in the law for the performance of a number of judicial functions on nonjuridical days. These include the issuance and execution of warrants for treason, felony, and breach of peace; and the sitting of a court to receive the verdict of a jury.

DIET, a term applied to the legislative bodies of certain states or nations. The term is commonly used as the English name for the legislatures of several foreign countries.

The first governmental body to be called a diet originated in the Frankish tribal councils (see FRANKS), which passed out of existence in the 10th century. The princes and nobles, both clerical and secular, of the Holy Roman Empire met in an imperial diet called the *reichstag*. By 1300 this body had acquired three principal components: the electors (who elected the king), the princes and nobles, and the town delegates. Among the most important sessions of the diet after it attained this structure were the diets of Worms (1521), Spires (1529), and Augsburg (1530), all of which had as their primary aim the suppression of the Protestant Reformation. By the Treaty of Westphalia (1648), the diet became merely an assembly of ambassadors of the German princely states, with very little power. After 1867 the diet evolved into a bicameral, representative legislature composed of the Bundesrat and the Reichstag (qq.v.).

DIET. See FOOD; NUTRITION.

DIEU ET MON DROIT (Fr., "God and my right"), the motto on the royal arms of Britain. It was first used by King Richard I of England as a battle cry in the battle of Gisors (1198), to signify his independence and defiance of all powers save that of God. It was subsequently adopted by Edward III and since then has served as the motto of England, except during the reigns of Queen Elizabeth and Queen Anne, who used *Semper eadem*, "Always the same".

DIEZ, FRIEDRICH CHRISTIAN (1794–1876), German philologist, born in Giessen, and educated at the universities of Giessen and Göttingen. He originated the scientific study of Romance philology and in 1823 became professor of Romance philology at the University of Bonn. Among his works are *Die Poesie der Troubadours* (1826), and *Grammatik der Romanischen Sprachen* (3 vols., 1838–42).

DIFFERDANGE, a town in the s.w. part of the grand duchy of Luxemburg, about 12 miles S.E. of the city of Luxemburg, and in the center of a coal and iron mining district. Pop. (1948) 15,179.

DIFFERENCE, in arithmetic and ordinary mathematics, the amount by which one quantity is larger or smaller in magnitude than another of the same kind. When the term difference is used in series and functions, it takes on a specialized meaning. In a series, such as the series of the squares of the whole numbers:

$$1, 4, 9, 16, 25, 36, \ldots.$$

the differences between consecutive terms yields a new series:

$$3, 5, 7, 9, 11, \ldots.$$

called a series of first differences. Taking the differences between the consecutive terms of this series results in a series of first differences of first differences, or a series of second differences:

$$2, 2, 2, 2, \ldots.$$

In a similar manner, series of third, fourth, or nth differences might be formed, depending upon the original series. Series of differences may be used to find the nth term, or the sum of the first n terms, of the original series.

The study of series of differences and their implications and uses is called the calculus of finite differences. Certain calculating machines (q.v.), particularly difference engines, are based upon the principle of differences. See ARITHMETICAL PROGRESSION.

DIFFERENTIAL. See AUTOMOBILE.

DIFFERENTIAL ANALYZER. See CALCULATING MACHINES.

DIFFERENTIAL CALCULUS. See CALCULUS.

DIFFERENTIAL EQUATION. See CALCULUS; EQUATION.

DIFFRACTION, a phenomenon of wave motion, in which a wave of any type is spread (instead of continuing to travel in a straight line) after passing the edge of a solid or opaque object or after passing through a narrow slit. As the waves spread, they interfere with each other (see INTERFERENCE), and alternately cancel out and reinforce each other. Diffraction of light can be observed if a photographic image of a small object is highly magnified. The image will be seen to consist of a central image surrounded by alternating rings of lightness and darkness caused by diffraction at the edges of the taking lens. Because of this effect the practical magnifying power of lenses is limited. When a number of extremely narrow slits are placed close together, white light passing through them will be spread out into a spectrum. Such an arrangement of slits is called a diffraction grating.

DIFFUSION, in physical science, the smooth and even flow of matter or energy from a position of high concentration to a position of lower concentration, so as to produce a homogeneous distribution. If one end of a rod is heated or electrically charged, the heat or electricity will diffuse from the hot or charged portion to the cool or uncharged portion. If the bar is made of metal, this diffusion will be rapid for heat, and almost instantaneous for electricity; if the bar is made of asbestos, the diffusion will be slow for heat and extremely slow for electricity. Diffusion of matter is in general even slower. If a lump of sugar is placed in the bottom of a cup of water, the sugar will dissolve and slowly diffuse through the water; but if the water is not stirred it may be weeks before the solution is close to homogeneity. Even diffusion of one solid in another is possible. For example, if gold is plated on copper, the gold will diffuse slowly into the surface of the copper; however, for an appreciable amount of gold to diffuse more than a microscopic distance would normally take thousands of years.

All of these types of diffusion follow the same laws. In all cases, the rate of diffusion is proportional to the cross-sectional area and to the gradient (of concentration, temperature, or charge). Thus, heat will travel four times as fast through a rod two inches in diameter as through a rod one inch in diameter; and when the temperature gradient is ten degrees per inch, heat will diffuse twice as fast as when the gradient is only five degrees per inch. The rate of diffusion is also proportional to a specific property of the substance, which in the case of heat or electricity is called conductivity (q.v.). The amount of material which diffuses in a certain time, or the distance which it traverses, is proportional to the square root of the time; thus, if it takes sugar one week to diffuse through water one inch from its starting point it will take four weeks to diffuse through two inches.

As distinguished from stirring, which is a process of mixing masses of material, diffusion is a molecular process, depending solely on the random motions of individual molecules. The rate of diffusion of matter is therefore directly proportional to the average velocity of the molecules. This average speed is greater for smaller molecules, in proportion to the square root of the molecular weight, and is greatly increased by rise of temperature. Metallic thorium, for example, diffuses rapidly through metallic tungsten at temperatures in the neighborhood of 2000° C. (3632° F.), and the operation of certain vacuum tubes is based on this diffusion.

If one molecule is four times as heavy as another, it will, in general, move half as fast, and its rate of diffusion will be half as great. Advantage can be taken of this difference to separate substances of different molecular weights, and in particular to separate different isotopes of the same substance. When a gas containing two isotopes is forced through a fine porous barrier, the lighter isotopes, which have a higher average speed, will pass through the barrier faster than the heavier ones. The gas with the greater concentration of lighter isotopes is then diffused through a series of such barriers for large-scale separation. This technique, known as the gaseous-diffusion process, is widely used in the separation of the fissionable uranium isotope U-235 from the non-fissionable U-238; see ATOMIC ENERGY AND ATOMIC BOMB. Another isotope-separation technique, called the thermal-diffusion process, was applied experimentally during World War II. In this process the separation depends upon thermal effects exhibited by some gases; when such gases are enclosed in a chamber subjected to a temperature gradient, the heavy isotopes tend to concentrate in the cool region. See ISOTOPES.

Diffusion processes are of great biological importance. For example, digestion is essentially a process of chemically changing food so that it will be able to pass, by diffusion, through the intestinal wall into the blood stream. "Shock", a condition which frequently follows surgery or injury, is a state in which the blood fluids have diffused excessively through the blood-vessel walls into the body tissues; treatment of such shock consists essentially of injecting into the remaining blood fluid chemicals, usually in the form of blood plasma or serum albumin, which so alter the blood that the diffusion tendency is reversed and fluids diffuse back into the blood vessels; see TRANSFUSION OF BLOOD. See also COLLOIDAL DISPERSION; OSMOSIS.

DIGESTION, the process of changing food chemically to prepare it for absorption by the tissues of the animal body. The digestive process is extremely complicated and varies widely in different animals, even among those which are closely related. In general, however, it involves the breaking down of complex organic compounds into simpler compounds which are soluble and which may therefore be readily absorbed by the tissues. In most animals this process involves catalytic reactions between ingested food and enzymes secreted by the body. The process of human digestion described below is typical in most respects of the digestion of vertebrates.

Digestion includes both mechanical and chemical processes. The mechanical processes include chewing, which breaks solid food up into small pieces, the churning action of the stomach, and the peristaltic action of the intestines. The churning and peristaltic actions serve the dual purpose of moving the food through the digestive tract and mixing it with various body secretions. Three basic chemical reactions take place in human digestion: the conversion of carbohydrates into simple sugars, or monosaccharides, such as glucose, levulose, and galactose; the breaking down of proteins into amino acids; and the conversion of fats into fatty acids and glycerol. These three reactions are accomplished by the action of a number of body secretions.

Digestion in man begins in the mouth. As soon as a bite of food is ingested, six salivary glands add their secretions to the material eaten. The saliva serves three purposes: it breaks down cooked starches into intermediate products such as dextrin and maltose; it serves to dissolve solid food and make it more susceptible to the juices of the lower digestive tract; and it stimulates the secretion of these juices.

When the food reaches the stomach it is subjected to the action of the gastric juice, which contains enzymes, chiefly pepsin and rennin, and dilute hydrochloric acid. Pepsin, which acts only in the presence of acid, breaks proteins down into simpler organic compounds such as peptones and proteoses. Rennin separates milk into liquids and solids. Lipase (an enzyme acting on fats) digests butterfat in the stomach. The other chief functions of stomachic digestion are to act on proteins and to prepare the partly digested food for subsequent digestion in the intestines. Some of the constituents of gastric juice do not react until exposed to the alkaline medium of the small intestine. Gastric juice is formed by the stomach even during periods of starvation, but its secretion is stimulated by the mechanism of swallowing and by the muscular churning motions of the stomach itself during digestion. The presence of food in the stomach stimulates the production of gastric secretions which in turn stimulate the production of digestive substances in the intestine.

The most important part of human digestion takes place in the small intestine. In this portion of the digestive tract most of the products are absorbed and the food is subjected to the action of three of the most powerful of the digestive fluids: the *pancreatic fluid,* the *succus entericus,* and the *bile.*

The pancreatic fluid, produced by the pancreas and introduced into the small intestine, contains a number of enzymes such as trypsin and erepsin, which split complex protein molecules into simpler components, the amino acids, from which, in turn, the body can build up the proteins of its own structure. Steapsin breaks down fats in the food; amylopsin breaks down starches into maltose, a disaccharide. Other enzymes further break down disaccharides, such as maltose, into monosaccharides, such as glucose. The secretion of pancreatic juice is particularly stimulated by the ingestion of proteins and fats.

The succus entericus is secreted by the walls of the small intestine. It contains a number of enzymes, and its function is to complete the work of the pancreatic juice by further breaking down the products of early digestion into simpler substances which are readily absorbed by the cells in the walls of the intestine. The flow of succus entericus is chiefly stimulated by the mechanical pressure of partly digested food in the intestine.

The role of the bile in digestion is not fully understood. This fluid, secreted by the liver and apparently flowing in response to small changes in the chemical composition of the blood during digestion, accelerates the emulsification and digestion of fats and to some extent of starches and proteins. From observation of cases of obstructive jaundice (q.v.), in which the flow of bile is inhibited, it is

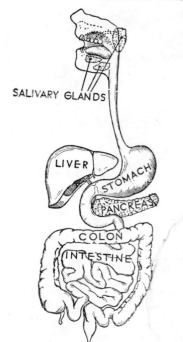

Organs of the digestive system of man

evident that the digestion of fats is ineffective without an adequate supply of bile.

Almost all of the products of digestion are assimilated into the body through the wall of the small intestine. This wall is able to absorb various nutritive substances selectively while rejecting other substances of very similar composition. The stomach and the large intestine or colon also have the ability to absorb water, certain salts, alcohol, and some drugs and crystalloids. The mechanism of assimilation is not well understood, but it is known that the intestinal walls pass amino acids and monosaccharides directly into the blood, and that fatty acids and related compounds are resynthesized into fats in the intestinal walls and pass into the blood via the thoracic duct.

See ENZYME; INTESTINE; METABOLISM; STOMACH.

DIGESTION IN PLANTS. See PLANT.

DIGGER WASP, any burrowing wasp, especially of the families Bembecidae and Sphecidae. The females of the family Bembecidae build their nests in sandy soil, close to each other, and occasionally feed flies to their larvae. Wasps of the family Sphecidae are solitary, each female building a nest and provisioning it with insects which she stings in

Peter Henderson & Co.

Foxglove, or digitalis, popular garden flower

such a way as to paralyze but not to kill them. The name digger wasp is sometimes extended to nonburrowing members of this family, such as the mud wasp or mud dauber, of the genus *Sceliphron*. This wasp, which is common in America, Europe, and Australia, builds nests of mud, often under the eaves of buildings.

DIGHTON ROCK, a large boulder on the bank of the Taunton River, opposite Dighton, Mass. An ancient inscription on the rock has been the subject of much antiquarian study. Various scholars have attributed Norse, Phenician, and Scythian origins to the inscription, but the belief most widely accepted today is that it is an American Indian carving.

DI GIACOMO, SALVATORE. See GIACOMO, SALVATORE DI.

DIGITALIS, a genus composed of about eighteen species of biennial or perennial Eurasian herbs of the Figwort family. They are commonly called foxgloves. The erect stems are three or more feet high and bear numerous large leaves at their bases. The stems terminate in long racemes of inflated bell-shaped flowers of various colors and markings. Foxgloves grow well in light, rich soil, either in exposed light or in partial shade. When once established, they are self-seeders. Purple-flowered, white-flowered, and yellow-flowered varieties are cultivated in America.

One species, *D. purpurea,* is famous for its medicinal uses. In the U.S. Pharmacopoeia, and in common usage, the term "digitalis" refers to the dried leaves of this species. The leaves of this foxglove, when about two-thirds of its flowers are opened, contain four important glucosides, of which three are heart stimulants and one a heart depressant. The three heart stimulants are *digitoxin,* $C_{34}H_{54}O_{11}$; *digitalin,* $C_{35}H_{56}O_{14}$; and *digitalein.* *Digitoxin* and *digitalin* are insoluble in water, the former being highly toxic and accumulative. *Digitalein* is soluble in water and may therefore be taken subcutaneously. The gastric disturbance often resulting from too large an oral dose of digitalis is caused by its heart depressant, *digitonin.*

Digitalis lengthens the diastole, the period of rest and nutrition of the heart muscle tissue, and thereby effectively causes the heart to obtain more rest even though it works harder under the influence of the drug. Digitalis also causes the heartbeat to become more regular and directly stimulates the cardiac muscle.

Overdoses and accumulation of digitalis in the body cause a condition known as *digitalism.* This condition results in gastro-intestinal disturbances, decrease in urine excretion, irregularity of heartbeat, paralysis of the heart, and eventually death.

DIHANG. See BRAHMAPUTRA.

DIHYDROXYBENZENE, one of three dihydric phenols found in or derived from resins and the sap of various plants, or prepared synthetically. Each has the formula $C_6H_4(OH)_2$. *o*-Dihydroxybenzene is called pyrocatechol, catechol, or pyrocatechin, and is sometimes used as a photographic developer. *m*-Dihydroxybenzene (resorcinol, resorcin), is an antiseptic obtained by treating asafetida, a gum resin, with potassium hydroxide. The proprietary antiseptic S.T. 37 is a derivative of this isomer. *p*-Dihydroxybenzene (hydroquinone, quinol) is a colorless, crystalline substance, soluble in water. It can be prepared from arbutin, a glucoside found in bearberry leaves. It is a strong reducing agent, often used as a photographic developer.

DIJON (Rom. *Divonense castrum*), capital of Côte-d'Or Department, E. France, situated in the western part of the Burgundian plain, at the junction of the Ouche and Suzon rivers. Dijon is 195 m. by rail s.e. of Paris.

It is important as a railroad center and has a port on the Burgundy Canal. The city is strategically located in a military sense, and is protected by fortresses. Dijon was the capital of the former duchy and province of Burgundy. The city is the site of the famous cathedral of St. Bénigne, built in the 13th century and named for the apostle of Burgundy, St. Benignus, who was martyred in Dijon in the 2nd century. The remains of Philip the Bold, Duke of Burgundy, and of Anne of Burgundy are contained in the vaults of the cathedral. Another 13th century church is Notre-Dame, of Burgundian-Gothic architecture. The remaining churches of importance are St. Michel, St. Jean, and St. Étienne, all dating from the 15th century. The town hall, built on the site of the old ducal palace, includes two towers, the kitchens, and the guardroom of the original structure. The 15th-century Palace of Justice is the former seat of the *parlement* of Burgundy. One of the great intellectual centers of France during the ducal occupancy, Dijon is still an important educational center. The university, founded in 1722, contains faculties of law, science, and letters. Industrial products of Dijon are machinery, automobiles, bicycles, hosiery, leather, tobacco products, flour, bakery products, mustard, soap, and brandy. In addition, the city contains large printing establishments, is a center of the wine trade of Burgundy, and has a considerable trade in wool and cereals. Pop. (1946) 100,664.

DIK-DIK or **DIG-DIG,** common name for several species of small East African antelopes (q.v.). They are about fourteen inches tall, and the males have straight horns about three inches long, ringed at the base. Their color is generally light brown. Dik-Diks are found throughout central Africa.

DIKE, in geology, a wall-like intrusion of igneous rock, cutting across other strata of pre-existing rocks, originally formed by a flow of molten rock into a fissure in which it cooled and solidified. A dike may be an inch to many thousand feet thick, and a few feet to many miles long. Frequently the rock material of the dike is harder than the surrounding rocks and as a result may be left standing by itself after the neighboring rock has weathered away. Similar intrusions of igneous rock which lie parallel to the enclosing layers are known as *sills*.

DIKE. See LEVEE.

DILL, an annual or biennial herb, *Anethum graveolens,* of the Parsley family. It grows wild in grainfields of S. Europe, England, and the United States, and is also cultivated as an herb. It has a strong, stimulating, aromatic taste, and is used extensively for flavoring pickles and sauces.

DILLON, JOHN (1851–1927), Irish statesman, born near Dublin, and educated at Catholic University Medical School. About 1879 he became a partisan of the movement for Irish home rule led by Charles Parnell (q.v.). Dillon was a member of Parliament from 1880 to 1883 and from 1885 to 1918. He was noted for the violence of his speeches on Irish questions; his criticism of the policies of the British government several times led to his imprisonment He co-operated with John Redmond in the direction of the Irish Nationalist Party and in 1918 became chairman of the party. In World War I he supported the British government's recruiting in Ireland but opposed conscription for Ireland. In the Parliamentary election of 1918 the Sinn Fein (q.v.) party defeated the Irish Nationalists and Dillon lost his seat.

DiMAGGIO, JOSEPH PAUL, popularly JOE (1914–   ), American professional baseball player, born in Martinez, Calif. In 1935, after three years with the San Francisco team of the Pacific Coast League, he became a member of the "Yankees", the New York American League team. His ability as a hitter and centerfielder soon made him a "Yankee" mainstay and the idol of "Yankee" fans everywhere. He batted .381 and .352 in 1939 and 1940 respectively, leading the American League, and in 1941 he hit safely in 56 consecutive games, establishing a new record. From 1943 to 1945, during World War II, DiMaggio served in the U.S. Army. He rejoined the "Yankees" in 1946 and retired following the 1951 season. His lifetime (13 seasons) major-league batting record is .325.

DIMENSION, FOURTH. See RELATIVITY; GEOMETRY: *Four Dimensional.*

DIMINUTIVE, a derivative form of a word denoting smaller size or greater youth than that denoted by the original word, and often with the added significance of affection, familiarity, or contempt. Every modern language possesses diminutives, and the most common method of their formation is by the addition of a syllable to the original word. In English the principal suffixes which form diminutives are -cule, -el, -et, -ette, -ie, -kin, -le, -let, -ling, -ock, -ule, and -y; as in mole*cule*, kern*el*, isl*et*, kitchen*ette*, bird*ie*, lamb*kin*, icic*le*, leaf*let*, gos*ling*, hill*ock*, caps*ule*, dog*gy*.

Diminutives often occur in proper names: *Perkins* is the diminutive of *Peters, Jenkins* of

Australian News & Info. Bureau

The dingo, of Australia

Johns; these have become, with usage, permanent and distinct surnames. In familiar or affectionate conversation, suffixes used as diminutives are sometimes affixed to Christian names; thus, *Peter* becomes *Peterkin, Gertrude* becomes *Gertie,* and *John* becomes *Johnny.* In Latin, diminutives almost invariably end in *lus, la,* or *lum.* The Italian and Spanish languages are particularly rich in diminutives, various suffixes supplying special shades and degrees of affection or disparagement; thus in Italian, *fratello,* the word for brother and itself a diminutive of the Latin *frater,* may become, in an excess of affection, *fratellinucciettinetto,* in which the diminution may be said to be carried to the sixth degree.

Diminutives are not always confined to nouns; *whitish* is the diminutive of the adjective *white;* and *tipple* and *scribble* are examples of diminutive verbs, formed from the original *tip* and *scribe.*

DIMNET, ERNEST (1869–   ), French abbé, lecturer, and writer, born in Trelon, and educated at Cambrai College, the University of Lille, and the Sorbonne. While head of the English department at the Collège Stanislas in Paris, he made frequent lecture tours of England and the United States. In 1923 he became Canon of the Cathedral of Cambrai. Among his writings are *Figures de Moines* (1908), *Les Sœurs Brontë* (1910), *The Art of Thinking* (1928), and *My New World* (1938).

DINANT, a town of Namur Province, Belgium, on the Meuse R. It is noted as a summer resort. In the Middle Ages Dinant was fa-

mous for its copperware, or "dinanderie". Present-day industries are the manufacture of paper, carpets, glassware, and metalware. In addition, Dinant contains breweries and tanneries. Black marble is quarried in the vicinity. A castle on a rock overlooking Dinant and the Gothic church of Notre Dame in the town date from the 11th and 13th centuries, respectively. Dinant dates from the 6th century, and has suffered greatly throughout its history from sieges. It was a wealthy city of Walloon Belgium, having a population of about 60,000, until it was besieged and sacked by Charles the Bold of Burgundy in 1466. Louis XIV of France captured Dinant in 1675 and the town was held by the French for nearly thirty years. During World War I, Dinant was partially destroyed by the Germans, but was restored after 1918. In 1940, during World War II, Dinant again suffered damage. Pop. (1948 est.) 6925.

DINAPUR or **DINAPORE,** town of Patna Division, Bihar State, Union of India, situated on the Ganges R., about 10 miles w. of the city of Patna. The town has a number of industrial establishments, manufacturing chiefly wood and iron products. Dinapur was at one time an important base of the British army. In 1857 it was a center of the Sepoy Mutiny. Pop. (1941) 40,057.

DINARIC ALPS, a mountain group in Yugoslavia, part of the East Alpine system, connecting the Julian Alps of N.E. Italy and N.W. Yugoslavia with the Balkan mountain system. They extend in a southeasterly direction to the Drin R. beyond the boundary of Albania, and rise to a height of more than 8000 ft. above sea level in Mt. Durmitor. The Dinaric Alps are characterized by massive limestone areas. The surface soil is thin, and many of the rivers rising in the group at high altitudes soon sink into cavities in the rocks and are lost until the waters reappear at lower levels along the Adriatic coast. A few rivers, such as the Narenta, flow to the sea in precipitous gorges. The Dinaric Alps have almost no natural passes and constitute a barrier between the Adriatic and the interior of Yugoslavia. Arable lands lie chiefly in scattered depressions and along the Adriatic coast.

DINGO, a wild dog, *Canis dingo,* found in Australia. It is about 2½ ft. long and 2 ft. high, with a reddish-brown coat and a bushy tail. Its ears are small and erect and it has a sharp muzzle. In the wild state dingos run in packs and frequently raid herds of sheep. They may, however, be domesticated if captured when young. The origin of the dingo is not entirely clear. Many authorities believe that marsupials are the only mammals native to the continent and that the dingos were brought to Australia by prehistoric migrants from Asia. Fossil remains of dingos have been discovered in deposits of the Pleistocene period in Australia, so that it is possible that the animals are truly indigenous. Dingos do not occur in Tasmania, New Zealand, or elsewhere.

DINGWALL. See ROSS AND CROMARTY.

DINKA or **DENKA,** a native people of the Sudan, Africa, and also the Nilotic language they speak. The Dinka inhabit both sides of the White Nile R. They are the most important of the Nilotic Negro groups, and are noted for their good physique, valor, and herds of cattle, sheep, and goats.

DINOCERAS. See UINTATHERIUM.

DINORNIS. See MOA.

DINOSAURIA, a large group of extinct reptiles which flourished in the Mesozoic era. During this period they were the dominant form of land animal life, and fossil remains of members of the group have been found in all parts of the world. The dinosaurs ranged in size from small animals approximately 2 ft. in overall length to gigantic beasts 80 ft. in length. In general the smaller species were the first to appear; the largest ones evolved later. The evolutionary history of the dinosaurs lasted throughout the entire Mesozoic era, with the earliest forms making their appearance in Triassic times and the most advanced species flourishing and finally dying off in the Cretaceous.

The dinosaurs exhibited great variety of form. The carnivorous species generally had long necks and walked or ran on their hind legs. A long, bulky tail served as a counterbalance for their necks and heavy bodies when they stood erect. The forelegs were small and weak, terminating in talonlike feet adapted for grasping. The herbivorous dinosaurs, in general, walked on four feet. Many later species were so heavy that they could not walk for any distance on dry land and therefore spent most of their lives in swamps and the shallow waters of lakes and seas where mud and water could buoy them up. Some even went into deep water. This hypothesis is strengthened by the fact that a number of the larger species had weak, pencil-like teeth adapted only for browsing on water plants. The dinosaurs have no modern descendants, but the crocodiles, their contemporaries, have persisted to the present day and now exhibit a mode of life similar to that of many of the dinosaurs. Some of the largest species had brains no larger than that of a modern dog, and the brain of the *Stegosaurus,* an animal the size of an elephant, was not larger than a walnut. An enlargement of the spinal cord in the hip, twenty times bigger than the brain, controlled the movements of the hind limbs and powerful tail.

Dinosaurs are classified in two orders, the Saurischia and the Ornithischia. The earliest saurischians were chiefly bipedal carnivorous animals belonging to the Theropoda, a group which includes the largest terrestrial animal of carnivorous habits, the *Tyrannosaurus.* This reptile, which lived toward the end of Mesozoic times, had an overall length of about 50 ft. and stood about 18 ft. high. Its massive head was about 4 ft. in length, and its mouth was armed with sharp teeth, some of which were almost a foot long. The *Tyrannosaurus* had a short neck, a heavy body, and a long tail. Other species of Theropoda included the giant *Allosaurus,* 35 ft. long, the *Megalosaurus,* the *Dicynodon,* and the *Anchisaurus.*

The four-footed herbivorous species of Saurischia are usually classified as Sauropoda. They include the *Brontosaurus,* the longest of all the dinosaurs; the *Brachiosaurus,* the heaviest and most bulky; the *Diplodocus,* and the *Cetiosaurus.*

The second order of dinosaurs, the Ornithischia, included only herbivorous species. The order includes the aquatic *Iguanodon* and a number of armored dinosaurs such as the *Stegosaurus.* Some species of ornithischians developed two horns above the eyes and a third at the end of the nose. Among these horned dinosaurs was the *Triceratops.* The *Protoceratops,* another horned species, was a small dinosaur approximately 9 ft. long. The eggs of this reptile have been found in Mongolia; they are about 9 in. in length, and are the only fossil dinosaur eggs ever to have been discovered. See separate articles on individual dinosaurs mentioned.

DINOSAUR NATIONAL MONUMENT, a national monument created in 1915, originally embracing an area of 80 acres in Utah, but enlarged in 1938 by the addition of 26,605 acres in Utah and 177,280 acres in Colorado, increasing the total area to 203,965 acres. It is noted for its deposits of fossil remains of prehistoric animal life, found chiefly in the shales and sandstones of the original 80-acre tract, and also for the scenic beauty of the canyons of the Yampa and Green rivers. The fossil remains discovered in the area are of great scientific interest, and include those of dinosaurs,

Smithsonian Institution

THE DINOSAURIA

Above: Museum model of Ceratosaurus, a dinosaur 20 feet long. Right: A gigantic Camarasaurus (70 feet long) modeled in clay. Below: Painting of Triceratops, a 25-foot long, horned dinosaur.

brontosaurs, allosaurs, flying reptiles, and other animals of remote geologic times. Fossil remains were uncovered in the region from 1909 to 1923 by an expedition of the Carnegie Museum of Pittsburgh. A skeleton of a brontosaurus unearthed in the area, 75½ ft. long and 20 ft. high, may be seen in that museum's Hall of Vertebrate Paleontology. Other institutions which have sponsored expeditions to the region have been the Smithsonian Institution and the University of Utah.

DINOTHERIUM, or DEINOTHERIUM, an extinct mammal belonging to the order Proboscidea, related to the elephant. Only fossil skulls of the dinotherium have been discovered, but the fact that these skulls are approximately 4½ ft. long and 3 ft. wide indicates that the animals must have been larger than modern elephants. A remarkable feature of the dinotherium was a pair of long, downward-curving incisors growing from its lower jaw.

DINWIDDIE, ROBERT (1693–1770), colonial lieutenant governor of Virginia (1751–58), born near Glasgow, Scotland. In 1754 he dispatched a force under the command of George Washington to the Ohio valley to prevent the French from taking possession of that region. Subsequently the French attack on Washington's detachment of Fort Necessity, on the present site of Pittsburgh, marked the beginning of the French and Indian War (q.v.). Dinwiddie played an active part in the campaigns of the war. After the war he became unpopular because he advocated taxation of the American colonies to help pay the cost of the conflict, and he was recalled in 1758.

DIO (or **DION**) **CASSIUS,** called COCCEIANUS (155?–235? A.D.), Roman historian and politician, born at Nicæa, in Bithynia. His maternal grandfather was the Stoic philosopher, Dion Chrysostomus. Dio Cassius held office in Rome under the emperors Commodus, Pertinax, Lucius Septimius Severus, and Marcus Aurelius Alexander Severus, twice (220 and 229) attaining the consulship. He is best known as the author of *Romaika,* a history of Rome in eighty books, written in Greek. Only eighteen of these books (37–54) are extant in their entirety, but fragments of many of the other books and epitomes by later writers have been preserved, and all are valued by modern historians as source material, especially for the history of the last years of the Roman Republic and the first years of the Empire.

DIOCESE (Gr. *dioikesis,* "administration"), the territory over which a bishop exercises ec-

clesiastical jurisdiction. The term occurs as early as the time of Demosthenes, to signify the treasury or department of finance. But in the organization of the Roman Empire introduced by Diocletian, the designation diocese was applied to the larger divisions, which were subdivided into provinces or eparchies. About the middle of the 5th century, the dioceses of the Empire were the East, Asia, Pontus, Thrace, Macedonia, Dacia, Illyria, Italy, Africa, Gaul, Spain, and Britain. The government of the Christian Church, as established by Constantine, adopted this division, and the term "diocese", as well as others borrowed from the government of the Roman Empire, passed over into ecclesiastical usage. The term was first applied in this sense to a collection of metropolitan churches or provinces (parishes), each under the charge of an archbishop. Later the term was applied to a single metropolitanate, or province, and finally it came to signify the local jurisdiction of any bishop of any rank.

DIOCLETIAN, in full GAIUS AURELIUS VALERIUS DIOCLETIANUS (245–313), Roman Emperor. He was born of humble parents in Dalmatia, and became an officer in the Roman army. When the Emperor Marcus Aurelius Numerianus died in 284, Diocletian's troops proclaimed him emperor. Carinus, the brother of Numerianus, contested his claim and defeated the forces of Diocletian in battle in Mœsia (285), but was killed by one of his own officers, and Diocletian's rule was assured. He was immediately faced with uprisings in many parts of the vast empire, and selected as his colleague a Pannonian officer, Marcus Aurelius Valerius Maximianus, better known as Maximian (q.v.), first (285) giving him the title of Cæsar, and later (286) the title Augustus. In order to obtain more assistance in defending and administering the empire, and also in order to assure a peaceful succession to the throne, Diocletian co-opted two more colleagues in 293, each with the title of Cæsar. He adopted one of them, Gaius Galerius Valerius Maximianus, better known as Galerius, as his son; Maximian adopted the other, Flavius Valerius Constantius (q.v.). The empire was divided into 101 provinces, grouped into thirteen larger divisions (called *dioceses*), and into four major parts, over each of which a Cæsar or Augustus was placed. All edicts were signed jointly by the four rulers, but the superior rank of the Augusti and the supremacy of Diocletian over the others were retained.

The fourfold division facilitated the maintenance of order, and victories over enemies of

Rome in Africa and in Persia extended the boundaries of the empire, which were everywhere strengthened and fortified. The administrative reorganization of the empire resulted in the centralization of control, on an equal basis, over all its vast territories, and correspondingly ended forever the primacy of Italy. Rome was no longer the capital city of the Roman Empire; its place was taken by Mediolanum (Milan) in Italy, the headquarters of Maximian; Nicomedia in N.W. Asia Minor, the capital of Diocletian; Augusta Trevirorum (Trier) in Germany, where the rule of Constantius was based; and Sirmium (Mitrovica) in Pannonia, the administrative center of Galerius. In spite of the fourfold division, organization was increasingly autocratic. Diocletian introduced Eastern ceremonies at his court, and adopted the appellation of Jovius (a form of the name Jupiter), assigning to Maximian that of Heraclius (from Hercules). His regulations were rigid and oppressive. Especially exacting was the so-called Edict of Diocletian (301), which fixed the maximum prices of commodities and wages throughout the empire; it was unenforceable and was soon abandoned. More lasting in their oppressive influence were the changes in the system of collecting taxes, which made civil officials responsible for payment of fixed sums, leaving office-holding in the hands of the most rapacious citizens and laying the basis for peonage and serfdom. Diocletian's reign is best remembered, however, for the renewed persecution of Christians, which he authorized beginning in 302. Three years later he abdicated his power, and forced Maximian to follow suit, leaving the succession, as he had planned, to Galerius and Constantius. Diocletian retired to his country estate at Salona, in Dalmatia.

DIODORUS SICULUS (1st cent. B.C.), Greek historian, born at Agyrium, in Sicily. He lived in the times of Julius Cæsar and Augustus, traveled in Asia and Europe, and lived a long time in Rome, collecting the materials of his great work, the *Bibliotheke Historike*. This was a history of the world, in forty books, from the Creation to the Gallic wars of Julius Cæsar. Of this great work, the first five books are extant in their entirety; the next five books are wholly lost; the next ten are complete; and of the remainder of the work, considerable fragments have been preserved in the *Excerpta* in Photius, and in the *Ecloga* prepared by command of the Byzantine emperor Constantine Porphyrogenitus.

DIOGENES (412?–323 B.C.), Cynic philosopher, born in Sinope, in Pontus. His father,

Icesias, a banker, was convicted of debasing the coinage, and his son, being implicated in the matter, was obliged to leave Sinope. He traveled to Athens, where he convinced the Cynic philosopher Antisthenes to take him as a disciple. Diogenes then plunged into a life of austerity and self-mortification. He wore coarse clothing, ate the plainest food, and accepted relief from the Athenians. He slept on the bare ground, in the open streets or under the porticoes. His eccentric life did not, however, lose him the respect of the Athenians, who admired his contempt of comfort. Practical good was the chief aim of his philosophy; and he did not conceal his disdain for literature and the fine arts. He laughed at men of letters for reading the sufferings of Odysseus while neglecting their own; and at orators who studied how to enforce truth but not how to practice it. He was seized by pirates on a voyage to Ægina and carried to Crete, where he was sold as a slave. When asked what business he was proficient in, he answered, "In commanding." He was purchased by a certain Xeniades of Corinth, who recognized his worth, set him free, and made him tutor to his children. According to a popular story, on one occasion Diogenes had an interview with Alexander the Great. The king opened the conversation with, "I am Alexander the Great," and the philosopher answered, "And I am Diogenes the Cynic." Alexander then asked him in what way he could serve him. "You can stand out of the sunshine," the philosopher replied. Alexander is said to have been so struck with the Cynic's self-possession that he went away remarking, "If I were not Alexander, I should wish to be Diogenes." Diogenes died at Corinth, according to tradition, on the same day as Alexander the Great. Diogenes was wholly concerned with practical wisdom and established no system of philosophy. (See CYNICS.) Certain literary works were early attributed to Diogenes, but they were recognized even in antiquity as being spurious.

DIOGNETUS, EPISTLE TO, name of an anonymous document written in defense of Christian beliefs and practices, probably in the 1st century A.D. It is one of a number of similar documents, designated collectively as apologetic literature, and is distinguished from them especially by its superior literary quality. Composed in the form of replies to questions put by one Diognetus, such as why Christians despise death and what god they worship, the Epistle rebuts with vigor contemporary accusations against the Christians, including the allegations that they were atheists and subverters of established governments. It stresses the practical side of Christianity, extolling godly living rather than correctness in theological dogma.

DIOMEDEA. See ALBATROSS.

DIOMEDE ISLANDS, two rocky islands in the Bering Strait, about halfway between Alaska and Siberia. They were discovered about 1728 by the Danish explorer Vitus Bering. Little Diomede (2.4 sq.m.) belongs to the U.S., and Big Diomede (11.3 sq.m.) to the Soviet Union. The two islands lie about one mile apart and lack harbor facilities. Between them runs the U.S.-Russian boundary line and the international date line. Fewer than 100 Eskimos are said to inhabit the islands.

DIOMEDES, a Greek legendary hero, the bravest, after Achilles, of all the Greeks who took part in the Trojan War. He vanquished Hector and Æneas, the most valiant of the Trojans. On returning to Argos, where he had succeeded to the throne after the death of Adrastus, he found that his wife had proved unfaithful in his absence; he then sailed away to Italy, and there married the daughter of King Daunus.

DION CASSIUS. See DIO CASSIUS.

DIONNE QUINTUPLETS (b. 1934), five Canadian girls, Cécile, Yvonne, Annette, Émilie, and Marie, born in Callander, Ont. to Oliva Dionne and his wife Elzire, then the parents of six other children. Born prematurely, the infants collectively weighed eleven and one-half pounds six days after birth. Such a multiple human birth is extremely rare, and the fact that the infants survived was unique in medical history. Dr. Allan Roy Dafoe (1883–1943), the Canadian physician who delivered the quintuplets and kept them alive, won great acclaim for his skill. From the moment of birth, the girls attracted world-wide attention. To prevent exploitation of the Dionne family, the Ontario government in 1935 designated the quintuplets wards of the state. By 1938 a trust fund for the girls totaling $600,000 had accumulated from gifts donated by people all over the world. Despite these unusual circumstances, the quintuplets enjoyed a normal childhood and adolescence. Émilie died in August, 1954, while residing in a Roman Catholic convent in Quebec.

DIONYSIA. See DIONYSUS.

DIONYSIUS, SAINT (fl. 3rd cent.), Pope from 259 until 268. After the persecutions of the Emperor Decius, beginning in 251, he reorganized the Church

DIONYSIUS OF HALICARNASSUS (1st cent. B.C.), Greek historian and critic, who lived in Rome during the reign of the emperor Augustus. Many of his critical works are extant, including *The Arrangement of Words, On Imitation,* and *Commentaries on the Attic Orators.* He is best known as the author of *Roman Antiquities,* a history of his adopted city to the year 264 B.C. Nine of the twenty books have been preserved in their entirety, and portions of the rest are extant or have been epitomized by later writers. While not authoritative by modern standards, his history is valued as a source dealing with a period little known from other works.

DIONYSIUS THE AREOPAGITE (1st cent. A.D.), one of the few Athenians who were converted by the preaching of the Apostle Paul (Acts 17:34). The celebrated Greek writings which bear his name and which laid the foundation for the mystical theology of the Church, were attributed to him after a fashion not uncommon in antiquity, but were not written by him. From the 6th century on, however, they were generally accepted as genuine, and exercised a great influence on the development of theology. In the Western Church they are first referred to in one of the *Homilies* of Gregory the Great.

DIONYSIUS THE ELDER (about 430–367 B.C.), Tyrant of the city of Syracuse, in Sicily. He was of humble birth, and worked as a government clerk before he seized power and became tyrant (Gr. *tyrannos,* applied to one who usurps power) in 405. Until 398 he maintained peace with the Carthaginians, who ruled a large part of the island of Sicily, but thereafter he conducted wars against them and against the Greek cities of southern Italy. His first campaigns (until 392) against the Carthaginians were victorious, and he made Syracuse the strongest power in southern Italy, capturing the city of Rhegium in 386. His later wars with Carthage were unsuccessful, and he lost the territory west of the Halycus River previously won by the Syracusans and their allies. Dionysius, however, made Syracuse one of the important powers of the ancient world. He made use of mercenary troops both as colonists and as fighters, and utilized Sicel allies in Sicily and Greek allies elsewhere to further his ends. Dionysius was also a patron of the arts and a playwright. He competed often at the dramatic festivals at Athens.

DIONYSIUS THE YOUNGER (4th cent. B.C.), Tyrant of Syracuse, son of Dionysius the Elder (q.v.), whom he succeeded in 367 B.C.

Ruins of the ancient Theater of Dionysus, in Athens. Inset: Marble throne in the front row of the theater, the seat occupied by the priest of Dionysus, a Greek dignitary.

He ruled at first under the supervision of Dion, his uncle, who served as regent. During this period, at Dion's request, the philosopher Plato visited Syracuse, attempting unsuccessfully to educate Dionysius to his ideals of kingship. At the behest of an envious courtier, Philistus, Dionysius banished Dion in 357. Dion raised an army, defeated Dionysius in battle, and drove him into exile. Dionysius returned to Syracuse in 346, seven years after Dion had been assassinated. His second period of rule was arbitrary and unpopular, and the people of Syracuse welcomed the intervention of the Corinthian general Timoleon, who captured Dionysius and sent him into exile at Corinth about 343 B.C.

DIONYSUS, a Greek nature god, probably of Thraco-Phrygian origin. In later Greek legend he was said to be the son of the chief Olympian god, Zeus, by Semele, who has been identified as a Phrygian earth-goddess. After Semele was destroyed by seeing Zeus in his full radiance, Dionysus was reared in the thigh of Zeus until he was full grown. Later he was cared for by a band of nymphs or, according to another tale, he journeyed throughout the world showing mortals how to raise vines. Although he was the god of all vegetation, he was especially worshipped as the god of the vine and as the god of wine, which, according to the poet Hesiod, he invented. His worship was characterized by frenzied orgies usually associated with intoxication. The use of phallic symbols, the tearing of wild animals into pieces, the eating of raw flesh, and savage dancing were also characteristic of his rites, especially in Thrace and Asia Minor. Greek drama (q.v., under DRAMA) originated in the early rites for Dionysus, and in historic times important festivals held in his honor included celebrations at Athens, during which great dramatic competitions were held. The most important of the Athenian festivals were the Great (or City) Dionysia in the spring and the Lenæa in the winter. After the 5th century B.C. Dionysus was also known to the Greeks as Bacchus (q.v.), under which name he was best known to the Romans.

DIONYSUS, THEATER OF, a structure in ancient Athens where dramatic presentations took place. It was built in the open air, in a bowl formed by the south side of the Acropolis. The original structure, made of wood, probably consisted only of the platform where the action of the play took place (Gr. *orchestra,* "dancing place") and the tiers of benches rising on the hillside. Later a stage building (*skene*) was probably added to accommodate the actors when they were not appearing in the orchestra. This theater was the location of the great theatrical competitions of the 5th century B.C., in which such illustrious playwrights as Æschylus, Sophocles, Euripides, and Aristophanes participated. About 330 B.C. the wooden structures were replaced by stone structures, and at a later period wings were added on each side of the *skene,* and a stage, encroaching on the *orchestra,* was built in front of the enlarged building. The Theater of Dionysus continued in use under Roman rule, and remains of both the wooden and stone structures have been discovered by modern archeologists.

DIOPHANTINE ANALYSIS, a method employed to find rational solutions of indeterminate algebraic equations, by means of squares and cubes of the unknown quantities. In this method the unknown quantities have no definite fixed values, but depend to some degree on assumption. This class of problems was first treated by Diophantus (q.v.), who was chiefly interested in solving equations of the second order. Examples of such problems are: to find two whole numbers (such as 3 and 4), the sum of whose squares is a square; and to find three whole numbers (such as 1, 5, and 7) the squares of which are in arithmetical progression. See FERMAT'S LAST THEOREM; INDETERMINATE EQUATION.

DIOPHANTUS (3rd cent. A.D.), Greek mathematician. He lived at Alexandria, Egypt, where he occupied himself chiefly with Diophantine analysis (q.v.), earning the title "Father of Algebra". He wrote the *Arithmetica,* of which only six books have survived of a reputed thirteen.

DIOPSIDE, a mineral of the pyroxene (q.v.) group, which crystallizes in the monoclinic system. It is essentially a calcium magnesium silicate, with a hardness of 5 to 6, and a specific gravity of 3.2. It is usually white, gray, yellow, or light green in color, but sometimes, owing to the presence of iron, it is dark green or nearly black. Diallage, a laminated variety of diopside, is usually of the darker shades. Diopside is a common mineral, often occurring in limestone and dolomite.

Transparent, oily, green crystals, especially those from St. Lawrence Co., N.Y., have been found sufficiently large and clear to be cut as gems.

DIORAMA. See PANORAMA.

DIORITE, name given to several closely related igneous rocks, usually gray or dark gray in color. They are crystalline, coarsely granular, and composed mostly of silica and alumina, with some iron oxides, lime, and magnesia. The most common species of diorite contain plagioclase feldspar and hornblende. Other diorites contain biotite, quartz, or various ferromagnesian silicates. Diorite is one of the commonest of all rocks.

DIOSCOREACEAE. See BRYONY; YAM.

DIOSCORIDES, PEDANIUS (fl. 1st cent. A.D.), a Greek physician, born in Anazarbus, in Cilicia. He accompanied the Roman armies as physician through many countries, and collected information on plants. He wrote *De Materia Medica,* a book which, until about 1600, was considered an authority on both botany and medicine.

DIOSCURI. See CASTOR AND POLLUX.

DIOSPYROS. See PERSIMMON; EBONY.

DIPHTHERIA, an acute and highly infectious disease, affecting children particularly, characterized by the formation of a false membrane in the passages of the upper respiratory system. The cause of the disease is an organism called the Klebs-Löffler bacillus, after the German pathologist Edwin Klebs (1834–1913), who discovered it in 1883, and F. A. J. Löffler, who isolated it in the following year.

The diphtheria bacilli enter the body through the mouth and nose and attack the mucous membranes, where they multiply and secrete a powerful toxin. Where the bacteria attack the walls of the nose and throat, gray-white exudate is formed, beginning about five days after exposure. This exudate increases in size and thickness, becoming a yellow false membrane which adheres to the mucous membrane and may block the air passages and cause asphyxiation. When such a blockage occurs, it is necessary to pass a metal tube through the mouth and into the trachea to permit the passage of air, an operation known as intubation. Even when the false membrane does not grow to this extent, victims of the disease sometimes die from the effects of the toxin absorbed from the bacilli. In nonfatal cases of diphtheria there is often an aftermath of paralysis of the eyes, legs, or one side of the body. Paralytic symptoms, however, are usually not permanent.

Prior to the development of diphtheria antitoxin in 1894 by P. P. E. Roux and E. A. Behring (qq.v.), the mortality from the disease averaged about 35 percent and was as high as 90 percent in cases of diphtheria of the larynx. The universal use of antitoxin in treatment has cut the mortality rate to approximately 5 percent. Inactive toxin-antitoxins and toxoids have also been developed, and have greatly reduced the incidence of the disease by making possible the immunization of children. Another weapon against diphtheria is the Schick test for determining whether an individual is susceptible to the disease; see SCHICK, BELA. By a program of testing, immunizing, and treatment with antitoxin, diphtheria has been brought under control in the U.S. and most other parts of the world.

DIPLODOCUS, one of the largest of the dinosaurs, of the suborder Sauropoda. It lived during the Jurassic period and inhabited what is now the western part of the United States. Fossil specimens indicate that the reptile attained lengths up to 87 ft., which would make it one of the longest of the known terrestrial animals. It was relatively slender, however, and somewhat less bulky than the Brontosaurus. The Diplodocus was a quadruped with a long neck, a low body, and a long tail. It had a small head with slender teeth and probably grazed in marshes and shallow water where buoyancy would support part of the weight of its great body. See DINOSAURIA.

DIPLOMACY, the art of managing the intercourse between nations and of adjusting their differences by negotiation. It arose out of the development of the great European powers and, as a uniform system, has until recently been confined chiefly to these powers. Its practical rules are embodied partly in international customs and usage and partly in treaties.

The management of the foreign intercourse of a nation is one of the chief functions of the executive head of the state. Formerly it was largely performed by the ruler in person, but it has in modern times passed into the hands of a class of officials, known as diplomatic agents. Under modern conditions the usual instruments of diplomacy are (1) the principal secretaries of state for foreign affairs; (2) regular diplomatic agents of various grades, ranging from ambassadors to chargés d'affaires; and (3) occasional embassies or agents of diplomatic intercourse appointed for the accomplishment of a specific purpose. See DIPLOMATIC AGENTS. Every diplomatic agent must be furnished with a letter of credence stating the general object of his mission, and requesting that full faith and credit be given to what he shall say on behalf of his government. Once a public minister enters the territory of the state to which he is sent, until he leaves the country, he is entitled to an entire exemption from the local jurisdiction, both civil and criminal.

Prior to the 15th century, diplomatic intercourse was conducted almost entirely by ambassadors and other special agents. But with the establishment of resident legations in that century, the practice of diplomacy was raised to a fine art which rapidly assumed commanding importance in European politics. At a period when international relations were based on personal and dynastic interests, and when statecraft was another name for intrigue, the role of the ambassador was second in importance only to that of the sovereign. There was no diplomatic profession, but the great posts in the service were sought after by the greatest persons in church and state. The institution by all the great powers of a trained diplomatic service in the 19th century, and the improvement in methods of communication, greatly reduced the previous wide discretion of ambassadors, and tended more and more to reduce them to the position of intermediaries, acting under instructions from their governments.

The methods of diplomatic action vary according to the magnitude of the interests involved and the nature of the emergency which calls them into play. For the settlement of questions vitally affecting several states, or such as involve the peace of a continent, or the general policy of the great powers of the civilized world, a general congress of international conference may be summoned. Examples of such conferences were the Congress of Westphalia, held in 1648 to settle the issues involved in the Thirty Years' War; the Congress of Vienna (1814–15), by which the problems arising out of the Napoleonic Wars were adjusted; The Hague Conferences (1899, 1907), for the promotion of the peaceful settlement of international differences among all civilized states; and the Conference of Algeciras (1906), for the settling of relations between European powers and Morocco.

One of the most important modern conferences was the Paris Peace Conference, following World War I. The first meeting was held in January, 1919, and led to the Treaty

United Nations

General Assembly of the United Nations, Paris, 1948. In this body the people of the world placed their hope for lasting peace through diplomacy.

of Versailles. There a new principle was introduced by U.S. President Woodrow Wilson in the first of the famous Fourteen Points, which declared for "open covenants openly arrived at". The very enunciation of this principle, although it was followed neither during the Conference nor by most of the Powers after that time, was of the greatest value in fixing the attention of the peoples of different countries upon the necessity of requiring from their diplomats a degree of responsibility for devious methods and secret agreements. Since World War I there has been a general tendency to force international diplomacy into the open where its movements may be observed by public opinion and the nations at large. See PEACE CONFERENCE. This feeling was especially strong in the U.S., where revelations of secret wartime diplomatic commitments between the belligerent powers did much to keep alive the agitation against traditional diplomatic methods. In practice, however, the old diplomatic machinery continued to function side by side with the League of Nations appartus which, as time went on, was increasingly confined to matters of minor international concern, such as the suppression of the drug traffic and the regulation of ocean fisheries. Member nations were required to register

treaties with the League, but there was still no assurance that diplomats had not contrived secret clauses. The period before World War II was marked by a wide range of diplomatic action. Chancellor Adolf Hitler personally conducted the aggressive German diplomacy which, by 1939, added Austria and Czechoslovakia to the Reich without provoking immediate war. In the almost unbroken succession of diplomatic crises of 1939, the most dramatic event was the signing, ten days before World War II began, of a non-aggression pact between Germany and the U.S.S.R.

The most notorious example of devious diplomatic methods in modern times was provided on Dec. 7, 1941, when Saburo Kurusu, special Japanese imperial envoy at Washington, answered with peaceful assurances an appeal from President Franklin D. Roosevelt to Emperor Hirohito, although Japan had commenced actual hostilities against the U.S. at Pearl Harbor several hours previously.

The most important diplomatic decisions of World War II were made in personal conferences by the chief executives of the anti-Axis powers. The meetings included those between Prime Minister Winston Churchill and President Franklin D. Roosevelt in mid-

Atlantic in 1941; and in 1943, between Roosevelt, Churchill and Generalissimo Chiang Kai-shek at Cairo, Egypt; and between Roosevelt, Churchill and Generalissimo Stalin at Teheran, Iran.

During World War II, emphasis was renewed on the traditional function of diplomacy of influencing foreign opinion. During the war, as many as forty belligerent nations, many of them represented by governments-in-exile with no formal relations with the U.S., maintained offices in the United States to distribute propaganda. At the conclusion of the European phase of World War II, the creation of the United Nations at San Francisco in 1945 revived aspirations toward a new diplomacy serving the ends of international justice. By 1947, most members of the United Nations had conceded diplomatic privileges to its secretary-general and his principal assistants.

For 300 years, until recent times, the language of diplomacy has been exclusively French. English, however, is now increasingly used as a common language between nations, and in the United Nations, French, English, and Russian are the three official languages of debate.

DIPLOMATIC AGENTS, in the widest sense, all the officers to whom the intercourse of the states with foreign powers is committed. As thus employed, the expression would include the foreign minister, or secretary of state for foreign affairs, and, in the United States, the Senate in the exercise of its constitutional function of approving treaties with foreign states, as well as the regular and occasional representatives of the government abroad. More properly, however, it has reference only to the latter class of officials, who, under instructions from the home government, carry on its intercourse with the nations to which they are accredited. For many centuries the diplomatic intercourse of states was carried on by occasional embassies, appointed for a particular purpose, and not until the 15th century were permanent and continuous diplomatic relations instituted by the establishment of resident embassies. By far the greater part of the international intercourse of the modern world is conducted through these regular diplomatic channels, though occasional embassies are still employed for special occasions, principally of a ceremonial character; and the foreign office, or department of state, of one government may, on occasion, communicate its views directly, by circular or otherwise, to the corresponding office of foreign states. The management of diplomatic intercourse in Europe has generally passed from the men of exceptional gifts or exceptional influence, selected at random for the service, to a professional class of trained diplomatic servants.

Formerly the term "ambassador" was applied to all accredited diplomatic agents, and it is sometimes still employed, interchangeably with "minister", as a general term to describe such agents of whatever rank. But the title is now strictly appropriate for only the highest class of diplomatic representatives. The process of classification began before the close of the 17th century, but did not receive international recognition until the beginning of the 19th century. In 1815 the eight principal powers represented at the Congress of Vienna agreed upon a gradation of diplomatic agents, who were thenceforth to rank as follows: (1) ambassadors, legates, and papal nuncios; (2) envoys, ministers, and others accredited to the sovereign; (3) chargés d'affaires accredited to the department of foreign affairs. At the Congress of Aix-la-Chapelle a further distinction was made between ministers plenipotentiary, who were accorded the second place, and ministers resident, who became an intermediate class between ministers of the second order and chargés d'affaires.

The United States long refused to recognize the classification of the European powers, and accredited all of its principal diplomatic agents as ministers plenipotentiary, i.e., ministers of full power and authority. In 1893, however, the President was authorized by act of Congress to appoint ambassadors of full rank and of equal grade and dignity with those which should be accredited by foreign powers to this country. In the United States there is no trained, professional diplomatic class. However, a distinction may be made between "career diplomats" and those who, without previous experience as envoys, have been appointed to important diplomatic posts. In recent years, the number of career diplomats in higher diplomatic posts has increased, and by 1948 comprised a majority of the 42 ambassadors and 15 ministers representing the United States in foreign countries.

In addition to the regular diplomatic representatives, a state may also employ agents of inferior rank who have a certain qualified diplomatic status, as officers in command of armed forces in foreign territory or commanders of ships of war. All of these enjoy some of the privileges and immunities which attach to the exercise of the diplomatic office. The distinction of the ambassadorial office, as the direct representative of a sovereign power, and the importance of the duties entrusted to it have combined to invest it with a peculiar sanctity. This has, in modern times, taken on the form of a privileged status attended with certain immunities, which a foreign minister enjoys in the country to which he is accredited. These may be briefly enumerated as follows: (1) exemption of the minister and a qualified exemption of his family from the local jurisdiction, both civil and criminal; (2) inviolability of his house, papers, and goods from search and seizure; (3) exemption of his personal effects from imposts and taxation; and (4) liberty of worship. These immunities are referred to the principle of extraterritoriality (q.v.).

DIPLOMATICS. See PALEOGRAPHY.

DIPLOPODA. See MYRIAPODA.

DIP, MAGNETIC. See MAGNETISM, TERRESTRIAL.

DIPNOI, a subclass or order of fishes, the lungfishes, which are characterized by the possession of air-breathing lungs as well as gills. The air bladder or lung of the Dipnoi opens into the esophagus and is filled with air which the fish swallows. The lungfishes live in marshes and seasonal streams and some species bury themselves for long periods in the mud in the bottom of dried-up brooks and rivers. The Dipnoi are often classified as an order of the Crossopterygii (q.v.), and, from the evolutionary point of view, may have been the ancestors of the amphibians. Members of the order were plentiful in earlier geological ages, but only three genera are extant today: *Ceradotus, Protopterus* (qq.v.), and *Lepidosiren.*

DIPPER, a small, gray, thrushlike bird, *Cinclus mexicanus,* of the family Cinclidae, inhabiting North America. It is sometimes called ouzel or water ouzel. It has short wings, a short, stout bill, and a very small tail. It frequents clear, pebbly streams and lakes, feeding chiefly on mollusks and aquatic insects. The dipper usually builds a domed nest of interwoven moss on a bank of a stream, and sometimes near or under a cascade. It is capable of diving under water, and moving about under the surface by means of its legs and wings. The name dipper is also given to several unrelated birds that are excellent divers, especially the blatherskite and the grebe (qq.v.).

DIPPER, in astronomy. See URSA MAJOR; URSA MINOR.

DIPPING NEEDLE, an instrument composed of a magnetized bar or needle like a compass

American Museum of Natural History
The extinct diprotodon

needle, suspended from its center of gravity and free to move in a vertical plane. The dipping needle is used to determine the inclination of the earth's magnetic field and to map it; see MAGNETISM, TERRESTRIAL. The line joining the points on the earth's surface where the dipping needle shows no inclination is called the aclinic line or the magnetic equator.

DIPROTODON, a genus of extinct, giant marsupials of the suborder Diprotodontia, related to the kangaroos. Fossils of these animals occur in Australia among Pleistocene deposits. Like the kangaroos, they lived on plants, but unlike them, they used all four legs for walking. The skull of the diprotodon is heavy and about three feet long; the entire animal is about the size of a rhinoceros. The only known species of this genus is *D.australis.* A related genus, *Nototherium,* bones of which are often found with those of the diprotodon, was also a giant marsupial. See MARSUPIAL.

DIPSACACEAE, a family of herbs, the Teasel family, in the order Rubiales. They have whorled or opposite leaves, and flowers in dense heads. Among the genera, most of which are found in temperate countries, are *Scabiosa* (q.v.) and *Dipsacus* (see TEASEL).

DIPSOMANIA. See ALCOHOLISM; INTOXICATION.

DIPSOSAURUS, a genus of small iguanid lizard. Only one species is known, *D. dorsalis,* commonly called the desert iguana, or keelbacked lizard, which inhabits the Colorado and Mohave deserts. It is herbivorous, and feeds exclusively on buds and flowers.

DIPTERA, one of the largest orders of insects, containing approximately 50,000 known species, including mosquitoes, midges, gnats (qq.v.), and true flies. Most species have a single pair of wings, but some are wingless. Members of the order are characterized by the possession of sucking, and sometimes piercing, mouth parts. Back of the wings most species are equipped with a pair of vestigial wings called halteres, which take the form of small stalks with knobs on their ends. Recent research has shown that the halteres are vibrated back and forth with great rapidity when the insect is in flight and by their motion act as stabilizers. All species of diptera undergo complete metamorphosis. The eggs of many species of diptera are known as nits, while the larvae are called maggots, bots, or wrigglers. The life habits of the various species of diptera vary widely. Some feed on nectar, some are scavengers, and some are bloodsuckers. Others live as internal or external parasites, while still others prey on other insects. See FLY.

DIR, a khanate of the North-West Frontier Province, Pakistan, situated to the N.E. of Swat. It commands the route between Chitral and Peshawar. Pop. (1951 est.) 148,000.

DIRAC, PAUL ADRIEN MAURICE (1902–), English mathematician and theoretical physicist, born at Bristol, and educated at Bristol and Cambridge universities. In 1932 he was appointed professor of mathematics at Cambridge University. In 1930 he was made a Fellow of the Royal Society, and in 1933 he shared the Nobel Prize in physics with Erwin Schrödinger. Dirac is well known for his researches in atomic structure and in quantum mechanics, and particularly for his development of the theory of the positron (q.v.). During World War II he conducted theoretical investigations of chain reactions. A member of the Institute for Advanced Studies in 1934–35, in 1946, and in 1947–48, he was invited to return in 1954, but because of delays in obtaining a visa his trip to the United States was postponed until 1955. His writings include *Principles of Quantum Mechanics* (1930).

DIRECTION FINDER. See RADIO AIDS TO NAVIGATION.

DIRECTORY, or (Fr.) DIRECTOIRE, the executive branch of the republican government established in France in 1795, in accordance with the constitution promulgated by the Convention (see CONVENTION, NATIONAL). The Directory, consisting of five members elected by both houses of the legislature, was in power from October, 1795, to November, 1799. In rotation, each of the

directors held the presidency for a three-month interval, and one director was replaced each year. As a result of incompetence and corruption within the Directory, the finances of the government became so strained that a proclamation of bankruptcy was issued early in 1796. The Directory thereupon sought to restore financial security by means of military conquest abroad, and appointed Napoleon Bonaparte (q.v.) to the command of its armies in Italy. He subsequently won a series of victories which augmented his own power and prestige, while the Directory itself was waning in influence at home. In 1799, military reverses abroad and an increasing number of counterrevolutionary uprisings at home combined to weaken the power of the Directory so greatly that, on November 9, Napoleon was able to seize power with little opposition. This action, which brought the Directory to an end, is known as the "coup d'état of the 18th Brumaire", the date according to the republican calendar proclaimed in 1792. See FRENCH REVOLUTION.

DIRECT PRIMARIES. See PRIMARY ELECTIONS.

DIRE DAWA, a city in E. central Ethiopia situated on the Franco-Ethiopian Railway, about midway between Addis Ababa, the Ethiopian capital, and the port of Djibouti, French Somaliland. Dire Dawa is the second-largest city of Ethiopia, and is a trade center. Pop. (1951 est.) 30,000.

DIRIGIBLE BALLOONS. See AIRSHIP.

DIRT BED, a deeply buried layer of soil, usually containing partially decayed twigs and leaves. One of the best-known dirt beds is a layer of argillaceous sands in the Jurassic rocks of southern England. Fossil remains of nearly thirty species of marsupials, including insectivorous, herbivorous, and carnivorous types, have been uncovered at Dorsetshire from these dirt beds. With them were found remains of fishes, crocodiles, and turtles. In the U.S., dirt beds exist in glacial deposits in the Mississippi basin.

DIS. See PLUTO (deity).

DISABILITY, in law, incapability of performing an act or of exercising a right, resulting from a lack of legal competence. Disabilities are classified in several ways, as *general*, when relating to incapacity to perform all legal acts of a certain class, and *specific*, when relating only to a single act; as *physical*, when resulting from physical or mental injuries or illnesses, and as *civil* or *legal*, when resulting from legal disqualifications. In the United States, minors and insane persons are said to be under general disability in that they have no legal capacity to make valid contracts, or enter into any other legal obligations; citizens under twenty-one years of age, in most States, are under specific disability of being ineligible to vote; and foreign-born citizens are legally ineligible for the Presidency, under the specific provisions of the Constitution of the United States. See WORKMEN'S COMPENSATION.

DISARMAMENT, the reduction and limitation of national military establishments either voluntarily through international agreement, or by compulsion as a result of conquest and subsequent peace terms. In recent history, conferences concerned with disarmament have treated it in three categories: as limitation of naval armament; limitation of land armament; and control over specific war weapons, such as military aircraft (see AIRPLANE; AIRSHIP), poison gas (see GAS WARFARE), and guided missiles (q.v.). In addition, some agreements have provided for the destruction of military fortifications on strategic territory, as, for example, the demilitarization of the United States-Canada frontier as a result of the Rush-Bagot Treaty of 1817.

The imposition of disarmament upon defeated powers by their conquerors has been a peace-treaty condition from ancient through modern history. It dates, in recorded history, as far back as the treaty which ended the Second Punic War, between Rome and Carthage, in 201 B.C. In modern times such disarmament was required by the *Articles séparés* (1808), following the Treaty of Tilsit (q.v.), by which Napoleon I compelled Prince William of Prussia to reduce his army to 42,000 men for a ten-year period and prohibited a militia.

The drastic disarmament of Germany after World War I by the Treaty of Versailles (q.v.) is one of the outstanding examples of compulsory disarmament. By the terms of the treaty, the size of the German army was fixed at 100,000 men and conscription was prohibited. The manufacture of munitions in Germany was very closely restricted and their export and import forbidden. The German general staff was abolished and the German navy was reduced. Maintenance of submarines and military aircraft was forbidden, and aircraft on hand at the time of the surrender were destroyed by order of the Allied powers.

There were, however, loopholes in the disarmament clauses. The treaty did not specifically mention military expenditures; by 1928, Germany was spending 7690 marks on each of 100,000 soldiers in contrast with 2313 marks spent on each of the 842,000 men in service in 1913. Educational and athletic organizations were forbidden to be militaristic; nevertheless, German youths were given military training in such organizations as, for example, the glider clubs with which Germany developed the science of glider warfare. German battleships were restricted in size, but German naval architects designed a class of pocket battleships, such as the *Deutschland*, launched in 1931, which were more powerful than ships of conventional size. Moreover, the treaty provided for a permanent inter-allied control commission to be stationed in Germany as surety that the disarmament conditions were fulfilled. German resentment resulted in the removal of the control commission in 1927 and its replacement by temporary committees which were supposed to examine German armament when so required by any member of the League of Nations. From that time on, inspection was almost nonexistent.

The results of voluntary disarmament have been equally unsuccessful. International disarmament provisions as a necessary condition for future peace were incorporated into treaties as long ago as the Treaty of Paris (1763), which ended the Seven Years' War (q.v.). The government of France tried unsuccessfully to initiate international disarmament conferences in 1831 and 1863. In 1899, Czar Nicholas II of Russia invited all nations with representatives accredited to his court to participate in discussions at The Hague, Netherlands, of a proposal to limit armaments at their levels of that year. The objections of Germany at the Hague Conference (q.v.), prevented formal compacts, though several resolutions in favor of disarmament were passed.

Several disarmament conferences were held in the period between the two World Wars, in the attempt to achieve mutual disarmament among nations. In 1921, influenced by public demand for disarmament, the United States invited Great Britain, France, Italy, and Japan to discuss, among other subjects, the reduction of their naval armament. The conference in Washington, D.C. (see WASHINGTON CONFERENCE) resulted in a treaty, signed in 1922, by which seventy capital ships were scrapped, including thirty belonging to the United States. The terms of the treaty also provided that, after 1931 (later amended to 1936), capital ships might be replaced according to a specified tonnage ratio allocated among the five nations.

The Washington conference was only partially successful. After the treaty took effect in 1923, the signatory nations began to compete in building vessels of 10,000 tons or less, which were not limited by the treaty. The building rivalry was so intense that the five principals met again in 1930, in London, to limit auxiliary war vessels and amend the Washington agreement. Italy, however, demanded parity with France and, when France refused, both nations withdrew. The other three powers limited their tonnages of cruisers, destroyers, and submarines. A clause authorizing construction by the signatories in excess of treaty limits, in case the navies of France or Italy should imperil their security, was inserted in the London Treaty.

Affirmations of their intent to reduce their military establishments and to keep peace were made by the signatories of the Locarno (q.v.) Pact and the Kellogg-Briand Pact (q.v.). In 1925 the League of Nations appointed a commission which, after a series of disagreements, finished the draft of a general disarmament treaty in 1930. The draft provided for limitation of military personnel, military aircraft, and total military expenditure; and for the acceptance of the naval limitations of the London treaty of 1930. However, even before the conference began, the various governments filed reservations to all the important provisions of the draft treaty.

The world was beginning to rearm when the first general disarmament conference was called to order at Geneva in 1932. Objections to the draft of the treaty were made almost immediately, notably by France, which refused to disarm unless guaranteed security, and by Germany, which demanded equality in armament with the other nations. No agreement was reached and, in 1933, Germany withdrew from the conference and resigned from the League of Nations. After several adjournments and reconvenings, and in the face of steadily increasing rearmament, the conference reached a deadlock and adjourned for the last time in 1934. At the end of the same year, representatives of the great naval powers met in London to discuss extension of the Washington naval treaty, which was to expire in 1936, and the London treaty of 1930. So many irreconcilable points of view were represented that this conference ended in failure except for minor agreements, and the limiting clauses of the 1922 and 1930 agreements were discontinued. By 1936, naval appropriations were, as a whole, larger than at any time since World War I. All talk of disarmament was abandoned and the great powers among the nations began an armament race which reached its climax in World War II.

Since the end of World War II, the United Nations has been empowered by its charter to plan for the reduction and regulation of armaments. The use of new weapons during the war, and atomic energy in particular, added complications beyond those of any previous disarmament proposals (see ATOMIC ENERGY AND ATOMIC BOMB: *Control of Atomic Energy*). In December, 1946, the General Assembly unanimously approved a resolution giving the Security Council responsibility for drawing a plan which, in addition to reducing armed forces, was to establish control over atomic energy and set up inspection and control agencies (referred to as an international police force) not subject to the veto.

The resolution was accepted by the Security Council and, in February, 1947, a Commission for Conventional Armaments was established to prepare the working plan for the limitation of armaments and armed forces, except for any matters related to atomic energy. In subsequent years the formulation of such a plan was repeatedly blocked by disagreements between the Western powers and the Soviet Union, mainly over the problem of integrating the regulation of atomic and conventional armaments. Compromise proposals were introduced in the General Assembly in 1951–52 with the aim of achieving this end; see UNITED NATIONS: *Regulation and Reduction of Armaments*. See also LEAGUE OF NATIONS; MILITARY PROGRESS; NAVAL TREATIES.

DISCHARGE, MILITARY, in the armed forces, a document presented to each soldier, sailor, and marine, on his leaving the service. Enlisted men cannot be discharged from the service until they have completed their terms of enlistment, except by order of the President, sentence of a general court-martial, certificate of disability, or writ of habeas corpus. However, enlistments may occasionally be terminated prematurely either "at own convenience" or "at convenience of the government".

The armed forces of the United States issue several kinds of discharges. The honorable discharge is most frequently issued, and is presented to those soldiers whose service records are good or excellent. The general discharge, a type of honorable discharge, is given to those whose records include offenses of a minor nature. Undesirable discharges are given to those who have demonstrated unfitness or misconduct while in the service. Discharges without honor, or bad conduct discharges, which may operate to deprive the recipient of some civil rights, are given only by an approved sentence of a summary or general court-martial and for more serious offenses. Dishonorable discharge is given only by an approved sentence of a general court-martial to those who commit grave crimes such as mutiny, desertion, murder, and rape; it is similar in effect to conviction for a felony, depriving the recipient of many civil rights.

DISCIPLES OF CHRIST, or CHRISTIANS, an American Protestant sect. Members of this body are often referred to colloquially as "Campbellites", an allusion to the founders of the sect, Thomas Campbell (1763-1854) and his son Alexander Campbell (q.v.), who had been Presbyterian ministers until their preachments incurred the censure of the church authorities. In 1809 Thomas Campbell issued his *Declaration and Address,* on the principles of which the new movement was founded one year later. In this document he declared that all true Christians should adhere to a single church, that the New Testament sufficed as a basis for Christian faith and behavior, and that the addition of creeds and formulations of faith was superfluous. In 1823 his son developed this view further in a periodical called *The Christian Baptist,* asserting that the new movement was aimed not at the organization of a new sect but at a return of all Christians to the tenets of the Gospel. The followers of the Campbells joined in 1832 with the followers of Barton Warren Stone, a former Presbyterian minister whose preachments were similar and who referred to his followers simply as "Christians".

The Church of the Disciples of Christ has grown rapidly in membership and scope of operations since its early days. In 1953 it claimed a world membership of nearly 2,000,-000 adherents worshiping in about 9000 churches, most of which were located in the United States and Canada. The Disciples maintain homes for children and for the aged, hospitals, and institutions of higher learning. In addition they carry on missionary work through mission schools located chiefly in the Far East, Africa, and South America. National headquarters of the Disciples are in Indianapolis, Ind.

The Discobolus (copy of the statue by Myron)

DISCIPLINE, CHURCH or **ECCLESIASTICAL.** See CHURCH DISCIPLINE.

DISCOBOLUS, in Greek antiquity, a term meaning a discus thrower. In Greek sculpture, the term *Discobolus* was applied specifically to a bronze statue, reputedly by the Greek sculptor Myron (q.v.), of a man in the act of throwing a discus. Of the lost original statue, three copies exist today, one in the Vatican Museum, Rome; one in the British Museum, London; and one in the Palazzo Lancelotti, Rome, considered the best.

DISCORD. See DISSONANCE.

DISCOUNT (Lat. *dis,* "away from"; *computare,* "to count"), in commerce, a deduction from the price of a commodity. Discounts are usually made in consideration of payment on delivery of merchandise, or of payment within a specified time limit. Special discounts given to purchasers of large quantities of merchandise are called quantity discounts. Trade discounts are given to wholesalers and other trade groups to cover the cost of performing specific functions, such as warehousing and merchandising.

In the United States, the Robinson-Patman Act of 1936, amending the anti-monopoly Clayton Act (q.v.) of 1914, makes unlawful in interstate trade special discriminatory discounts given to some purchasers and not to others. The principal objective of this provision is to protect smaller concerns from price discrimination in favor of their larger competitors.

In finance, discounts are premiums or considerations given on the purchase of promissory notes, bills of exchange, or other forms of negotiable commercial paper in advance of their maturity dates. Such discounts comprise deductions from the face value of the discounted paper and are made at the time of purchase. The principal agencies engaged in discounting commercial paper are commercial banks and, in a few countries, financial institutions which specialize in that practice. When discounted paper is again put into circulation by a bank or discount house and is discounted again, it is said to be rediscounted.

As the holders of discounted bills and notes, at the time they fall due, receive the full face value of the commercial paper they present for payment, the practice of discounting bills and notes, is in effect, a means of extending credit in the form of loans, and the discounts are regarded as advance collections of interest on the loans. Rates for discounting and rediscounting commercial paper are established by commercial banks and discount houses in accordance with the relative demand for and supply of funds. In countries in which the banking system is organized on a centralized basis (see BANK AND BANKING), discount and rediscount rates are determined in large part by the central banks; in the United States, these rates are established in part by the Federal Reserve Banks.

DISCRIMINATION, in common law, an improper distinction made in serving patrons by one engaged in a public or common calling, such as a common carrier. It is the legal duty of everyone engaged in such a calling to serve all persons in the order in which they present themselves. Further than this, however, the common-law duty does not extend.

Under the common law, a common carrier is not permitted to transport one man's goods in preference to those of another, but is not forbidden to carry for favored individuals at an unreasonably low rate, or even gratis. The earliest statute on this subject is the act of the British Parliament known as the Railway Clauses Consolidation Act of 1845. Its main purpose was to prohibit a common carrier from charging more to one person for the carriage of freight than it charged at the same time to others for the same kind of service. This legislation has served as a model for various Federal and State statutes in the United States. The most important legislation on the matter is that known as the Interstate Commerce Act (q.v.), enacted in 1887 and subsequently amended. Under its provisions, common carriers are required to make just and reasonable charges for transportation and are forbidden to exercise undue and unreasonable preferences or discrimination. The Interstate Commerce Commission has charge of the enforcement of the provisions of this act.

The enactment of the Robinson-Patman Act in 1936 by Congress was another step taken to eliminate discrimination in commerce. Under its provisions, no seller of commodities in interstate commerce is permitted to discriminate in price between different purchasers of goods of like grade and quality, where such goods are sold for use, consumption, or resale within the United States or any of its territorial possessions.

Recently, various States have enacted considerable legislation to combat discrimination in the field of civil rights. Many States have broadened and codified the rules against discrimination and have extended them considerably. In New York, as in a number of other States, a Civil Rights Law has been in existence for a number of years. This law prohibits discrimination of any kind against any person in any place of public accommodation, resort, or amusement, because of race, creed, or color. Many States also have enacted laws making it unlawful for any employer to discriminate against any applicant for a job, otherwise qualified, because of race, creed or color.

Similar legislation has been passed making it unlawful for an employment agency to inquire as to the race, creed, or color of any applicant for a prospective job, and prohibiting the dissemination of advertisements by hotels and resorts in which discriminatory references are made as to the type of patronage solicited. Recently, also in New York State, legislation has been enacted prohibiting colleges and other institutions of higher learning from discriminating against applicants for admission because of racial or religious reasons.

DISCUS THROWING, an athletic sport, in which the individual competing athletes hurl a disk-shaped object called a discus, of specified weight and dimensions, to the greatest possible distance from a fixed mark. This sport was one of the five contests comprising the pentathlon in the Olympic games of the ancient Greeks. The discus used by them was a circular piece of stone or metal about 8 or 9 inches in diameter and weighing from 4 to 5 pounds. The Greek *discobolus* (q.v.), or

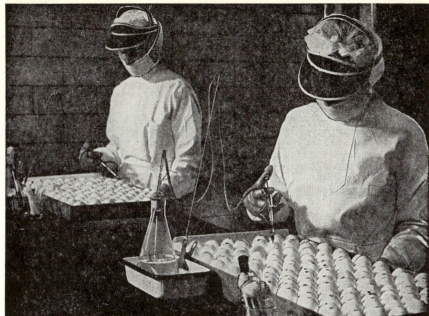

E. R. Squibb & Sons

TREATMENT OF DISEASE

*Above: In modern laboratory, chicken eggs
are inoculated with the virus of influenza
to produce influenza antitoxin.*
*Right: In the 13th century, St. Louis of
France treating a sick man. Little was then
understood concerning the causes of disease.*

thrower, employed a rigidly stylized technique.
The sport was generally neglected from ancient
times until the late 19th century. In 1896 it
was revived, when the Olympic games were
reinstituted, and since then it has flourished
all over the world. The modern discus consists of a circular wooden frame rimmed by a
metal band, with small brass plates set into
the center of the frame to assure an accurate
weight of at least 4 pounds, 6.4 ounces. Throwing technique has lost its original rigidity of
style. Since its 19th-century revival it has improved greatly, as evidenced by the fact that,
whereas the 1896 Olympic record was only 95
feet 7.5 inches, in 1949 a world's record was
set by Fortune Gordien (U.S.A.) at 186 feet,
11 inches.

DISEASE, a departure from the normal
state of well-being of a plant or animal organism. It is characterized by malfunction of the
vital processes, accompanied by marked symptoms and definite physical signs. It may be

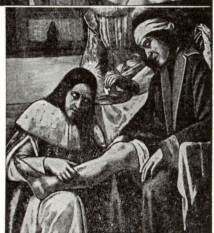

caused by the invasion of the body by macro-
scopic or microscopic parasites, by deficiencies
in nutrition, by congenital deficiencies, or by
damage caused by foreign matter or harmful
radiation.

In primitive societies, disease was often regarded as a visitation of the supernatural, an
affliction either sent by a divinity or invoked
by witchcraft. In such societies, medicine men
and witch doctors learned the rudiments of
therapeutics by rough experiment and, in par-

ticular cases, often made discoveries in advance of civilized medicine; as, for example, the finding of the antimalarial properties of cinchona bark and quinine, and the palliative astringent properties of "toad venom", or ephedrine. Hippocrates, in the 5th century B.C., was the first to recognize that disease is governed by natural laws. He regarded disease as disorder of the four humors (q.v.), or vital fluids, of the body. In the 2nd century B.C., Asclepiades taught that the internal pores or passageways of the body controlled the flow of the humors, and that their malfunction, interfering with the humoral flow, could be cured by a system of physical exercise resembling athletic training. The study of physiology and its application to the study and cure of disease began with Galen (about 2nd century A.D.). He regarded the elements of the living body as hot, cold, wet, and dry, and by an ingenious attribution of the same elemental principles to the character of drugs, made some progress in the development of an empirical pharmacology. Little further progress was made until the 16th century, when Paracelsus identified the characteristics of diseases by various "signatures", and in assigning similar signatures to chemical agents, instituted the first rude beginnings of chemotherapy. A few years later, the studies of Vesalius in anatomy laid the foundations of modern pathology.

During the next two centuries the study of disease changed from abstract philosophizing to a careful observation of symptoms and of the effects of disease in the human organism. Knowledge of physiology advanced greatly, and its lessons were extended to pathology. William Harvey discovered the circulation of the blood and opened the way to the study of diseases of the circulatory system; Edward Jenner discovered the connection between smallpox and cowpox and, by introducing the process of vaccination, laid the foundations of serum and vaccine therapy and of immunization.

In the 19th century, the discoveries of Charles Darwin removed the last barriers to the consideration of disease as having application to the entire animal kingdom, and opened the way to the study of human diseases by observation of their effects on laboratory animals. About the same time numerous investigators established the connection of microorganisms with the causation of disease; their work, culminating in the discoveries of Louis Pasteur and Robert Koch, laid the foundation of the germ theory of disease. Koch formulated four postulates for the identification of a specific microorganism as the cause of a disease: the organism must be recovered from the lesions of the disease; it must be cultivated in pure culture; inoculation with the pure culture in a healthy animal or human being must produce the typical form of the disease; and the organism must be recovered from the lesions of the disease so produced.

In the early years of the 20th century, application of the germ theory disclosed many of the causative organisms of common diseases, including bacteria, protozoa, and filtrable viruses (qq.v.), and led to the discovery of methods of prevention and cure. The infectious diseases were identified and combated by quarantine, prophylaxis, and antisepsis; carriers, such as the rodent fleas responsible for the spread of bubonic plague and typhus, were found and attacked, as were intermediate hosts, such as the mosquitoes harboring malaria and yellow fever. Not all diseases, however, were found to be caused by microorganisms. Hereditary deficiencies cause diseases such as hemophilia (see BLOOD) and certain forms of heart disease, and deficiencies in diet cause a group of disorders known as deficiency diseases. With the decline of the germ diseases in morbidity and mortality (respectively, disease rate and death rate in a population; see VITAL STATISTICS), the neoplastic diseases (see CANCER) rose in relative frequency to be second only to diseases of the heart and circulatory system; diseases of unknown etiology, such as epilepsy (q.v.), and degenerative diseases (see GERIATRICS), also became more prominent. After World War II, and the development of atomic power and new radioactive isotopes, diseases caused by exposure to hard radiation, before then caused only by excessive exposure to radium and X-rays, became increasingly important.

In general, diseases are classified as functional and organic. In organic diseases, pathological changes or lesions are evident in the organ affected. In functional diseases, no pathological change is to be found in the organ giving rise to the symptoms. This classification is somewhat vague. Diabetes, for example, which was once thought to be a functional disease of the kidney, was later found to be an organic disease of the pancreas, and reclassified. Some medical authorities maintain that all so-called functional diseases are reflex reactions to organic diseases in distant organs; others contend that true functional diseases exist, especially those of psychosomatic origin (see PSYCHOSOMATIC DISEASES).

For study and specialization, however, diseases are classified according to the organ or system of organs affected; as, for example, diseases of the eye, of the circulatory system, of the gastro-intestinal system, of the genito-urinary system, of the brain and central nervous system, or of the endocrine glands.

See ANTIBIOTIC; CORTISONE; DISEASES OF ANIMALS; DISEASES OF PLANTS; INFECTIOUS DISEASES; MEDICINE; NEOPLASMA; OCCUPATIONAL DISEASES; PATHOLOGY. See also separate articles on specific diseases, such as: ARTHRITIS; INFANTILE PARALYSIS; PSITTACOSIS; TUBERCULOSIS; UNDULANT FEVER; and articles on diseases of the various organs, such as: EYE, DISEASES OF THE; HEART, DISEASES OF THE. For mental diseases, see PSYCHOLOGY, ABNORMAL. See also ENDEMIC DISEASES.

DISEASED MEAT. See BOTULISM; PTOMAINES; PYEMIA.

DISEASES OF ANIMALS, maladies of any description which affect animals, particularly farm and domestic animals such as cattle, horses, poultry, and dogs. Animal diseases can be subdivided into six groups: (1) bacterial diseases, (2) virus diseases, (3) diseases caused by internal parasites, (4) diseases caused by external parasites, (5) nutritional diseases, and (6) poisonings.

Common bacterial infections of animals include anthrax, which attacks cattle, horses, sheep, and goats, and to a lesser extent dogs, cats, birds, and men. Tuberculosis is another common animal disease, particularly in cattle. Brucellosis, infection with several varieties of *Brucella*, causes so-called contagious abortion of cattle and hogs and undulant fever in man. Johne's disease, the paratuberculosis of cattle, results from infection by a bacillus. Pullorum disease of chickens, caused by a germ which forms a toxin, is a serious source of loss to U.S. poultrymen. Other bacterial diseases of animals include glanders, bovine mastitis, swine erysipelas, tularemia, blackleg, and the shipping fever of cattle.

One of the most serious of the virus diseases of animals is equine encephalomyelitis, or sleeping sickness, frequently fatal to both horses and men. Cattle plague, or rinderpest, and foot-and-mouth disease, both of which are caused by viruses, are among the most destructive of cattle diseases on a world-wide scale, but have been largely kept out of the U.S. by quarantine. Virus diseases of hogs include swine influenza and hog cholera. (The infective agents of cholera in other animals and in man are bacteria.) Hog cholera has caused losses as high as $65 million in the U.S.

in a single year. Other common virus diseases of animals include rabies and psittacosis, both of which can be transmitted to man.

All animals are susceptible to attack by internal parasites, which include both one-celled microscopic protozoa and various worms. Dourine in horses, coccidiosis in fowl, and Texas fever or cattle tick fever in cattle are all caused by protozoan infestation. Various types of flukes, tapeworms, and Nematodes, a group known scientifically as helminths, are found in the intestines and other internal organs of domestic animals. Many types of birds, mammals, and even fish are subject to malaria (of types different from those which attack man), but domestic animals are not commonly affected by malaria.

A common disease that attacks cattle, horses, dogs, and swine is mange, which is caused by several varieties of microscopic mites that live in the animals' skins and cause swellings, loss of hair, and lesions. Among the most troublesome of several flies which attack livestock is the botfly, which, in its larval form, burrows in the mucous membranes of the nose, throat, stomach, and intestines of equines. The maggot of the heel fly, often called the cattle grub, burrows deeply into many parts of the bodies of cattle. The annual U.S. loss from cattle grubs has been estimated as high as $100,-000,000. Ticks, lice, and fleas are also common external parasites found on a number of domestic animals which cause much damage.

In recent years it has been discovered that animals suffer from a number of forms of deficiency diseases, including those caused by lack of minerals in the diet and those caused by lack of vitamins. Rickets caused by vitamin-D deficiency is found in cattle, poultry, and other animals. The milk fever of cattle is characterized by a deficiency of calcium, although the exact cause of the disease is not known. Phosphorus deficiency in cows and other farm animals can often be detected when the beasts chew on bones and other organic material in an effort to supplement their regular diet. Deficiencies of salt, iodine, or sulfur, or of manganese or other trace elements in animals' diets can also cause sickness.

In all parts of the United States there are a number of native plants that are toxic when eaten by domestic animals. Among those which cause the largest losses of livestock are the larkspurs, crotalaria, the chokecherry, locoweed, some types of milkweed, and horsebrush. Selenium, which is found in the soil in some parts of the Middle West, is sometimes absorbed by animals through herbage on which they graze. Selenium poisoning causes loss of hair, lameness due to foot lesions, and the halting of hoof growth.

The causes of several additional diseases which attack animals are unknown. Among these diseases are the periodic ophthalmia, or periodic blindness, of horses; and avian leukosis, which causes paralysis, anemia, and bone deformities in poultry.

The annual loss from all forms of animal diseases in the U.S. amounts to approximately $500,000,000. The diseases of animals represent a public-health problem as well as an economic one, since a number of these diseases can be transmitted from animals to men. Among the diseases so transmitted, in addition to those mentioned in this article, are tuberculosis and trichinosis.

See separate articles on many of the diseases mentioned. See also DOG, DISEASES OF; VETERINARY MEDICINE.

DISEASES OF PLANTS, deviations from the normal growth and development of plants caused by unfavorable environmental conditions or by the attack of viruses or parasites. Primary injuries by insects or higher animals are not regarded as plant diseases.

A large number of plant diseases are caused by the large protein molecules known as viruses. They include the mosaic diseases, which attack many varieties of plants, causing a regular pattern of yellow spots to appear on the leaves. Tobacco and bean plants are particularly subject to mosaic disease. Viruses also cause some types of chlorosis, a disease of green plants characterized by a reduction of the amount of chlorophyll in the leaves or by total absence of chlorophyll. Peach yellows, causing the premature ripening of peaches, is a virus disease, as is little peach, a disease delaying ripening of the fruit. Leaf roll in potatoes is also caused by a virus. Virus diseases of plants are infectious and may be transmitted by contact, by insects, or by infected seeds. For this reason sterilization of hands and tools, disposal of diseased plant material, and disinfection of seed are necessary precautions in avoiding the spread of such diseases.

Plants are subject to attack by parasites of several different kinds, all of which cause disease. Parasitic bacteria are responsible for the disease of fire blight which affects apple and other fruit trees, and roses and other ornamental shrubs. Plants suffering from fire blight look as though their twigs had been scorched or burned. One form of bean blight (which particularly affects kidney beans), cucumber wilt, gladiolus scab, and the soft rot of irises are also caused by bacteria. Crown gall is a bacterial disease. Another type of parasite is typified by the slime molds or myxomycetes (q.v.) which cause club root in cabbage and powdery scab in potatoes.

The majority of plant diseases result from parasitic infestation by various fungi. Damping-off, stem rot, grape mildew, leaf spot, and a number of other wilts, blights, and cankers are caused by fungi. Large bracket fungi attach themselves to trees and bring on rotting of both sapwood and heartwood. Other fungus diseases include wheat rot, smuts, rusts, mildews, and anthracnose (q.v.).

Nematodes of the order Telogonia (threadworms) are also parasitic on plants, causing certain typical diseases. One species enters the bulbs of such plants as narcissus, phlox, and hyacinth, and causes dwarfing of the foliage when the plant grows. Another nematode is parasitic on more than 500 species of plants, producing irregular root knots or galls, which sap the vitality of the growing plant. Yet another nematode enters the leaves of such greenhouse plants as chrysanthemums and begonias, killing the foliage.

Among the strangest disease-causing parasites are certain of the higher plants which feed on other plants, producing disease or death. These parasites include the dodder and the mistletoe (qq.v.).

Plant diseases caused by environmental factors are often called physiological diseases. Deficiencies of food elements in the soil are responsible for one group of these diseases. Lack of nitrogen produces yellowing and stunting of plants, and lack of iron or magnesium will result in chlorosis. The disease called sand drown of tobacco is also caused by magnesium deficiency. Other trace-element (q.v.) deficiencies also have adverse effects. An excess of food material in the soil may also cause disease. If the soil is oversupplied with nitrogen, plants will grow lushly, but the quality of their fruit will be impaired and they may lack the hardiness to withstand the cold of winter. Excess soil acidity will also produce disease symptoms in most plants, although certain plants such as rhododendrons and huckleberries require acid soils for best growth. Drought, excess water, excess of lime or acidity, high and low temperatures, industrial gas, and smoke are also responsible for physiological diseases of plants.

For diseases of specific plants, see articles on the plants in question.

DISLOCATION, in medicine, the displacement of the bones making a joint. A partial

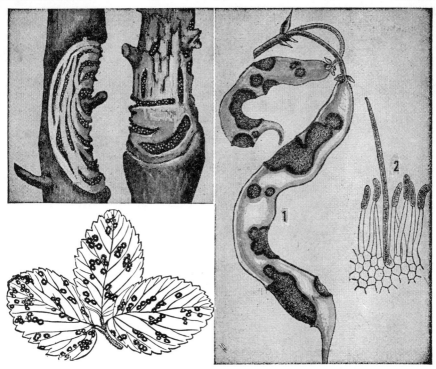

DISEASES OF PLANTS. *Left: Top, European apple-tree canker; bottom, strawberry leaf spot. Right: 1, French bean canker; 2, fungus causing the disease (much enlarged).*

or incomplete dislocation is called a subluxation. It is possible to dislocate almost any articulated joint in the human skeleton, but certain dislocations, such as those of the jaw, knee, shoulder, and finger bones, are more frequent than others. The ease of dislocation from a wrench or twist depends on the shape of the bones involved and on the amount of strength in the ligaments which hold the joints in place. Dislocations of the wrist and the ankle are comparatively rare, since the wrist joint is held firmly in place by ligaments, and the shape of the bones of the ankle make displacement difficult. These joints are, however, subject to sprain (q.v.) or strain. The treatment for all types of dislocation is to move the bones back into proper relation with each other, a process known as reduction. Dislocations should be reduced as quickly as possible to avoid immobility of the joint or other permanent harm. The contraction of muscles sometimes makes reduction difficult unless the patient is anesthetized.

DISMAL SWAMP, a marshy region of S.E. Virginia and N.E. North Carolina, extending from about 7 miles S.W. of Portsmouth, Va., to the vicinity of Albermarle Sound, and covering an area of 750 sq.m. Through it runs the Dismal Swamp Canal, 22 m. long, connecting Chesapeake Bay with Albermarle Sound. Lake Drummond, 7 m. long, in the midst of the swamp, is the setting of "The Lake of the Dismal Swamp" by the Irish poet Thomas Moore. A large part of the swamp is heavily timbered and noted for hunting and fishing. The Dismal Swamp is of historical interest as a former part of the Virginian estate of George Washington.

DISNEY, WALT(ER E.) (1901–   ), American cartoonist and producer of animated motion-picture cartoons, born in Chicago, and educated at the Chicago Academy of Fine Arts. In 1923 he established, in Hollywood, Calif., the Disney Studio for the production of motion pictures. His first venture in this new enterprise was *Alice in Cartoonland,* a film which combined the movements of a living

Walt Disney Productions
Walt Disney

actress with those of animated cartoon figures. Disney followed this experiment with *Oswald the Rabbit* (1926), his first animated cartoon without living actors. In 1928 he began to produce *Mickey Mouse* and *Silly Symphony* cartoons in sound. Several of the animal characters created for the Mickey Mouse series, particularly Donald Duck and the dog Pluto, became the subjects of other Disney comedies. In 1938 Disney produced his first full-length animated film, *Snow White and the Seven Dwarfs.* His other full-length films include *Pinocchio* (1940), *Fantasia* (1940), *Bambi* (1942), *The Three Caballeros* (1944), *Make Mine Music* (1946), *Melody Time* (1948), *Cinderella* (1950), *Peter Pan* (1953), and *The Vanishing Prairie* (1954). He produced a series of films specifically for television in 1954.

DISORDERLY CONDUCT, in criminal law, behavior tending to disturb the peace or shock public morality. Disorderly conduct is made an offense only by statute or ordinance. At common law there was no offense known as "disorderly conduct", although misconduct constituting a public nuisance was indictable. The term is now used mainly in municipal ordinances to describe certain minor offenses below the grade of misdemeanors. It is applied generally to the use of abusive language in public, causing a crowd to collect in a public thoroughfare, and to similar offenses which tend to create a breach of the peace. The punishments for disorderly conduct are usually small fines, or small jail sentences, or in some cases both.

DISPENSATION, in Christian ecclesiastical law, release by competent authority from ob-

servance of a law. It differs from absolution in that it not only permits an otherwise illegal act, but validates its consequences. The power to grant dispensations was based on St. Peter's authorization by Christ to bind and loose (Matt. 16). Until claimed as an exclusive pontifical prerogative by Pope Innocent III, dispensation was also practiced as a matter of right by the lower dignitaries of the hierarchy, including especially the bishops. Thereafter, it was exercised by the lower dignitaries only by virtue of the power delegated to them and within the limits which were defined by the popes.

In the Middle Ages, when the church had vast temporal power and the jurisdiction of the ecclesiastical courts (q.v.) extended to virtually all social relationships in a number of countries, the right to grant dispensation had great significance. After the Reformation most social relationships were regulated by the secular state, and ecclesiastical dispensations declined in importance. Today, in the Roman Catholic Church, dispensations are granted principally in connection with such matters as religious vows and marriages with noncommunicants, in specific cases, and in matters of fasting and abstinence. In the Protestant Church dispensations are virtually obsolete, but survive in a few relatively insignificant connections, as in England, where the Anglican Church may grant a clergyman permission to hold two benefices simultaneously, and exempt affianced couples from publishing banns prior to marriage.

DISPERSAL, in botany, a term applied to the scattering of seeds, pollen, and spores by wind, water, and animals. This scattering assures the growth of new plants in a favorable environment, often far from the parent plant. Some of the methods of dispersal are based upon fundamental aerodynamical and mechanical principles. For example, the maple-tree fruit has two wings which spin the fruit as it falls, carrying it far from the mother tree. The hard seeds of some fruit, such as cherries, may pass through the digestive tracts of animals which eat them, and into the earth with excretion. Coconut palms have multiplied in many regions from seeds carried from their native lands by ocean currents. The seeds of many other plants have appendages adapted to the efficient dispersal of seeds. See Coco De Mer; Maple; Seed.

DISRAELI, Benjamin, 1st Earl of Beaconsfield (1804–81), British statesman and novelist, born in London, and educated at private schools at Blackheath and Walthamstow. He was the son of Isaac D'Israeli (q.v.), a wealthy Jewish man of letters who, in 1817, had his children baptized in the Church of England. From the age of seventeen to twenty, Benjamin Disraeli was apprenticed to the law in a London office. During the same period he speculated in stocks and suffered heavy financial losses. Primarily in order to pay off his debts, he began writing novels, the first of which, Vivian Grey, appeared with some success in 1826. He continued to write novels in a fanciful, romantic vein, and frequented fashionable salons and dressed in an eccentric, foppish manner. In 1830 he traveled in Spain, the Balkans, Turkey, and the Levant. On his return he decided to enter politics, and from 1832 to 1835

stood unsuccessfully for Parliament, first as a Radical, and three times as a Tory.

Despite these defeats he won a reputation through a series of pamphlets, tracts, and letters to *The Times* of London, in which he set forth the foundation of his conservative philosophy. At the elections held when Queen Victoria came to the throne in 1837, he finally won a seat in the House of Commons but, at his maiden speech, nearly ruined his career because his extravagant phraseology and eccentric garb provoked derisive laughter from his fellow members. He slowly won a reputation in Parliament, but was refused a cabinet post in 1841 in Sir Robert Peel's Conservative ministry. Disraeli labored to win support for a policy which championed factory workers against the rich Whig

American Museum of Natural History

POLLEN AND SEED DISPERSAL. *Left, top: Bee carrying apple pollen from flower to flower. Left, bottom: Tree fruits dispersed by wind. 1, maple; 2, linden; 3, elm; 4, ailanthus; 5, black locust; 6, ash. Right: Hairy cat-tail seeds are also borne by the wind.*

Benjamin Disraeli

manufacturers, and which regarded the Crown, the aristocracy, and the church as the custodians of civil liberties. His novels *Coningsby, or the Younger Generation* (1844) and *Sybil, or the Two Nations* (1845), expressing his views, increased his prestige in Parliament, especially with the "Young England" group. When Peel was engaged in the effort to repeal the Corn Laws (q.v.) in 1846, Disraeli's eloquent attacks on his party's chief won him leadership of the Tory protectionists, but the divided Conservative Party lost power until 1852. During this period, in 1847, Disraeli supported the Liberal prime minister Lord John Russell when Russell's government lifted the ban excluding adherents of the Jewish faith from Parliament. In 1852 Disraeli became chancellor of the exchequer under the Earl of Derby and held the same office in the succeeding Derby ministries of 1858–59 and 1866–68.

As leader of his party in the House of Commons in 1859, Disraeli introduced but failed to carry a reform bill extending the franchise, but later succeeded in getting passed the much more democratic Reform Act of 1867. When Lord Derby retired the next year, Disraeli became prime minister, but his government was defeated in 1868 and he spent six years in bitter Parliamentary opposition to Prime Minister William Ewart Gladstone. After the elections of 1874 he was able to form a strong majority government backed by the partisan sympathy of Queen Victoria, of whom he became an intimate

friend. His prime ministership was marked by many notable events. He promoted legislation against Roman Catholic tendencies in Church of England ritual in 1874. In 1875 he took personal responsibility for borrowing £4,000,000 to purchase for the government the shares in the Suez Canal owned by the Khedive of Egypt. He further emphasized his "imperial" policy by creating for Queen Victoria in 1876 the title of "Empress of India", the title of emperor being retained by succeeding British monarchs until 1948. He became Earl of Beaconsfield in 1876. His most spectacular triumph came in 1878 at the Congress of Berlin (q.v.), which redrew the boundaries of eastern Europe after the defeat of Turkey in the Russo-Turkish War of 1877–78. During the war Disraeli had been concerned with preventing Russia from gaining strategic advantages across Britain's lifeline to the East and had sent the British fleet to the Dardanelles, in February, 1878. As British plenipotentiary at the Congress of Berlin, he contrived by brilliant diplomatic maneuvering to deprive Russia of many of the advantages of victory, and returned to England claiming to have won "peace with honor". His government fell in 1880 and he spent the remaining year of his life in writing and furthering his conservative political philosophy. The Primrose League, so called after Disraeli's favorite flower and dedicated to his political ideas, was founded in 1883. Its members pledged themselves to the "maintenance of religion, of the estates of the realm, and the imperial ascendancy of Great Britain". The League survived into the 20th century largely as a female auxiliary of the Conservative party.

Disraeli's writings include *Vindication of the British Constitution* (1835), and the novels *The Young Duke* (1831), *Henrietta Temple* (1837), *Venetia* (1837), *Tancred, or the New Crusade* (1847), *Lothair* (1870), and *Endymion* (1880).

D'ISRAELI or **DISRAELI,** ISAAC (1766–1848), English author, born at Enfield. He was the son of Benjamin D'Israeli, a Jewish refugee who came to England from Venice in 1748, and who amassed a fortune as a merchant. Benjamin D'Israeli planned a business career for his son, but was persuaded to allow Isaac to follow literary and scholarly pursuits. Isaac spent the remainder of his life in quiet study. He wrote several novels, but his popularity as a writer was due mainly to such books of research and criticism as *Curiosities of Literature* (6 vols., 1791–1834), which in spite of its inaccuracy contains many interesting literary and historical anecdotes. In 1802 he married Maria Basevi, and had four sons, one of whom was Benjamin Disraeli (q.v.), later Earl of Beaconsfield. In 1817 Isaac D'Israeli and his children were baptized in the Anglican Church. His writings include *Calamities of Authors* (1812–13), *Quarrels of Authors* (1814), *Genius of Judaism* (1833), and *Amenities of Literature* (3 vols., 1841).

DISSECTION. See ANATOMY.

DISSOCIATION, in chemistry, the breaking up of compounds into simpler constituents, especially under the influence of heat and pressure. The term is usually applied only to those reactions which are reversible; that is, to those reactions in which the final products are capable of reforming the original substance by changing the equilibrium of the reaction. Dissociation therefore differs from decomposition (q.v.) for in decomposition no implications as to the behavior of the final products are assumed.

By heating phosphorus pentachloride in a glass vessel, its dissociation into phosphorus trichloride and chlorine gas can be readily observed, because of the green color of the chlorine:

$$PCl_5 = PCl_3 + Cl_2$$

Even more striking is the dissociation of nitrogen tetroxide, N_2O_4, which is a faintly colored gas, into the brownish-red oxide of nitrogen, NO_2, by the application of heat:

$$N_2O_4 = 2NO_2$$

In the case of both phosphorus pentachloride and nitrogen tetroxide, lowering of the temperature causes a recombination of the products of dissociation into their original forms, and a consequent disappearance of the colors. The extent to which a compound may be dissociated is strongly influenced by the temperature of the reaction, and by the pressure exerted upon the reactants. In the case of nitrogen tetroxide, the application of a moderate degree of heat causes only a small fraction of the original amount to change; but as the temperature is raised, the dissociation fraction increases. This is plainly shown by the darkening of the gas. Increased pressure causes the dissociation fraction to diminish, as is indicated by the gradual disappearance of the color. Careful experiments, carried out at a temperature of 50° C., have shown that at that temperature, nitrogen tetroxide is almost completely dissociated if the pressure is very low; when subjected to a pressure of about 500 millimeters of mercury, only half of the tetroxide is changed. See also ELECTROLYTIC DISSOCIATION.

DISSONANCE, in music, a combination of tones which strikes the ear harshly; in particular, two tones which when struck together seem to repulse each other and to produce upon the ear the effect of two distinct sounds rather than a single blended sound. The term "discord" is often used synonymously with "dissonance", but a distinction exists between the two. "Discord" is the more general term, denoting any harsh or jarring combination of sounds that cannot be analyzed musically. The term "dissonance" is applied to definite musical intervals (q.v.), such as the intervals of the major second and the major seventh and all augmented or diminished intervals which leave the ear unsatisfied when they are struck, and, to satisfy the ear, must be harmonically resolved (see HARMONY) into a combination of tones known as a "consonance". A discord may contain a number of dissonances; a dissonance cannot contain a discord.

DISTEMPER, an acute and dangerous disease of dogs, analogous to influenza in human beings. In general it attacks animals between two months and one year old, although it sometimes occurs in older dogs. The disease frequently ends in death, and even when the victim recovers from distemper, chorea and other nervous diseases often follow.

The primary cause of distemper is a filtrable virus (q.v.), but often the disease is complicated by secondary bacterial infections. Distemper is extremely contagious and it is believed that the infecting virus is transmitted by air-borne water droplets inhaled by the animal. The first symptoms of the disease are a rise in temperature, shivering, sneezing, lassitude, and discharges from the mouth and nose. As the attack continues there may be pneumonia, convulsions, chorea, and paralysis. The course of distemper is normally about four weeks, if the animal lives, and in the later stages the victim may be extremely weak.

Two forms of inoculation have been used successfully both for immunization against distemper and for its treatment. In one, vaccine is administered, followed by a dose of living virus; in the other, antidistemper serum is employed in place of vaccine. Immunization by either method is usually performed after the puppy is three months old, as earlier inoculation may not produce complete immunity. The treatment given a dog suffering from distemper usually consists of inoculations of antidistemper serum and careful nursing. The sick dog should be kept warm, dry, and quiet, and should be fed small amounts of such easily digested foods as milk, raw eggs, and beef broth. During convalescence, overeating and overexercise should be avoided.

As the result of the discovery in 1954 of several new strains of the distemper virus authorities claim that the vaccine must be modified periodically to include the viral types currently infecting dogs.

DISTILLATION, the process of heating a liquid until its more volatile constituents pass into the vapor phase, and then cooling the vapor to recover such constituents as a liquid. The first change is known as vaporization and the second as condensation. In industrial and laboratory practice, distillation differs from evaporation and from drying only in that the vapor is condensed. In all three cases the purpose of the operation is to separate a mixture of several components by taking advantage of their different volatilities. In evaporation and in drying, the object is to obtain the less volatile constituent, and the more volatile constituent (usually water) is discarded; in distillation on the other hand, the principal object of the operation is to obtain the more volatile constituent in pure form. For example, the removal of water from glycerin (by vaporizing the water) is called evaporation, but the removal of water from alcohol (by vaporizing the alcohol) is called distillation, although similar apparatus is employed in both cases.

When the difference in volatility (and hence in boiling point) between the two constituents is great, complete separation may be easily accomplished by a single distillation. For example, sea water, which contains about 4% of dissolved solids (principally common salt), may be readily purified by vaporizing the water, condensing the steam thus formed, and collecting the product, distilled water. This product is, for most purposes, equivalent to pure water, although actually it contains some impurities in the form of dissolved gases, the most important of which is carbon dioxide.

When the boiling points of the constituents of a mixture differ only slightly, complete separation cannot be achieved in a single distillation. An important example is the separation of water, which boils at 212° F. (100° C.), and alcohol, which boils at 173° F. (78.5° C.). If a mixture of these two liquids is boiled, the vapor which rises is richer in alcohol and poorer in water than the liquid from which it came, but it is not pure alcohol. If one desires to concentrate a 10% solution of alcohol (such as might be obtained by fermentation) to ob-

tain a 50% solution (a common strength for whiskey), it is necessary to redistill the distillate once or twice, and if industrial (95%) alcohol is desired, many redistillations are required.

Fractional Distillation. If a portion of the distillate is returned from the condenser and made to drip down through a long tower onto a series of plates, and if the vapor as it rises on its way to the condenser is made to bubble through this liquid at each plate, the vapor and liquid will interact so that some of the water in the vapor condenses and some of the alcohol in the liquid vaporizes. The interaction at each plate is thus equivalent to a redistillation, and by building a tower with a sufficient number of plates, 95% alcohol can be obtained in a single operation. Moreover, by "feeding" (inserting) the original 10% alcohol solution gradually at a point in the middle of the column, virtually all of the alcohol may be stripped from the water as it descends to the lowest plate, so that no alcohol need be wasted.

This process is known as rectification, fractionation, or fractional distillation, and is very common in industrial usage, not only for simple mixtures of two components, such as alcohol and water in fermentation products or oxygen and nitrogen in liquid air, but for highly complex mixtures, such as those found in coal tar and petroleum. The type of tower most frequently used is a "bubble tower", in which the plates are arranged horizontally a few inches apart and the ascending vapors are forced to rise through bubble caps in each plate and then bubble through the liquid. The plates are baffled so that the liquid flows from left to right on one plate, then overflows onto the plate below, and there flows from right to left. If the interaction between liquid and vapor is incomplete, or if frothing and entrainment occur so that some of the liquid is carried up by the vapor to the plate above, five actual plates might be required to do the work of four theoretical plates (four redistillations). An inexpensive equivalent of a bubble tower is a "packed column" in which the liquid flows down over a packing of earthenware rings or bits of glass tubing.

The only disadvantage of fractional distillation is that a fraction (which may be about one half) of the condensed distillate must be *refluxed,* that is, returned to the top of the tower and eventually boiled over again, and more heat must therefore be supplied. On the other hand, the continuous operation made

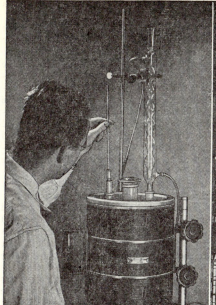

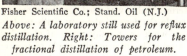

Fisher Scientific Co.; Stand. Oil (N.J.)

Above: A laboratory still used for reflux distillation. Right: Towers for the fractional distillation of petroleum.

possible by fractionation allows great heating economies, for the outgoing distillate may be used to preheat the incoming feed.

When the mixture consists of many components, they are drawn off at different points along the tower. Industrial distillation towers for petroleum often have over 100 plates, with as many as ten different fractions being drawn off at suitable points. Although it is not possible, starting with a mixture as complex as petroleum, to obtain pure components with a tower of practical size, the fractions produced, such as kerosene and gasoline, are pure enough for practical purposes. Towers with more than 500 plates have been used for the separation of isotopes (q.v.) by distillation.

Theory of Distillation. In the simplest mixture of two mutually soluble liquids, the volatility of each is undisturbed by the presence of the other. In such a case, the boiling point of a 50–50 mixture, for example, would be half way between the boiling points of the pure substances, and the degree of separation produced by a single distillation would depend only on the vapor pressure (that is, on the volatility) of the separate components at this temperature; see BOILING; BOILING POINT.

This simple relationship was first stated by the French chemist F. M. Raoult (1830–1901) and is called Raoult's law. Raoult's law holds only for mixtures of liquids which are very similar in chemical structure, such as benzene and toluene. In most cases wide deviations occur from this law, and these deviations must be determined experimentally. Thus, the volatility of alcohol in dilute aqueous solution is several times as great as predicted by Raoult's law. In extremely concentrated alcohol solutions, the deviation is even more striking: the distillation of 99% alcohol produces vapor which has *less* than 99% alcohol. For this reason, alcohol cannot be concentrated by distillation beyond 97%, even by an infinite number of distillations; see ALCOHOL.

When one component is only slightly soluble in the other, its volatility is abnormally increased. For example, fusel oil (amyl alcohol), a common impurity in freshly fermented alcohol, is slightly soluble in water, and is normally less volatile than water. However, in aqueous solution it is extremely volatile. For this reason it rises above the lowest plates of an alcohol distillation tower, but condenses at the level where fairly pure alcohol is being formed. It thus collects near the middle of the tower, and may be drawn off in comparatively pure form for further purification as a valuable by-product.

Steam Distillation. When two insoluble liquids are heated, each is unaffected by the presence of the other (so long as they are agitated so that the lighter does not form an impenetrable layer over the heavier), and vaporizes to an extent determined only by its own volatility. Such a mixture, therefore, always boils at a temperature lower than that of either constituent, and the percentage of each constituent in the vapor depends only on its vapor pressure at this temperature. This principle may be applied to distill, at temperatures below their normal boiling points, substances which would be damaged by overheating if distilled in the usual fashion. For example, the normal boiling point of pure aniline is about 184° C. (363° F.), and of impure aniline somewhat higher. However, a mixture of water and aniline boils at 98° C. (208° F.), and the vapor rising from this mixture contains about one aniline molecule to every fifteen water molecules, or about one third aniline by weight. It is thus possible to purify aniline by distillation at a low temperature simply by blowing steam through it.

Vacuum Distillation. Another method of distilling substances at temperatures below their normal boiling points is by partially evacuating the still. Thus aniline may be distilled at 100° C. by removing 93% of the air from the still. This method is as effective as steam distillation, but somewhat more expensive. The greater the degree of vacuum, the lower is the distillation temperature. When the distillation is carried on in a practically perfect vacuum, the process is called *molecular distillation.* This process, which is now regularly used industrially for the purification of vitamins and certain other unstable products, was perfected during World War II. The substance is placed on a plate in an evacuated space, and heated. The condenser is a cold plate, placed as close to the first as possible. Most of the material passes directly across the space between the two plates, and very little is lost.

Sublimation. When a solid substance is distilled, passing directly into the vapor phase and back into the solid state without a liquid being formed at any time, the process is called sublimation. Sublimation does not differ from distillation in any important respect, except that special care must be taken to prevent the solid from clogging the apparatus. Rectifica-

tion of such materials is impossible. Iodine is regularly purified by sublimation.

Destructive Distillation. When a substance is heated to a high temperature to decompose it into several valuable products, and these products are separated by fractionation in the same operation, the process is called destructive distillation. The only important applications of this process are the destructive distillation of coal for coke, tar, gas, and ammonia, and the destructive distillation of wood for charcoal, acetic acid, acetone, and wood alcohol. The latter process has been largely displaced by synthetic processes for making the various by-products. The cracking of petroleum is essentially identical with destructive distillation, though not usually so called.

Stills. Technically, the term *still* is applied only to the vessel in which liquids are boiled during distillation, but the term is sometimes applied to the entire apparatus, including the fractionating column, the condenser, and the receiver in which the distillate is collected. The term still is also extended to cover apparatus for destructive distillation or cracking. The term retort is sometimes used for a still, and the term alembic was used for the same apparatus in the days of alchemy. Stills for laboratory work are usually made of glass, but industrial stills are generally made of iron or steel. Where iron would contaminate the product, copper is often employed, and small stills for the production of whiskey are frequently made of glass and copper.

DISTILLED LIQUORS, beverages of high alcoholic content, produced by distillation, formerly called ardent spirits or aqua vitae (q.v.). They may be made from other beverages of lower alcoholic content, such as brandy from wine or applejack from hard cider, or from fermented mixtures originally containing large proportions of carbohydrates, such as rum from molasses or whiskey from grain mash. The earliest alcoholic beverages were products of simple fermentation which, at most, yields about 12% alcohol. The first mention of distillation on record was made by Abul Kasim, an Arabian physician, in the 10th century. At first only wine was distilled, but soon afterward other fermented products were employed. The process of distillation not only concentrates the alcohol, but also removes a large portion of the unpleasant-tasting impurities from the beverage. If rectification (purification by repeated or by fractional distillation) is carried too far, however, all of the flavoring elements are removed with the impurities, and pure alcohol is produced. Consequently, in the distillation of potable liquors, the process is only partially completed, and the remaining impurities are removed by filtration of the liquors through charcoal and by aging in charred wooden barrels. During aging, the impurities, which consist mostly of a mixture of higher alcohols, are in part oxidized to acids which react with the remaining alcohols to form pleasantly flavored esters. The amount of flavoring material remaining in the finished beverage is less than one half of one percent; the remainder consists of water, and alcohol ranging from 80 proof for mild whiskies to 150 proof or more for strong brandies and rums. Many cordials and liqueurs (q.v.) are made by distilling mixtures of alcohol and flavoring agents. See ABSINTHE; ALCOHOL; BRANDY; DISTILLATION; FERMENTATION; LIQUORS, FERMENTED AND DISTILLED; RUM; WHISKEY.

DISTILLED WATER. See DISTILLATION.

DISTOMUM. See FLUKE.

DISTRIBUTION, in economics, a term applied to two different, but related, processes: the division among the members of society, as individuals, of the national income and wealth; and the apportionment of the value of the output of goods among the factors or agents of production, namely, labor, land, capital (qq.v.), and management. The division or apportionment of this value takes the form of monetary payments, consisting of wages and salaries, rent, interest (qq.v.), and profit. Wages and salaries are paid to workers; rent is paid for the use of land and certain kinds of physical objects; interest is paid for the use of capital; and profit is realized by the owners of business enterprises as a reward for risk-taking; see NATIONAL INCOME.

Recipients of these payments do not receive equal parts of the total. The formulation of the economic laws governing the division of the total of these payments into their various forms and relative portions constitutes the central problem of economic theory in the sphere of distribution.

Economists have not agreed in formulating these economic laws. Different schools of economists have defined them differently at various times; see ECONOMICS. A large body of authoritative opinion maintains that inequalities in income result, in great part, from the operation of the law of demand and supply; see SUPPLY AND DEMAND. In this view, for example, an overproduction of cotton will result, through a consequent fall in the price of cotton, in a decrease in the income of cotton growers; and it will also tend to result in an increase in the real income, or purchasing power, of the purchasers of cotton, who can buy it more cheaply than would otherwise be possible. Similarly, when capital is abundant and the demand for it is low, interest rates tend to fall; as a result, the relative share of the national income of creditors tends to decrease, while that of borrowers tends to rise. Variations in the relative share of the national income of workers are also explained in terms of the operation of the law of demand and supply: when labor is plentiful, wage rates tend to fall; when labor is scarce, as in wartime, wages tend to rise. And, finally, inequalities in income among workers are explained by the relative abundance or scarcity of their skills: skilled workers, less numerous than unskilled workers, receive higher wage rates; and workers with rare skills are paid at a higher rate than workers with skills found in abundance.

Economists recognize, however, that the distribution of the national income is influenced by a number of factors in addition to the operation of demand and supply. These factors include the practice of some monopolies and cartels of creating artificial scarcities and fixing prices, collective bargaining by unions and management, and social-reform legislation such as social-security and minimum-wage and maximum-hour laws. Such factors tend to increase the income of one group or another above the level it would reach through the unimpeded operation of the law of demand and supply. Taxation is also an important factor affecting income distribution.

In commerce, distribution refers to the physical movement of commodities into the channels of trade and industry.

DISTRIBUTION OF ANIMALS. See GEOGRAPHICAL DISTRIBUTION OF ANIMALS.

DISTRIBUTION OF PLANTS. See GEOGRAPHICAL DISTRIBUTION OF PLANTS.

DISTRIBUTIVE LAW, a basic law in arithmetic and algebra, symbolized by the following relationship:

$$a(b + c + d) = ab + ac + ad$$

This law states that the multiplication of a compound term (an arithmetic sum of any number of single terms) by a simple multiplier is equal to the arithmetic sum of the terms formed by multiplying the simple multiplier by each of the terms of the compound term. The signs of each of the terms formed are subject to the normal sign laws of multiplication (q.v.) and addition.

DISTRIBUTOR. See AUTOMOBILE: *Ignition,*

DISTRICT ATTORNEY, in the legal system of the United States, the public prosecuting officer within a defined district. In some States, he is called county attorney or state's attorney. The office of district attorney is one of great importance in the administration of the criminal law, including the investigation of charges of crime, the gathering of evidence against alleged criminals, the submission of criminal charges to the grand jury, and the drawing of indictments, as well as the supervision of the several stages of the criminal prosecution and the actual trial of the accused.

As jurisdiction over crimes is divided in the United States, between the Federal and State courts, the Federal government has one set of district attorneys, and each State has an entirely different set for the same territory. The former are appointed by the President and are deputies of the Attorney General of the United States, to whom they are required to make report of their official acts. They are appointed for the several judicial districts into which the United States is divided, and are charged with prosecuting offenses against the Federal government as well as with conducting government civil actions.

In most of the States, a district attorney is elected in each county. His most important duties are discharged in prosecuting criminals in the State courts, but he also serves as the prosecuting officer in the county court of the county in which he was elected. In some States, he is subject to the control of the Attorney General.

Under the common law, the prosecution of criminal offenses was left to the initiative of the persons injured or other private persons representing them, and in England it was not until 1879 that the state undertook that duty in any effective or systematic way. By act of Parliament in that year, and in 1882, a new department was created under a director of public prosecutions, with functions and powers like those of the district attorney in the United States. See CRIME; CRIMINAL PROCEDURE.

DISTRICT OF COLUMBIA, the Federal District of the United States, coextensive with the City of Washington (q.v.), the National Capital. It is situated about 30 miles s.w. of the center of Baltimore, Md., on the E. bank of the Potomac R. The river separates the District from Virginia. The District of Columbia forms an enclave in the State of Maryland, and is rectangular in shape, its one irregular side being that along the Potomac. Its greatest width, measured along the s.E. boundary, is about 9 m. The length of the

N.E. boundary is approximately 10 m. Except for a number of swampy areas contiguous to the river, the terrain is hilly and gently rolling, with an extreme elevation of about 420 feet above sea level. The Anacostia R., a tributary of the Potomac, traverses the southeastern portion of the district. Rock Creek, a smaller tributary of the Potomac, flows across the N. central portion. Area of the District, 69.2 sq.m., including about 8 sq.m. of water surface; population (1950) 802,178.

The District of Columbia contains, in addition to the urban areas surrounding the Capitol, numerous suburban communities. Georgetown, the most important suburb, is the site of Georgetown University (q.v.), one of several outstanding institutions of higher learning in the District. Prominent among others are George Washington University, Catholic University of America, Howard University, and American University (qq.v.). The District has a free public-school system, with separate schools for Negro and white children. Attendance throughout a full school year is compulsory for all children between the ages of seven and sixteen. Public schools in the district number about 160. In 1952–53 these schools had an enrollment of about 90,000 students, of whom approximately 34,000 were junior and senior high school students.

The District of Columbia is the seat of the Federal government, and the carrying on of the work of a multitude of governmental departments and agencies is the chief activity of the District. The principal industries are the production of goods and services for local or Federal government consumption. Transit facilities of the District include a network of motorbus and trolley-car systems. The District has three modern airports, and is serviced by a number of railway systems, including the Baltimore and Ohio, the Pennsylvania, and the Chesapeake and Ohio.

By the terms of Article I of the Constitution of the United States, executive and legislative authority in the District of Columbia is vested in the Congress of the United States. The denial, implicit in this provision, of the franchise, of a voice in the local government, and of representation in Congress to permanent residents of the District was deliberate on the part of the Founding Fathers, who sought thereby to establish safeguards against the development of undue local influence in Federal affairs. However, the initial Congressional legislation dealing with local government, the charter (1802) that incorporated the City of Washington, author-

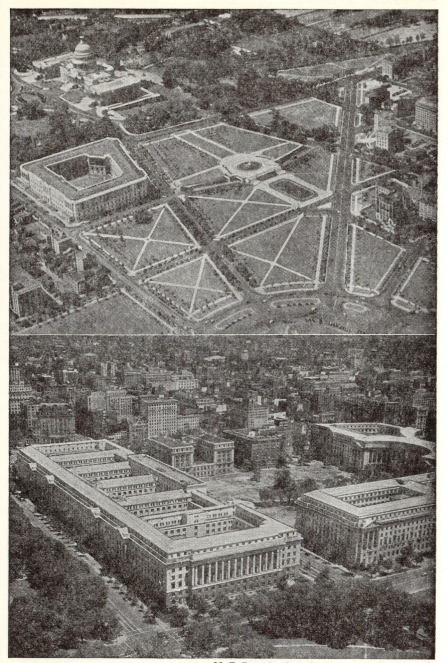

M. E. Browning from Gendreau, N.Y.; Pix-Weinstein
IN WASHINGTON, DISTRICT OF COLUMBIA
Top: Avenues and parks at Union Station plaza. The Capitol is shown at upper left.
Bottom: Government buildings seen from top of Washington Monument, looking northeast.

Screen Traveler from Gendreau

Cherry blossoms blooming in the spring outline Washington Monument in Washington, D.C.

ized a city council, elected by the residents. Congress subsequently extended popular control in the District; for example, in 1871 it granted the voters representation in the House of Representatives.

The present form of government of the District of Columbia was established by Congressional legislation adopted in 1878. By the terms of this enactment, which in effect abolished the right of suffrage in the District, the District of Columbia became a municipal corporation, the administrative control of which was vested in three commissioners appointed by the President of the United States for three-year terms. Two of these commissioners, all of whom must be approved by the Senate, must be civilians; the third must be an officer, with the grade of captain or higher, of the Corps of Engineers of the U.S. Army. Although the Board of Commissioners controls the police, fire, health, and a number of other departments of the District, it has, in general, less authority than that vested in the governing authorities of large American cities. The board, for example, cannot levy taxes on real estate and personal property in the District or collect license fees. Local taxes are levied by Congress and are payable directly to the U.S. Treasury Department. Income from taxation is usually sufficient to defray from 78 to 82% of local expenses; the balance is appropriated by Congress. The judicial system of the District consists of a municipal court, a police court, a juvenile court, a small claims court, a district court of the United States, and a United States court of appeals.

The territory now comprising the District of Columbia was ceded to the government of the United States by the State of Maryland in 1788. In the following year, the State of Virginia ceded another tract, consisting of about 30¾ sq.m. on the w. side of the Potomac, making the site of the projected district a square, 10 m. on a side. A legislative enactment, adopted by Congress in 1790, authorized President George Washington to appoint three commissioners charged with making necessary surveys, purchasing lands from private owners, and providing public buildings. In 1791, Congress adopted another bill, approving the ceded territory as the permanent seat of government of the United States. The enclave, first known as the Territory of Columbia, contained only two municipal corporations, the towns of Georgetown and Alexandria. In 1846, Alexandria and the remainder of the territory on the w. side of the Potomac were returned, by an act of Congress, to the State of Virginia. Georgetown retained its status as a separate municipal corporation within the District until 1871, when it was merged with Washington and a Territorial form of government for the entire District was adopted. Three years later, the present form of government was adopted on a temporary basis, and was permanently established by Congress in 1878.

DITHYRAMB, in ancient Greece, originally an orgiastic hymn sung in honor of the god of wine Dionysus by revelers attired as satyrs, as they danced about his altar to the accompaniment of music on an aulos or flute. Later, the dithyramb was composed in honor of other gods, including Apollo and Athena, and sung at festivals in their honor. At Athens there were annual contests at the Greater Dionysia, Lesser Dionysia, Panathenæa, Thargelia, and Lenæa (see GREEK FESTIVALS) between choruses of singers of dithyrambs from the various Greek tribes. In the earliest period (6th century B.C.), the prize for the best performance was an ox; in the 5th century B.C. and later, a tripod. The subject of the dithyramb was the birth and life of the god celebrated. About 600 B.C. the Lesbian poet Arion wrote dithyrambs of a tragic rather than a laudatory nature; and about 536 B.C., the Greek poet Thespis (fl. 6th century B.C.) wrote dithyrambs to be sung by a chorus and a leader, and also introduced passages to be sung by one person alone; out of this practice the Greek tragedy reputedly arose (see DRAMA: *Greek Drama*). After the development of tragedy, the dithyramb was still composed independently by important poets, including Bacchylides and Pindar (qq.v.); only fragments of the dithyrambs written by these poets have been preserved. In modern times, the term "dithyramb", by extension, serves to designate poetry of a wild, impassioned nature, and also speeches delivered in an ardent and unrestrained manner.

DITMARS, RAYMOND LEE (1876–1942), American naturalist, born in Newark, N.J., and educated at the Barnard Military Academy, New York City. After serving for five years as assistant curator of entomology at the American Museum of Natural History, he was appointed curator of reptiles at the New York Zoological Park in 1899, and curator of mammals in 1910. He was a corresponding member of the Zoological Society of London, and a fellow of the New York Zoological Society. During his lifetime he was considered the world's outstanding herpetologist. He wrote *The Reptile Book* (1907), *Strange Animals I Have Known* (1931), *Reptiles of North America* (1936), *Book of Living Reptiles* (1936), and *Making of a Scientist* (1937).

DIVER, the name given to several water-birds, especially the black-throated loon, the grebe, and the blatherskite (qq.v.). They are remarkable for their great skill in diving and swimming. Many hunters assert that these birds, after seeing the flash of a rifle, can dive before the shot reaches them.

DIVER'S DISEASE. See BENDS.

DIVIDEND, in corporation law, a fund appropriated out of the profits of a corporation and distributed among its stockholders; also the share of the fund received by a stockholder. Dividends are usually declared periodically—quarterly, semianually, or annually—by the corporation's directors. The action of a board of directors with respect to the declaration or nondeclaration of dividends is usually final and conclusive upon the stockholders and is only subject to review by the courts in the event that the action is willful, arbitrary, or capricious.

Dividends are distributed on a proportional basis; the fractional share of the total dividend received by a stockholder is equal to the proportional share of the company's stock owned by him. Holders of the preferred stock of a company have generally a prior right to the payment of dividends over holders of common stock, and, if their stock so provides, are paid at a fixed periodic rate; see STOCK. Preferred dividends may be cumulative or noncumulative: cumulative dividends are dividends which, if not paid for one or more periods, constitute charges on the profits of succeeding periods, and must be paid at a future date before dividends may be distributed on common stock; noncumulative dividends, if omitted, do not constitute charges on future profits. Dividends may take the form of additional shares of stock or of the right to purchase stock for a fixed sum per share; such dividends are called stock dividends.

The term dividend is also applied to the assets of a bankrupt or insolvent business which are distributed among its creditors during the course of its liquidation. The term is also used in insurance to signify the sum appropriated out of profits for distribution among policy holders whose policies so provide; such dividends may be applied to the reduction of a premium coming due.

DIVINATION, the practice of attempting to acquire hidden knowledge and insight into events, past, present, and future, through the direct or indirect contact of human intelligence with the supernatural. The practice was formerly closely allied with religion among pagan, Hebrew, and Christian peoples; nowadays it persists chiefly among superstitious persons.

Contact with the supernatural is usually sought through a psychic medium, i.e., a person supposedly endowed with supernormal receptivity. In direct divination, the medium acquires knowledge through direct contact with the unknown. The oracle (q.v.), a medium, or diviner, who figured prominently in the beliefs of a number of ancient peoples, including those of Babylonia and Greece, typified the mediumistic method. Oracles employed various techniques in establishing contact with divinity. Some, like the oracle at Delphi (q.v.), passed into a trance and, in this condition, uttered divine messages. Others practiced oneiromancy, or divination by dreams, and necromancy (q.v.), the art of securing revelations from the souls of the dead. The direct method of divination is closely approximated in many of the practices of modern spiritualism (q.v.).

The accomplishment of indirect or artificial contact with the supernatural depends on the interpretation by a medium of the behavior of animals and natural phenomena, which might convey messages from the supernatural. Common artificial or inductive means of divination in antiquity were the casting of lots; haruspication, or the inspection of animal entrails; and ornithomancy, the study of the activity of birds. The forms of inductive divination best known today include astrology, the study of the influences of the planets; crystallomancy, or crystal-gazing; bibliomancy, the interpretation of secret messages from books, especially from the Bible; numerology, the study of numbers; and the practices of reading palms, tea leaves, and cards.

DIVINE COMEDY, THE, or (It.) LA COMMEDIA DIVINA, an epic poem by Dante Alighieri (q.v.), begun about 1307 and finished about 1314. The poem is considered one of the greatest of all works of literature. It is an account of Dante's imaginary journey through hell, purgatory, and heaven; its three sections are correspondingly named *il Inferno, il Purgatorio,* and *il Paradiso.* Each section contains thirty-three cantos, or divisions, except for the first section, which has, in addition, a canto serving as a general introduction. The poem is written in *terza rima* (q.v.), and was the first composition of artistic merit in this popular verse form. Dante intended the poem to be a popular work for his contemporaries, and wrote it in Italian rather than Latin, the language in which medieval works of literature were usually composed. He named the poem *La Commedia* ("The Comedy") because it ends happily, in heaven; the adjective *divina* ("divine") was first added to the title in an edition of the poem which appeared in 1555.

The Divine Comedy is unlike other epic poetry (q.v.), for a greater portion of the poem is theological and philosophical dissertation, rather than narrative action. The incidents which occur during the course of the journey are used as examples or explanations of the theme of the poem, which is designed to show the rewards and penalties meted out after death as the result of one's behavior in life. Dante drew from history or from among his contemporaries the characters who appear in his work: the Roman poet Vergil is Dante's guide through hell and purgatory, and Beatrice Portinari (q.v.) leads him through heaven.

The Divine Comedy became so celebrated in Italy that, by the 15th century, nearly every Italian city had established a professorship for the study of the work; in the centuries following the invention of printing, almost 400 Italian editions were published, illustrated by such artists as Sandro Botticelli, Michelangelo, John Flaxman, and Gustave Doré. Gioacchino Antonio Rossini and Robert Schumann set parts of the poem to music. It has been translated into more than twenty-five languages; notable English translations were made by the English poet Lord Byron and the American poet Henry Wadsworth Longfellow.

DIVINE RIGHT or **DIVINE RIGHT OF KINGS,** the ancient doctrine that sovereigns are representatives of God and derive their right to rule directly from Him. The concept was derived from the theocracies of the East. Before the Reformation the king was considered God's representative in all secular matters; after the Reformation, in Protestant countries he filled this function in religious matters also. According to the doctrine, a ruler's power is not subject to secular limitation; he is responsible only to God, and not to his subjects. In the 17th century the doctrine was supported by the English Royalists against the Parliamentarians, who maintained that the exercise of political power springs from the will of the people. The opponents of divine right included John Milton, Algernon Sidney, and James Harrington, and its chief supporters were Thomas Hobbes, Claudius Salmasius, and Sir Robert Filmer, whose *Patriarcha or*

The Natural Power of Kings Asserted (1680) contains a complete exposition of the theory. The settlement of the crown on William and Mary in 1689, after the Glorious Revolution of 1688, ended the English controversy. In France the doctrine of Divine Right had many supporters until the French Revolution settled the issue.

DIVING, the act of plunging into water head foremost, usually as a preliminary to swimming or other aquatic sport. Surface diving, used in lifesaving, is the act of plunging under the water, while swimming, by lowering the head, at the same time kicking the legs and making an upward stroke with the arms. Fancy diving is the performance of dives involving a take-off, usually from a springboard, a maneuver in the air, and an entry either feet or head foremost into the water.

Fancy dives are classified into three types: the *layout,* in which the body must not be bent, and the arms are kept straight and the feet together; the *pike,* in which the body is bent at the hips, and the knees are kept rigid; and the *tuck,* in which the body is compactly bunched, while the diver clasps his ankles with his hands. The *swan dive,* or *swallow dive,* is a layout dive which is executed with the head bent backward, the back slightly hollowed, and the feet held together so that they form a straight line from the hips to toes. As the diver springs upward, he spreads his arms to the sides at shoulder height and holds them there until he is near the water; then he swings them forward over his head, maneuvering his hands so that they break the water before the rest of his body. In the *jackknife,* a pike dive, the diver bends at the hips, generally at the highest point of the dive, clasps or touches his ankles, and then straightens before he enters the water. Somersault dives, in which the diver executes a somersault before entering the water feet first, are usually pike dives; when more than one full revolution is made, the dive is more easily done as a tuck. The *full gainer,* or *Mollberg,* is a back somersault which begins from a front take-off; after completing the maneuver, the diver enters the water feet first. The *half gainer,* or *Isander,* begins from a front take-off, but at the highest point of the dive the diver turns in a back half-somersault, and straightens to enter the water head first. Either the full or half gainer may include a jackknife. All fancy diving is based on combinations or variations of these types, which may be modified by twists or other intricate movements in the air.

Fancy diving was first made a competitive sport in England in 1905. Since then, international diving contests have become subject to regulations made by the International Amateur Swimming Federation; in the U.S., the Amateur Athletic Union regulates competitive diving. The following heights are international standards for diving boards used in contests: for springboards, 1 meter (3 ft., 3 in.) or 3 meters (9 ft., 9 in.); for firm boards or platforms, 3–5 meters (9 ft., 9 in.–16 ft., 3 in.), 5–8 meters (16 ft., 3 in.–26 ft.), or 8–12 meters (26 ft.–39 ft.). Boards higher than 10 meters (32 ft., 6 in.) are rarely used in actual practice. In principle, the height of the board should be no more than twice the depth of the water, which should be at least 6 feet. Water need be no more than 15 feet deep for any height of diving board.

DIVING, or DEEP-SEA DIVING, the act of entering the water and remaining below the surface for the purpose of making observations or of working, either with or without mechanical aids. Diving without such aids has been practiced since ancient times in the harvesting of pearls and sponges, and various devices to supply the diver with air and thus permit him to prolong his stay under water have been tried since at least the 4th century B.C. It has been stated that Alexander the Great of Macedon made a descent in a machine that was probably a primitive form of diving bell, and Aristotle mentions devices that enabled divers to breathe while under water. Practical diving apparatus, however, was not developed until the 18th century.

Diving Bells. In 1717 Edmund Halley devised the first practical diving bell. It was a wooden chamber, open at the bottom, with glass windows in the top to admit light. Air was supplied to the men working inside the bell from exterior, movable, wooden air barrels fitted with leather tubes. Water was kept out of the upper part of the bell by the pressure of air inside it. The modern diving bell is a steel chamber supplied with compressed air through a hose. Except for specialized purposes such as leveling the sea bottom for the construction of piers and jetties, ordinary open diving bells are little used. They are not practical for use at depths of more than 60 ft., and they limit the movements of the divers in them to a few square feet. Several closed diving bells which maintain normal atmospheric pressure inside and rely on structural strength to withstand the pressure of the water have also been devised for underseas exploration, notably the bathysphere (q.v.), which was invented by the American scientist Charles William Beebe. The bathyscaphe (q.v.), a type of submarine vessel capable of descending to great depths, was developed by the Swiss physicist Auguste Piccard.

Diving Suits. From the 17th century on, numerous attempts were made to perfect a diving helmet or diving suit which would permit a diver to move about freely under water. The first successful device of this kind was devised by the Anglo-German inventor Augustus Siebe (1788–1872) in 1819. Siebe's "open" diving suit consisted of a leather jacket to which was fitted a metal helmet. An air pump at the surface forced air into the helmet through a flexible hose. This suit utilized the principle of the diving bell; it did not entirely exclude water but simply kept the water level below the diver's chin by air pressure. In 1830 Siebe introduced what is essentially the modern closed diving suit. This modern suit is made of rubberized fabric, is airtight and watertight, and covers the diver entirely. Valves on the diver's helmet permit him to regulate the pressure of air inside the suit and thus regulate his buoyancy. Auxiliary equipment of modern diving dress includes heavily weighted shoes to aid the diver in standing upright on the bottom, and other weights on the back and chest. A rope which also contains telephone wires connects the diver with the surface and permits him to talk with his tenders, and, in emergencies, to signal them by jerking the rope.

The ordinary diving dress has two serious limitations. The first is that the diver must drag unwieldy lengths of air hose and life line as he moves about the bottom, and the second that the pressure on the diver increases as his depth increases. To avoid these difficulties several forms of diving armor have been invented. These are jointed metal suits of very heavy construction which have sufficient structural strength to withstand great water pressures. The air pressure within the armor, therefore, can be normal. The air supply for diving armor can be pumped from the surface or can be self-contained to give the diver greater mobility. A self-contained air supply consists of a pressure cylinder of mixed oxygen and air and a regeneration chamber filled with caustic soda. Exhaled air is passed through the regeneration chamber, which removes carbon dioxide, and then is combined with oxygen and air from the cylinder and rebreathed. The air supply of such a self-contained unit is limited, varying from 45 minutes to 2 hours.

Wide World Photos

FANCY DIVING

Above: Stroboscopic photograph showing a back dive, half twist, forward one and a quarter somersault. Right: Double swan dive.

In recent years several kinds of special-purpose diving apparatus have been developed. One such device is a light and simple helmet which can be worn by a diver in a bathing suit. The diver wears a weighted belt or weighted shoes and the helmet rests like a yoke on his shoulders. This type of diving helmet is widely used in diving for sport and for scientific exploration of coral reefs. During World War II, members of underwater demolition teams, which cleared away mines and other underwater obstacles prior to amphibious landings, were equipped with lightweight breathing masks operating on the same principle as the self-contained diving suit. These masks permitted their users to swim under water for half an hour or longer. A similar device, called a "Mommsen lung", is employed

Austral. News & Info. Bur.; U.S. Navy Photo

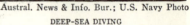

DEEP-SEA DIVING

Above: Pearl diver about to be lowered into the water off the coast of Australia.
Left: A diver seen through the plate-glass window of his diving helmet. Valve at left of his chin is for regulating air pressure.

to enable crew members to escape from damaged submarines.

Equipment. Because of the difficulty of working under water with ordinary hand tools, divers usually employ pneumatic hammers, drills, wrenches, and other implements. Cutting and welding are carried out with standard torches. Because in many waters daylight penetrates only a few feet beneath the surface, it is necessary to supply artificial light for divers to work by. High-power incandescent electric lights are usually employed.

Depth of Working. For divers working without mechanical aids, a depth of about 60 ft. is the practical limit of working. Native pearl divers of the Indian Ocean, the East Indies, and the South Sea Islands are credited with reaching depths of 100 ft. in individual dives. Such trained "skin divers" commonly remain submerged from 50 to 80 seconds at depths of about 40 ft. For ordinary diving operations in conventional suits, depths of about 150 ft. and pressures of about 70 lbs. per sq.in. are the practical limit. The greatest depth at which work was performed by divers was 275 ft., during the salvage of a sunken U.S. submarine off Honolulu. These dives were made in conventional diving suits, and the divers withstood pressures of 122 lbs. per sq.in. A diver wearing self-contained armor has worked extensively on a sunken ship in 240 ft. of water off the coast of Newfoundland.

For the harmful effects of air pressure on divers, see BENDS.

DIVING BEETLE, common name for any predaceous aquatic beetle of the family Dytiscidae. They are oval, flattened beetles with long hind legs covered with hairs, well adapted for swimming. When at rest in the water, the adults hang head downward with only the tip of the body protruding. When diving, the beetles carry a supply of air under their wing covers. The segmented larvae of these beetles are longer than the adults and are often called water tigers. When they are about to enter the pupal stage the larvae dig small cells in the earth near the water, in which they pass the pupal period. Many of the species of diving beetles are large and feed not only on other insects but even on small fish. Among the common species of the family are *Dytiscus fasciventris,* which grows to a length of an inch or more and has a greenish-black body with yellow markings on the thorax, and *D. harrisii,* which resembles the aforesaid species but which reaches a length of more than 1½ in. Another common species, *Cybister fimbriolatus,* is intermediate in size between these two beetles and has a brownish body with prominent yellow markings on the thorax and the edges of the wing cases.

DIVISION, one of the four fundamental operative processes in arithmetic, the reverse of multiplication. Division is the process of determining how many times one number, *b,* must be added to itself to give another number, *a.* The number divided, *a,* is known as the *dividend.* The number by which it is divided, *b,* is called the *divisor.* The result, *c,* is known as the *quotient.* In mathematical symbols:

$$a \div b = c$$

The symbol between the two first terms is called the division sign. Other notations for division are: $\frac{a}{b}$, a/b, $b\overline{)a}$, and $a:b$, in which a is the dividend and b is the divisor. If the divisor is contained in the dividend an integral (or whole) number of times, then the division is said to be exact. If the division is not exact, then the fraction by which the quotient exceeds a whole number or zero is called the remainder. Division by zero is not defined in elementary arithmetic because it does not yield a single-valued solution, and attempts to divide by zero may yield fallacious results. The reciprocal of a number is the quotient obtained by using that number as divisor and the number one as dividend.

The sign of the quotient is determined by the signs of the dividend and the divisor. If the signs of the latter are different, the quotient is negative; if the signs are the same, the quotient is positive. The usual check for the correctness of a division is to multiply the quotient by the divisor; the result should equal the dividend. Division of very large numbers, and series of successive divisions, are easily performed by the use of logarithms or calculating machines (qq.v.).

DIVISION, in military organization, a body of troops, usually consisting of two or more infantry or artillery brigades, to which are attached a number of auxiliary and special troops of the other arms, in such a proportion as to make it capable of independent action. The strength and composition of a division varies in times of peace and of war, according to the purposes and functions of the division. In most cases a division ranges from 14,000 men, including about 10,000 infantrymen and about 3000 artillerymen, to 21,000 men. A division is normally commanded by a major general.

The so-called "streamlined" divisions of the U.S. Army in World War II were of two kinds:

DIVING BEETLE. *Left to right: Male, larva, and female of beetle of the genus Dytiscus.*

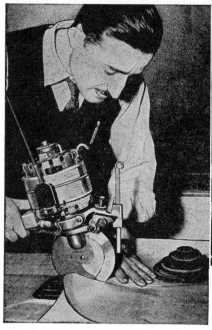

Port of N.Y. Authority

OCCUPATIONAL DIVISION OF LABOR
In clothing manufacture worker at left cuts cloth; worker above sews the parts together.

square and triangular. Square divisions were organized on the basis of two infantry brigades of two regiments each, and one artillery brigade of three regiments. Triangular divisions were organized on the basis of three regiments of infantry, each of which was usually supported by one battalion of artillery. See MILITARY ORGANIZATION.

DIVISION OF LABOR, in economics, the separation of the work involved in production and trade into processes performed by different workers or groups of workers. The separation may occur on several bases, the most frequent being geographical, or territorial, and occupational. Geographical division of labor may develop from the occurrence of raw materials in one part of the world and the establishment of manufactories which use them in another. Thus, crude rubber produced in the Far East is compounded, vulcanized, and manufactured into auto tires and other products in the United States; and iron ore mined in the Mesabi Range, Minnesota, is used in the manufacture of steel in Chicago, Detroit, Cleveland, Pittsburgh, and other cities. Geographical division of labor may take the form of the localization of the manufacture of component parts of a finished product in various places. Thus, the window glass and tires made in Pittsburgh and in Akron,

respectively, are used in the manufacture of automobiles which are produced chiefly in Detroit.

Separation of the productive process into individual operations, each performed by different groups of workers, is called occupational, or technical, division of labor. As an illustration of this type of separation may be cited the manufacture of the automobile, which consists of thousands of parts, each one requiring a number of distinct processes. Many of these parts are manufactured in plants devoted solely to the production of those particular items, and within these plants the productive process is divided among many different groups of workers, each of whom has a specialized task to perform. The outstanding advantage resulting from technical division of labor is greater productivity. If each of the approximately 647,000 workers employed in 1952 in the United States in the production of automobiles were required to perform all the operations involved, it is obvious that the total production of autos would be infinitely less than the approximately 4,300,000 which came off the assembly line. Greater productivity results from several factors, among which the most important are a marked increase in individual and collective efficiency due to specialization and resulting increase in

Netherlands Info. Bur.; B. F. Goodrich Co.

GEOGRAPHICAL, DIVISION OF LABOR

Crude rubber is collected in the Dutch East Indies (right) and sent to the United States for the manufacture of rubber tires (above).

skill; economy in training of workers, especially with respect to time; economy resulting from the continuous use of tools which would otherwise remain idle during part of the working time as workers move from process to process; and the development of highly productive, specialized tools, machinery, and equipment.

Division of labor has been a feature of production from the earliest times. In primitive society, men hunted, trapped, fished, and fought; and women managed their households and tended crops. As civilization developed, a division of labor took place on a vocational basis: the performance of different economic activities by separate groups of producers. Thus, for example, with the development of tools, utensils, and productive techniques, handicrafts and agriculture were carried on by separate groups. The separation of handicrafts and agriculture accompanied and was developed by the growth of cities. Vocational division of labor became more widespread during the Middle Ages as a result of the development of the guilds (q.v.).

During the later Middle Ages, technical division of labor appeared for the first time on an important scale, in connection with a widespread increase in the production of articles for sale. Subsequently, the Industrial Revolution (q.v.) of the latter part of the 18th and the first part of the 19th centuries created the modern factory system of production and thereby gave a tremendous impetus to the development of technical and geographical division of labor. The division of labor in modern industry into many thousands of individual processes and skills has given rise to the science of industrial management, with its many complex technical, organizational, and personnel problems.

DIVORCE, in modern law, a dissolution of marriage, by public authority, at the instance of one of the parties, for a cause that has arisen since the establishment of the connubial relation. Divorces are usually granted by courts under general laws. A judicial declaration that two persons who have gone through the form of contracting marriage are not husband and wife, as when one of the parties was already married, is not a divorce; nor is the term divorce properly applied to an annulment of marriage for a cause that antedates the marriage, as impotence or fraud. Again, a judicial separation that merely relieves the parties of some of the duties and suspends some of the rights connected with the connubial relation is not a divorce, for divorce dissolves the connubial bond itself.

Jurisdiction. Divorce being a decree of a court, the first essential is that the court have jurisdiction of the subject matter. In the United States, the place of marriage confers no jurisdiction. The location of the marriage *status* is that of the domicile of the parties. When husband and wife make their home in the same State, that State has jurisdiction. When they live separately the husband's domicile determines the jurisdiction, because, in law, the domicile of a wife is that of her husband. But when a wife is living apart from her husband, in another State, and makes her home there, she is said to have acquired a *separate* domicile for the purpose of securing a divorce; and the courts of the State in which she resides may take jurisdiction in such a case.

Aside from these general considerations, statutes in many States require residence therein for a definite period of time, usually from six months to a year, before the courts will take jurisdiction; but no State can, by statute, assume jurisdiction over something outside its boundaries. Thus, a statute that permitted a wife to secure a divorce in a State in which no domicile had ever been acquired would not be recognized outside of that State; and one who secured a divorce under such circumstances, and remarried in another State,

would be guilty of bigamy. All divorce actions must be begun by the service of process on the other spouse. The method of service, whether personal or by publication, is regulated by statute in each State.

Unlike an action for damages at law, a divorce is never granted solely upon the default of the defendant. The plaintiff must prove his case; that is, he (or she) must produce before the court legal evidence, showing the existence of the necessary facts upon which a divorce is granted according to the law of the State wherein the action is brought. A divorce trial is usually held before a judge but not before a jury. However, it is customary in many cases for the court to appoint a referee to take testimony and make a report to the court. Sometimes the court, on its own motion, may direct that certain issues be tried before a jury. The right of either party to demand a jury trial exists in some States.

The marriage relation is dissolved when the final decree is made. According to the law of many States, the final decree of divorce forbids the defendant to remarry, or to remarry within a certain period. Some States permit the defendant to remarry at once. If a divorced party remarries contrary to a decree forbidding it, he is subject to punishment for contempt of court, but such violation of the court's decree does not affect the validity of the divorce. A divorced person who is forbidden to remarry by the laws of the State that granted his divorce sometimes remarries in another State. Whether he is subject to punishment for contempt of court if he returns to the State which granted the divorce, is a moot question. Some courts have held he cannot be punished, on the ground that the contempt of court was committed outside of its jurisdiction.

In a divorce action, the court may direct a husband to pay the wife sufficient money to enable her to employ counsel to prosecute or defend the action, and may also grant her temporary alimony. The final decree of divorce may grant the wife alimony to be paid by the husband at stated periods, and may also award the custody of children to either or both parties, and make suitable regulations as to visiting of the children by either party.

Grounds for Divorce. The grounds for divorce vary from State to State. In South Carolina, divorce was not recognized by law until 1949; in New York, the only ground for divorce is adultery, and the adultery must be without the connivance or collusion of the plaintiff; also the plaintiff must not be guilty of adultery. Adultery is a ground for divorce in practically all the States; some provide that it must be without the connivance of the other party; some that the plaintiff must be innocent; some provide that it is no ground if forgiven. Another ground is impotence; in many States, however, it is a valid ground only if present at the time of the marriage. Other grounds for divorce are desertion, failure of a husband to support his wife, habitual drunkenness, cruelty, habitual manifestations of violent temper, incurable insanity, confinement in an asylum for a long period of time, pregnancy at the time of marriage which was unknown to the husband, concealment of a loathsome disease at the time of marriage or contraction of one after marriage, membership in a religious society forbidding cohabitation, conviction of a felony, and imprisonment for life.

The Supreme Court, in a ruling in 1942, ostensibly overruled a long line of previous decisions and held that there could be no attack upon the validity of divorce granted by a State having jurisdiction of the parties, in the courts of any other State. This decision was predicated upon the doctrine that under the Federal Constitution each State is required to give full faith and credit to the judicial decrees of every other State. In 1945, this general principle was considerably limited and clarified by a decision of the Supreme Court, which held that the question as to whether the State granting the divorce had jurisdiction was still subject to review and attack in the courts of any other State. If such reviewing court finds that no proper domicile was established by the party obtaining the divorce, the decree does not have to be recognized by a State under the full faith and credit clause of the Constitution, because the State granting the divorce is assumed never to have had proper jurisdiction.

Statistics. The first divorce census in 1887 showed 27,919 divorces, or 0.5 divorces per 1000 persons of population. In 1910, the number of divorces stood at 83,045, or 0.9 per 1000 persons. Divorces in 1915 numbered 104,298 or 1.0 divorces per 1000 persons. By 1920, this figure had risen to 170,505 (1.6 per 1000 population). The increase in the next five years was not so great, and the figure in 1925 was 175,449 (1.5 per 1000 population). The 1930 figure, 191,591 (1.6 per 1000 persons) showed a slight decrease from the 1929 figure, 201,468 recorded divorces.

By 1934, the 1929 figure had been topped, with 204,000 divorces (1.6 per 1000 popula-

tion), and in 1940 the figure was as large as 264,000 or 2.0 per 1000 pop. From 1925 to 1940, there were about 3,312,000 U.S. divorces. Since 1940, the number of divorces has shown an upward trend. A considerably sharper increase followed the termination of World War II in 1945; the peak year was 1946 with 626,000 divorces. The number decreased gradually thereafter; in 1953 it was about 390,000.

Divorce in Other Countries. The status of divorce in countries where Protestantism is the prevailing faith is the result of a long evolutionary development. This development began, in part, in the Reformation, which, although it continued to invest marriage with religious sentiment, rejected the Roman Catholic doctrine that marriage is indissoluble. It results, partly, also, from philosophic and political theories which hold that marriage is pre-eminently a civil contract and therefore subject to dissolution for sufficient cause. These views were strongly emphasized by the leaders of the French Revolution of 1789, and became increasingly current throughout the world in the 19th and 20th centuries. An extreme application of these theories, in the view of some historians, took place in Russia, following the revolution of 1917 and the disestablishment of the Greek Orthodox Church. Marriage and divorce were easily arranged and consisted primarily of an official recording of the essential facts for purposes of vital statistics and for the establishment of legal responsibility with respect to children. In 1944, however, the Soviet government made it necessary for citizens seeking divorce to have recourse to the courts.

In countries where Roman Catholicism is the dominant religion and canon law prevails, as in Spain and Italy, and among Catholics the world over, the traditional Catholic attitude toward divorce obtains. However, the Catholic Church permits separation of one spouse from the other because of unnatural sexual congress, cruelty, infidelity, and the taking of vows in connection with entry into a religious order. Among grounds for the annulment of marriages among Catholics, are impotence prior to marriage, and consanguinity. Notwithstanding the strict interdiction of divorce by Catholicism, and the provisions established by the Catholic Church for separation and the annulment of marriages, large numbers of Catholics in the United States and other countries procure divorces in the courts. Such divorces are often obtained with the approbation of Church authorities in order to protect the civil rights of the injured party, although they are not recognized as divorces in the eyes of the Church.

Divorce on various grounds is recognized among peoples of the Mohammedan and Buddhist faiths. In India, the status of divorce among the Hindus varies from caste to caste, some permitting, others forbidding it. Prior to 1898, the Japanese attitude toward divorce was derived from a code of law formulated by the Chinese sage Confucius; the Confucian code permitted men to divorce women because of barrenness and lasciviousness, among other reasons. A new code, adopted in 1898 and amended in 1914, modernized the Japanese attitude toward divorce, making it essentially similar to that in the United States. Since about 1913, the Chinese attitude toward divorce has also been essentially modern. In general, it may be said, the tendency in the world today is toward the establishment of marriage and divorce as primarily civil relationships. See MARRIAGE; FAMILY.

DIX, DOROTHEA LYNDE (1802–87), American philanthropist and reformer, born at Hampden, Maine. About 1820 she established a school for girls in Boston, and served as head of the school during the ensuing fifteen years. She became interested in conditions in almshouses and prisons in 1841, when she began visiting such institutions in Massachusetts, and set about securing legislation for their improvement. Through her activities, institutions for the insane and destitute were founded in twenty States and in Canada. Her efforts also resulted in drastic reforms in prison and almshouse conditions in European countries. During the Civil War she served with the Union Army as superintendent of women nurses. Her writings include *The Garland of Flora* (1829) and *Prisons and Prison Discipline* (1845).

DIX, DOROTHY. See GILMER, ELIZABETH MERIWETHER.

DIX, JOHN ADAMS (1798–1879), American statesman and soldier, born in Boscawen, N.H., and educated at Brown University. He served in the War of 1812, remained in the army until 1828, and was secretary of state of New York from 1833 to 1839. He was a U.S. senator from 1845 to 1849, and later was appointed secretary of the treasury by President James Buchanan. During the Civil War he served in the Union Army with the rank of major general, and in 1863 he was given command of the military Department of the East. From 1866 to 1869 he was U.S. minister to France. In 1872 he was elected governor of New York State and served for one term,

failing of re-election in 1874. Dix was the author of *Resources of the City of New York* (1827), *A Winter in Madeira and A Summer in Spain and Florence* (1850), and *Speeches and Occasional Addresses* (2 vols., 1864).

DIXIE, the name of a song composed in 1859 by the American minstrel and song writer Daniel Decatur Emmett (1815–1904). The words of the song touch on life in the Southern States, popularly known as Dixie. The song was sung for the first time at a performance of Bryant's Minstrels, at Mechanics' Hall, New York City. It speedily became popular, especially in the South. It was sung at the inauguration of Jefferson Davis as President of the Confederate States of America, at Montgomery, Ala., in February, 1861; during the Civil War it was the principal war song of the Confederate soldiers. The song is often played and sung today throughout the United States. Two alternative sets of words for the song were written during the Civil War period. One, by the Confederate General Albert Pike, favored the cause of the South; it appeared in the Natchez *Courier* in May, 1861. The second, written by T. M. Cooley, favored the cause of the North. Neither version achieved any lasting popularity.

DIYARBEKIR, capital of the il of the same name, Turkey in Asia. The town is situated at the head of navigation on the Tigris R., about 470 miles S.E. of Ankara, with which it is connected by rail. Diyarbekir was originally a Roman colony, known as *Amida;* it eventually came under Persian control, and in 1515 was taken by the Turks. The town is surrounded by black basalt walls, and contains many mosques and a number of Christian churches. Its industries include the manufacture of silk and cotton fabrics, of iron and copper ware, and the processing of grains and tobacco. Farming, the raising of livestock, and mining are the principal occupations of the il. Area, 5742 sq.m.; pop. (1950) 294,618. Pop. of town (1950) 45,495.

DJIBOUTI, or JIBUTI, port and capital of French Somaliland, and terminus of the Franco-Ethiopian railroad. In a recent year approximately 1360 merchant vessels entered the port. The principal imports are cotton goods, coal, cattle, and sugar; exports are coffee, hides, and salt. Pop. (1953 est.) 27,723.

DNEPRODZERZHINSK, city in the Dnepropetrovsk Region of the Ukrainian Soviet Socialist Republic. It is situated on the Dnieper R., about 20 miles N.W. of the city of Dnepropetrovsk, in a district rich in mineral resources, notably coal and iron ore. The city

Ewing Galloway

A miller's water wheel in the Dnieper River at a village near the city of Kiev

is an important center of the metallurgical industry of the Soviet Union, and contains large iron and steel works, engineering works, plants for the manufacture of machinery and railway rolling stock, and chemical works. Pop. (1939) 147,829.

DNEPROPETROVSK, formerly EKATERINO-SLAV, name of a Region and of its administrative center, in the Ukrainian Soviet Socialist Republic. The Region lies within the rocky steppe formed by an eastern extension of the Carpathian Mts.; it is rich in coal, in iron, manganese, and other metallic ores, and in water power, supplied by the Dnieper R., which traverses Dnepropetrovsk from N. to S. The mineral resources of the Region furnish the raw materials for a variety of heavy industries, including, besides mining, the manufacture of iron and steel, aluminum, machinery and machine tools, tractors and other agricultural machinery, railway rolling stock, ball bearings, and chemicals. Power for these industries is generated at the hydroelectric station at the Dneprostroi Dam across the Dnieper, above Zaporozhe. These and other heavy industries are operated as a single producing unit, called the Dnieper Industrial Combine. Heavily mechanized collective farms in the Region produce wheat, rice, beets, and fruit; cattle, sheep, and goats are raised.

The city of Dnepropetrovsk, founded in 1786 by the statesman Grigori Potemkin, on the site of a former Polish castle, is situated on the Dnieper, about 45 miles N. of Zaporozhe. It is one of the most important metallurgical-manufacturing centers of the Soviet Union. In addition to steel mills and foundries, it also contains sawmills and flour mills. Pop. of city (1946 est.) 500,000.

DNIEPER RIVER (Russ. *Dnepr*), a river and important traffic artery of the Soviet Union, about 1400 m. long. It is the third longest river of Europe, being exceeded in length by the Volga and Danube rivers. The Dnieper rises about 140 miles W.S.W. of Moscow in the Valdai Hills of the Smolensk Region, Soviet Russia, and flows in a general southerly direction to empty into the Black Sea, about 12 miles beyond Kherson, in the Soviet Ukraine. The estuary of the Dnieper forms part of a large marshy region, of which another part is formed by the mouth of the Bug R. The Dnieper is navigable throughout its entire course, and is entirely free of ice about nine months of the year.

The Dnieper drains an area of about 202,000 sq.m. The upper course of the river lies partly through hilly country and skirts the eastern end of the Pripet Marshes. The middle and lower reaches pass through the fertile agricultural and highly industrialized areas of the Ukraine. A part of the lower course of the river traverses the rocky steppe of the Dnepropetrovsk (q.v.) Region, where the Dnieper attains its greatest breadth, about 1¼ m., and where rapids extend for about 25 m. and the river falls about 155 ft. The chief tributaries of the Dnieper are the Berezina, Pripet, Sozh, and Desna rivers. Kiev, capital of the Ukrainian Soviet Socialist Republic, is the principal city situated on the Dnieper. Other important cities on the river include, from S. to N., Kherson, Zaporozhe, Dnepropetrovsk, Dneprodzerzhinsk, Mogilev, and Smolensk.

In ancient times, the Dnieper was an important commercial artery between the northern and southern parts of eastern Europe. The Greeks called the river *Borysthenes*; the

Doberman pinscher

Romans, *Danapris;* the Turks, *Uzi* or *Uzu;* and the Tatars, *Eksi.* Various Italian geographers of the Middle Ages called the river the *Elice, Lerene, Luosen,* and *Lussem.*

In later times, as the size of ships was increased, the commercial importance of the Dnieper decreased, principally because of the impossibility of navigating the rapids above Zaporozhe. In the 19th century, navigation was facilitated following the construction of a number of channels through the rapids. However, the problem of making the entire river navigable was not solved until 1932, when the great Dneprostroi Dam above Zaporozhe was completed. The dam raised the water level above the rapids sufficiently high to allow vessels to pass over them in safety. Construction of a canal linking the Dnieper with the Bug R. in the south, and the construction of canals in the north linking the Berezina and Pripet rivers with the Dvina and Niemen rivers, respectively, made the Dnieper the principal link in a continuous waterway from the Black to the Baltic seas.

As a result of these improvements, about 6% of the total tonnage borne annually over the inland-waterways system of the Soviet Union before World War II was transported over the Dnieper. Lumber, grain, metals, and machinery were among the chief articles of transport. An increase in the above percentage was anticipated following the completion of canals linking the Dnieper with the Oka and Volga rivers. During World War II (q.v.), major battles were fought on the banks of the Dnieper between the German and Soviet armies.

DNIESTER RIVER (Russ. *Dnestr,* Rom. *Nistru,* anc. *Tyras* or *Danastris*), a river of the Soviet Union, about 850 m. long. It rises in the Carpathian Mts., about 5 miles w. of Drogobych in the Ukrainian Soviet Socialist Republic, and flows in a general southeasterly direction, partly along the eastern boundary of the Moldavian Soviet Republic, to empty into the Black Sea, about 20 miles w. of Odessa. The river's broad estuary comprises several arms which form a marshy lagoon, called the Dniester Liman. The numerous tributaries of the Dniester are small meandering streams. The average width of the river is 500 to 750 ft.; its maximum width is about 1400 ft. For about 70 days during the winter a large part of the Dniester is frozen.

The Dniester drains an area of about 29,700 sq.m., and is an important traffic artery for the shipment of grain, vegetables, sunflower seeds, cattle and cattle products, and lumber, all of which are produced in the Dniester basin. The most important city on the river is Tiraspol.

Before the Soviet Union acquired Bessarabia from Romania, during World War II, the Dniester formed part of the boundary between Romania and the Soviet Union. During World War II, large-scale battles were fought on the banks of the river between the German and Romanian invaders of the Soviet Union and the country's defenders.

DOBBY. See Loom.

DOBELL, Sydney Thompson (1824–74), English poet and critic, born at Cranbrook, Kent, and privately educated. His enthusiasm for the cause of oppressed nations led him to write the long dramatic poem *The Roman* (1850), concerning the struggles of the Italians in their attempts to unify their country. The poetry of Dobell belongs to the "spasmodic school", a term applied to certain writing of the time because of its skeptical and restless quality. His works include the dramatic poem *The Balder* (1854) and *England in Time of War* (1856).

DOBERMAN PINSCHER, a working dog which originated at Apolda, Thüringen, Germany, where it was first bred about 1890 from the German shepherd dog, the rottweiler, the black and tan terrier, and the German pinscher. The Doberman pinscher takes its name from its first breeder, Louis Dobermann. It was employed at first as a watch dog and later was trained to act as a police dog and a war dog. Characteristics of the breed are a wedge-shaped head; dark eyes ranging from brown to black in color and having an alert, courageous expression; a well-muscled neck; and a smooth, hard, close-lying coat which is black, brown. or blue in color. Males are from twenty-five to twenty-eight inches high at the shoulders; bitches, from twenty-four to twenty-six. The male weighs from sixty-five to seventy-five pounds. The Doberman pinscher has an elegant appearance, and is obedient, loyal, and especially fond of children. The breed became popular in the United States about 1921.

DOBROGEA. See DOBRUJA.

DOBRUJA or **DOBRUDJA** (Romanian, *Dobrogea*), region of N.E. Bulgaria and S.E. Romania, fronting the Black Sea and bounded on the N. and W. by the Danube R. The Dobruja region is generally fertile; major crops are cereal grains, beets, grapes, mulberries, fodder plants, and tobacco. Romania acquired northern Dobruja from Bulgaria in 1878 by the terms of the Treaty of Berlin following the Russo-Turkish War of 1877–78. Southern Dobruja was ceded to Romania under the terms of the Treaty of Bucharest following the Balkan Wars of 1912–13. The latter acquisition was upheld by the Treaty of Neuilly in 1919. Southern Dobruja, comprising about a third of the region's area, was returned to Bulgaria in Sept., 1940, by the Treaty of Craiova. After 1949 Bulgarian Dobruja was included within the Bulgarian provinces of Ruse and Stalin. Romanian Dobruja constituted a Romanian province until 1952. Area of Bulgarian Dobruja, 2971 sq.m.; pop. (1940) 318,772. Area of Romanian Dobruja, 5998 sq.m.; pop. (1948) 503,217.

DOBSON or **DOBSON FLY.** See CORYDALIS.

DOBSON, (HENRY) AUSTIN (1840–1921), English author, born at Plymouth. In 1856 he became a clerk in the marine department of the British Board of Trade; from 1884 to 1901 he was principal clerk. In 1873 a collection of his poems that had previously appeared in periodicals was published in book form under the title *Vignettes in Rhyme*. He was one of the leaders of the movement which introduced such French verse forms as the rondeau, the triolet, and the ballade into English poetry. Among his works, which include both poetry and prose, are *Proverbs in Porcelain* (1877), *At the Sign of the Lyre* (1885), *Eighteenth Century Vignettes* (1892–96), and *The Paladin of Philanthropy* (1899); and the biographies *Fielding* (1883), *Steele* (1886), *Goldsmith* (1888), *Samuel Richardson* (1902), *and Fanny Burney* (1903).

DOCK, any of several types of harbor structure used for the loading, unloading, or repair of ships. In accurate usage the term "dock" applies either to the water channel in which a ship is berthed beside a pier, or to a dry

dock in which a ship is placed for repairs. In common U.S. usage the term is applied to piers and quays.

In harbors which have a large tidal range, ships are usually berthed in *wet docks*. These docks are basins, accommodating a large number of vessels, which can be shut off from the rest of the harbor by movable gates that hold the water in the dock at the high-tide level. Wet docks are a necessity in most of the ports of the British Isles and in other localities where the height of the tide is more than about 10 ft. Among the great ports of the world equipped with wet docks are London, Liverpool, Cardiff, and Aberdeen in the British Isles; Havre, Bremerhaven, and Antwerp in Europe; and Bombay and Calcutta in India. The London wet-dock system is the largest in the world, and the combined length of its quays and piers amounts to about 45½ miles.

In most seaports of the U.S. the rise and fall of the tide is sufficiently small to permit the use of *tidal docks*. Such docks, which are almost universally used in this country, consist of a series of rectangular water spaces between piers projecting out from the shore into the river or harbor. In some ports, ships are berthed around the edge of open *tidal basins*, where they are also subject to the rise and fall of the tide. New York harbor, the largest harbor of any kind in the world, has approximately 1000 miles of dockage, including the length of shoreline and of the harbor's 2000 piers.

For the repair of ships, *dry docks* are universally employed. These are structures into which the ship can be floated and which are then closed and pumped free of water, leaving the ship resting on props and shores at the bottom of the dock. There are two kinds of dry docks: *graving docks,* fixed basins of masonry timber; and *floating dry docks,* usually made of steel. Floating dry docks have certain advantages over graving docks in that they can be built more quickly and economically than fixed docks and also can be built at a distance from their final location, and towed into place. During World War II large numbers of floating docks were built and towed overseas (or shipped in sections), for use at advanced naval bases. The disadvantage of floating docks is that in general they cannot accommodate the largest passenger vessels and battleships. The largest commercial floating dock in the world is located at Southampton, England. It is 860 ft. in length, 130 ft. in breadth, and will accommodate ships with a draft of 38 ft. The world's largest graving

Port of N.Y. Authority; British Information Services

Top: Dock space in harbor of New York City. City skyline is seen from New Jersey side of the Hudson River. Bottom: Piers and quays in the extensive wet-dock system of London.

dock, completed in 1945 at Cape Town, South Africa, is 1250 ft. long, 156 ft. wide, and 48 ft. in depth. See HARBOR; PIER.

DOCK, common name for several plants of the genus *Rumex* of the Buckwheat family. Other plants in this genus are called sorrel, the difference not being clearly defined. Sorrel generally includes low-growing plants in the subgenus *Acetosa* which have a sour herbage; whereas dock generally includes plants of the subgenus *Lapathum,* which are taller, and have herbage which is not acid, or only slightly so.

Plants of this genus include about 100 species of biennial and perennial herbs. Of the 30 or more species found in North America, about one third have been introduced from Europe. They have stout tap roots, or running rootstocks, and their lanceolate leaves, with smooth, and sometimes wavy margins, are placed alternately on the stems. The greenish flowers, which have no petals, are arranged in whorled panicles. The fruits are red or brown triangular nuts enclosed in leathery sepals. Most of these plants are troublesome weeds found in fields and pastures.

The great water dock of Europe, *R. hydrolapathum,* which grows to a height of 6 feet, is used for landscaping, and the root extract of *R. conglomeratus* has been used for dyeing. See also CANAIGRE.

Sorrels are perennial herbs which spread by running rootstocks. Their fleshy sour leaves are often shaped like spearheads. Some sorrels, notably *R. acetosa,* the garden sorrel, are cultivated in the United States. Their leaves are edible, and are used in soups and to flavor salads.

DOCTOR FISH. See SURGEON FISH.

DOCTOR OF THE CHURCH, a posthumous title conferred on Christian teachers by a declaration of the Pope or of the Sacred Congregation of Rites. The title originated in 1295, when Pope Boniface VIII bestowed it upon the four early theologians St. Ambrose, St. Augustine, St. Jerome, and St. Gregory the Great, whom he designated the great Doctors of the Latin Church. During that ceremony, Pope Boniface declared that the prerequisites for designation as Doctor of the Church included eminent learning and heroic sanctity. St. Thomas Aquinas (q.v.) and St. Francis de Sales (q.v.) are among the twenty-five theologians who have since been named Doctors.

DOCTRINE. See DOGMA.

DODD, WILLIAM EDWARD (1869–1940), American historian, born at Clayton, N.C., and educated at Virginia Polytechnical Institute and the University of Leipzig. He was professor of American history at Randolph-Macon College from 1900 to 1908 and then at Chicago University until 1933, when he was appointed ambassador to Germany. He returned to the U.S. in 1937, and wrote *Ambassador Dodd's Diary, 1933–38* (1941) in which he denounced the German Nazi government. Among his other writings are *The Life of Jefferson Davis* (1907), *Statesmen of the Old South* (1911), *Expansion and Conflict* (1915), *Woodrow Wilson and His Work* (1920), and *Lincoln or Lee* (1928). With Ray Stannard Baker he edited *The Public Papers of Woodrow Wilson* (1924–26).

DODDER, common name for plants of the genus *Cuscuta,* family Convolvulaceae. Dodder is also called love vine, strangleweed, goldthread, and hell-bind. It is one of the few higher plants that are parasitic on other plants. It has yellowish or reddish threadlike twining stems and no leaves or chlorophyll. The young plant attaches itself on germination to surrounding vegetation by means of sucking organs, called *haustoria,* through which it takes nourishment from the host.

Several species of dodder are common in Europe and the U.S. They are annuals, with small white, pink, or yellow flowers, which appear from summer to autumn, and they produce an abundance of seeds from July until frost. Dodder is especially harmful to clover, alfalfa, and flax, and is also found on ornamental plants. Commercial clover and alfalfa seed is always specially treated to avoid the possibility of contamination by dodder seed.

DODECANESE or **DODECANESUS,** a group of about fifty islands and islets situated

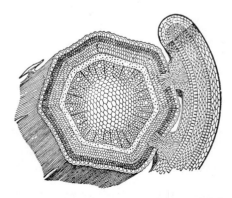

Cross section of a parasitic dodder (right) with haustoria embedded in stem of hop vine

in the S.E. part of the Ægean Sea, off the coast of Asiatic Turkey. The group comprises the southern Sporades (q.v.). Area, 1036 sq.m.; pop. (1951) 121,074. Only fourteen of the group are permanently inhabited. Of these, the most important are Rhodes, Cos or Kos (qq.v.), and Karpathos. The largest, both in area and population, is Rhodes, which contains the city of Rhodes, the capital of the group. The other inhabited islands (1940 census figures) are Kalymnos (area, 41 sq.m.; pop., 11,864), Leros (21 sq.m.; pop., 6131), Syme (22 sq.m.; pop., 4083), Nisyros (16 sq.m.; pop., 2605), Patmos (13 sq.m.; pop., 2428), Kastelorrizon (4 sq.m.; pop., 800), Astypalaia (37 sq.m.; pop., 1791), Kasos (25 sq.m.; pop., 1322), Chalke (11 sq.m.; pop., 702), Telos (24 sq.m.; pop. 1085), and Lipsos (6 sq.m.; pop., 873).

Agriculture is the chief industry of the Dodecanese, with the largest yields being produced in Rhodes and Cos. The leading crops are olives, grapes, oranges, and other fruits, and vegetables and tobacco. Sheep, oxen, horses, mules, and pigs are raised. The sponge-fishing industry is important in several of the islands, particularly in Calymnos and Symi. Among the principal manufactures of the group are olive oil, decorative pottery and tiles, carpets, silk, tobacco products, leather goods, and wine.

Greeks comprise the overwhelming majority of the population. Episcopal sees of the Greek Orthodox Church are situated on the islands of Rhodes, Leros, Cassos, and Cos. Administrative authority is vested in a governor general appointed by the government.

Buffalo Museum of Science
Museum model of the extinct dodo

Only twelve islands were included in the Dodecanese group in antiquity, hence the name (Gr., "twelve islands"). Settled by the ancient Greeks, several of the group, especially Rhodes, figured prominently in Hellenic civilization for many centuries. The islands subsequently became Roman dominions and, following the division of the Roman Empire, part of the Byzantine Empire. In 1522 the Dodecanese were seized by the Turks, who retained control until the successful invasion of Rhodes in 1912 by the armed forces of Italy. The Turkish government formally ceded the group to Italy in 1924. During World War II, German troops occupied the Dodecanese, but surrendered to a British force on May 8, 1945. The British government gave control of the islands to Greece on March 31, 1947. In June, 1947, by the terms of the Italian peace treaty, the group was ceded to Greece.

DODECATHEON. See COWSLIP.

DODGSON, CHARLES LUTWIDGE, also known as LEWIS CARROLL (1832–98), English mathematician and author, born at Daresbury, Cheshire, and educated at Rugby and at Oxford University. From 1855 to 1881 he was a member of the mathematics faculty at Oxford. He was the author of various mathematical treatises, including *Euclid and his Modern Rivals* (1879). Under the pseudonym Lewis Carroll, he wrote *Alice's Adventures in Wonderland* (1865) and its sequel *Through the Looking Glass* (1871), as well as *Phantasmagoria* (1869), *The Hunting of the Snark* (1876), and *Sylvie and Bruno* (1889).

Alice in Wonderland, which has made the name Lewis Carroll famous throughout the world, was originally written for Alice Liddell, the daughter of the dean of Christ Church, Henry George Liddell. On its publication with illustrations by Sir John Tenniel, the work became immediately popular as a story for children. Its subsequent appeal to adults was based upon Carroll's ingenious mixture of fantasy and realism, irony and absurdity. The names of its characters, such as the March Hare, the Mad Hatter, and the Cheshire Cat have become familiar in everyday speech.

DODO, common name applied to a flightless bird, *Raphus cucullatus,* belonging to the order Columbiformes (q.v.), and now extinct. The dodo formerly inhabited the forests of Mauritius (q.v.). About the size of a turkey, the bird had a large, hooked bill, undeveloped wings and tail, and short, thick, yellow legs. It laid a single, large egg in a ground nest made of grass. The dodo was first reported in

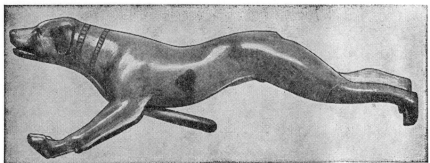

Metropolitan Mus. of Art; Gaines Food Co.

Above: Ancient Egyptian ivory carving of a dog. If the rod is pressed toward the dog's belly, the lower jaw opens.
Right: The boxer, related to the bulldogs.

1598 by Dutch colonizers, who characterized it as a sluggish bird and unafraid of man. Dodos were last observed in 1681. The speedy extinction of the species is attributed in part to domestic animals imported to the island by the settlers; such animals as hogs escaped to the woods and multiplied, and they destroyed many of the eggs. The name "dodo" is derived from a Portuguese word meaning "simple-minded". In present-day usage the word "dodo" is applied colloquially to simple-minded persons unable to adjust to new situations and ideas.

DODONA, the most ancient of Greek shrines, located in the interior of Epirus, about 50 miles E. of Corcyra (modern Corfu). It was sacred to Zeus and his consort Dione. Priests of the temple interpreted as responses from Zeus the rustling of a great oak tree, the activities of doves in its branches, the clanging of brazen pots hung from its branches, and the murmur of a fountain in the environs. Both Homer and Hesiod mention Dodona, and its oracle was among the most respected of antiquity. Greeks from many cities, and even non-Greeks (as Crœsus, King of Lydia) consulted the oracle. The shrine was destroyed in warfare by the Ætolians in 219 B.C., but was probably restored thereafter. Modern archeologists have found scattered remains at the site.

DOE. See DEER.

DOE, JOHN, and **ROE,** RICHARD, in law, originally the names respectively of fictitious plaintiffs and fictitious defendants in common-law actions of ejectment. By extension, these names have come to be used in law to refer to a party whose identity is unknown or is concealed. The most frequently used is *John Doe,* and in criminal actions, proceedings against an alleged offender whose identity is unknown are sometimes called *John Doe* proceedings.

DOEBIRD. See CURLEW.

DOG, a name given to members of several species of the family Canidae, particularly the domestic dog, *Canis familiaris.* Dogs are four-footed carnivores with compact bodies and slender legs. Each forefoot bears five nonretractile claws and each hind foot bears four. The head of the dog is constricted to form a muzzle. Characteristically the bodies, heads, and legs are covered with thick hair. In the true dog each jaw has six incisors, two canines, and eight premolars. The upper jaw carries two molar teeth on each side and the lower jaw carries three.

Though dogs are carnivorous and subsist

M.G.M.; U.S. Coast Guard; Stand. Oil Co. (N.J.)

WORKING DOGS. *Above: A Saint Bernard dog in scene from a motion picture. This type of dog often accompanies monks in the Swiss Alps in search of persons lost in storms. Left: German shepherd with United States Coast Guardsman, patrolling beaches during World War II. Below: Team of Eskimo dogs hitched to sledge, in northwestern Canada.*

chiefly on red meat when they are in the wild state, they also eat reptiles, fish, insects, and some forms of vegetable matter. They are gregarious in habit and usually hunt in packs. Most species mature in about two years and have an average life span of ten to twelve years, although individuals may live to an age of more than twenty.

WILD DOGS. The genus *Canis* contains a number of wild species, several of which are known as wild dogs. Among them are the Australian dingo (q.v.), *C. dingo*; the wild dog of Burma, *C. rutilans*; and the Siberian wild dog, *C. alpinus*. The coyote (q.v.), *C. latrans*, of the western U.S. is also sometimes called a wild dog. The wild dogs of India, the dhole and buansu, belong to a related genus, *Cuon,* and differ from the true dogs in that they have one less molar on either side of the lower jaw. Some other members of the family Canidae are also called dogs, including the fox dog, and the raccoon dog, *Nyctereutes procyonides,* which is found in Japan and China and resembles a small raccoon.

DOMESTIC DOGS. The extraordinary variety shown by the various breeds of *C. familiaris* is strong evidence of the length of time that the dog has been bred selectively as a domestic animal. Neolithic remains indicate that dogs shared human habitations in prehistoric times, and Egyptian monuments of about 3000 B.C. show pictures of several well-defined breeds of dogs. It is impossible to be certain of the ancestry of the domestic dog, but it is extremely likely that the species arose from selective breeding of the wolf, *Canis lupus,* and crossing with other wild members of the genus.

The many breeds of domestic dogs are grouped today into two broad general classes: sporting dogs, or dogs useful for hunting, and nonsporting dogs. A more detailed grouping divides all dogs into six divisions, as follows (for information concerning each group or breed mentioned, see the individual articles under the name of each group or breed).

Sporting Dogs are the dogs known also as "gun dogs" or "field dogs" (q.v.), used in the sport of hunting. The group comprises the following breeds and varieties of breeds: the griffon and the pointer, including the English or American pointer and the German shorthaired pointer; the retriever, including the Chesapeake Bay, curly or curly-coated, flat-coated, golden, and Labrador retrievers; the setter, including the English, Gordon, and Irish setters; and the spaniel, including the American water, Brittany, Clumber, cocker,

field, Irish water, English springer, Welsh springer, and Sussex spaniels.

Sporting Dogs of the Hound Type comprise mainly hunting dogs that follow their quarry by scent, but include also a few breeds of hound that follow quarry by sight. The principal breeds of hound are the Afghan hound, basset hound, beagle, bloodhound, borzoi or Russian wolfhound, dachshund, Scottish deerhound, Norwegian elkhound, foxhound, greyhound, otterhound, saluki, whippet, and Irish wolfhound.

Working Dogs comprise dogs useful for such practical tasks as herding, pulling carts or sleds, carrying packs, guarding, and assisting police in pursuing and catching criminals. The principal breeds of working dogs are the Alaskan malamute, Belgian sheepdog, boxer, briard, collie, Eskimo dog, German shepherd dog, great Dane, great Pyrenees dog, komondorok, kuvasz, mastiff, Newfoundland dog, old English sheepdog, Samoyede, Shetland sheepdog, Siberian husky, and Saint Bernard dog.

Terriers are small or medium-sized dogs originally used for hunting small furred game, but now kept chiefly as pets. The terrier group includes the Airedale, Bedlington, bull, Dandie Dinmont, fox, Irish, Kerry blue, Manchester, Norwich, Scottish, Sealyham, Skye, Staffordshire, and Welsh terriers, and the schnauzer.

Toy Dogs are small dogs, or miniature varieties of larger dogs, used principally as pets. The group includes the Chihuahua, Italian greyhound, Mexican hairless dog, the papillon, miniature pinscher, Pomeranian, pug dog, toy Manchester terrier, toy poodle, and Yorkshire terrier.

Nonsporting Dogs are dogs used mainly as companions. Among the breeds of this group are the Boston terrier, the English and the French bulldog, the Chow Chow, the Dalmatian, the Keeshonden, the poodle, and the schipperke.

DOGBANE, common name for plants of the genus *Apocynum* of the family Apocynaceae. The dogbane of N. America, *A. androsaemifolium,* called variously the spreading dogbane, wild ipecac, American fly-trap, or honey-bloom, is a perennial shrublike herb containing a poisonous milky juice. It grows to a height of from 1 to 4 feet. The plant has widely branching stems and opposite, slightly pointed leaves. The small, well-shaped flowers are pink and numerous, and are borne in clusters. Dogbane grows in open, barren places from Georgia to Canada. The bark of the root is valued for its emetic, diaphoretic, and tonic properties. Canadian or Indian hemp, *A. cannabium*, which is found throughout western U.S., was used by the American Indians as a source of fiber for making rope.

DOG DAYS. See CANIS MAJOR.

DOG, DISEASES OF, maladies affecting dogs, particularly the domestic dog, *Canis familiaris*. Among the commonest and most destructive of dog diseases are distemper and mange (qq.v.). Hydrophobia (q.v.), known also as rabies, occurs less often, but is a very dangerous disease both to dogs and to man.

Blacktongue, a disease which chiefly attacks dogs in middle age or old age, is caused by a deficiency of B vitamins, particularly of nicotinic acid, as is pellagra in man. It is characterized by inflammation of the tongue and the inside of the mouth and similar symptoms in the intestinal tract, accompanied by vomiting and diarrhea. During the course of the disease the tongue frequently becomes blue-black in color. The prevention and treatment of blacktongue depends on diet. Dried yeast is prescribed by veterinarians for animals suffering from the disease. The use of yeast, fresh meat, milk, and salmon in the dog's normal diet has been found to be a good preventive measure.

Fits or convulsions in dogs can arise from a number of causes, including foreign bodies or parasites in the intestinal tract, indigestion, violent exercise or excitement, and teething in puppies. In these attacks the dog will usually become rigid, make chewing motions, froth at the mouth, and fall to the ground kicking spasmodically. When fits occur, veterinarians recommend removing the animal to a quiet place and not feeding it for a day after the attack has passed. *Running fits* or *fright disease,* in which the animal runs around and barks wildly and seemingly exhibits great excitement or fear, is a malady of obscure origin which is sometimes mistaken for rabies. It is believed that diet may play some part in this disease, since it seems to be more common in dogs that have been fed largely on cereals and breadstuffs than in dogs that have had plenty of meat in their diet.

Dogs are subject to a number of internal parasites including protozoa, flukes, and worms. The most destructive of these parasites are the *hookworms,* small roundworms with sharp, hooklike teeth, with which they fasten themselves to the animals' intestines. These worms draw a large quantity of blood from the host and cause symptoms of anemia, such as loss of weight and pallor of the mucous membranes of the mouth. A number of drugs have been used to control hookworms, of which the most effective are tetrachloroethylene and *n*-butyl chloride. Various species of *tapeworms* are also found in the intestines of dogs. These flattened worms attach themselves to the intestinal walls and in some cases grow to a length of 16 ft. The symptoms caused by tapeworm infestations vary, but usually include diarrhea and other digestive disturbances. The drug used for treatment is arecoline bromide, a strong purgative. Dogs are also subject to heartworms, nematodes which are transmitted by the bites of mosquitoes and fleas, and which infest the valves of the heart and the pulmonary artery. A dog suffering from heartworms becomes tired easily and may collapse after exercise and exhibit other symptoms of bad circulation. Heartworms have been treated successfully by injections of various antimony compounds. Other types of worms which attack the lungs, kidney, and eyes are less common but are sometimes encountered in dogs.

Of the external parasites which attack dogs, ticks are the most dangerous, not only for the harm that they do to dogs but because they transmit spotted fever and tularemia (qq.v.) which are highly dangerous to humans. In regions which are infested with ticks, dogs may be kept free of ticks by dipping them twice weekly in a solution of soap and derris powder. Tweezers are used to remove ticks to avoid the possibility of infection.

DOGE (Lat. *dux,* "leader"), title of the chief magistrate of the former republics of Venice and Genoa. At the time (697 A.D.) of its institution in Venice, the office was filled by popular vote. The early doges were vested with executive authority, the power to convoke the *Concio,* or popular assembly, and the authority to appoint various officials. Attempts by later doges to make the office hereditary met with strong opposition from the people. In 1032, legislation confirming the antidynastic principle was adopted, prohibiting appointment or nomination of a successor by a doge. Additional legislation adopted at the same time provided further checks on the doge's powers. Thereafter his acts were subject to review and approval of a privy council of two and a larger council of prominent citizens called the *Pregadi,* or Senate. Other restrictions on the doge's authority followed, as in 1172, when the *Maggior Consiglio,* or Greater Council, was created. This body, consisting of about 480 members appointed for one-year terms by special electors, was granted extensive powers, including the right to appoint electors and various other important officials. In addition, the powers of the *Concio* were restricted, the privy council was enlarged, and election of the doge became the responsibility of eleven electors chosen from the nobility. These measures represented the first stages of a process which culminated, early in the 14th century, in the centralization of political power in the hands of a few aristocratic families. In 1310, the Council of Ten (q.v.) became the governing authority of Venice. Thereafter, the doge's functions were chiefly ceremonial. On the overthrow of the republic in 1797, the office was abolished.

In the Republic of Genoa, the first doge was elected for life by popular vote, in 1339. The Genoese doges enjoyed unrestricted power until the conquest of the republic, in 1396, by the French. For more than a century afterward the rulers of Genoa were puppets, dominated alternatively by France and Milan. Following the liberation of Genoa, in 1528, by Andrea Doria, the doge's term of office was limited to two years. The new constitution also restricted the office to members of the nobility, who gradually acquired complete control of the republic. In 1797, when Genoa was again occupied by the French, the office was abolished. It was reinstituted for a brief period from 1802 to 1805.

DOGE'S PALACE, THE (It. *Palazzo Ducale*), the former official residence of the doges (see DOGE) of Venice, Italy, and one of the best examples of medieval architecture in Europe. Construction of the edifice, fourth of a series (the previous buildings having been destroyed by fire) dating from about 814, was begun at Venice in 1309 by the doge Pietro Gradenigo (1249–1311). Most of it was completed by the middle of the 15th century, although certain additions, including the Renaissance staircase leading from the interior court to the upper loggia, were added later. Among the most imposing features of the palace are the south and west façades, dating from the first half of the 15th century. The façades have a total of 35 arches, which form a long first story, or loggia. This is surmounted by a traceried arcade, with 71 columns. The massive walls of the upper two stories are relieved by balconies, arched windows, and surface patterning in red Verona marble and white Istrian stone. The entire building is profusely decorated by finely ex-

Façade of the Doge's Palace in Venice

ecuted sculpture. Outstanding points of interest in the palace include the Hall of the Greater Council, where the meetings of the *Nobili* were held; the Bridge of Sighs (built in 1660), linking the palace with the adjoining prison; and the torture and execution chambers used during the Inquisition. The walls and ceilings of the more important rooms of the palace are adorned with works by the great 16th-century Venetian painters Vecelli Titian, Paolo Veronese, and Il Tintoretto.

DOG FENNEL. See FEVERFEW; MAYWEED.

DOGFISH, or DOG SHARK, common name for any of a number of small sharks, particularly members of the families Carchariidae (q.v.), Squalidae, and Scylliorhinidae. The dogfishes differ from most other sharks in that most species are oviparous and have the habit of feeding and hunting in groups rather than singly. The most common dogfish is the spiny dogfish, *Squalus acanthias*, which is found in coastal waters on both sides of the North Atlantic. This shark is a slender fish about 4 ft. in length and has a spiny protuberance in front of each of its dorsal fins. A similar species, *S. suckleyi*, native to Californian waters, is also known as the spiny dogfish. The smooth dogfish, *Cynias canis*, is a larger species common in the North Atlantic. The name spotted dogfish is given to two spotted species, the 2-ft. rough hound, *Scyllium canicula*, and the nurse hound, *Scyllium catulus*, both of which are found in the Atlantic. Dogfish are seldom used for food, but are sometimes caught for their livers, which are a source of vitamins A and D. See FISH; SHARK.

DOGGER BANK, an extensive flat sandbank near the middle of the North Sea, between England on the w. and Denmark on the E. It has an average breadth of about 40 m., and stretches N.E. and S.W. for a distance of about 160 m. The depth is generally less than 120 feet, and toward the English coast is little over 50 feet. The bank is noted for codfishing. In 1781 a naval engagement was fought there between English and Dutch fleets. In 1904 the Russian Baltic squadron, under Admiral Rozhdestvenski, by mistake fired upon a British fishing fleet and killed two men. The incident was settled by arbitration, with Russia paying damages. In 1915, during World War I, a British fleet under the command of Vice-Admiral Sir David Beatty defeated a German fleet commanded by Rear Admiral Franz von Hipper in the Battle of the Dogger Bank.

DOG GRASS, common name for any of several grasses, especially couch grass (q.v.) or dog bent (see BENT GRASS).

DOGMA, originally an opinion or proposition put as a positive assertion, its truth being supposed to have been previously shown. In theology, the term signifies a doctrine defined by the Church and advanced, not for discussion, but for belief.

The first attempt to give a connected view of Christian dogma was made in the 4th century by St. Augustine, who in his *Encheiridion* and other works compiled and discussed the whole body of doctrine held by the Church, though without scientific arrangement. The contributions to doctrinal theology, or dogmatics, made in the 5th, 6th, and 7th centuries were isolated statements rather than organized bodies of doctrine.

In the East, in the 8th century, the dogmas of the Greek Church were gathered and codified by John of Damascus, and his work may be considered the first systematically arranged treatise on dogmatics. Many theologians of the Western Church have since given exhaustive study to the subject, especially St. Thomas Aquinas, whose works Pope Leo XIII designated as the norm of modern dogmatic theology.

Because the dogmatic method easily degenerates into an insistence upon the validity of groundless opinions, the term *dogma* has come to be frequently used, in everyday speech, for assertion without proof.

DOGMATISM, in philosophy, the promulgation of a doctrine or theory without preliminary examination of the conditions and limits of knowledge and without regard for contradictory evidence. If, for example, a philosopher accepts a judgment regarding ultimate reality without inquiring whether such reality can actually be known in accordance with a logically tenable theory of knowledge, and without taking account of all relevant empirical data, he is generally considered a dogmatist. The assertions that evolution is false because the Bible does not mention it and the assertion that God does not exist because He cannot be found in a laboratory are both dogmatic. Thus, dogmatism properly refers to the theory of knowledge according to which a belief is held, rather than to the content of the belief itself. In the 18th century the German philosopher Immanuel Kant inaugurated the modern era of critical thought by declaring that previous philosophies had been insufficiently critical of the capabilities of human reasoning and had attempted to know what was actually unknowable; Kant then tried to define rigorously the limits within which knowledge is possible. Certain modern philosophies, notably some schools of pragmatism and positivism (qq.v.), have also been called dogmatic because they base truth on a narrow interpretation of valid experience and so exclude too much evidence from consideration. See EPISTEMOLOGY; CRITICAL PHILOSOPHY.

DOGRIBS, a North American Indian tribe of Athapascan stock, inhabiting an area between the Great Bear and Great Slave Lakes in the Northwest Territories, Canada.

DOG ROSE, common name for a wild rose, *Rosa canina*, native to Eurasia. It grows wild in Europe and the eastern part of the United States as a shrub or bush. It has stout, hooked prickles and bears mostly single, pink or white flowers. Because of its hardiness, it has been widely used in Europe as a stock for grafting. See ROSE.

DOG SALMON. 1. A salmon, *Oncorhynchus keta*, common on the Pacific coast of northwestern U.S. and Japan. It resembles the quinnat (q.v.), but has no spots on its fins and is smaller. It is often called keta. A similar species found in Alaska, the humpbacked salmon, *O. gorbuscha,* is also called the dog salmon. **2.** The name given to any adult male salmon while it is swimming upstream to its breeding place or spawning at the breeding grounds. These males die soon after spawning. See SALMON.

DOG SHARK. See DOGFISH; TOPE.

DOG'S-TAIL GRASS, common name for any grass of the genus *Cynosurus,* native to Europe and Asia. *C. cristatus,* the crested dog's-tail grass, is a perennial, growing in tufts 1 to 2 feet high. Its herbage is thin and of insufficient quantity for good hay, but its deep roots make it drought resistant. It is important in pastures and lawns, and is used in the manufacture of Leghorn hats. Another common name, goldseed, is due to its small, shiny, yellow seeds.

DOG STAR. See CANIS MAJOR; SIRIUS.

DOGWOOD, common name for plants of the genus *Cornus.* About 25 species of dogwood occur in Europe, Asia, and North America. They are nearly all showy shrubs or small trees which brighten the spring, fall, and winter landscapes of many parts of Europe and N. America. A few, such as *C. canadensis,* are herbs; and some, such as *C. nuttalli,* are trees growing to a height of 75 feet or more. The native flowering dogwood, *C. florida,* is rarely more than 30 feet tall. In the early

Flower of the dog rose

Blossoms of native flowering dogwood

spring its "blossoms", consisting of dense heads of small, inconspicuous greenish flowers, each head surrounded by four prominent, white, blunt-ended bracts, are a familiar sight in the Atlantic Coast States. In the fall it bears red leaves and scarlet fruits.

C. alba, the Tatarian dogwood of w. Asia, grows to a height of 10 feet. It has blood-red branches, creamy-white inflorescences, and white or bluish fruits. *C. amomum,* the silky dogwood, is a purple-branched shrub found from Massachusetts to Tennessee. It has a yellowish inflorescence and blue fruits. The red osier dogwood, *C. stolonifera,* which spreads by means of underground stems, grows from Newfoundland to Virginia. It has dark red branches and white or blue fruits. *C. racemosa,* found from Maine to Georgia, has gray branches and produces attractive white inflorescences in early summer. It has red stems and bears white fruits in the fall. *C. rugosa* has purple branches and bears creamy-white inflorescences. The blood-twig dogwood, *C. sanguinea,* is the common European species. It has dark red branches and its leaves are deep red in the fall. The cornel or cornelian cherry, *C. mas,* is a large European shrub which bears red, edible fruits in late summer.

Oil extracted from the fruit of the blood-twig dogwood is used for making soap in France. The hard, white, fine-grained wood of *C. nuttalli,* which grows in the Pacific Northwest, is used for inlaying and turning.

A leguminous tree of the West Indies, *Piscidia erythrina,* is known as dogwood. Poison sumac is sometimes improperly called poison dogwood.

DOGWOOD FAMILY, or CORNACEAE, a family in the order Umbellales, consisting of 16 genera and 90 species, found mainly in temperate regions. The Cornaceae are usually trees or shrubs, and rarely herbs. *Cornus* and *Nyssa* are the two main genera.

DOHNÁNYI, ERNÖ (1877–), Hungarian pianist, composer, and conductor, born in Pressburg. He was a pupil (1885–94) in piano and harmony of Carl Forstner, in Pressburg; later he studied at the Royal Academy of Music, Budapest, and with Eugen d'Albert. As a pianist he toured in Europe, Great Britain, and the United States from 1897 to 1908. He became director of the Budapest Conservatory in 1919, and conducted the Budapest Philharmonic Orchestra. In 1926 he came to New York City to conduct a number of concerts for the State Symphony Orchestra. In 1931 he became general director of the Hungarian National Radio. He lived in the United States after 1948 and taught at Florida State College. Among his compositions are orchestral works, including two symphonies, two piano concertos, two violin concertos; the opera *The Tower of Voivod* (1922); the comic operas *Tante Simona* (1912) and *The Tenor* (1929); *Concertina for Harp and Orchestra* (1952); chamber music, including three string quartets; music for piano; and songs.

DOISY, EDWARD ADELBERT (1893–), American biochemist, born at Hume, Ill., and educated at the University of Illinois and at Harvard University. In 1923 he became professor of biochemistry at the St. Louis University School of Medicine, and in 1924 became director of the department of biochemistry at St. Mary's Hospital. He is best known for his researches with female sex hormones, blood buffers, antibiotics, and vitamin K. He shared the Nobel Prize in medicine in 1943 (with Henrick Dam, q.v.) for his discovery of the chemical nature of vitamin K. He was a coauthor of *Sex and Internal Secretions* (1939).

DOLCI or **DOLCE,** CARLO or CARLINO (1616–86), Florentine painter. He is best known for his small religious paintings, usually representing a single figure, half figure, or head. He is also noted for his portraits. Among his works are "Andrew Praying before his Crucifixion" and "Ecce Homo" (both in the Pitti Gallery, Florence), "Christ Blessing the Bread and Wine" (Cathedral of Pistoja), "St. Cecilia" (Dresden Gallery), "Magdalen" (Munich Gallery), and a self-portrait at the age of 56 and the portrait "Archduchess Claudia" (both in the Uffizi Gallery, Florence).

DOLE, SANFORD BALLARD (1844–1926), American statesman and lawyer, born in Honolulu, Hawaii, and educated at Oahu College (Hawaii) and Williams College (Mass.). From 1884 to 1887 he sat in the Hawaiian legislature, and was active in securing the Constitution of 1887. When the monarchy of Queen Liliuokalani was overthrown in 1893, he was elected first president of the Republic of Hawaii. In 1898, after the attempt of President Grover Cleveland to restore the queen, Dole went to Washington to use his influence in favor of annexation. Hawaii was adopted as a territory of the United States in 1900, and President William McKinley appointed Dole first territorial governor. In 1903 he became U.S. district court judge in Hawaii and served until his retirement in 1915.

DOLERITE, a rock of coarse basaltic composition. See BASALT.

DOLICHOS, a genus of twining plants, chiefly tropical, in the leguminous subfamily Papilionoideae. Several species are grown for food, forage, and cover crops in the tropics. Two species are grown in gardens of the U.S. for their wistarialike flowers. *D. lablab,* called the hyacinth bean, bonavist, or lablab, a perennial grown as an annual, has large tripartite leaves and reddish-purple flowers. *D. lignosus,* the Australian pea, is also a perennial, and has rosy-purple or white flowers and much smaller leaves. Other important species are *D. lubia,* a native of Egypt; *D. biflora* (horse gram), a native of India; and *D. sphaerospermus* (calavana, or dark-eyed pea), a native of the West Indies. See BEAN.

DOLL, a miniature figure, usually representing a baby. It is one of the oldest toys in human use, common to all times and nations. Dolls were known to the Asiatics, the Egyptians, and the Arabs as long ago as the 18th century B.C. Evidence of their use has been found in Egyptian, Greek, and Roman remains, where figures of clay, bone, wood, ivory have been found buried in children's graves. The American Indians fashioned dolls in the image of deities, and such toys, carved out of wood, were regarded as sacred objects. The Keres Indians of Laguna used, for their ceremonial offerings, dolls that were merely rounded pieces of wood, resembling prayer sticks. The Eskimos have long made

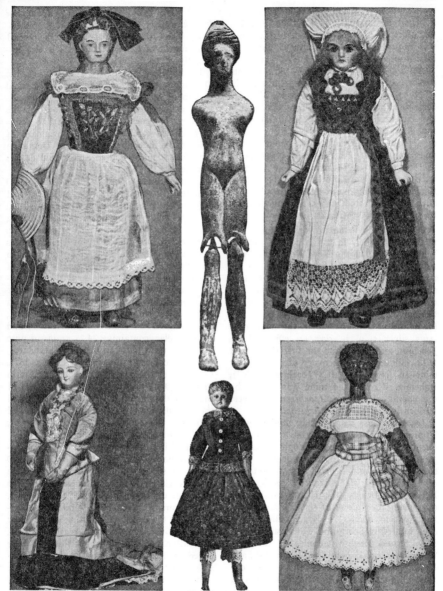

New-York Historical Society; Boston Museum of Fine Arts

DOLLS. *Top, left to right: Hungarian, 19th century; Greek, 4th century B.C.; Swedish, 20th century. Bottom: American dolls made in the 19th century.*

dolls out of bone, ivory, or animal teeth, dressed in fur and hide. Among the Mohammedans and Hindus, dolls with elaborate costumes were given to brides as wedding presents. In Europe, early in the Christian Era, dolls were made in the likeness of saints and were often used in representations of the scenes of the Nativity, especially at Christmastime. During the 17th and 18th centuries, such representations of the manger, the animals, and the magi and their followers reached a height of ingenuity and elaboration. The manufacture of dolls on an industrial scale was begun in the 19th century. Wood fell into disuse as a material and, from about 1860, dolls were made with kid or cloth bodies, and with heads of papier-mâché or china, and later of a hard wax. Many of these dolls had human hair, eyes that opened and shut, and an apparatus that imitated the sound of the human voice. Dolls made of rags, plastic materials, rubber, papier-mâché, and china, and stuffed dolls with bisque heads are common toys. Germany led in the production of dolls until World War II; after that time an increasing number of dolls were produced in the United States, England, France, Italy, and the Netherlands.

DOLLAR, the name of various coins formerly or currently in use in certain parts of Europe, Asia, and the New World; and specifically the standard value, or unit of account, in the monetary systems of Canada and the United States. The word dollar is derived from *daler,* Low German form of the German *thaler.* The latter word is an abbreviation of *Joachimsthaler,* the name of a large silver coin, bearing an effigy of St. Joachim, and struck for the first time about 1518, following the discovery of a rich silver mine in Joachimsthal ("Joachim's dale"), Bohemia. Because the mine was owned by the counts of Schlick, *Joachimsthaler* were frequently also called *Schlicksthaler.*

Joachimsthaler were widely used in what is present-day Germany, and were subsequently called dollars by English-speaking people. Later, Spanish coins, equal in value to eight reals and bearing a representation of the famous Mediterranean rocks called Pillars of Hercules (see HERCULES, PILLARS OF), were called *pieces of eight, pillar dollars,* and *Spanish dollars*; a large, milled, silver coin, minted in Spain and widely used in the Spanish and English colonies of the New World, was called *peso duro* in Spanish, and *hard dollar* in English. From this usage probably arose the modern practice of identifying the coins of a number of Latin American countries, such as the peso of Mexico, as dollars. An Austrian silver coin, bearing the image of the Empress Maria Theresa and issued since 1780 for use in trade, is known as the *Maria Theresa dollar* or *Levant dollar.* In the latter part of the 19th century the British government began minting silver coins for use in the crown colonies of Hong Kong and the (Malay) Straits Settlements; these

coins were called *Hong Kong dollars* or *British dollars,* and *Straits dollars,* respectively. The Chinese *yuan,* issued by the central government of China since 1914, is also frequently called a dollar.

In the latter part of the 19th century, the Dominion of Canada adopted the decimal system of coinage; dollars, cents, and mills were defined as the denominations of the country's currency, and a dollar of 2.58 grains of gold was established as the standard of value of its monetary system. The Dominion government made United States gold dollars legal tender in Canada.

UNITED STATES DOLLAR. The Continental Congress, in the year 1786, after it had adopted the decimal system of coinage, fixed the legal value of the dollar then circulating in the States, at 375.64 grains of pure silver. The first dollars minted in the United States were issued by the Federal government in Philadelphia in 1794, following passage of the Coinage Act of April 2, 1792. That enactment provided for two standards of value: a silver dollar "of the value of a Spanish milled dollar the same as is now current", containing 371.25 grains of pure silver; and a gold dollar, containing 24.75 grains of pure gold. The ratio between these two standards, called the coinage ratio, was expressed as 15:1. Congress, in 1834, increased the coinage ratio to 16.002:1 by decreasing the gold content of the gold dollar. In 1837 Congress increased the metallic content of the gold dollar and decreased the content of the silver dollar, making the coinage ratio about 15.98:1.

In revising the coinage law in 1873, Congress authorized the minting of dollars of 420 grains of silver, 900 fine; these coins were issued exclusively for use in trade with the Far East, and became known as *trade dollars.* At the same time, Congress omitted authorization for the continued minting of the silver dollars provided for in the legislation of 1837. Thereafter, no silver dollars of this type were issued until 1878, when passage of the Bland-Allison Act provided for resumption of their coinage. In 1887, Congress terminated the minting of *trade dollars.* A Congressional enactment in 1900 established the gold dollar as the monetary standard of value in the United States, thereby fixing the legal value of legal-tender paper money in terms of the metallic gold dollar. Following passage of the Gold Reserve Act of 1934, the gold content of the dollar was reduced to 59.06% of its former content, all gold coins and certificates were made the property of the Federal government, and the coinage of gold dollars was discontinued (see DEVALUATION). At that time, about 321 million gold dollars were in circulation in the United States. In 1953 there were 491,517,862 silver dollars in circulation. See MONEY: *Monetary System of the United States*; BIMETALLISM; FOREIGN EXCHANGE; MINT.

DOLLARFISH. See HARVEST FISH.

DOLLFUSS, ENGELBERT (1892–1934), Austrian statesman, born in Texing, Lower Austria. He was educated at the Universities of Vienna and Berlin, and received a degree in political economy from the latter university. Dollfuss was a leading member of the Christian Socialist Party. In 1931 he became president of the Federal Railways, and the following year minister of agriculture and forestry. In 1932 he was appointed chancellor. To resist Nazi efforts to undermine the independence of Austria and forcibly incorporate it into Germany, Dollfuss made an alliance with the Heimwehr (Home Guard), a private fascist army led by Prince von Stahremberg and reported to have received arms and money from Mussolini. Following Hitler's coming to power in Germany, President Miklas of Austria, in March, 1933, invested Dollfuss with extraordinary powers. Dollfuss immediately dissolved the parliament, abolished freedom of speech, the press, and assembly, and dissolved the Communist Party and the Schutzbund (armed defense body of the Social Democratic Party). In June he outlawed the National Socialist Party (Nazis). In February of the following year, in protest against Heimwehr raids on their centers and press, the workers of Vienna, led by the Social Democrats, declared a general strike. Civil war broke out. Dollfuss, using the Heimwehr, crushed the strike after several days of fighting that resulted in more than a thousand casualties. He then dissolved the Social Democratic Party and called a rump parliament which voted a new constitution establishing a "Christian German Federal State on a corporative basis". During the unsuccessful Nazi putsch of July 25, 1934, Dollfuss was assassinated.

DÖLLINGER, JOHANN JOSEPH IGNAZ VON (1799–1890), German Catholic theologian and historian, born at Bamberg, Bavaria, and educated at the lyceum for philosophy and Catholic theology in that city. He was ordained a priest in 1822 and four years later became professor of theology at the University of Munich. In 1844 he represented his university in the second chamber of the Bavarian legislature. In *Die Reformation* (1846–48) and *Luther* (1851) he vehemently attacked the Reformers and their work. Döllinger delivered two addresses in Munich in 1861 which were regarded as hostile to the temporal sovereignty of the Pope; he attempted to justify his position in *Kirche und Kirchen, Papstthum und Kirchenstaat* (1861). When the Vatican Council issued a decree affirming the doctrine of papal infallibility in 1869, Döllinger refused to accede to the doctrine. In the following year he organized a meeting of theologians at Nuremberg which publicly repudiated the doctrine, and later organized the Old Catholic movement. In 1871 Döllinger was excommunicated by the Archbishop of Munich. He presided over joint conferences of theologians of the Old Catholic, Eastern, and Anglican churches, which were held at Bonn, Germany, in 1872, 1874, and 1875, for the purpose of formulating plans for church unity. His other writings include *Past and Present of Catholic Theology* (1863), *Universities Past and Present* (1867), and *Geschichte der Moralstreitigkeiten in der Römisch-Katholischen Kirche seit dem 16. Jahrhundert* (1899).

DOLLY VARDEN TROUT, a char (q.v.), *Salvelinus malma*, named for the Dolly Varden, a gaily-printed muslin dress popular from 1865 to 1870. These trout are olive green with orange or red spots, and are two or three feet long; they weigh from five to twelve pounds. They are native to the streams of the Pacific Northwest of the United States, Canada, and Alaska. See TROUT.

DOLMEN, or CROMLECH, in archeology, a type of prehistoric chamber consisting of several huge unhewn stone slabs, or megaliths, set edgewise in the earth and supporting a flat capstone which serves as a roof. Dolmens are found particularly in the British Isles where they occur in large numbers in Ireland, Wales, Devonshire, and Cornwall; in northwestern France, especially in Brittany; and in Spain. They are also found in northern Africa, in Syria, and in other countries ranging as far east as Japan. Dolmens were sometimes covered with immense artificial hillocks or tumuli, but at times the covering of earth reached only the capstone. Sometimes the mound enclosing the dolmen was of great size, as that of Sidbury Hill, Wiltshire, which was 170 feet high and 316 feet along the slope. Archeologists now believe that dolmens were burial chambers. They are known to have served also as altars,

Dolmen in Cornwall, England

as in Guernsey, where they were used by the Druids for their religious rites.

DOLMETSCH, ARNOLD (1858–1940), French musician and musical antiquarian, born at Le Mans. He studied the violin with Henri Vieuxtemps at Brussels, and also at the Royal College of Music, London. He became a collector of obsolete types of musical instruments, including stringed instruments such as the viol and the viola da gamba; keyboard instruments such as the virginal, spinet, harpsichord, and clavichord; and wind instruments. From 1902 to 1909 he was employed by the piano manufacturers Chickering & Sons, of Boston, Mass., principally to make instruments of obsolete keyboard types and to restore or repair old specimens. In 1914 he established a factory of his own at Haslemere, Surrey, England, for making and repairing all types of obsolete instruments. From 1925 to 1940 he gave annual festivals at Haslemere of chamber music of the 16th to the 19th centuries, at which the music was played on obsolete instruments principally by him and by members of his family. He was also the leader of the Dolmetsch Trio, which gave recitals of early music. Dolmetsch edited much old music and was the author of *The Interpretation of the Music of the Seventeenth and Eighteenth Centuries* (1915).

DOLOMITE, a common mineral with the formula $CaMg(CO_3)_2$, occurring chiefly in rock masses as dolomitic limestone, but occurring sometimes in veins. It has a hardness of $3\frac{1}{2}$ to 4, and sp.g. 2.85. It is usually colorless, white, pink, or flesh-colored, but may be brown, black, or green, depending on the impurities present. In the United States it is found at many localities in Vermont, Rhode Island, New Jersey, and New York. Good crystals of dolomite have been obtained from the deposits at Joplin, Missouri. When treated with sulfuric acid, dolomite yields calcium sulfate (gypsum) and magnesium sulfate (Epsom salts). Calcined dolomite is extensively employed as a lining for Bessemer converters in the production of steel from pig iron.

Some varieties of dolomite are called bitter spar or pearl spar. The name dolomite is sometimes given to any rock composed chiefly of massive dolomite, or of any combination of magnesium and calcium carbonates. Compare CALCITE; MAGNESITE; LIMESTONE.

DOLPHIN, common name for cetaceans of the family Delphinidae, closely related to the porpoises, commonly but incorrectly called fish. They are native to all seas and some large rivers. These aquatic mammals travel in schools and are very graceful swimmers and divers. Dolphins feed on small fish and have many small, sharp teeth. The snout of the dolphin is a distinct, flattened beak about six inches long to which the skull drops sharply. The top of the head has a single, crescent-shaped blowhole, and there is usually a conspicuous, triangular fin on the back. Dolphins are usually under 10 feet in length.

The common dolphin, *Delphinus delphis,* sometimes called porpoise, occurs in the Mediterranean Sea and in the North Atlantic Ocean. It is about 7 feet long, black on top and white on bottom. This dolphin has about

200 sharp teeth, and its dorsal fin is about 9 inches high. A pure white dolphin, *D. sinensis,* occurs in the Chinese sea, and an allied species *D. peronii,* is native to the south seas. In the waters off the eastern coast of North America, the bottlenose (q.v.) or bottle-nosed dolphin, *Tursiops truncatus,* is often seen. Among other dolphins are the bouto, an inhabitant of South American coastal waters, the tucuxi, which occurs in the rivers of the Amazon valley, and the beluga (q.v.). See CETACEA.

The coryphene, a true fish, is also called dolphin. See CORYPHENE.

DOMAGK, GERHARD (1895–   ), German chemist, born in Lagow, and educated at the University of Kiel. He was professor of chemistry at the University of Münster, becoming in 1925 a member of the Pathological Institute there. In 1927 he was made director of the I. G. Farbenindustrie research institute in Elberfeld. He discovered prontosil, the forerunner of sulfanilamide, the "wonder drug" used in combatting various infectious diseases. For this discovery he was awarded the Nobel Prize for physiology and medicine in 1939, but was forbidden to accept it by the Hitler government, which had been angered in 1935 by the award of a Nobel Prize to an anti-Nazi. In 1947 he was awarded the Nobel gold medal. See SULFA DRUGS.

DOME, in architecture, a roof, usually hemispherical in form, although at times ovoid, pointed, or bulbous, constructed on a circular or, rarely, on an elliptical base. The term is almost synonymous with "cupola", and the two words are often used interchangeably. A dome may be constructed of a variety of materials, including wood, stone, metal, concrete, and tile; it may be built in a single thickness or consist of two or even three shells. It may rise directly from a substructure or be raised upon a drum, and it may

be crowned with a lantern of stone or wood, or be without one.

The dome was first developed as roofing over the circular huts of the ancient peoples of the Mesopotamian region. Representations of such dwellings and domes are found in Assyrian bas-reliefs dating from the 8th and 7th centuries B.C. The dome was also used in Persia from early times through the Sassanian period, which culminated in the middle of the 7th century A.D. The domes of the Assyrians and Persians, on palaces as well as on ordinary dwellings, were sometimes of low hemispherical and sometimes of high ovoidal form; they were usually constructed of brick and were supported by solid walls. The principles of the dome were characteristic of Mycenean beehive tombs, but the dome, with the arch (q.v.), was abandoned in classical Greek architecture. The Romans learned the construction of the dome from the Etruscans, and developed it into a form that exerted great influence on the architecture of succeeding periods. The most noteworthy of the Roman domes is that of the Pantheon (q.v.), built between 110 and 125 A.D. by order of the Emperor Hadrian. The largest masonry dome in the world, it is hemispherical in shape, measuring 144 ft. in diameter, and rests upon a continuous wall; light is admitted by means of a great circular opening in the top of the dome, the *oculus* or "eye". The Roman hemispherical dome was used in early Christian times for roofing mausoleums and baptisteries. The dome (about 325 A.D.) of the mausoleum of the church of Santa Constanza, Rome, is notable because it was the first dome not supported by a continuous wall, but instead by a series of twelve arches borne on a double circle of columns.

The dome was easily constructed over a circular room, which it naturally fitted, but from early times builders were concerned with the

Common dolphin of the Mediterranean Sea and North Atlantic Ocean

problem of erecting a dome over a square or octagonal room or building. The problem was strikingly solved by Byzantine architects (see BYZANTINE ART: *Architecture*) of the 6th century A.D. in the construction of the dome of the church of Saint Sophia (q.v.) or Santa Sophia, in Constantinople. The weight of this dome, which is 100 ft. in diameter and rises 180 ft. above the floor of the church, is supported not by a circular wall, as the dome of the Pantheon is supported, but by four piers, one in each corner of the square area covered by the dome. From the upper part of each pier extends a triangular segment of masonry termed a pendentive; the pendentives join and form four round arches, which span the sides of the square. The dome is supported on the arches, its weight being transferred to the piers through the pendentives. The lower part of the dome of St. Sophia has a circle of forty windows, with buttresses between them; from this construction was derived the dome supported on a drum, often pierced with windows.

By the use of pendentives, domes could be constructed not only over square areas but over areas of any shape; an additional advantage was that the floor space beneath the dome was unenclosed. The dome of St. Sophia was widely imitated in Italy and in France and in the lands conquered by the Mohammedans, including India, Persia, Turkey, Egypt, North Africa, Sicily, and Spain. Notable examples of the Byzantine type of dome are the dome of the church (now cathedral, begun 1063) of St. Mark, Venice, and that of the church of Saint Front (begun 1120), Perigueux, France. Mohammedan builders did not use the circular form of dome but developed the pointed dome, the ovoid dome, and (in Persia, about the 15th century) the swelling or bulbous dome. The Mohammedan domes of India are particularly notable, and include those of structures in Delhi and Bijapur, dating from the 16th and 17th centuries, and the famous alabaster dome of the mausoleum Taj Mahal, at Agra (q.v.).

The dome of the Pantheon at Rome served as an example for the domes built on many churches in Italy during the Renaissance. Such domes were usually constructed over the part of the church floor known as the "crossing", where the transept of the church crossed the nave. The type of support used, however, was of Byzantine origin, with pendentives; between the pendentives and the dome a drum was generally constructed, and the top of the dome was usually crowned by a stone lantern of great weight. Architects constantly strove to build domes large enough for impressive external appearance, but were constantly faced by the problem of a dome weighing so much that, with the additional weight of the lantern at its apex, it caused the base of the entire structure to spread. One solution to the problem was to re-enforce the dome's base by wooden beams held together in a chain; another was to build domes with two or more shells instead of with one shell. In the dome with two shells, the smaller inner dome usually supported the weighty lantern, thus making possible the construction of a far larger outer shell, which gave the external appearance sought. Among the most notable of Renaissance domes is that of Santa Maria del Fiore Cathedral, Florence, completed by the Italian architect Filippo Brunelleschi in 1431. The dome has two shells, and is about 137 ft. in interior diameter and over 300 ft. high. Though generally called a dome, this structure is technically a vault (q.v.), for it is octagonal in shape rather than hemispherical. Perhaps the most famous of all Renaissance domes is that of the basilica of St. Peter's, Rome, designed by the Italian architect Michelangelo and completed (1590) after his death. It has two shells

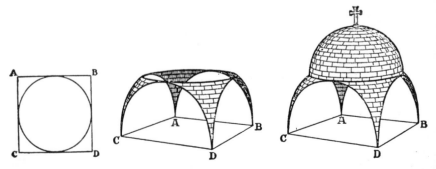

Drawings showing how pendentives are used to support a circular dome over a square room

Canadian Pacific Railway

THE DOME. *Left: Interior of the Pantheon in Rome, showing the oculus at top of dome.*
Right: Top, Brunelleschi's dome, Florence; bottom, bulbous Mohammedan dome in Delhi.

of brick, the inner supporting the lantern; like Brunelleschi's dome, it is about 137 ft. in interior diameter. Another important Italian dome of this period is that of the church of Santa Maria della Salute, Venice (completed 1631), designed by the Venetian architect Baldassare Longhena (1604–32). It has two shells, the inner of masonry and the outer of timber, and is 80 ft. in interior diameter.

Among the most notable domes constructed outside of Italy after the Renaissance are that of St. Paul's Cathedral (1675–1710), London, 102 ft. in interior diameter, designed by the English architect Sir Christopher Wren; that of the church of Les Invalides (1706), Paris, 92 ft. in interior diameter, designed by the

French architect Jules Hardouin-Mansart; and that of the Pantheon (1735), Paris, 74 ft. in interior diameter, designed by the French architect Jacques Soufflot. Each of these domes has three shells, the second of which supports the lantern.

The dome has been widely used in the United States for State capitols, beginning with the construction (completed 1798) of the dome for the capitol of Massachusetts, designed by the American architect Charles Bulfinch (q.v.). The dome of the Capitol at Washington, D.C., 90 ft. in interior diameter, is made of cast iron and was designed and completed (1865) by the American architect Thomas U. Walter (q.v.). Large libraries are often built with domes. That of the Library of Columbia University, New York City, is 80 ft. in diameter; that of the public library of Melbourne, Australia, is 124 ft. Domes of glass and steel are often used for the buildings of expositions and for large conservatories. The Hayden Planetarium (q.v.), New York City, has an outer dome 81 ft. in diameter and an inner dome 75 ft. in diameter. The outer dome holds the weight of the inner, upon the surface of which images of the celestial bodies are projected by stereoscope lanterns for purposes of study.

DOMENICHINO, IL (1581–1641), Italian painter, born in Bologna. His real name was Domenico Zampieri. He studied at the Accademia degli Incamminati of the Caracci (q.v.) brothers at Bologna, under Agostino Carracci; and later with Annibale Carracci in Rome. Il Domenichino is considered after Guido Reni the most distinguished pupil of the Carracci, and one of the best painters of the Eclectic or Bolognese School of painting. Among Il Domenichino's works are the paintings "Madonna of the Rosary" and "Adam and Eve" (Gallery of Bologna), "Diana and Nymphs Hunting" (Borghese Gallery, Rome), and "Communion of St. Jerome" (the Vatican); the fresco "Death of Adonis" (Loggia of the Giardino Farnese, Rome); and frescoes in the abbey of Grotta Ferrata, Rome. The Louvre, Paris, possesses a large number of his works.

DOMESDAY BOOK, or DOMESDAY, a document embodying the results of a statistical survey of England carried out by order of William the Conqueror. The survey, made in 1086, was an attempt to register the landed wealth of the country in a systematic fashion, with a view to determining the revenues due to the king. The previous system of taxation was of ancient origin and had become obsolete. By listing all feudal estates, both lay and ecclesiastical, the *Domesday Book* enabled William further to strengthen his authority by exacting oaths of allegiance from all tenants on the land, as well as from the nobles and churchmen on whose land the tenants lived. The survey was executed by groups of officers called *legati,* who visited each county and conducted a public inquiry. The set of questions which these officers asked of the town and county representatives comprised the *Inquisitio Eliensis;* the answers to these questions supplied the information from which the *Domesday Book* was compiled. The term "Domesday" is a corruption of Doomsday (the day of the final judgment), and the work was so named be-

cause its judgments as to levies and assessments were final and irrevocable.

Of the two volumes in the original manuscript, the first and larger one, sometimes called the *Great Domesday,* included information on all of England, with the exception of three eastern counties (Essex, Suffolk, and Norfolk) and several northern counties. The surveys of the three eastern counties made up the second volume, which was known as the *Little Domesday.* These manuscripts were frequently used in the medieval law courts, and in their published form they are occasionally used today in cases involving questions of topography or genealogy. The two volumes were first published in 1783; an index was published in a separate volume in 1811; and an additional volume, containing the *Inquisitio Eliensis* and various surveys of counties not covered in *Domesday,* was published in 1816.

DOMESTIC ECONOMY, art and science of home management, the subject of a course taught at various educational levels in the schools of the United States. Known also as domestic science, home economics, or household arts, the course usually includes the study of nutrition, cookery, dressmaking, home furnishing and management, domestic finance, child care, hygiene, and handicrafts. Domestic economy was introduced as a formal subject in American education about 1870, when it became a recognized course in the curriculum of the State agricultural colleges. Along with manual training for boys, the course for girls was introduced into public schools during the eighties. It is now taught in elementary and high schools, colleges, universities, normal schools, and vocational, technical, and trade schools. Training for teachers of domestic science is given in most universities, agricultural schools, and teachers' colleges. By the Smith-Lever Extension Act of 1914, extension work in home economics, offered under the auspices of State universities and agricultural colleges, is subsidized by the U.S. government; by the Smith-Hughes Act of 1917, Federal funds are provided for the teaching of home economics in vocational schools. The teaching of domestic economy has also been adopted in the school systems of Canada and of Europe.

DOMESTIC SCIENCE. See DOMESTIC ECONOMY.

DOMICELLA. See LORY.

DOMICILE, the legal residence of a person. Though used in common speech as synonymous with "home" or "place of abode", in the strict legal sense domicile denotes the place which the law will hold to be a man's residence; and this may or may not coincide with the place where he in fact usually or habitually resides. It is a doctrine of modern law that every person shall have a definite location in some jurisdiction, to which his legal rights and obligations may be referred and by which his legal status, public and private, is determined. The name and the notion of domicile, as well as the necessity for it, are comparatively recent and arise from the modern conception of law as being of territorial rather than of personal obligation. Formerly the important question was that of nationality, it being conceived that every person was entitled to be judged and to have his rights and obligations determined by the law of his national allegiance rather than by that of his actual domicile. But the triumph of the principle that the authority of a state extends to every individual within its borders, irrespective of his nationality or citizenship, and that it is in the main confined to those limits, has given a new importance to the question of domicile.

Three kinds of domicile are now generally recognized: domicile by birth, by choice, and by operation of the law. The first is determined by the place of nativity, the second is acquired by a man's own volition, and an illustration of the third is the domicile of a wife, being that of her husband and acquired by her at the time of marriage. A child, of course, has the domicile of his parents and is considered incapable of changing his domicile of his own accord, but he follows any change in the domicile of the parents. When the father of a family dies, the domicile of his children and widow continues to be that of his last residence until a new one is acquired.

In its relation to private rights and obligations the general rule may be laid down that the law of the place of domicile governs in contracts relating to personal property and in the matter of wills and bankruptcy; while, on the contrary, in matters relating to real estate the law or the place of its situation (*lex rei situs*) prevails. See CITIZEN; SUBJECT.

DOMINIC, SAINT (1170–1221), Roman Catholic theologian, born at Calaroga, Spain. According to legend, even in his childhood he revealed extreme asceticism and religious devotion. At the age of seventeen he entered the University of Palencia where he studied theology and philosophy. He was known for his acts of piety and renunciation, on one occasion offering to become a slave to the Moors in exchange for the liberation of a widow's only son. In 1195 he became canon of Osma in Castile and was soon actively engaged in local ecclesiastical reforms. He accompanied his superior, Diego d'Azevedo, Bishop of Osma, on a religious mission to Rome in 1203, and on his way back to Spain was overwhelmed by the clerical abuses and the prevalence of the Albigensian heresy (see ALBIGENSES) which he observed in the Languedoc province of France. In Montpellier he encountered three papal legates who had been sent out by Rome to suppress the heretics, but at the sight of the pomp and sybaritism of these ecclesiastical envoys, he recommended setting the notable example of humility and self-denial as the most efficient means of defeating the Albigenses. Thereupon he and the Bishop of Osma set out to preach against the heretics throughout the Languedoc, and the following year founded at Prouille his first institution, an asylum for poor girls who were in danger of changing their faith through the inducements offered them by rich adherents of the new belief. Dominic continued his campaign against the heretics for ten years, but failed to suppress them despite various miracles which he brought about on his tours through the Languedoc. The Catholic Church finally launched a crusade of extermination against the Albigenses under the leadership of Simon de Montfort (q.v.), and Dominic's part in this war was limited to prayer for the success of the Catholic arms, and urgent labor for the conversion of the people. In 1216 he founded in Toulouse the first house of the Dominican Order (see DOMINICANS), and thereafter devoted his life to the order. He is credited with numerous miracles, and was canonized by Pope Gregory IX in 1234. His feast day is August 3rd.

DOMINICA, one of the Windward Islands of the British West Indies, situated about midway between the islands of Martinique and Guadeloupe, and constituting a separate colony. It is about 29 m. long from N. to S., and has an extreme width of 16 m. The terrain is mountainous, with a number of elevations in excess of 4000 ft. above sea level. Mt. Diablotin (5314 ft.) is the highest peak. The island has numerous volcanic phenomena, notably hot springs and Boiling Lake. Subterranean gases and fumes frequently arise from the waters of this lake. Luxuriant vegetation, including valuable stands of timber on the mountain slopes, is also a feature of the terrain. The soil is fertile and well watered, yielding a wide variety of crops, including coconuts, citrus fruits, cocoa beans, bananas, and vanilla. The chief manufactured products are rum, lime juice and oil, bay oil, and copra. Annual precipitation of rain attains more than 160 inches in some parts of the island, but the climate is generally healthful. Temperatures range between a maximum of 86° F. in the hot season, which extends from August to October, and a minimum of 72° F. in the cool season. The population consists of Negroes, who are the predominant group, people of French and English origin, and a small group of Carib Indians. The capital and chief town is Roseau (pop. in 1946, 9752).

Dominica was discovered and named by Christopher Columbus on November 3, 1493, during his second voyage to the New World. In 1632 the island was colonized by the French, who retained possession of it until their expulsion in 1756 by the British. The French subsequently invaded the island on a number of occasions, notably in 1805. Throughout the greater part of its history under British rule, Dominica was a presidency of the Leeward Islands. In 1940 it was transferred to the Windward Islands group of the British West Indies, and established as a separate colony. Area, 304 sq.m.; pop. (1952 est.) 57,017.

DOMINICAN REPUBLIC (formerly SANTO DOMINGO), a republic of the West Indies, comprising the eastern portion (about two thirds) of the island of Hispaniola. It is bounded on the w. by Haiti, on the E. by Mona Passage which separates it from Puerto Rico, and on the s. by the Caribbean Sea. The Dominican Republic is generally triangular in shape, with an extreme length E. and w. of about 235 m., and a maximum width, in the w., of about 165 m. Its frontier with Haiti is 193 m. long. A number of adjacent islands, notably Beata and Saona islands, are possessions of the Dominican Republic. The capital and principal city is Ciudad Trujillo (q.v.). Other important cities are Santiago de los Caballeros, San Pedro de Macoris, and Puerto Plata. The Dominican Republic is composed of nineteen major political units, which are termed provinces, and one district, containing the national capital. Area, 19,129 sq.m.; pop. (1953 est.) 2,290,800.

Physical Features. The Dominican Republic is predominantly mountainous. About four fifths of the country is occupied by a series of massive ranges, extending generally parallel in

Left: The modern Hotel Jaragua in Ciudad Trujillo, capital of the Dominican Republic. Below: View of the harbor of the city.

Dom. Info. Cen.; Pan Amer. World Air.

a N.W. and S.E. direction. Loma Tina, 10,300 ft. above sea level, is the highest mountain in the West Indies. Between the Cibao mountain range and the Sierra de Monte Christi, a parallel range to the N., is the Valley of Cibao, one of the most fertile and best watered areas of the country. The coastal plain E. and W. of Ciudad Trujillo is another fertile region. Among the numerous streams of the Dominican Republic are the Yaqui del Norte, Yasica, and Nagua rivers, in the N., and the San Juan, Jalina, Ozama, and Yuma rivers, in the S. The principal lake is the salt-water Lake Enriquillo, about 27 m. long and 8 m. wide, situated 25 m. inland from the S.W. coast. The coast line of the Dominican Republic, about 1015 m. in length, is irregular and indented by many bays forming natural harbors, notably Caldera Bay in the S.W. and the Bay of Samana in the N.E. Among other harbors are those of Ciudad Trujillo, San Pedro de Macoris, and Azua.

Climate. The country has a semitropical climate, tempered by the prevailing easterly winds. Temperatures above 74° F. are registered in the lowlands throughout the year. During the summer months, temperatures range between 80° F. and 95° F. in these regions. The highlands are considerably cooler. Annual precipitation averages about 120 inches, with the heaviest rainfalls occurring N. of the central uplift, known as the Cordillera Central. The wet season extends from June to November. Tropical hurricanes occur occasionally.

Flora and Fauna. The vegetation of the Dominican Republic, like that of the other islands of the West Indies, is extremely varied and luxuriant. Among the species of indigenous trees are mahogany, rosewood, satinwood, grugru palm, fustic, logwood, cypress, ironwood, pine, oak, and cacao. Many species of useful plants and fruits are common, including rice, tobacco, cotton, sugar cane, pimento, yam, banana, pineapple, mango, fig, orange, grape, breadfruit, and apple. The only noteworthy mammal among the indigenous fauna is the agouti (q.v.). Wild dogs, hogs, and cattle are abundant, and there are numerous reptiles, notably snakes, lizards, and caymans. Waterfowl and pigeons are the predominant birds.

Production, Industry, and Commerce. The Dominican Republic is chiefly an agrarian country. Cultivable lands total about 9900 sq.m., of which approximately 37% is in production. The chief crop is sugar cane, grown mainly in the coastal region around Ciudad Trujillo. More than half of the sixteen cen-

Dominican Information Center

Planting banana roots, in a valley in the interior of the Dominican Republic

trals, or plantations, that comprise the bulk of the industry, are controlled by American corporations. The total yield of raw sugar in 1952–53 amounted to 693,000 short tons, giving the Dominican Republic a leading position among the sugar-producing countries of Latin America. The crop next in importance, by value, is cacao, production of which totaled 33,070 short tons in 1952–53. Other leading crops, with yields in 1952–53, are coffee (29,172 short tons) and tobacco (14,300 short tons). Agricultural production also includes such crops as corn, rice, yucca, beans, sweet potatoes, oranges, and bananas. Cattle and hogs are raised, mainly for local consumption.

The principal manufacturing industry of the island is the processing of sugar cane. Raw sugar, molasses, and refined sugar are the chief products of this industry. The other manufacturing industries are small-scale enterprises, producing largely for the domestic market. The chief products include cigars, cigarettes, matches, straw hats, hides, shoes, chocolate, beverages, cotton textiles, furniture, cement, tiles, fertilizer, soap, and peanut oil.

The country contains deposits of gold and copper. Gypsum, petroleum, rock salt, and iron, silver, and platinum ores are also found.

In 1952, the foreign trade of the Dominican Republic was valued at $194,405,000. Exports, consisting predominantly of sugar, cacao, and coffee, represented $115,015,000 of this total. The leading markets, in the order of importance, for Dominican products were the United States, the United Kingdom, Canada, Puerto Rico, Spain, and Belgium. The bulk of the imports, which consisted mainly of cotton textiles, iron and steel products, food, machinery, and petroleum, came from these countries, with the United States furnishing over two thirds, by value, of the total. Virtually all of the waterborne commerce of the Dominican Republic is transported in foreign-flag vessels.

Communications. The Dominican Republic in 1951 had 900 m. of railroad lines. Most of these are narrow-gauge lines, situated on the large plantations, and are privately owned. The remainder provides connections between Puerto Plata, Santiago de los Caballeros, and the Samana Gulf port of Sanchez. All of the major towns and cities of the country are linked by a system of trunk highways, one of which, at Elias Piñar on the Haitian border, links with a Haitian highway extending to Port-au-Prince. The highway system in 1951 had a total length of 2008 m., more than half of which are inferior roads. Connections between the Dominican Republic and foreign points are provided by passenger vessels and by five air lines.

People, Language, and Religion. About 60 percent of the population of the Dominican Republic consists of persons of mixed Indian, European (chiefly Spanish), and Negro origin. Negroes comprise about 12 percent of the population, and the remainder is European in origin, principally Spanish. Spanish is the official language of the country, but many of the inhabitants speak English. The Roman Catholic Church is the predominant religious denomination. The Church maintains an archdiocese at Ciudad Trujillo.

Education. The Dominican Republic has a free public-school system, with compulsory attendance for children between the ages of seven and fourteen. In 1951 there were 2698 primary, secondary, vocational, and other schools, maintained chiefly by public funds. Student enrollment (1951) in these schools totaled 260,325. The chief institution of higher learning is the University of Santo Domingo, at Ciudad Trujillo, founded in 1538. According to official Dominican estimates, the ratio of illiterates was reduced from 750 per 1000 of population, in 1930, to about 57 percent of all persons 10 years of age and older, in 1950.

Government. The government of the Dominican Republic is based on the constitution of 1942. By the terms of this document, executive power is vested in a president, elected for a five-year term. He is assisted by a cabinet consisting of twelve secretaries of state. Legislative authority is vested in a senate composed of twenty members and a chamber of deputies of forty-five members, all of whom are elected for five-year terms. The judicial system consists of a supreme court of justice, three courts of appeal, and various minor courts. The supreme court is composed of a president and eight judges, who are selected by the senate, and a procurator-general, who is appointed by the president.

History. Prior to the establishment of the Dominican Republic, the region now occupied by that country was under various sovereignties for varying periods (see HISPANIOLA). Dominican independence was secured from Haiti in 1844. Pedro Santana, one of the revolutionary leaders, became the first president of the Dominican Republic. His administration and that of Manuel Jiménez, who succeeded him in 1848, were marked by popular unrest and frequent boundary disputes with Haiti. Although a number of reforms and improvements were accomplished during the administration of Buenaventura Báez, who succeeded Jiménez in the presidency, the nation continued to be torn by political strife. This state of affairs was reflected chiefly in a political grouping led by Santana, who advocated return to Spanish rule, and a rival movement led by Báez, who advocated annexation of the country to the United States. Santana seized power in 1858. and three years later proclaimed annexation of the country to Spain. In 1863–4, a general revolt, aided by the Haitians, developed against Spanish authority. Military reverses and diplomatic representations from the United States forced the Spanish government to withdraw its forces and to annul the annexation. The second Dominican Republic was proclaimed in February, 1865.

In 1869, Báez, then president of the Second Republic, negotiated a treaty of annexation with representatives of the United States government. However, the United States Senate refused to ratify this document. Political turmoil continued throughout the remainder of the 19th century, notably during the presidency (1882–99) of Gen. Ulises Heureaux, who was assassinated.

Because of mounting Dominican indebtedness to a number of European nations, some of which threatened intervention, the Dominican government in 1905 negotiated an agreement with the United States, turning over to the latter the administration and control of its customs department. In exchange, the United States undertook to adjust the foreign financial obligations of the Dominican government. By the terms of a treaty, ratified in 1906, this arrangement became effective for a fifty-year period. Successive revolts and changes of administration occurred during the ensuing decade. American attempts, including armed intervention, to pacify the rebellious Dominican factions culminated on November 29, 1916, when naval forces of the United States occupied the country and established a military government. Partial control of the Dominican Republic was restored to its people in 1922, with the establishment of a provisional government. In March, 1924, a constitutional government assumed control of the country, and later that year the American occupation ended.

The outstanding development of the subsequent period was the dictatorship established by General Trujillo Molina (see TRUJILLO MOLINA), head of the Dominican Party. Elected to the presidency in 1930, he forcibly eliminated all political opposition, thereby acquiring absolute control of the nation. He relinquished the presidency to one of his lieutenants in the Dominican Party in 1938, but resumed this post again in 1942. Meanwhile (1935), settlement of a 91-year-old boundary dispute with Haiti was announced. Various border incidents occurred during 1937, however. According to Haitian reports, thousands of Haitian peasants, who had crossed into the Dominican Republic in search of land and work, were forcibly expelled by Dominican troops. In the course of these incidents, the reports stated, several thousand men, women, and children were killed. The resultant dispute between Haiti and the Dominican Republic was settled amicably in 1938.

In 1940 the United States government terminated its administration of the Dominican customs department. In December, 1941, shortly after the United States entered World War II, the Dominican government declared war on Japan, Germany, and Italy. The Dominican Republic subsequently became a charter member of the United Nations. Resumption of the multi-party system in Dominican politics was announced by President Trujillo in May, 1945. Two oppositionist and several progovernment parties were subsequently established. In 1946 the government announced that a national election would be held in May, 1947. Oppositionist activity was severely curbed during the ensuing campaign.

President Trujillo was re-elected by an overwhelming majority, and the Dominican Party won every seat in the Senate and all except two seats in the chamber of deputies.

The Dominican Congress granted (March, 1948) President Trujillo extraordinary powers, including authority to promulgate decrees on all matters connected with national security. In April the Republic participated in the 9th Inter-American Conference, held at Bogotá, Colombia, and became a signatory of the charter of the Organization of American States. Early in 1949 the government launched a three-year public-works program aimed at increasing supplies of pure water, improving roads and harbors, and encouraging the tourist trade.

An abortive uprising organized by a small party of invading revolutionaries took place in Puerto Plata Province on June 16, 1949. Shortly thereafter the Trujillo regime accused the Cuban, Guatemalan, and Costa Rican governments of encouraging anti-Trujillo activities. In December Congress enacted legislation granting President Trujillo power to declare war (without consulting Congress) on countries aiding plotters against the Dominican Republic.

Early in 1950 the Haitian government formally protested to the Council of the Organization of American States that the Trujillo regime had given overt help during the previous year to Haitian revolutionaries. An investigating committee found the Dominican Republic guilty of interfering in the internal affairs of Haiti. In February Congress, at the president's request, repealed the law vesting him with the power to declare war. President Trujillo and the president of Haiti settled most of the differences between their countries during the first half of 1951.

In July, 1951, President Trujillo announced that he would not be a candidate for re-election in 1952. The Dominican Party promptly nominated his younger brother and secretary of state for war, marine, and aviation Gen. Hector Bienvenido Trujillo Molina (1908–). He was unopposed in the election, which took place in May, 1952.

Former President Trujillo was appointed foreign minister on March 1, 1953. In June the government signed a military-assistance pact with United States. Anti-Trujillo demonstrations, the first in several years, took place in July in the city of Santiago. As a result several cabinet ministers were replaced; however, the Trujillo family remained firmly in control of the government.

Four stringent laws aimed at American sugar interests became effective in January, 1954.

DOMINICANS, or FRIARS PREACHERS, a Roman Catholic order which received its pontifical letters in 1205, and adopted the Rule of St. Augustine, with certain modifications, in 1216. It was founded at Toulouse, France, by St. Dominic (q.v.) for the purpose of counteracting, by means of preaching, teaching, and the example of austerity, the heresies prevalent at the time. The necessity for such an order became apparent to Dominic during his early attempts to convert the Albigenses, and he, together with a group of sixteen disciples, resolved to devote his life to the organized salvation of the souls of the heretical and the ignorant. The first institutional act of this group was the founding in 1205 of an asylum for the wayward daughters of the poor in Toulouse. However, Dominic and his disciples were refused recognition as an order by the Apostolic See until 1216, when Pope Honorius III granted them the necessary papal confirmation and various special privileges, including the right to preach and hear confessions everywhere, without local authorization. The Dominicans differed from older orders by their insistence on absolute poverty, rejecting the possession of even community property, and becoming, like the Franciscans (q.v.), a mendicant order dependent on charity for their daily subsistence. The first house of the order was at the church of St. Romain at Toulouse, from which, in 1217, Dominic sent some of his disciples to spread the movement in Spain and other parts of France. The order was introduced into England within six years and a house was founded at Oxford. There the Dominicans acquired the name of "Black Friars", from the habit which they wear outside the convent when preaching and hearing confessions—a black coat and hood over a white woolen garment. By the end of the century fifty friaries were functioning in England, and the order had established houses in Scotland, Ireland, Italy, Bohemia, Russia, Greece, and Greenland.

In accordance with the declared purpose of their foundation, the Dominicans have always been known as dedicated preachers and as combatants against any departure from the teaching of the Catholic Church. In this capacity they were entrusted with the conduct of the Inquisition as an ecclesiastical enterprise; and even in Spain, after the Inquisition became virtually a department of civil government, a Dominican was usually at its head. The office of master of the sacred palace, cre-

ated for St. Dominic in 1218, and subsequently endowed with great privileges by Pope Leo X, has always been held by a member of the order, and since 1620 the censorship of books has been one of its functions. In 1425 the permission to hold property was granted by Pope Martin V to certain houses, and extended by Pope Sixtus IV to the entire order in 1477.

Dominicans have held many high Church offices, and four Popes (Innocent V, Benedict XI, Pius V, and Benedict XIII) and more than sixty cardinals have belonged to the order. Apart from their specific work, the Dominicans have done much for the development of art; Dominican cloisters have produced such distinguished painters as Fra Angelico and Bartolommeo della Porta (qq.v.). Their contributions to literature have been chiefly in the fields of theology and scholasticism, in which they number such important writers as St. Thomas Aquinas, author of the standard work on dogmatic theology; St. Albertus Magnus, the "father" of scholastic philosophy; and Raymond of Peñaforte, codifier of canon law. The important medieval encyclopedia *Speculum Majus* was the work of a Dominican, Vincent of Beauvais; and the German mystics Johannes (Meister) Eckhart, Johannes Tauler, and Heinrich Suso were Dominicans, as was Savonarola (q.v.). In the later Middle Ages the order was equaled in influence only by the Franciscans, the two brotherhoods dividing the major influence in the Church, and often in the Catholic states, and arousing frequent hostility on the part of the parochial clergy whose rights had been invaded by the friars. The Dominicans played the leading part in the evangelization of South America; the first American saint, Rose of Lima, was a Dominican. In 1805 they introduced their order into the United States, where they now have twenty monasteries. Missionary work still remains one of the important Dominican functions, and the order maintains missions in Annam, Tongking, and China, and in Iraq and Kurdistan. The head of the entire order is the general, whose term of office is twelve years; since 1273 the residence of the general has been at the Santa Maria Sopra Minerva in Rome. The order is divided into 52 provinces, each with a provincial at its head.

The Dominican nuns, founded in 1205 before the male branch of the order was established (1216), nevertheless called themselves the "Second Order of St. Dominic". A third order was founded by St. Dominic in 1220, to provide a constant supply of lay defenders of the Church against the assaults of the Albigenses and other militant innovators. Dominic gave it the name "Militia of Jesus Christ" and pledged its members to defend the Church with their arms and their possessions. This body was joined, toward the close of the 13th century, with the "Brothers and Sisters of the Penance of St. Dominic", another lay group vowed to piety, which was under the direction of the First Order. This amalgamation formed the body which finally came to be known as the "Third Order of St. Dominic".

DOMINOES, a game introduced in Europe in the 18th century and played by two or more persons, using 28 oblong pieces, of ivory, bone, or wood, called *dominoes*. Originally, the pieces had ivory faces, backed by ebony; they are thought to have been named on the basis of their resemblance to the hood called a *domino*. Each domino, called also a *piece* or a *man*, is divided in half, with a combination of spots, or *pips*, at each end. One man is blank; the remainder are numbered downward from double six, i.e., 6-6, 6-5, 6-4, 6-3, 6-2, 6-1, 6-0; 5-5, 5-4, 5-3, 5-2, 5-1, 5-0, and so on through all the other numbers. Before the game starts, the 28 pieces are turned face downward and intermixed, the right to make the first play usually being determined by drawing for the highest domino. Then, according to the particular variation of the game about to be played, the entire number, or a certain proportion, of the dominoes is selected, one at a time, by the respective players. Each player sets his dominoes up on edge so that they cannot be seen by his opponents. The stock or reserve is formed by whatever dominoes are not drawn. The first player *poses* (places) one man face upward on the table, and the second player must place against it *a match,* i.e., a piece out of his hand corresponding in pips at one end with the piece laid down. Then the next player must in turn match from his hand a domino to meet the new combination of pips, there being always two ends for which he may select a match. Doubles, or dominoes with the same number of spots at both ends, are posed *à cheval* (crosswise) rather than lengthwise. In certain variations of the game, the play of a double gives rise to one or two additional branches available for matching. If a player has no number to match either end, he *passes,* and the next player takes his turn. In a *draw game* (a game in which less than the whole number of dominoes is dealt) a player, in his turn, may *draw* on the stock up to, but never including, the last two dominoes. He may thus exhaust the stock even when he has a match; this practice is occasionally good strategy, especially when the opponent is blocked. The game proceeds until one of the players wins by setting out the last of his dominoes, or until no player can match at either end. In the latter case, the winner is the player with the smallest number of pips on his remaining dominoes, or, in the case of an equality of pips, the player with the fewest dominoes. Other variations of the game which have been popular are *matador,* similar to the draw game; the *block game; muggins,* or *all fives; all threes; Sebastopol;* the *Bergen game;* and *domino pool.*

DOMITIAN, or in full TITUS FLAVIUS DOMITIANUS AUGUSTUS (51–96 A.D.), Roman Emperor, second son of the Emperor Vespasian, and brother of the Emperor Titus, whom he succeeded in 81 A.D. In the early years of his rule he was a conscientious and capable administrator, but he was unable to maintain peace on the borders of the Empire and suffered a humiliating defeat at the hands of the Dacians under Decebalus. In 84 A.D., probably actuated by jealousy, he recalled Gnæus Julius Agricola, his general in Britain, who was in the midst of a successful military campaign. Four years later Domitian ruthlessly crushed a revolt led by Antonius Saturninus, his general in Germany. Following these incidents his reign was characterized by terror. He was murdered by an ex-slave with the encouragement of his wife Domitia.

DOMREMY-LA-PUCELLE, a village of Vosges Department, E. France, on the Meuse R., 7 miles N. of Neufchâteau. It is the birthplace of Joan of Arc, from whom its name, (Fr. *La Pucelle,* "the Maid") is derived. The cottage where Joan was born still remains. A number of memorials throughout the town are dedicated to the Maid of Orleans, the most important of which is the modern basilica of Le Bois Chenu, situated on the hill where she is supposed to have received the spiritual mission to deliver her country from the enemy. The village was freed from all taxes by Charles VII in honor of Joan of Arc, and enjoyed this privilege until the Revolution. A yearly pageant representing the life of Joan is given by the people of the village. Pop. (1946) 185.

DON, a river of the Russian Soviet Federal Socialist Republic, about 1300 m. long. It rises about 140 miles S.S.E. of Moscow, in

Lake Ivan, flows in a general southeasterly direction to a point about 50 miles w. of Stalingrad, and then flows in a southwesterly direction, emptying, about 25 miles w. of Rostov, into the Sea of Azov. The three mouths of the river form a delta with an area of about 130 sq.m.

The Don drains an area of about 166,000 sq.m. Most of the land in the Don basin comprises fertile steppes. A region N.W. of the delta, rich in coal and iron ore and highly industrialized, is called the Donbas. The chief tributary of the Don is the Donets R.; other tributaries, from N. to S., include the Veronezh, Khoper, Medveditsa, and Manych rivers. Rostov is the chief port and principal city situated on the Don. Other important cities on the river include Novocherkassk, Shakhty, and Voronezh.

The Don varies in breadth from about 500 to approximately 1900 ft. Shallow reaches are numerous, and the depth varies from 4 to about 70 ft. The river is navigable for some 800 m., but during the winter the greater part of the Don is frozen; in the spring, melting snow and ice swell the Don, especially its lower reaches. In June the river begins to subside and in August most of it is usually so shallow that navigation, in large part, is halted.

The Don was long an important traffic artery from the Black Sea and Caucasus regions of old Russia to the central part of the country. After the revolution of 1917, and following the inception of economic planning on a national scale, the commercial importance of the river was increased as a result of its integration with other important waterways. In the N., the Yepifan Canal was constructed to link the Don with the Upa R., a feeder stream of the Oka R. The Oka is a tributary of the Volga, which, in turn, is connected with Moscow by another canal. In the S.E. the Volga-Don Canal, approximately 60 m. long, connects the Don with the Volga s. of Stalingrad.

Ancient Greek geographers considered the Don, which they called the *Tanais,* a part of the boundary between Europe and Asia. Later, Tatar invaders of Europe called the stream the *Tuna* or *Duna.* In the Middle Ages, serfs, fleeing from the oppression of Muscovite princes in the north, settled in the Don basin; their descendants became known as the Don Cossacks (see COSSACKS). During World War II (q.v.), major battles were fought on the banks of the Don between the Germans and the Russians.

DONATELLO (1386?-1466), Italian sculptor, born in Florence, the son of a wool comber. Donatello's real name was Donato di Niccolò di Betto Bardi. Nothing is known of his boyhood or of his early training in sculpture; but it has been established that when he was seventeen he assisted the noted Florentine sculptor Lorenzo Ghiberti (q.v.) in constructing and decorating the famous bronze doors of the baptistery of the church of San Giovanni, Florence; and that Donatello was also an associate of the noted sculptor Filippo Brunelleschi (q.v.), with whom he reputedly visited Rome in the early years of the 15th century in order to study the monuments of antiquity.

His career may be divided into three periods. The first or formative period comprised the years before 1425. His work of these years is marked by the influence of Gothic sculpture, but also shows classical and realistic tendencies. Among his sculpture of this period are the statues "St. Mark" (Church of Or San Michele, Florence), "St. George" (Museo Nazionale, Florence), "John the Evangelist" (Opera del Duomo, Florence), and "Joshua" (campanile of the cathedral, Florence). The second period extended from 1425 to 1443 and is in general characterized by Donatello's reliance on the models and principles of the sculpture of antiquity. From 1425 to 1435 Donatello worked together with the Florentine sculptor and architect Michelozzo on a number of projects, including the monument to Pope John XXIII (baptistery, Florence) and the monument to Bartolomeo Aragazzi (cathedral of Montepulciano). In their joint work Michelozzo executed the architectural designs and also helped in the making of the bronze castings; Donatello executed most of the statues. From 1433 to 1434 Donatello was in Rome, where he executed a number of works, notably the Ciborium in the sacristy of the basilica of St. Peter, decorated with reliefs of two "Worshiping Angels" and "Burial of Christ". He spent the following nine years in Florence; the most noted work of this period is his bronze statue "David" (Museo Nazionale, Florence), the first nude statue made in the Renaissance. In his third and culminating period, Donatello broke away from classical influence and in his work emphasized realism and the portrayal of character and of dramatic action. Notable examples of his sculpture of this period are "Miracles of St. Anthony" (basilica of Sant' Antonio, Padua): "Gattamelata" (in the square before the basilica of Sant' Antonio, Padua), the first bronze equestrian statue since ancient times; and "Judith and Holofernes" (Loggia dei Lauzi, Florence).

Donatello's sculpture influenced the sculpture of Florence and northern Italy of the 15th century; it was one of the influences that stimulated the development of realism in Italian painting, notably in the work of the great Paduan artist Andrea Mantegna (q.v.). Donatello is generally considered one of the greatest sculptors of all time and the founder of modern sculpture. He had many pupils, the most important of whom was Desiderio da Settignano (q.v.).

DONATI, GIOVANNI BATTISTA (1826–73), Italian astronomer, born in Pisa. He became professor at the Royal Institute and director of the observatory in Florence. He discovered six comets, one of which bears his name, and determined the gaseous composition of comets by means of the spectroscope. He wrote *Intorno alle Strie degli Spettri Stellari* (1860). See DONATI'S COMET.

DONATI'S COMET, a comet (q.v.) discovered by Giovanni Donati at Florence on June 2, 1858. When the comet was nearest the earth its tail had an apparent length of 50°, more than half the distance from the horizon to the zenith, and corresponding to the enormous linear size of 45,000,000 miles. The period was estimated at more than 2000 years, so that it will not return until about the year 4000.

DONATISTS, a dissident North African sect of the early Christian Church, holding that the validity of the sacraments depended on the sinless character of the minister. It was formed as a result of the consecration in 311 A.D. of Cæcilian as bishop of Carthage. Felix, bishop of Aptunga, who had consecrated Cæcilian, was believed to be a *traditor*, i.e., one of those ecclesiastics who had been guilty of betraying their offices by handing over their copies of the Bible to the oppressive forces of the emperor Diocletian. An opposition group of seventy bishops, led by Secundus, bishop of Tigisis and primate of Numidia, formed itself into a synod at Carthage and declared the consecration of Cæcilian invalid. They held that the Church must exclude from its membership persons guilty of mortal sin, and that therefore no sacrament could rightly be performed by a *traditor*. The synod excommunicated Cæcilian when he refused to appear before it, and in his place consecrated the *lector* Majorinus. Four years later Donatus the Great became bishop of Carthage on Ma-

"St. George," sculpture by Donatello

jorinus' death, and the sect took its name from him. As a result of the Emperor Constantine's desire to settle the dispute, it was submitted to various ecclesiastical bodies and in 316 to the emperor himself, and in each case the consecration of Cæcilian was upheld. Constantine at first attempted to suppress the Donatists by force, but in 321 he adopted a policy of tolerance; his son Constans instituted a regime of persecution. In 411 a conference between the Donatist and Catholic bishops was held at Carthage, for the purpose of arriving at a final settlement of the dispute. The decision, confirmed by the Emperor Honorius, was once again adverse to the Donatists. As a result, they were deprived of all civil rights in 414, and, in the following year, their assemblies were banned under penalty of death. The sect then began to decline; the Vandal invasions of the 5th century and those of the Saracens in the 7th completed its destruction.

DON CARLOS. See CARLOS.

DONCASTER, county borough in the West Riding of Yorkshire, England, on the Don R., 32 miles s. of York. It is a coal-mining and railroad center, and has a considerable trade in farm produce. Manufactured products include locomotives and railway cars, linen, woolens, sacking, wire, agricultural machinery, chocolate, and wallpaper. The Doncaster horse races have been annual events since 1615. The famous St. Leger race, which originated in 1776, is run each September. Doncaster was the *Danum* of the Romans and the *Dona Ceaster* of the Saxons. It suffered severely during the Danish invasion of England. It received municipal rights from Richard I in 1194, and was created a county borough in 1927. Pop. (1951 est.) 81,896.

DONCELLA or **DONZELLA. 1.** Name of several brightly colored, spiny-finned fishes native to the West Indies and Florida. They include fish of the family *Ophidiidae,* the sand cusks or cusk eels, of which *Ophidion marginatum* is the most common. This eel-like species occurs as far north as New York. The genus *Platyglossus,* of the family Labridae (the wrasses), is also included in the doncellas, as is the ladyfish, *Bodianus rufus.* See WRASSE.

2. Two species of tropical hardwood trees, *Byrsonima spicata* and *B. cuneata* of the Barbados-cherry family.

DONEGAL, northernmost county of the Republic of Ireland, bounded on the N. and W. by the Atlantic Ocean. It is mountainous and boggy, and has many small lakes and rivers. The coast line is long and deeply indented; numerous islands are offshore. The soil is not fertile; small crops of wheat and barley are grown in cultivated areas. About 35% of the land is in pasture, however, and cattle, sheep, and poultry are extensively raised. The chief manufactures are linens, muslins, and woolens, including the well-known Donegal homespun. The county has sandstone and granite quarries, and important deep-sea and salmon fisheries.

Donegal in ancient times was called Tyrconnell, and sometimes O'Donnell's country. Along the coast are many ruins of castles, including that of the early northern Irish kings, situated at the head of Lough Swilly, and Kilbarron Castle, situated near the town of Ballyshannon (pop. in 1946, 2514). The county seat is Lifford (pop. in 1946, 476); other important towns are Letterkenny (2848) and Buncrana (2729). Area of the county, 1865 sq.m.; pop. (1951 est.) 131,511.

DONELSON, FORT. See FORT DONELSON NATIONAL MILITARY PARK.

DONETS, or DONETZ, a river rising in the Central Russian Highland and flowing in a general southeasterly direction through the eastern Ukraine, joining the Don R. about 60 miles N.E. of Rostov-on-Don. It is about 670 m. long and is navigable during high water to Izyum, in Kharkov Region. The famous Donets Coal Basin (also called the Donbas) occupies an area, between the s. bank of the river and the Sea of Azov, 230 m. long from E. to W. and 50 m. wide. This area is one of the leading centers of the Soviet Union for coal mining and heavy industry. Three quarters of the basin lies within the political boundaries of the Ukraine (q.v.).

DONIZETTI, GAETANO (1797–1848), Italian operatic composer, born at Bergamo. He studied music at the Naples Conservatory and at the Liceo Filarmonico, Bologna. During his career he composed 65 operas and operettas. His first work was *Enrico di Borgogna,* which he wrote in 1818; it was not until he had his thirty-third opera, *Anna Bolena* (1830), produced that he became widely known. Donizetti's musical style was considerably influenced by that of Gioacchino Rossini, and is characterized by brilliant and graceful melodies, designed chiefly for the use of singers of vocal virtuosity. His most important works are the grand operas *Lucia di Lammermoor* (1835), his most popular work, and *Linda di Chamounix* (1842); and the light operas *L'Elisir d'Amore* (1832), *La Fille du Régiment* (1840) and *Don Pasquale* (1843).

DON JUAN, in Spanish literature, legendary hero of a story found in the folklore of various European lands. The Spanish tale recounts the hero's seduction of the daughter of the commander of Seville. Don Juan, after killing the father of the girl in a duel, visits a statue of the commander and ironically invites it to a feast, whereupon the statue comes to life, seizes the hero, and drags him off to hell. Variations of the story have occurred in the literature of countries throughout the world, and its hero has become a universal symbol of sensuality.

The first formal literary treatment of the story was the play *El Burlador de Sevilla y Convidado de Piedra*, attributed to the Spanish dramatist Tirso de Molina and printed in 1630 at Barcelona. About 1657, traveling Italian actors performed the story as a pantomime in France, where it was later dramatized by several French playwrights. These adaptations led the French dramatist Molière to write *Don Juan ou le Festin de Pierre* (first acted in 1665), in which he added comic effects to the tale. The theme appeared in England in Sir Aston Cokain's *Tragedy of Ovid* (1669), and later in Thomas Shadwell's *The Libertine* (1676). The story and the character of the hero was greatly changed and used by such later writers as Lord Byron in *Don Juan* (1818–24) and George Bernard Shaw in *Man and Superman* (1903). A modern dramatic treatment of the story, *Don Juan Tenorio* by José Zorilla, is produced annually in every large city in Spain.

The theme of Don Juan has attracted many composers, but by far the finest musical treatment is the operatic masterpiece by Mozart, *Don Giovanni* (1787, libretto by Lorenzo de Ponte).

DONKEY, domestic ass. See Ass.

DONNE, JOHN (1573–1631), English poet, lawyer, and divine, born in London. At the age of eleven, he entered Hart Hall, Oxford University, where he studied for three years. According to some accounts, he spent the next three years at Cambridge University. He began the study of law at Lincoln's Inn, London, in 1592. About two years later, he relinquished the Roman Catholic faith, in which he had been brought up, and joined the Anglican Church. His first poems, a number of unpublished satires, were written during this period of residence in London. In 1596, possibly as a result of his friendship with Henry Wotton (q.v.), whom he had met at Oxford, he joined the naval expedition which Robert Devereux, 2nd Earl of Essex, led against Cádiz, Spain. On his return to England, Donne was appointed private secretary to Sir Thomas Egerton, Keeper of the Great Seal. His secret marriage, in 1601, to Egerton's niece, Anne More, resulted in his dismissal from this position and in his confinement, for a brief period, in prison. Meanwhile, he had written *Of the Progress of the Soul*, a long philosophical poem (published in 1633).

During the next few years, he made a meager living as a lawyer, serving chiefly as legal

John Donne

counsel for Thomas Morton, an anti-Catholic pamphleteer. Donne's principal literary accomplishments during this period were *Divine Poems* (1607) and *Biathanatos* (published 1644). His next work, *Pseudo-Martyr* (1610), in opposition to the Roman Catholic Church, won him the friendship of King James I. In 1615, at the urging of King James, Donne became a priest of the Anglican Church. He was appointed royal chaplain later that year. In 1616 he received livings at Keyston, Huntingtonshire, became rector of Sevenoaks, Kent, and was appointed divinity reader at Lincoln's Inn. He soon attained eminence as a preacher, delivering sermons that are regarded as the most brilliant and eloquent of his time. Meanwhile, he continued to write poems, among them *Cycle of Holy Sonnets* (1618). In 1621, James I appointed him dean of St. Paul's Cathedral, a post he held until his death. Donne's friendship with Izaak Walton (q.v.), who later wrote his biography, began in 1624. During his final years, Donne delivered a number of his most notable sermons, including *Death's Duel* (1631).

His poetry is characterized by complex imagery and irregularity of form. Rejecting the conventional imagery of his predecessors, largely derived from medieval philosophy, he frequently expressed his ideas in language drawn from the new scientific knowledge of the Renaissance. His love poetry, often cynical and sensuous, represents a reaction against the sentimental Elizabethan sonnet, and influenced the development of the Cavalier School of English poets. The religious poets of the 17th century sometimes referred to as "the metaphysical poets"), such as Henry Vaughan and George Herbert, drew their inspiration from Donne's imagery and spirituality. Renewed interest in Donne's work developed during the first quarter of the 20th century, and such poets as T. S. Eliot and W. H. Auden were greatly influenced by his style.

In addition to those already cited, Donne's works include *Juvenilia, or Paradoxes and Problemes* (1633), a collection of essays; *Catalogus Librorum Aulicorum* (1650), a bibliography satirizing numerous authors; *Essays in Divinity* (1651); *Devotions Upon Emergent Occasions* (1623–24); *Letters to Several Persons of Honour* (1651); and six collections of sermons.

DO NOTHINGS, derisive name for members of the Constitutional Union Party (q.v.).

DONOVAN, WILLIAM JOSEPH (1883–), known as "Wild Bill", American lawyer and soldier, born in Buffalo, N.Y., and educated at Columbia University. He began the practice of law in Buffalo in 1907. During World War I, he served in several important posts, including that of colonel of the 165th Infantry ("the fighting 69th"); he was awarded the Congressional Medal of Honor, among other decorations.

After World War I, Donovan was U.S. district attorney for the Western District of New York (1922–24); assistant attorney general of the U.S. (1924–25); and assistant to the U.S. attorney general (1925–29). He was counsel to the Association of the Bar of the City of New York, and to the New York and Bronx County Bar associations in the investigation of alleged bankruptcy malpractices in the city of New York. The Republican Party named him candidate for lieutenant-governor of the State of New York in 1922, and candidate for governor in 1932. In World War II, after serving as co-ordinator of information in 1941, he was, in 1942, appointed director of the Office of Strategic Services under the Joint U.S. Chiefs of Staff, and served in that capacity throughout the war. In 1943 he was appointed brigadier general, and promoted to major general in 1944. After the war, he resigned from the army to resume his law practice in 1945. During the 1948 occupation crisis in Berlin, Donovan went to that city as an unofficial observer. In 1953 he became ambassador to Thailand; he resigned this post in 1954.

DON QUIXOTE, or in full *The History of Don Quixote de la Mancha,* a satirical novel and one of the masterpieces of world literature, by Miguel de Cervantes Saavedra (q.v.), originally published in two parts (1605 and 1615). According to tradition, Cervantes began to work on *Don Quixote* while serving a term in prison. His purpose in writing the book was, in his own words, "to diminish the authority and acceptance that books on chivalry have in the world and among the vulgar". His intention was not so much to burlesque Spanish knight-errantry, which was at that time no longer practiced, as to put an end to the affected and absurd literary romances of chivalry which still enjoyed wide influence and popularity.

Don Quixote has had an enormous influence on the development of prose fiction; it has been translated into all modern languages and has appeared in some 700 editions. Its first publication in English was in a translation by Thomas Shelton in 1612. It has been the subject of a variety of works in other fields of art, including operas by Giovanni Paisiello, Jules Massenet, and Manuel de Falla, a tone poem by Richard Strauss, and a number of paintings by Honoré Daumier.

DOOLEY, MR. See DUNNE, FINLEY PETER.

DOOLITTLE, HILDA (1886–), American poet, born in Bethlehem, Pa. For a brief period following World War I she was prominently identified with the Imagist (see IMAGISM) school of poetry, a movement led by the American poet Ezra Pound and the British poet Richard Aldington, which was characterized by its melodic free verse. She generally used the initials "H.D." as her pseudonym. Her writings include *Heliodora* (1924), *Collected Poems* (1925), *Hedylus* (1928), *Tribute to Angels* (1945), and *Flowering of the Rod* (1946).

DOOLITTLE, JAMES HAROLD (1896–), American aviator and army officer, born in Alameda, Cal., and educated at the University of California and the Massachusetts Institute of Technology. He served in World War I as a cadet in the aviation section of the Signal Corps and as a gunnery and flight instructor; after the war he became chief of experimental flying for the Army Air Corps at McCook Field, Dayton, Ohio. He resigned from the U.S. Army in 1930. From 1922 to 1935 Doolittle accomplished several notable aviation feats, including the establishing of what was at the time (1932) ·a new world's record speed, for land planes, of 252.68 miles per hour. In 1940 he was recalled to active army duty. In World War II he led a force of United States planes in a bombing attack upon Tokyo in 1942, the first United States air raid upon Japan proper; for this achievement he was promoted to the rank of brigadier general. The same year he was placed in command of the United States aviation forces taking part in the invasion of North Africa, and in 1944 was commanding general of the Eighth Air Force, stationed in the United Kingdom. He became a lieutenant general in 1944 and retired in 1945 to become president of a civil aviation company.

DOOMSDAY BOOK. See DOMESDAY BOOK.

DOOR, a movable barrier, of wood, iron, bronze, or other material, for closing and opening the entranceway or doorway (q.v.) to a building, apartment, or room. A door usually turns on hinges; sometimes it turns on pivots or is moved by sliding. In its commonest form a door consists of a single part or "leaf" hung to one door jamb; if the entranceway is more than four feet wide the door may consist of two leaves which meet at the middle of the entranceway. In a double-swing door the leaves are each hung on separate hinges and swing either in or out. Wide doorways in the interior of buildings and such wide exterior doorways as those of barns and railroad cars may be closed by *sliding* doors, rolling on metal rails. In some cases, as in garages, doors roll down to close, and up to open. *Storm* doors are temporary doors, set outside of an entrance doorway, generally during the winter months, to provide added protection against the elements. In place of storm doors, modern buildings use either two sets of permanent entrance doors with a vestibule or lobby between them, or *revolving* doors, consisting of four leaves placed at right angles to each other and revolving on a pivot in a cylindrical enclosure. Fireproof doors may be wholly of metal or of wood covered with sheet iron, tin, or copper.

In ancient times in Palestine, Syria, and Mesopotamia wooden doors were often covered with sheets of metal in which ornamental patterns in relief were worked. A notable example of doors of this type was the double door, or gate, to the palace of the Assyrian king Shalmaneser III (859–825 B.C.) at Balawat, northern Mesopotamia, now Iraq. The door consisted of two leaves, each 27 ft. high and over 8 ft. wide, adorned with bands of sheet bronze ten inches high and ornamented with reliefs of battle scenes and figures; the British Museum contains many of these bands. The doors of ancient Greece and Rome were generally of wood and were paneled. No examples of the ordinary house doors of the period are extant; but wall paintings and reliefs of the ancient city of Pompeii contain representations of doors which closely resemble the ordinary doors of today. The doors of important edifices of ancient classic times were chiefly of bronze. Among extant examples of Roman bronze doors are those of the Pantheon (110–125 A.D.), and of the basilica of the Lateran, and the basilica of Saints Cosmas and Damian. In Italian Romanesque buildings, bronze doors were made of thin metal hammered into low relief and applied to paneled frames of wood. Examples of such doors dating from the 11th and 12th centuries and earlier are to be found in churches in Rome, Pisa, Verona, Amalfi, Ravello, and elsewhere.

The doors of the Gothic cathedrals of the late 12th century were usually made of wood, their sole decoration consisting of their hinge plates of wrought iron. In the late Gothic period the wood door itself was intricately carved; the carving of wooden doors became more and more elaborate in Renaissance times, as seen, for example, in the carved wooden doors (1540) of the church of St. Maclou, Rouen, France, attributed to the French sculptor Jean Goujon. Bronze doors in simple classic style, cast in solid bronze and then chiseled and finished by hand, came into vogue in Italy with the doors (set up in 1336) for the south side of the baptistery at San Giovanni, Florence, by the Italian sculptor Andrea Pisano. Doors of like nature, world-famous for their workmanship, were constructed during the Renaissance by the Italian sculptor Lorenzo Ghiberti for the north doorways (1424) and the east (1447) of the baptistery; by the Florentine sculptor and architect Filarete for the basilica of St. Peter, Rome; and by the Florentine sculptor Lucca della Robbia for the sacristy of the cathedral of Florence. Modern bronze doors often follow the Italian Renaissance models.

DOORA. See ANDROPOGON; DURRA.

DOORWAY, in architecture, the opening in a wall designed to give access to, or exit from, a room, enclosure, or building. It may or may not be provided with a door (q.v.) or doors. The vertical sides of the opening are its *jambs*, the beam or stone which spans the top of a square doorway is its *lintel,* and

THE DOORWAY IN ARCHITECTURE

Above, left: Ancient Greek ruin, Mycenae.
Above: Cathedral of St. Mark, in Venice.
Left: Altamura cathedral, southern Italy.
Below: "Red door" of Notre Dame in Paris.

the undersurface of the lintel is the *soffit*. The woodwork which surrounds an interior doorway is collectively the *door casing*, and the portions of this casing which are visible on either side of the wall constitute the *trim*. It has been customary in all ages to frame or enclose the opening with some form of architectural adornment. The form of the doorway is determined by the architectural style of the building in which it is placed. In Egypt it was always rectangular, surmounted by a prominently projecting cornice. In Babylonia and Assyria, the doorway was arched, made of brick, and often decorated with faïence (q.v.) and flanked with protecting colossi. The Persians largely imitated the Egyptians in their style of doorways, but surrounded them with banded architraves (q.v.). The primitive Greeks used chiefly a square doorway constructed of huge, often unwrought, stone, with heavy lintels; the Lion Gate of Mycenæ is a famous example. The Hellenic Greeks confined themselves to the rectangular doorway and evolved a type of which the most perfect example is the doorway of the Erechtheum in Athens. The Roman doorways were sometimes arched, but more often rectangular as in the Pantheon. In the usual Roman type, the doorway was surrounded by a banded architrave and surmounted by a cornice the ends of which were sometimes supported on carved consoles or brackets. In the early Christian style, doorways were of small artistic importance. Those of Byzantine buildings were, however, often of magnificent proportions and appearance, as in the church of Saint Sophia (q.v.), Constantinople, and the church of Saint Mark's (q.v.), Venice.

Romanesque Doorways. In the 11th and 12th centuries was developed an entirely new type of doorway, which, originating almost simultaneously in Lombardy and France, spread through Europe. In this type, the doorway was formed by a series of arches successively diminishing from the exterior face of the walls, the innermost and smallest arch inclosing a rectangular opening under a lintel, above which was a lunette or a *tympanum* sculptured in relief. Shafts in the angles of the recessed jambs supported the successive arches, which were richly carved. In Italy, elaborate canopies on columns often sheltered the entrance to this type of doorway. In France, figure sculpture was frequently used in the decoration of the doorway, as in the great portals of Saint-Gilles and Saint-Trophime at Arles, in Provence.

Gothic Doorways. About the beginning of the 12th century, the French builders began to develop the pointed portals, singly or in groups of three, with more stylized and more thoroughly architectural sculpture, as in the cathedrals of Chartres and Bourges, and the Abbey of St. Denis. From these were developed the magnificent Gothic doorways, of which the 13th-century masterpieces are at Notre Dame, Paris, and the cathedrals of Amiens and Rheims. To secure sufficient depth for the increased sculptural adornments, and to allow the doorway to become in itself a porch in which the worshiper might pray before entering the church, these portals were made to form gabled structures projecting beyond the face of the wall. Medieval conceptions of the history of the universe are represented in the sculptures of these cathedral doorways, which thus acquire remarkable importance in the history of art. Only seldom is their value in this respect equaled outside of France. In Italy there are a few fine examples of such doorways, notably at the cathedrals in Verona, Perugia, and Altamura; and in Germany, in the portals of the cathedrals of Freiburg and Nuremberg.

Renaissance Doorways. During the Renaissance the style of doorways returned to classic simplicity, in three principal types: **(1)** The arched doorway framed in rusticated masonry, i.e., blocks of stone beveled at their edges to emphasize the joints, as in the Pitti Palace in Florence and the Farnese Palace, Rome. (2) The square-headed or arched doorway flanked by pilasters or columns bearing an entablature (q.v.) with or without a pediment, as in the San Giobbe, Venice. (3) The square-headed doorway framed by a banded architrave bearing an entablature or pediment, often with consoles, as in the Massimi Palace in Rome. The French developed monumental variations of these types in the 17th and 18th centuries. The German Renaissance doorways are low and broad, often adorned with fantastic and grotesque sculpture, as in the Heidelberg Castle.

In modern doorways the historical styles are generally followed, often with ingenious modifications, as in the French Gothic portals of the Riverside Church in New York City, and the Romanesque doorway of Trinity Church, Boston.

DOPPLER, CHRISTIAN JOHANN (1803–53), Austrian physicist and mathematician, born in Salzburg, and educated at Salzburg and Vienna. He was a professor successively at the Technical Institute at Prague and at the Polytechnicum of Vienna, and became director of the Physical Institute of Vienna University in 1850. He described Doppler's Principle (q.v.) in his monograph, *Über das Farbige Licht der Doppelsterne* (1842). He also wrote *Dissertations on Optics* (1843), *Three Dissertations on the Theory of Undulations* (1846), and *Polarization, Galvanoelectric and Electric* (1849).

DOPPLER'S PRINCIPLE, a law of physics stating that the apparent frequency of any emitted wave, such as a wave of light or sound, varies as the source approaches or moves away from the observer. The principle takes its name from the physicist Christian Doppler who first stated it in 1842. Doppler's principle explains why, if a source of sound of a constant pitch is moving toward an observer, the sound seems higher in pitch, while if the source is moving away it seems lower. This change in pitch can be heard by an observer listening to the whistle of an express train from a station platform or another train. The lines in the spectrum (q.v.) of a luminous body such as a star are similarly shifted toward the violet if the distance between the star and the earth is decreasing and toward the red if the distance is increasing. By measuring this shift, the relative motion of the earth and the star can be calculated.

DOR or **BONGO,** a tribe of Negroes living in the Bahr el Ghazal lowlands of Anglo-Egyptian Sudan (q.v.) in N.E. Africa, and similar to the Dinka and Niam-Niam stocks. The members of the tribe are industrious and amicable. Their leading occupation is agricultural, and they are noted for their work in iron and wood. The women of the tribe tattoo the upper part of their bodies and wear rings and straws through their nostrils and lips.

DORA, SISTER. See PATTISON, DOROTHY WYNDLOW.

DORCAS GAZELLE, a common gazelle, *Gazella dorcas,* of North Africa, Syria, and Palestine. These animals are about two feet high and are fawn-colored, except for the ears, rump, abdomen, and inner side of the legs, which are white. Both sexes of dorcas gazelles have slender, ringed horns about nine inches long. In the Sahara, Arabs call these gazelles *rhezal* and *hemar.*

DORCHESTER, a part of the city of Boston, Mass. Prior to 1870 it was a separate town. Older than Boston, and at one time the largest town of the Massachusetts Bay Colony, Dorchester was settled in 1630 by Puritans from Dorsetshire, England. In 1633 the settlers organized there the first township form of government in New England. The first free school in America to be supported by a public tax was established in Dorchester in 1639. Notable landmarks include a house built in 1640, and the old graveyard in which are the graves of William Stoughton and Richard Mather

(qq.v.), and that of Barnard Capan (d. 1638), said to be the oldest marked grave in the U.S. The Dorchester Historical Society maintains a library and a museum in the James Blake house (1648). In 1776, Gen. Washington fortified Dorchester Heights, and forced the British evacuation of Boston.

DORCHESTER, BARON. See CARLETON, SIR GUY.

DORDOGNE, inland department of s.w. France, formed in 1790 from parts of the ancient provinces of Périgord, Saintonge, Limousin, and Angoumois. Highlands, more than 1300 ft. above sea level, are in the northern part of the department. The northeast and central portions consist of barren plateaus which slope toward an area of pine forests, known as the Double, in the west. In the valleys of the Dordogne, Isle, and Vézère rivers, which cross the department from E. to w., are fertile farm lands. Grapes, tobacco, wheat, corn, and potatoes are the principal crops, and walnuts, chestnuts, cider apples, and plums also are grown. Cattle, sheep, hogs, and poultry are raised. The mineral resources of the department include lignite, cement, clays, building stone, and peat. The leading manufactured products of Dordogne are leather and foodstuffs. Wine, truffles, chestnuts and fruits, poultry and livestock, and various minerals are exported. Important relics of prehistoric cave dwellers have been found in Dordogne. The department is noted also for its excellently preserved châteaux. A château of the 14th century and one dating from the 16th century, both within the same fortifications, are located at Bourdeilles. The château of Biron (11th century) is famous for its chapel of late Gothic and early Renaissance workmanship. At Cadouin are the remains of a Cistercian abbey, of note for its Romanesque chapel and its cloister in flamboyant style. A Romanesque church is situated at St. Jean-de-Côle, as is a château of the 15th to 18th centuries. The capital of Dordogne is Périgueux (q.v.). Area of department, 3550 sq.m.; pop. (1953 est.) 394,000.

DORDOGNE, a river of central and s.w. France, formed by the union of the Dor and the Dogne on the plateau below Mont Dore. The river flows westward for about 300 m., through the departments of Corrèze, Lot, Dordogne, and Gironde, to Bec d'Ambès, 13 miles N. of Bordeaux. There, along with the Garonne R., it enters the Gironde estuary. The two important tributaries of the Dordogne are the Vézère, which joins it in the department of Dordogne, and the Isle, which joins it at Libourne, Gironde Department, the head of navigation for seagoing ships.

DORDRECHT or **DORT,** town in South Holland Province, the Netherlands, on an island in the Merwede R. (the lower Meuse), 12 miles s.e. of Rotterdam. The town has a good harbor and a considerable trade in wine. Lumber is imported from Scandinavia and North America. Industrial establishments in Dordrecht include sawmills, sugar refineries, gristmills, shipbuilding yards, and factories producing chocolate, cigars, metalware, glass, and cordage. Dordrecht was founded in 1018 by Count Dirk III of Holland, and during the Middle Ages it was the commercial center of the country and a member of the Hanseatic League (q.v.). The town was formerly on the mainland, but became an island as a consequence of a river flood in 1421. In 1572 the first assembly of the independent states of Holland (see NETHERLANDS, THE) was held at Dordrecht, and in 1618–19 the city was the meeting place of the Synod of Dort, which affirmed the doctrines of John Calvin (see DORT, SYNOD OF). An architectural feature of Dordrecht is the 14th-century Church of Our Lady (Groote Kerk), which contains carved stalls by Jan Terween Aertsz. The Dordrecht Museum contains a number of paintings by famous masters. Pop. (1953 est.) 73,610.

DORÉ, (PAUL) GUSTAVE (1833–83), French illustrator and painter, born in Strasbourg. He was a precocious artist; at the age of fifteen he was regularly employed as an illustrator for the periodical *Journal pour Rire.* He is best known for his book illustrations, which are characterized by dramatic action against weird and gloomy backgrounds; the drawing, due to his insufficient training, is often faulty. Among the books which he illustrated were editions of the works of Rabelais (1854), Balzac's *Contes Drolatiques* (1856), Dante's *Inferno* (1861), Cervantes' *Don Quixote* (1863), La Fontaine's *Fables* (1866), Milton's *Paradise Lost* (1866), Ariosto's *Orlando Furioso* (1880), and Poe's *Raven* (1883). Among his paintings are "Battle of the Alma" (1855), "Paolo et Francesca da Rimini" (1863), and "Neophyte" (1868).

DORIANS, one of the three principal peoples of ancient Greece. According to legend, they took their name from Dorus, the son of Hellen, who settled in Doris, which was always regarded by the Dorians as their mother country. Dorians invaded and occupied Crete, and Laconia, Argolis, and Corinth in the Peloponnesus. Only in Laconia do the invaders seem to have kept themselves separate from the conquered tribes, and the Spartans were always regarded as the representatives of the unmixed Dorian blood. In Greek legend this conquest of Peloponnesus was related to the mythical return of the Heraclidæ, or descendants of Heracles, and placed about 1104 B.C. It is probable that the migrations took place during the 12th and 11th centuries B.C., or even earlier. From Peloponnesus the Dorians colonized the s.w. corner of Asia Minor and the neighboring islands, and planted settlements in Sicily and s. Italy. For Doric dialect, see GREEK LANGUAGE.

DORIC ORDER, in architecture, one of the three major styles of ancient Greek columns and entablatures. See COLUMN; ENTABLATURE.

DORMOUSE, any of the small, arboreal rodents comprising the family Muscardinidae. The members of this family, widely distributed through Europe, Asia, and Africa, are distinguished from other rodents by several features of internal structure. Most of them are small; the species *Muscardinus avellanarius* of Europe and Asia, called the common dormouse in England, is about the size of a mouse.

Unlike *M. avellanarius, Glis glis,* found in central and southern Europe, grows to a length of nearly seven inches, the tail not included. This species, called the edible dormouse, is eaten in Europe in the season just before hibernation, when the animal is very fat. Another large dormouse is the particolored lerot or garden dormouse, *Eliomys guercinus.* Africa's dormice include *Graphiurus ocularis,* a large gray form with a tufted tail. China's *Typhlomys cinereus* is conspicuous because of its feathery tail. India has the spiny dormouse, *Platacanthomys lasiurus,* named for its rough, spiny coat.

The dormice have large ears and long tails, usually bushy. Their fur is generally soft and fine. A general resemblance to squirrels, more or less marked in different genera and species, is heightened by the fact that dormice sit up on their hind legs and hold their food in their forepaws. Unlike squirrels, dormice are nocturnal. Their food includes nuts and acorns, and also insects such as aphids, weevils, and caterpillars. The species living in cool climates hibernate; the name dormouse is probably derived in part from *dorm,* an English dialect word for doze, and indirectly from the French *dormir,* to sleep. The dormouse is called the sleepiest of the hibernators, for its winter sleep may last six months. During this period, as with all true hibernators, its temperature

American Museum of Natural History

Dormouse (Glis glis)

drops sharply and respiration is slow. Its winter nest may be a bird's nest refurbished with a soft lining of moss, and occasionally with a roof added. During the dormouse's hibernation period the animal often falls prey to the weasel.

The dormouse builds a nest for its young, usually four in a litter. The average female has two litters a year. The young are born blind, but soon open their eyes, and in a remarkably short time are mature enough to become independent.

DORSETSHIRE or **DORSET**, county of southern England, on the English Channel between Devonshire and Hampshire. The surface of the county is irregular, with high chalk hills in the central area. Among the numerous small rivers draining toward the coast are the Frome, the Char, and the Stour. The Dorsetshire coast has many summer resorts, including Lyme Regis, Charmouth, Bridport, Weymouth, Lulworth, and Swanage. To the east, south of Poole Bay, is the Isle of Purbeck, which supplies a marble much used for buildings in England and a white pipe-clay exported to the potteries of Staffordshire. The Isle of Portland, to the west, supplies a widely used white freestone. The principal industries of Dorsetshire are farming and stock raising. The county is noted for its Devon, Shorthorn, and Hereford cattle, and for its butter, cheese, and cream. The chalk downs provide pasturage for many sheep. Dorsetshire possesses a number of prehistoric ruins of barrows and cromlechs, and many evidences of Roman occupation, notably the remains of a huge amphitheater at Dorchester. Among the ruins left from Anglo-Saxon times are those of Corfe Castle, a seat of the Saxon kings of Wessex, situated on the Isle of Purbeck. Dorsetshire has served as the setting for literary works by Jane Austen, William Wordsworth, William Barnes, and Thomas Hardy. The county seat is Dorchester. Area of county, 973 sq.m.; pop. (1951 est.) 291.157.

DORT. See DORDRECHT.

DORTMUND, city of the State of North Rhine-Westphalia, West Germany, on the Emscher R., 73 miles N.N.E. of Cologne. It is in the heart of the Ruhr coal fields and near extensive iron-ore deposits. Dortmund is connected with Emden and the North Sea by the Dortmund-Ems canal, 170 m. long, opened in 1899. With the development of the modern iron industry in the Ruhr, the city became an important rail and manufacturing center. Leading products are iron and steeel, steel rails, railway cars and locomotives, mining machinery, wire and cables, and sewing machines. Dortmund was in early times a free imperial city. About the middle of the 13th century it joined the Hanseatic League (q.v.). Four of Dortmund's churches are noteworthy: St. Reinoldi, with fine stained-glass windows; St. Mary, in Romanesque style, dating from about 1150; St. Peter; and the cloistered Dominican Church. The town hall, built in the 13th century and restored in the 19th, contains a valuable antiquarian collection. After World War II, Dortmund was included in the British zone of occupation. Pop. (1950) 500,516.

DORT, SYNOD OF, the most important legislative council held (1618–19) by the Reformed Dutch Church. It was called by Prince Maurice of Orange, as President of the Council of State of Holland, to settle the theological differences between the Arminians (Remonstrants) and the Calvinists. The religious argument between the Arminians and the strict Calvinists had by this time become a subject of controversy between opposing political forces in Holland. Adherents of the House of Orange supported the Calvinists while the Arminians found their support in the republican-inclined middle class, led by Jan van Olden Barneveldt and Hugo Grotius (q.v.), both of whom had been imprisoned by Prince Maurice before the synod was called. The council held 154 formal sessions, from Nov. 13, 1618, to May 9, 1619; deputies from Switzerland, England, Scotland, the Palatinate, Hesse, Nassau, East Friesland, and Bremen attended by invitation. Of the Dutch delegates, only those from Utrecht were Arminians, and they were refused seats at the synod. Simon Episcopius and other Arminian leaders were called before the Synod to defend their views. After having been given a brief hearing, they were dismissed, judged in their absence to be ecclesiastical rebels, and deprived of all offices. The "Canons of the Synod of Dort", which were adopted at the 136th session, April 23, 1619, are a reaffirmation of Calvinist doctrine and consist of five main points: (1) Divine Predestination; (2) Death of Christ (limited atonement); (3) Corruption of Man; (4) Irresistible Grace; (5) Perseverance of the Saints. Arminians were required to approve the condemnation of their leaders and the doctrinal decisions; those who refused were banished from the church. See ARMINIANISM.

DORUS. See DORIANS.

DORY. See BOAT.

DORY. 1. Common name for fish of the genus *Zeus*, typifying the family Zeidae of the order Acanthopterygii. These fish have large eyes, and are colored olive-brown with two dark patches on each side. The body is compressed and has numerous spines, particularly along the top. The dory projects its mouth outward to catch the small fish upon which it feeds. Dorys are sometimes as long as twenty-two inches, and may weigh up to eighteen pounds. They are native to the moderately deep waters of tropical and temperate seas. The most common of the dorys is the John Dory (q.v.). **2.** Local name in the Great Lakes region for the walleyed pike. See PIKE PERCH.

DOS PASSOS, JOHN RODERIGO (1896–), American author, born in Chicago, and educated at Harvard University. His first novel, *One Man's Initiation—1917* (1920), was followed by *Three Soldiers* (1921), which brought him both critical and popular recognition. In *Manhattan Transfer* (1925) he introduced several experimental innovations in the novel form: he interrupted the narrative at irregular intervals with selected newspaper headlines, popular-song lyrics, and short biographical sketches of notable figures of the day. These techniques were perfected, and their use expanded, in his subsequent novels. The central theme of his writings is the inevitable corruption of individual character by the excessive commercialism of contemporary civilization. His later novels include *The 42nd Parallel* (1930), *1919* (1932), *The Big Money* (1936), *Adventures of a Young Man* (1939), *Number One* (1943), *The Great Design* (1948), and *Chosen Country* (1951). The first three of these were incorporated into a trilogy entitled *U.S.A.* (1937) and the second three into *District of Columbia* (1952). *Three Plays* (1934) consists of *The Garbage Man* (1926, produced as *The Moon is a Gong*), *Airways, Inc.* (1929), and *Fortune Heights* (1933). He also wrote a volume of poetry, *A Pushcart at the Curb* (1922), and the nonfiction works *The Ground We Stand On* (1941), *The Pros-*

pect *Before Us* (1950), and *The Head and Heart of Thomas Jefferson* (1954).

DOSTOEVSKI, FËDOR MIKHAILOVICH (1821–81), Russian novelist, born in Moscow, and educated at the School of Military Engineers, St. Petersburg. He was commissioned in the army in 1841, but served only three years and thereafter made literature his profession. His first novel, *Poor Folk,* won instant recognition when it was published in 1846, and he became a member of an advanced literary circle. Despite poverty and incipient epilepsy, he produced several novels in rapid succession. However, they disappointed the critics and public, and he quarreled with liberal men of letters, notably Ivan Turgenev (q.v.), over their attitude toward his works. He associated with the Petrashevski circle, a group of young revolutionary theorists. In the wave of repression that followed the revolts of 1848 throughout Europe, members of the Petrashevski circle were seized. Dostoevski and his comrades were tried in 1849, and he was sentenced to four years of hard labor in Siberia and life servitude in the army ranks. As an added punishment, the authorities read a false sentence of death to the young men, and made bogus preparations to carry it out. Dostoevski learned his real sentence only after he had watched the firing squad make ready to exe-

Fëdor Dostoevski

The dotterel

cute him. The ordeal aggravated his epilepsy and for the rest of his life he suffered seizures of disabling intensity. He served four years in a penal settlement at Omsk and an additional year as an army private in Siberia, until Czar Alexander II restored his commission. Dostoevski was not, however, permitted to return from exile until 1859. During the period of his punishment, he gave up his early socialist and internationalist convictions and became devoutly religious and nationalistic. In 1861, in his novel *The House of Death,* he recorded his sympathy with the oppressed serfs and with the criminals whom he had known in prison. Despite his hostility to revolutionary atheism, his views continued to excite official suspicion, and his magazine *Vremya,* which he founded in St. Petersburg with his brother Mikhail, was for a time suppressed. He was burdened with debts and family obligations, and his poverty was made hopeless by a neurotic compulsion to gamble. In addition, he was exploited by his publishers. Nevertheless he continued to write, and produced the great novels of his later period, most of which were written at great speed under extreme financial pressure. In 1867 he fled to Germany to escape his creditors but continued gambling there. In 1871 he returned to Russia, where he gradually won some financial security as an influential conservative journalist. During his later years he enjoyed national fame and European homage. The prestige of his works has increased since his death, and modern critics rank Dostoevski among the greatest masters of the novel. His novels include *Poor Folk* (1846), *Letters from the Underworld* (1864), *Crime and Punishment* (1866), *The Gambler* (1867), *The Idiot* (1868–69), *The Eternal Husband* (1870), *The Demons* (or *The Possessed,*

1871), *A Raw Youth* (1875), *The Brothers Karamazov* (1880), and *Stavrogin's Confession* (suppressed chapter of *The Possessed,* trans. 1922).

DOTO. See NUDIBRANCHIA.

DOTTEREL, a reddish plover, *Eudromias morinellus,* inhabiting the northern parts of Europe and Asia. It breeds in the Alps, Scandinavia, and Siberia, and on the approach of winter migrates to the countries surrounding the Mediterranean Sea and to areas of similar climate. It is sometimes seen in Great Britain, but is now very rare there, because it has been hunted excessively. See PLOVER.

DOU, DOW, or **DOUW,** GERARD (1613–75), Dutch painter, born at Leiden. He was a pupil of Rembrandt. His early career was devoted chiefly to portraiture, but he is known principally for his later work, in genre painting. His paintings are small and are characterized by minute detail, skillful chiaroscuro, and life-like effect. Among his paintings are "The Poulterer's Shop" (National Gallery, London), a self-portrait (Metropolitan Museum of Art, New York City), "The Dropsical Woman" (Louvre, Paris), and "The Young Mother" (Hague Gallery).

DOUAI or **DOUAY,** town in the department of Nord, N. France, on the Scarpe R. It was held by the counts of Flanders from the 7th century until 1384, when the dukes of Burgundy took it; it then passed to the Hapsburgs, and was finally awarded to France in 1713 by the Treaty of Utrecht. Several famous seats of learning were established in Douai during the 16th and 17th centuries. Philip II of Spain established a university there in 1562; Cardinal William Allen established a seminary for English Catholics, banned by Queen Elizabeth's Thirty-nine Articles of 1563; and English Benedictines and Franciscans established seminaries there in 1568. The university was confiscated in 1793 during the French Revolution. The Douay Bible (see BIBLE), the first vulgate text for English-speaking people, was translated in the town by Cardinal Allen and other alumni of Oxford University. In World War I the Germans captured Douai, but caused little damage to its large library, scientific and archeological museum, and historical buildings. The manufacturing establishments of Douai include ironworks, glass and chemical works, sugar and salt refineries, breweries, and flax mills. The trade, largely water-borne, is principally in building materials and agricultural products. Pop. (1946) 35,509.

DOUAY. See DOUAI.

DOUBLE BASS, the largest and lowest-pitched instrument of the violin family. It originally had three strings, but the modern double bass has four tuned in E_1 (E on the first line below the bass staff), A_1 (first space of the staff), D_1 (third line), and G (fourth space). The notes of the double bass sound an octave lower than written. The instrument has a range of about three octaves extending upward from E_1. Some instruments have a fifth string, adding one below the E-string and extending the range downward to the C three full octaves below middle C. The double bass is essentially an orchestral instrument, rarely being used for solo performances. The first orchestral use of the double bass on record occurred about 1555; it was then one of the twenty instruments, the others being violins, of the orchestra of Catherine de Médicis, led by the Italian violinist Baltazarini (d. about 1587). Virtuosi on the double bass have included Joseph Kämpfer (fl. latter part of 18th century), Domenico Dragonetti (1763–1846), Giovanni Bottesini (1821–89), and Serge Koussevitzky (q.v.).

DOUBLE COCONUT. See COCO DE MER.

DOUBLEDAY, ABNER (1819–1893), American army officer born in Ballston Spa, N.Y., and educated at the U.S. Military Academy. Some authorities credit Doubleday with the creation of the modern game of baseball (q.v.); it is said that in 1839, while attending school at Cooperstown, N.Y., the young man inaugurated the diamond-shaped field and definite playing positions.

Doubleday served in the U.S. Army during the Mexican War (1846–48). He fired the first gun from Fort Sumter in response to the Confederate attack in 1861, at the beginning of the American Civil War. He was appointed a brigadier general of volunteers and placed in command of the defenses of Washington in 1862, and was promoted to major general in the same year. He fought in many battles of the Civil War, including Bull Run, Antietam, and Fredericksburg. On the first day of the battle of Gettysburg (July 1, 1863), he commanded the Union troops in the field for several hours after his superior officer, Maj. Gen. John Reynolds, had been killed. After the Civil War he continued to serve, as a colonel, in the regular U.S. Army until his retirement in 1873. He wrote *Reminiscences of Forts Sumter and Moultrie in 1860–61* (1876) and *Chancellorsville and Gettysburg* (1882).

DOUBLE ENTRY. See BOOKKEEPING.

DOUBLE PERSONALITY or **SPLIT PERSONALITY,** a condition in which an individual at different times shows two or more distinct personalities. The comparable condition in which more than two personalities are shown is called *multiple personality*. Every neurosis involves some degree of personality division, since conflict or inner disunity is the essence of neurosis. But only in special cases do the different parts of the individual alternate so completely that the other personalities may not even be remembered by the dominant one. Schizophrenia (q.v.) literally means "split mind", but it is actually in hysteria (q.v.) that the most striking examples of double or multiple personality are found. See PSYCHOLOGY, ABNORMAL.

DOUBLE STARS, stars which appear to the naked eye to be a single body but which are actually composed of two stars. When the two stars merely appear to be close together, although one is actually much farther from the earth than the other, they are known as *optical double stars*. Stars that are actually close together in space are called *physical double stars*. Double stars which revolve around a common center of mass are called *binary stars*.

Playing the double bass

Telescopic observation serves not only to find double stars but also to determine their types. Repeated observations will show whether the stars show a regularly repeated change in the apparent distance between them (in which case they are binaries), or whether the apparent distance between them changes at a constant rate over a long period of time (in which case they are optical doubles). When both components of a binary star emit the same kind of spectral light, it is possible to determine the fact that the pair is a double star by means of the spectroscope, even though the components are so close together that they cannot be separated optically by the largest telescope. When one component moves away from the earth and the other approaches it as they revolve in their orbit, the spectrum lines from the receding star will be shifted toward the red, while those from the advancing star will be shifted toward the violet (see DOPPLER'S PRINCIPLE). The spectra of such stars will show double lines. Pairs of this type are known as *spectroscopic binaries*.

Another type of double star is the so-called *eclipsing variable*. Stars of this type are composed of bright and dark components. When the orbit of the components is such that the dark star eclipses the bright one as seen from the earth, the intensity of the light coming from the star will fluctuate regularly.

The discovery of optical double stars was announced by Sir William Herschel in 1781, and spectroscopic doubles were first observed in 1889 by E. C. Pickering. Eclipsing variables were first observed in the 17th century, but the explanation of their variation was not advanced until comparatively recently. Recent studies indicate that approximately one out of every eighteen stars of magnitude 9 or brighter is double.

DOUBS, department of E. France, bounded on the E. and S.E. by Switzerland. Doubs is traversed by the Doubs R., which rises in the N.E. of the department; by the Dessoubre, a tributary of the Saône; and by the Loue. With the exception of "the plain", a low range of hills extending from the N.W. border to the Doubs R., the surface is mountainous, being crossed by four parallel ranges of the Juras. The climate is cold and damp, and the winters are severe. Pine, walnut, and fruit trees thrive; mines of iron and coal are worked; and gypsum, building stone, lime, and marble are abundant. The trade is principally in iron, horses, cattle, and dairy products. Doubs Department was formed in 1790 from part of the old province of Franche-Comté and from the principality of Montbéliard. The capital is Besançon (q.v.). Area, 2031 sq.m.; pop. (1953 est.) 324,000.

DOUC. See LANGUR.

DOUGHERTY, DENIS J., CARDINAL (1865–1951), American Roman Catholic prelate, born in Girardville, Pa., and educated at St. Charles Seminary, Overbrook, Pa. In 1903 he was appointed bishop of Nueva Segovia, Philippine Islands, and was the first American to occupy that post. He was made bishop of Jaro, P.I., in 1908. In 1915 he became bishop of Buffalo, and three years later was made archbishop of Philadelphia. He was created cardinal in 1921. Pope Pius XI appointed Cardinal Dougherty papal legate to the International Eucharistic Congress at Manila, P.I., in 1937.

DOUGHERTY, PAUL (1877–1947), American marine painter, born in Brooklyn, N.Y. He studied art in various European cities, including Paris, London, and Florence. Among his works are "Sun and Storm" (National Gallery, Washington, D.C.), "A Freshening Gale" (Albright Art Gallery, Buffalo, N.Y.), "October Seas" (Metropolitan Museum of Art, New York City), and "The Land and the Sea" (Corcoran Gallery, Washington, D.C.). He was a brother of the American actor Walter Hampden.

DOUGHTY, CHARLES MONTAGU (1843–1926), English poet, explorer, and scholar, born in Suffolk, and educated at Caius and Downing colleges, Cambridge University. He studied geology, archeology, and philology in Norway, Greece, Spain, North Africa, and the Near East until he was thirty-three, and then embarked on a hazardous journey into the interior of Arabia. He left Damascus with a pilgrim caravan in November, 1876, and after many adventures and discoveries he reached Jidda in August, 1878. *Travels in Arabia Deserta* (1888), his account of this journey, contained a mass of scientific observation but was also used as the vehicle for Doughty's theories on the English language. He wrote in a style which he hoped would restore to written English the simplicity of its origins in Anglo-Saxon and in Chaucerian and Elizabethan writers. *Travels in Arabia Deserta* was almost disregarded for fifteen years but Doughty continued his experiments in language, notably in the form of epics and verse drama. His works in verse include *The Dawn in Britain* (6 vols., 1906), *Adam Cast Forth* (drama, 1908), *The Cliffs* (1909), *The Clouds* (1912), and *Mansoul, or the Riddle of the World* (1920).

DOUGHTY, THOMAS (1793–1856), American painter, born in Philadelphia, Pa. He was self-taught as an artist. Doughty was one of the earliest of the Hudson River school of painters (see PAINTING, AMERICAN). The subjects of his works are mostly river scenes. Among his paintings are "A View of the Schuylkill" (Edinburgh Museum), and "On the Hudson" and "A River Glimpse" (Metropolitan Museum of Art, New York City).

DOUGLAS, seaport and capital of the Isle of Man, on the E. coast, 75 miles N.W. of Liverpool, England, across the Irish Sea. It is situated at the common mouth of the Dhoo and the Glass rivers, and is noted as a summer resort, and as the principal packet station of the Isle of Man, with daily sailings to and from Liverpool and seasonal connections with Belfast and Dublin, Ireland, and with Glasgow, Scotland, and Fleetwood, Heysham, and Barrow in Lancashire, England. Pop. (1951 prelim.) 20,288.

DOUGLAS, noble Scottish family prominent in the history of Scotland and England for more than 700 years. The historic titles held by the family, those of the Black Douglases (earls and marquises of Douglas) and of the Red Douglases (earls of Angus) were merged and were held in modern times by the marquises and dukes of Hamilton. Other modern titles of the family include the marquess of Queensberry (q.v.) and the earl of Morton.

The origin of the family is lost in legend, part of which attributes the foundation of the Douglases to Sholto Douglas in 770. The rise of the Douglases may be attributed to their part in the incessant wars of medieval Scotland, and to the fact that their principal estates were close to the English border, involving them constantly in warfare between England and Scotland.

The most important members of the Douglas family were the following.

1. WILLIAM OF DOUGLAS (fl. 1200), the first Douglas recorded in authentic history, who was a *witness of charters* in 1175, in the century after the kingdom of Scotland was founded by the amalgamation of the four original tribal kingdoms of the Scots, Picts, Britons, and Angles. His holding was in Lanark, in the Vale of Douglas (Gaelic *dubh glas,* "dark water"), from which he seems to have derived his name. The Douglas-Home branch of the family still retains Douglasdale as its seat in Lanarkshire.

2. ARCHIBALD or ERKENBALD (d. about 1240), son of William, and the first to attain knighthood. He was granted manors in Northumberland for war service to Edward III.

3. SIR WILLIAM OF DOUGLAS, called "the Hardy" (d. 1298), who first formally assumed the title of Lord of Douglas. William the Hardy twice broke his sworn allegiance to Edward I of England. He commanded the forces of John de Baliol (q.v.), King of Scotland, at Berwick castle, and was imprisoned when it fell to the English under Edward. He was released and his Scottish estates were restored, but in 1297 he joined the rising of Sir William Wallace (q.v.) and died a prisoner in the Tower of London.

4. SIR JAMES DOUGLAS, LORD OF DOUGLAS (1286–about 1330), called "the Good", and by the English "the Black Douglas", son of the 1st Lord, educated at Paris. His offer of allegiance to Edward I was refused and he joined Robert Bruce in his coronation at Scone in 1306 and became his greatest captain in the subsequent wars. He fled to the highlands with Bruce after the battle of Methven. Douglas is said to have won 57 of his 70 battles. Three times he destroyed English garrisons in his own castle of Douglas; on one such occasion (1307) the butchery was so notorious as to be called "The Douglas Larder". He was knighted by Bruce on the battlefield of Bannockburn (1314). Invading Yorkshire in 1319, he defeated an army raised by the archbishop of York and the bishop of Ely in a battle known as "Chapter of Myton". Until 1327, his constant raids across the border made "the Black Douglas" dreaded in English homes. After he had laid waste the north of England, he returned to Scotland, and in 1329 the dying Bruce commissioned him to take his heart to the Holy Land. Douglas reached Spain with the embalmed heart but fell fighting the Moors. Since that time, a human heart has been worn on the Douglas coat of arms.

5. SIR ARCHIBALD DOUGLAS (about 1296–1333), half-brother of "the Black Douglas". He defeated Edward de Baliol at Annan in 1332 and was appointed regent of Scotland for King David II. He was killed shortly afterward when he invaded England and was defeated at Halidon Hill.

6. JAMES DOUGLAS, 2nd EARL OF DOUGLAS AND MAR (about 1358–88), conqueror of Hotspur (see PERCY, SIR HENRY). In 1373, he married Lady Isabel Stewart, daughter of Robert II. In 1385 he made war on England with French assistance. At the battle of Otterburn (1388), the Scots captured Hotspur and his brother but Douglas was killed. The battle is celebrated in the English ballad *Chevy*

Chase and the Scottish ballad *The Battle of Otterburn.*

7. ARCHIBALD, 3rd EARL OF DOUGLAS, LORD OF GALLOWAY (about 1328–1400), called "the Grim", and also "the Black Douglas". He was the illegitimate son of Sir James. In 1389, he invaded England. Between wars with the English, he imposed order on the wild chieftains of the border and the western marches. During his lifetime, the power of the "Black Douglas" house was greater than that of the crown and Douglas was able to marry his daughter to the heir of Robert III and two sons to the king's daughters.

8. ARCHIBALD, 4th EARL OF DOUGLAS, 1st DUKE OF TOURAINE, (1372–1424), called "the Tyneman" (loser), son of Archibald the Grim, married to a daughter of Robert III. With the regent of Scotland, the Duke of Albany, he was suspected of complicity in the murder of Robert's heir, the Duke of Rothesay, but the alleged plotters were exculpated by the Scottish parliament. In 1402, he raided England and was captured by the Percy family. He fought at Shrewsbury (1403) with Hotspur against the English king Henry IV and was captured in turn by Henry. In 1412, he visited Paris, formed a personal alliance with John the Fearless, Duke of Burgundy, and led 10,000 Scots against the English in 1423. He was given a French duchy. He died in action in a battle with the English at Verneuil.

9. ARCHIBALD, 5th EARL OF DOUGLAS and 2nd DUKE OF TOURAINE (about 1391–1439), son of the 4th Earl. He fought against the English at Beaugé (1421), and carried home James I of Scotland from captivity in England.

10. WILLIAM, 6th EARL OF DOUGLAS (about 1423–40), and **13.** DAVID OF DOUGLAS, sons of the 5th Earl. They were taken as boys before the young King James II, subjected to a mock trial, and summarily beheaded in the courtyard of Edinburgh Castle. This judicial murder broke the power of the "Black Douglas" and the honors of the family were dispersed.

11. JAMES, 9th and last EARL OF DOUGLAS (1426–98), brother of the 8th Earl. He raised arms against James II as his brother's murderer, but submitted to the king when his allies fell away. He gained a papal dispensation to marry his brother's widow in order to keep the Douglas lands intact. In 1455, he rebelled again. He and his three brothers, the lords ORMOND, MORAY and BALVANY were routed on the Esk by a kinsman, the "Red Douglas", 4th Earl of Angus. Moray was killed and Ormond captured and executed. The Earl and Balvany escaped to England, where the Earl was later employed by Edward IV to induce the western highlanders to league themselves against the Scottish king. He was captured while raiding across the border from England and confined to a priory in Galloway, where he died. The Douglas castles were dismantled and the Douglas honors were distributed among their rivals, chiefly to the earls of Angus (the "Red Douglas").

12. ARCHIBALD, 6th EARL OF ANGUS (about 1489–1557), son of George, master of Douglas, who was killed at Flodden Field. In 1514 he married Margaret Tudor, queen dowager, widow of James IV of Scotland, and sister of Henry VIII of England. His marriage led to jealousy and civil war, during which the regent of Scotland, John Stewart, Duke of Albany, besieged the queen and seized her young son, James. Douglas briefly enjoyed supreme power when he defeated James Hamilton, 1st Earl of Arran, but in 1522 Albany banished him to France for high treason. Douglas returned to Scotland under the protection of Henry VIII in 1525, called a parliament and assumed control of his royal stepson, James V. For three years Angus was all powerful, but in 1528 Queen Margaret obtained a divorce and roused Albany to opposition. James escaped from Angus's tutelage and, when Angus was forced to flee to England, revenged himself on the Douglases. In 1537, James had Janet, Lady Glamis, who was Angus's sister, burned at the stake. In 1542, on the death of James, Angus returned and was made lord lieutenant of the south of Scotland; in 1545 he defeated the English at Ancrum Moor. Lady Margaret Douglas (1515–78), his only surviving legitimate child, married Matthew Stewart, 4th Earl of Lennox, and became the mother of Lord Darnley (q.v.), husband of Queen Mary and father of King James VI of Scotland, who became James I of England.

13. WILLIAM DOUGLAS, 1st MARQUIS OF DOUGLAS, 11th EARL OF ANGUS (1589–1660), son of the 10th earl. He joined the Marquis of Montrose (q.v.) in warfare against the Covenanters (q.v.) and was defeated with him at Philiphaugh in 1645. He was imprisoned in Edinburgh Castle and released only upon signing the Covenant. His son, WILLIAM DOUGLAS, 1st Earl of Selkirk (1635–94) became 3rd Duke of Hamilton in 1660 after his marriage to Anne, Duchess of Hamilton in her own right. He and succeeding dukes of Hamilton became male heirs of the main line of the House of Douglas.

14. LADY JANE DOUGLAS (1698–1753), a

sister of the 1st Duke. She secretly married Col. John Stewart (or Steuart), by whom she had twin sons in Paris in her 51st year. At the death of the Duke of Douglas, the surviving child, Archibald James Edward Stewart (or Steuart) became heir to the dukedom, and to the Douglas estates which would otherwise have reverted to the Hamilton family. In 1769, the legitimacy of the twins was contested by the Hamiltons in the Scottish courts, which, after six years, decided against the child. The decision was reversed two years later by the House of Lords, and young Archibald Stewart inherited Douglasdale and the Douglas estates. He was created Baron Douglas of Douglas in the English peerage in 1790. He left no sons, but a daughter married the 11th Earl of Home, whose descendants represent the main Douglas line on the female side.

DOUGLAS, GAWIN or GAVIN (1474?–1522), Scottish poet and ecclesiastic. He was the son of Archibald Douglas, fifth earl of Angus. After being educated for the priesthood at St. Andrews University, he was made provost of St. Giles, Edinburgh, in 1501. From that time until 1513, he devoted himself to his ecclesiastical duties, to writing poetry, and to translating from the classics. After the marriage of his nephew, Archibald Douglas, sixth earl of Angus, to the widowed Queen Margaret of Scotland in 1514, he was appointed archbishop of St. Andrews. However, the chapter voted against Douglas, and the prior, who was the poet's enemy, expelled him. Pope Leo X appointed him bishop of Dunkeld in 1515, but Douglas became involved in the political quarrels of the time and, before he could be consecrated, he was imprisoned for a year by the regent, the Duke of Albany. In 1516 he was consecrated bishop of Dunkeld; he was deprived of his see in 1520 after his nephew fell out of favor with the queen. He went to London to ask Henry VIII of England for aid, and died there of the plague.

Douglas' poetry includes the allegories *The Palice of Honour* and *King Hart*, and *Conscience*. He is best known for his translation of Vergil's *Aeneid,* which was the first translation of a classical work into English.

DOUGLAS, SIR JOHN SHOLTO. See QUEENSBERRY, JOHN SHOLTO DOUGLAS, MARQUIS OF.

DOUGLAS, LLOYD CASSEL (1877–1951), American clergyman and novelist, born in Columbus City, Ind., and educated at Wittenberg College and Hamma Divinity School, Springfield, Ohio. In 1903 he was ordained a Lutheran minister and made pastor of Zion Church, North Manchester, Ind. For the next thirty years, except for the period 1911–15, when he was director of religious work at the University of Illinois, he served as pastor of various congregations in the U.S. and Canada. After 1933 he gave all his time to writing and lecturing. His novels, which deal with the Christian themes of self-sacrifice, brotherhood, and faith, proved to be highly popular. *The Robe* (1942), based on the life of the Roman soldier who received Christ's robe after the crucifixion, was one of the best sellers of all time. Among his other works are *Magnificent Obsession* (1929), *Precious Jeopardy* (1933), *Green Light* (1935), *White Banners* (1936), *Disputed Passage* (1939), *Invitation to Live* (1940), *The Big Fisherman* (1948), and *A Time to Remember* (autobiography, 1951).

DOUGLAS, NORMAN (1868–1952), British writer, born in Tilquhillie on the Deeside, Scotland. He was educated chiefly at the *Gymnasium* in Karlsruhe, Germany, specializing in science and languages. From 1893 to 1896 he was with the British Foreign Office, serving as an undersecretary at the British Embassy in St. Petersburg from 1894 to 1896. Douglas' first published works were treatises on zoology contributed to various periodicals. His literary reputation was established by his novel *South Wind* (1917), a tale of the cosmopolitan inhabitants of a mythical Mediterranean island on which an enervating climate and an unconventional type of morality prevail; the distinguishing feature of the novel is its satire on modern life and morality from the viewpoint of hedonistic philosophy. Douglas' other writings include *Unprofessional Tales* (under pseudonym "Normyx", 1901), *Siren Land* (1911), *Fountain in the Sand* (1923), *Old Calabria* (1928), *One Day* (1929), *Goodbye to Western Culture* (1930), *Looking Back* (2 vols., 1933), *Late Harvest* (1946), and *Footnote on Capri* (1952).

DOUGLAS, STEPHEN ARNOLD (1813–61), American politician, born at Brandon, Vt., and educated in schools at Brandon and at Canandaigua, N.Y. He practiced law in Illinois, where he became successively public prosecutor, member of the legislature (1836), secretary of state (1840), and judge of the supreme court (1841–43). He was elected to the U.S. House of Representatives in 1843, and became an outstanding spokesman for a policy of national expansion. He advocated the annexation of Texas, supported the war with Mexico, and opposed compromise with Great Britain in the Oregon dispute, holding

Stephen A. Douglas

to the Democratic Party slogan "Fifty-four Forty or Fight". He became chairman of the committee on territories in the House, and when elected to the Senate in 1847 was chosen head of its committee on territories. In this capacity he was in charge of legislation by which Minnesota, Oregon, New Mexico, Utah, Washington, Kansas, and Nebraska were constituted as Territories, and Texas, Florida, Wisconsin, Iowa, Minnesota, California, and Oregon were admitted to the Union as States. He opposed ratification of the Clayton-Bulwer Treaty (q.v.) and advocated the annexation of Cuba. With Henry Clay, he was mainly responsible for the Missouri Compromise of 1850 (q.v.). However, he brought about the reopening of the entire slavery question in 1854 by incorporating in the bills which established the Territories of Kansas and Nebraska the principle of "popular sovereignty", providing that the inhabitants of those territories might decide whether or not slavery should be permitted within their borders.

In the course of his campaign for election of candidates to the State senate to insure his selection as U.S. senator from Illinois, he was opposed by Abraham Lincoln, and the two candidates met in a momentous series of debates on the slavery issue. Douglas won the nomination for the U.S. Senate in that campaign, but Lincoln's candidates gained more popular votes and Lincoln emerged with a national reputation. In 1860, Douglas and Lincoln were opponents for election to the U.S. Presidency. Douglas had won the Democratic nomination, but Southern Democratic delegates seceded and nominated John C. Breckenridge. Douglas lost the election, winning 12 electoral and 1,375,157 popular votes, as against 180 electoral and 1,866,352 popular votes for Lincoln. When the Civil War broke out, he gave Lincoln loyal support. He died in Chicago while on a commission from the President to rally the Northwest to the cause of the Union.

DOUGLAS, WILLIAM ORVILLE (1898–), American jurist, born in Maine, Minn., and educated at Whitman College, Walla Walla, Wash., and at Columbia University, New York City. He was admitted to the New York bar in 1926 and was a member of the law faculty of Columbia University from 1925 to 1928 and of Yale University from 1928 to 1934. Douglas served on various Federal commissions, including the Securities and Exchange Commission, of which body he was chairman from 1936 to 1939. In 1939, by nomination of President Franklin D. Roosevelt, he became an associate justice of the U.S. Supreme Court. Douglas was noted for his liberal views on social and economic questions. He wrote *Strange Lands and Friendly People* (1951), *Beyond the High Himalayas* (1952), *North from Malaya* (1953), and *An Almanac of Liberty* (1954).

DOUGLAS FIR, common name of a large coniferous tree, *Pseudotsuga taxifolia,* belonging to the Pine family. It is sometimes called Douglas Spruce, but it not closely related to either the firs or the spruces. The Douglas fir sometimes reaches a height of 300 ft., and commonly grows to 200 ft. in height and 6 ft. in diameter. It is the most important timber tree of the western U.S. and is particularly common in the States of Oregon and Washington. Douglas fir lumber, usually known as Oregon pine or yellow fir, amounts annually to about one quarter of all the lumber produced in the U.S.

DOUGLASS, FREDERICK (1817?–95), assumed name of FREDERICK AUGUST WASHINGTON BAILEY, American Negro Abolitionist orator and writer, born in Tuckahoe, Md. He was the son of the Negro slave Harriet Bailey and a white man, and was largely self-educated. Cruel treatment instilled in him a hatred of slavery; he failed in an attempt to escape in 1836 but two years later he succeeded and reached New Bedford, Mass., where he assumed the name of Douglass.

His career as an Abolitionist began dramatically in 1841 at an antislavery convention in Nantucket, Mass., where his impromptu address to the convention revealed him to be an orator of great eloquence. As "a recent graduate from the institution of slavery with his diploma on his back", he was forthwith engaged as an agent of the Massachusetts Anti-Slavery Society. His speeches in the following years in the northern States and his work for the Underground Railroad (q.v.) did much to further the cause of the Abolitionists and made his name a symbol of freedom and achievement among the slaves in the South.

So impressive were Douglass' oratorical and intellectual abilities that opponents refused to believe he had been a slave and alleged that he was an impostor foisted on the public by the Abolitionists. In reply, Douglass wrote *Narrative of the Life of Frederick Douglass, An American Slave* (1845), which he revised twice in later years; in final form, it appeared in 1882 under the title *Life and Times of Frederick Douglass.*

In 1845, Douglass, at the urging of his friends, went to England to escape the danger of seizure under the fugitive slave laws. His lectures in the British Isles on the slavery question in the United States aroused sympathy for the Abolitionists' cause and enabled him to raise sufficient funds to purchase his freedom. After returning to the United States in 1847, Douglass became the "station-master and conductor" of the Underground Railroad in Rochester, N.Y., where he also established the Abolitionist newspaper *North Star*, which he edited until 1860.

During these years he became friendly with John Brown (q.v.), and approved, at first, of Brown's strategy of destroying "the money value of slave property" by training a force of men to help large numbers of slaves escape to freedom in the North via the Underground Railroad. In 1859, however, when Douglass learned, on the eve of the raid on Harpers Ferry, that it was Brown's intention to seize the Federal arsenal there, he objected on the ground that an attack on the arsenal would be tantamount to an assault on the U.S. government and would prove disastrous, and withdrew from further participation. Brown and his followers felt that Douglass had deserted them at a critical moment.

After the raid, fearing reprisals by the government, Douglass fled to Europe, where he

Nature Magazine

Left: A Douglas fir tree. Right: Branch of the tree, showing cones.

Frederick Douglass

stayed for six months. On his return to the United States, he campaigned for Abraham Lincoln during the Presidential election of 1860 and, following the outbreak of the Civil War, helped raise a regiment of Negro soldiers, the Massachusetts 54th. After the war, Douglass, as a recognized leader of and spokesman for the former Negro slaves, fought for enactment of the 13th, 14th, and 15th Amendments to the U.S. Constitution. He became U.S. marshal for the District of Columbia (1877–81), recorder of deeds for the District of Columbia (1881–86), and U.S. minister to the Republic of Haiti (1889–91). Douglass is accounted the greatest American Negro orator and one of the great orators of the United States.

DOUKHOBORS. See DUKHOBORS.

DOUMA. See DUMA.

DOUMER, PAUL (1857–1932), French statesman and 13th president of the French Republic, born at Aurillac. After seven years as a Radical member of the Chamber of Deputies (1888–95), he became minister of finance in the Léon Bourgeois cabinet (1895–96). From 1897 to 1902 he was governor general of French Indo-China. Re-entering the Chamber of Deputies in 1902, he became head of the budget commission, and, in 1905, president of the Chamber. In 1906 as the candidate of the moderate and reactionary

parties, he lost the presidential election to Armand Fallières. In 1909 he again headed the budget commission but failed of re-election to the Chamber the following year. Representing Corsica, he entered the Senate in 1912, opposed the policies of Briand's war cabinet and joined that of Paul Painlevé as minister without portfolio (1917). In the cabinets of Aristide Briand (1921–22 and 1925–26) he was minister of finance, and, in 1927, he was made president of the Senate. On May 13, 1931, he was elected president of France. He was assassinated by Paul Gorgoulov, a Russian, on May 7, 1932.

DOUMERGUE, GASTON (1863–1937), French statesman, born at Aigues-Vives, and educated at the Faculté des Droits, in Paris, where he studied law. From 1888 until 1893 he was a colonial magistrate in French Indo-China and in Algeria. In 1893 he was elected deputy from Nîmes, as a Radical-Socialist, acting as secretary of the Chamber of Deputies in 1895–96 and as vice-president in 1905–06. Between 1902 and 1910 he held various cabinet offices, serving as minister for the colonies (1902–05), minister of commerce (1906–08), and minister of public instruction (1908–10). In 1910 and 1912 Doumergue was elected to the Senate. He became prime minister in 1913, holding both that office and the portfolio of foreign affairs until 1914. During World War I he was minister of the colonies from 1914 to 1917, when he was sent to Russia on a diplomatic mission. In 1917 he re-entered the Senate, serving as its president in 1923–24, after which he was president of France until 1931. He was the twelfth president, and the first Protestant to hold that office. In 1931 he retired from public life, but was recalled to the premiership for a brief period in 1934.

DOURO (Sp. *Duero;* anc. *Durius*), a river of Spain and Portugal. It rises in Soria Province, N. central Spain, and empties, after a total course of about 485 m., into the Atlantic Ocean near Porto (Oporto), Portugal. Its general course is westward to the boundary of Portugal, southwestward as the Spanish-Portuguese boundary for about 60 m., and again westward, across Portugal, to its mouth. Navigation on the river is possible into Spain, but hampered by rapids, and by floods which occasionally occur in the lower reaches. The mouth of the river is obstructed by sand bars which permit only vessels of small draught to enter. At Leixões, N. of the mouth of the Douro, a harbor accommodating seagoing vessels has been constructed. The river yields fish, and, in Portugal, serves to carry to market the wines of the Paiz do Vinho region.

DOUROUCOULI or **DURUKULI,** a common name for monkeys of the genus *Aotus*, in the family Cebidae. These small monkeys, native from Nicaragua to Argentina, eat insects, birds, and fruits. They hunt for their food at night, and for that reason are called night apes. The body of the douroucouli is about nine inches long and it has a long, bushy tail of about fourteen inches. It has a short face, huge eyes, and a nose more prominent than that of any other American monkey. Its fur is soft and light gray with a brown stripe down the back.

DOVE, a common name for any bird of the pigeon family, usually restricted to the smaller varieties. The turtle dove, *Turtur auritus*, common to Europe and Asia, but not found in North America, was sacred to the ancient Israelites and most Mediterranean peoples. The dove, which became a Christian symbol of simplicity and gentleness, is even now referred to as the bird of peace.

Doves are common in all parts of the U.S. Thirteen species of doves are native to North America. The mourning dove, *Zenaidura macroura*, the most common variety in the U.S., appears in rural districts and is named for its call, which is low, sweet, and melancholy. It has a brown body with bluish-gray wings, and its white-tipped, short outer tail is banded with black. The Inca dove, *Scardafella inca*, with its scaled brown and black plumage and grayish-pink breast, the ground dove, *Columbigallina passerina*, and the white-winged dove, *Melopelia asiatica*, are native to the extreme southern States of the U.S. See COLUMBIFORMES; PIGEON.

DOVEKIE or **DOVEKEY. 1.** A short-billed auk, *Alle alle*, also called the rotche or sea dove. Its upper parts are black with white streaks, its neck, sides, and upper breast are brown, and its lower breast and stomach are white. The dovekie is about eight inches long. This species breeds in the Arctic coasts, especially Iceland, Greenland, and Spitsbergen. In the winter, dovekies occur as far south as Long Island, and sometimes even in South Carolina. Dovekies float in flocks on the open sea and dive for their food. **2.** Another common name for the black guillemot, *Cepphus grylle*, also of the Auk family. These birds are thirteen inches long and entirely black except for the upper portions of their wings, which are white. This species is found from central Labrador to Nova Scotia and Maine. In the winter the birds appear as far south as New Jersey. Black guillemots float on water like ducks and dive for fish which they spear with their sharp, black bills. See AUK; AUKLET; GUILLEMOT.

DOVER, capital of the State of Delaware and county seat of Kent Co. It is situated in the central part of the State, on St. Jones R., 48 m. by rail s. of Wilmington. The city is the commercial center of a rich agricultural region, noted for its apples, peaches, grapes, straw-

U.S.D.I., Fish & Wildlife Service
Left: Turtle dove. Right: Mourning dove in a nest with its young.

British Information Services

Shakespeare's Cliff, famous landmark of the chalk cliffs of Dover

berries, and poultry. Industrial products of Dover include canned and dried fruits, flour, rubber products, automobile bodies, mattresses, wood products, silk hosiery, and electrical equipment. One of the noteworthy points of interest in the city is the State House, constructed between 1787 and 1793, and the second oldest State Capitol still in use in the United States. Among other notable edifices are Christ Church, built in 1734, and the Presbyterian Church, built in 1791. Delaware State College, a coeducational school of higher learning for Negroes, is situated near the city. Dover was laid out in 1717. In 1777 it became the capital of the State, replacing New Castle. Dover was incorporated as a town in 1829, and as a city in 1925. Pop. (1950) 6223.

DOVER, seaport and municipal borough of Kent County, England, on the Strait of Dover, at the mouth of the Dour R., 76 m. by rail E.S.E. of London. It is the point on the English coast nearest to France, 21 m. distant. Dover has an excellent harbor, through which passes a great volume of freight and passenger traffic to and from Calais and Dunkirk, France, and Ostend, Belgium. Industries in the town include the manufacture of paper, flour, and iron castings.

On the east height of the Dover chalk cliffs, 375 ft. above sea level, is Dover Castle, one of the largest and most notable examples of me-

dieval fortification in existence as an intact unit. The castle, which has been altered at various times in accordance with changing military requirements, is said to predate the Roman invasion. It contains the remains of a Roman lighthouse, or *pharos,* and the ancient fortress-church St. Mary in Castro, a unique specimen of Roman-British architecture. On the citadel heights, north of the castle, is a restored circular church of the Knights Templars. In High Street are the central hall and other remnants of the Maison Dieu founded in the 13th century by Hubert de Burgh as a hospice for pilgrims from all lands. The Dover museum (1849) contains many historical relics. Outside the town hall hangs a bell taken from Antwerp, Belgium, by the Germans during World War I and used as an air-raid warning at Zeebrugge; it was later presented to Dover by the Belgians.

In World War I, Dover was subjected to German attacks by submarines and aircraft in 1914, and was bombed frequently in 1916. In 1917–18, attempts were made by sea and air to damage the harbor, which served as the base for the flotilla known as the Dover Patrol. The patrol not only safeguarded English and Allied traffic in the Strait of Dover, but prevented the passage of German submarines from the North Sea to the English Channel by maintaining a barrier of moored mines across the 21 miles of the strait. The monitors and siege-gun units of the Patrol provided the main artillery support for the left flank of the British army in Flanders. The patrol also attacked Zeebrugge on April 23, 1918, and sank ships in the Belgian harbor to block German traffic. The exploits of the Dover Patrol are commemorated by memorials at Dover and at Cape Gris-Nez, France; and a memorial, provided by popular subscription in England, has been erected at Fort Hamilton, Brooklyn, overlooking the New York City harbor.

During World War II, Dover was repeatedly subject to German air raiding, as well as to shelling by German guns entrenched at Cape Gris-Nez. Thousands of homes and other buildings were damaged.

Dover was an important port as far back as Roman times, when it was called *Dubris*. The Normans called it *Dovore;* the French, *Douvres*. It was famous as one of the Cinque Ports (q.v.). During the Middle Ages, Dover Castle was frequently besieged in civil wars and foreign invasions, and the town was regarded as the key to England. Pop. (1951 est.) 35,217.

DOVER PATROL. See DOVER.

DOVER, STRAIT OF, strait separating England from France and the European continent, and connecting the English Channel and the Atlantic Ocean with the North Sea. Its limits on the English coast are defined as the promontories of Dungeness and South Foreland; on the French coast, as those of Cape Gris-Nez and Calais. The strait is known to the French as *Pas de Calais*. It is 20 to 27 m. wide and 6 to 162 ft. deep. Near the center of the strait are the Ridge Shoals, over 8 m. long, where the depth is 10 to 24 ft. Both the English and French shores are formed by chalk cliffs; their corresponding strata show that in prehistoric times a land connection existed at that point. The strait is one of the busiest maritime routes in the world. Frequent proposals have been made in the 20th century for the construction of a tunnel under the strait, and engineering surveys of an England-to-France route have been made.

DOVRE FJELD or **DOVREFJELD,** part of the central mountainous plateau of Norway, s.w. of Trondheim. The elevation, in general, ranges from 2650 to 3600 ft. above sea level, but Snehætten, the loftiest peak, reaches an altitude of nearly 7600 ft. The Dovre Fjeld is crossed by the Oslo-Trondheim railroad.

DOW, GERARD. See DOU, GERARD.

DOW, HERBERT HENRY (1866–1930), Amer-

ican chemist, born in Belleville, Ont., Canada, and educated at the Case School of Applied Science in Cleveland, Ohio. In 1889 he founded the Midland Chemical Company in Michigan. Later, he founded the Dow Process Company and the Dow Chemical Company, and served as president and general manager of the latter until his death. He developed many new chemical processes, including a method of extracting bromine and magnesium (qq.v.) from sea water. Virtually all of the world's supply of metallic magnesium is produced by this method. During World War I, Dow was a member of the advisory committee of the Council of National Defense. In 1930 he was awarded the Perkin Medal by the Society of Chemical Industry.

DOWDEN, EDWARD (1843–1913), Irish critic, poet, and educator, born at Cork, and educated at Trinity College, Dublin. He was professor of English literature at Trinity from his twenty-fifth year until his death, but lectured extensively elsewhere, notably at Oxford in 1889, at Trinity College, Cambridge, from 1892 to 1896, and at Princeton University in 1896. He is best known for his work as a Shakespearean critic. The publication of his *Shakespeare, His Mind and Art* (1875) gave him a wide academic reputation, and he later became noted as well for his studies of 19th-century poets. His work includes *Studies in Literature* (1878), *Life of Shelley* (1886), *Introduction to Shakespeare* (1893), *A History of French Literature* (1904), *Robert Browning* (1904), *Michel de Montaigne* (1905), and *Essays: Modern and Elizabethan* (1910). His *Collected Poetical Works* (2 vols.) and *Letters* appeared in 1914.

DOWER, in law, tne common-law right of a wife to a one-third interest for life in the real estate of her deceased husband. Dower attaches only in those cases in which the husband was possessed of an absolute fee in real property, inheritable by the issue of the marriage. The law of the place where the property is located governs the right of dower. Dower still exists in most States of the U.S., usually by reason of statutes which, frequently, have modified or changed the common-law rules. It has been completely abolished in New York and in a number of other States.

DOWIE, JOHN ALEXANDER (1847–1907), religious leader, born in Edinburgh, Scotland, and educated at Edinburgh University. He studied for the Congregationalist ministry and, after he was ordained, became pastor of a church in Alma, South Australia. Believing that he could cure disease by prayer, he went to Melbourne and established the Divine Healing Association of Australia and New Zealand. In 1888 he came to the U.S., where he attracted many followers and, in 1896, organized the Christian Catholic Church in Zion. Dowie proclaimed himself Elijah the Restorer in 1901, and, using money contributed by his followers, bought a tract of land on the western shore of Lake Michigan, where he founded Zion City. The city's population was composed entirely of supporters of Dowie, who ruled almost as a dictator. Branches of the Christian Catholic Church were established throughout the world. In 1903 Dowie was ridiculed in New York City when he led his "hosts" there to regenerate the city, and he was attacked by a hostile mob in London a year later. In 1906 the inhabitants of Zion City deposed him on charges of fraud, tyranny, and polygamy.

DOWITCHER, a bird, *Limnodromus griseus,* of the Sandpiper (q.v.) family. Although it is not a snipe, it is commonly called the long-billed snipe or red-breasted snipe. Its plumage is gray in the winter, and brown in the summer. The bill is from 2 to $2\frac{1}{2}$ inches long, and the over-all length of the bird varies from 10 to 12 inches. The dowitcher occurs from the Arctic coast of North America to Alaska and northwestern Canada in the summer, and from Florida and Mexico to northern South America in the winter.

DOWN, county of Northern Ireland. The coastline, on the Irish Sea, is low, rocky, and indented by many bays. The greater part of Down consists of low hills and many bogs, though the Mourne Mountains, in the south, rise to 2796 ft. above sea level in the peak Slieve Donard. The county is drained by the Lagan R. in the north, and the Bann and the Newry in the west. The soil is chiefly rocky loam. The principal crops are oats, potatoes, and turnips. The growing of flax, once important in the county, has been practically abandoned. Hogs, sheep, and poultry are raised; and the county is especially noted for the breeding of race horses. Manufactures in County Down include linens, woolens, hosiery, leather, and thread. Downpatrick (pop., 1951 prelim., 3878) is the county seat; Bangor is the largest town. Area, 951 sq.m.; pop. (1951 prelim.) 241,105.

DOWNING, H(AROLD) H(ARDESTY) (1886–), American educator and mathematician, born in Lexington, Ky., and educated at the University of Kentucky and the University of Chicago. In 1908 he joined the faculty of the University of Kentucky as an instructor in mathematics. He was appointed assistant professor in 1910, associate professor in 1927, and professor in 1931. From 1947 to 1952 he served as head of the department of mathematics and astronomy. He wrote *A Brief Course in Analytic Geometry* (with P. P. Boyd, 1947).

DOWNING COLLEGE, a college of Cambridge University (q.v.), founded in 1800 by Sir George Downing, and opened in 1821. Study in the college is restricted to English law and medicine. The faculty consists of one master and two professors; the student body numbers about 120.

DOWNING STREET, a street in the West End of London, England. It was named in honor of Sir George Downing, secretary of the treasury in 1667. The official residence of the prime minister, where cabinet meetings are frequently held, is located at No. 10. Also located on Downing Street are the residence of the chancellor of the exchequer and both the Foreign Office and the Colonial Office. The term "Downing Street" is frequently used as a synonym for the British Government.

DOWNS, a term generally applied to hillocks of sand thrown up by the sea or wind along the shore of a sea or other body of water; and also a general name for any undulating tract of upland too light in soil for cultivation but covered with grass fit for grazing sheep. Specifically, the term is applied to the system of undulating chalk hills in England, s. of the Thames R. Best known as the Downs in England are the North Downs, in Surrey and Kent counties, and the South Downs, in Sussex County. Both ridges extend from a series of hills, the Western Downs, in the chalk area of Dorsetshire and Hampshire. The North Downs, reaching from Farnham to the English Channel between Dover and Folkestone, are 95 m. long, and are broken by a series of deep gaps made by streams. The South Downs, from Petersfield to the Channel at Beachy Head, are 65 m. long and also are breached by the courses of streams. The highest point of the North Downs is Leith Hill, 965 ft. above sea level; that of the South Downs, Butser Hill, 889 ft. above sea level. Smooth, rolling lines are characteristic of the Downs. The sides of the hills are wooded; the uplands are covered with good grazing sod for sheep. The English Downs enclose a wooded district called the Weald (q.v.).

DOWNY MILDEW, common name for fungi of the family Peronosporaceae. They are parasites which live in the fleshy parts of plants, and many of them destroy valuable fruits and vegetables. Important genera are *Albugo,* the white rust of the mustard family; *Phytophthora,* producing potato rot; *Plasmopara,* one species of which, *P. viticola,* is the grape mildew; and *Peronospora,* several species of which are common parasites on many vegetables. See FUNGI; MILDEW.

DOWRY, property which the wife brings to the husband as her marriage portion. Though recognized at the common law and often forming in England an important element in the arrangement known as a marriage settlement, it is almost unknown in the United States, except in Louisiana. In that State, as in most countries which have adopted the system of the Civil Law (q.v.), it constitutes a distinct as well as an important form of property. It is given to the husband, who has exclusive control and administration of it during marriage, to be employed in defraying the expenses of the family. The wife cannot deprive the husband of its control. On the other hand, he is not allowed to alienate real estate which comes to him as dowry. Dowry is to be distinguished from dower, or the common-law right of the wife in the real estate of her husband, with which it is sometimes confused. See DOWER.

DOWSING ROD. See DIVINING ROD.

DOWSON, ERNEST CHRISTOPHER (1867–1900), English writer, born at Lea, Kent. He was a prominent member of the Aesthetic Movement, formed by a small group of English poets and artists of the 1890's as a reaction against Victorianism. He wrote polished, delicate lyrics, of which the most famous is *Non sum qualis eram,* better known by its refrain, "I have been faithful to thee, Cynara, in my fashion." Among his other works are two novels, written in collaboration with Arthur Moore, *A Comedy of Masks* (1893) and *Adrian Rome* (1899).

DOXOLOGY (Gr. *doxologos,* "praising"), a hymn offering praise to God. Doxologies are found in the Bible in such verses as Rom. 16:27, Eph. 3:21, and Jude: 25. The *lesser* and *greater* doxologies are two responsive forms which originated in the 4th century and are now used in the Roman Catholic and Anglican liturgies. *Gloria Patri* is the name of the lesser doxology: "Glory be to the Father, and to the Son, and to the Holy Ghost; as it was in the beginning, is now, and ever shall be, world

without end. Amen." The greater doxology, *Gloria in excelsis Deo,* is an early-Church expansion of the song of the angels in Luke 2:14. In the Roman Catholic Church, the lesser doxology is recited in all responsories of the breviary (q.v.) and at the end of all but two psalms and canticles, the *Te Deum* and the *Benedicte.* It is omitted in seasons of mourning and in Masses said for the dead. The greater doxology occurs in the Roman Catholic Mass, except during Advent and Lent (qq.v.) and in Mass for a special intention. In the Anglican liturgy, the lesser doxology appears at the end of psalms and canticles, and the greater doxology is repeated at all times in the communion service.

The last stanza of a hymn by the English bishop Thomas Ken, beginning "Praise God from Whom all blessings flow", is commonly called *The Doxology* in Protestant churches.

DOYLE, SIR ARTHUR CONAN (1859–1930), British physician, novelist, and detective-story writer, born in Edinburgh, and educated at Stonyhurst College and the University of Edinburgh. From 1882 to 1890 he practiced medicine in Southsea, England. *A Study in Scarlet,* the first of sixty-eight stories featuring his famous fictional detective, Sherlock Holmes, appeared in 1887. Doyle was so speedily successful in his literary career that about five years later he abandoned his medical practice to devote his entire time to writing.

The Holmes stories, of which some of the best-known are *The Sign of the Four* (1889), *The Adventures of Sherlock Holmes* (1891), and *The Hound of the Baskervilles* (1902), made Doyle internationally famous. His remarkable literary versatility brought him equal fame for his historical romances, such as *Micah Clarke* (1888), *The White Company* (1890), and *Sir Nigel* (1906).

He served in the Boer War as a physician, and on his return to England wrote *The Great Boer War* (1900) and *The War in South Africa; Its Causes and Conduct* (1902), for which he was knighted in 1902. During World War I, he wrote *History of the British Campaign in France and Flanders* (6 vols., 1915–20) as a tribute to British bravery.

After the death of his eldest son in the war, he became an advocate of spiritualism (q.v.) and toured Australia, Africa, and the U.S. in the interest of his new belief. During the last part of his life, he wrote extensively on spiritualism, including such books as *A New Revelation* (1918) and *History of Spiritualism* (2

Sir Arthur Conan Doyle

vols., 1926). Among his other works are poems, and the plays *The Fires of Fate* (1909) and *The Poison Belt* (1913). His autobiography, *My Memories and Adventures,* was published in 1924. See PSYCHICAL RESEARCH.

D'OYLY CARTE, RICHARD (1844–1901), English operatic impresario, born in London, and educated at University College there. At the age of seventeen he left school to enter his father's business of music publishing and musical-instrument making, and to study music. He opened a concert agency in 1870, and began to produce light operas, introducing into England Offenbach's *Whittington* and Lecocq's *Giroflé-Girofla.* He soon became interested in promoting English light opera, and, in 1875, produced the first Gilbert and Sullivan operetta, *Trial by Jury,* at the Opéra Comique Theatre. In 1878, D'Oyly Carte, Sir William Schwenck Gilbert (q.v.), and Sir Arthur Sullivan (q.v.) formed the Comic Opera Company to present the operettas of Gilbert and Sullivan. In the same year, in New York, they introduced *The Pirates of Penzance,* which they produced in London in 1880. From 1881 until 1896 they produced operettas at the Savoy Theatre, established by D'Oyly Carte especially for the presentation of the works of Gilbert and Sullivan. After these two ceased to collaborate in 1896, D'Oyly Carte continued, at the Savoy Theatre, the production of works by other authors and composers and revivals of the works of Gilbert and Sullivan.

Beginning in 1913, Rupert D'Oyly Carte (1876–1948), son of Richard, directed the D'Oyly Carte Opera Company, which appeared in the United States in 1934, 1936, 1939, 1947–48, and 1950–51.

DRACAENA. See DRAGON TREE.

DRACHMANN, HOLGER HENRIK HERHOLDT (1846–1908), Danish writer, born at Copenhagen. He became known as one of the leaders of the modern movement in Danish literature. His works include the volumes of poetry *Muffled Melodies* (1875), *Songs by the Sea* (1877), and *Motley Leaves* (1901); the plays *Once Upon a Time* (1885) and *Brav-Karl* (1897); and the novels *On a Sailor's Word* (1878), *With a Broad Brush* (1887), *The Sacred Fire* (1899), and *Dädalus* (1900).

DRACO (Lat., "dragon"), a circumpolar constellation situated in the northern hemisphere, just below the celestial pole. The star Etamin or γ Draconis, a second-magnitude star and the brightest in the constellation, was the principal object of measurement used by James Bradley (q.v.) in 1729 in discovering the aberration of light.

DRACO. See DRAGON.

DRAFT ACT. See CONSCRIPTION; SELECTIVE SERVICE.

DRAFTING or **ENGINEERING DRAWING,** the process of representing topography, engineering works, buildings, and pieces of machinery by means of conventionalized drawings. The techniques of drafting are an important part of all types of engineering and manufacturing and also find application in such diverse fields as architecture and geology.

The fundamental purpose of an engineering drawing is to convey the exact shape and dimensions of the object represented. An ordinary perspective drawing gives no information about hidden details of the object and is not drawn to scale. The technique of conventional drafting is to use two or more projections to represent solid objects; see DESCRIPTIVE GEOMETRY. These projections are views or plans of the object and are not complete in themselves, but when taken together they represent every shape and dimension of the object.

The primary view or projection of an engineering drawing is the *front view* or *elevation,* which usually shows the side of the object which has the largest dimensions. Above the elevation the draftsman draws the *top view* or *plan,* which shows the object from directly above. When these two views are not sufficient, other views are added: a *side view* or *side elevation; auxiliary views,* based on special points of view outside the object and designed to show external details that are not otherwise clear; and *sections* or *sectional views,* which represent the object as partly cut away to show internal detail. Each line in an engineering drawing represents a contour or a meeting of two surfaces. Unbroken lines represent visible contours and surface junctions, and dotted lines invisible ones. The drawing in addition indicates the exact dimensions of all lines necessary to define the object exactly.

A number of special conventions are used in electrical, topographic, architectural, and other forms of drafting to give information that will be needed by the user of the drawing. In electrical drafting, such conventions include stylized signs to indicate circuit components such as condensers and microphones; in topographic drafting, conventional signs are used to show types of land and elevations and depressions of the land; and in architectural and mechanical drafting, conventional linings, shadings, and crosshatchings indicate different kinds of structural materials. When practical, engineering drawings are drafted to be precisely the same size as the object presented. Drawings of small parts or details of machinery, however, are frequently drawn with all dimensions enlarged in a given ratio, whereas maps and drawings of large engineering works are reduced similarly. The ratio of enlargement or reduction of a drawing is known as its *scale,* and is always marked on the drawing.

The reading of engineering drawings requires training in the conventional representation used. For this reason, during World War II, when millions of unskilled workers were employed by defense plants, new drafting techniques were developed to show with greater simplicity the details of construction and assembly of complex machines. Machine drawings were made in true or in isometric perspective to show the parts of a machine as they actually looked when assembled. "Exploded" drawings showed all the parts separated, but in proper size and proper relative positions. Stacks of transparent drawings bound as books were used to represent the entire assembly of a complex device from its exterior to its innermost parts. These types of simplified drawings are now widely used as a supplement to conventionalized engineering drawings.

DRAFT RIOTS, in United States history, the mob violence incited in New York City, from July 13 to July 16, 1863, during the Civil War, by opponents of conscription (q.v.) and individuals sympathetic to the Confederate cause. Because of the traditional hostility of the American people to compulsory military service, the Federal government had relied, during the early stages of the war, on the volunteer system of obtaining recruits for the Union armies. The pressing need for more soldiers compelled Congress to pass (March 3, 1863) legislation, known as the Enrollment Act, which imposed liability for military duty on virtually all able-bodied males between 20 and 45 years of age. Opponents of President Lincoln's administration and policies vigorously attacked the bill, criticizing with particular emphasis a provision which enabled draftees to obtain exemption from service by supplying a substitute or by the payment of $300. As the date for enforcement of the act approached, dissatisfaction with this provision, called "The Rich Man's Exemption", became widespread among the poor sections of the population of New York City.

Although no disturbances occurred on Saturday, July 11, when the draft began, its resumption on the following Monday was marked by the rapid mobilization of an unruly crowd, which soon attacked and burned the draft headquarters. The crowd kept fire apparatus from the building, and flames shortly spread to the entire block. Attempts by the New York police and a small detachment of U.S. Marines to disperse the rioters provoked the mob to intensified violence. The rioters, joined by additional thousands of sympathizers, roamed freely through the city, destroying property and committing other outrages. These were directed especially against Negro citizens, who, in the opinion of the mob, were responsible for the Civil War. Many were lynched, and on Monday afternoon the rioters sacked and burned the Colored Orphan Asylum, a charitable institution housing nearly 800 Negro children.

The rioting subsided late Monday night, but was resumed with even greater violence on Tuesday, July 14. Police, aided by small detachments of troops stationed in and near the city, made vain attempts to disperse the mobs. More Negroes were murdered, Negro neighborhoods were burned, and general pillaging took place. Unrestrained rioting continued until July 15, when military detachments reached the city from Pennsylvania and from West Point, N.Y. Temporary sus-

Metropolitan Museum of Art

Left: Saint George slaying the dragon, an English legend symbolizing triumph of good over the powers of evil.
Above: A dragon insignia on the robe of a Chinese emperor. In China the dragon is regarded as a symbol of good fortune.

pension of the draft was announced the same day. By Thursday, July 16, law and order had been restored. Estimated fatalities during the three days of violence totaled more than 1000. More than 50 large buildings were destroyed by fire, and property damage approximated $2,000,000.

DRAFTS, or DRAUGHTS. See CHECKERS.

DRAGO, LUIS MARÍA (1859–1921), Argentine jurist, statesman, and author, born in Buenos Aires. He was trained as a lawyer. In 1902–03, he was foreign minister of Argentina and later became a member of the Permanent Court of Arbitration at The Hague, Netherlands. Drago is famous mainly because of his support of the principle of international law known as the *Drago Doctrine*. In 1902, Great Britain, Germany, and Italy sent armed naval units to blockade several Venezuelan ports because the government of Venezuela had refused to pay claims arising from international loans. Drago, in a note to the U.S. Department of State, enunciated the doctrine that public debt in the form of bonds, owed by a sovereign American state to citizens of a European state, must not be collected by armed intervention of a European state on American territory. He desired this principle to be accepted as a corollary to the Monroe Doctrine (q.v.).

The Drago Doctrine was proposed to the Hague Conference (q.v.) of 1907, where the nations represented accepted it in a modified form. They agreed that the government of one state shall not use armed force to recover debts due from the government of another state until after the debt has been submitted to international arbitration and the debtor state has obstructed the formulation of a compromise or has failed to carry out a decision against it. Among Drago's works are *La Literatura del Slang* and *Colección de Fallos en Materia Civil y Commercial*.

DRAGON, in mythology, a reptilic monster similar in form to a crocodile and usually represented as having wings, huge claws, and a fiery breath. In the folklore of antiquity, particularly that of nations infested by venomous reptiles, the dragon symbolizes destruction and evil. This conception is found, for example, in the Creation Epic (q.v.) of Babylonia. One of the central figures of the legend is the goddess Tiamat, dragonlike personification of the Oceans, who headed the hordes of chaos and whose destruction was prerequisite to an orderly universe. In the sacred writings of the ancient Hebrews, the dragon frequently represents death and evil. Christian mythology inherited the Hebraic conception of the dragon, which figures in all of the important apocalyptic literature of the Bible and appears in later Christian traditions (see GEORGE, SAINT). In Christian art, the dragon is the symbol of sin. It is often represented as crushed under the feet of saints and martyrs, symbolizing the triumph of Christianity over paganism.

Although the dragon appears as the embodiment of evil in certain mythologies, it is more generally credited with beneficent powers. The ancient Greeks and Romans believed that dragons had the ability to understand and to convey to man the secrets of the earth. Partially as a result of this conception of the monster as a benign, protective influence, and partially because of its fearsome qualities, it was adopted as a military emblem. The Romans adopted it as such in the 1st century A.D., inscribing the figure of a dragon on the standards carried into battle by the cohorts. The folklore of the pagan tribes of northern Europe contained both beneficent and terror-inspiring dragons. In the *Nibelungenlied* (q.v.), Siegfried kills a dragon, and one of the principal episodes of *Beowulf* (q.v.) deals with a similar achievement. The ancient Norsemen adorned the prows of their vessels with carved likenesses of dragons. Among the Celtic conquerors of Britain the dragon was a symbol of sovereignty; the legendary monster was also depicted on the shields of the Teutonic tribes that later invaded Britain; and it appeared on the battle standards of British kings as late as the 16th century. Subsequently it was inscribed on the armorial bearings of the Prince of Wales.

The dragon also figures in the mythology of various Oriental countries, notably Japan and China. It is deified in the Taoist religion, and was the national emblem of the Chinese Empire. Among the Chinese people, the dragon is traditionally regarded as a symbol of good fortune.

DRAGON, or FLYING DRAGON, any small, brilliantly colored, arboreal lizard of the genus *Draco,* or related genera, inhabiting the East Indies and southern Asia. They are distinguished from all other lizards by their winglike folds of skin, supported by five or six hind ribs, which form a parachute and help buoy up the lizards as they jump from limb to limb. They are capable of traveling long distances in this manner, resembling the flying squirrels in their method of aerial flight. *D. volans,* a native of Malaya, has a brilliant metallic luster on its upper surfaces, varied by bands and spots; the parachute and the throat appendage of the male of this species are orange.

The Komodo monitor (q.v.), the largest living lizard, is also called Komodo dragon.

DRAGON BIRD. See UMBRELLA BIRD.

DRAGONET, a common name for marine fish of the genus *Callionymus,* especially *C. draco,* inhabiting the temperate coasts of Europe and the tropical seas of the Orient. Dragonets are usually classified in the same family with the gobies, but some authorities give them separate family rank. Their tiny gill openings are located close together near the back of the head. Dragonets have no air bladder. The sexes vary greatly in appearance: the females are dull in color, and the males are brilliantly colored, especially during the mating season. Small shellfish form the bulk of their diet.

DRAGONFISH, a fish of the genus *Pegasus,* inhabiting Oriental and Australian seas. It is covered with bony plates, movable except near the tail, and has large, fanlike, pectoral fins. It has prominent eyes, and a greatly prolonged, toothless snout. *P. volans* is frequently seen dried as a curiosity, and is sometimes depicted on ornamental boxes made in China. The dragonet (q.v.) is also sometimes called dragonfish.

DRAGONFLY, the common name of any predaceous insect of the order Odonata. This order is usually divided into two principal suborders: the Zygoptera, or damsel flies, which hold the wings above the body when resting; and the Anisoptera, the true dragonflies, which hold the wings spread when resting. Members of both suborders have large heads with very large eyes and relatively short antennae. They have mouths adapted for biting and two pairs of elongated membranous wings. The abdomen is relatively very long.

Dragonfly (Anax junius) on a flower

The insects' legs are located far forward on the body and are seldom used for walking. The damsel flies are generally smaller and weaker in flight than the true dragonflies. Both types are known by a number of popular names such as darning needle, devil's-darning-needle, snake feeder, and horse doctor.

The dragonflies undergo incomplete metamorphosis during their development. Some species simply drop their eggs into the water or attach them to the stems of aquatic plants, but others, including all the damsel flies, make slits in the stems of plants at or below the water line and there deposit elongated eggs. The eggs of all species hatch into *nymphs*, which mature in the water, feeding on various forms of aquatic life. Nymphs of some of the larger species will attack even small fish. Dragonfly nymphs have a special extensible lower jaw called the mask, with which they seize their prey. The length of time which dragonflies spend in nymphal form varies from one to three or more years, and during this period the nymph molts ten or more times. When nymphs have fully matured they leave the water and undergo metamorphosis into the adult form.

Approximately 2700 species of dragonflies are known, and members of the order are found in all temperate and tropical regions of the world. Common U.S. species of Zygoptera include the ruby-spot, *Hetaerina americana,* which has white wings and a red body in the male, and the black-wing, *Calopteryx maculata,* which has black wings in the male and brown wings in the female. Among the common species of Anisoptera found in this country are members of the genus *Gomphinae,* with black bodies striped with green or yellow, and *Anax junius,* which has clear wings and a green head and thorax. The latter species is one of the most widely distributed of dragonflies. It is found in Asia, in the Pacific islands, and in the Western Hemisphere as far north as Alaska and as far south as Costa Rica.

Most temperate-zone species of dragonflies have wingspreads of 2 to 3 in., but tropical species sometimes reach 7½ in. The largest known dragonfly lived in Carboniferous times and had a wingspread of 2 ft.

DRAGONHEAD, common name for plants of the genus *Dracocephalum* of the Mint family. The plants bear blue, purple, or white two-lipped flowers in whorls. They are easily raised from seed or cuttings, but have no great horticultural value because their flowers quickly wither in the sun. *D. bullatum,* a perennial

herb which bears bright blue flowers, is sometimes grown in shady corners of rock gardens.

DRAGON ROOT, common name for a tall herb, *Arisaema dracontium,* of the Arum family. In America it is sometimes called green dragon. It has a tuberous rootstock and bears orange-red berries within greenish, flowerlike bracts. It is closely related to the jack-in-the-pulpit (q.v.), *A. triphyllum,* and to the cuckoo-pint, *A maculatum,* a common European arum.

DRAGON'S BLOOD, an oleoresin, usually dark red in color, derived from several species of trees, particularly *Calamus draco.* Dragon's blood is used extensively as a resist in photoengraving (q.v.) and is also sometimes employed for coloring varnishes and lacquers. Other trees which yield dragon's blood include the dragon tree (q.v.) and some species of the genera *Croton* and *Eucalyptus.*

DRAGON'S-MOUTH. See SNAPDRAGON.

DRAGON TREE, a tree, *Dracaena draco,* belonging to the Lily family, and found only in the Canary Islands. The tree has long, narrow leaves and clusters of white flowers. Dragon trees grow to enormous dimensions. The trunk of a tree at one time growing in Tenerife measured 70 ft. in height and 45 ft. in circumference. The trees are supposed to be extremely long-lived, and the specimen mentioned above is believed to have been 5000 years old. Dragon trees exude a type of oleoresin which was formerly sold as dragon's blood (q.v.).

DRAINAGE, the removal of excess water from the soil by means of canals, drains, ditches, or other structures which collect the water and carry it away. The term drainage is also applied to the large-scale reclamation of marshes and underwater land by means of a combination of drainage ditches and dikes, sometimes assisted by pumps.

In large-scale drainage where improvement of outlet facilities is essential to the protection of adjacent property, it is customary to improve natural stream channels to provide required discharge capacity and to excavate main and lateral drains as open ditches or canals to convey the effluent from farm drainage systems to these improved channels. Such connecting drains commonly follow the natural surface drainage pattern of the area; they thus intercept normal surface run-off which takes place during periods of excessive rainfall.

Small-scale drainage is often practiced by farmers and other land owners who wish to remove surface water from arable fields or to improve water-laden soil. Properly constructed drainage systems can also prevent erosion and gullying of land on slopes by catching the surface water before it reaches the slope. The essential principle of any type of land drainage is to provide an open, adequate, and readily accessible channel through which the surface or subsoil water can flow. For this purpose open ditches are sometimes used, but they are not always satisfactory because they may become choked with sediment and vegetation. Underground drains are usually employed, particularly on land that is to be plowed. Such drains are of two kinds, *French drains* and *pipe drains*. A French drain consists of a ditch partly filled with large stones which are covered with soil to the level of the surrounding ground. The stones, being irregular, leave a channel through which water can flow along the ditch. French drains are often unsatisfactory, as fine soil seeps into the spaces between the stones and clogs the passages. The pipe used in drainage may be of porous earthenware sections which are laid end to end in the bottom of a ditch, with the spaces between the sections covered but not closed; it may be perforated metal pipe; or it may take any of a number of other forms designed to receive water from the surrounding soil and to be self-cleaning in so far as possible. The flow in a pipe drain is swifter than in a French drain and is less subject to interruptions which are caused by choking of the drain by earth and roots. The particles of earth filled in around the pipe in the trench should be large enough so that they will not flow into the pipe, yet small enough so that the finer surrounding soil will not, in turn, flow into the backfill material and clog it.

In draining comparatively flat land, it is common practice to lay along one side of the plot a main drain to which are connected a number of transverse laterals. The laterals are often set parallel to the main drain, coming together to join it at the lower end of the field. Local conditions of soil and terrain govern the spacing of laterals and the depth at which they are placed. Laterals may be from 15 to 300 ft. apart and from 2 to 4 ft. below the surface.

A type of temporary drain called a mole drain is common in Europe and used to some extent in the U.S. This kind of drain is often constructed by dragging a steel ball or other heavy object through the soil at the proper depth, leaving an open drain below ground. Such channels eventually become filled in, but may be effective for as long as five years, and may be easily reopened.

To prevent water from higher ground from reaching lower areas, catchment or interception drains are frequently built. They consist of ditches or underground drains placed across the slope which catch water and carry it away before it reaches the low ground.

The drains discussed above all operate by gravity, but in the drainage of low-lying areas it is not always possible to set the outlet of the drain low enough to obtain a natural flow of water. This situation occurs in many areas in Holland, in the fen country of England, and in many small areas throughout the world, such as at some airports in river-bottom areas near large cities in the United States. Where gravity flow is impossible, the water from the drainage system is pumped away into streams or canals, the level of which is often higher than that of the drained land. The difficulty of drainage in low areas is increased by the fact that drained land frequently settles as its moisture content is lowered. In the English fens this sinking has amounted to an average of 18 inches. Where the soil rests on a water-bearing foundation such as gravel, subsurface drainage may be provided by pumping water from wells, thus lowering the water level in the soil.

Drainage in the U.S. In 1950 a total of 102,688,331 acres of land in the United States was serviced by drainage enterprises administered by private corporations, co-operatives, State governments, and the Federal government. Besides the land drained by such enterprises, considerable acreage is drained by private owners.

In 1953 a total of 1,560,377 acres of farm and ranch land was drained. Much of this drainage was accomplished by means of group-enterprise projects, whereby several owners, treating their individual properties as a single unit, installed drainage systems extending through their farms. More than two fifths of the total drainage-enterprise area is in Louisiana, Minnesota, Indiana, and Michigan. Drainage is extensively practiced also in Ohio, Illinois, Iowa, Florida, and Texas. The various State governments have taken a prominent place in drainage enterprises, because in 1850 the Federal government gave the States sovereign rights over swampland. During the latter part of the 1930's the Works Progress Administration and the Civilian Conservation Corps, both Federal agencies, did much drainage work. The Secretary of the Army, under the Flood Control Act of De-

DRAISINE

DRAISINE `# DRAISINE# DRAISINE

cember, 1922, was authorized to investigate and to construct and operate channel and major drainage improvements as directed by the Congress. The Soil Conservation Service in many sections assists farmers with on-farm drainage improvements. The Bureau of Reclamation carries out drainage projects on Federal Reclamation Projects in the seventeen western States.

Drainage Abroad. Holland has one of the best known and most extensive systems of drainage and land reclamation in the world. The greater part of the country is low and flat and must be protected by dikes against inundation by the sea. The soil was originally marshy, and there were many lakes, but owing to drainage and the pumping off of the drained water by windmills the land has been made arable. In 1923 Holland began its largest project, the reclamation of 550,000 acres of land from beneath the waters of the Zuider Zee. This project, although interrupted by World War II, is now about one-third complete. The process of reclamation, known as poldering, consists of creating large enclosed lakes by building dikes, and then pumping the lakes dry.

A large area of eastern England between the cities of Cambridge and Lincoln, known as the Fens, has been reclaimed from marshland. The reclamation, which like that of Holland has continued for centuries, has been accomplished by extensive drainage, the building of dikes, and by rechanneling the rivers of the area to prevent silting. In addition, between 60,000 and 70,000 acres have been retrieved from the sea.

Other large drainage and reclamation programs of recent years have been carried out in the Pontine Marshes in Italy and in the Salonika Valley at the mouth of the Vardar River in Greece. See RECLAMATION.

DRAISINE. See BICYCLE.

DRAKE, SIR FRANCIS (1545?–96), English navigator, born near Tavistock, Devonshire. He received his early education under the direction of Sir John Hawkins, a relative. Apprenticed on a coasting vessel before he was twenty years old, Drake rapidly advanced through various grades to the rank of captain. In 1567 he commanded the *Judith,* one of a squadron of vessels which Hawkins led against Spanish shipping in the Gulf of Mexico. The squadron was attacked by a Spanish fleet in the harbor of Vera Cruz and, except for Drake's ship which escaped to sea, was destroyed. Following his return from this ill-fated venture, Drake was granted (1570) a

privateer's commission by Queen Elizabeth. He made voyages to the West Indies in that and the following year, mainly for the purpose of planning future operations against the Spaniards. In 1572 he organized a squadron of three vessels and embarked again for the Caribbean region. Accomplishments of this expedition included the capture of Nombre de Dios, on the Isthmus of Panama, the destruction of the nearby town of Porto Bello, and the acquisition of considerable plunder, notably thirty tons of silver. Before weighing anchor for England, Drake led a party across the Isthmus of Panama to a point overlooking the Pacific Ocean (then called the South Sea), becoming the first English commander to see the Pacific. He solemnly resolved to "sail once in an English ship in that sea".

Drake's exploits and achievements on this expedition brought him fame and wealth. From 1573 to 1576 he commanded the naval phase of military operations, led by Walter Devereux, Earl of Essex, against the Irish rebellion of that year. In 1576 he obtained from Queen Elizabeth secret approval and support of a projected expedition against the Pacific-coast colonies of Spain, then a friendly power. The expedition, composed of Drake's ship the *Pelican,* and the *Elizabeth,* both vessels of 100 tons burden, and three smaller ships, sailed from Plymouth with 166 men on December 13, 1577. Drake reached the Brazilian coast early the following April. After a delay of more than four months, during which he abandoned two out of his original five vessels, and tried and executed a mutineer, he sailed southward. The squadron entered the Strait of Magellan on August 21, 1578, and completed the passage sixteen days later. In a furious storm that arose shortly thereafter, one of the vessels was lost with all hands. Drake's ship, renamed the *Golden Hind,* became separated from the *Elizabeth,* which returned to England. Drake cruised northward, plundering Spanish towns and shipping along the South American coast. Continuing northward in search of a passage to the Atlantic, he reached a point off the N.W. coast of what is now the State of Washington, before cold weather forced him to turn back. He stopped for refitting in a small inlet on the coast of present-day California, which he named New Albion and claimed for Queen Elizabeth. Late in July, 1579, he began the westward crossing of the Pacific. He arrived at the Moluccas, or Spice Islands, on November 4, at Celebes on December 10, and at Java on March 11, 1580. Sailing from Java about two weeks later, he crossed the Indian Ocean and, on June 15, rounded the Cape of Good Hope. The *Golden Hind* dropped anchor in Plymouth harbor about September 26, 1580, completing the first circumnavigation of the world by an English vessel. Despite Spanish diplomatic protests against Drake's raids, Queen Elizabeth boarded his ship at Plymouth and knighted him. He was elected mayor of Plymouth in 1581.

Drake resumed his naval career in 1585, on the recurrence of hostilities with Spain. Placed in command of a fleet of twenty-five ships, he won a succession of victories, including the capture of Santiago in the Cape Verde Islands, Santo Domingo (now Ciudad Trujillo, Dominican Republic), and St. Augustine (in what is now the State of Florida). His next exploit, a raid on the port of Cadiz, Spain, on April 19, 1587, ranks among the most brilliant achievements in British naval history. Leading a fleet of thirty vessels into Cadiz harbor, he destroyed approximately 10,000 tons of shipping, most of which had been destined for the Armada (q.v.). He later characterized this victory, which was accomplished without damage to his fleet, as "singeing the King of Spain's beard". In 1588, shortly before the arrival of the Armada in English waters, Drake was promoted to the rank of vice-admiral and placed in command of one of the three divisions of the English fleet. He defeated part of the Armada off Gravelines in the subsequent fighting, and pursued remnants of it northward. In 1589 he participated in the English expedition against the Spanish and Portuguese coasts. Although he won several victories, including the destruction of Vigo, he failed to accomplish his objective, the capture of Lisbon. Drake's final venture, a joint raid with Sir John Hawkins against the Spanish West Indies, was unsuccessful. His death, caused by dysentery, occurred off Porto Bello during the West Indies expedition. He was buried at sea.

DRAKE, JOSEPH RODMAN (1795–1820), American poet, born in New York City. In collaboration with Fitz-Greene Halleck (q.v.) he wrote satirical verse for the New York *Evening Post*, under the joint pen name *Croakers & Co.* His best-known poems are "The Culprit Fay", an imaginative story about the love of a fairy for a mortal girl, and the highly patriotic lyric "The American Flag", both of which were published in *The Culprit Fay and Other Poems* (1835).

DRAKENSBERG, or QUATHLAMBA, mountain range in the Union of South Africa, parallel to the E. coast and forming the E. boundary of Basutoland and the Orange Free State. It is the highest portion of the eastern scarp of the South African plateau. Among its peaks are Mont-aux-Sources, 10,761 ft. above sea level, the highest mountain in the Union of South Africa, and Giant's Castle, 9600 ft. The Drakensberg Mountains are crossed by rail at two points, Van Reenan Pass (5400 ft.) and Laing's Nek (4100 ft.).

DRAKE UNIVERSITY, a coeducational, nonsectarian institution of higher learning, located in Des Moines, Iowa. It was founded in 1881. In co-operation with the city of Des Moines it maintains a municipal observatory. Among its schools and departments are arts and science, business, journalism, fine arts, law, pharmacy, speech and dramatics, teaching, and theology. In 1953–54 the enrollment was 4850, including 2100 full-time students; the faculty numbered 160.

DRAMA (Gr. *dran,* "to act"), a literary composition in either verse or prose, intended to be performed by actors upon a stage, and usually in the form of a narrative told by the action and dialogue of characters portrayed by the actors.

A drama is usually divided into several acts, which, for more effective telling of the story, are often divided into scenes. Each act marks a stage in the development of the story; successively the acts introduce the characters and elements of the plot, develop the story to its climax, and finally resolve the principal theme, problem, or conflict of the play by means of a conclusive event known as the "catastrophe" or "denouement". Some plays have only one act; others have many scenes but no formal act divisions.

Three ancient principles of dramatic construction have at various times exercised great influence on dramatic writing. These principles, known as the three "unities", were originated by the Greek dramatists of the 5th century B.C. and set down in the following century by Aristotle in his *Poetics.* The "unity of time" requires that the events presented in a play must cover a period of no more than 24 hours; the "unity of place" requires that these events must happen within a single locality; and the "unity of action" requires that no events or characters be introduced which are inconsistent with the central theme or mood of the play. The unities were often observed in periods of classical influence, as in 17th-century France by Jean Baptiste Racine and his contemporaries; but were ignored by playwrights in periods of romantic or realistic influences. Shakespeare ignored

Top, right: Stone carving of a mask worn by character in an ancient Greek drama. Above: Ancient Roman bas relief depicting a scene from a comedy. Left: Masks worn in traditional Japanese dramas.

the deeper sufferings of humanity. Generally in a tragedy the leading character is brought to an end of a calamitous nature because of some passion or weakness of his own. However, the hero of a tragedy is often of admirable character and, in many cases, before his tragic end, achieves an understanding of the forces with which he has been contending and an inspiring growth of his inner self. Comedy, on the other hand, generally deals with the light and amusing side of life and usually has a happy ending. Comedy often deals with the follies and absurdities of human beings and sometimes has a satiric purpose. In general, the object of a tragedy is to excite the deeper emotions; of a comedy, to excite mirth.

Among the various types of comedy is the *comedy of manners*, the purpose of which is to satirize the weaknesses of the upper classes, usually of the contemporary period; this form of comedy had its greatest vogue in the 17th and 18th centuries and is still written today. Other important types of comedy are the

the unities of time and place, shifting the time and localities in his play freely; and he frequently ignored the "unity of action" by introducing into a tragedy a comic scene, such as the grave-digging scene in *Hamlet*. Most modern playwrights are not bound by the classical unities, preferring for each play the method of construction best suited to its theme or narrative.

The principal types of the drama are tragedy and comedy, terms which originated in ancient Greek times. Tragedy deals with serious themes and is concerned especially with

CNS Photo

Above: Actors performing a scene from the Chinese play entitled, "Jade Hall Spring." Above, right: Scene from a French medieval farce (15th-century woodcut). Right: Illustration for "Abraham and Mary," play by the German dramatist Roswitha, who wrote in the 10th century (from an early engraving).

comedy of humors, a satiric form of comedy popular in England in the 17th and 18th centuries; and sentimental comedy, a form of comedy developed in England in the 18th century, which had for its purpose the reform of public morals. Other forms of comedy are *farce,* in which the emphasis is on a complicated and extravagant plot; *burlesque,* which is a broad travesty of a serious work; and the *vaudeville,* a set theatrical piece, rarely seen today, in which pantomime or dialogue is combined with light songs and with dancing.

Many types of drama do not fall precisely into the category of either tragedy or comedy. Among these types are the *historical* and the *romantic drama,* in which the emphasis is respectively on the historical or romantic element of the story, although the general atmosphere may be tragic. The term *melodrama,* in modern usage, is applied to a play in which romantic and exciting situations, and incidents of a sensational nature are stressed at the expense of characterization. *Pantomime* and *ballet* (qq.v.), each of which contains various elements of the drama, are derived from the drama.

GREEK DRAMA. Both Greek tragedy and comedy originated in the religious ceremonies in honor of the god of wine Dionysus, or Bacchus (q.v.). The principal feature of these ceremonies consisted of a dance around the altar of the god by fifty men clad as satyrs, who sang or recited in chorus as a dithyramb (q.v.). In 536 B.C. the Greek poet Thespis (q.v.) wrote dithyrambs to be sung or recited by the chorus with responses made to the chorus by a leader or "responder", thus creating through dialogue an elementary and limited form of drama. The range of these early plays was greatly extended by the playwright Aeschylus, who in his tragedies added a second actor, making possible dialogue of a more dramatic nature and also the beginnings of dramatic action. The playwright Sophocles added still a third actor. In the work of these two playwrights and that of Euripides, all of whom flourished in the 5th century B.C., Greek tragedy reached its highest development. In general, a Greek tragedy consisted of a prologue, which comprised the first act; and of a number of episodes which were separated from each other by lyric passages sung by the chorus, generally of 48 persons; and terminated in *exodos*, a scene following the final song of the chorus. The tragedies of the Greek playwrights of the 5th century B.C. were generally written and performed in tetralogies or groups of four.

According to Aristotle, tragedy was intended to provide a *catharsis*, or release of the emotions of pity and terror in the spectator, and thereby to induce in him a mood of serenity. In addition, Greek tragedy usually had religious and ethical significance. In the dramas of Aeschylus, *Nemesis*, or "divine vengeance", an essential element in the plots of all Greek tragedy, is a religious mystery which may not be questioned. The plays of Sophocles emphasized ethical problems, and *Nemesis* is brought about in them by violation of ethical laws. With Euripides, however, Greek tragedy became a means of portraying human dilemmas and conflicts without reference to religious or ethical interpretation. In his tragedies, *Nemesis* is not based on religion or ethics but is simply an inexplicable source of human catastrophe and sadness.

The development of Greek comedy was parallel to that of tragedy. The rude jests with which the songs of some Dionysiac festivals were enlivened led to the creation of dramatic compositions of an outspoken and often licentious nature. The history of Greek comedy which, like tragedy, centered at Athens, is commonly divided into three periods: that of Old Comedy (5th century, B.C.); Middle Comedy (4th century B.C.); and New Comedy (4th and 3rd centuries B.C.). Well-known writers of the first period were Crates, Eupolis (both of the 5th century B.C.), and Cratinus (520?–423 B.C.). Aristophanes, the greatest of all Greek writers of comedy, and in many respects the greatest of all time, also belongs to the first period. Through the medium of comedy, Aristophanes attacked the social and political abuses of his time with a boldness of wit and audacity of personal satire. The comedies of Aristophanes were organized in a manner similar to that of tragedy, and had a chorus of 24; they made use of a type of a choral ode known as the *parabasis*, in which the audience was directly addressed. In Middle Comedy, represented chiefly by the work of Antiphanes (408?–334 B.C.), the speech was more restrained than in Old Comedy, and the satire, still largely political, was aimed at classes rather than individuals; in Middle Comedy the chorus disappeared from Greek drama. New Comedy, of which Menander and Philemon are the best-known writers, found its subject matter no longer in political questions, but in the complications of life in a society which had lost its simplicity and much of its virtue.

ROMAN DRAMA. Roman drama was largely an imitation of Greek drama. It consisted in the main of comedy. The two important masters of Roman comedy were Plautus and Terence, both basing their plays on the Greek comedy of the last period. The plays of the former are marked by rough vigor and broad jocularity; those of the latter are more refined in both characterization and wit. Roman comedy introduced one innovation into dramatic form: the prologue ceased to be the first act of the play and became an explanatory scene or speech preceding the play proper. The most important writer of Roman tragedy was Lucius Annæus Seneca, among whose nine tragedies are *Hercules Furens, Phædra,* and *Troades.*

DRAMA OF INDIA. Like Greek drama, Indian drama had its origin in the dances and songs of popular religious festivals. Indian drama, however, has no tragedy and makes far more of the motive of romantic love than does the Greek. A prominent feature of Indian plays is their use of different types of languages for the speech of different types of characters; gods, heroes, and men of high position use the Sanskrit language, whereas men and women of low degree speak various forms of the group of vernacular languages of India known as Prakrit.

Indian drama reached its highest development in the period between the 4th and the 9th centuries A.D. India's greatest dramatist was Kālidāsa, who flourished in the 5th century A.D.; his best-known play is *Çakuntala,* a heroic drama of love. He was also the author of *Vikramorvasî* ("The Hero and the Nymph"). Next in importance among Indian dramatists was Bhavabhuti, who flourished in the 8th century; two of his three plays concern the adventures of Rama, the hero of the Sanskrit epic *Ramayana*. Several other Indian dramas are founded on this epic.

Among other notable plays of India are the *Mricchakatika* ("The Little Clay Cart"), a ten-act drama of social life, ascribed to a Hindu monarch named Sudraka, but more likely written by the Sanskrit poet Dandin; and *Ratnavali* ("The Pearl Necklace"), a romantic play supposedly written by King Sriharsha (7th century).

CHINESE DRAMA. Compared to other forms of Chinese literature, Chinese drama is of comparatively recent origin. It began in the 6th century A.D. but did not become firmly established in China until the 8th century, when it was stimulated by the efforts of an emperor of the T'ang dynasty, Ming Huang, who established an acting school known as the "Pear Garden". Chinese drama reached its highest development in the Yuan or Mongol period (1280–1368); however, the most renowned of all Chinese plays *Pi Pa Chi* ("Story of the Guitar"), belongs to a later period.

Chinese plays are classified not as tragedies and comedies, but as *Wen*, "civil" plays, which deal with the ordinary aspects of life and tend to be comic; and *Wu*, "military" plays, which deal with combats and other types of violent deeds. Chinese drama has as its purpose the glorification of virtue. Music and singing are a part of all Chinese plays. Costumes are elaborate, but stage settings are simple and make little attempt at realism; simple properties are used and are brought upon the stage during the performance by the property man, in full view of the audience. Women's parts are taken by men.

MEDIEVAL DRAMA, EUROPEAN. In early medieval times, the Roman Catholic Church condemned dramatic performances of all kinds. In the Church itself, however, an elementary form of drama was developing out of the liturgy. Among the earliest examples of Church drama are those which, toward the end of the 10th century, grew out of the Easter service. At this service, priests representing holy women engaged in dialogue concerning the resurrection of Christ, with other priests representing angels. From such a beginning the liturgical drama developed into short dramatic scenes or plays in Latin presenting episodes from the life of Christ and performed by the clergy, principally at Easter and Christmas. Later, the subject matter was broadened to include tales from the lives of the saints; comic characters, chiefly devils, were introduced, and laymen began to take part in the performances. After a time, the liturgical drama developed into full-fledged plays which, because of the increasingly large audiences, were given on the steps of the church. These plays were of two types, the *miracle plays* and the *mysteries* (qq.v.). Subsequently these dramatic representations were produced and performed by the guilds of the various European cities and towns. A third form of medieval drama, the *moralities* (q.v.) developed from the miracle plays and mysteries. Out of these three types of medieval drama and also out of certain medieval secular parodies of church plays (see FARCE), the modern drama developed. Many characteristics of the miracle plays and mysteries survive in the Passion play, performed, in recent years, in Oberammergau, Bavaria, and in *Veronica's Veil,* performed in Union City, New Jersey.

ITALIAN DRAMA. The medieval religious drama attained considerable development in Italy. Its principal form was the *Rappresentazione Sacra* (15th century), which grew out of the Italian mystery play, and was produced chiefly in connection with festivities in honor of St. John the Baptist. A notable example of this type of drama is *Abramo e Isaaco* by Feo Belcari (fl. 15th century).

The Renaissance gave a new stimulus to drama in Italy. The drama of this period took two principal forms, the popular improvised drama known as the commedia dell'arte (q.v), and the literary form which aimed at reviving the classical type of drama. Among the plays of this period based on classical models are the tragedy *Sofonisba* (1515) by Giovanni Giorgio Trissino (1478–1550) and the pastoral drama *Aminta* by Torquato Tasso. In the 16th century, also, a type of comedy modeled after the plays of Plautus was written, notably by Lodovico Ariosto and Niccolò Machiavelli. In the 17th century, a reaction took place against classical drama; among the works of this period were the comedies *Tancia* (1612) and *Fiera* (1618) by Michelangelo Buonarroti, nephew of the great artist Michelangelo. At the beginning of the 17th century Ottavio Rinuccini (1562–1621) wrote the words for *Dafne,* a melodrama or play with music, the music of which was composed by Jacopo Peri; *Dafne* was the progenitor of a new form of art, the opera (q.v.), which achieved great popularity in Italy in the 17th and 18th centuries. Among writers of librettos of high literary quality for melodramas and operas were Apostolo Zeno (1668–1750) and Metastasio.

Among the notable lyric dramas of the latter, set to music by various composers, are *Didone Abbandonata* (1723) and *Atilio Regolo* (1750).

The foremost names in 18th century Italian drama are those of Carlo Goldoni, Carlo Gozzi, and Conte Vittorio Alfieri. Goldoni, often called "the Italian Molière", is the greatest of writers of Italian comedy; his play *La Lacondiera* is still performed. Gozzi's contribution to Italian drama was to give literary form to the *commedia dell'arte*. Alfieri wrote tragedies which followed classical models, especially in their observance of the three dramatic unities; his plays were attacks on tyranny and sought to revive a spirit of national pride in Italy. Among his tragedies are *Filippo II* and *Saul*. Among the important Italian dramatists of the 19th century were Giovanni Battista Niccolini (1782–1861), author of *Arnaldo da Brescia* and of other plays; Paolo Giacometti (1816–82), among whose works is *Michelangelo;* Alessandro Manzoni, a writer of romantic dramas with powerful characterization, including the tragedies *Il Conte di Carmagnola* (1820) and *Adelchi* (1822); Paolo Ferrari (1822–89), author of popular comedies in Modenese dialect, two of which, *La Medicina d'una Ragazza Ammalata* and *Il Codicillo dello Zio Venanzio* are still played. Giuseppe Giacosa (1847–1906) was a writer of naturalistic dramas, including *Luise* (1883). Others of the naturalistic, later known as the veristic school, were Marco Praga (1863–1929), among whose plays are *La Moglie Ideale* (1890) and *La Porta Chiusa* (1913); and Giovanni Verga (1840–1922), who is famous for his short story *Cavalleria Rusticana*, later dramatized (1884) and then the libretto of an opera.

The most important Italian playwrights of the 20th century were Gabriele D'Annunzio (see ANNUNZIO, GABRIELE D'), writer of lyrical and heroic romantic tragedies, including *Citta Morte* (1898), *Francesca da Rimini* (1902) and *La Nave* (1908); and Luigi Pirandello, author of plays of experimental form and daring philosophic questioning of established ethical and social values, including *Così È Se Vi Pare* (1918), *Sei Personaggi in Cerca d'Autore* (1921), and *Come Tu Mi Vuoi* (1930). Other Italian dramatists of recent times are Antonio Fogazzaro, Roberto Bracco (1862–1943), and Sem Benelli, who is known chiefly for *La Cena delle Beffe* (1909) and *L'Amore dei Tre Re* (1909), which is the libretto of an opera, as well as a play.

SPANISH DRAMA. The late 16th and early 17th centuries marked the most brilliant period of Spanish drama. Among the dramatists of this era were Miguel de Cervantes, author of the tragedy *La Numancia;* Juan de la Cueva de la Garoza (about 1550–about 1610), Cristóbal de Virués (1550–1610), Bartolomé Leonardo Argensola, and Juan Ruiz de Alarcón y Mendoza. Tirso de Molina of this period is notable for his drama *El Burlador de Sevilla y Convidado de Piedra*, in which the character of Don Juan (q.v.) was for the first time used in a play. The two greatest of Spanish dramatists, Lope de Vega and Calderón de la Barca, also belong to this period. At a time when critics were insisting that playwrights follow the rules of the classical drama, Lope de Vega disregarded nearly all classical principles in writing his vigorous dramas. He was reputedly the author of more than 1800 plays. Calderón de la Barca gave expression in his dramas to some of the loftiest of Spanish ideals, devotion to the king, to the church, and to personal honor; he is also noted for his religious plays, the *autos sacramentales*.

Among important Spanish dramatists of the 19th and 20th centuries were José Echegaray y Eizaguirre, among whose works are *El Gran Galeoto* (1881); Gregorio Martínez Sierra, among whose plays are *Canción de Cuna* (1911) and *Reino de Dios* (1915); the Quintero brothers, Serafin Álvarez and Joaquín Álvarez, among whose plays, written in collaboration, are *Malvaloca* (1912) and *La Calumniada* (1919); Benito Pérez Galdós, author of *Mariucha* (1903), *Santa Juana de Castilla* (1918), and of other plays; and Jacinto Benavente y Martínez, whose dramatic works, characterized by realism and satire, include *La Otra Honra* (1924) and *Pepa Doncel* (1928).

FRENCH DRAMA. The 17th century in France was notable for both the revival of classical drama and the development of comedy to its highest point. The two principal writers of tragedy, in which the three dramatic unities were strictly observed, were Pierre Corneille and Jean Baptiste Racine. Both playwrights, among the most illustrious France has ever produced, were concerned mainly with the conflict between human inclination and will. In Corneille's dramas the protagonists are men; in Racine's, women. Of the two playwrights, Racine wrote with the greater warmth and naturalness. Among the dramas of Corneille are *Le Cid* (1636 or 1637), *Horace* (1640), and *Polyeucte* (about 1642); among those of Racine are *Phèdre* (1677) and *Athalie* (1691). To this period also belongs Molière, one of the greatest writers of comedy in the

J. Arthur Rank; French Embassy, Information Division

Top: Lawrence Olivier as "Henry V," in a modern motion-picture presentation of the play by Shakespeare. Bottom, left: Heroine of the play "Phèdre," by Racine (from an engraving). Right: Actors of the Comédie Française in Molière's "Le Misanthrope."

history of the drama. Among his plays, which have seldom been excelled for wit and understanding of life are *Les Précieuses Ridicules* (1659), *Le Misanthrope* (1666), *L'Avare* (1668), and *Tartuffe* (1669). In the 18th century the chief writers of French tragedy were Voltaire, who wrote *Zaïre* (1732), and Crébillon, the elder, author of *Catilina* (1748). The most notable writers of comedy in this period

were Pierre de Marivaux, author of *Le Jeu de l'Amour et du Hasard* (1730), and Pierre Augustin Caron de Beaumarchais, author of *Le Barbier de Séville* (1775).

The 19th and 20th centuries were periods of rich dramatic production in France. Among the notable dramatists of the 19th century were Victor Marie Hugo, author of *Hernani* (1830); Alfred de Musset, *On ne Badine pas avec l'Amour* (1834) ; Comte Alfred Victor de Vigny, *Chatterton* (1835) ; Alexandre Dumas, père, *Kean* (1836) ; Augustin Eugène Scribe, *Le Verre d'Eau* (1840) ; Alexandre Dumas, fils, *La Dame aux Camélias* (1852) ; Émile Augier, *La Gendre de Monsieur Poirier* (with Jules Sandeau; 1854) ; and Henri Meilhac and Ludovic Halévy, in collaboration, *Froufrou* (1869).

To these may be added: Octave Feuillet, *Le Sphinx* (1874) ; Henry François Becque, *Les Corbeaux* (1882) ; Victorien Sardou, *La Tosca* (1887) ; Georges de Porto-Riche, *Amoureuse* (1891) ; Alfred Jarry, *Ubu Roi* (1896), and Edmond Rostand, *Cyrano de Bergerac* (1898).

Among the notable playwrights of the first two decades of the 20th century were Eugène Brieux, *La Robe Rouge* (1900) ; Paul Ernest Hervieu, *Connais-toi* (1909) ; Rostand, *Chantecler* (1910) ; Guillaume Apollinaire, *Les Mamelles de Tirésias* (1917) ; and Charles Maurice Donnay, *La Chasse à l'Homme* (1919). Belgian drama, usually regarded as a branch of French drama, is represented principally by the work of Maurice Maeterlinck, among whose plays are *Pelléas et Mélisande* (1892) and *L'Oiseau Bleu* (1909).

Among French playwrights important after 1920 were Tristan Bernard, *Triplepatte* (1906) ; Charles Vildrac, *Le Paquebot Tenacity* (1920) ; Jean Jacques Bernard, *Martine* (1922) ; Jules Romains, *Knock, ou le Triomphe de la Mèdecine* (1923) ; Paul Raynal, *Le Tombeau Sous l'Arc de Triomphe* (1924) ; Sacha Guitry, *Mozart* (1925) ; Edouard Bourdet, *La Prisonnière* (1926) ; Marcel Pagnol, *Topaze* (1928) ; Henry Bernstein, *Mélo* (1929) ; Jean Giraudoux, *Amphitryon 38* (1929) ; Jean Cocteau, *La Machine Infernale* (1934) ; Armand Salacrou, *L'Inconnue d'Arras* (1935), François Mauriac, *Les Mal Aimés* (1945) ; Albert Camus, *Caligula* (1944), and Jean Paul Sartre, *Huis Clos* (1945).

GERMAN DRAMA. German drama did not begin to have a national character until the 18th century, which produced three of Germany's most important dramatists: Gotthold Ephraim Lessing, Johann Christoph Friedrich von Schiller, and Johann Wolfgang von Goethe. Among the plays of Lessing are *Miss Sara Sampsòn* (1755), *Minna von Barnhelm* (1763), and *Nathan der Weise* (1779) ; among those of Schiller are *Die Räuber* (1781), *Die Jungfrau von Orleans* (1801), and *Wilhelm Tell* (1804). Among the plays of Goethe are *Götz von Berlichingen* (1773), which inaugurated the romantic school of drama in Germany; *Torquato Tasso* (1790), and his

famed *Faust* (1st part, 1808; 2nd part, 1832).

German drama was romantic in theme until about 1880. Among the most important romantic dramatists of the 19th century were Heinrich von Kleist, whose works include *Penthesilea* (1808) and *Die Hermannschlacht* (1821) and the Austrian playwright Franz Grillparzer, *Das Goldene Vlies*, a trilogy, (1822). A notable playwright of the 19th century in Germany, who wrote realistic plays, was Georg Büchner, *Dantons Tod* (1835). From 1880 until World War I a new type of play, the naturalistic drama, (see NATURALISM) dominated the German stage. The most important playwright of this period was Gerhart Hauptmann. Among his plays are the powerful naturalistic dramas *Vor Sonnenaufgang* (1889), *Die Weber* (1892), *Fuhrmann Henschel* (1898), and *Gabriel Schillings Flucht* (1912) ; he was also the author of the romantic fantasies *Hanneles Himmelfahrt* (1892) and *Die Versunkene Glocke* (1896). Other important playwrights of the period were Hermann Sudermann, who wrote *Ehre* (1891), *Heimat* (1893), and *Das Glück im Winkel* (1895); Frank Wedekind, *Frühlings Erwachen* (1891) and *Erdgeist* (1895) ; the Austrians Arthur Schnitzler, *Anatol* (1893), and Hugo von Hofmannsthal, *Elektra* (1903) ; and Walter Hasenclever, *Der Sohn* (1914). With the drama *Bettler* (1912) by Reinhard Johannes Sorge (1892–1916), expressionist drama (see EXPRESSIONISM) became important in Germany. To the expressionist school, which was the leading dramatic movement in Germany from shortly before World War I to about 1933, belonged Georg Kaiser, *Von Morgens bis Mitternachts* (1916), *Gas I* (1918), and *Gas II* (1920) ; and Ernst Toller *Die Wandlung* (1919) and *Masse Mensch* (1920). Among other important German dramatists of the 20th century were Franz Werfel, *The Goat Song* (1921) and *Juarez and Maximilian* (1926) ; and Fritz von Unruh, *Heinrich von Andernach* (1925) and *Zero* (1932).

No German playwright of importance emerged during the period when Germany was ruled by the National Socialist (Nazi) Party, 1933 to 1945.

CZECH DRAMA. Before World War I Czech drama consisted mainly of realistic comedies and historical dramas, of little literary merit. Among the playwrights of this period were Joseph K. Tyl (1808–56), in one of whose plays occurs the national air of Bohemia, "Where is My Home?"; and Wencelas Kličpera (1792–1859), who wrote more than fifty comedies and tragedies. The most important

Czech dramatist of the period was Jaroslav Hilbert (1871–1936), who modeled his plays chiefly after those of Henrik Ibsen. Among Hilbert's plays are *O Boha*, "Of God" (1898), and *Psanci*, "The Outlaws" (1900). Hilbert's *Michael* (1935) was also a notable Czech drama after World War I. The most important Czech dramatists of the post-World War I period were Karel Čapek, *R.U.R.* (1921), and his brother Josef. The brothers in collaboration wrote the internationally famous play *Ze Života Hmyzu*, "The Insect Play", also known as *The World We Live In* (1923). Another important Czech dramatist who flourished after World War I was František Langer (1888–   ), *Jizdni Hlidka*, "The Cavalry Watch" (1935).

HUNGARIAN DRAMA. Among the important Hungarian playwrights of the 19th and 20th centuries were Ferenc Herczeg (1863–   ), *Bizánc*, "Byzantium" (1904), and *Kék Róka* (1917); Melchior Lengyel (1880–   ), *The Great Chieftain* (1907); Ernö Vajda (1887–   ), *Fata Morgana* (1924); and Ferenc Molnár, *The Devil* (1907), *Liliom* (1909), and *The Good Fairy* (1930).

SCANDINAVIAN DRAMA. The first notable Scandinavian dramatist was the Dane, Ludvig Holberg, whose comedies did much to supplant the trivial plays from the French and German which prevailed upon the Danish stage in the 18th century; he is often referred to as "the Molière of Denmark". Among his comedies, produced between 1723 and 1754, are *Ulysses of Ithaca* and *Witchcraft*. In the first half of the 19th century, Adam Gottlob Oehlenschläger inaugurated a new era in Danish drama with plays that drew their subject matter from Norse mythology. Among his dramas are *Baldur hin Gode* (1808) and *Nordens Gudur* (1819), an epic cycle drawn from the Norse saga, the *Edda*. The most important development in Scandinavian drama came in the second half of the 19th century. The Norwegian dramatist, Björnstjerne Björnson, was noted both for his plays based on Norwegian legend and for his problem plays. Among his works are the trilogy *Sigurd the Bastard* (1862), *The Newly Married* (1865), and *Beyond Human Power* (1883). The greatest of Norwegian playwrights was Henrik Ibsen, who, after writing the poetic and philosophical plays *Peer Gynt* (1866) and *Brand* (1867), turned to the writing of searching and realistic dramas on contemporary ethical and social problems, which profoundly influenced the drama of the entire civilized world, marking a turn in dramatic art from the superficial, so-called "well-made", play to the play dealing seriously with reality. Among his many dramas are *A Doll's House* (1879), *Ghosts* (1881), and *Hedda Gabler* (1890). The Swedish writer August Strindberg, was one of the most important of modern dramatists; his work also had strong influence on the drama outside his native land, particularly on the plays of the expressionist dramatists of Germany and on the plays of the American dramatist Eugene O'Neill. Among Strindberg's plays are *The Father* (1887), *Lady Julia* (1888), and *A Dream Play* (1902).

DUTCH DRAMA. In the Netherlands in the 16th and 17th centuries, a number of playwrights, including Joost van den Vondel, brought about a post-Renaissance revival of drama. The later Dutch stage largely imitated the contemporary French drama. Of modern Dutch dramatists, Herman Heijermans was the most distinguished. Among his plays are *Ghetto* (1899) and *Op Hoop van Zegen*, "The Good Hope" (1900).

RUSSIAN DRAMA. Russian drama had its beginnings in the middle of the 18th century in the work of Aleksandr Petrovich Sumarokov, whose most important play was the comedy *The Usurer* (1768). In the 19th century the vogue in Russia was successively for dramas of middle-class life in imitation of similar German plays; patriotic plays; plays after French classic models; and melodramas and romantic plays. A play which was an exception to the general trends of 19th century Russian drama was the satire in verse on Russian officialdom *Gore ot Uma* "The Misfortune of Being too Clever" (1821) by Aleksandr Sergeevich Griboedov. Historical drama on the Shakespearean model was introduced into Russia by Alexander Sergeevich Pushkin in his tragedy *Boris Godunov* (1831). Other important playwrights of the 19th century were Nikolai Vasilievich Gogol, *Revizor*, "The Inspector General" (1836), a brilliant satire on Russian bureaucracy; Ivan Sergeevich Turgenev, *A Month in the Country* (1853), a play which emphasized poetic atmosphere rather than conflict; and Aleksandr Nikolaevich Ostrovski, *The Storm* (1860) and *The Snow Maiden* (1873). The most important Russian dramatist of the late 19th and early 20th centuries was Anton Pavlovich Chekhov, whose plays are characterized by poetic atmosphere, emotional tension, and profound psychological understanding. Among his plays are *The Seagull* (1896), *The Three Sisters* (1901), and *The Cherry Orchard* (1904). Other important dramatists of this period were Maxim Gorky,

The Lower Depths (1902), Count Leo Tolstoi, *The Power of Darkness* (1889) and *The Living Corpse* (1911); and Leonid Nikolaevich Andreev, *Life of Man* (1906) and *He Who Gets Slapped* (1915).

After the Revolution of 1917, dramatic activity increased greatly over what it had been in czarist days. Among the important dramatists of the post-Revolutionary period were Gorky, *Dostigaev and Others* (1933); Mikhail Afanasievich Bulgakov (1891–1940), *Days of the Turbins* (1926) and *Molière* (1936); Rodion Mikhailovich Akulshin (1896–), *A Window Open on the Village* (1927); Valentine Petrovich Kataev (1897–), *Squaring the Circle* (1928) and *Lonely White Sail* (1938); Aleksandr Nikolaevich Afinogenov (1904–41), *Fear* (1931) and *Spain, We Salute Thee* (1936); and Konstantin Simonov, *The Russian People* (1942).

BRITISH DRAMA. The drama of medieval England consisted of mysteries, miracle plays, and moralities, at first generally written by ecclesiastics and also acted by them. Notable in English medieval drama is the cycle known as Coventry Plays (q.v.), which was performed in the town of Coventry annually in the 16th century. One of the best known of English morality plays is *Everyman* (printed 1529). Early English comedy originated about the middle of the 16th century. It was derived in part from the moralities and, more particularly, from classical comedy. Nicholas Udall's *Ralph Roister Doister* (about 1553), considered the earliest of English comedies, was an adaptation of the comedy *Miles Gloriosus* by Plautus. In 1561 appeared the first English tragedy, a play in blank verse, *Gorboduc or Ferrex and Porrex*, by Thomas Norton and Thomas Sackville; *Gammer Gurton's Needle* (1566), the first native English farce, is attributed to the clergyman William Stevenson (d. 1575).

The development of the drama was rapid in England during the latter part of the 16th century, culminating in the work of William Shakespeare. Among the dramatists who wrote during Shakespeare's early years were John Lyly, *Alexander and Campaspe* (1584); Thomas Kyd, *The Spanish Tragedy* (1592); Thomas Nash, *Summers Last Will* (1592); George Peele, *King Edward the First* (1593); Thomas Lodge, *The Wounds of Civile War* (1594); and Robert Greene, *The Honorable History of Friar Bacon and Friar Bungay* (1594). The greatest of them was Christopher Marlowe, who was second only to Shakespeare in his mastery of dramatic blank verse. Among

Marlowe's dramas are *Tamburlaine the Great* (acted about 1587) and *The Tragedy of Dr. Faustus* (published, 1601).

The greatest of all English dramatists and generally considered to be the foremost dramatic genius the world has ever produced was William Shakespeare, whose plays dominated the English stage in the late 16th and early 17th centuries. He wrote for a theater which employed only the slightest of scenic accessories, but brought the drama to its highest perfection. His comedies, historical plays, and tragedies exemplify the depth, sublimity, refinement, and variety of which the drama is capable. (For plays of Shakespeare, see SHAKESPEARE, WILLIAM.)

The best of Shakespeare's contemporaries were Ben Jonson and the two collaborators, Francis Beaumont and John Fletcher. Jonson, like Shakespeare, wrote both comedy and tragedy; his work shows more classic influence than does that of Shakespeare. Jonson was a noted writer of a form of entertainment known as the *masque* (q.v.), which was popular at the courts of English royalty and nobility in the 16th and 17th centuries. Among his plays are *Every Man in His Humour* (1598) and *Volpone* (1605). Beaumont and Fletcher in collaboration wrote approximately fifty comedies and tragedies, including the comedy *The Knight of the Burning Pestle* (1607) and the tragedy *The Maid's Tragedy* (about 1611). Other important playwrights of the 17th century were George Chapman, who collaborated with Ben Jonson and John Marston in *Eastward Hoe* (1605); Thomas Dekker, who wrote the *Shoemaker's Holiday* (1600) and collaborated with Philip Massinger on *The Virgin Martyr* (1621); John Webster, *The Duchess of Malfi* (about 1614); John Ford, *'Tis Pity She's a Whore* (1633), and James Shirley, *The Cardinal* (1641) a tragedy, and *The Contention of Ajax and Ulysses* (1659) a masque.

In September, 1642, a month after the outbreak of the civil war between Parliament and the King, when power was held by the Puritans, Parliament passed an ordinance which forbade the performance of any kind of theatrical entertainment. From 1642 until the Restoration (1660) the theaters of England were closed and the drama, except for masques and other performances given privately, almost entirely ceased to exist. With the Restoration, however, the English theaters were reopened and the drama achieved a popularity greater than ever before in its history.

THEATRE GUILD PRODUCTIONS
Above: A family scene in Eugene O'Neill's comedy, "Ah, Wilderness."

Right: "The Good Earth," dramatization of Pearl Buck's book on Chinese farm life.

The principal writers of tragedy of the period 1660 to 1800 were John Dryden, *Aurengzebe* (1676) and *All For Love* (1678); Nathaniel Lee, *The Rival Queens* (1677); Thomas Otway, *Venice Preserved* (1682); and Joseph Addison, *Cato* (1713). The period, however, was distinguished mainly for its comedy, principally the comedy of manners; this form of play pictured the life of the upper classes and, in reaction against Puritanism, was often licentious in tone. The most important writer of Restoration comedy was William Congreve, whose graceful and witty dialogue has seldom been equaled in the English theater. Among his plays are *Love for Love* (1695) and *The Way of the World* (1700). Other important writers of comedy of the time were Thomas Shadwell, *The Sullen Lovers* (1668); William Wycherley, *The Plain Dealer* (produced about 1674); Sir John Vanbrugh, *The Provoked Wife* (produced 1697); and George Farquhar, *The Beaux' Stratagem* (1707). A little later in the period came Susanna Centlivre, *The Busy Body* (1709); Colley Cibber, *Nonjuror* (1717); and John Gay, *The Beggar's Opera* (1728). The two outstanding writers of comedy of the latter part of the 18th century were Oliver Goldsmith, *She Stoops to Conquer* (1773), and Richard Brinsley Sheridan, *The Rivals* (1775), *The School for Scandal* (1777) and *The Critic* (1779).

Little drama of importance was written in England in the 19th century until toward the end of that period. Among the dramatists of the first part of the century were James Sheridan Knowles, *The Love Chase* (1837), Edward George Bulwer-Lytton, *The Lady of Lyons* (1838), and Thomas William Robertson, *David Garrick* (1864) and *Caste* (1867). The last two decades of the century were marked by the rise of drama dealing with social issues. The most important dramatists of this period were Arthur Wing Pinero, *The Magistrate* (1885) and *The Second Mrs.*

Theatre Guild

"Porgy," a play about Charleston water-front life by DuBose and Dorothy Heyward, produced in 1927. George Gershwin used the play as the basis for his opera, "Porgy and Bess."

Tanqueray (1893); George Bernard Shaw, *Widower's Houses* (1892) and *Mrs. Warren's Profession* (1893); and Henry Arthur Jones, *Michael and His Lost Angel* (1896) and *Mrs. Dane's Defence* (1900). The comedy of manners was exemplified during this period by Oscar Wilde's, *Lady Windermere's Fan* (1892) and *The Importance of Being Earnest* (1895).

In the first decade of the 20th century, George Bernard Shaw began to attain international recognition as the foremost modern writer of plays in English. His dramas, characterized by witty dialogue and brilliant satire of generally accepted ideas, continued the late-19th-century concern of English dramatists with critical examination of social and economic conditions. Other dramatists of the time who showed this analytical tendency were Harley Granville Granville-Barker, *Waste* (1907); and John Galsworthy, *Strife* (1909) and *Justice* (1910). The same period was marked by the rise to importance as a playwright of Sir James Matthew Barrie with a number of plays characterized by whimsical comedy and fantasy, including *Peter Pan*

(1904) and *Alice-Sit-By-the-Fire* (1905). A realistic play of great power was *The Tragedy of Nan* (1909) by John Masefield.

Among the notable plays written by English dramatists after 1909 were *The Madras House* (1910) by Granville-Barker; *Pygmalion* (1912), *Heartbreak House* (1917), and *Saint Joan* (1923) by Shaw; *Dear Brutus* (1917) by Barrie; *Abraham Lincoln* (1918) by John Drinkwater; *Mr. Pim Passes By* (1919) by Alan Alexander Milne; *The Circle* (1921) and *The Constant Wife* (1927) by William Somerset Maugham; *A Bill of Divorcement* (1921) by Clemence Dane; *Loyalties* (1922) by Galsworthy; *Spring Cleaning* (1923) by Frederick Lonsdale; and *Journey's End* (1928) by Robert Cedric Sheriff.

To these may be added *The Barretts of Wimpole Street* (1930) by Rudolf Besier; *The Good Companions* (1931, with Edward Knoblock) by John Boynton Priestley; *Victoria Regina* (1935) by Laurence Housman; *The Ascent of F 6* (1936) by W.H. Auden and Christopher Isherwood; *The Corn is Green* (1938) by Emlyn Williams; *The Winslow*

Boy (1947) by Terence Ratigan; *The Cocktail Party* (1950) by T. S. Eliot; *I Am a Camera* (1951) by John van Druten; and *Venus Observed* (1952) by Christopher Fry.

The early 20th century was marked by activity in the Irish drama. This took the form of a movement for encouraging the writing and producing of plays based on Irish themes, initiated principally by the Irish poet and playwright William Butler Yeats. The movement culminated in the founding of the Irish National Theatre Society which in 1904 acquired the Abbey Theatre (q.v.), in Dublin, thereafter a center for the production of Irish drama. The most significant of the dramatists who contributed plays to the Abbey Theatre was John Millington Synge, *The Playboy of the Western World* (1907). Other playwrights who were important in the Irish drama in the first two decades of the 20th century, and whose works were produced mainly at the Abbey Theatre, were Yeats, *Deirdre* (1907); Lady Augusta Gregory, *The Rising of the Moon* (1907); Lord Dunsany, *The Glittering Gate* (1909); St. John Greer Ervine, *John Ferguson* (1914); and Lennox Robinson, *The Whiteheaded Boy* (1916). The most significant Irish playwrights after 1920 were Sean O'Casey, *Juno and the Paycook* (1924) and *Within the Gates* (1933); Denis Johnston, *The Moon in the Yellow River* (1931); Paul Vincent Carroll, *Shadow and Substance* (1937); and Michael Macliammoir, *Ill Met by Moonlight* (1946).

AMERICAN DRAMA. The first permanent playhouses in the American colonies were the Southwark Theatre, erected in Philadelphia in 1766, and the John Street Theatre, built in New York City in 1767. The plays presented there and, later, elsewhere in the colonies, were of British authorship. The first tragedy written by an American and the first American play to be given a professional production in America was *The Prince of Parthia* by Thomas Godfrey, Jr. It was produced at the Southwark Theatre, Philadelphia, in 1767. The first play by an American on an American theme to be professionally produced was *The Contrast* by Royall Tyler, which appeared at the John Street Theatre, New York City, in 1787. This play contained a low-comedy character, "Jonathan", modeled after the native Yankee or New England type, and was the first play ever produced in America to portray a native type of character. This was followed by many "Yankee plays", dealing with American character types, which soon superseded the British plays in popularity. Other important American

playwrights of the late 18th and early 19th centuries were William Dunlap, the first American writer to adopt playwrighting as a profession, who wrote or adapted between fifty and sixty plays; and John Howard Payne, noted for his tragedy *Brutus, or The Fall of Tarquin* (1818).

In the two decades following 1820, a number of great British actors visited the United States, and the interest the American people took in their performances greatly stimulated interest in drama itself. Among these actors were Edmund Kean, Charles John Kean, Junius Brutus Booth, William Charles Macready, and Clara Fisher. The production of American drama received a more lasting impetus, however, when the American actor Edwin Forrest offered money prizes for new plays by American authors, and himself put on the stage as producer a number of new American plays. Among these were *Metamora* (1829) by John Augustus Stone and *The Gladiator* (1829) by Robert M. Bird. The first successful social satire by an American was *Fashion, or Life in New York* (1845), by the American actress and playwright Anna Cora Mowatt. One of the most popular plays of the mid-century, and one that became among the most successful in the annals of the American theater, was the dramatization by George L. Aiken (1830–76) of the novel *Uncle Tom's Cabin* by Harriet Beecher Stowe. The play, produced in 1852, had a run of 300 consecutive performances, a record at the time, and is occasionally played today.

Among the noted playwrights of the second half of the 19th century were the Irish-born actor and playwright Dion Boucicault, *The Octoroon* (1859) and *The Colleen Bawn* (1860); and John Brougham (1810–80), also an Irish actor and playwright, who was the author of approximately 100 plays. Others were John Augustin Daly, famous for melodramas such as *Under the Gaslight* (1867); Albert Marshman Palmer, *The Two Orphans* (1873); Steele Mackaye, *Hazel Kirke* (1880); Bronson Crocker Howard, *The Henrietta* (1887) and *Shenandoah* (1888); and William Hooker Gillette, the actor and playwright, famous for *Secret Service* (1895) and his dramatization of the Conan Doyle stories *Sherlock Holmes* (1899). David Belasco, both as playwright and producer, strongly influenced the American drama in the direction of literal and elaborate realism. Among the plays which he wrote alone or in collaboration were *The Girl I Left Behind Me* (1893) and *The Heart of Maryland* (1895); his career extended through the first quarter of the 20th century, with such successful plays as *The Girl of the Golden West* (1905) and *Laugh, Clown, Laugh* (1923). The work of Augustus Thomas also spanned the end of the 19th and the first two decades of the 20th centuries; among his plays are *In Mizzoura* (1893), *The Hoosier Doctor* (1897), *The Witching Hour* (1907), and *The Copperhead* (1918).

The first decade of the 20th century was marked by interest among American playwrights in the economic, social, and ethical problems of the country. Among the outstanding playwrights of this period were Charles Klein, *The Music Master* (1904); George H. Broadhurst, *The Man of the Hour* (1906); Clyde Fitch, *The Truth* (1907) and *The City* (1909); William Vaughan Moody, *The Great Divide* (1906); Eugene Walter, *The Easiest Way* (1908); Percy Mackaye, *The Scarecrow* (1908); and Edward B. Sheldon, *Salvation Nell* (1908). George Michael Cohan, who wrote, produced, and acted in his own plays, was the author of many highly popular musical comedies of the period, including *Forty-Five Minutes from Broadway* (1905) and *The Yankee Prince* (1909), and of many plays, including *Get-Rich-Quick Wallingford* (1910) and *Seven Keys to Baldpate* (1913). Among the outstanding plays produced during and immediately following World War I were *Children of Earth* (1915) by Alice Brown; *The Unchastened Woman* (1915) by Louis Kaufman Anspacher; *Lightnin'* (1918) by Winchell Smith and Frank Bacon; and *Déclassé* (1919) by Zoë Akins.

The first decades of the 20th century were also notable in the history of the American drama for the formation of three amateur acting groups: "The 47 Workshop" of Harvard University, founded in 1905 and directed until 1924 by the American educator George Pierce Baker; the Washington Square Players, founded in New York City in 1916; and the Provincetown Players (qq.v.) established in Provincetown, Mass., in 1915 and in New York City in 1916. In Professor Baker's "47 Workshop" his students of dramatic composition, among whom were many who later became famous playwrights, including Philip Barry, Sidney Howard, Eugene O'Neill, and Edward Sheldon, tried out their plays, often of an experimental and noncommercial nature. The aim of the other two groups was to produce for the general public plays of an artistic nature which were free of the conventionalities and restrictions of the commercial theater. The example of all three groups

was of great influence in the formation of the so-called "Little Theatres" with similar aims, all over the United States. The Washington Square Players, which produced chiefly one-act plays, was the nucleus for the formation of the Theatre Guild (q.v.), established in 1919 for production of full-length plays of artistic merit. The subsequent activities of the Theatre Guild served to raise the level of the entire American drama. The Provincetown Players group, which lasted until 1929, is especially notable for its productions of the earlier works of Eugene O'Neill, the world famous American playwright, who was thereby first brought to the attention of the public.

Outstanding American playwrights of the three decades succeeding World War I are grouped below in alphabetical order, with characteristic works of each given. For further consideration of these dramatists and their place in American drama, consult the articles on many of the individual writers.

Maxwell Anderson, *What Price Glory* (1924, with Laurence Stallings), *Winterset* (1935), and *Joan of Lorraine* (1946); Philip Barry, *The Philadelphia Story* (1939) and *Without Love* (1942); Samuel Nathaniel Behrman, *Brief Moment* (1931), *No Time for Comedy* (1939), and *Jane* (1952); Clare Boothe, *The Women* (1936) and *Margin for Error* (1939); Marc Connelly, who in collaboration with George S. Kaufman wrote *Dulcy* (1921), *Beggar on Horseback* (1924), and other plays, and alone wrote *The Green Pastures* (1930); Rachel Crothers, *Let Us Be Gay* (1929) and *Susan and God* (1937); Russel Crouse and Howard Lindsay, *Life With Father* (1939); Edna Ferber, who in collaboration with George S. Kaufman wrote *The Royal Family* (1927) and *Dinner at Eight* (1932); Rose Franken, *Claudia* (1941) and *The Hallams* (1948); Susan Glaspell, *The Verge* (1921) and *Alison's House* (1930); Ruth Gordon, *Over Twenty-One* (1944); Paul Green, *In Abraham's Bosom* (1926), *The House of Connelly* (1931), and *The Lost Colony* (1937); Moss Hart, who collaborated with George S. Kaufman in *Once in a Lifetime* (1930), *You Can't Take It With You* (1936), and other plays, and alone wrote *Lady in the Dark* (1941) and *Light Up the Sky* (1948); Ben Hecht, *The Front Page* (1928) and *Twentieth Century* (1932), both with Charles MacArthur; Lillian Hellman, *The Children's Hour* (1935), *Watch on the Rhine* (1941), and *The Autumn Garden* (1951); Sidney Coe Howard, *They Knew What They Wanted* (1925) and *The Silver*

Cord (1926); Garson Kanin, *Born Yesterday* (1946); George S. Kaufman, *The Butter and Egg Man* (1925); George Kelly, *The Showoff* (1924); *Craig's Wife* (1925); Sidney Kingsley, *Men in White* (1933), *Dead End* (1935), and *Detective Story* (1949); Jack Kirkland (1901–   ), who dramatized (1933) the novel, *Tobacco Road* by Erskine Caldwell; Joseph Kramm, *The Shrike* (1953); John Howard Lawson, *Processional* (1925); Arthur Miller, *Death of a Salesman* (1949); Clifford Odets, *Awake and Sing* (1935), *Waiting for Lefty* (1935), *Golden Boy* (1937), and *The Country Girl* (1950); Eugene O'Neill, *Anna Christie* (1921), *The Hairy Ape* (1922), *Strange Interlude* (1928), *Mourning Becomes Electra* (1931), and *The Iceman Cometh* (1946); Samson Raphaelson, *The Jazz Singer* (1925); Elmer Rice, *The Adding Machine* (1923), *Street Scene* (1929), *Counsellor-at-Law* (1931), and *Dream Girl* (1945); Lynn Riggs, *Green Grow the Lilacs* (1931); William Saroyan, *The Time of Your Life* (1939) and *The Beautiful People* (1942); Robert Emmet Sherwood, *Reunion in Vienna* (1931), *Abe Lincoln in Illinois* (1938), and *There Shall Be No Night* (1940); John Steinbeck, *Of Mice and Men* (1937) and *Burning Bright* (1950); Dan Totheroh, *Wild Birds* (1925); John Wexley, *The Last Mile* (1930) and *They Shall Not Die* (1934); Thornton Nevin Wilder, *Our Town* (1938) and *The Skin of our Teeth* (1942); and Tennessee Williams, *A Streetcar Named Desire* (1947) and *The Rose Tattoo* (1951).

For additional information on many of the playwrights mentioned in the body of this article, see separate articles.

DRAMA, capital of the department of the same name in N.E. Macedonia, Greece. The principal industry is tobacco processing. Area of department, 1349 sq.m.; pop. (1951) 119,009. Pop. of city (1951) 32,895.

DRAMATIC ARTS, AMERICAN ACADEMY OF, a training school for acting in the theater and in motion pictures, founded by Franklin H. Sargent in New York City in 1884, and chartered by the regents of the University of the State of New York in 1899. Its curriculum consists of two six-month terms during which classes are held in vocal and speech training, vocal expression, pantomime, make-up and stage costuming, dancing and stage deportment, fencing and stage dueling, radio technique, and modern and standard drama. During the second term, the class is organized as a stock company and offers several public performances. In 1953–54 there

were 300 full-time students enrolled, and the faculty numbered 20.

DRAMMEN, capital and seaport of the county of Buskerud, s. Norway, situated at the joining point of the Drammen R. with the fjord of the same name. The city is about 30 miles s.w. of Oslo, the capital of Norway. It is a railroad junction, and an export center for one of Norway's richest forest districts. Important industries are the processing of wood pulp, cellulose, paper, and other lumber by-products; the mining of zinc, nickel, and cobalt; shipbuilding; and salmon fishing. Pop. (1950) 27,297.

DRAPER, ANDREW SLOAN (1848–1913), American educator and lawyer, born in Westford, N.Y., and educated in Albany, N.Y. He was New York State superintendent of public instruction (1886–92) and was in charge of the public schools of Cleveland, Ohio (1892–94). In 1894 he became president of the University of Illinois, a post which he occupied for the next ten years. In 1904 he was appointed the first New York State commissioner of education and served in that capacity until his death. He was the author of many books on education, including *American Schools and American Citizenship* (1891), *Public School Pioneering in New York and Massachusetts* (1892), and *Conserving Childhood* (1909). He was editor in chief of *Self-Culture for Young People* (10 vols., 1906).

DRAVA, or DRAVE (German, *Drau*), an important affluent of the Danube R. It rises s. of the Hohe Tauern Alps in the s.w. part of the Austrian Tirol, and flows through the Pusterthal (the longest longitudinal valley of the Alps) toward Lienz, Austria, where it is joined by the Isel R. It then flows eastward through Maribor, a town of Slovenia, Yugoslavia, traversing the N. tip of that country, and is joined by its principal branch, the Mur, near Kaposvár, a Hungarian town on the Yugoslav border. The Drava forms the boundary between Hungary and Yugoslavia from Varaždin to a point above Osijek, and then, turning southeast, joins the Danube about 10 m. below Osijek. In the first part of its 450-mile course, the Drava is a mountain torrent. From Villach, Austria, to Osijek, Yugoslavia, it is navigable by rafts only; from Osijek to its mouth, a distance of 100 m., it is navigable by small steamers. At its mouth the Drava is 1055 ft. wide and 20 ft. deep.

DRAVIDIAN, the name applied to the short, dark, indigenous peoples, probably of Negroid affinities, who inhabited the southern part of the Indian peninsula prior to the ad-

Canadian Pacific Railway
*Dravidian architecture: ornately sculptured
tower of the Minakshi temple, Madura, India*

vent of the Aryans (see ARYAN RACE AND LAN-
GUAGES; CASTE). The present-day Dravidians
are much intermixed racially; Caucasian and
other stocks are strongly represented in the
total Dravidian population of about 60,000,-
000. Similarly, the culture of the Dravidians
is heterogeneous. Totemism, kinship in the female line, and other primitive customs are
encountered among some segments of the
Dravidians, while a high state of civilization,
embracing a literature and architectural skill,
exists among other Dravidian groups.

Properly, the term Dravidian is applied today to language rather than to race, the former having remained comparatively pure.
The Dravidian languages are agglutinative.
They form an isolated group of languages,
comprising the principal forms of speech in
southern India and northern Ceylon. The
principal Dravidian languages are Tamil
(spoken by over 18,000,000 persons), the

Malayalam (spoken by about 6,800,000 persons), the Kanarese (spoken by about 10,500,-
000 persons), and the Telugu (spoken by
about 23,500,000 persons). Such works of
Dravidian literature as exist in the several languages are comparatively modern, despite the
antiquity of the Dravidian civilization. Various compositions of the Tamil tongue are attributed to the legendary sage Agastya, who is
said to have lived before Christ; but these
works, comprising treatises and writings on
grammar, can hardly be dated prior to the
10th century A.D. Probably not far removed
from the same date are the *Kintamani,* a romantic poem of some 15,000 verses, and the
Naladiyar. The latter, a moralistic poem, was
translated into English by Alexander Pope.
About the 12th century, the Tamil poet Kam-
bar made a version, or adaptation, of the
Sanskrit epic *Ramavana,* and in the 16th century, Ati-vira-Rama Pandya, a native king,
wrote poetic works of merit. In the 18th century, the Tamil poet Tayumanavar flourished,
and an Italian Jesuit missionary named Beschi
wrote prose and poetry in the Tamil language.
In the Telugu language the oldest extant work
is a version of the Sanskrit epic *Mahabharata,*
written by Nannaya Bhatta in the 12th century A.D. A poet named Kesava wrote in the
Kanarese in the 12th century, and in the
Malayalam language there are various works
based upon the Sanskrit.

DRAVIDIAN ARCHITECTURE, a term
designating the Hindu or Brahman architecture of southern India. Notable examples of
the architecture are the temples of the cities
of Chillambaram, Ramisseram, Madura, Tar-
putry, Vellore, Perore, Tanjore, and Con-
jeveram. The temples are distinguished by
gopuras, or gateways with lofty towers ornamented with numerous sculptured figures.

DRAYTON, MICHAEL (1563–1631), English poet, born at Hartshill, Warwickshire. He
settled in London in 1590, and a year later
wrote his first volume of poems, *The Harmony
of the Church,* a poetical rendering of scriptural passages. This work offended the Archbishop of Canterbury, and almost the entire
edition was publicly burned. Soon thereafter
he wrote *Idea; the Shepherd's Garland* (1593),
consisting of nine pastoral poems, and *Idea's
Mirror* (1594), a collection of love sonnets.
Drayton's historical poem *The Baron's Wars*
(published in a shorter form as *Mortimeriados*
in 1596) was printed in 1603. The first part of
Polyolbion (1622), a patriotic description of
England, was published in 1613. His *Nymph-
idia, the Court of Faery* (1627), a poem of

imaginative fancy, and his *Ballad of Agincourt* (in *Poems Lyric and Pastoral,* 1605), are considered his greatest works. Among his other writings are the historical poems *Piers Gaveston* (1593), *Matilda* (1594), and *Robert, Duke of Normandy* (1596); *Poems Lyrical and Pastoral* (about 1606); and *The Muses' Elizium* (1630).

DREAMING, the act of experiencing apparent sensations and events during sleep, trance, or other unconscious states. Dreams may be confined to a single sensation but more often include incidents and whole chains of connected events in which the dreamer seems to take part. Among the most important characteristics of dreams are their seeming reality and their usually fantastic content.

Many hypotheses have been advanced concerning the causes and mechanism of dreaming. Until recently dreams were sometimes believed to represent, either directly or symbolically, events which would take place in the future, or visitations by ghosts or other spirits; see DIVINATION.

One of the most modern explanations of dreams is that of the psychoanalytic school, who believe that dreaming represents the activity of a part of the mind called the unconscious (q.v.). According to psychoanalytic theory, dreams represent the imaginative fulfillment of wishes and desires which are repressed in the conscious mind during periods of wakefulness. In young children the wish-fulfillment of dreams is readily apparent (for example, the child will dream that he has been given a box of candy or a new toy), but in adults, in whom repressions are stronger and more deeply seated, the wish or desire is clothed in symbols. The interpretation of these dream symbols, which recur again and again, with modifications, in the dreams of different individuals, is one of the techniques of psychoanalysis.

Although it is difficult to observe dreams by any objective method, psychologists have reached certain conclusions about them. It is almost certain that actual external stimuli are incorporated into the fabric of dreams, and it is probable that dreams are frequently the drowsy interpretation of such stimuli. Observation leads to the hypothesis that in some instances dreams take place very rapidly. A sleeper who has been sprinkled with a drop or two of water may wake in a few seconds, but in the meantime may have dreamed of a long and complicated sequence of events leading up to a violent rainstorm or a fall into a lake. Some psychologists believe that all human beings dream when asleep, although many people do not remember their dreams when awake or recall only fragments of them. By systematically attempting to remember dreams on awaking in the morning, an individual can train himself to remember the greater part of his dream. Little is known about the dreams of lower animals.

DRED SCOTT CASE, a case which came before the U.S. Supreme Court in 1856–57, and which involved determination of the constitutionality of the Missouri Compromise (q.v.), and of the legal right of a Negro to become a citizen of the United States. Dred Scott was a slave owned by a Dr. Emerson of Missouri. In 1836 Scott had been taken by his master to Ft. Snelling, in what is now Minnesota, then a territory in which slavery was expressly forbidden according to the terms of the Missouri Compromise. While still on free territory, Scott had been allowed to marry a woman who was also a slave owned by Dr. Emerson. In 1838, Scott, his wife, and a child born to them on free soil were taken back to Missouri. Some ten years later Scott sued for freedom for himself and his family on the grounds that residence in free territory released him from slavery, and established his status as a freeman. The Supreme Court of Missouri, however, ruled in 1852 that upon his being brought back to territory where slavery was legal, the status of slavery reattached to him and he had no standing before the court. In 1854, the case was brought before the Federal Circuit Court, which took jurisdiction but held against Scott. The case was taken on appeal to the Supreme Court of the United States, where it was argued at length in 1855 and 1856, and finally decided in 1857. The decision handed down by a majority vote of the court was to the effect that there was no power in the existing form of government to make citizens of Negro slaves or of Negroes descended from slaves, and that at the time of the formation of the Constitution they were not, and could not be, citizens in any of the States. Accordingly, Scott was still a slave and not a citizen of Missouri, from which it followed that he had no right to sue in the Federal courts. The chief importance of the case, however, lay not so much in the actual decision as in the views expressed by the majority of the court and delivered by Chief Justice Roger Brooke Taney as *obiter dicta.* These opinions went beyond the actual point to be settled to the extent of asserting that Scott, having originally been a slave, and therefore a mere chattel, might, according to the law of

Doubleday & Co.

Theodore Dreiser

Missouri, be taken, like any other chattel, anywhere within the jurisdiction of the United States; that the Missouri Compromise was in violation of the Constitution; and that slavery could not be prohibited by Congress in the territories of the United States. The case, and particularly the court's *dicta* aroused intense bitterness among the Abolitionists, widened the breach between the North and South, and was among the incidents that led to the Civil War.

DREISER, THEODORE (1871–1945), American novelist and journalist, born at Terre Haute, Indiana, and educated at the University of Indiana. He began newspaper work as a reporter on the Chicago *Daily Globe* in 1892, and was dramatic editor and traveling correspondent of the St. Louis *Globe Democrat* in 1892–93, and traveling correspondent of the St. Louis *Republic* in 1893–94. His career as a novelist began in 1900 with *Sister Carrie,* which he wrote in the intervals between work for various magazines. Public outcry against the novel for its realistic treatment of sexual problems caused the publisher to withdraw it temporarily from public sale. Dreiser continued writing, and was managing editor of *Broadway Magazine* from 1906 to 1907, and editor in chief of Butterick publications from 1907 to 1910. By the time his second novel, *Jenny Gerhardt,* was published in 1911, Dreiser's work had found influential support-

ers, including Frank Norris, H. G. Wells, and Hugh Walpole, and he was able to devote himself entirely to literature. His work continued to excite controversy. In *The Financier* (1912) and *The Titan* (1914), he drew a harsh portrait of a type of ruthless businessman. In *The Genius* (1915) he presented a study of the artistic temperament in a mercenary society. This last novel increased his influence among young American writers, who acclaimed him leader of a new school of social realism. Dreiser's real fame, however, did not come until 1925, when his *American Tragedy* had great popular success. The novel was dramatized, and it was made into a moving picture. Although Dreiser's style was regarded by some critics as clumsy and awkward, he was generally recognized as an American literary pioneer. Sinclair Lewis (q.v.) hailed his *Sister Carrie* as "the first book free of English literary influence." Toward the end of his career Dreiser devoted himself largely to promoting his radical political views. He had visited the Soviet Union and, in *Dreiser Looks at Russia* (1928) avowed his sympathy for that country. Six months before his death, it was announced that he had become a member of the U.S. Communist Party. His last novel, *The Bulwark,* was published in the year following his death. His other work includes *Plays of the Natural and Supernatural* (1916), *A Hoosier Holiday* (1916), *Twelve Men* (1919), *A Book About Myself* (1922), *The Color of a Great City* (1923), *Moods* (verse, 1926), *Chains* (1927), *A Gallery of Women* (1929), *Dawn* (1931), *Tragic America* (1932), and *America Is Worth Saving* (1941).

DRENTHE, province of the Netherlands, bordering Germany on the N.E. The principal towns are Assen, the capital, and Hoogeveen (q.v.). The province is for the most part a sandy plateau, marshy and with little vegetation. Only about one eighth of the surface is under cultivation. Buckwheat, potatoes, and small crops of rye, oats, and beans and peas are grown; cattle, sheep, and pigs are raised; and peat is dug. Considerable portions of the province have been forested with firs. Area, 1029 sq.m.; pop. (1950) 285,079.

DRESDEN, capital of the former State of Saxony, East Germany, situated along the Elbe R., about 100 miles s. of Berlin and 65 miles E.S.E. of Leipzig. The city is composed of several quarters, notably Altstadt and Friederichstadt, on the s. bank of the Elbe, and Neustadt, Antonstadt, and Alberstadt, on the N. bank. Five bridges, including two railway bridges, link the N. and s. divisions of the city. Famous squares of Dresden include the Theaterplatz, the Altmarkt, and the Schlossplatz, all in the Altstadt. This quarter of Dresden also contains the Brühl Terrace, a fine promenade along the Elbe. The principal park of the city is the Grosser Garten. Dresden has long been known for its churches. Noteworthy among these is the Roman Catholic Hofkirche, a structure in rococo style constructed between 1739 and 1751. The Protestant Sophienkirche, an edifice with twin spires, dates from the 14th century. The Church of Our Lady, dating from early in the 18th century, is surmounted by a stone cupola 311 feet in height. One of the most prominent of the secular edifices in Dresden is the former royal palace, the Georgenschloss, built (1530–35) in the German Renaissance style and restored between 1890 and 1902. Other buildings are the Prinzen-Palais, built in 1715; the Hoftheater, a Renaissance-style structure which serves as the Dresden opera house; the Rathaus, a huge building in the German Renaissance style, surmounted by a 400-foot octagonal tower; the Albertinium, formerly the arsenal of Dresden and later a museum of oriental and classical antiquities; and the Zwinger, an incompleted palace. The Zwinger contains the Dresden Picture Gallery, one of the foremost institutions of its kind in the world. It has more than 2500 paintings, including such works by masters of the Italian, Flemish, and Dutch schools as Raphael's "Madonna di San Sisto", Corregio's "La Notte", Titian's "Venus", Rembrandt's "Portrait of Himself with Wife Sitting on His Knee", and Rubens' "The Boar Hunt". Among other features of the Zwinger museum are a collection of about 350,000 engravings and drawings, exhibits of works by modern painters, and a valuable collection of casts depicting the development of sculpture from ancient to modern times. The Zwinger also has zoological, mineralogical, and other scientific exhibits. The Johanneum Museum contains one of the most complete historical collections in Germany and specimens of porcelain from all parts of the world. The Green Vault, in the Georgenschloss, has collections of precious stones; of gold, amber, ivory, and silver art objects; and of weapons. Dresden also has extensive educational facilities, including various schools of higher learning.

The city is one of the principal commercial and industrial centers of eastern Germany, and is serviced by a wide network of railway systems and by water-borne carriers operating on the Elbe. Among the broad variety of industrial products manufactured in Dresden are precision, surgical, and musical instruments, china, perfumes, gold and silver ornaments, cameras, soap, leather goods, paper, agricultural machinery, beer, distilled liquors, chemicals, straw hats, artificial flowers, and gloves. Dresden porcelain, to which the city gives its name, is manufactured chiefly at Meissen (q.v.), about 15 miles to the N.W.

Founded around the close of the 12th century, Dresden first attained prominence in 1270, when it became the seat of government of Henry the Illustrious, margrave of Meissen. Wenceslaus II of Bohemia acquired control of the town after Henry's death (1288). Bohemian rule was superseded by the margraves of Brandenburg. The margrave of Meissen regained Dresden early in the 14th century. In 1485 it was acquired by Albert III, Duke of Saxony, who made it the capital of his dominions. Numerous improvements were accomplished in Dresden during the next few centuries, notably in the reign (1694–1733) of the elector Frederick Augustus I. Severe damage was done to the city during the Seven Years' War and the Napoleonic Wars. In 1813 Napoleon established headquarters in Dresden. Later that year he won his last great victory in and around the city.

Dresden expanded considerably during the second half of the 19th century, particularly between 1880 and 1900. In the final year of World War II, the city was severely damaged by major British and American air raids, the worst of which occurred on February 14 and 15, 1945. Dresden was taken by the armed forces of the Soviet Union in May, 1945, and following World War II was included in the Soviet zone of occupation. Pop. (1946) 467,966.

DRESS. See COSTUME.

DRESSLER, MARIE, stage namé of LELIA KOERBER (1873–1934), American actress, born in Cobourg, Ontario, Canada. Her first stage appearances were made in operatic roles, and she toured with the Bennett and Moulton Opera Co. She made her New York stage debut in 1886 and played leading comedy roles for many years in that city. In 1906 she attained her first great popular success as leading woman of the theatrical company of the comedian Joseph M. Weber. Later, she became famous as a star in musical comedy, her greatest success being the leading role of *Tillie's Nightmare* (1910).

Her first motion picture was *Tillie's Punctured Romance,* in which she was starred with Charlie Chaplin in 1916. After 1926, she played only in motion pictures, first as a comedienne in such films as *Caught Short* and *Reducing,* and later as a dramatic actress in such films as *Anna Christie, Dinner at Eight, Tugboat Annie,* and *The Late Christopher Bean.* In 1931 she received the award of the Academy of Motion Picture Arts and Sciences as the best actress of the year for her performance in *Min and Bill.* Her autobiography, *The Life Story of an Ugly Duckling,* was published in 1924.

DREW, name of a famous American family of actors. Among the more prominent members of the family were: **1.** JOHN DREW (1827–62), born in Dublin, Ireland. He made his stage debut at the Bowery Theater, New York City, in 1846. He later became noted for his portrayal of comic Irish roles, notably that of Sir Lucius O'Trigger in Richard Brinsley Sheridan's *The Rivals.* After many successful tours, he became one of the managers of the Arch Street Theater, Philadelphia, Pa., in 1853, and there organized a famous stock company in which he played leading roles opposite his wife, Louisa Lane Drew. He toured England with great success in 1855, and Australia in 1859. **2.** LOUISA LANE DREW (1820–97), born in London, England, the daughter of a London actor. She made her stage debut in 1827 as the young Duke of York in a Philadelphia production of Shakespeare's *Richard III.* She became a child star and, later, a leading lady, notably as Lady Teazle in Sheridan's *The School for Scandal* and as Mrs. Malaprop in Sheridan's *The Rivals,* her most famous role. She married John Drew in 1850 and later assisted him in managing the Arch Street Theater, of which, from 1861 to 1893, she was sole manager as well as leading lady. The three Drew children, John, Sidney, and Georgiana, all became actors; Georgiana, who married Maurice Barrymore (q.v.), became the mother of Lionel, Ethel, and John Barrymore (qq.v.). **3.** JOHN DREW (1853–1927), born in Philadelphia, Pa., the eldest son of John and Louisa. He made his stage debut in 1873 with his mother's company; two years later, he joined Augustin Daly's stock company in New York City, and was the company's leading man from 1879 to 1892. During this period, he played opposite Ada Rehan (q.v.), notably in Shakespeare's *The Taming of the Shrew* and *As You Like It,* and in *The School for Scandal.* In 1892 he left Daly's company and became a star, under the management of Charles Frohman (q.v.), in *The Masked Ball* by Clyde Fitch. He starred in both classic and contemporary plays for Froh-

man and, after the latter's death in 1915, continued to star under various managements, chiefly in contemporary plays in which he played bantering, semi-ironical society roles. He was touring in Sir Arthur Wing Pinero's *Trelawney of the Wells* at the time of his death.

DREW UNIVERSITY, formerly DREW THEOLOGICAL SEMINARY, a coeducational institution, located in Madison, N.J., and conducted under the auspices of the Methodist Episcopal Church for the training of its ministers. Although many of its courses are devoted to theology, the university also offers a broad range of secular subjects. In 1953–54 the enrollment was 723, including 593 full-time students; the faculty numbered 60. In the same period the university endowment was $8,278,000 and the library contained 208,000 volumes.

DREXEL, ANTHONY JOSEPH (1826–93), American banker and patron of art and music, born in Philadelphia. At the age of thirteen he entered the banking house later known as Drexel & Co., established in Philadelphia by his father, Francis Martin Drexel. In 1885 he became nominal head of the banking system which included Drexel, Morgan & Co. of New York City, and Drexel, Harjes & Co. of Paris. In 1864, Drexel, with George W. Childs, bought the Philadelphia *Public Ledger.* He contributed buildings and equipment worth more than $2,000,000 toward the founding of the Drexel Institute of Art, Science and Industry, now the Drexel Institute of Technology, in Philadelphia, and later established an endowment fund of more than 2½ million dollars.

DREXEL INSTITUTE OF TECHNOLOGY, a coeducational institution located in Philadelphia, Pa., and founded in 1891 by Anthony J. Drexel as the Drexel Institute of Art, Science, and Industry. The purpose of the institution is to train men and women in the arts and sciences as applied in industry. The work of the Institute is divided among three schools: Engineering, Domestic Science and Arts, and Secretarial. Drexel was one of the first schools to adopt the co-operative plan, whereby students combine academic work with experience as employees in selected businesses and industries. In 1953–54 the enrollment was 6567, including 2693 full-time students, and the faculty numbered 461.

DREYFUS, ALFRED (1859–1935), French artillery officer, famous as the victim of a notorious miscarriage of justice, born in Alsace of a Jewish family. After being educated at the École Polytechnique, the French military school at Paris, he became a captain in an artillery regiment in 1889 and three years later was appointed to the general staff. In 1894 Dreyfus was accused of having written an anonymous letter, a *bordereau* ("schedule"), giving French military information to the German military attaché at Paris. Despite scanty evidence, a secret court-martial condemned Dreyfus to public degradation and life imprisonment, and he was sent to Devil's Island. A storm of agitation and propaganda against the Jews broke out in France as a result of the court's decision.

In 1896 Lt. Col. Georges Picquart, head of the intelligence department of the French War Office, uncovered information which seemed to absolve Dreyfus and implicate an infantry officer, Maj. Marie Charles Ferdinand Walsin Esterhazy, as the writer of the *bordereau*. The heads of the general staff, however, refused to reopen the case; instead, Picquart was replaced as head of the intelligence department by a Lt. Col. Henry, and sent on a dangerous mission to Tunisia.

Shortly afterward, Mathieu Dreyfus, the prisoner's brother, accused Esterhazy of the crime in a letter to the minister of war. Auguste Scheurer-Kestner, vice-president of the French Senate, began to agitate for the release of Dreyfus, and the ministry of war was forced to court-martial Esterhazy in 1898. He was, however, acquitted.

The Dreyfus case became the most important political issue of the time in France, and the conflict between the prisoner's supporters and opponents led almost to civil war. The nationalists regarded the condemnation of Dreyfus as a necessary vindication of the army's honor, and anti-Semitic elements used every possible means to prevent his release. At the same time, the Liberals and Socialists and many prominent intellectuals, notably Georges Clemenceau, Anatole France, and Émile Zola, fought for revision of the 1894 decision.

In 1898 the newspaper *l'Aurore* published an open letter by Zola in which, under the heading J'Accuse ("I accuse"), the novelist charged the general staff and the government with obscuring the truth in the Dreyfus affair. Zola was tried for libel and sentenced to a fine and imprisonment, but he fled to England. Public demand for a new trial increased to such an extent that Jacques Cavaignac, then minister of war, had to defend the position of the army by reading to the Chamber of Deputies the ministry's proofs of Dreyfus's

Alfred Dreyfus

guilt. Six weeks later, however, Col. Henry confessed that he had forged the ministry's principal documentary evidence; he was arrested, and committed suicide in his cell. The scandal forced the reorganization of the general staff and the dismissal of Esterhazy, though the war ministry continued to insist that Dreyfus was guilty. Esterhazy went to England, where he admitted that he had written the original *bordereau*. The French premier, Eugène Brisson, a month before the Dreyfus issue caused the fall of his cabinet, laid the case before the Court of Cassation, the highest court of appeal in France.

The court ordered a new court-martial in 1899, and Dreyfus was brought back to France. He was tried at Rennes and, to the amazement of the public, was again found guilty. The court-martial sentenced him to a ten-year imprisonment but, ten days after the conclusion of the trial, the government overruled the court's decision and granted him a full pardon. The agitation continued, however, and, in 1900, to conclude the matter peaceably, the government passed a bill giving amnesty to all the participants in the case.

Six years later, the Court of Cassation again reviewed the decision and nullified the Rennes court-martial. The court held that the evidence presented at Rennes was forged; that Dreyfus could not have known the information given in the *bordereau*, and that the court-martial had not permitted the giving of testimony which would have established Dreyfus' innocence.

Dreyfus was reinstated in the French army with the rank of major in 1906, but he resigned a year later. Repercussions of the case persisted, and in 1908 Dreyfus was shot and wounded by an anti-Semitic journalist. During World War I he re-entered the army and was promoted to the rank of lieutenant-colonel and made an officer of the Legion of Honor. After the war he lived in retirement in Paris.

The Dreyfus affair influenced the course of history both in and outside of France. The victory of the supporters of Dreyfus resulted in a staunchly Republican government and the decline of the French monarchist and nationalist movements. In addition, opposition to the anti-Semitic attitude of the French church occasioned the passage of the Separation Law of 1905, which disestablished the Roman Catholic Church as the state church of France and dissolved the French monasteries and convents.

The anti-Semitic outbreaks occurring after the first Dreyfus trial had the effect of giving strong initial impulse to modern Zionism. The Austrian Jewish writer Theodor Herzl (q.v.), founder of the movement, thereby became convinced of the necessity for a Jewish national homeland.

DRILL. See BABOON.

DRILL, a cutting tool for making round holes in wood, metal, rock, or other similarly hard material. Tools for drilling holes in wood are commonly known as bits, as are certain specialized types of tools used in rock drilling.

The most common tool for drilling wood is the *auger bit*, which is provided with single or double helical cutting surfaces and is revolved by a cranklike *brace*. A number of special forms of wood bits are also employed, including the *expanding bit*, which has a central guide screw and a radial cutting arm that can be adjusted to drill holes of different sizes.

For drilling metal, *twist drills* are usually employed. A twist drill is a cylindrical rod with two spiral flutes cut around the rod. The flutes meet at the point of the drill in an angle which is usually between 118° and 120°. Twist drills are made in sizes from a few thousandths of an inch in diameter to an inch, and the diameter of the drill governs the size of the hole produced. When a larger-diameter hole is required the drilled hole is enlarged by means of a boring tool. Twist drills are rotated either by hand in

geared *hand drills* or *breast drills*, or by motor-driven drilling devices. The simplest form of drilling machine is a small, hand-held electric motor with a chuck which grasps the drill. For precise work and for larger drills a *drill press* is employed. This machine consists of one or more motor-driven spindles, usually vertical, with chucks at the lower ends for holding drills. The spindle can be raised or lowered by means of a hand wheel or lever. An adjustable metal table below the spindle holds the work to be drilled. Hand-rotated or power-rotated twist drills can be used for drilling in glass, plastics, and ceramics, as well as in metal.

Small, shallow holes in stone, concrete, brick, and similar materials are usually drilled by hand with a *star drill*, a steel rod with an x-shaped cutting point. In use, the point is held against the object to be drilled and the other end of the rod is struck with a hammer or sledge. The drill is revolved slightly after each stroke. Similar *rock drills* powered by pneumatic hammers are used to drill holes larger in diameter, such as those used for the placement of explosive charges in mining and quarrying.

A new technique for drilling extremely small holes in hard substances is the use of an electric spark. By means of sparks, holes of less than a thousandth of an inch in diameter have been made in diamonds used for wire-drawing dies.

DRILL, any of several small gastropod mollusks, which bore through the shells of other mollusks and suck out their juices. A common drill of the waters off the eastern coast of the U.S. is *Urosalpinx cinerea*, which destroys huge numbers of oysters. Drills lay eggs in small vase-shaped capsules which are often found in groups attached to the undersurface of stones. They live in tide pools and in weedy borders of rocky shallows. See BORER.

DRIMYS. See WINTER'S BARK.

DRIN, or DRINI (anc. *Drilo*), a river rising in Lake Ohrid, on the Albanian-Yugoslav border, and flowing N. through S.W. Yugoslavia, and N. and then W. through N. Albania, emptying into the Adriatic Sea after a winding course of about 170 m. In Albania it is known as the Black Drin.

DRINKER, PHILIP (1894–), American educator, born in Haverford, Pa., and educated at Princeton and Lehigh universities. In 1922 he joined the faculty of the Harvard University School of Public Health as an instructor in ventilation and illumination. He was assistant professor in that field from 1926 to 1931 and associate professor of industrial hygiene from 1931 to 1936, when he became professor. He is coauthor of *Industrial Medicine* (with W. I. Clark, 1935) and *Industrial Dust* (with T. Hatch, 1936).

DRINKWATER, JOHN (1882–1937), English poet, playwright, and critic, born at Leytonstone, Essex, and educated at Oxford High School. He worked as an insurance clerk for twelve years, during which he wrote poetry, and in 1913 became manager-producer of the Pilgrim Players, which grew into the Birmingham Repertory Theatre. He used historical themes for many plays of his own authorship, the most successful being *Abraham Lincoln* (1918). He wrote many critical works, including *William Morris* (1912); *Swinburne* (1913); *The Pilgrims of Eternity: Byron— A Convict* (1925); *Mr. Charles, King of England* (1926); *Oliver Cromwell: A Character Study* (1927); and *Charles James Fox* (1928). Among his plays are *Mary Stuart* (1921), *Oliver Cromwell* (1921), *Robert E. Lee* (1923), *Robert Burns* (1925), *Bird-in-Hand* (1928), and *Midsummer Eve* (1932). His *Collected Poems* was published in 1923, and his *Collected Plays* in 1925. *Inheritance* (1931) and *Discovery* (1933) are autobiographical works.

DRIVER ANT, ARMY ANT, FORAGING ANT, or **LEGIONARY ANT,** any blind, nomadic ant of the subfamily Dorylinae, found in the tropical rain forests of the Americas, Asia, and Africa. The name "driver ant" is sometimes restricted to members of the genera *Anomma* and *Dorylus* and the name "legionary ant" to members of the genus *Eciton*; but members of all these genera are also called "army ants" or "foraging ants".

These ants are organized in colonies of from 100,000 to 150,000 individuals. They build no permanent homes, but move from place to place, finding shelter in hollow trees or under branches. At night the colony forms itself into a large cylindrical cluster around the queen and the larvae. In the daytime the entire colony moves forward either in a swarm or in a long column to find food. The ants devour any form of insect life they find in their way, and will attack and eat small mammals and even domestic animals that are penned or tied up and thus are unable to escape. The columns of driver ants on the march may move as fast as 2 ft. per minute and be as long as 1000 ft.

Recent studies of the habits of the driver ants show that many species, if not all, alternate periods of nomadic life with periods during which the colony stays in one place. When the larvae of the colony enter the pupal state, the foraging worker ants return to the cluster each evening, but after the pupae hatch the entire colony resumes its wanderings, nesting in a different place each night.

Army ants have loosely been credited with intelligence because of the precise organization of their columns. Scientific observation of their habits, however, shows that the leaders of columns start out quite at random and that the ants that follow the leaders simply follow blindly the chemical traces left by them. See ANT.

DRÔME, a department of S.E. France, bounded on the w. by the Rhone R. and drained by several of its tributaries, the most important of which are the Drôme and the Isère. In the E. section of the department a spur of the Alps contains peaks rising to nearly 8000 ft. Smaller ranges stretch westward to the Rhone valley. Agricultural activities, centered in the river valleys, include the growing of wheat, oats, potatoes, truffles, mulberries, walnuts, grapes, olives, and figs, and the raising of cattle, sheep, and silkworms. Minerals of economic importance, mined in the mountainous areas, are lignite, lead and zinc ores, building stone, and clay. Drôme is noted for the manufacture of silk. Other industrial products are bricks, tiles, pottery, porcelain, flour, woolen and cotton goods, paper, hats, confectionery, and leather boots. In addition to the capital, Valence (q.v.), the principal towns of the department are Romans and Montélimar (qq.v.), Crest (pop. in 1946, 3821), and Die (2502). Area, 2533 sq.m.; pop. (1953 est.) 275,000.

DROMEDARY. See CAMEL.

DRONE. See BAGPIPE; BEE.

DRONE FLY, a widely distributed fly, *Eristalis tenax*, of the family Syrphidae. Its larvae, frequently called rat-tailed maggots, live in putrefying carcasses of animals, and breathe by means of an elongated anal projection bearing spiracles at the tip. The adult fly resembles the honeybee, and this resemblance gave rise to the widely held but false theory that honeybees may be born from filth or decaying bodies. See SYRPHUS FLY.

DRONGO or **DRONGO SHRIKE,** any arboreal, oscine bird of the family Dicruridae, widely distributed throughout Africa, Australia, and southeastern Asia. They have bills similar in appearance to those of the shrikes, with bristles at the base which enable the birds to catch insects while on the wing. Their plumage is glossy black; the tail has ten feathers and is forked. The drongos are active, pugnacious birds, and are usually seen in flight.

DROP FORGING. See FORGING.

DROPSY, EDEMA, or OEDEMA, a condition caused by an abnormal accumulation of diluted lymph in the tissues or body cavities. In medical terminology, dropsy is usually employed with a qualifying phrase, such as "abdominal dropsy", "acute dropsy", or "famine edema". It is often a result of stagnation of the circulation and may be caused by any condition which obstructs the veins or the lymphatics, or interferes with absorption of fluids from the tissues into the circulatory system. Present-day treatment of dropsy includes the administration of the newly developed drug Diamox, which stimulates kidney excretion of excess sodium, potassium, and water. In 1954 physicians reported that the blood plasma substitute known as dextran is effective in the treatment of stubborn cases of the disease.

DROPWORT, common name for a perennial Eurasian herb, *Filipendula hexapetala*, of the Rose family. It has the panicles of delicate reddish or whitish flowers, and fernlike leaves. It is 2 to 3 feet tall and is found in north temperate regions. Meadowsweet, common name for species of the genus *Spiraea* (q.v.), is sometimes applied to the genus *Filipendula*.

Dropwort also refers to plants of the genus *Oenanthe* of the Parsley family. The water dropwort is the European poisonous herb *O. crocata*.

DROSERA. See CARNIVOROUS PLANTS.

DROSOPHILA, a genus of small flies, commonly called fruit flies, belonging to the family Drosophilidae. The most important species is the red-eyed pomace fly, *D. melanogaster*, also called the sour fly or vinegar fly. It has a yellowish body marked with black, and can often be observed on open baskets of fruit in the summer. The larvae of this species feed on overripe fruit, vinegar, stale beer, and similar fermenting substances. The importance of *D. melanogaster* lies in two characteristics which make the species an ideal subject for genetic experiments: it has exceptionally large chromosomes, and it can produce a large new generation of flies in a period of about two weeks. Much of the most valuable data on heredity is derived from the study of this genus. See FRUIT FLY; HEREDITY; MORGAN, THOMAS HUNT.

DROWNING. See RESPIRATION, ARTIFICIAL.

DRUG ADDICTIONS, morbid cravings for any of a number of habit-forming drugs, especially opium and its derivatives. Other drugs which tend to develop addiction in users are alcohol, Benzedrine, barbiturates, bromides, cocaine, and hemp derivatives such as hashish, bhang, and marijuana. Such drugs include both stimulants and sedatives. Some authorities regard tobacco, tea, coffee, and maté as habit-forming. Addiction to mild drugs, without physiological deterioration, is usually called habituation.

The most serious addictions are those to cocaine, opium, morphine, and heroin. If any of these drugs is used daily over a period of about a month, the user will develop the typical cravings of the addict. Many addictions are no fault of the addict, as they may be caused by the medical administration of the drug to allay pain. Physical symptoms of such drug addiction include sallowness of complexion and a coated tongue. The addict, deprived of the drug, is conscious of itching or irritability of the skin, and is emotionally depressed. Continued use of the drug increases his tolerance for it, and larger doses must be taken to gain even temporary relief from discomfort. His need grows so great that he will steal or commit acts of violence to obtain a supply of the drug.

The cure for such drug addiction commences with sudden withdrawal of the drug, or, in severe cases, with gradual withdrawal over a period of one to three weeks. The addict immediately develops unpleasant symptoms known as withdrawal symptoms, which may include vomiting, diarrhea, pains and tremors, restlessness, and mental disturbance. Treatment of these symptoms is an important part of the cure, and they gradually disappear as the patient returns to health. In cases of long addiction it may not be possible to withhold the drug from the patient entirely, and a small daily dose must be permanently allowed. In any case, withdrawal must be followed by a long period of care, education, and psychotherapy.

The number of drug addicts in the U.S. reached a peak about the beginning of the 20th century. Most of the addicts formed the drug habit through the use of patent medicines containing habit-forming drugs. Regulation of the composition and sale of patent medicines and of the drug trade in general brought about a substantial annual decrease in the number of addicts until World War II, when the trend was reversed. After the war crime syndicates smuggled large quantities of drugs into the country and sold them especially to adolescents and school children.

Some forms of drug addiction seemingly have little effect on the physical condition of the users. The Indians of the South American Andes chew the leaves of the coca plant, from which cocaine is derived, to lessen fatigue, and show none of the common symptoms of addiction. See separate articles on each of the drugs mentioned. See also NARCOTICS.

DRUIDISM, the religious faith of ancient Celtic inhabitants of Gaul (q.v.) and the British Isles. It flourished from the 2nd century B.C. until the 2nd century A.D., but in parts of Britain which the Romans did not invade, druidism survived until it was supplanted by Christianity two or three centuries later. The tenets of this religion included a belief in the immortality of the soul, which, upon the death of an individual, was believed to pass into the body of a new-born child. According to the writings of Julius Cæsar, which are the principal source of information on this subject, the followers of druidism believed themselves descended from a Supreme Being, and, in common with the Romans, worshiped such deities as Mercury, Apollo, and Mars.

The function of priests, religious teachers, judges, and civil administrators were performed by *druids,* supreme power being vested in an archdruid. Three classes of druids existed: prophets, bards, and priests. They were assisted by prophetesses, or sorceresses, who did not enjoy the powers and privileges of the druids. The druids were also versed in astrology, magic, and the mysterious powers of plants and animals; they held the oak tree and the mistletoe, especially when the latter grew on oak trees, in great reverence; and they customarily conducted their rituals in oak forests. Modern archeologists believe it probable that the druids used as altars and temples the ancient stone monuments known as dolmens (q.v.), which are found throughout the areas where druidism flourished.

The druids led their people in resisting the Roman invasions, but their power was weakened by the rebelliousness of the Gallic warriors, who were envious of their political authority. The superior military strength of the Romans, combined with subsequent conversions to Christianity, led to the disappearance of the religion. See CELTIC PEOPLES.

DRUM, a musical percussion instrument consisting of a hollow cylinder or hemisphere of wood or metal, over each end of which, or sometimes over one end only, a skin or vellum called the "head" is held taut by means of mechanical contrivances such as cords, hoops, and screw rods. The drum is played by beating the head or heads with a stick or sticks. The principal types of the drum are the bass drum, a large drum which is held so that its heads are in a perpendicular position and is played by striking the heads with a ball-end stick; the snare drum (q.v.), or side drum; and the kettledrum (q.v.). The trap drum, used extensively in theater orchestras and dance bands, is a bass drum to which a cymbal has been attached; each instrument is played by means of a separate stick operated by a foot pedal. With the exception of the kettledrum, drums cannot be perfectly tuned and hence are of use only to mark the rhythm in music; the kettledrum participates in the orchestral harmony. Drums of various forms were used in ancient India and Egypt. Various primitive tribes use a type of drum generally called a tom-tom in religious ceremonies, for transmitting signals, and in war. The drum was known to the ancient Greeks and Romans, mainly in the form of the tympanum, which resembled a small modern kettledrum though it could not be exactly tuned. Greek and Roman drums were used chiefly in the worship of the nature goddess Cybele and the god of wine Bacchus. The drum was introduced into western Europe by the Romans.

DRUM or **DRUMFISH,** any of several fishes of the family Sciaenidae, capable of making a noise under water resembling the roll of a muffled or distant drum. *Pogonias cromis,* the salt-water drum of the Atlantic coast of the U.S., has been known to exceed 100 pounds in weight, but ordinarily weighs less than 50 pounds. It is a heavily built fish, with large scales arranged in diagonal rows and a large number of short barbels hanging from the lower jaw. It frequents bays and shallow coastal waters in search of mollusks, upon which it feeds. It is commonly encountered in the oyster beds near New York City, and destroys annually a vast number of cultivated oysters, crushing into fragments hundreds more than it eats.

A South Atlantic variety of drumfish, *Pogonias curbina,* is known by the Brazilians as curbina, meaning "croaker". *Aplodinotus grunniens,* also called thunderpumper, sheepshead, and croaker, is a related fish of the lakes and streams in the Mississippi valley. In the South it is highly prized as a food fish.

Other species of drums are the red drum of the South Atlantic and the Gulf States, *Sciaenops ocellata,* and the black drums, mostly of the Old World, of the same genus.

York Corp.; Netherlands Info. Bur.; Joe Glazer

DRUMS. *Above: African native beating hollow-log signal drum (from painting). Below, left: Bushman of Dutch East Indies with tom-tom. Right: Snare and trap drums in an American dance band.*

DRUM, or TYMPANUM. See EAR.

DRUMMOND, SIR ERIC, 16th EARL OF PERTH, 12th VISCOUNT STRATHALLAN (1876–1951), British diplomat, educated at Eton. He entered the British Foreign Office in 1900, serving as private secretary to the undersecretary of state for foreign affairs (1906–10), as précis writer to Foreign Secretary Sir Edward Grey (1908 and 1910–11), as one of the private secretaries of Prime Minister Asquith (1912–15), and as private secretary to Foreign Secretary Arthur James Balfour (1916–19). He attended the Paris peace conferences with Balfour, was secretary general of the League of Nations from 1919 to 1933, and organized the secretariat of the League. He was British ambassador to Italy from 1933 to 1939, and chief adviser on foreign publicity to the British Ministry of Information in 1939–40. In 1946 he became deputy leader of the Liberal Party in the House of Lords.

DRUMMOND OF HAWTHORNDEN, WILLIAM (1585–1649), Scottish poet, born at Hawthornden, near Edinburgh, and educated at the University of Edinburgh. He studied law for two years at Bourges and Paris. After returning to Scotland, he wrote his first poem, *Teares on the Death of Meliades* (1613), an elegy on Henry, Prince of Wales. In 1616 appeared his volume *Poems: Amorous, Funerall, Divine, Pastorall: in Sonnets, Songs, Sextains, Madrigals.*

Drummond was one of the masters of the Petrarchan sonnet in English, but is best known to modern readers for his notes on the visit paid him in the winter of 1618–19 by Ben Jonson, which were discovered long after the death of both men and were printed in 1842 as *Conversations;* and for *The Cypresse Grove* (1623), an essay on death. His other works include *Forth Feasting: A Panegyricke to the King's Most Excellent Majesty* (1617), *History of Scotland During the Reigns of the Five Jameses* (1655), and many political pamphlets which were suited, by expediency, to the temper of the times.

DRUNKENNESS. See INTOXICATION; TEMPERANCE.

DRUPE. See FRUIT.

DRURY LANE THEATRE, a London playhouse situated in Russell Street, not far from Drury Lane. The original building was constructed in 1663 by Thomas Killigrew, who had been granted a royal patent authorizing him to organize a theatrical company. The theater was originally named the Theatre Royale, and Killigrew's company was known as the King's servants. In 1665 Nell Gwyn, who subsequently became England's foremost actress and the mistress of Charles II, made her stage debut at this playhouse. It was destroyed by fire in 1672, and was rebuilt from designs made by Sir Christopher Wren, reopening in 1674. In 1709 it was closed as a result of financial difficulties, but it reopened soon afterward under the management of the actor Colley Cibber and his associates. David Garrick, one of the greatest actors of all time, took over the management in 1747, appearing at the head of a famous company which included the popular actresses Peg Woffington and Kitty Clive. Garrick was replaced as head of Drury Lane by the dramatist Richard Brinsley Sheridan in 1776. Among the many plays which Sheridan produced at this playhouse was his own masterpiece, *School for Scandal.* The second structure was replaced in 1791, but the new one burned in 1809 and was superseded three years later by the building which still stands on the site. After the completion of the new building, the owners met with financial difficulties until the celebrated Edmund Kean appeared there in 1814 as Shylock, and subsequently in a number of other Shakespearean roles. Under the management (1879–96) of Sir Augustus Harris, the Drury Lane also housed many pantomimes, pageants, and other spectacular presentations, and it is still used primarily for these purposes today.

DRUSES, a religious sect, probably of Kurdish, Persian, and Arab stock, living chiefly in Lebanon and s.w. Syria. Specifically, they are most numerous in the following regions: the Shuf and Metn districts of Lebanon, the Hauran (Anti-Lebanon Mts.) and Mt. Hermon districts of s.w. Syria, and Djebel Druse (Jebel Druze) in s. Syria. These areas lie in mountainous terrain, traversed by numerous rivers. The Druses are an industrious people, and have terraced the mountainsides with rich soil brought from the valleys. Mulberries and olives are grown in quantity, and silk is manufactured.

The Druses can be differentiated from other inhabitants of the region only because of their religion, which has completely dominated their habits and customs. The basis of the Druse religion is that at various times God has been divinely incarnated in a living person, and that His last, and final, such incarnation was in the person of al-Hākim, the sixth Fatimid caliph, who announced himself at Cairo about 1016 A.D. as the earthly incarnation of God. In 1017 the new religion found an apostle in Hamza ibn 'Ali ibn Ahmad', a Persian mystic, who became Hākim's vizier. Hamza gave the religion form and content, and co-ordinated its various dogmas into a single, acceptable creed. The religion probably derives its name from Muhammad ibn-Ismail al-Darazi, one of the first missionaries and followers of Hākim.

The Druses believe that in Hākim a final appeal was made to man to redeem himself; and that God, in the appearance of Hākim, would again return to establish the primacy of His religion. The religion itself is an outgrowth of Mohammedanism, but is admixed with Judaism and Christianity. The Druses believe in one God whose qualities cannot be understood or defined, and who renders impartial justice. They do not believe in proselytizing. The seven cardinal principles to which they adhere are: (1) veracity in dealing with each other; (2) mutual protection and resistance; (3) renunciation of other religions; (4) belief in the divine incarnation of Hākim; (5) contentment with the works of God; (6) submission to His will; and (7) separation from those in error, and from demons. They believe in the transmig_ation of souls, with constant advancement and final purification. The teachings demand abstinence from wine and tobacco, and from profanity and obscenity. The Druses do not pray, fast, or feast, and, with exception of the Āquils, a privileged class, do not hold religious services. In order to protect their religion and not divulge its secret teachings, they worship as Moslems when among the Moslems, and as Christians when among Christians. Jesus Christ is acknowledged by the Druses as one of the divine incarnations.

Politically, the Druses are divided into two parties, the Jumblatiehs and the Yezbekiehs. These two parties live in almost constant strife except when faced with common danger.

In 1588 the Druses were conquered by the Turks under Sultan Murad III; but in the beginning of the 17th century they recovered their independence under Emir Fakru'd-din Maan II and reached the height of their power. Around the middle of the 17th century, after the death of Fakru'd-din by assassination, the Druse regime crumbled. In 1773 the Druses attempted, unsuccessfullly, with the aid of the Russians, to acquire their independence from the Turks. In 1860 a conflict broke out between the Maronites, a Syrian Christian sect, and the Druses, in the course of which several thousand Maronites were killed and large numbers driven from their homes. European powers intervened to protect the Christians, a French force occupying the Lebanon for nearly

a year. A Christian governor general was appointed administrator in 1864, and a large measure of autonomy was conferred on the Lebanon. This marked the end of the political importance of the Lebanese Druses, who until 1918 remained an aloof, conservative community. However, the Syrian Druses were engaged periodically in struggles against Turkish rule until 1910, mainly on the question of taxes and military service. During World War I most of the Druses remained neutral. On Sept. 1, 1918, an armed force of Syrian anc' Lebanese Druses, led by Sultan Pasha el Atrashi, gave assistance to Faisal I (later king of Syria), who helped the British capture Damascus. Late in 1920 the Druses entered into negotiations with the French, who controlled Syria by mandate (established April 25, 1920, and approved by the League of Nations, July 24, 1922), and on March 4, 1921, an agreement was concluded by the terms of which Djebel Druse was granted autonomy. In April, 1925, the Druses petitioned the French authorities for a hearing to discuss French breaches of the agreement. On July 11, 1925, Gen. Sarrail, the high commissioner for the French mandate, ordered his delegate at Damascus to summon the Druse representatives. On arrival the petitioners were seized and exiled by the French to Palmyra, precipitating a Druse revolt led by Sultan Pasha. This revolt gave impetus to the independence struggles of Syria and Lebanon (qq.v.). Because of the Druse practice of conforming outwardly to the faith of the people among whom they live, it is difficult to make an estimate of the number of Druses living outside of Syria and Lebanon. There were 15,000 in Israel, according to the 1951 census. Pop. (in Syria and Lebanon) about 160,000.

DRUSUS, the name of a distinguished Roman family. Among its more important members were the following. **1.** MARCUS LIVIUS DRUSUS (d. 91 B.C.). He was tribune in 91 B.C., and as spokesman for the aristocrats attempted to restore to members of the senate the right to sit as jurors (*judices*) in the law courts, which had been transferred to the *equites* ("knights", actually the propertied group in Rome) by the legislation of Gaius Gracchus. In order to accomplish this purpose, Drusus proposed to admit three hundred of the knights to the senate, doubling the membership of that body; to grant the franchise to non-Roman Italian allies; and to decrease the price of grain distributed to the people. These and other proposals were passed, but were subsequently declared invalid because they had been enacted as a single measure. Shortly after the rejection of his proposals Drusus was assassinated, and a rebellion of the Italian allies broke out (see SOCIAL WAR). **2.** NERO CLAUDIUS DRUSUS GERMANICUS, known also as DRUSUS SENIOR (38 B.C.–9 B.C.), younger son of Livia Drusilla by her first husband (Tiberius Claudius Nero). He was the brother of the Emperor Tiberius, and stepson of the Emperor Augustus. He served as a general under Tiberius against the Rhæti and Vindelici in 15 B.C., and from 13 until 10 B.C. he was governor of the three Gallic provinces. In 9 B.C. he held an army against the German peoples of the Elbe region, penetrating farther than previous Roman armies. He died after a fall from his horse. Germanicus Cæsar and the Emperor Claudius (qq.v.) were his sons.

DRYAD (Gr. *drys,* "tree"), in Greek mythology, a nymph of the trees and the forests. According to popular belief each tree had its own dryad, who came to life with it, watched its growth, and died when it fell. The dryad was sometimes conceived as dwelling in her tree (she was then often called hamadryad, from Gr. *hama,* "together with"; *drys,* "tree"), sometimes as merely living near it. The name is also employed in a general sense for nymphs who dwell in the forest without association with particular trees. See NYMPHS.

DRYBURGH ABBEY, a ruined abbey, in Berwickshire, Scotland, 5 miles E.S.E. of Melrose, on the Tweed R. It contains the tomb of Sir Walter Scott and his son-in-law John Gibson Lockhart. The abbey was founded in 1150 by King David I of Scotland.

DRYDEN, JOHN (1631–1700), English poet, dramatist, and critic, born of a Puritan family at Aldwinkle, Northamptonshire, and educated at Westminster School and at Trinity College, Cambridge University. About 1657 he went to London as clerk to his relative, Sir Gilbert Pickering, who was Oliver Cromwell's chamberlain. Dryden's first important poem was *Heroic Stanzas* (1659), written in memory of Oliver Cromwell, but after the Restoration he became a Royalist and celebrated the return of Charles II in two poems, *Astraea Redux* (1660) and *Panegyric on the Coronation* (1661). In 1663 he married Lady Elizabeth Howard, daughter of the Earl of Berkshire and sister of his patron, Sir Robert Howard.

In 1662, Dryden began to write plays as a source of income. His first attempts, including the comedy *The Wild Gallant*, failed, but *The*

John Dryden

Rival Ladies, a tragi-comedy written in 1664, was a success. During the next twenty years, he became the most prominent dramatist in England. His comedies, including *An Evening's Love, or the Mock Astrologer* (1668), *Ladies à la Mode* (1668), and *Marriage à la Mode* (1672), are broad and bawdy; one of them, *The Kind Keeper, or Mr. Limberham* (1678) was banned as being indecent. His early heroic plays, written in rhymed couplets, are extravagant in style and full of pageantry; among them are *The Indian Queen* (with Sir Robert Howard, 1664), *The Indian Emperor, or the Conquest of Mexico by the Spaniards* (1665), and *Almanzor and Almahide, or the Conquest of Granada* (1670). One of his later tragedies in blank verse, *All for Love* (1678), a version of the story of Antony and Cleopatra, is considered his greatest play and one of the masterpieces of Restoration tragedy.

In his poem *Annus Mirabilis* (1667), he wrote of the events in the "Wonderful Year", 1666, chiefly of the English victory over the Dutch in July and of the Great Fire of London in September. In 1668 he wrote his most important prose work, the *Essay of Dramatick Poesie,* on which is based his pre-eminent position as a critic.

He was appointed poet laureate and historiographer in 1670. In 1681 he wrote his first and greatest political satire, *Absalom and Achitophel,* a poem in heroic couplets ridiculing the Whig attempt to make the Duke of Monmouth (q.v.), rather than the Duke of York, successor to King Charles II. His other great verse satires, all written in 1682, are *The Medall,* the second part of *Absalom and Achitophel* (in collaboration with Nahum Tate), and *Mac Flecknoe.*

Though Dryden had defended his adherence to Protestantism in the poem *Religio Laici* (1682), he became a Catholic in 1685, presumably because James II, an avowed Catholic, came to the throne in that year. The poet then wrote *The Hind and the Panther* (1687), in defense of his new faith. The revolution of 1688 and the resulting succession of the Protestant king William III, however, did not change his religious views, though he lost his laureateship and his pension because of them.

He returned to writing for the stage, but without much success. He then began a new career as a translator, the most important of his translations being *The Works of Vergil* (1697). During the same period he wrote one of his greatest odes, *Alexander's Feast* (1697), which, like an earlier ode, *Song for St. Cecilia's Day* (1687), was written for a London musical society and set to music. In 1699 he wrote the last of his published works, verse adaptations from Chaucer, Boccaccio, and Ovid, under the title *Fables, Ancient and Modern;* this volume included, as its prose preface, one of his most important critical essays. He was buried in Westminster Abbey.

DRY DOCK. See DOCK.

DRY FARMING, the production of farm crops without irrigation in areas of limited rainfall. Dry-farming practices are generally adopted in regions where the soil is good but annual rainfall is 20 in. or less, or where the larger part of the annual rainfall does not fall during the growing season. Successful crop production is achieved under these conditions by careful conservation of all the water in the soil and by the selection of crops which do not require a large amount of water. The scant rainfall of dry-farming regions is usually conserved by killing of weeds and maintenance of a *mulch,* or cover of earth or decaying vegetable matter which will inhibit erosion, runoff, and evaporation. Crops suitable for dry farming include sorghums, corns, and some varieties of wheat. Dry farming has been practiced for many thousands of years, particularly in the Deccan region of India. In the U.S., dry farming was begun in Utah in 1863 and is now practiced in a number of other States. Other dry-farming regions are found in Africa, Australia, and the U.S.S.R.

DRY ICE. See CARBON DIOXIDE.

DRYOPE, in Greek legend, the daughter of Dryops, King of the Dryopes, a tribe of Thessalian origin which settled in Eubœa. Dryope won the love of the god Apollo, who visited her in the form of a tortoise one day while she was playing with her dryad friends. Later, after bearing Apollo a son, she was carried away by the dryads and transformed into a poplar.

DRY POINT, in art, the process of engraving on metal by means of a needle, usually of the type used in etching (q.v.), but more obliquely ground and sometimes pointed with a diamond. The process of dry point differs from line engraving (q.v.) in that the needle is used instead of the tool called a "burin"; dry point differs from etching in that no acid is used in the engraving process. In dry point, the scratches of the needle cause a certain amount of turning up and accumulation of the metal beside the cut; this roughness is known as the "bur". As the bur holds more ink in printing than does a scratch made by other tools used in various forms of engraving, it gives to prints made by the dry-point process a characteristic line, richer and softer than that produced in etching and line engraving. The process of dry point is often used to finish a plate previously etched, because its use makes unnecessary a recoating of the plate with varnish and an additional application of acid. The term "dry point" is applied also to the needle used in the process, and to both the engraving made by the needle and to the print made from the engraving.

DRY ROT, the decay of seasoned wood caused by the attacks of any of a number of species of saprophytic fungi, particularly *Merulius lacrymans, Coniophora cerebella,* and *Poria incrassata.* These fungi penetrate to the interior of timbers and consume the wood fibers, leaving the timbers porous, although they may appear sound on the surface. The name *dry rot* comes from the powdery appearance of the decayed wood, but is otherwise misleading, since the fungi need water to live, and dry rot appears only in wood which has been exposed to moisture. The best method of preventing dry rot in any type of wood construction is to avoid dampness. Where dampness is unavoidable, as in the case of outdoor construction, creosote or other compounds may be used to protect timbers; see FUNGICIDE.

The term *dry rot* is also sometimes applied to the decay of living trees caused by bracket fungi.

DRY STOVE. See GREENHOUSE.

DRY TORTUGAS, a group of ten coral keys or islets, situated in the Gulf of Mexico about 70 miles w. of Key West, and comprising part of Monroe Co., Fla. Among the principal islets, all of which are low and partially covered with mangrove bushes, are Bird Key, Loggerhead, East Key, and Garden Key. The last-named islet is the site of Fort Jefferson National Monument (q.v.). During and for a period after the American Civil War, Fort Jefferson was utilized by the Federal government as a prison for political offenders and captured Confederate troops. One of its inmates was Samuel A. Mudd, the physician who treated John Wilkes Booth following the assassination of President Lincoln. A marine biological station, maintained by the Carnegie Institute of Washington, is situated on Loggerhead Key. The entire group is a bird sanctuary, established by the Federal government in 1908.

DUALIN. See DYNAMITE.

DUALISM, in philosophy, the theory that the universe is explicable only as a whole composed of two distinct and mutually irreducible elements. In Platonic philosophy the ultimate dualism is between "being" and "non-being", i.e., between ideas and matter. In the 17th century, dualism took the form of belief in two fundamental substances, mind and matter. René Descartes, whose interpretation of the universe exemplifies this belief, was the first to emphasize the irreconcilable difference between thinking substance (mind) and extended substance (matter). The difficulty created by this view was to explain how mind and matter interact, as they apparently do in human experience. This perplexity caused some Cartesians to deny entirely any interaction between the two, and to assert that mind and matter were inherently incapable of affecting each other, and that any reciprocal action between the two was caused by God, Who, on the occasion of a change in one, produced a corresponding change in the other; see OCCASIONALISM. Other followers of Descartes came to deny the truth of dualism altogether, propounding the doctrine of monism (q.v.).

In recent years, reaction against the monistic aspects of the philosophy of idealism has to some degree revived dualism. One of the most interesting defenses of dualism is that of William McDougall (q.v.), who divides the universe into spirit and matter and maintains that there is good evidence, both psychological and biological, of the spiritual basis of physiological processes. Henri Berg-son (q.v.) in his second great philosophic work, *Matter and Memory*, likewise takes a dualistic position, defining matter as what man perceives with his senses and possessing in itself the qualities that man perceives in it, such as color and resistance. Mind, on the other hand, reveals itself as memory, the faculty of storing up the past and utilizing it for modifying our present actions, which otherwise would be merely mechanical. However, in his later writings Bergson abandons dualism and comes to regard matter as an arrested manifestation of the same vital impulse which composes life and mind.

Dualism also has an ethical aspect; namely, in the recognition of the independent and opposing principles of good and evil. This dualism is exemplified in Zoroasterianism (q.v.) and in the Manichean heresy (q.v.).

DUANE, JAMES (1733–97), American jurist, born in New York City. He attained prominence as a lawyer prior to the outbreak of the American Revolution and, though an opponent of republicanism, was elected (1774) to the Continental Congress. As a member of that body, in which he served for ten years, he helped to draft the Articles of Confederation. He became the first mayor of New York.

DUANE, WILLIAM JOHN (1780–1865), American lawyer and public official, born in Clonmel, Ireland, the son of William Duane. He was brought to the U.S. at the age of sixteen. After his admission to the bar in 1815, he practiced law in Philadelphia and became active in politics and public projects. In 1833 he was appointed secretary of the treasury by President Andrew Jackson, but was dismissed later in the year for refusing, without authority from Congress, Jackson's demand that he transfer government deposits from the United States Bank to private banks.

DU BARRY, MARIE JEANNE BÉCU, COMTESSE (1743 or 1746–93), mistress of Louis XV of France, born in Vaucouleurs. She was the illegitimate daughter of Anne Bécu and a tax collector whose name is unknown. As a child, she was taken to Paris by her mother, and educated at the convent of Sainte-Aurore. When she was fifteen, she left the convent and worked as a lady's maid and then as an assistant in a millinery shop. She became a courtesan, and in 1764 Chevalier Jean du Barry, who operated a Paris gambling house, made her his mistress. In 1768 she attracted the attention of Louis XV and became his official mistress. For the sake of appearance, she went through a marriage ceremony with

Marie Jeanne Bécu du Barry

Comte Guillaume du Barry, the brother of Jean, and was presented at court in 1769.

Comtesse du Barry wielded great influence over the king and the French court until the death of Louis XV in 1774. She spent vast sums of money on clothes and entertainment, but her political intrigues were unimportant compared with those of her predecessor, Mme. de Pompadour (q.v.). Louis XVI banished her from the court when he came to the throne in 1774, and she lived afterward in her château at Luciennes, France. When the French Revolution began, she fled to England. In 1793 she returned to France, where she was arrested and tried by the Revolutionary Tribunal for having conspired against the republic. She was condemned to death and guillotined.

DUBINSKY, DAVID (1892–   ), American labor leader, born in Brest-Litovsk, Poland. While serving an apprenticeship in a bakery in Lodz, Poland, owned by his father he became an active trade unionist. In 1909 he was seized by the czarist police because of his union activities and exiled to Siberia. He soon managed to escape, however, and in 1911 made his way to the United States. Five years later he was naturalized. Settling in New York City, Dubinsky learned the cloak-cutting trade and joined the International Ladies Garment Workers Union (q.v.). He held various positions of leadership in Local 10 of the union, rising (1921) to the post of manager-secretary. In 1929 he was elected vice-president of the I.L.G.W.U. He advanced to the presidency in 1932 after three years as general secretary-treasurer. A brilliant administrator and militant anticommunist, he led the I.L.G.W.U. to many impressive victories during the next two decades, vastly increasing its membership and influence. Dubinsky was a stanch supporter of the New Deal during this period and was a founder of the American Labor Party (1936), the Liberal Party (1944), and Americans for Democratic Action (1947).

DUBLIN, county of Leinster Province, Republic of Ireland, in the w. central section of the island, and adjoining the Irish Sea. The terrain is generally flat, except in the extreme s. portion. This region contains the N. extremities of the Wicklow Mountains. Noteworthy peaks of the range within the county are Glendoo (1919 ft.) and Two Rocks (1699 ft.). The county coast line, about 70 m. long, is indented by a number of creeks and bays, notably Dublin Bay, formed by Howth Peninsula. Dublin Bay receives the waters of the Liffey R., the only stream of consequence in the county. Several islands, including Lambay Island and Ireland's Eye, are attached to the county for administrative purposes. The county has numerous small farms, the chief products of which are cattle, oats, and potatoes. The fishing industry is important, producing valuable catches of salmon, brill, cod, haddock, sole, plaice, and oysters. Industrial production is confined largely to Dublin (q.v.), capital of the Republic of Ireland and administrative center and chief seaport of the county. Among the principal towns are Dun Laoghaire (q.v.), Balbriggan (pop. in 1946, 2537), and Skerries (2305). Area, 356 sq.m.; pop. (1951) 693,022.

DUBLIN (Gaelic, *Baile Atha Cliath,* "Town of the Ford of the Hurdles"), capital, county borough, and seaport of the Republic of Ireland, and administrative center of Dublin Co., in Leinster Province. It is at the mouth of the Liffey R., on Dublin Bay, an inlet of the Irish Sea. The city, about 8350 acres in area, occupies a generally flat site, which is bisected in an E. and W. direction by the Liffey. The river is spanned by ten bridges, notably O'Connell's Bridge, which links the main thoroughfares of the city. Except in its s.w. portion, where the streets are narrow and crooked, Dublin is well laid out, with broad avenues and spacious squares. These are especially numerous in the S.E. and N.E. quarters, which also contain many stately old mansions. Circular Drive, a boulevard about 9 m. long, extends along what was the periphery of the city at the end of the 19th century. Since that time, the city limits have been considerably extended. The port area, confined to the lower reaches of the Liffey, has a number of quays and basins accessible to vessels drawing up to 23 feet of water. Two canals, the Royal (96 m. long) and the Grand (208 m. long), provide connections between the port area and the N. and S. branches of the Shannon R. The city is serviced by steamship lines operating to Cork, in Eire, to Belfast, Northern Ireland, and to various ports in England, Scotland, and France, and by four railway systems, which provide connections with all important points in Ireland. Local transportation is afforded by an electric-tramway system. Dublin contains several notable suburbs, including Rathmines and Rathgar (pop., about 45,000), where are the homes of many of the wealthy business men of Dublin; and Glasnevin, where Joseph Addison, Jonathan Swift, Richard Brinsley Sheridan (qq.v.), and other celebrities once resided. In the cemetery of Glasnevin lie the remains of the Irish patriots Daniel O'Connell and John Philpot Curran (qq.v.).

Dublin contains many noteworthy points of interest, both historic and contemporary. Most of the historic edifices are situated in the old section of the city, on the N. side of the Liffey. Dublin Castle, the nucleus around which the modern town developed, formerly housed the offices of the British viceroy of Ireland. Although most of this structure, which occupies a ridge overlooking the river, was completed in the 16th century and later, parts of it date from early in the 13th century. In the vicinity of the castle is the Protestant cathedral of Christ Church, founded in 1038 by the Christianized Danish king Sigtryg, and rebuilt in 1870–77 according to the original design. St. Patrick's Cathedral, not far from Christ's Church, is the largest of the many churches in Dublin and the center of the Protestant faith in Ireland. It is sometimes called the "Westminster of Ireland". The cathedral, a Gothic structure, was founded in 1190 and rebuilt between 1220 and 1260. The remains of Jonathan Swift, once dean of St. Patrick's, are interred in the cathedral. Among the Roman Catholic churches are St. Mary's, the cathedral on Marlborough Street, and also St. Saviour's, St. Augustine's and St. Kevin's. The University of Dublin (see DUBLIN, UNIVERSITY OF) and the Bank of Ireland building, formerly the Irish House of Parliament, also are in the old section of Dublin. Among other public buildings of the city are the Customs House, the National Library, the Museum of Science and Art, the National Gallery, the Four Courts (seat of the high courts of Eire), and Leinster House, seat of Dáil Eireann, the parliament of Eire. Dublin also has a number of notable monuments. One of the best known of these is Nelson's Pillar, a stone column, more than 100 feet high, surmounted by a statue of the British naval hero Horatio Nelson. Numerous other statues commemorate famous Irish citizens, including Daniel O'Connell, Edmund Burke, the Duke of Wellington, and Oliver Goldsmith.

In addition to the University of Dublin, the city contains University College, a division of the National University of Eire. The city has several excellent libraries, notably the library of the University of Dublin, with more than 442,000 volumes; the Irish Academy Library; and the National Library. Other cultural institutions include the Museum of Science and Art, which contains numerous Irish antiquities; the National Gallery, which has valuable collections of painting and sculpture; and the Abbey Theatre (q.v.).

The principal unit of the Dublin park system is Phoenix Park, in the western environs of the city. About 7 m. in circumference, the site of this park encompasses part of the Liffey R. valley. Besides recreational facilities, Phoenix Park contains zoological gardens, several conservatories, an arboretum, and the residence of the president of Eire.

Dublin is predominantly a commercial city, the trading center and natural outlet of the adjoining agricultural region. Livestock, agricultural products, and local manufactures constitute the principal exports, and a wide variety of commodities is imported. The chief manufacturing industries of the city are brewing and whiskey distilling. Other important products are biscuits, poplin, leather goods, wood products, flour, glass, clothing, boots and shoes, cigarettes, and sugar. Some shipbuilding is carried on, and the city has a number of foundries and automobile-assembly plants.

The first known settlement on the site of Dublin was called *Eblana*, a name that is found in the writings of the 2nd-century Alexandrian geographer Ptolemy. The town next appears in history as *Dubh-linn* (Gael., "Black Pool"), the inhabitants of which won (291 A.D.) a military victory over the armed forces of Leinster. *Baile Atha Cliath*, the present official name, which refers to the ford of hurdles, or wattled frames, that once spanned the Liffey R. near the town, is be-

Irish Tourist Association

The University of Dublin, Eire. The bank of Ireland is seen at left.

lieved to have been applied to the settlement at a later date.

Dublin has often figured prominently in Irish history. Its inhabitants were converted to Christianity about 450 by Patrick, later the patron saint of Ireland. The town was captured in the 9th century by the Danes. The rebellious Irish wrested control of Dublin from the Danes on a number of occasions during the next three centuries, notably in 1052, 1075, and 1124. In 1171 the Danes were expelled by the Anglo-Normans, led by King Henry II of England. He held his court in Dublin in the following year, and later made the town a dependency of the English city of Bristol. English overlordship in Dublin remained unchallenged until 1534, when the Irish patriot Thomas Fitzgerald (q.v.) laid brief siege to the city in the course of the rebellion he fomented against English rule.

The Royalists seized Dublin Castle during the early stages of the Great Rebellion (q.v.), precipitating an indiscriminate massacre of the Protestant section of the population. In order to avoid reprisals by Irish followers of Oliver Cromwell, the city was surrendered to English Parliamentary forces in 1647. The city again became a stronghold of Catholicism after the Restoration (1660). James II established his headquarters there in 1689, following the occupation of the British throne by

William III. After William's victory at the Battle of the Boyne, he participated in a ceremony of thanksgiving at St. Patrick's Cathedral.

Dublin remained quiescent under British control until the Irish insurrection of 1798, during which an attempt to seize the city ended in failure. A second attempt in 1803, led by Robert Emmet (q.v.), also ended disastrously. Further abortive insurrections occurred in Dublin in 1847 and in 1867. Dublin was the scene of some of the most severe fighting of the Irish rebellion of 1916, and of the revolution of 1919 to 1921, which resulted in the establishment of the Irish Free State. Pop. of Dublin County Borough (1951) 522,183.

DUBLIN, UNIVERSITY OF, also known as TRINITY COLLEGE, the oldest and leading institution of higher learning in Eire. The first University of Dublin was established in 1320 in connection with St. Patrick's Cathedral, but lacked an endowment and never functioned successfully, finally shutting its doors with the dissolution, by Henry VIII, of the cathedral foundation. The present foundation was chartered by Queen Elizabeth in 1591 as "the mother of an university" with the title of "the College of the Holy and Undivided Trinity, near Dublin". It was expected that other colleges would be formed about this nucleus, and that a university of the English type would eventually develop in its place. This expectation was never realized, and Dublin University retains to the present day the capacity to function as both a college and a university. The Corporation of Dublin donated to the University the grounds and the ruins of the confiscated All Hallows monastery, and a building fund was raised by local subscription. James I, during his reign, endowed the institution with £400 a year and the revenue of various estates in Ulster; and the English army in 1601 commemorated its victory over the Spanish at Kinsale by subscribing £1800 to establish a library for the college. Chiefly with these contributions, the foundation of the present college was laid. Its original constitution has been revised several times, although some of the original statutes are still in effect. Under the present system a provost appointed by the crown is at the head of the college. Entrance to the college is by examination, and there is an additional examination to rank the entrants according to scholarship. The majority of students enter the liberal arts course, but there are courses leading to degrees or licenses in divinity, music, law, medicine, education, commerce, agriculture, and engineering. The degrees of SC.D. and LITT.D. are conferred on holders of the B.A. who have achieved distinction in science or literature respectively. The general course of study usually extends over four years and is patterned after the methods of Oxford and Cambridge universities; the students are known as junior freshman, senior freshman, junior sophisters, and senior sophisters. Women have been admitted to classes and have been eligible for degrees since 1904.

The University of Dublin possesses a number of valuable collections. The library contains over 442,000 volumes, as well as a notable collection of old Irish manuscripts, including the rare *Book of Kells* containing the Gospels. The college also has museums of natural philosophy, zoology, geology and mineralogy, engineering, pathology, and materia medica; magnetic and astronomical observatories; and an herbarium, a botanical laboratory, and botanical gardens. Among those at various times connected with the institution are George Berkeley, Jonathan Swift, Edmund Burke, Thomas Sheridan, and Oliver Goldsmith. In 1952–53 the enrollment was 2171 and there were 161 members of the faculty.

DU BOIS, W(ILLIAM) E(DWARD) BURG-HARDT (1868–   ), American Negro author,

educator, and sociologist, born at Great Barrington, Mass., and educated at Fisk and Harvard universities and the University of Berlin. He was professor of Greek and Latin at Wilberforce University from 1894 to 1896. In 1897 he became professor of economics and history at Atlanta University, where he initiated and for the next thirteen years directed a program of historical and racial studies. From 1910 to 1932 he was director of publications of the National Association for the Advancement of Colored People, of which he was cofounder, and edited its magazine, *Crisis.* He was an organizer of the first Pan-African Congress, which was held in Paris during the Versailles Peace Conference, in 1919. He returned to Atlanta University in 1933 and headed its department of sociology until 1944. From 1940 to 1944 he edited the *Phylon Quarterly Review.* In 1944 he became the first Negro to be elected a member of the National Institute of Arts and Letters. In 1945 he served as special consultant at the founding conference of the United Nations at San Francisco. From 1944 to 1948 he was director of special research for the N.A.A.C.P. His many writings include *The Suppression of the African Slave Trade* (1896), *The Souls of Black Folk* (1903), *John Brown* (1909), *Darkwater* (1920), *The Gift of the Black Folk* (1924), *Black Reconstruction* (1935), *Color and Democracy* (1945), *The World and Africa*

Nat'l. Assn. for Advancement of Colored People

W. E. Burghardt Du Bois

(1947), and *In Battle for Peace* (1952). He edited the *Encyclopedia of the Negro* (1946).

DUBUQUE, county seat and port of entry of Dubuque Co., Iowa, situated on the Mississippi R., opposite the Wisconsin-Illinois boundary. It is served by six railroads, and is a river port. Dubuque is an important market for agricultural produce, and is the center of a large wholesale and jobbing trade and of the lead and zinc mining industry of the Northwest. It contains railway repair shops, large sash and door factories, flour and lumber mills, pork-packing houses, iron and brass foundries, breweries, and factories manufacturing hardware, leather, furniture, bricks, engines, boilers, steel ship hulls, barrels, brooms, dry batteries, plumbing supplies, clothing, oil tanks, agricultural implements, and boots and shoes. The city is the see of a Roman Catholic archbishop, and the site of Loras and Clarke colleges (Roman Catholic), for men and women, respectively, and of the University of Dubuque (Presbyterian), which was originally a German theological seminary and became a university in 1920. Wartburg Seminary (Lutheran) is located in the city, and one of the three Trappist monasteries in the U.S. is 14 miles s.w. of Dubuque.

The oldest city in the State, Dubuque was named in honor of Julien Dubuque, a French-Canadian who settled there in 1788 and to whom a monument has been erected. The first permanent settlement dates from 1833. Pop. (1950) 49,671.

DU CANGE, CHARLES DU FRESNE, SIEUR (1610–88), French scholar, born at Amiens, and educated at the Jesuit college there, and at Orléans, where he studied law. He later devoted himself to philology, history, and linguistics. In 1647 he became treasurer of Amiens but, because of a plague, left his native town in 1668 for Paris, where he continued his studies until his death. Among his works are *Histoire de l'Empire de Constantinople sous les Empereurs Français* (1657), *Glossarium Mediæ et Infimæ Latinitatis* (1678), *Glossarium ad Scriptores Mediæ et Infimæ Græcitatis* (1688), and *Histoire de l'État de la Ville d'Amiens, et de ses Comtes* (published posthumously in 1814).

DUCCIO DI BUONINSEGNA (1255?–1319?), Italian painter, born in Siena. He was probably a pupil of Guido da Siena, and reputedly received training in art from a Byzantine master, possibly at Constantinople. Duccio was, after Giotto, the foremost Italian artist of the late medieval period in Italy and the founder of the Sienese school of painting.

His work brought to perfection the art of medieval Italy as influenced by Byzantine art (q.v.). Duccio's paintings are characterized by precise drawing and skillful composition, a decorative quality akin to that of the mosaic, and by deeper emotional feeling than that of the Byzantine models which he followed. His most famous work is the altarpiece executed for the cathedral of Siena. Its front panel, 14 feet long and 7 feet high, represents a Madonna enthroned and surrounded by a host of angels and saints and by the Apostles; the reverse of the panel contains 26 scenes from the life of Christ, painted on the type of golden background characteristic of Byzantine art. The panel is now in the museum of the cathedral of Siena. Among other works generally attributed to him are "Madonna with the Three Franciscans" and "Madonna with Four Saints" (Siena Gallery), "Madonna and Child" and "Transfiguration" (National Gallery, London), and a triptych, "The Crucifixion" (Buckingham Palace, London).

DU CHAILLU, PAUL BELLONI (1831–1903), American explorer, born in France, probably in Paris. He spent his youth in the colony of Gabon, French Equatorial Africa, with his father, a French trader. In 1852 he migrated to the United States, where he became a naturalized citizen. He led an expedition, sponsored by the Philadelphia Academy of Natural Sciences, to central Africa in 1855. He returned to the U.S. in 1859, bringing with him many rare birds and animals unknown to science until that time, and including the first gorillas ever seen in the U.S. His account of the expedition, *Explorations and Adventures in Equatorial Africa* (1861), aroused controversy because it conflicted with geographical, zoological, and ethnological theories held before that time. To prove the truth of his account, he led a second expedition to Africa in 1863 and, in addition to confirming his first report, verified rumors concerning a race of pygmies which inhabited the African forests. He returned in 1865 and wrote the account of his second expedition, *A Journey to Ashango Land* (1867). From 1871 to 1874, he traveled in northern Europe; his account of these travels is *The Land of the Midnight Sun* (1881). Among other books written by him are *Stories of the Gorilla Country* (1868), *The Country of the Dwarfs* (1871), and *The Viking Age* (1889).

DUCHESNE, PÈRE. See HÉBERT, JACQUES RENÉ.

DUCK, common name for the female of any of a number of species of water birds of the

U.S.D.A., Bureau of Animal Industry

DUCKS. *Top: Left, male goldeneye in flight; right, eider duck's nest with ducklings. Bottom: Left, Peking ducks, common domestic birds; right, shoveler, a fresh-water duck.*

family Anatidae. The males, usually more brilliantly colored than the females, are properly called drakes, but in ordinary usage they are often also termed ducks. Ducks are closely related to swans and geese, but differ from them in that their necks and legs are shorter and that their legs are covered with scales on the front rather than on the back. The legs are placed far back on their bodies and are not efficient for walking, but enable the birds to swim powerfully. The plumage is dense, soft, and water-repelling. Most species have spoon-shaped or shovel-shaped bills. The majority nest on the ground, although some species make their homes in hollow stumps or trees. The nests of all species are characteristically lined with down and small feathers plucked from the breasts of the parent birds. A number of species are migratory, nesting in the summer as far north as the Arctic Circle and wintering in the temperate, subtropical, and tropical regions. The diet is varied and includes small fish and invertebrates as well as seeds, berries, and roots.

Three subfamilies of ducks are generally recognized: the Anatinae or fresh-water ducks, the Fuligulinae or sea ducks, and the Merginae or mergansers. A number of breeds are raised domestically. Among the most important are the Peking duck, an all-white breed originated in China; the mallard, a native duck with a chestnut breast, a white ring around the neck, and a green-black head; and the Muscovy duck, a crested species native to tropical America.

For descriptions of various species of ducks see BLACK DUCK; BLATHERSKITE; BLUEBILL; BUFFLEHEAD; CANVASBACK; EIDER; GOLDENEYE; MALLARD; MERGANSER; PINTAIL; SHELᴅʀᴀᴋᴇ; Tᴇᴀʟ; Wɪᴅɢᴇᴏɴ; Wᴏᴏᴅ Dᴜᴄᴋ.

DUCKBILL. See Pʟᴀᴛʏᴘᴜs.

DUCK-BILLED CAT. See Pᴀᴅᴅʟᴇғɪsʜ.

DUCK HAWK. See Hᴀᴡᴋ.

DUCKING STOOL, a device formerly used in Great Britain and parts of the United States for the punishment of women convicted as common scolds. It was constructed on a see-saw principle, with the center balancing post placed at the edge of a pond or stream. One half of the cross plank extended over the water, and to this end of the plank was attached a chair, into which the convicted woman was tied. The chair was lowered into the water, and its occupant completely submerged by raising the opposite end of the plank. The ducking stool was raised and lowered by officers of the court, and the number of duckings to be given was pronounced by the sentencing judge. A ducking stool was used at Leominster, England, as late as 1809 and is preserved in the Priory Church there.

DUCKWORTH, Gᴇᴏʀɢᴇ Eᴄᴋᴇʟ (1903–), American classical philologist, born in Little York, N.J., and educated at Princeton University. He served as a classics instructor at Princeton in 1924–25 and at the University of Nebraska from 1926 to 1928. In 1929 he returned to Princeton. He was assistant professor of classics from 1930 to 1940, associate professor from 1940 to 1945, and Giger professor after 1945. His works include *T. Macci Plauti Epidicus* (1940), *The Complete Roman Drama* (1942), and *The Nature of Roman Comedy* (1952).

DUCLAUX, Pɪᴇʀʀᴇ Éᴍɪʟᴇ. See Dᴀʀᴍᴇs-ᴛᴇᴛᴇʀ.

DUCOMMUN, Éʟɪᴇ (1833–1906), Swiss journalist, born in Geneva. He devoted most of his life to furthering the cause of peace, and edited and contributed to many pacifist journals, including *Revue de Genève, Progrès,*

Early American ducking stool (old woodcut)

Helvétie, and *États-Unis d'Europe.* In 1891 he organized the International Bureau of Peace at Berne. He received the Nobel Peace Prize, with Albert Gobat, in 1902.

DUCTILITY. See Mᴇᴛᴀʟs: *Physical Properties.*

DUCTLESS GLANDS. See Hᴏʀᴍᴏɴᴇ.

DUDEVANT, Bᴀʀᴏɴɴᴇ. See Sᴀɴᴅ, Gᴇᴏʀɢᴇ.

DUDLEY, market town and county and parliamentary borough of Worcestershire, England, 8 m. by rail ɴ.ᴡ. of Birmingham. The city was known as Dudelei in medieval times. Industrial establishments of present-day Dudley are coal mines, limestone and dolerite quarries, ironworks, brass foundries, and brickworks. The lime quarries of Dudley have disclosed excellent specimens of Silurian fossils. Pop (1953 est.) 61,420.

DUDLEY, Lᴏʀᴅ Gᴜɪʟᴅғᴏʀᴅ. See Gʀᴇʏ, Lᴀᴅʏ Jᴀɴᴇ.

DUEL (Lat. *duellum,* "combat between two", old form of *bellum,* "war"), a prearranged combat with deadly weapons between two persons, generally taking place under formal arrangements and in the presence of witnesses, called seconds, for each side. The usual cause of a duel is injury or offense given by one person to the other; in most cases, the challenged person has the right to name the time, place, and weapons.

The duel, in the modern sense, did not occur in the ancient world; the famous single combats of antiquity, such as that between Achilles and Hector (q.v.), happened during the course of national wars. Modern dueling derived directly from the legal, judicial combat used to decide controversies, such as guilt for crimes and ownership of disputed land, in Teutonic countries during the early Middle Ages; such combat was first legalized by Gundebald, king of the Burgundians, in 501 ᴀ.ᴅ. (See Bᴀᴛᴛʟᴇ, Wᴀɢᴇʀ ᴏғ.) The custom of judicial combat spread to France, where it became prevalent, particularly from the 10th to 12th centuries; even the Church authorized it to decide the ownership of disputed church property. The Normans brought this form of duel to England in the 11th century. As late as 1817, an English court authorized a judicial combat between the accuser and accused in a case of murder.

Dueling to avenge one's honor, however, has never been legalized and its history has, instead, been marked by laws against it. The custom became popular in Europe after a famous affair between Francis I of France and Charles V of Spain. When Francis declared war on Spain in 1528, abrogating a treaty be-

THE DUEL IN MEDIEVAL FRANCE

Above: The duel of honor was popular with the nobility but did not have the sanction of judicial authority. Right: The judicial duel was held in the presence of the court to decide controversies over legal matters (15th-century manuscript illustrations).

tween the two countries, Charles accused the French ruler of ungentlemanly conduct and was challenged by him to a duel. Though the duel did not take place, because of the difficulty in making arrangements, the incident so influenced European manners that gentlemen everywhere thought themselves entitled to avenge supposed slights on their honor by similar challenges.

Dueling became particularly popular in France and occasioned so many deaths that Henry IV, in 1602, declared in an edict that participation in a duel was punishable by death. Similar edicts were issued by Henry's successors, though they were rarely enforced with any strictness. The various French republican governments also outlawed dueling, making it an offense against the criminal code. Duels, however, still occur in France, though they are rarely fatal.

Under the imperial regime in Germany, dueling was a recognized custom in the army and navy, though each affair was subject to approval by a so-called council of honor. The German student *Mensuren,* or duels, were famous elements of German university life and were regarded as a form of sport. Every university had *Verbindungen,* or dueling clubs, and membership in them was an honor. Restrictions on dueling, however, were in force even during the Empire, and the 1928 criminal code of the Weimar Republic made dueling an offense punishable by imprisonment.

The duel was exceedingly popular in England, particularly during the Restoration (q.v.), as a reaction against the Puritan morality of Oliver Cromwell's protectorate, and in the reign of George III (1760–1820), during which 91 deaths resulted from 172 encounters. Numerous legislative enactments during the 17th and 18th centuries had little effect on curbing the practice. Though the English common law holds killing in a duel to be murder, juries rarely convicted in dueling cases until the custom ceased to be popular during the reign of Victoria. The British articles of war were amended in 1844 to make participants in a duel subject to general court-martial; since that date, dueling has become almost extinct in the British Army.

In the U.S., duels were common from the time of the first settlement, a duel occurring at Plymouth in 1621. Such combats under all sorts of conditions and with every variety of weapon were frequent during the 18th and early 19th centuries; they were usually fatal. In 1777, Button Gwinnett (q.v.) was killed in a duel, and one of the most famous American victims of a duel was Alexander Hamilton, who was killed by Aaron Burr in 1804. The District of Columbia outlawed dueling in 1839, and, since the American Civil War, all the States have legislated against dueling, with punishments ranging from disqualification for public office to death.

By the beginning of the 20th century, dueling was almost universally prohibited by law as a criminal offense. The major factors in the suppression of dueling, however, have been social changes and social disapproval. The greatest of these social changes has been the decline of the aristocracy, since dueling was a custom reserved for the upper classes. In addition, organizations were formed to force social disapproval, notably a British association founded in 1843 and an international league founded by European aristocrats in 1900.

DUE PROCESS OF LAW, law as administered through courts of justice in accordance with established and sanctioned legal principles and procedures, and with safeguards for the protection of individual rights. It is frequently defined as the "law of the land", an expression used for the first time in the sense of due process in the great charter of English liberty, the Magna Carta (q.v.).

As determined by custom and law, due process is a guarantee of civil and other rights. It includes, among many other things, provision for insuring an accused person a fair and public trial before a competent tribunal, the right to be present at his trial, and the right to

be heard in his own defense; the doctrine that the provisions of criminal statutes must be drawn so that reasonable persons can be presumed to know when they are breaking the law; and the principles that taxes may be imposed only for public purposes, that property may be taken by the state only for public use, and that the owners of property so taken must be fairly compensated.

DUERO. See DOURO.

DUFAY, GUILLAUME (1400?–74), Flemish composer, born probably at Chimay, Hainaut. From 1428 to 1437 he was a singer in the papal chapel, Rome, and from 1442 to 1449 lived in Paris, where he became a priest. Subsequently he was canon in the Cathedral of Cambrai. Dufay was one of the early masters of counterpoint (q.v.), especially four-part music, and many reforms in musical notation are attributed to him. Among his compositions are magnificats, masses, motets, and songs.

DUFFY, FRANCIS PATRICK (1871–1932), American Roman Catholic clergyman, born in Cobourg, Ontario Province, Canada, and educated at St. Michael's College, Toronto; St. Joseph's Seminary, Troy, N.Y.; and Catholic University, Washington, D.C. He taught at the Grammar School of St. Francis Xavier College in New York City (1893–94) and received the degree of Master of Arts at that college in 1894. Two years later he was ordained. During the Spanish-American War he served as unofficial chaplain at Montauk Point, Long Island. From 1898 to 1912 he was professor of logic and metaphysics at St. Joseph's Seminary, Dunwoodie, N.Y., after which he became rector and organizer of the parish of the Church of Our Savior in New York City, retaining this post until 1919. He served as chaplain of the 165th Infantry (formerly the 69th Regiment of the New York National Guard) during World War I, attaining the rank of lieutenant colonel, and was awarded several military decorations, including the Distinguished Service Cross. The French government honored him with the rank of chevalier of the Legion of Honor. Father Duffy became pastor of Holy Cross Church in New York City in 1920 and acted in that capacity until his death. He was associate editor of the *New York Review* (1905–10) and wrote *Father Duffy's Story* (1919). A statue of Father Duffy was erected in Times Square, New York City, and was unveiled in May, 1937. Two years later, that part of Times Square which surrounds the statue was renamed Duffy Square.

DUFOURSPITZE, one of the ten summits of Monte Rosa (q.v.), and the highest peak in Switzerland. Its elevation is 15,217 ft. above sea level.

DU FRESNE, CHARLES. See DU CANGE.

DUFY, RAOUL (1877–1953), French painter and decorative artist, born in Le Havre, and educated there and at the École Nationale des Beaux-Arts, Paris. He was greatly influenced by the Impressionists (see IMPRESSIONISM) early in his career. In 1905 he met the French painter Henri Matisse, then leader of the group of painters called *les Fauves* ("wild beasts"); see FAUVIST. His canvases executed between 1905 and 1909 reflect the Fauvist influence. In 1909 he began to study the techniques of cubism (q.v.), but his paintings in this style were not generally well received. He had won praise meanwhile for his work in the graphic and decorative arts. The book illustrations for *Le Bestiaire* (1911), by the French poet and novelist Guillaume Apollinaire, are particularly noteworthy. Dufy was well known also as a designer of textiles, tapestries, and ceramics.

Gaiety, freshness, and the imaginative use of flat planes and luminous color distinguish his style, particularly after 1920. Outdoor scenes and activities at fashionable resorts are among his favorite subjects. Following a visit to the United States in 1950 he executed a series of water colors based on impressions of New York and Boston. Dufy is represented in many leading museums of the United States and Europe. Some of his best-known paintings are *Regatta at Le Havre, Antibes, Races at Ascot,* and *Boulevard at Nice.*

DU GARD, ROGER MARTIN. See MARTIN DU GARD, ROGER.

DUGGAR, BENJAMIN MINGE (1872–   ), American botanist, born in Gallion, Ala., and educated at Alabama Polytechnic Institute and at Harvard and Cornell unversities. From 1912 to 1927 he was research professor of plant physiology at Missouri Botanical Gardens and at Washington University, both in St. Louis. In 1927 he became professor of physiological and economic botany at the University of Wisconsin, and in 1943 professor emeritus. Later, while serving as consultant in mycological research and production at Lederle Laboratories, Inc., he was a codiscoverer of the antibiotic aureomycin.

DUGONG. See SIRENIA.

DU GUESCLIN, BERTRAND (1320?–80), Constable of France, born near Dinan, Brittany. He was known as "the Eagle of Brittany", and was one of the most celebrated French soldiers of his age. He joined the forces of Charles de Blois, Duke of Brittany, in 1342, and later fought in the war against the invading English. In 1356 he relieved Rennes, which was besieged by the Duke of Lancaster, and with his help the city held out until the truce of Bordeaux, in June, 1357. Later, Du Guesclin entered the service of the French kings, serving first under John II and then under Charles V, and was made lieutenant of Normandy and Count of Longueville in 1364. He was taken prisoner at the battle of Auray (1364) but was ransomed and became commander of one of the Grand Companies, which he led into Spain to aid Henry of Trastamara, later Henry II (q.v.), King of Castile, against Henry's half-brother Pedro the Cruel (q.v.). For his great services in establishing Henry upon the throne of Castile, Du Guesclin was made Constable of Castile and Duke of Molinas. In 1370 he was made Constable of France and for ten years was active and successful in driving the English from the south and west of the country. In 1373 he seized and held most of the strongholds in the Duchy of Brittany. He died while besieging the fortress of Châteauneuf-de-Randon.

DUHAMEL, GEORGES (1884–   ), French physician and writer (pen name Denis Thévenin), born in Paris, and educated at the University of Paris. While studying medicine he associated himself with such writers as Jules Romains and Charles Vildrac in the founding of a literary circle known as the *Abbaye.* This group established a printing press at Créteil and published the works of its members, including Duhamel's first published work, a volume of verse entitled *Des Légendes, des Batailles* (1907). Two subsequent books of poetry, *Selon Ma Loi* (1910) and *Les Compagnons* (1912), established Duhamel as a master of the verse medium. He also wrote several plays during this period; among those which were staged were *La Lumière* (1911) and *Dans l'Ombre des Statues* (1912). From 1914 to 1918 he served with the French Army as chief of a surgical unit. His war experience provided him with material which he used with vivid effect in the widely read novels *Vie des Martyrs* (1914–16; translated as *The New Book of Martyrs,* 1918) and *Civilisation* (1918), the latter of which was awarded the Goncourt Prize. His numerous additional writings include the two series of novels *Cycle de Salavin* (1920–32) and *Chronique des Pasquier* (1936); and many volumes of essays, including *Scènes de la Vie Future* (1930), a warning against the machine age, which was translated as *America, the Menace* (1931). After the outbreak of World War II he demonstrated his ardent anti-Nazi sentiments in such works as *Why France Fights* (1940) and *Lieu d'Asile* (1945). The novel *Cry Out of the Depths* (1954) is a penetrating study of a French collaborationist during the German occupation. Duhamel was named permanent secretary of the Académie Française in 1942, but resigned four years later.

DUIKER or **DUIKERBOK,** any of the small African antelopes of the subfamily Cephalophinae. They have large eyes and ears and two small, straight spikes on their convex foreheads, usually with a small tuft of stiff hairs between the spikes. Duikers rove in herds in the dense forests of South Africa and eat berries and small fruit.

The subfamily Cephalophinae is divided into three genera. In the genus *Cephalophus* the most numerous species is *C. grimmi,* which is variable in color and is about twenty-six inches tall. It roams throughout the southwestern forests of Africa, as do the banded duiker, *C. doriae,* and the wood antelope, *C. sylvicultor.* Another member of this genus is the blaubok. The second genus, *Guevei,* contains the blue duikers, pygmy antelopes of the Natal forests in southeastern Africa. They are generally about thirteen inches tall and bluish gray in color. The third genus, *Sylvicapra,* contains only one species, *S. grimmia,* found throughout South Africa. See ANTELOPE.

DUISBURG, city and port of North Rhine-Westphalia, West Germany, near the Belgian border, and at the confluence of the Ruhr and Rhine rivers, about 15 miles N. of Düsseldorf. Duisburg was formed in 1929 when the cities of Duisburg-Ruhrort and Hamborn were merged, and the site has become one of the largest river harbors in the world. Duisburg was known as *Castrum Deutonis* to the Romans, and as *Dispargum* under the Frankish kings. In the 12th century it ranked as an imperial free town, and joined the Hanseatic League in the 13th century. The Church of St. Salvator, constructed in the 15th century and containing the tomb of the geographer Mercator, is a notable example of Gothic architecture. Duisburg is the center of the Westphalian coal and iron trade and has large imports from the Americas and Sweden. Exports from the city are iron ore and coal, grain transported from other points, and the many commodities manufactured locally, such as steel and brass foundry products, machinery, chemicals, textiles, plate glass, soap, starch, sugar, margarine, and malt products. Duisburg is connected with Dortmund by the Rhine-Herne canal, and in turn with German North Sea ports via the Dortmund-Ems canal. The city was one of many in the Westphalia-Saar Basin region heavily bombed by the British in World War II. Following the war the city was included in the British zone of occupation. Pop. (1950) 410,783.

DUKAS, PAUL (1865–1935), French composer, born in Paris. He studied at the Paris Conservatory and in 1888 won the second prize in the competition for the Prix de Rome. In 1909 he became a teacher of composition at the Conservatory and in 1928 its director. Dukas' reputation as a composer rests principally on two works: the orchestral scherzo *L'Apprenti Sorcier* (first performance, 1897), a brilliant piece of program music based on a ballad by Goethe; and the opera *Ariane et Barbe Bleue,* one of the most important of modern French operas, performed in leading opera houses in Europe and the United States. Among other works by Dukas are the overtures *King Lear* (1883) and *Polyeucte* (1892), the *Symphony in C* (1896), the ballet *La Péri* (1912), the *Sonata in E-flat Minor* (1901) for piano, and the *Sonnet de Ronsard* (1924) for voice and piano.

DUKE UNIVERSITY, a coeducational institution of higher learning, located in Durham, N.C. The institution was founded as a secondary school in 1838, in Randolph County, N.C., and was granted power to confer degrees in 1852. It took the name of Trinity College in 1859 and moved to its present location in 1891. In 1924, through the liberal endowment of James Buchanan Duke, its facilities were extended and it attained the status of a university. The enlarged institution took the name of its benefactor as a condition of the endowment, but Trinity College remains a component undergraduate school for men. In addition, the university includes the co-ordinate Woman's College, a graduate school, and schools of engineering, law, forestry, nursing, divinity, and medicine. Among the periodicals issued by the university press are *Law and Contemporary Problems, Journal of Parapsychology, Duke Mathematical Journal,* and *The South Atlantic Quarterly.* In 1953–54 there were 4766 students enrolled, all attending classes full time; the faculty numbered 621, and the library contained 1,085,000 volumes.

DUKHOBORS (Russ. *dukhobortsy,* "spirit wrestlers"), name applied to a nonconformist sect of Russian peasantry. They were so called as early as 1785 by the priests of the Russian Orthodox Church, who employed the term disparagingly to describe the Dukhobors as fighters against the spirit of God. The Dukhobors were content for a considerable time to accept the term at its literal significance and use it as their name, but eventually they decided to call themselves "Christians of the Universal Brotherhood". Basing their belief on the premise that all human beings were brothers and equals, they refused to acknowledge any worldly ruler or to participate in military service, and, in consequence, were banished in 1840 to the Caucasus near the Turkish border. They built this sterile territory into a flourishing community, but in 1887 Czar Alexander III introduced universal conscription into the Caucasus and Dukhobors were subjected to violent persecution. Their sufferings were eventually alleviated through the efforts of the Russian writer Leo Tolstoi and of the Society of Friends in England, and in 1898 they were permitted to emigrate to British territory. In the summer of that year, 1126 members of the sect sailed for Cyprus, where the community intended to settle. However, sufficient money later became available to take two other parties, totaling over 4000, to Canada in January, 1899; these were eventually joined by the Cyprus party, and by about 2000 other Dukhobors from the Caucasus, totaling in all some 7500 members of the sect. The Canadian government granted them territory in the provinces of Saskatchewan and Assiniboia, and in 1902 they were joined by their leader, Verigin, who had just been released from exile in Siberia. Except for some disagreements with the Canadian government, occasioned from time to time by the Dukhobor refusal to accept any authority but that of their leader, or of his son and successor Peter Verigin, the sect has lived peacefully and has developed flourishing communities in Canada. In recent years, Dukhobor colonies have settled in Mexico and in various parts of Russia.

DULCAMARA. See BITTERSWEET.

DULLES, JOHN FOSTER (1888–   ), American statesman, born in Washington, D.C., and educated at Princeton and George Washington universities and at the University of Paris. He began to practice law in New York City in 1911, and subsequently became known as an authority on international law. In 1945 he was a member of the U.S. delegation to the founding conference of the United Nations at San Francisco, and he later served as a U.S delegate to the U.N. and as an adviser at meetings (1945 and 1947) of the Council of Foreign Ministers. He was appointed U.S. senator from New York in 1949 to complete the unexpired term of Senator Robert F. Wagner. As U.S. ambassador-at-large, Dulles negotiated the terms of the Japanese peace treaty signed in 1951; See WORLD WAR II: *Peace Treaties.* Dulles became secretary of state in the cabinet of President Dwight David Eisenhower in January, 1953. He wrote *War or Peace* (1950).

DULSE, or DILCE, common name for several edible red algae which grow on rocky marine coasts. It is used as a food or condiment in several parts of the world, especially the Orient. Purple seaweeds of the genus *Porphyra,* sometimes called laver, are the most widely used for this purpose. *P. laciniata* is grown in large quantities in Japan. *Rhodymenia palmata,* which is eaten in the British Isles and in other northern countries, has a purple, leathery frond. *Iridaea edulis,* eaten in s.w. England and Scotland, has a succulent, dull-purple frond. Compare CARRAGEEN.

DULUTH, county seat of St. Louis **Co.,** Minn., and port of entry. It is situated at the western extremity of Lake Superior, on the N. bank of the estuary of the St. Louis R., opposite Superior Wis., and about 150 miles N.E. of Minneapolis. Duluth is the third largest city in Minnesota and, in terms of volume of cargo handled, the leading port on the Great Lakes. Duluth and Superior share an excellent natural harbor, 19 sq.m. in area and almost completely landlocked. Entrance to the harbor is afforded by broad channels through Minnesota and Wisconsin points, enclosing the harbor. Vessels drawing up to 22 feet of water have access to all parts of the port, including the estuary of the St. Louis R. The site of Duluth, 62.3 sq.m. in area, occupies ground which slopes upward from the lake and river fronts to an elevation of 600 feet. A modern boulevard, Skyline Parkway, extends along the crest of this bluff for a distance of 25 m., providing an unobstructed view of Lake Superior and the city. Among points of interest in Duluth are the Civic Center, comprising the City Hall, the Court House, and the Federal Building; the Public Library; the John Jacob Astor Trading Post, near the s.w. city limits, a replica of the stockade and blockhouses established in that vicinity early in the 19th century by the noted fur trader; the Aerial Lift Bridge, 510 ft.

Duluth Chamber of Commerce

Downtown Duluth, Minnesota. Wisconsin shore is seen across Lake Superior in background.

long, which spans the Minnesota Point entrance to the Duluth-Superior harbor; the Zoological Gardens; and Minnesota Point, site of a United States Naval Training Station and a United States Coast Guard Station. The city has more than 100 churches.

Duluth has various educational and cultural facilities including a modern public-school system, sixteen parochial schools, and a junior college. Schools of higher learning are the Duluth Branch of the University of Minnesota, with 1150 students (1953) and the College of St. Scholastica, a Roman Catholic school for women, founded in 1912. Among the cultural institutions are the Children's Museum and Art Center, which contains natural history, ethnological, and industrial exhibits; the Bible House, with an outstanding collection of old Bibles and religious art objects; and the Duluth Symphony Orchestra. Three daily newspapers, one in the Finnish language, are published in the city.

The Duluth park system comprises more than 3200 acres, and has facilities for swimming, boating, fishing, golf, and other recreational activities. Superior National Forest, the largest in the United States, is easily accessible from the city. Duluth is the coolest large city in the United States during the summer season (having then a mean temperature of about 63°F.) and is popular as a summer resort.

Duluth attained pre-eminence as an inland port primarily because of its proximity to the Vermilion, Cuyuna, and Mesaba iron ranges,

the sources for most of the iron ore produced in the United States. Virtually all of the ore from these ranges is transported by rail to the port for transshipment to points east. The port is also the center of a region producing vast amounts of grain, which ranks second only to iron ore among cargoes moving through the city. In addition, large amounts of coal are received at the port. The port is equipped with extensive cargo-handling facilities, including seven iron-ore-loading docks with a total storage capacity of nearly 820,000 tons, 25 grain elevators with a capacity of nearly 50,000,000 bushels, 21 coals docks, 46 general-cargo piers, and a cement elevator. Duluth harbor is open to navigation from about the middle of April to the middle of December, when it is usually closed by ice. Rail connections with important Canadian and American points are provided by eight major railway systems, including the Great Northern, the Northern Pacific, and the Canadian National. Four of the systems operate lines to the iron-ore fields. In a recent year, more than 53,000,000 tons of water-borne cargo were moved through the port of Duluth.

Next to shipping, the most important industry of Duluth is manufacturing. The city produces a broad variety of products, notably steel and iron, cement, paper, leather products, food products, machinery, flour, lumber, railway equipment, glass products, and textiles.

French fur traders were active in the vicinity of what is now Duluth as early as

1660. In 1679, Sieur Duluth, the French explorer from whom the city takes its name, visited the region. Although John Jacob Astor established a trading station near the site of Duluth in 1817, the first permanent settlement was not founded until 1853. Four years later Duluth received its charter as a town. In 1870 it was incorporated as a city, its population then being about 3130. By 1900 the population of Duluth had increased to 52,969. Pop. (1950) 104,511.

DULWICH, district and parliamentary division in the s. part of Camberwell Borough, London, England, 4 miles s.e. of Saint Paul's Cathedral. The division, which forms a suburb of London, is the site of Dulwich College and of Alleyn's School, both of which developed from the College of God's Gift, founded in 1619 by the actor Edward Alleyn. The college contains a notable art gallery, bequeathed by Sir P. F. Bourgeois in 1811. Pop. (1931) 60,643.

DUMA, in Russian history, the lower house of parliament of the Russian Empire, established (Oct. 30, 1905) by Czar Nicholas II during and as a result of the Revolution of 1905. See RUSSIA: *History.* Under the ukase of March 5, 1906, the parliament consisted of the old Council of the Empire, which was converted into the upper house; and the Duma, or lower house. According to the ukase, no law could be passed without the consent of the assembly, but in practice this principle was rendered ineffective by political maneuvers. The members of the Duma were chosen by *electors,* who in turn were elected in six curias, or subdivisions: large landowners, small landowners, capitalists, middle class, laboring class, and peasantry. Each group was represented according to its political influence in the Empire, rather than according to its relative size. Thus, in the first Duma, the large land-owning class, which numbered about 200,000, chose 2594 electors, whereas the 70,000,000 peasants chose only 1168. Demands of the Duma, such as to have the widespread persecution of the Jews brought to an end, were ignored by the government. When shortly the Duma began to criticize governmental policy and action, it was promptly dissolved, after having been in existence for 73 days. The second Duma was convened in the following year (1907). The government had meanwhile declared a large number of the liberal and socialist electors of the first Duma ineligible, and consequently the second Duma was more conservative. Nevertheless, the second Duma was also dissolved, after 103 days, for opposing the arrest of several members by the Czar's police. For the third Duma, which sat from 1907 to 1912, the electorate was considerably changed. Polish districts lost two thirds of their representation, and that of the peasantry and the workers of the large cities was diminished. The fourth Duma, composed almost entirely of land owners, retired military officers, and members of the clergy, convened in 1912, served through World War I, and was replaced by the Provisional Government during the Revolution in 1917.

DUMAS, ALEXANDRE, known as DUMAS PÈRE (1803–70), French novelist and playwright, the son of the French general Alexandre Dumas, born at Villers-Cotterets, France. He had little formal education. He worked as a clerk, first to a notary and then in the service of the Duke of Orléans, studying French history in his spare time. The performances in Paris of an English Shakespearean company, headed by Charles Kemble, inspired him to write for the theater. His first works to be produced were the vaudevilles *La Chasse et l'Amour* (1825) and *La Noce et l'Enterrement* (1826), both written in collaboration with other authors. The Comédie-Française produced his play *Henri III et Sa Cour* in 1829, and an earlier work, the romantic drama, *Christine,* in 1830. These plays established Dumas' reputation as a dramatist. They were followed by numerous works for the theater, for which he is best known in France, and by the historical novels for which he is even more famous outside of France (see MONTE-CRISTO,

Alexandre Dumas, père

The Count of; Three Musketeers, The). He was a prolific writer, and about 1200 volumes were published under his name. Although many of these works were the result of collaboration or were the production of a fiction factory in which hired writers completed or executed his ideas, almost all of the writing bears the unmistakable imprint of his personal genius and inventiveness. His earnings were enormous but scarcely sufficient in his later years to sustain his extravagant style of living, which involved the maintenance of an estate called Monte-Cristo and a horde of attendant parasites, or to compensate for the losses incurred in the operation of a theater devoted chiefly to his own plays and of several newspapers. He died in comparative poverty. His works include the plays *Antony* (1831), *Teresa la Tour de Nesle* (1832), *Angèle* (1833), *Catherine Howard* (1834), *Don Juan de Marana* (1836), *L'Alchimiste* (1839), *Lorenzino* (1842), and *L'Orestie* (1856), as well as numerous dramatizations of his own fiction; and the novels *Le Capitaine Paul* (1838), *John Davis, le Capitaine Pamphile* (1840), *Les Trois Mousquetaires* (1844), *Vingt Ans Après* (1845), *Dix Ans Plus Tard ou le Vicomte de Bragelonne* (1848–50), *Le Comte de Monte-Cristo* (1844), *La Reine Margot* (1845), *Le Chevalier de Maison-Rouge* (1846), *Mémoirs d'un Médecin* (1848), *Olympe de Clèves* (1852), *Les Mohicans de Paris* (1854), and *Les Compagnons de Jéhu* (1857).

DUMAS, Alexandre, known as Dumas fils (1824–95), French playwright and novelist, born in Paris. He was the natural son of Alexandre Dumas père. His first literary work was a volume of poetry, *Péchés de Jeunesse* (1847). The following year his first novel, *La Dame aux Camélias,* appeared, and his subsequent dramatization of this work, produced in 1852, established him as a success in the theater. Thereafter he enjoyed a prolific and rewarding career as a playwright, usually selecting for his themes some controversial aspect of sexual morality. His works include the novels *Tristan le Roux* (1849), *Henri de Navarre* (1850), *Diane de Lys* (1851, dramatized 1853), *La Dame aux Perles* (1854), and *L'Affaire Clémenceau* (1866); and the plays *Le Demi-Monde* (1855), *La Question d'Argent* (1857), *Le Fils Naturel* (1858), *Un Père Prodigue* (1859), *L'Ami des Femmes* (1864), *Monsieur Alphonse* (1873), *La Princesse de Bagdad* (1881), and *Francillon* (1887).

DUMAS, Jean Baptiste André (1800–84), French chemist, born in Alais. He became a tutor at the École Polytechnique in Paris in 1823, and then professor of chemistry in the Athenaeum. He founded the École Centrale des Arts et Manufactures. Later, he was professor of chemistry at the Sorbonne. He was made a member of the Académie des Sciences in 1832, and became its perpetual secretary in 1868. From 1849 to 1851 he was minister of agriculture and commerce.

Dumas showed that the molecular weight of certain organic compounds is directly proportional to the vapor density of the compound, and, using this principle, he devised a valuable method for determining molecular weights. He formulated a theory on substitution, after observing that the properties of certain organic compounds were little changed when their hydrogen was replaced by an equivalent quantity of chlorine. Dumas also devised a method for the quantitative determination of nitrogen in organic substances (see Analysis, Organic). He wrote *Traité de Chimie Appliquée aux Arts* (8 vols., 1828–45) and *Leçons sur la Philosophie Chimique* (1837).

DU MAURIER, Daphne (1907–), English author, born in London, and educated privately in Paris. She is the daughter of the actor-manager Sir Gerald du Maurier, about whom she wrote *Gerald, a Portrait* (1934). Her work is characterized by colorful backgrounds, usually historical, and by melodramatic action. Among her other writings are *The du Mauriers* (1937); the novels *Jamaica Inn* (1936), *Rebecca* (1938), *Frenchman's Creek* (1941), *Hungry Hill* (1943), *Parasites* (1950), *My Cousin Rachel* (1952), and *Mary Anne* (1954); the play *The Years Between* (1945); and the collection of short stories *Kiss Me Again, Stranger* (1953).

DU MAURIER, George Louis Palmella Busson (1834–96), English artist and novelist, born in Paris, and educated in Paris and at University College, London. He became an analytical chemist in Bucklersbury, but in 1856 left for the Paris Latin Quarter to devote himself to painting. Later he continued his artistic training in Antwerp. While there he lost the sight of one eye, but was able to continue using his talents as a graphic artist. In 1858 he began drawing for *Punch's Almanac.* His caricatures for *Punch, One Week,* and the *Cornhill Magazine,* in which he satirized the middle and upper classes, are of historical value in portraying the fashionable social life of his time. He illustrated *Ballads* and *Henry Esmond* by William Makepeace Thackeray; and works by Henry James, George Meredith, and Elizabeth Gaskell. He wrote and illustrated the novels *Peter Ibbetson* (1891) and *Trilby* (1894), both of which were successfully dramatized; the former was used as a theme for an American opera by Deems Taylor.

DUMBARTON OAKS, a former private estate in Washington, D.C., now owned by Harvard University. In 1944 it was the site of the conversations, conducted by representatives of the United States, China, Great Britain, and the Soviet Union, which resulted in the Dumbarton Oaks Proposals. These constituted the basic plan from which the Charter of the United Nations (q.v.) was developed at the San Francisco Conference in 1945. The estate was deeded to Harvard in 1940 by Robert Woods Bliss, a former ambassador to Argentina, and his wife. Among its notable features are a library and art collection consisting of early Christian, Byzantine, and medieval works, used for advanced research by students of the university.

DUMFRIES, county town and river port of Dumfriesshire, Scotland, on the River Nith, 9 m. from its mouth in the Solway Firth, and about 73 miles s.s.w. of Edinburgh. The town is built on rising ground surrounded, except toward the sea, by undulating hills. Manufactures in Dumfries include tweeds, hosiery, gloves, and neckties. The town is a market for livestock and hareskins. Oilseed cake, beans, and fertilizers are imported. Amalgamated with Dumfries since 1929 is Maxwelltown, on the opposite bank of the Nith. Three bridges and a railway viaduct link the two localities. One of the connecting bridges is a massive stone structure, constructed in 1280 by order of Devorguila, the mother of John de Baliol (q.v.). In the chapel of the Greyfriars monastery, also built by order of Devorguila, Robert Bruce killed Red John Comyn (q.v.). The churchyard of St. Michael's in Dumfries is the burial place of Robert Burns; other places associated with the Scottish poet include the house in which he died, and the Theatre Royal, where several of his prologues and epilogues were enacted. In the neighborhood of the town are Lincluden Abbey, described by Burns as "an old ruin in a sweet situation", and the ruins of Carraverock Castle, which is said to be the Ellangowan of Sir Walter Scott's novel *Guy Mannering.* Dumfries is believed to occupy the site of an ancient British fortress. It has been a royal burgh since the time of William the Lion (q.v.). Pop. (1951 prelim.) 26,320.

DUMFRIESSHIRE, border county of Scotland. It has 21 m. of coast line on the Solway Firth, toward which its surface slopes from the northern portion, which is mountainous. The county contains extensive tablelands and rich bottom lands. Near the Solway are tracts of moss land, such as Lochar Moss and Nutberry Moss, which were once under water but have been reclaimed through drainage. The county is divided into three districts (Nithsdale, Annandale, and Eskdale) by the rivers Nith, Annan, and Esk, which run N. and S. The principal lakes are Loch Skene in the N., a group around the town of Lochmaben, and Loch Urr in the W. The raising of cattle and exporting of cattle and cattle products to England is the principal industry. At Langholm (pop., 1951 prelim., 2403) and Annan (4631) are distilleries; at Dumfries (q.v.) the county seat, and at Langholm are woolen and hosiery mills. Salmon fisheries are located along the Solway Firth and the Nith and Annan rivers. Lead is mined at Wanlockhead; limestone is quarried at Keir and Carmertrees. The coal deposits at Sanquhar and Rowanburn were once worked but are no longer considered of economic importance. Among the antiquities of Dumfriesshire are the ruins of Roman stations at Birrens (q.v.) and the Castle of Carlaverock near Dumfries. Area of county, 1073 sq.m.; pop. (1953 est.) 87,100.

DUMONT, ALBERT. See SANTOS-DUMONT.

DUMONT D'URVILLE, JULES SÉBASTIEN CÉSAR (1790–1842), French naval officer and explorer, born at Condé-sur-Noireau, Normandy. In 1820, on an expedition to the Grecian Archipelago, he recognized a then recently unearthed Greek statue, now known as the "Venus de Milo", as an ancient masterpiece and secured its acquisition by the French government. In 1822 he served aboard the *Coquille,* which circumnavigated the globe. Three years later he was given command of the vessel, renamed the *Astrolabe,* and was commissioned to find traces of the lost explorer Count de la Pérouse (q.v.). Between 1826 and 1829 d'Urville traversed the southern Australian coast, charted parts of New Zealand, and visited New Guinea, New Caledonia, and other islands in the western Pacific. At Vanikoro Island, in the Santa Cruz group, north of the New Hebrides, he found evidence that la Pérouse and the ship's company had been massacred by natives. On d'Urville's return, he was promoted to the rank of full captain. He embarked with the *Astrolabe* and *Zélée* in 1837, on an expedition to the South Polar regions. In 1838 he discovered Palmer Land, and then Joinville Island off its northern extremity. He refitted in Talcahuano, Chile, made explorations of the New Guinea

Jean Henri Dunant

and Borneo coasts, and in 1840 sailed from Hobart, Tasmania, for the Antarctic, where he discovered a coast which he called Adélie Land. This proved to be part of the continental mass and represents the French claim to the Antarctic continent. D'Urville Sea, off Adélie Land, and Cape d'Urville, Netherlands New Guinea, bear the explorer's name. D'Urville was appointed a rear admiral on his return from the Antarctic, and wrote accounts of his various voyages.

DUM PALM. See DOOM PALM.

DUNA. See DVINA, SOUTHERN.

DUNABURG. See DAUGAVPILS.

DUNANT, JEAN HENRI (1828–1910), Swiss philanthropist and founder of the Red Cross, born in Geneva. Moved by the condition of the wounded he saw while traveling near the battlefield of Solferino in 1859, during the Franco-Austrian War, he wrote a book, *Un Souvenir de Solferino* (1862), suggesting that neutral organizations be established to aid wounded soldiers in time of war. His idea was supported by the Société Genevoise d'Utilité Publique, and in 1863 an international conference was held in Geneva. The Geneva Convention (q.v.) of 1864, planned by the meeting of 1863, established the permanent International Red Cross which was endorsed by ten governments. In 1901 Dunant shared the first Nobel Peace Prize with Frédéric Passy. Dunant devoted his entire fortune to charity. Among his writings are *L'Esclavage*

chez les Musulmans et aux États-Unis de L'Amérique (1863), *Fraternité et Charité Internationales en Temps de Guerre* (1864), and *La Rénovation de l'Orient* (1865).

DUNBAR, WILLIAM (1460?–1520?), Scottish poet, educated at St. Andrews University. He became a Franciscan friar and, after travels in England and France, was attached in 1500 to the court of James IV of Scotland. Dunbar was the outstanding Scottish poet influenced by the work of Chaucer. The robust humor, imagination, sharp satire, and invective of his poetry are shown best in *The Dance of the Sevin Deidly Synnis* (between 1503 and 1508). Among his other poems are *The Thrissill and the Rois,* composed in honor of Margaret Tudor and James IV of Scotland, *The Golden Targe, Lament for the Makaris, Flyting of Dunbar and Kennedie, The Twa Maryit Wemen and the Wedo,* and *Orisone.*

DUNBARTONSHIRE, county in the western midlands of Scotland. In the north and northwest portions are the Highlands, containing peaks rising from 2000 to 3200 ft. above sea level, and many scenic lakes, including Loch Lomond. In south Dunbartonshire the Kilpatrick Hills rise to 1300 ft. above sea level. Along the Clyde and Leven rivers in the south are the Lowlands, the location of many farms and dairies. The principal crop is oats. Sheep and cattle graze on the hills. Because of the purity and softness of the water of the Leven, many plants for the bleaching, dyeing, and printing of cloths and yarns have been built along the river. Other industries of Dunbartonshire are shipbuilding (see CLYDE-BANK), distilling, brewing, and coal mining. Found in the shire are the ruins of forts and mounds built by prehistoric peoples and the ruins of a wall built from the Firth of Forth to the River Clyde by order of the Roman emperor Antoninus Pius. In the Highlands are the glens where the Macgregors, the Macfarlanes, and other medieval Scottish clans made their homes, and from which they raided their neighbors in the Lowlands. The county seat is Dumbarton. Area of county, 244 sq.m.; pop. (1953 est.) 166,400.

DUNCAN, the name of two kings of Scotland. **1.** DUNCAN I (d. 1040), a grandson of King Malcolm II, whom he succeeded in 1034. Before his accession to the throne he was ruler of the kingdom of Strathclyde. Macbeth, who ruled the kingdom of Moray (q.v.) and served Duncan as a general, killed Duncan and became king of Scotland. The tragedy *Macbeth* by Shakespeare is based upon the struggle between the two kings. **2.** DUNCAN II

(d. 1094), son of Malcolm III by his first wife, and grandson of Duncan I. In 1093, after being held for some time as a hostage in Normandy, he deposed his uncle Donald Bane from the Scottish throne. Duncan ruled a year before he was killed by emissaries of Donald Bane, who was then restored to the throne.

DUNCAN, Isadora (1878–1927), American dancer, born in San Francisco. She is noted for her creation of new dance techniques based largely on the dances of the ancient Greeks. Her dancing was characterized by free and flowing movements expressive of deep inner emotion and intended to portray the movements of such natural forces as waves, winds, birds, and insects. At first she met strong opposition, chiefly from adherents of the ballet (q.v.), with its conventions and restrictions, but eventually her kind of dancing came into wide favor. It had great influence on the Russian ballet, and also became the progenitor of a new type of dancing, popular today, known as "interpretive dancing" (see Dancing: *Interpretive Dancing*). She established schools near Berlin (1904), in Paris (1914), in Moscow (1921), and in other localities, and toured Europe and America in dance recitals with her pupils, who were known as "Duncan dancers". Her personal life was tragic, being marked by an unfortunate marriage terminated by divorce; the death of two children by drowning; early poverty, and in her last years, great financial difficulties; and her own death in an automobile accident. She is the author of an autobiography, *My Life* (1926–27).

DUNDEE, royal and parliamentary burgh, and seaport of Angus, E. Scotland, on the Firth of Tay, 59 m. by rail N.E. of Edinburgh. Dundee, the fourth-largest city of Scotland, extends for more than 4 m. along the water front; its docks, accessible in all tides, are about 12 m. from the North Sea. Town Churches, housing three separate churches (St. Mary's, St. Paul's, and St. Clement's) under the same roof, is one of Dundee's interesting landmarks. The city was built as a royal burgh by William the Lion about the year 1200. In 1889, Queen Victoria granted city status to Dundee, through royal charter. Products manufactured in the city are iron castings, machine tools, lumber, coarse linen and jute fabrics, boots and shoes, meal, flour, confectionery products, and ale. In addition, bleaching and dyeing is carried on. Dundee was formerly important as a whaling and seal-fishing center. Pop. (1953 est.) 177,200.

DUNDEE, Viscount. See Graham, John.

DUNDONALD, Thomas Cochrane, 10th Earl of. See Cochrane, Thomas.

DUNEDIN, capital of Otago Province, South Island, New Zealand, situated on Otago Harbor, 15 m. from the Pacific Ocean. The city was founded in 1848 under the auspices of the Free Church of Scotland, the site having been selected because of its fine harbor. Dunedin increased in importance, especially after 1861, when the discovery of gold in the neighborhood attracted thousands of settlers from Australia. Dunedin is the seat of Otago University, containing faculties of arts, medicine, chemistry, and mineralogy; and a teachers' training college. The city is a rail center. Industry is chiefly the manufacture of woolen goods. Gold mining, sheep and cattle raising, and the processing of dairy products are the principal occupations in the surrounding region. Most of these commodities are exported; coal, timber, and manufactured goods are the leading imports. Pop. (1953) 97,900.

DUNE VEGETATION, plants which grow on dunes. Although dune vegetation is commonly regarded as being composed only of *xerophytes* (plants specially adapted to grow under conditions of severe drought or high salt concentration), *mesophytes* (plants water availability) are commonly found upon adapted to grow under conditions of medium dunes, thriving even on those that have been established for centuries.

Both the absence of water and the instability of the sand in a dune make the initial establishment of vegetation difficult. Upon such shifting areas, the most successful species are those able to withstand submergence because of their underground stems, which root at frequent intervals and so extend over wide areas. Sand weeds of the genus *Ammophila,* which are common beach plants (q.v.), are the best-adapted dune plants. They are found throughout the northern hemisphere and are often planted to aid in preventing dunes from moving. Among woody plants capable of growing on dunes are various species of small willows; shrubby cherries and sumacs are also abundant in many dune areas of the United States.

DUNFERMLINE, city and royal burgh in the county of Fife, Scotland, 3 m. from the N. shore of the Firth of Forth and about 16 m. by rail N.W. of Edinburgh. The city is cut from N. to S. by Pittencrieff glen, a deep ravine at the bottom of which flows the stream Lyne Burn. Dunfermline dates from about the 9th century, when the Culdees, early Celtic monks, maintained an abbey on the site. In 1070

Malcolm Canmore, king of Scotland, and Margaret, his queen, were married there. King Robert Bruce of Scotland granted the city a royal charter in 1322. In Dunfermline Abbey, next to Iona, are said to be interred most of Scotland's royal dead.

The American industrialist Andrew Carnegie, born in Dunfermline in 1835, donated to the city a public library, public baths, the estate of Pittencrieff park and glen, and a trust fund of some £750,000 for the maintenance of the park, the endowment of a theater, and the promotion of the general interests of the townspeople. Dunfermline is now the headquarters of all Carnegie trusts in Scotland. The chief occupation in the city is the manufacture of fine Damask table linen. Other industries are bleaching and dyeing, and the manufacture of brass and iron castings, pottery, ale, soap, and cordage. Numerous coal mines are in the vicinity of Dunfermline. Pop. (1953 est.) 45,300.

DUNG BEETLE. See SCARAB.

DUNKERS. See CHURCH OF THE BRETHREN.

DUNKIRK (Fr. *Dunkerque*), a seaport in the department of Nord, France, on the Strait of Dover, 28 miles N.E. of Calais. It is connected by railway and canal with the principal coal, industrial, and agricultural centers of Belgium and France. Dunkirk is a leading seaport of France, and is the headquarters of large herring and codfishing fleets. The harbor, which is approached by a natural roadstead, is accessible to the largest vessels. Industries in Dunkrik include the manufacture of soap, starch, beer, beet sugar, cordage, and leather. The town also contains metal foundries, distilleries, flour and saw mills, petroleum refineries, and shipyards. Dunkirk owes its origin to a church built in the 7th century by St. Eloi, patron saint of goldsmiths, in the midst of sand dunes; hence the town's name, meaning "Church on the Dunes". Historically Dunkirk shared the fortunes of Flanders, coming successively under Burgundian, Austrian, and Spanish rule. It was taken by the English in 1658, and sold by Charles II to France in 1662. By the Treaty of Utrecht in 1713 the French were compelled to destroy the fortifications of Dunkirk, which were restored, however, in 1783. In World War I the port was the object of constant attacks by the Germans, principally by air, because of its importance as an antisubmarine base. In World War II, during the Battle of France, May-June, 1940, Dunkirk was the site of one of the great military feats of history, when over 335,000 men were evacuated by small British craft, while under constant German fire and air attack. Though successful in saving an army, the evacuation represented one of the great Allied disasters of the war. Pop. of town (1947) 10,575.

DUN LAOGHAIRE or **DUNLEARY,** formerly KINGSTON, a seaport in County Dublin, Republic of Ireland, situated on the s. side of Dublin Bay, 15 miles S.E. of the city of Dublin. The town received the name of Kingston in 1821 in honor of a visit by King George IV. Dun Laoghaire was merely a fishing village prior to the construction of its large harbor between 1817 and 1859. The harbor covers about 250 acres, and varies in depth from 10 to 28 ft. according to the tide. Cattle, lead ore, and granite are exported; coal, iron, timber, corn, and foodstuffs are the chief items of import. Fishing is still an important occupation of the townspeople. Pop. (1946) 44,674.

DUNLAP, WILLIAM (1766–1839), American playwright, painter, and art historian, born at Perth Amboy, N.J. He studied art in London under Benjamin West in 1784, and, after painting for a time, turned to writing plays. Dunlap was the first American professional playwright, and is called the "Father of Am(rican Drama" (see DRAMA: *American Drama*). His first successful play was *The Father of an Only Child* (1789). Thereafter he wrote or adapted sixty additional plays, among which are *Leicester* (1794) and *Fontainville Abbey* (1795). In 1796 he became one of the managers of the John Street Theatre, New York City, and two years later became sole director of the New Park Theatre in the same city. In 1805 bankruptcy ended his managerial career and in 1816 he resumed his career as a painter. He became one of the foremost American painters of religious subjects. In 1826 he was one of the founders of the National Academy of Design. Among his paintings are "Calvary", "Christ Rejected", and "Bearing of the Cross' Dunlap was the author of *History of the American Theatre* (1832) and *History of the Rise and Progress of the Arts of Design in the United States* (1834), both important sources for the study of early American culture.

DUNMORE, JOHN MURRAY, 4th EARL OF (1732–1809), Scottish colonial governor in North America. He was a member of the British House of Lords from 1761 to 1770 as a representative peer of Scotland. In 1770 he was appointed governor of New York, and in 1771 he became governor of Virginia. He dissolved the Virginia House of Assembly in 1772, in 1773, and again in 1774 upon its resolution to observe June 1, the day of the closing of the port of Boston (see BOSTON PORT BILL), as a time of public fast. A war between the Indians and Virginians in 1774, which he is said to have incited, is called Dunmore's War. In April, 1775, he removed a part of the powder stores from Williamsburg to the British warship *Magdalen*. Thereupon the colonists organized an armed resistance, under the leadership of Patrick Henry. During a session of the colonial legislature in June, a riot occurred, and Dunmore transferred the seat of government to the British man-of-war *Fowey*, 12 miles off Yorktown. The colonial burgesses declared that he had abdicated, and vested a committee of safety with executive powers. Dunmore equipped a flotilla, with which he unsuccessfully attacked Hampton. He burned Norfolk on Jan. 1, 1776. Later that year, driven by the Americans from his station on Gwynn's Island, Chesapeake Bay, he sent his fleet to the West Indies, and returned to England. From 1787 to 1796 he was governor of the Bahamas.

DUNN, OSCAR JAMES (1820–71), American Negro soldier and politician, born a slave in Louisiana. At the age of twenty-one he escaped from his owners. He served in the Union Army during the Civil War and became a captain in a regiment of Negro troops, but resigned his commission when an incompetent white man was placed over him as major. After the war he took an active part in the reconstruction measures in Louisiana and became lieutenant governor in 1868. He was the first Negro to hold an important public executive office in the United States.

DUNNE, FINLEY PETER (1867–1936), American humorist, born in Chicago, Ill. He was on the editorial staff of the Chicago *Evening Post* and Chicago *Times-Herald* from 1892 to 1897, and editor of the Chicago *Journal* from 1897 to 1900. He first attracted attention while on the *Times-Herald* with the publication of a series of sketches concerning the opinions and adventures of a humorous, prolix, Irish saloonkeeper called "Mr. Dooley". These were subsequently (1898) collected into a book, *Mr. Dooley in Peace and in War*, which enjoyed a wide popularity in America and England, and established "Mr. Dooley" as a household character. Mr. Dooley's adventures were continued in *Mr. Dooley in the Hearts of his Countrymen* (1898), *Mr. Dooley's Philosophy* (1900), *Mr. Dooley's Opinions* (1901), *Observations by Mr. Dooley* (1902), *Dissertations by Mr. Dooley* (1906), and *Mr. Dooley Says* (1910).

DUNNING, WILLIAM ARCHIBALD (1857–1922), American educator and historian, born in Plainfield, N.J., and educated at Columbia University. He joined the faculty of that institution in 1886 and became professor of history, and political philosophy in 1904. From 1894 to 1903 he was also managing editor of the *Political Science Quarterly*. Dunning was president of the American Historical Association in 1913. His writings include *Essays on the Civil War and Reconstruction* (1898); *Reconstruction, Political and Economic* (1907); and *The British Empire and the United States* (1914).

DU NOÜY, PIERRE LECOMTE (1883–1947), French scientist, born at Paris, and educated at the Sorbonne. While an officer in the French army in 1915, he became acquainted with Alexis Carrel (q.v.), the famous French scientist, and through him became devoted to science. From 1920 to 1927 he was an associate member of the Rockefeller Institute in New York. After 1927 he conducted research at the Pasteur Institute in Paris, leaving in 1937 to become a director of the École des Hautes Études at the Sorbonne. In 1917 he formulated an equation to calculate the time required for complete healing of surface wounds. This was the first time that a biological process was completely described by a mathematical equation. Du Noüy wrote *Biological Time* (1937), and *Human Destiny* (1947).

DUNSANY, EDWARD JOHN MORETON DRAX PLUNKETT, 18th BARON (1878–   ), Irish poet, dramatist, and novelist, born in London. He was educated at Eton College and at Sandhurst, and served in the Boer War and World War I. In 1940–41 he was Byron Professor of Literature at Athens University, Greece. His works, characterized by mysticism and fantasy and drawn frequently from Celtic and Oriental mythology, include *The Gods of Pegana* (1905), *The Sword of Welleran* (1908), *A Dreamer's Tales* (1910), *Tales of War* (1918), *Unhappy Far-Off Things* (1919), *The King of Elfland's Daughter* (1924), *The Charwoman's Shadow* (1926), *Fifty Poems* (1929), *My Ireland* (1937), *Jorkens Has a Large Whiskey* (1940), *Guerrilla* (1944), and *The Year: A Poem* (1946); and the plays *The Glittering Gate* (1909), *The Gods of the Mountain* (1911), *A Night at an Inn* (1916), *If* (1921), *Alexander and Three Small Plays* (1925), *Plays for Earth and Air* (1937), and *A Glimpse from a Watch Tower* (1946).

DUNSINANE, one of the Sidlaw Hills, in the E. of Perthshire, Scotland, 7 miles N.E. of

Perth. It rises 1012 feet above sea level, and overlooks the Carse of Gowrie and the Tay valley. It is located in the area in which took place the action of Shakespeare's play *Macbeth*. On the summit of Dunsinane are the remains of "Macbeth's castle". Birnam Wood, where Macbeth was defeated by Siward, Earl of Northumbria, is located nearby.

DUNS SCOTUS, JOHN (1265?–1308?), Scottish scholastic theologian and philosopher, born in Duns, Scotland. He was also known as *Doctor Subtilis* (Lat., "the cunning teacher"), a title which was accorded him for his dialectic skill in his defense of the doctrine of the Immaculate Conception. He entered the Franciscan Order, and studied at Oxford, where, after about 1290, he lectured on the *Sententiæ* of Peter Lombard. He spent some time in Paris, returned to Oxford, and then went again to Paris, where by 1302 he became a lecturer and received his master's license. He was subsequently transferred to Cologne, where he died.

In his system of philosophy, Duns Scotus established the necessity of revelation on the ground that reason alone cannot demonstrate clearly and simply that the highest end of human existence is the intuition of God. Revelation is necessary, in addition to instinctive knowledge or philosophy, to enable man to know the fullness of truth, and, on the basis of this knowledge, to fulfill his eternal destiny. Revelation therefore supplements and perfects natural knowledge, and consequently no contradiction can exist between them. The object of theology is God, by reason of his Godliness, whereas philosophy treats of God only in so far as He is the first cause of things. Theology is a practical science, directed not so much toward the dissipation of ignorance as toward the furtherance of man's salvation. The incorruptibility and immortality of the human soul, Duns Scotus held, is a truth of faith, which cannot be demonstrated by reason. He was a realist in philosophy, and yet maintained that universals need not be differentiated to become individuals; see NOMINALISM. Individuality is original, and the universal, while pre-existing in God's plan, has real existence only in the individual; by abstraction, the human mind takes from the individual the ideal of the universal. The supreme function of mind is, in the philosophy of Duns Scotus, not thought, as in that of Thomas Aquinas, but will; and he maintained his position by pointing out that thought presupposes the exercise of will in attention. Will is free, he taught, and not determined by motives. This concept is true not only of men, but of God, Who therefore does not, as Thomas Aquinas asserted, command an action because He sees it to be good, but makes it good by commanding it.

Duns Scotus' beliefs had many adherents, but during the Renaissance the "Dunsmen", or followers of Duns, "raged in every pulpit" against the revival of classicism, and brought their name into such disrepute as obstructionists and cavilers that the term "dunce" became synonymous with "sophist", "pedant", and, finally, "blockhead". The most famous of Duns Scotus' works are his philosophic grammar, his commentaries on the Bible and Aristotle, and his commentary on the *Sententiæ* of Peter Lombard (12 vols., 1639).

DUNSTABLE or **DUNSTAPLE,** JOHN (1370?–1453), English mathematician and composer, born probably at Dunstable, Bedfordshire. Practically nothing is known of his life and, until the end of the 19th century, little was known concerning his work. At that time, however, works by Dunstable were found in libraries at Oxford, Modena, Bologna, Rome, and Dijon. Especially important in giving musicologists information of Dunstable's achievements were his compositions, which formed part of a collection of six manuscript volumes of 15th-century music discovered by the German church musicologist Franz Xaver Haberl in the cathedral of Trento, Italy. Through such discoveries, it was established that Dunstable was the leading English composer of the early 15th century, and that the art of music, particularly of church music, was well developed in England at that time. Dunstable was reputedly the first composer to write instrumental accompaniments to church music and the first to write elaborate music about a cantus firmus. Among his works are masses, motets, antiphons, and songs, including the three-part song *O Rosa Bella*.

DUNSTAN, SAINT (925?–988), English prelate and statesman, born near Glastonbury, and educated by Irish pilgrims. Accused of practicing black arts, he was expelled from King Athelstan's court. After a serious illness, he became a monk and lived as a hermit until Edmund, Athelstan's successor, recalled him to court and appointed him abbot of Glastonbury about 943. He rebuilt the abbey, and under his administration it became a famous school. After Edred succeeded to the throne, Dunstan was virtually ruler of the kingdom and instituted policies of political unification, the establishment of royal authority, and religious reforms. When Edwy became king in 955, Dunstan fell into disfavor for opposing his marriage and was banished from the country. He was recalled by Edwy's successor, Edgar, in 958, and became successively Bishop of Worcester (958), Bishop of London (959), and Archbishop of Canterbury (961). He was again the most influential figure in the kingdom and introduced monastic reforms based on a strict observance of the Benedictine rule; he rebuilt churches, and promoted education. On the death of Edgar, Dunstan succeeded in placing Edgar's son Edward on the throne, but with the latter's murder in 975, Dunstan's public career ended and he retired to Canterbury.

DUNTON, THEODORE WATTS-. See WATTS-DUNTON.

DUODENUM. See INTESTINES.

DUPLEIX, MARQUIS JOSEPH FRANÇOIS (1697–1763), French colonial administrator, born at Landrecies. His father, a shareholder in the French East India Company, appointed him to a seat in the superior council at Pondicherry, French India, in 1720. Ten years later he became superintendent of French affairs at Chandernagore in Bengal. In 1742 he was appointed governor general of all the French possessions in India. The increase and discipline of his army, and his improvements in the defenses of Pondicherry, had already begun to alarm the English East India Company, when war broke out in Europe between France and England (1742). An attack on the English at Fort St. David failed, but Dupleix's military ability and courage were eminently displayed in the defense of Pondicherry (1748), which the British admiral Edward Boscawen attacked in force for five weeks without success. Dupleix had formed the project of founding a French empire in India, but his military designs were frustrated by the energy and military genius of the British generals Robert Clive and Henry M. Lawrence. The struggle continued until 1754, when Dupleix was recalled and repudiated by Louis XV, who desired peace with England. Dupleix died in obscurity, having spent his personal fortune in carrying out his policies.

DU PONT, name of a family of American industrialists of French ancestry, famous as the founders and major stockholders of E. I. du Pont de Nemours and Company, Inc., the largest manufacturer of chemical products and explosives in the world. Among the more famous members of the family were the following.

Pierre Samuel du Pont de Nemours

1. PIERRE SAMUEL DU PONT DE NEMOURS (1739–1817), French economist, born in Paris. His name was originally Dupont; he changed the form and later added "de Nemours" to avoid confusion with innumerable other Duponts in France. Only he and his sons used the full name. Du Pont was educated by his mother, and in his early twenties became a friend and disciple of François Quesnay (q.v.), leader of a group of economic theorists. The supporters of Quesnay's theories took the name of physiocrats (see ECONOMICS) from du Pont's book explaining Quesnay's doctrines, *Physiocratie, ou Constitution Naturelle du Gouvernement le Plus Avantageux du Genre Humain* (1768). Du Pont was made editor of the physiocrats' journal, *Les Ephémérides du Citoyen,* in 1768, but his articles favoring reforms, such as the abolition of slavery and of governmental restrictions on the country's economic life, aroused the government's anger, and he was forced to leave France. After traveling in Germany, Sweden, and Poland, where he served for a time as secretary of the Polish Council of Public Instruction, he was recalled to France in 1774 by Anne Robert Jacques Turgot (q.v.), who in that year became comptroller general of King Louis XVI. Two years later, Turgot was forced to resign, and du Pont left the government service. He returned at the request of Jacques Necker, who became finance minister in 1776. In 1782 he was entrusted by the Comte de Vergennes, then foreign minister, with the negotiations with England which led to Great Britain's recognition of U.S. independence in the following year, and the negotiation of a commercial treaty between France and England in 1786. The district of Nemours elected him to the States-General in 1789 and later to the Constituent Assembly, of which he was twice president. After the Assembly was dissolved (see FRANCE: *History*), he opened a printing and publishing business in Paris. His reactionary and Royalist views, particularly his defense of Louis XVI, led to his imprisonment by the Convention, and he narrowly escaped being guillotined. In 1799 he and his sons emigrated to the U.S., where he hoped to establish a colony in Virginia; the colony never materialized. Du Pont was well received in the United States. Thomas Jefferson, then president, asked him to prepare a plan for national education; the plan was not adopted in the U.S., but parts of it were later incorporated into the French education code. When Napoleon Bonaparte began to welcome the refugees from the French Revolution back to France, du Pont, in 1802, returned. He played an important role in the negotiations for the purchase of Louisiana from France by the U.S. and, later, was appointed president of the Paris Chamber of Commerce. After the defeat of Napoleon I, he became secretary of the provisional government preparing for the return of Louis XVIII to the French throne, but Napoleon's escape from Elba in 1815 forced him to take refuge with his sons in the U.S., and there he remained. Among his works were *Observations sur les Effets du Commerce des Grains* (1770), *Mémoires sur la Vie et les Ouvrages de Turgot* (1782), and *Philosophie de l'Univers* (1796).

2. VICTOR MARIE DU PONT DE NEMOURS (1767–1827), French diplomat, later American industrialist, the elder son of Pierre Samuel, born in Paris. He entered the French diplomatic service in 1787 as attaché to the French legation in the U.S., became first secretary of the legation in 1795, and, in the same year, was appointed French consul in Charleston, S.C. After returning to France, where he was for a time aide-de-camp to the Marquis de Lafayette, then commanding the French National Guard, he resigned from the government service. In 1799 he emigrated with his father to the U.S., where he was later naturalized. For a time he was a member of the Delaware legislature and a director of the Second Bank of the United States.

3. ÉLEUTHÈRE IRÉNÉE DU PONT DE NEMOURS (1771–1834), Franco-American industrialist,

the younger son of Pierre Samuel, born in Paris. He became a pupil of Antoine Laurent Lavoisier (q.v.) in 1787, and entered the royal powder mills at Essonne, where he was trained in the manufacture of gunpowder in order to succeed Lavoisier, eventually, as superintendent of the mills. When the French Revolution broke out, du Pont left the mills, and took charge of his father's printing business in Paris in 1791. He was a Royalist and, eight years later, emigrated with his father to the U.S. Noting the poor quality of gunpowder then manufactured in the U.S., he decided to manufacture explosives. He returned to France to get plans and models of French gunpowder machinery and to obtain financial support. In 1802 he began to manufacture gunpowder near Wilmington, Del. So successful were his operations that, at the time of his death, the du Pont factory was the largest of its kind in the U.S.

4. SAMUEL FRANCIS DU PONT (1803–65), American naval officer, the son of Victor Marie, born in Bergen Point, N.J. When he was twelve years old, he was appointed a midshipman in the U.S. Navy by President James Madison. By 1842, du Pont had reached the rank of commander, and in 1845 he was designated to assist in the organization and administration of the newly established U.S. Naval Academy at Annapolis. During the war between the U.S. and Mexico (1846–48), he commanded a ship, and in 1861 he was given command of the Federal fleet which was blockading the South Atlantic. In 1863 du Pont was ordered to attack Charleston, S.C. The Federal ships attacked and were repulsed with great losses; when the admiral was ordered to attack again, he refused on the ground that his forces were insufficient. He was relieved of his command and retired from active duty. Du Pont's name is commemorated in the city of Washington, D.C., by Congressional order in 1882; one of the most important traffic circles in the city was named Du Pont Circle, and a statue of him was erected there.

DUPRÉ, JULES (1811–89), French landscape painter, born in Nantes. His father was a manufacturer of porcelain, and young Dupré's earliest art training was received in decorating porcelain objects. Subsequently he studied art under various masters in Paris, where he was particularly influenced by the paintings in the Louvre of the Dutch landscape painters Meindert Hobbema and Salomon van Ruisdael. Dupré also admired the work of the contemporary French landscape artist Théodore

Rousseau, and became a member of the Barbizon School (q.v.) of painting, with which Rousseau was identified. A trip to England in 1834 enabled Dupré to study the paintings of John Constable, an experience which also helped to form his mature and individual style.

Dupré became one of the leaders of the Barbizon group, and is considered one of the founders of the modern French school of landscape painting. His work in general expresses the gloomy, the dramatic, and the tragic in nature; it is characterized by vivid and sharply contrasting colors, often applied in thick coatings (impasto). Among his paintings are "Morning" and "Evening" (both in the Louvre, Paris), "River Scene" (Tate Gallery, London), "Hay Wagon" and "The Old Oak" (Metropolitan Museum of Art, New York City), and "Barks Fleeing Before a Storm" (Art Institute of Chicago).

DUQUESNE, a city of Allegheny Co., Pa., situated on the Monongahela R., 10 miles S.E. of Pittsburgh. Duquesne is the site of one of the largest steel plants in the U.S. Other industries are the manufacture of cement, chemicals, and drugs. Duquesne was founded in 1885, incorporated as a borough in 1891, and chartered as a city in 1917. Pop. (1950) 17,620.

DURA MATER. See BRAIN.

DURAN, CAROLUS (1837–1917), French painter, born in Lille. He was also known as Auguste Émile Carolus-Duran; his real name was Charles Auguste Émile Durand. He studied at the Lille Academy of Art and at the École Suisse, Paris; his extensive copying of paintings of the old masters in the Louvre, particularly those of Lenoardo da Vinci and Velasquez, also helped form his style. Duran was chiefly a portrait painter and his best work is characterized by lifelike quality and vivid coloring. He was also a notable teacher; among his pupils were the American painters John Singer Sargent and Will Hicok Low. In 1905 Duran was elected a member of the French Institute and appointed director of the French Academy in Rome. Among his works are many portraits of women and children; portraits of contemporary personages, including Charles Gounod, Louis Pasteur, and Gustave Doré; and the paintings "The Assassination" and "Lady with a Dog" (both in the Lille Museum), "The Lady with the Glove" and "Evening on the Loire" (both in the Luxembourg Museum, Paris), and "Gloria Mariæ Medici" (decoration for a ceiling in the Louvre, Paris).

DURAND, ASHER BROWN (1796–1886), American engraver and painter, born in South Orange, N.J. He had instruction from the American engraver Peter Maverick, but was largely self-taught. He established his reputation as an engraver in 1823 with "The Signing of the Declaration of Independence" after the painting by the noted American artist John Trumbull. Subsequently Durand executed over fifty engraved portraits of contemporary personages, including General Andrew Jackson, Henry Clay, and a number of American Presidents. After 1835 he devoted himself chiefly to painting, at first executing principally figure pieces and portraits but subsequently specializing in landscape painting, chiefly of scenes along the valley of the Hudson River and in New England. With Thomas Cole he was the originator of the Hudson River school of painting (see PAINTING, AMERICAN). He was one of the founders of the National Academy of Design in 1828, and was its president from 1845 to 1861. Among Durand's works are the engraving "Ariadne" after the painting by the American artist John Vanderlyn; and the paintings "The Wrath of Peter Stuyvesant" (New York Historical Society), "Franconia Notch" (New York Public Library), "Mountain Forest" (Corcoran Gallery, Washington, D.C.), and "In the Woods" (Metropolitan Museum of Art, New York City).

DURAND, WILLIAM FREDERICK (1859–), American mechanical engineer, born at Bethany, Conn., and educated at the United States Naval Academy. He was professor of marine engineering at Cornell University from 1891 to 1904, and professor of mechanical engineering at Stanford University from 1904 to 1924. In 1945 he was awarded the medal of the American Society of Mechanical Engineers for his researches in hydrodynamics and aerodynamics. He wrote *Fundamental Principles of Mechanics* (1889), *Practical Marine Engineering* (1901), and *Hydraulics of Pipe Lines* (1921).

DURANGO, capital of the State of the same name in N. central Mexico. The S. and N. portions of the State are traversed by the western range of the Sierra Madre Mts. The climate in this region is cool, with moderate rainfall. On the plateau, which extends N. and E. from the base of the mountains, the climate is warm, with very little precipitation. The largest rivers are the Nazas and the Mezquital. In the mountains are important mineral deposits and extensive grazing ranges for livestock. The plateau contains fertile areas in which wheat, cotton, corn, tobacco, sugar cane, and grapes are grown. Durango is one of the principal mining regions of Mexico, noted for the production of silver, iron, copper, gold, tin, coal, cinnabar, and sulfur. The most important deposits of silver ore are located in the San Dimas district, which contains the famous Candelaria mine. The Cerro del Mercado, a hill near the city of Durango, is estimated to contain 300,000,000 tons of unusually pure iron ore.

The capital city, Victoria de Durango, or Durango, is situated in a fertile valley among the spurs of the Sierra Madre, 670 m. by rail N.W. of Mexico City. It is an important mining and commercial center, and contains iron foundries, cotton and woolen mills, sugar refineries, flour mills, tanneries, and tobacco factories. Durango was founded in 1563. In Spanish colonial times it was the capital of the province of Nueva Viscaya, which included the present States of Chihuahua and Durango. Other important towns are El Oro (pop. in 1940, 1800), and Guanaceví (2512). Area of State, 47,679 sq.m.; pop. (1950) 629,874. Pop. of city (1940) 33,412.

DURANT, WILL, in full WILLIAM JAMES (1885–   ), American philosopher and author, born in North Adams, Mass., and educated at St. Peter's College, Jersey City, and Columbia University. From 1907 until 1911, he taught Latin and French at Seton Hall College, South Orange, N.J. In 1917, he taught philosophy at Columbia University. He directed the Labor Temple School in New York City from 1914 until 1927, and became professor of philosophy at the University of California in Los Angeles in 1935. He wrote *The Story of Philosophy* (1926), *Transition* (1927), *On the Meaning of Life* (1932), *The Tragedy of Russia* (1933), *The Story of Civilization:* Part I, *Our Oriental Heritage* (1935), Part II, *The Life of Greece* (1939), Part III, *Caesar and Christ* (1944), Part IV, *The Age of Faith* (1950), and Part V, *The Renaissance* (1953).

DURAZZO. See DURRËS.

DURBAN, principal seaport of Natal Province, Union of South Africa, and one of the largest cities of the Union. It was established as a township in 1835 and named after Sir Benjamin D'Urban, governor of the Cape of Good Hope. Durban lies on the Bay of Natal, the Indian Ocean, about 40 miles S.E. of Pietermaritzburg, the capital of Natal. Port Natal, the name sometimes given to the harbor of the city, formerly was accessible only to small craft. However, a protective sea wall and pier were constructed, forming a channel entrance with an average depth of 35 to 40 ft. This entrance is kept free of silt and sand-

banks by the tide and by dredging operations. The harbor possesses a floating dock, a graving dock, and coal-loading facilities capable of handling five ships simultaneously. Nearby is the largest grain elevator in South Africa, with a storage capacity of 42,000 tons. The discovery of gold in 1884–86 in Natal was largely instrumental in the growth of Durban. Exports are chiefly coal, corn, wattle bark, wool, and sugar. Coastal whaling activities are centered in Durban, and most of the oil obtained is used in local soap factories. Pop. (1951) 475,026.

DURCHMUSTERUNG. See ARGELANDER; ASTRONOMY.

DÜREN (anc. *Dura* or *Duria*), town of North Rhine-Westphalia, West Germany, on the right bank of the Roer R., 19 m. by rail E. of Aachen and about 25 miles S.W. of Cologne. The Gothic church of St. Anna, said to contain a portion of the head of the saint, is the objective of many pilgrimages to Düren. The local museum has a natural-history collection, an art gallery, and many objects of antiquity. Iron castings, machinery, needles, textiles, paper, carpets, sugar, and alcoholic beverages are the principal products of Düren. After World War II, Düren was included in the British zone of occupation. Pop. (1946) 27,653.

DÜRER, ALBRECHT (1471–1528), German painter and engraver, born in Nuremberg. As a boy he worked with his father, a goldsmith; from 1486 to 1489 he studied in Nuremberg with the German painter Michel Wohlgemuth. From 1490 to 1494 Dürer traveled, studied, and worked in various parts of Europe, including Colmar, Basel, and Venice. After his return to his native city in 1494, he worked in Wohlgemuth's studio until 1497, when he established one of his own.

Dürer's career may be divided into three periods. In the first, comprising the years 1494 to 1505, he was under the influence of the German painter and engraver Martin Schongauer and the Italian artists Andrea Mantegna and Jacopo de' Barbari. Notable among Dürer's works of this period are two portraits of his father (1490 and 1497), two of himself (1498 and 1506), and the portrait "Hans Dürer" (1500); the painting "The Adoration of the Magi" (1504); and a number of engravings on copper, including "Adam and Eve" and "The Prodigal Son". The period was also marked by his execution of three masterly sets of woodcuts, the "Apocalypse" series (16 blocks, published 1498); the "Great Passion" series (12 blocks, executed in 1500)

Metropolitan Museum of Art

EXAMPLES OF THE WORK OF ALBRECHT DÜRER. *Left: "Hieronymus Holzschuher," portrait.*
Right: "Christ Appearing to the Magdalen," a woodcut from the "Small Passion" series.

and the "Life of the Virgin" series (16 blocks, executed in 1504–05). Dürer's second period included the years between 1505 and 1520. From 1505 to 1507 he had a studio in Venice. In that city, through his study of Greek and Roman art and of the work of the Venetian masters of painting, particularly Giovanni Bellini, Dürer's work lost the angularity and stiffness hitherto characteristic of the work of the German school of art. The most important works produced by Dürer during his Venetian stay are the altarpiece "Feast of Rose Garlands", commissioned by German merchants living in Venice for their chapel in the church of San Bartolommeo; and "Christ Crucified" (1506, now in the Dresden Gallery). In 1507 Dürer returned to Nuremberg. Among the notable works he executed from 1507 to 1520 were the altarpieces "Adoration of the Trinity" (Vienna Museum) and "Adam and Eve" (Prado, Madrid); a number of portraits, including "Charles the Great" and "Emperor Sigismund" (1510, both in the Germanic Museum, Nuremberg); his copper-engraving masterpieces "St. Jerome in his Study", "The Knight", and "Melancolia" (1514); a number of single woodcuts, and the woodcut series "Small Passion" (37 blocks, 1509–10). From 1512 to 1519 Dürer was court painter to the Holy Roman Emperor Maximilian I, for whom he made twenty-four of

the blocks for a series of ninety known as "Triumphal Arch". Dürer also executed the woodcut series "Triumphal Procession" and made marginal pen-and-ink drawings for the emperor's prayer book. After the death of Maximilian, Dürer became court painter to his successor, Charles V.

During a stay in the Netherlands in 1520, Dürer studied the paintings of early Flemish masters, particularly Hubert and Jan van Eyck. The rich and subtle colors in the paintings of Dürer's third period, from 1521 to 1528, are largely due to the influence of the work of the van Eycks. Among the paintings of Dürer's third period are the portraits "An Unknown Man" (Boston Museum of Fine Arts), "Hans Imholf" (Madrid Museum), and "Hieronymus Holzschuher" (National Gallery, Berlin); the paintings "Madonna and Child with St. Anne" and "Virgin and Child" (both in the Metropolitan Museum of of Art, New York City); and the work which is generally recognized as his masterpiece in painting, "The Four Apostles" (1526, Munich Gallery). In this third period he also executed his portraits in the medium of copper engraving of the great German religious reformers Erasmus and Melanchthon (1526), who were among his many distinguished friends. In addition to his many paintings and engravings, all through his career he made numerous drawings in pencil, pen, charcoal, chalk, and other mediums. A collection of over 100 of his drawings is in the Albertina, Vienna; other notable collections are in the British Museum and in Berlin.

Dürer is the most important and the most representative of all German artists. He was the most prominent engraver of his time and by most critics is considered one of the greatest in history. He was the foremost master of the woodcut and one of the earliest masters of the process of etching (q.v.).

DURESS, in law, illegal compulsion applied to a person to force him to commit an act he would not otherwise do. It may consist of physical restraint or violence, or of threats; the latter is called duress *per minas*. Violence or threats directed against the spouse or children of a person in order to compel him to perform a particular act also constitute duress. The courts formerly held that, to constitute duress, threats had to be of sufficient strength to overcome the resistance of a person of average firmness. They now tend to take into consideration such factors as the age, sex, and physical state of the person compelled.

DURHAM, county seat of Durham Co., N.C., situated 22 miles N.W. of Raleigh and 75 miles E.S.E. of Winston-Salem. The city is one of the most important centers of the tobacco industry in the U.S., producing about 20% of all cigarettes manufactured. Other leading industries include the manufacture of hosiery and cotton goods. Durham is the site of Duke University (q.v.) and North Carolina College (founded 1910). Six miles N.W. of the city is Bennett Place Memorial, which marks the scene where, on April 26, 1865, Gen. Joseph E. Johnston surrendered all Confederate armies remaining in the field to Gen. William T. Sherman. Durham was settled about 1855 and incorporated in 1869. Pop. (1950) 71,311.

DURHAM, a maritime county of N.E. England, situated between the Tees and the Derwent rivers. It is drained principally by the Derwent, Wear, and Tees rivers. In addition to the county town, Durham, the leading cities are the municipal boroughs of Stockton-on-Tees, Hartlepool (qq.v.), and Jarrow, and the county boroughs of Darlington, Gateshead, Sunderland, West Hartlepool, and South Shields (qq.v.). In the W. part of the county are large wasteland areas. The E. section of the county contains rich coal fields, and is fertile, particularly in the river valleys. Oats, wheat, barley, potatoes, turnips, and

rutabaga are grown, and sheep are raised, the Teesdale and Weardale breeds being particularly well known. Durham is one of the leading coal-mining counties in England. Shipbuilding is another important industry, the yards on the Derwent, a tributary of the Tyne R., ranking second to those on the Clyde R. In addition, marble, slate, and fire clay are quarried, and machinery, locomotives, trolley cars, tools, chemicals, glass, earthenware, and fertilizer are manufactured.

Durham was once an outpost of the Romans. Later, it became a part of the Saxon Kingdom of Northumbria. After the Norman conquest it obtained the privileges of a county palatine, and for many years its affairs were administered by the bishops of the see at the town of Durham. The area was at various times harassed by the Danes. In 1536 Henry VIII stripped the bishops of much of their judicial power, and in 1646 the palatinate was abolished. It was revived after the Restoration and continued until 1836, when an act of Parliament removed all temporal jurisdiction and privileges from the bishopric. Area (including county boroughs), 1015 sq.m.; pop. (1951 est.) 1,463,416.

DURHAM, JOHN GEORGE LAMBTON, 1st EARL OF. See LAMBTON, JOHN GEORGE.

DURIAN or **DURION,** a fruit tree, *Durio zibethinus,* of the Chocolate family, found in the East Indian islands. It is a tall tree, with leaves resembling those of the cherry and with large bunches of pale-yellow flowers. The fruit, also called durian or durion, is about the size of a coconut and has a hard, thick rind covered with soft spines. The cream-colored meat is flavorsome, but has a bad odor. The fruit contains ten or twelve seeds each as large as a walnut. When roasted, the seeds taste like chestnuts. In the Indian markets, the durian commands a higher price than any other native fruit. One tree yields about 200 fruits each year.

DURKIN, MARTIN P. (1894–   ), American labor leader and government administrator, born in Chicago, Ill., and educated in the Chicago public schools. In 1917, following six years of apprenticeship, he became a journeyman steam fitter. He served in the U.S. Army during World War I, and in 1921 was elected business manager of the Chicago local of the Steamfitters Union. Appointed director of labor for the State of Illinois in 1933, he held this post until September, 1941. Later in 1941 he was elected secretary-treasurer of the United Association of Journeymen and Apprentices of the Plumbing and Pipe Fitting

Industry of the United States and Canada. He became president of that organization, an affiliate of the American Federation of Labor, in 1943. Though an active, registered Democrat, Durkin was appointed secretary of labor by President Dwight David Eisenhower in January, 1953. He resigned from this post in September of the same year, and resumed the presidency of the Plumbing and Pipe Fitting union.

DUROCHER, Leo (Ernest) (1906–), American professional baseball player and manager, born in West Springfield, Mass., and educated there in the public schools. He joined the New York "Yankees", an American League club, in 1928 as an infielder. His brash self-confidence and competitive spirit soon earned him the nickname "Lippy". Transferring to the National League in 1930, he played for three seasons with the Cincinnati "Reds". In 1933 he was traded to the St. Louis "Cardinals" and as a member of that team he won recognition as a star shortstop. In 1937 he joined the Brooklyn "Dodgers". He became manager of the Brooklyn club the next year. Under his management the "Dodgers" won (1941) their first National League championship in twenty-one years. Durocher was named manager of the New York "Giants" in July, 1948. His team won the National League pennant in 1951 and in 1954. In the World Series of the latter year, he led the "Giants" to victory over the Cleveland "Indians", winning four straight games. In 1947 he married the American actress Laraine Day (1920–).

DURRA, Dourra, Doora, or Grain Sorghum, a variety of *Sorghum vulgare* (see Andropogon; Sorghum), grown extensively in s. Asia and n. Africa. It was introduced into the United States in 1874. It is a medium-sized plant, having narrow leaves and a dry, pithy stalk, and bearing hard, round grains. Durra is a relatively nonsweet sorghum and is grown for its grain and as an animal forage. Although its meal does not make good bread, it is excellent as a substitute for rice in puddings, and is prepared for food in various other ways.

DURRES (It. *Durazzo*), capital and port of Durrës Prefecture, Albania, situated on the Adriatic Sea, about 20 miles w. of Tiranë (*Tirana*). The ruins of a Byzantine citadel lie within the town, which is partially encircled by walls originally built as embattlements. The harbor, once of great importance, is slowly filling up with silt and sandbanks. On the sea front of the town is a long quay with rows of old cannon. The town is the seat

National Museum & Automobile Old Timers
Charles Duryea's first automobile

of a Greek Orthodox metropolitan and, since the 5th century, of a Roman Catholic archbishop.

Durrës is tne ancient Epidamnus, founded about 625 B.C. by Corcyræns and Corinthians from Greece. The Romans, who seized it in the 4th century B.C., changed the name to Dyrrachium. The town has figured prominently in many wars, from ancient to modern times. In 1501 the Turks captured the town, and it was occupied by them for more than 400 years, until 1913. In 1915, during World War I, it was taken by the Serbs and later occupied by the Italians. It was taken by the Austrians in 1916, subjected to Allied naval and air attacks in 1918, and reoccupied by the Italians. In 1939, Italian troops used Durrës as a point of disembarkation in the invasion of Albania. In the course of the Italian invasion of Greece, during World War II, the town was subjected to heavy aerial bombardment by the British in order to destroy Italian lines of communication. Olive oil, grain, tobacco, livestock, and hides are the chief products of both the town and prefecture of Durrës. Pop. of town (1945) 14,031; of prefecture (1941) 90,243.

DURUY, Victor (1811–94), French historian, born at Paris, and educated at the École Normale Supérieure. He became professor of history in the Collège Henri IV at Paris in 1833 and was minister of education from 1863 to 1869. He did much to improve primary education in France and worked to make it free and compulsory. He is the author of many histories, the most famous being *Histoire du Peuple Romain* (7 vols., 1879–85).

DURYEA, Charles Edgar (1862–1938), American inventor and manufacturer, born near Canton, Ill., and educated at Gittings Seminary, La Harpe, Ill. He became interested in motor-carriages as early as 1884, and in 1891 he began construction of an automobile which was successfully tested in 1892. Many consider this machine the first American automobile, although other machines, such as that of Elwood Haynes, are said by some authorities to have antedated it. Duryea invented the spray carburetor in 1892 and was the first to use pneumatic tires on his cars, in 1893. In 1895 a Duryea car driven by his brother Frank won the first American automobile race, and in the same year he and his brother organized the Duryea Motor Wagon Company for the manufacture of automobiles. In 1900 he organized the Duryea Power Company for the production of an improved car. He retired from automobile manufacture in 1914.

DUSE, ELEONORA (1859–1924), Italian actress, born at Vigevano. Her father was a strolling player and she made appearances with his company as a young child. In 1873 she attracted favorable attention when she appeared in Verona as Juliet in *Romeo and Juliet*, but did not achieve widespread recognition as an actress until her appearance in *Les Fourchambault* by Émile Augier, in Naples, 1878. The following year the noted Italian actor Cesare Rossi engaged her as his leading lady, and her work with this company in subsequent years gave her an international reputation. In Rossi's company and her own she made tours of Europe, Egypt, and the United States; she appeared in New York City for the first time in 1893, at the Fifth Avenue Theatre, in *La Dame aux Camélias* by Alexandre Dumas, fils. From 1878 to about 1897 her principal roles were those of Marguerite Gautier in *La Dame aux Camélias*; Magda in *Heimat* (*Magda*) by Hermann Sudermann; Santuzza, a role she created, in *Cavalleria Rusticana* by Giovanni Verga; and Hedda in *Hedda Gabler* and Ellida in *The Lady from the Sea*, both by Henrik Ibsen. In 1897 she began a close friendship with the Italian playwright Gabriele D'Annunzio, and thereafter, until her retirement from the stage in 1909 because of ill health, she devoted herself principally to acting and promoting interest in his plays, particularly *La Gioconda* and *Francesca da Rimini*. Financial losses suffered during World War I caused her to return to the stage in 1921 and for three years she toured Italy and played in England and the United States, in spite of failing health. She died in April at Pittsburgh, Pa., and was

buried at her summer home in Asolo, Italy.

Duse was considered one of the leading actresses of her time, in the opinion of some critics being superior even to the renowned French actress Sarah Bernhardt. Duse's reputation was due to her sympathetic portrayal of the sufferings of human beings, her power to convey powerful emotion, and her sense of realism, touched, however, by a poetic spirit.

DÜSSELDORF, capital of the State of North Rhine-Westphalia, West Germany, and former capital of a government district of the same name, North Rhine Province, Prussia (liquidated after World War II). It is situated on the Rhine R., near Dortmund, Essen, Cologne, and other German industrial cities in the Ruhr, and is 55 miles E. of both the Belgium and Netherland borders. Heinrich Heine, the famous German poet and literary critic, was born in Düsseldorf in 1795. Düsseldorf received the official status of a town in 1288 from Count Adolf of Berg. Its castle was for a long period the residence of the counts, and later the dukes of Berg. The city became the capital of the Napoleonic grand duchy of Berg in 1805; in 1815, along with the duchy, it became a part of Prussia. Düsseldorf attained importance as an industrial center in the Ruhr after 1870. The chief industrial establishments are engaged in the manufacture of castings and other metal products, machinery and machine tools, chemicals and dyes, paper and paper products, textiles, technical and scientific instruments, musical instruments, furniture, glass, porcelain, enamel, fire clay, cement, and beer. In addition, the city contains a large printing and publishing industry. Düsseldorf has been damaged many times during wars. After World War I the city was occupied by Allied forces from 1921 to 1925. During World War II Düsseldorf suffered its greatest damage as a result of aerial bombardment. At the end of World War II Düsseldorf was included in the British zone of occupation in Germany. Pop. (1950) 500,516.

DUST, fine particles of organic and inorganic substances suspended in the atmosphere. Among the substances found in dust are animal and vegetable fibers, pollen, silica, bacteria, and molds. In cities where much coal and oil is burned, the atmospheric dust contains a large number of smoke particles and tarry soot particles.

No part of the lower atmosphere is entirely free from dust, although the concentration varies widely according to the locality. In an industrial city there may be more than fifty million particles per cubic inch of air, but in the middle of the ocean or in high mountains the count may fall to a few thousand per cubic inch. The size of dust particles varies from about half a micron (.00002 in.) to several times this size. Because of their extremely small size, dust particles remain suspended in the air for long periods of time. A dust particle of the same density as water and one micron (.000039 in.) in diameter will take more than a day to fall ten feet. In this time it can be carried hundreds of miles by even a moderate wind. The most remarkable demonstration of the distances which dust particles may travel was given by the dust cloud thrown up by the eruption of Krakatoa (q.v.) in 1883. Clouds of volcanic dust from this eruption were carried several times around the world and gave rise to brilliantly colored sunsets in many countries from 1883 to 1886.

Atmospheric dust has two important physical properties: its ability to scatter light of short wave lengths (see COLOR), and its ability to serve as nuclei for the condensation of water vapor. Mist, fog, and clouds would never occur if it were not for the presence in the air of particles around which water droplets can condense.

The heavy concentration of dust in the air over large cities is a serious problem, because as much as 2000 tons of dust per square mile may fall annually in such areas. Dust is also a problem in flour and sugar mills, and in coal mines, where a concentration of inflammable particles constitutes an explosion hazard. Silica particles in dust are destructive to machinery, and to polished surfaces such as the facets of semiprecious stones, because of their hardness; they can also be injurious when inhaled (see SILICOSIS). To obtain dust-free air in manufacturing plants and other places where dust may cause contamination or damage, air filters have been devised, using either cloth or water as filtering medium. Dust and smoke may be removed from exhaust stacks of industrial plants by such devices as the Cottrell precipitator (q.v.). See SMOG.

DUST BOWL, common name applied to a large area in the southern part of the Great Plains region of the U.S., much of which suffered extensively from wind erosion during the 1930's. The area included parts of Kansas, Oklahoma, Texas, New Mexico, and Colorado, and comprised a total of approximately 96,-000.000 acres.

Several factors were responsible for the devastation of the Dust Bowl: the character of the soil, the climate, and the types of agriculture practiced. Much of the soil is loessal and was originally deposited by the wind (see DEPOSIT); an additional large quantity of soil is outwash, carried down from the Rocky Mountains by rainwater. In its primitive state, however, it was covered with hardy grasses which held the soil in place in spite of the long recurrent droughts and occasional torrential rains characteristic of the region.

In the thirty years before World War I, a large number of homesteaders settled in the area, many of whom planted wheat and row crops instead of employing the land for grazing. The acreage devoted to wheat in one part of the Dust Bowl region tripled between 1914 and 1919 and increased more than fifty percent more in the next decade. This expansion in wheat growing was partly due to the high prices current during the war and partly to the availability of tractors, harvester-threshers, and other machinery for large-scale farming.

In 1935 about half of the Dust Bowl area was cropped and half was devoted to intensive cattle raising. Both of these forms of farming left the soil exposed to the danger of erosion by the winds that constantly swept over the gently rolling land. The grass covering the cropland was plowed under, and the grass of the grazing land was cut short and trampled into the ground by large herds of cattle. A series of crop failures from 1930 to 1935 aggravated the dangers of erosion. Beginning in the early 1930's, the region suffered a period of severe droughts and the soil began to blow away. The organic matter, clay, and silt in the soil was carried for hundreds of miles by the winds (in some cases darkening the sky on the Atlantic coast), while sand and heavier materials drifted against houses, fences, and barns. In many places 3 to 4 inches of topsoil were blown away, and sand and silt dunes 4 to 10 feet in height were formed. In one area in the heart of the Dust Bowl it was estimated that eighty percent of the land suffered from wind erosion during the drought years, with forty percent being severely eroded. The combined effect of crop failure and loss of the productive soil ruined a large number of farmers. Many thousands of families emigrated westward, while about a third of the remaining families had to accept government relief.

Beginning in 1935 intensive efforts were made by both Federal and State governments to develop adequate programs for soil con-

Soil Conservation Service

Roots of tree exposed by erosion of soil over a twenty-year period, a dramatic example of the devastation in the Dust Bowl area of the United States

servation and for rehabilitation of the Dust Bowl. The measures taken have included the seeding of large areas in grass; a three-year rotation of wheat, sorghum, and fallow; the introduction of contour plowing, terracing, and strip planting; and, in areas of greater rainfall, the planting of long "shelter belts" of trees to break the force of the wind. By 1940 the area subject to dangerous wind erosion had been reduced from about 50,-000,000 acres to less than half that figure, and in subsequent years it was reduced still further. See CONSERVATION; EROSION.

DUTCH BORNEO. See BORNEO; NETHERLANDS INDIES; REPUBLIC OF INDONESIA.

DUTCH EAST INDIA COMPANY. See EAST INDIA COMPANY.

DUTCH EAST INDIES. See NETHERLANDS INDIES; REPUBLIC OF INDONESIA.

DUTCH ELM DISEASE, disease of elm trees, caused by the fungus *Ceratostomella ulmi.* The disease is characterized by gradual yellowing of the leaves and defoliation. Eventually the infected tree dies. The fungus is transmitted from diseased trees to healthy elms by various bark-beetle carriers, notably the species *Hylurgopinus rufipes,* native to the United States, and the smaller European bark beetle, *Scolytus multristriatus.* See BARK BEETLE. Elm-bark beetles are highly susceptible to D.D.T. The disease may be controlled by thorough spraying of the trees with this insecticide. In addition, all dead elm wood which might serve as breeding material should be removed from the controlled area.

DUTCH GUIANA. See SURINAM.

DUTCH LANGUAGE, a member of the western group of the Germanic branch of Indo-European languages. It is the language of the inhabitants of the Netherlands, the northern half of Belgium, the northern part of the department of Nord, France, and the Netherlands overseas territories. Cape Dutch, or Afrikaans, spoken in South Africa, is, although an independent tongue, to a large extent identical with "High" Dutch. The name Dutch is derived from the word *Dietsch,* meaning the vernacular, as distinguished from Latin. Dutch belongs to the Low Frankish division of Low German and is very closely related to Flemish, with which it is now nearly identical in its written form. Like English, the language may be divided into three main periods, as follows.

(1) Old Dutch, extending to about 1100. The only important, extant monument of this period is a translation of the Psalter.

(2) Middle Dutch, extending from 1100 to 1550. The language during this period underwent changes in sounds and inflections; no standard written form was at first recognized, and each writer used his own dialect. In the 13th century a determined effort was made to

establish a literary Dutch, the leader in the movement being Jacob van Maerlant (1235?–1300). The use of dialects, however, continued to prevail.

(3) Modern Dutch, extending from 1550 to the present day. The most important single event in the history of the language during this period was the publication (1619–37) of the *Statenbijbel*, the authorized version of the Scriptures, which did much to spread this form of Dutch in the Low Countries. The effect of this translation was similar to that of Luther's version of the Bible in High German, in establishing a standard of language and orthography that was generally recognized as authoritative. During the 18th century, efforts were made to purify the language by the elimination of all foreign influences, and the language and Dutch literature suffered in consequence. A more conservative view prevailed during the next century, and Dutch achieved a greater freedom and range of expression. In more recent years, efforts have been made to reform Dutch orthography and to effect uniformity of usage in the Netherlands and Belgium.

DUTCH LIQUID. See ETHYLENE CHLORIDE.

DUTCH LITERATURE. The earliest examples of Dutch literature extant today are the works of Heynrik van Veldeken (fl. about 1200), who wrote a *Life of St. Servatius,* based on a Latin source, an *Eneïde* (Aeneid) after a French source, and various love songs. In the middle of the 13th century a number of epics were produced, including Klaas van Haarlem's *William of Orange* (1211–17) and Dederic van Assenede's *Floris and Blanchefleur* (about 1250). The language achieved a high level of literary perfection after 1250 with the work of Jacob van Maerlant, called the father of Dutch literature, who wrote didactic poetry, romances of chivalry, treatises on history and government, and a *Rhyme Bible* based on the *Biblia Scholastica* of Petrus Comestor. However, the period which followed Maerlant witnessed the corruption of the language under the Burgundian domination of the Netherlands (1363–1477), and the assimilation of French words and forms. The restoration of the Dutch language to creative usage was initiated by Dirk Volkertszoon Coornhert (1522–90), and Philip van Marnix (1538–98). Their contributions led directly to the Golden Age of Dutch literature. Coornhert, who wrote poetry, drama, and prose, is best known for his *Zedekunst, dat is Wellevens Kunst* (1586). Marnix is the author of one of the most acrimonious satires ever directed against the

Catholic Church, *Biëncorf der Heiligher Roomscher Kercke.*

The Golden Age which occupied most of the 17th century in Dutch literature is marked by intellectual independence, an emphasis on Humanist values, and the suppression of foreign terms and idioms from the language. Jacob Cats (1577–1660), known as "Father" Cats, enjoyed wide popularity as a poet. His writings, characterized by the expression of homely moral precepts and workaday philosophy, include *Houwelijck* (1625), *Spieghel van den Ouden ende Nieuwen Tijdt* (1632), *Trou-Ringh* (1637), and an autobiographical volume of reminiscences, *Ouderdom, Buytenleven en Hofgedachten op Zorgh-vliet* (1656). Pieter Hooft (1581–1647), in contrast, reflects the Renaissance spirit; his works are on a high cultural and intellectual level, and include the tragic dramas *Geeraerd van Velsen* (1613) and *Baeto* (1626), which owe their inspiration to Seneca; a comedy, *Warenar* (1617), adapted from Plautus' *Aulularia;* and the historical studies *Henrik de Grote* (1626) and the unfinished *Nederlandsche Historien* (1628–47). Gerbrand Bredero (1585–1618) was one of the founders of the Amsterdam Theater; he first wrote romantic plays but he achieved his greatest success in low-comedy farces; these include *Klucht van de Koe* (1612), *Klucht van Symen ender Soelighyd* (1612–13), *Klucht van den Molenaer* (1613), *Het Moortje* (1616), and *De Spaansche Brabander* (1617). Joost van den Vondel (1587–1679) was the

Netherlands Information Bureau
Jacob Cats

Netherlands Information Bureau

Gerbrand Bredero

greatest, and one of the most prolific, poets of the Golden Age. His chief contribution to literature consists of 24 poetic dramas, modeled on the classical form. Some of the lyrics in these plays are among the finest in the Dutch language. His plays include *Gysbreght van Aemstel* (1637), *Maeghden* (1639), *Joseph in Dothan* (1640), *Jeptha* (1659), and *Adam in Ballingschap* (1664). His masterpiece *Lucifer* (1659), which concerns itself with the revolt of the angels against God, was for many years the subject of literary controversy in which one school of critics held that *Lucifer* had served the English poet John Milton as a model and source for his *Paradise Lost*. Constantijn Huygens (1596–1687), father of the famous mathematician Christian Huygens (q.v.), possessed a brilliant facility with language and a mastery of form. His collected poems, *Korenbloemen,* were published in 27 volumes (1658–72); he is also the author of the play *Tryntje Cornelis* (1659) and of a translation (1634) of the poetry of John Donne. The latter part of the 17th century witnessed the gradual slackening of this renascence. Pieter Langendijk (1683–1756), one of the important writers of the first half of the 18th century, is the author of comedies which are still performed in the Netherlands. His works include *Het Wederzijds Huwelijks Bedrog* (1712–14), *Krelis Louwen of Alexander de Groote op het Poeettemaal* (1715), and *De Wiskenstenaars of 't Gevluchte Juffertje* (1715). Other noteworthy writers of

this period were Justus van Effen (1684–1735), who imitated the English reviews with his *Hollandsche Spectator* (1731–35), and Lucas Rotgans (d. 1710), a dramatist and the author of the epic *Willem III.*

The last quarter of the 18th century is marked by a movement known as the "Verlichting" or "enlightenment", which was opposed to the rules and forms of the almost outmoded classicism. Two women were among the distinguished contributors to this movement, Betje Wolff-Bekker (1738–1804) and her friend Aagje Deken (1741–1804), whose joint work produced a number of novels in letter form, among them *Sara Burgerhart* (1782) and *Willem Leevend* (1784–85). Rhijnvis Feith (1753–1824), in contrast, wrote the sentimental romances *Julia* (1783) and *Ferdinand en Constantia* (1785); didactic poems, as *De Ouderdom* (1803); and a number of songs still in use as church hymns. Hieronymus van Alphen (1746–1803) wrote on esthetics, and translated one of the standard works of the time, Riedel's *Theory of Fine Arts,* providing a valuable original preface for the Dutch reader. Willem Bilderdijk (1756–1831) became the hero of a political and religious movement called the *"Réveil".* His works include the epic poem *De Ondergang der Eerste Wereld* (1810), religious poetry such as *Gebed* (1796) and *Boetzan* (1826), and the famous *Ode van Napoleon* (1806) and *Afscheid* (1810). Johannes Kinker (1764–1845) was a philosopher, critic, and philologist best known for his attacks on the sentimental school of writing. Adriaan Loosjes (1761–1818) in his *Maurits Lijnslager* produced a forerunner of the historical novel. Frederik Helmers (1667–1813) is the author of the famous patriotic poem *De Hollandsche Natie* (1812).

The 19th century opened inauspiciously with writing marked by conventionality, lack of originality, and an emphasis on form. Van der Palm (1763–1841), an orator, is the author of the most familiar work of this period, *Geschied-en-Redekunstig Gedenkschrift van Nederlands Herstelling* (1816). Isaak da Costa (1798–1860) was a disciple of Bilderdijk; his works include *Bezwaren tegen den Geest der Eeuw* (1823), an attack on liberalism; *Hagar* (1848), a Biblical poem; and the historical poem *De Slag bij Nieuwpoort* (1859). The prose writing of this period includes the literary criticism of Jacob Geel (1789–1862), collected in the volume *Onderzoek en Phantasie;* and the historical novels of Jacob van Lennep (1802–68) and of Jan Frederik Oltmans (1806–54), both of whom reveal the influence of Sir Walter Scott. Everardus Johannes Potgieter (1808–75), apart from his own creative writing, was the founder, in 1837, of the review *De Gids*, which served as an organ for the romantic movement. His works include *Jan, Jannetje, en hun Jongste Kind* (1842), in which the Holland of three different generations is compared; *Het Rijksmuseum* (1844), in praise of 17th-century Holland; and a quantity of scholarly, abstruse poetry. Nikolaas Beets (1814–1903), one of the most famous writers of this period, owes his reputation to a single work, *Camera Obscura* (1839), a gently humorous reflection of the life and manners of middle-class society. Pieter Hasebroeck (1812–96), writing under the pseudonym of Jonathan, and Johannes Kneppelhout (1814–85), whose pseudonym was Klikspaan, both produced works which resemble Beets' *Camera Obscura*. Anna Louise Geertruida Bosboom-Toussaint (1812–86), whose name is also importantly associated with the romantic movement and *De Gids*, is the author of ncvels influenced by the English romantics; her works include *Het Huis Lauernesse* (1840), a cycle dealing with the adventures of Robert Dudley in the Netherlands (1845–55), and the fictionalized diary *Majoor Frans* (1874). Petrus Augustus de Genestet (1829–61) was a Protestant minister who enjoyed popularity as a poet of both religious and secular subjects, and Josephus Albertus Alberdingk Thym (1820–89) was a Catholic romantic. Conrad Busken Huët (1826–86), a theologian and pastor who resigned from his church to devote himself to literary criticism, served with Potgieter on the staff of *De Gids* and in 1872 founded his own newspaper in Batavia, the *Algemeen Dagblad van Nederlandsch Indië*. His essays and reviews have been collected in 25 volumes under the title *Literarische Fantasien en Kritieken* (1881–88).

Eduard Douwes Dekker (1820–87), who wrote under the pseudonym of Multatuli, anticipated the revolutionary movement in Dutch letters by some twenty years. He won immediate fame with the novel *Max Havelaar* (1860), which castigated the Dutch bourgeoisie for its un-Christian and profiteering treatment of the Javanese natives. His style was simple, and free from the formalism which had become a literary standard of the language, and the success of his work did much to emancipate the next generation of writers from meaningless restrictions.

The renascence of the 1880's is generally dated from the first issue (October, 1885) of a review called *De Nieuwe Gids*, which was so named to mark its secession from the values and standards of the old *Gids* and to announce its intention of supplanting that outmoded periodical. The leaders of the "Eightiers", as the new movement was called, were the poets Willem Kloos (1859–1938), Albert Verwey (1865–1937), Lodewijk van Deyssel (pseudonym of Karel Alberdingk Thym, 1864–), and Frederik van Eeden (1860–1932). The poetry of Kloos, *Verzen* (1894), which had first been published in *De Nieuwe Gids*, revolutionized literary diction. Albert Verwey, who was one of the first editors of *De Nieuwe Gids*, served as the mentor of the younger "Eightiers", and in 1905 founded a new monthly, *De Beweging*, which in turn became the rallying point of another generation of literary rebels; his works include a literary history, *Het Leven van Potgieter* (1903), and *Proza* (1925), a ten-volume collection of his prose writings. Van Deyssel was the prophet of the movement, coining its slogans and credos and proving their validity in his writings, which include the novels *De Kleine Republiek* (1886) and *Een Liefde* (1887), and a quantity of critical writing for *De Nieuwe Gids* and the *Tweemaandelijksch Tijdschrift*. Van Eeden, one of the founders of *De Nieuwe Gids*, was also one of the most versatile members of the movement, functioning as a poet, critic, novelist, and dramatist with equal facility. His works include the tale *De Kleine Johannes* (1887), the novel *Van de Koele Meren des Doods* (1900), the dramatic poem *De Broeders; Tragedie van het Recht* (1894), the long philosophic poem *Het Lied van Schijn en Wezen* (1895–1910), and the plays *Ijsbrand* (1908) and *De Heks van Haarlem* (1915).

The reaction against the "Eightiers" was led by C. S. Adama van Scheltema (1877–1924), a socialist who opposed their narrow preoccupation with "art for art's sake" and believed in art for the many rather than the few; his own poetry resembles folk art. He expounded his theories on poetry in *Grondslagen eener Nieuwe Poezie* (1908). Henriëtte Roland Holst (1869–) identified her poetry with the voice of communism and social rebellion; her works include *Sonnetten en Verzen in Terzinen Geschreven* (1895), *De Nieuwe Geboort* (1902), *Opwaartsche Wegen* (1907), and *De Vrouw in het Woud* (1912). Herman Gorter (1864–1927) wrote *Mei* (1889), one of the great poems of modern Dutch literature. Pieter Cornelis Boutens (1870–1943) was one

Netherlands Information Bureau

Menno ter Braak

of the most distinguished poets of his generation. His works include *Verzen* (1898), *Praeludiën* (1902), *Stemmen* (1907), *Liederen van Isoude* (1919), *Bezonnen Verzen* (1931), and *Honderd Hollandsche Kwatrijnen* (1932). Of the novelists of this period, Louis Couperus (1863–1923), the author of *Eline Vere* (1889), *Majesteit* (1893), *Wereldvrede* (1895), and *De Boeken der Kleine Zielen* (1901–03), won an international reputation. Jacobus van Looy (1855–1930), less known outside of Holland, was a writer of imagistic prose who was also a talented oil painter. His works include an autobiographical novel of his boyhood, *Jaapje* (1917). Marcellus Emants (1848–1923) was a novelist, poet, and playwright. His prose works, chiefly studies of neurotic characters, include *Een Nagelaten Bekentenis* (1894), *Waan* (1905), and *Liefdeleven* (1916); his best play is *Domheidsmacht* (1904). Herman Heijermans (1864–1924) was one of the most successful playwrights of the Dutch theater; his numerous social dramas include *Ghetto* (1898), *Het Zevende Gebod* (1899), *Op Hoop van Zegen* (1900), and *Ora et Labora* (1903).

After World War I, a reaction to the overintellectualized literature of the early 1900's was led by Hendrik Marsman (1890–1940), who championed the cause of "vitalism", based on the theory that the poet is merely a member of, and spokesman for, the masses. The organ of the Marsman group was first *Het Getij*, then *De Vrije Bladen;* the contributors to these periodicals included Jan Slauerhoff, Hendrik de Vries, Jan Engelman, and Anthonie Donker. These writers, in turn, aroused the reaction of another group, consisting of Menno ter Braak, Charles E. du Perron, and Simon Vestdijk, whose work was published in the periodical *Forum* and who argued that the "vitalists" were becoming too stylized and obscure. The Forum group had a strong influence on the youngest generation of Dutch writers. Recently a group of these young writers, under the influence of the French literary movement known as surrealism, initiated a reaction against the literalness of the Forum school.

DUTCH NEW GUINEA. See NEW GUINEA.

DUTCH PAINTING, a school of painting founded at Haarlem in the late 15th century by Albert van Ouwater. The most famous exponents of the movement as it existed at that time were Dierik Bouts and Lucas van Leyden. Despite the efforts of this group, Dutch painting was then still chiefly derivative of Flemish art, and it did not develop any significant individual characteristics for nearly a hundred years. The Dutch achieved their political independence in 1564, and that year may be said more accurately to mark the awakening of Dutch art and national consciousness. The 17th century marks the golden age of Dutch painting. Haarlem remained the chief center of art, although there was an important school at Amsterdam. The overthrow of Spain and Catholicism abated the demand for religious paintings, and such specialized modern forms as the portrait, genre, landscape, and still life came into popularity. Among the 17th-century Dutch painters the chief masters in portraiture were Frans Hals and Rembrandt; the latter was equally great in landscape painting and produced light effects which are considered unique among the accomplishments of painters. In genre painting the most important were Adriaen van Ostade, Gerard Terborch, Gerard Dou, Jan Steen, and Pieter de Hooch. Jan Vermeer stands apart in the perfection of his still lifes, genre paintings, and allegorical subjects. The Dutch were the first to take up landscape and animal painting as arts in themselves. Their greatest landscapists were Jacob van Ruisdael, and Meindert Hobbema; in animal painting Philips Wouwerman, Paul Potter, Adriaen van de Velde, and Albert Cuyp were pre-eminent. In marine painting, the most important work was done by Willem van de Velde, the Younger, and Ludolf Backhuysen. In the 18th century, Dutch art declined, and it was not until the 19th century that a new group of artists, al-

PAINTINGS OF THE DUTCH SCHOOL. *Top: "The Mother," by Pieter de Hooch. Bottom, left: "The Concert," by Gerard Terborch. Bottom, right: "Portrait of a Rabbi," by Rembrandt.*

though lacking the genius of their predecessors, restored Dutch painting to some prestige. The latter-day school includes the work of Jozef Israels, the peasant painter, Jacob and Willem Maris in landscape, Anton Mauve in animal subjects, and Hendrik Willem Mesdag in marines. Vincent van Gogh is the most famous and original artist of this period. See articles on many of the individual artists.

DUTCH REFORMED CHURCH. See RE-FORMED CHURCHES.

DUTCH WARS, name applied by historians to three naval wars of the 17th century. **1.** FIRST DUTCH WAR (1652–54), between Great Britain under the Commonwealth and the United Provinces (Holland), caused by trade rivalry. A blockade of the United Provinces by the British fleet resulted in a peace favorable to Great Britain. **2.** SECOND DUTCH WAR (1664–67), between Great Britain under King Charles II and the United Provinces, also caused by trade rivalry. The United Provinces were ineffectively supported in the war by King Louis XIV of France. Each side won naval victories. The terms of the Peace of Breda, concluding the war, favored the Dutch, but formally granted to Great Britain the Dutch colony of Nieuw Amsterdam (New York), which had been seized by the British. **3.** THIRD DUTCH WAR (1672–74), between Great Britain under King Charles II, supported by King Louis XIV of France, and the United Provinces, first under the leadership of Jan De Witt, later under William of Orange. The war was a phase of a general European struggle caused by the expansionist ambitions of King Louis XIV. It was preceded by the secret Treaty of Dover (1670) forming an alliance between Charles II and Louis XIV. The conflict was unpopular in England, and after several defeats at sea Great Britain withdrew from the war. Later Britain re-entered the war, against France, however, and as the ally of the United Provinces and Spain.

DUTCH WEST INDIA COMPANY, a trading company incorporated by the States-General of the Netherlands in 1621 to share world trade with the Dutch East India Company (see EAST INDIA COMPANY). In return for subsidies to the state, the West India Company was granted a monopoly of trade in America and Africa, with the right of colonizing and of maintaining armed forces. The armed forces were used to enforce the sovereign rights of the company wherever possible, and to plunder the various Spanish and Portuguese settlements in America and Africa. The

colonizing activities of the company were notable for the settlement of New Netherlands (later New York), Surinam, and Curaçao. In Brazil, the company took Bahia in 1623, but later lost it to the Spanish and Portuguese. The company was established at Pernambuco and elsewhere in Brazil until 1661, when it resigned all rights in the country.

The trading career of the Dutch West India Company was not so successful as that of its sister company, the Dutch East India Company. In 1674 it dissolved in financial difficulties. A new company lasted until 1794, when it collapsed in the course of the French invasion of the Netherlands. Another West India Company, formed in 1828, was unsuccessful.

DUTCH WEST INDIES. See CURAÇAO; SURINAM.

DUTIES. See CUSTOMS DUTIES.

DUTRA, ENRICO GASPAR (1885–   ), Brazilian soldier and statesman, born in Cuiabá, Mato Grosso, and educated at the Escola Militar do Rio Pardo, the Escola Militar do Baia Vermelha, and the Escola de Estado-Maior. He became a second lieutenant in the Brazilian Army in 1910, and subsequently rose through the various officer grades until he was appointed a general of division in 1935. From 1936 to 1945 he served as minister of war, and played a decisive role in the planning of such Brazilian military operations in World War II as the sending of a Brazilian expeditionary force to participate in the Italian campaign and the establishment of Allied air bases in Brazil. Dutra was elected president of Brazil in December, 1945, with the support not only of his own Social Democratic Party but also of the Labor Party, led by his predecessor in office, Getulio Dornelles Vargas (q.v.). A Constituent Assembly met two months after Dutra's election and drafted a new constitution, which was adopted on September 17, 1946. One week later, the Brazilian congress convened for the first time in nearly a decade. Other notable events of Dutra's regime include the meeting of the Inter-American Defense Conference at Rio de Janeiro, which in September, 1947, resulted in the signing of a mutual aid and defense treaty by most of the nations of the Western Hemisphere. In October, 1947, the publication of an article in a Russian periodical attacked Dutra as a tool of the United States. The refusal of the Soviet government to accept responsibility for the article resulted in the severance of diplomatic relations between Brazil and the U.S.S.R. Dutra left office following the election of Getulio Vargas in October, 1950. He was given the rank of marshal of the army in 1952.

DUTTON, CLARENCE EDWARD (1841–1912), American geologist, born in Wallingford, Conn., and educated at Yale University. After serving in the Civil War, he became identified with geological surveys for the United States government. He investigated the Charleston earthquake of 1886, discovering a method for determining the depth of focus of an earthquake, and publishing important observations on the nature and speed of earthquake wave motion. After studying volcanic regions of Hawaii, California, and Oregon, he announced in 1906 his theory that volcanism is caused by radioactivity. He wrote *Hawaiian Volcanoes* (1884), *The Charleston Earthquake of 1886* (1886), and *Earthquakes in the Light of the New Seismology* (1904).

DUTTON, IRA, also known as BROTHER JOSEPH (1843–1931), American Trappist monk, born at Stowe, Vermont. He was brought up in the Protestant faith. During the Civil War he served as a lieutenant, and subsequently worked as a printer and drug clerk. After being converted to Roman Catholicism, he entered the Trappist monastery at Gethsemane, Ky., where he was admitted to the order as a lay member. He spent the remaining 45 years of his life in the leper colony at Kalaupapa on the Hawaiian island of Molokai, and in 1889 succeeded Father Damien (q.v.) in ministering to the spiritual and temporal needs of the lepers. As a signal of respect to Brother Joseph's lifework, in 1908 the U.S. Atlantic fleet, on its tour of the world, passed in review off the coast of the leper settlement. Brother Joseph died in Honolulu, to which he had been removed for an operation on his eyes.

DUTY. See CUSTOMS DUTIES; EXCISE TAX.

DUVAL, FRANÇOIS. See FONTENAY-MAREUIL.

DUVENECK, FRANK (1848–1919), American painter, etcher, sculptor, and art teacher, born in Covington, Ky. He studied with the German painter Feodor Dietz in Munich. In 1878 Duveneck established an art school in Munich and later taught at Florence. He was a notable art teacher; among his pupils were the American painters John W. Alexander, William M. Chase, and John Twachtman. After 1888 Duveneck was a permanent resident of Cincinnati, where he occupied himself mainly with teaching. Among his works are a series of etchings of Venetian scenes (1880–85); a bronze monument to his wife (1888), the original of which is in the English cemetery in Florence and marble replicas of which are in the Metropolitan Museum of Art, New York

City, and in other American museums; a bust of Charles W. Eliot (Harvard University); and the paintings "Portrait of an Old Woman" and "The Circassian" (both in the Metropolitan Museum of Art, New York City), and "Whistling Boy" and "Young Man with a Ruff" (both in the Pennsylvania Academy of Fine Arts, Philadelphia).

DU VIGNEAUD, VINCENT (1901–   ), American biochemist, born in Chicago, and educated at the universities of Illinois and Rochester. In 1932 he became professor and head of the department of biochemistry in the school of medicine at George Washington University. In 1938 he assumed a similar position at the Cornell University Medical College. Most of du Vigneaud's researches were on hormones, vitamins, amino acids, insulin, and the synthesis of penicillin. His formula of biotin, proposed in 1942, was confirmed by synthesis in 1943. He wrote *Trail of Research in Sulfur Chemistry and Metabolism and Related Fields* (1952).

DUYKER. See DUIKER.

DVINA, NORTHERN (Russ. *Dvina Syevernaya*), a river in N. Soviet Russia, formed by the union of the Sukhona, the Yug, and the Luza rivers, and emptying into the White Sea after a northwesterly course of about 470 miles. Its main tributaries are the Vychegda, Vaga, and Pinega rivers. After its juncture with the Pinega, just below Arkhangelsk, the Dvina divides into three branches, which form a delta about 3 miles wide. The Dvina is frozen from October until May, but during the warmer months is navigable from its confluence with the Vychegda R. to the White Sea, a distance of about 400 miles. The river provides a variety of edible fish.

DVINA (Russ. *Zapadnaya Dvina; Ger. Düna;* Lettish *Daugava*), also called SOUTHERN DVINA or WESTERN DVINA, river of the Soviet Union, rising in the Valdai Hills (q.v.), and flowing s.w. to Vitebsk, a town in White Russia, then N.w. through Latvia, emptying into the Gulf of Riga, 8 m. below the city of Riga. The Dvina is 640 m. long. During normal weather conditions it has a maximum depth of about 30 ft. and a maximum width of about 1400 ft. Spring floods, however, cause the river to become as much as 45 ft. deep, and a mile wide. The Dvina falls about 800 ft. in its course to the Gulf of Riga. Because of rapids and shallows it is used mainly for floating timber and for rafting. During the winter months the Southern Dvina is frozen.

DVINSK. See DAUGAVPILS.

Anton Dvořák

DVOŘÁK, ANTON (1841–1904), Czech composer, born in Nelahozeves (Mühlhausen), Bohemia. As a child he learned to play the violin and often entertained the guests at his father's inn. In 1855 he studied music with Anton Liebmann in Zlonice, and in 1857 became a student at the Organ School, Prague. After completing his studies there he became a member of the concert band of Komzák and later of the orchestra of the National Theatre, Prague, with which the band was merged. He had begun to compose while still at school, but it was not until 1873, when his cantata *Hymnus* was performed with great success, that Dvořák received marked public recognition. From 1873 to 1884 he composed a number of notable works, including his first series of *Slavonic Dances* (1878), and his reputation rapidly grew. In 1884 he made the first of nine trips to England. There he made many successful appearances as a conductor and composed much music. From 1892 to 1895 he was director of the National Conservatory of Music of America, New York City. During his stay in the United States he acquired a great liking for Negro spirituals and American Indian music. Two of his most famous works, the *Symphony in E Minor*, known as "The New World" symphony and the *Quartet in F*, known as the "American" quartet, were both composed in the United States in 1893; though these works do not contain actual themes from Negro or American Indian music, they have melodies that in structure and spirit are strongly akin to the melodies of these types of music. After Dvořák's return to Bohemia in 1895, he composed extensively, mainly symphonic poems and operas, and in 1901 became director of the Prague Conservatory. The day of his funeral was a day of national mourning throughout Bohemia.

Dvořák's early works were influenced by the music of Schubert and Beethoven, and all through his career he was influenced to some extent by the work of Richard Wagner. However, in Dvořák's most mature and characteristic compositions he drew on Czech and Slavonic folk music for material, and these works reflect both his national and racial consciousness. He is regarded as one of the most important European composers of the 19th century and as the leading Czech composer of his time. Among his pupils were the noted Czech composers Josef Suk and Vítězlav Novák. In addition to the works mentioned above, among Dvořák's compositions are eight symphonies (1865–93); the oratorios *Stabat Mater* (1876–77) and *The Specter's Bride* (1884); the overtures *In Nature's Realm* (1891) and *Carnival* (1891); chamber music, including the *Dumka Trio* (1890–91) and the *String Quintet, Op. 97* (1893); music for the piano, including the well-known *Humoresque* (1894); the symphonic poems *The Wood Dove* (1896) and *Heroic Song* (1897); and the operas *Vanda* (1875), *The Jacobin* (1887–88), and *Armida* (1902–03).

DVORSKY, MICHEL. See HOFMANN, JOSEF CASIMIR.

DWALE. See BELLADONA.

DWAMISH. See SALISH or SALISHAW.

DWARF, in zoology and anthropology, an undersized and often deformed animal, particularly an undersized human being under fifty inches in height. The term midget is sometimes applied to particularly small dwarfs. A dwarf differs from a pygmy (q.v.) in that the latter term is applied to people whose shortness of stature is a racial trait and not the result of pathological conditions.

Cretinism (q.v.), a result of a disease of the thyroid gland, is the cause of most dwarfism seen in Europe and the United States. Other causes of dwarfism are Mongolism (a congenital disease with symptoms similar to those of cretinism), achondroplasia (a disease characterized by great shortness of the extremities as a result of absorption of cartilaginous tissue during the fetal stage), spinal tuberculosis, and deficiency of the secretion of the pituitary gland or of the ovary. Most human dwarfs display traces of rickets (q.v.), a nutritional disorder of bone formation, although in some instances dwarfs show no signs of the disease and are physically well proportioned. Formerly dwarfs were attractions in the entourages of kings. The growth of any part of the human body may be restricted by suitable mechanical devices, and the Romans practiced artificial dwarfing of children by such means in order to obtain court jesters. Perhaps the best known of all dwarfs was General Tom Thumb (see STRATTON, CHARLES SHERWOOD), but other dwarfs have been smaller, some being less than two feet in height when fully grown. The hunchbacked dwarfs at the court of Philip IV of Spain were immortalized by the great Spanish painter Velasquez (q.v.). Dwarfs are now often exhibited to the public for profit.

Stories of dwarfs are familiar in the folklore of nearly every tribe on earth, though the greatest development of these myths seems to be among the peoples of N. Europe. The dwarf Alberich in Wagner's opera *Siegfried* is a well-known example. A theory has been advanced that the superstitious belief in dwarfish "brownies" in some parts of England is a survival from ancient times, when a small, dark race of aborigines inhabited the country.

DWARF SNAKE, any small, slender serpent of the genus *Calamaria*, inhabiting southeastern Asia, or of related genera in the subfamily Colubrinae, inhabiting both the Old and New World. *Haldea striatula*, usually included in this group, although considered by some authorities to be more closely related to the water snakes (Natricinae), is common in the southern part of the U.S. It is a harmless snake, less than a foot long when fully grown, brown on its upper surface and yellow or reddish on its under surface, with a chestnut band across its head.

DWIGHT, THEODORE WILLIAM (1822–92), American educator and jurist, born at Catskill, N.Y., and educated at Hamilton College and Yale University. He became professor of law at Hamilton College, where he established a school of law. In 1858, he was appointed professor of municipal law at Columbia College, and there he became the founder and administrator of the Law School. He participated in the New York Constitutional Convention in 1867 and in 1874 he was appointed to the New York Commission of Appeals. He was author of *Trial by Impeachment* (1867).

DWIGHT, TIMOTHY (1752–1817), American clergyman and educator, born at Northampton, Mass., grandson of the elder Jonathan Edwards, and educated at Yale College. He was a chaplain in the army during the Revolutionary War, and pastor at Greenfield, Conn., from 1782 to 1795. In the latter year he was chosen president of Yale College and filled the position till his death. He was author of *Theology, Explained and Defended* (5 vols., 1818–19), and *Travels in New England and New York* (4 vols., 1821–22).

DYAKS, or DAYAKS, the name applied to the aborigines of Borneo, particularly to the pagan tribes of the interior. The Dyaks are divided into six groups: the Punans, Klemantans, and Kenyahs, who represent the oldest Dyak elements of Borneo; and the Kayans, Muruts, and Ibans (known as Sea-Dyaks), who are later arrivals. Physically, many Dyaks tend toward the Occidental rather than the Oriental races. However, clear anthropological groupings are difficult, if not impossible, due to the long admixture of Chinese, Malay, and Negrito stock. The Ibans, or Sea-Dyaks, probably the latest of the Dyak arrivals to Borneo, and long famous as pirates and conquerors, alone of the Dyak groups inhabit the coastal region. They bear great ethnological similarities to the Malays, who came to Borneo in the 12th century. The Ibans were converted to Mohammedanism by the Malays (maintaining at the same time vestiges of pagan worship), intermarried with the Malays, and undoubtedly influenced the Malay language, which is thought to contain many words of Iban derivation. The other Dyak groups, especially the Kayans and Punans, have maintained their ancient customs, habits, and religious beliefs to a much greater extent. They follow a polytheistic pagan worship that incorporates a system of major and minor gods. The exact form of worship and nomenclature of the respective gods varies from tribe to tribe.

The Dyak practice of head-hunting (q.v.), rooted for the most part in religious beliefs, is rapidly dying out. The Ibans, formerly the most notorious of the head-hunters, have dropped the custom more quickly than the other tribes, probably because, living on the coast, they are in more direct contact with European civilization and law.

The Dyaks are skilled craftsmen, making fine cloth and excellent steel weapons. They are efficient in the use of the blowpipe and are noted for the construction of serviceable bamboo suspension bridges. Rice cultivation,

A Dyak tribesman dressed for battle

hunting, and the gathering of wild fruit are their main means of subsistence. See BORNEO.

DYAS. See PERMAIN SYSTEM.

DYCK, SIR ANTHONY VAN. See VANDYKE, SIR ANTHONY.

DYEING, the process of coloring textile fibers and other substances so that the coloring matter becomes an integral part of the fiber or substance rather than a surface coating. *Dyes* or *dyestuffs* are chemical compounds, chiefly organic, which have a chemical or physical affinity for fibers and which are "fast", i.e., tend to retain their color in the fiber under exposure to sunlight, water, detergents, and wear. *Pigments* (q.v.) are insoluble coloring compounds.

History. Dyeing is an ancient art, and was practiced in Egypt, Persia, China, and India thousands of years before the birth of Christ. Little is known about the dyes used in those times, but it is probable that they included madder as a red dye and indigo as a blue. In the early days of the Roman Empire, garments dyed with Tyrian purple were worn by the imperial family and the nobility. This dye, which was prepared from the secretions of certain mollusks, was extremely valuable, and as late as the 4th century A.D., cloth colored with this dye was literally worth its weight in gold. Because of the value of the dyestuff, the mollusks that provided it were virtually exterminated in Roman times. The art of dyeing was greatly stimulated by the discovery in the 13th century of a purple dye, archil, made from a species of lichen. Northern Italy, where the discovery was made, became the center of dyeing in Europe. In the 16th century, explorers brought back a number of dyestuffs such as cochineal and logwood from the Americas, and these new materials were incorporated in the dyers' art. Among the other important natural dyes were quercitron, weld, fustic, brazilwood, safflower, and indigo (q.v.). The 19th century saw the development of the first synthetic dye, mauve, an organic compound derived from coal tar, which was discovered by William Henry Perkin (q.v.) in 1856. From that time to the present a great number of synthetic and artificial dyes have been developed, and the use of natural dyes has virtually ceased.

Many thousands of dyes and a number of dyeing processes have been developed. The dye and process used in a given operation depends on three factors: color, cost, and colorfastness.

Dyes are classified in a number of ways. They are broadly classified as direct dyes if they have the property of coloring fibers placed directly in the dye solution, and as indirect dyes if preliminary or subsequent treatment of the fiber is needed to produce a fast color. Dyes are also classified chemically according to their structures (see DYESTUFFS), and as what are commonly called acid and basic dyes. Acid dyes contain acidic groups, such as the sulfonic and carboxyl groups, and form salts with bases. The basic dyes are those which will form salts with acids.

The chemical characteristics of textile fibers determine the dyes and dyeing methods which can be used for coloring them. Wool and silk, which are proteins, will form salts with either acid or basic dyes and hence can be dyed directly by either type. Wool dyes more easily than silk. Cotton, on the other hand, will react only with acid dyes and cannot be dyed directly by the basic dyes.

The dyeing of synthetic fibers depends upon

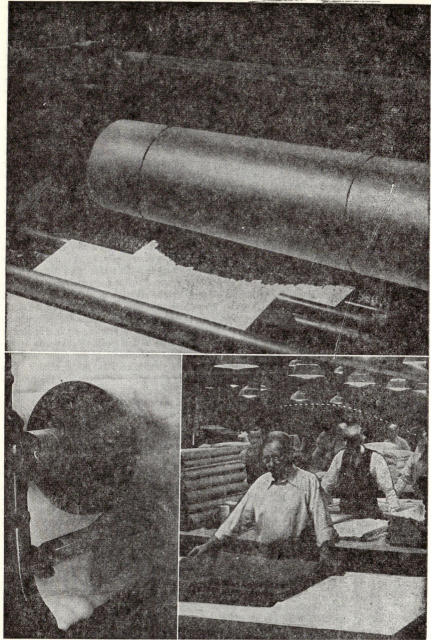

Bradford Dyeing Assn.

OPERATIONS IN A DYEING PLANT. *Top: Dyeing cloth by "color padding," process in which dye solution is forced through cloth as it passes between rollers. Bottom: Left, washing cloth in soap and water after dyeing; right, folding finished cloth for shipping.*

their composition. Viscose rayon and cuprammonium rayon, being essentially cellulose, can be directly dyed with the same compounds used for cotton. Acetate rayon (see CELANESE) requires the use of special dyes and indirect processes. Some types of nylon (q.v.) can be dyed directly with modified silk dyes, but in general the compounds and techniques employed are similar to those employed for cellulose acetate fibers. New synthetic fabrics usually require new types of dyes. Fabrics made of glass fiber cannot be dyed, because of the inert nature of the material, and are colored with metallic salts while the glass is molten, before the fibers are spun.

Indirect Dyeing. Among several processes for indirect dyeing, the simplest involves the pretreatment of the textile material with a *mordant,* followed by immersion in the dye bath. The action of the mordant permits the dye to act on the fiber. Formerly tannin was much used as a mordant, because it allowed the use of basic dyes with cotton fabrics. The most generally used mordant-dyeing process at present involves three steps: the treatment of the fabric with a solution containing the salt of a metal; a second bath containing ammonia; and a dye bath. The ammonia acting on the salt produces insoluble metal hydroxides, which remain in the fibers and which react with the dye solution to produce colored compounds known as *lakes,* which are also stable and insoluble. In the chrome dyeing of wool, the fabric is first directly colored with a soluble dye, and then treated with sodium dichromate, which combines with the dye to form a chrome lake in the fibers.

A number of dyes are insoluble compounds, and must be chemically altered before they can be used for the coloring of fabrics. In *sulfur dyes* and *vat dyes* the insoluble dye is first chemically reduced to a soluble *leuco compound.* The fabric is immersed in a solution of the leuco compound, and then exposed to air to reoxidize the compound, forming the insoluble dye in the fiber. Sulfur dyes are reduced in a solution of sodium sulfide, and vat dyes in a sodium thiosulfate solution.

Another technique of indirect dyeing involves the actual formation of the dye chemical within the fibers themselves. Such *developed dyes* are passed through two or more baths of compounds which react with each other to create the appropriate dyestuff. A similar system is used in the production of dyes in photographic emulsions in color photography (q.v.).

Dyeing Processes. Textiles may be dyed at any stage during their manufacture. Yarn or thread is dyed for the weaving of patterned fabrics and high-quality solid-color cloths. For less expensive solid-color fabrics, the cloth is dyed "in the piece", i.e., after weaving. Colored designs can also be formed on woven cloth by several processes of selective dyeing. Dyeing machinery is in general simple in operation. For acid dyes, vats of Monel metal and other acid-resisting alloys are commonly employed, and stainless steel vats are used for basic or neutral dye baths. When thread or yarn is dyed, it is usually wound on perforated spindles, through which the dye solution is forced under pressure to insure that the dye penetrates to all parts of the spools of yarn. Cloth dyed in the piece is usually run backwards and forwards over a set of rollers in the dye bath a number of times to insure even dyeing.

Three methods are employed for pattern dyeing. In *direct printing,* the cloth is run over a copper roller which has a design etched to correspond to the pattern. The dye, thickened by the addition of some substance such as starch or gelatin, is transferred to the cloth, as in the intaglio processes for printing on paper. The *reserve printing* method is similar except that a dye-repelling substance is applied to the cloth from the roller, and the cloth is then placed in the dye bath. This method is used, for example, for the production of white polka dots on a colored ground. For *discharge printing,* the cloth is first dyed and then printed with a chemical that will oxidize or reduce the dye, leaving a pattern.

See DIAZO COMPOUNDS; DYESTUFFS; PHTHALEIN DYES; TEXTILE PRINTING.

DYER'S-BROOM, a Eurasian shrub, *Genista tinctoria,* of the Pea family. It is a slander plant, often reaching 3 feet in height, and has striped branches. Its multiflowered inflorescence is born in terminal clusters. The variety *plena* is prized for its double flowers. The tops of dyer's-broom were formerly used in Europe for a yellow dye (see BROOM). Dyer's-broom is also called greenwood, dyeweed, whin, and woadwaxen.

DYESTUFFS, any of a large group of chemicals, almost exclusively organic in nature, which are used for the coloring of textiles, inks, food products, and other substances.

The color properties of organic compounds depend upon their structure. In general, the colored compounds used as dyes are unsaturated organic chemicals. The quality of possessing color is particularly noticeable in compounds containing certain well-defined chemically unsaturated groupings. These groups are known as *chromophores* (color bearers). The chromophores are not all equally effective in producing color. Dyestuffs, however, in addition to being colored, must be capable of entering and coloring cloth fibers or other substances. It has been found that certain other chemical radicals have the property of anchoring the colored compound effectively. These radicals, known as *auxochromes*, are acidic or basic in nature and give rise to the acid and basic dyes; see DYEING. In the case of some compounds the addition of an auxochrome group changes a colorless compound into a colored one in addition to acting as an anchor.

The basic "raw materials" of synthetic dyes are compounds such as benzene, anthracene, phenol, and naphthalene, which are derived from the destructive distillation of coal; see COAL TAR; ANILINE. For this reason synthetic dyestuffs are often popularly known as coaltar dyes. In many instances they are similar in structure to natural substances which were used in the dyeing art before the introduction of synthetics. From the basic materials, *intermediates* are manufactured by a number of chemical processes. In general these processes involve the substitution of specific elements or chemical radicals for one or more of the hydrogen atoms in the basic substance. Many dye intermediaries are known, from which a far larger number of dyes can be produced by further chemical treatment.

Dyestuffs can be classified according to their use (see DYEING) or by their chemical structure. The chemical classification is generally made according to the nucleus of the compound. Among the more important dye groups are the azo dyes (see DIAZO COMPOUNDS), which include butter yellow and Congo red; the triphenylmethane dyes, which include magenta and methyl violet; the phthalein dyes (q.v.); the azine dyes, which include mauve; and the anthraquinone dyes, which include alizarin. Indigo is a vat dye, occurring in nature in the crystalline glucoside indican. An important new group of dyes are the phthalocyanine dyes, which are blue or green in color and resemble chlorophyll in chemical structure. Of all the groups of dyes the azo dyes are the most generally useful and widely employed.

DYING DECLARATION. See DECLARATION, DYING.

DYNAMITE, an explosive, usually consisting of a mixture of nitroglycerine or nitrostarch (qq.v.), sodium nitrate, and an absorb-

ent, such as wood flour, sawdust, or charcoal, to cushion the nitroglycerine from shock. Dynamite was invented in 1866 by Alfred Nobel (q.v.), who used diatomaceous earth (q.v.) for the absorbent. Because of the comparative safety with which dynamite can be handled and manufactured (being much more stable than nitroglycerine or most other explosives which explode with a force comparable to its own), and because of its high shattering power, it has become the most widely used nonmilitary explosive in the U.S. and most other parts of the world. The nitroglycerine is often mixed with ingredients which depress its freezing point, so that the dynamite may be used under conditions of low temperature. The strength of a quantity of dynamite depends upon its nitroglycerine content, which usually ranges from ten to seventy-five percent of the mixture. Oxidizing agents are included in most dynamites used in the U.S. in order to reduce the amount of carbon monoxide and other poisonous fumes produced when the mixture explodes.

Various types of dynamite are manufactured according to the uses for which they are intended. The most powerful of the dynamites is blasting gelatine. When this material is mixed with wood flour and potassium nitrate, a product known as gelatine dynamite results. This water-resistant material is the most common explosive for underwater uses. A nonfreezing dynamite, useful at low temperatures, is a mixture of nitrostarch, oxidizing agents, and absorbent. For quick-acting, powerful explosions, an explosive called straight nitroglycerine dynamite, a mixture of nitroglycerine and a combustible absorbent, is used. Ammonia dynamites, which consist of the same materials as nitroglycerine dynamites with part of the nitroglycerine replaced by ammonium nitrate, are relatively safe to handle.

Dynamite is generally manufactured in sticks or cartridges about eight inches long and from one to three inches in diameter. These cartridges are fired by detonating caps, inserted under the paper covering of the dynamite stick. See DETONATOR; EXPLOSIVES.

An indication of the widespread use of dynamite in the U.S. may be gathered from the fact that in a recent year over 300,000,000 pounds of it were manufactured and sold in the U.S. About seventy-five percent of the dynamite manufactured in the U.S. is used in mining.

DYNAMOELECTRIC MACHINERY, devices for converting mechanical energy into

Du Pont Co.; Standard Oil Co. (N.J.)

Above: Precision dynamiting. In preparing to build a dam for a hydroelectric project on the Saguenay River, Canada, attempts to build a preliminary structure to hold back the water failed because of the torrential rush of the stream. Engineers overcame the difficulty by building a dam in final form on its side, completely out of water. They then placed dynamite charges under the supports, and the resulting blast shown above dropped the huge structure accurately into place, effecting a perfect dam.

Left: Placing a wired detonating cap into the end of a large stick of dynamite.

is the principle of magnetic induction discovered by the English scientist Michael Faraday in 1831. If a conductor is moved through a magnetic field, or if a conductor is held in a varying magnetic field, a current is set up or induced in the conductor. The converse of this principle is the principle of magnetic reaction, first observed by the French physicist A. M. Ampère in 1820. If a current is passed through a conductor located in a magnetic field, the field exerts a mechanical force on it.

The simplest of all dynamoelectric machines is the disk dynamo developed by Faraday. It consists of a copper disk which is mounted so that part of the disk is between the poles of a horseshoe magnet. When the disk is rotated a current is induced between the center of the disk and its edge by the action of the field of the magnet. The disk can be made to operate as a motor by applying a voltage between the edge of the disk and its

electrical energy, or electrical energy into mechanical energy, by electromagnetic means. A machine which converts mechanical energy into electrical energy is called a generator or dynamo, and a machine which converts electrical energy into mechanical energy is called a motor.

Two related physical principles underlie the operation of generators and motors. The first center, causing the disk to rotate because of the force produced by magnetic reaction.

Because the magnetic field of a permanent magnet is not strong enough to operate a practical dynamo or motor, electromagnets are universally employed. Both motors and generators consist of two basic units, the *field*, which is the electromagnet with its coils, and the *armature*, the structure which supports the conductors that cut the magnetic field and carry the induced current in a generator or the exciting current in a motor. The armature is usually a laminated soft-iron core around which conducting wires are wound in coils.

D.C. Generators. When a movable armature revolves between a pair of stationary field poles, as shown in the accompanying diagram, the current in the armature moves in one direction during half of each revolution and in the other direction during the other half. To produce a steady flow of unidirectional or direct current (d.c.) from such a device it is necessary to provide a means of reversing the current flow outside the generator once during each revolution. This reversal is accomplished by means of a *commutator,* a split metal ring mounted on the shaft of the armature. The two halves of the ring are insulated from each other and serve as the terminals of the armature coil. Fixed *brushes* of metal or carbon are held against the commutator as it revolves, connecting the coil electrically to external wires. As the armature turns, each brush is in contact alternately with the halves of the commutator, changing position at the moment when the current in the armature coil reverses its direction. Thus there is a flow of unidirectional current in the outside circuit to which the generator is connected. Direct-current generators are usually operated at fairly low voltages to avoid the sparking between brushes and commutator that occurs at high voltage. The highest potential commonly developed by such generators is 1500 volts.

A number of refinements have been made in the structure of modern d.c. generators. The armatures now in use usually consist of a large number of windings set in longitudinal slits in the armature core and connected to appropriate segments of a multiple commutator. This type of armature is called a drum armature. In an armature having only one loop of wire the current produced will rise and fall depending on the part of the magnetic field through which the loop is moving. The drum armature always has one loop of wire moving through the high-intensity area of the field, and as a result the current induced in the ar-

mature windings is virtually constant. Fields of modern generators are usually equipped with four or more electromagnet poles to increase the size and strength of the magnetic field. Sometimes smaller interpoles are added to compensate for distortions in the magnetic flux of the field caused by the magnetic effect of the armature.

Direct-current generators are commonly classified according to the method used to provide field current for energizing the field magnets. A series-wound generator has its field in series with the armature, and a shunt-wound generator has the field connected in parallel with the armature. Compound-wound generators have part of their fields in series and part in parallel. Both series-wound and compound-wound generators have the advantage of delivering comparatively constant voltage under varying electrical loads. A *magneto* is a small d.c. generator with a permanent-magnet field.

D.C. Motors. In general, d.c. motors are similar to d.c. generators in construction. They can, in fact, be described as generators "run backwards". When current is passed through the armature of a d.c. motor, a torque is generated by magnetic reaction, and the armature revolves. The action of the commutator and the connections of the field coils of motors are precisely the same as those used for generators. The operation of motors differs, however, because the revolution of the armature induces a voltage in the armature windings. This induced voltage is opposite in direction to the outside voltage applied to the armature, and hence is called *back voltage* or *counter e.m.f.* (electromotive force). As the motor rotates more rapidly, the back voltage

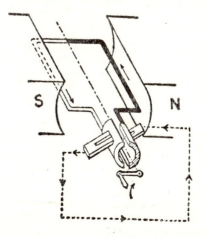

rises until it is almost equal to the applied voltage. The current is then small and the speed of the motor will remain constant as long as the motor is not under load and is performing no mechanical work except that required to turn the armature. Under load the armature turns more slowly, reducing the back voltage and permitting a larger current to flow in the armature. The motor is thus able to receive more electric power from the source supplying it and to do more mechanical work.

Because the speed of rotation controls the flow of current in the armature, special devices must be used for starting d.c. motors. When the armature is at rest it has virtually no resistance, and if the normal working voltage is applied a large current will flow, melting the armature windings. The usual means of preventing the armature from burning out in this way is the use of a *starting resistance* in series with the armature to lower the voltage until the motor begins to develop an adequate back voltage. As the motor picks up speed the resistance is gradually reduced, either manually or automatically.

The speed at which a d.c. motor operates depends upon the strength of the magnetic field acting on the armature. The stronger the field, the slower is the rate of rotation needed to generate a back voltage large enough to counteract the applied voltage. For this reason the speed of d.c. motors can be controlled by varying the field current.

A.C. Generators (Alternators). As stated above, a simple generator without a commutator will produce an electric current that alternates in direction as the armature revolves. Such alternating current (a.c.) is advantageous for electric power transmission (q.v.) and hence most large electric generators are built to supply a.c. In its simplest form, an a.c. generator differs from a d.c. generator in only two particulars: the ends of its armature winding are brought out to solid unsegmented *slip rings* on the generator shaft instead of to commutators, and the field coils are energized by an external d.c. source rather than by the generator itself. Low-speed a.c. generators are built with as many as 100 poles, both to improve their efficiency and to attain more easily the frequency desired; see ELECTRICITY. Alternators driven by high-speed turbines, however, are often two-pole machines. The frequency of the current delivered by an a.c. generator is equal to half the product of the number of poles and the number of revolutions per second of the armature.

It is often desirable to generate as high a voltage as possible, and rotating armatures are not practical in such applications because of the possibility of sparking between brushes and slip rings and the danger of mechanical failures which might cause short circuits. Alternators are therefore constructed with a stationary armature within which revolves a rotor composed of a number of field magnets. The principle of operation is exactly the same as that of the a.c. generator described, except that the magnetic field (rather than the conductors of the armature) is in motion.

The current generated by the alternators described above rises to a peak, sinks to zero, drops to a negative peak, and rises again to zero a number of times each second, depending on the frequency for which the machine is designed. Such current is known as *single phase a.c.* If, however, the armature is composed of two windings, mounted at right angles to each other, two current waves will be produced, each of which will be at its maximum when the other is at zero. Such current is called *two-phase a.c.* If three armature windings are set at 120° to each other, current will be produced in the form of a triple wave, known as *three-phase a.c.* A larger number of phases may be obtained by increasing the number of windings in the armature, but in modern electrical-engineering practice three-phase a.c. is most commonly used and the three-phase alternator is the dynamoelectric machine typically employed for the generation of electric power. Voltages as high as 13,200 are common in alternators.

A.C. Motors. Two basic types of motors are designed to operate on alternating current, *synchronous motors* and *induction motors.* The synchronous motor is essentially a three-phase alternator operated in reverse. The field magnets are mounted on the rotor and are excited by direct current, and the armature winding is divided into three parts and fed with three-phase a.c. The variation of the three waves of current in the armature causes a varying magnetic reaction with the poles of the field magnets, and makes the field rotate at a constant speed which is determined by the frequency of the current in the a.c. power line. The constant speed of a synchronous motor is advantageous in certain devices such as electric clocks; however, in applications where the mechanical load on the motor varies, synchronous motors cannot be used, because if the motor slows down under load it will "fall out of step" with the frequency of the current and come to a stop. Synchronous motors can be made to operate from a single-

Westinghouse

DYNAMOELECTRIC MACHINERY. *Alternating-current generators at Hoover Dam, California, convert water power into electricity. Output of each generator is 115,000 horsepower.*

phase power source by the inclusion of suitable circuit elements which cause a varying magnetic reaction.

The simplest of all electric motors is the *squirrel-cage* type of induction motor used with a three-phase supply. The field of the squirrel-cage motor consists of three fixed coils similar to the armature of the synchronous motor. The rotating armature consists of a core in which are imbedded a series of heavy conductors arranged in a circle around the shaft and parallel to it. With the core removed, the armature conductors resemble in form the cylindrical cages once used to exercise pet squirrels. The three-phase current flowing in the field windings generates a rotating magnetic field, and this field induces a voltage in the conductors of the cage. The magnetic reaction between the rotating field and the current-carrying conductors of the armature makes the armature turn. If the armature is rotating at exactly the same speed as the magnetic field, no currents will be induced in it; in operation the speeds of rota-

tion of the armature and the field differ by about 2 to 5 percent. This speed difference is known as slip. Motors with squirrel-cage armatures can be used on single-phase a.c. by means of various arrangements of inductance and capacity which alter the characteristics of the single-phase voltage and make it resemble a two-phase voltage. Such motors are called *split-phase motors* or *condenser motors* (or *capacitor motors*) depending on the arrangement used. Single-phase squirrel-cage motors do not have a large starting torque, and for applications where such torque is required *repulsion-induction* motors are used. A repulsion-induction motor may be of the split-phase or condenser type, but has a manual or automatic switch which allows current to flow in the armature when the motor is starting and short-circuits the armature after it begins to rotate. Repulsion-induction motors are so named because their starting torque depends on the repulsion between the field and the armature and their torque while running depends on induction. Series-wound induction motors with commutators, which will operate on either a.c. or d.c., are called *universal motors*. They are usually made only in small sizes.

Miscellaneous Machines. For special applications several combined types of dynamoelectric machines are employed. It is frequently desirable to change from d.c. to a.c. or vice versa, or to change voltage of a d.c. supply, or the frequency or phase of an a.c. supply. The most direct method of accomplishing such changes is to use a motor operating from the available type of electric supply to drive a generator delivering the current and voltage wanted. *Motor generators,* consisting of an appropriate motor mechanically coupled to an appropriate generator, can accomplish any of the indicated conversions. A *rotary converter* is a machine for converting alternating to direct current, using separate windings on a common rotating armature. The a.c. supply voltage is applied to the armature through slip rings, and the d.c. voltage is led out of the machine through a separate commutator. A *dynamotor*, which is usually used to convert low-voltage d.c. to high-voltage d.c., is a similar machine which has separate armature windings.

Pairs of machines known as *selsyns, autosyns,* or *synchros* are used to transmit torque or mechanical movement from one place to another by electrical means. They consist of pairs of motors with stationary fields and armatures wound with three sets of coils similar to those of a three-phase alternator. In use, the armatures of selsyns are connected electrically in parallel to each other but not to any external source. The field coils are connected in parallel to an external a.c. source. When the armatures of both selsyns are in the same position relative to the magnetic fields of their respective machines, the currents induced in the armature coils will be equal and will cancel each other out. But when one of the armatures is moved, an unbalance is created which will cause a current to be induced in the other armature. The magnetic reaction to this current will move the second armature until it is in the same relative position as the first. Selsyns are widely used for remote control and remote indicating instruments where it is inconvenient or impossible to make a mechanical connection. See ELECTRICITY.

DYNAMOMETER, an apparatus used to measure the mechanical power developed by an engine or other prime mover. Such apparatus is either of the absorption or transmission type. Absorption dynamometers absorb all of the mechanical power output of the engine they are measuring. This mechanical power is converted by frictional drag into heat; the dynamometer then measures (by some form of spring balance and a tachometer) the frictional power, or measures (by a calorimeter) the total heat produced. The results obtained are converted into units of power such as watts or horsepower. The friction for absorption dynamometers may be furnished by cords, belts, or wooden blocks tightened around the engine output shaft or pulley, by liquid or air in a closed container around the shaft, or by a magnetic drag. The Prony brake is an example of an absorption dynamometer.

In transmission dynamometers, the power furnished to the device passes on to an external load. In one device of this type, called the torsion dynamometer or torquemeter, a shaft is inserted between the engine and its load. This intermediate shaft is constrained, and twists through an angle dependent upon the force that the engine develops. The dynamometer is usually calibrated in such a manner that, when its reading is multiplied by a tachometer reading, the power of the engine in horsepower is obtained directly.

DYNE. See C.G.S. SYSTEM.

DYSENTERY, an acute or chronic disease of the large intestine of man, characterized by frequent passage of bloody mucous stools and by ulceration of the walls of the intestine. The disease may be a result of amebic (see AMEBA) or bacillary (see BACTERIA) infection.

Amebic dysentery, also called amebic colitis, intestinal amebiasis, and entamebiasis, is caused by a parasite, *Entameba histolytica,* found in stools of infected persons. The ameba is characterized by its motility when observed in a fresh stool specimen, and by the structure of its stained nucleus.

Amebic dysentery is endemic in tropical countries. It is the most common type of dysentery in the Philippine Islands, the Malay Archipelago, and the West Indies, but also occurs in outbreaks in almost all temperate countries. The most recent outbreak in the United States occurred in Chicago during the late summer and fall of 1933.

The disease is caused by the ingestion of freely motile or encysted forms of *E. histolytica.* Amebic dysentery is most commonly spread by water or uncooked food contaminated with feces from infected persons. Uncooked vegetables are a common source of infection, especially in tropical countries where untreated human feces is used as a plant fertilizer. Flies, which may carry the amebic cysts on their feet, spread the ameba from the feces of infected persons to food. The disease is also spread by *carriers,* people who suffer no ill effects from the disease but pass large numbers of the encysted parasites in their feces, whence contamination may occur.

Amebic dysentery may result in perforation of the walls of the intestine, and in abscesses of the liver and lungs. Various drugs, including emetine (q.v.), arsenicals such as carbarsone, and iodine-containing preparations such as yatren, anayodin, and quinoxyl, have been useful in treating the disease. According to medical reports in 1954, considerable success in controlling the disease is obtained by the administration of a new drug, called Camoform; the drug is effective also in the treatment of chronic carriers of the disease.

Bacillary dysentery is caused by certain non-motile bacteria (q.v.) of the Shigella group. This disease is also most prevalent in the tropics, but epidemics and sporadic outbreaks are common in all parts of the world. The stool passed in bacillary dysentery differs from that of amebic dysentery by the presence in the latter of *E. histolytica,* and the presence in the former of the dysentery bacteria and large phagocytic (pus) cells. Simultaneous infections by both amebae and bacteria may occur. Bacillary dysentery is spread by contaminated water, milk, and food. Feces from active cases and from healthy carriers contain immense numbers of the disease-producing bacteria. Flies, which may carry the bacteria on their feet or in their saliva and feces and deposit them on food, are one of the most important means of dissemination of bacteria; ants are also believed to spread the disease. It is easily spread from a single infected individual or a carrier to many people, and is therefore a constantly present danger to the public health.

Besides dehydration produced by loss of water in the feces, bacillary dysentery may also cause arthritis and perforation of the bowel. General debility may also result from vitamin deficiencies resulting from improper digestion and absorption of food. Sulfa-drug therapy has proved excellent in curing acute cases. Vaccine therapy has proved more successful in chronic cases.

DYSMENORRHEA. See MENSTRUATION.

DYSPROSIUM, a metallic element, one of the rare-earth (q.v.) family of elements. Its symbol is Dy, atomic number 66, atomic weight 162.46, valence 3. Dysprosium usually occurs as the white oxide, Dy_2O_3, dysprosia, with erbium and holmium, two other rare-earth elements. It is 45th in abundance among the elements in the earth's crust. Its compounds are found in gadolinite, xenotime, euxenite, and fergusonite in Norway, U.S., Brazil, India, and Australia. Its salts are yellow or yellow green, the most common being a chloride, $DyCl_3$, a nitrate, $Dy(NO_3)_3 \cdot 5H_2O$, and a sulfate, $Dy_2(SO_4)_3 \cdot 8H_2O$. The salts of dysprosium have an extremely high magnetic susceptibility, higher than that of any other substance except metals such as iron. The element was discovered in 1886 by P. E. Lecoq de Boisbaudran (1838–1912), who separated one of its compounds from crude holmia. There are no commercial uses for compounds of dysprosium.

DYTISCUS, or DYTICUS. See DIVING BEETLE.

DZUNGARIA. See SUNGARIA.

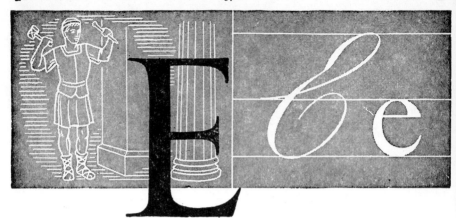

E, the fifth and most frequently used letter of the English alphabet. Its form was derived without alteration from the fifth letter of the classical Latin alphabet, which had adapted it from the Greek letter epsilon (E ε). The letter evolved from the Phenician ⋺ , which in turn had developed from the Egyptian hieratic ⊔ and the earlier hieroglyph ⊓ , the ultimate origin of the letter.

Its modern English name is pronounced as the first syllable of the word *even.* In the other languages which use the Roman alphabet, such as French and Spanish, the name of this letter rhymes with the word *may;* this sound was also originally the sound of long *e* in English. *E* is always long in modern English when doubled, as in *eel* and *keep,* and also when followed by a silent *e* after an intervening single consonant, as in *complete,* and *extreme.* Silent *e* serves also to lengthen other vowels when they precede it and are separated from it by a single consonant, as in *late, fire, bone,* and *rule.* Short *e* is most commonly pronounced as in *get* and *bell,* but changes somewhat when followed by an r, as in *there.* In such words as *slipped* and *over, e* has the quality of a mere voice glide.

Among the many uses of the letter *e* are the following. As a Roman numeral, capital E stands for 250 or, in the form Ē, for 250,000. As an abbreviation, capital E may stand for such personal names as Edward, Ernest, and Emily, and for such terms as East, Eastern, Earth, Easter, and English. Capital E symbolizes, in logic, the universal negative propo-

sition, and in physics, energy, electromotive force (voltage), or the lowermost layer of the ionosphere. Small *e* may be used as an abbreviation for the stage direction *entrance,* for the coefficient of impact or for elasticity in engineering, and for the eccentricity of a curve in mathematics. In music, E is the name of the third note in the natural scale (C) and the fifth in the relative minor scale (A minor). Italicized *e* symbolizes the electrical charge of an electron or proton in physics.

e, in mathematics, a number of great importance, comparable only to π (the ratio of the circumference of a circle to its diameter) in the wide variety of its applications. Unlike π it has no simple geometrical interpretation. Like π, it is a transcendental number, i.e., it cannot be expressed exactly in terms of any finite algebraic equation, nor of any finite fraction. It can, however, be approximated to any desired degree of accuracy by any one of a number of infinite series, of which one of the simplest is

$$1 + \frac{1}{1} + \frac{1}{1 \times 2} + \frac{1}{1 \times 2 \times 3} + \cdots$$

The approximate value of *e* is 2.71828182845-904523536.

In mathematics, *e* appears as the base of natural logarithms. In physics and biology, it appears in the so-called exponential function, e^x, the only function having a rate of growth equal to its size (in the language of calculus, the only function having a derivative equal to itself), and therefore the fundamental function for equations describing growth and many other processes of change. In geometry, e is a necessary component of the formulas for many curves, such as the catenary, the shape assumed by a cord suspended from its extremities. In the study of imaginary numbers, e appears in the extraordinary equation $e^{\pi i} = -1$, where i is the imaginary number $\sqrt{-1}$. e appears constantly in the theory of probability. For example, if a large number of letters are written and the corresponding envelopes addressed, and the letters are then fitted at random into the envelopes, the probability that every letter will go into a wrong envelope is $\frac{1}{e}$. e also appears in formulas for calculating compound interest. Even in pure theory of numbers, e crops up. Thus, the number of prime numbers in the first N numbers (if N is very large) is given by the expression $\frac{N}{\log N}$ where log N is the natural logarithm of N, and therefore a function of e. Compare Pi.

EA or **EN-KI** (Sum., "Lord of the Earth"), a deity of Sumerian origin, constituting with Anu and Bel (qq.v.) the supreme triad of the Babylonian pantheon. He was worshiped chiefly at Eridu (q.v.), one of the earliest Mesopotamian cities. Ea was the creator of mankind, patron god of civilization, healer of the sick, and bringer of arts and sciences. He was likewise the god of fresh water; as such he was conventionally represented with the head of a man and the body of a fish, and dwelt in Apsu, the nether sea, from which springs and rivers flowed.

EADMUND. See Edmund.

EADWINE. See Edwin.

EAGLE, common name for a number of the largest members of the Hawk family in the order Falconiformes. The term is loosely used; some buzzards of the same family and some hawks are larger than the smaller eagles. Like other members of the Hawk family, the eagle is characterized by a hooked beak, and by well-developed legs and feet with the toes equipped with long, curved talons. Its keenness of vision and the strength which it displays in flight are remarkable. The bird soars to great heights, from which it swoops down suddenly to seize its prey either in the air or on the ground. To a limited extent, the eagle has been used in falconry (q.v.).

From ancient times the eagle has been regarded as a symbol of courage and power because of the altitudes to which it flies, because of the great size of the larger species, and because of the inaccessibility of the mountain heights in which some species nest. In Roman myths the eagle is associated with Jupiter. It was the emblem of certain Roman legions, and of France under the Bonapartes, of Germany, of the Russian and Austro-Hungarian empires, and of the United States.

The golden eagle, *Aquila chrysaëtos*, is distributed through most of the Northern Hemisphere. In North America it is seen as far south as Mexico, although it is most common in the Rocky Mountain area and in the mountains of the Pacific Coast; east of the Mississippi it is relatively rare. The male grows to an average length of about thirty-three inches from the tip of the beak to the tip of the tail, and has a wingspread of six and one-half to seven feet. The female is larger by several inches. It is characteristic of the genus that the legs down to the toes are feathered. The plumage is dark brown shading to a sooty color on some parts, with irregular bands or mottling of a grayish color on the tail. The head and the back of the neck are covered with slightly longer feathers of a tawny hue. The name golden eagle probably is derived from the bright yellow of the beak and feet. Compared with that of other species, the beak is relatively short, but has the typical curve beginning below the fleshy base.

By preference the golden eagle builds its nest on a high ledge or rock. The nest is large and coarse, built of sticks or twigs. The female lays two, and occasionally three, eggs. Usually the nest is built at a considerable distance from other eagle nests, for one pair of birds and their young consume extraordinarily large quantities of food, and need an extensive area for their hunting ground. The diet of this species consists mainly of small birds and mammals. Legends crediting eagles with carrying off children greatly exaggerate the bird's strength; experiments have proved that no eagle can rise into the air with a load greater than eight or ten pounds. Occasionally, however, the golden eagle carries off a new-born lamb.

Another member of the genus *Aquila* is *A. heliaca*, the imperial eagle of Asia and S.E. Europe; it is smaller and darker than the golden eagle. The much smaller, spotted eagles, *A. maculata* and *A. clanga*, are found in central and southern Europe, and the dwarf eagle, *A. pennata*, is found in southern Europe and in India and Africa. *A. vindhiana* and *A. rapax* are the tawny eagles of India and Africa, respectively.

Sea Eagles. The sea eagles or ernes inhabit

Nature Mag.; Amer. Mus. Nat. Hist.; Australian News
& Info. Bur.; N.Y. Zoological Soc.

*Above: Left, northern bald eagle; right, white-
tailed sea eagle. Right: Head of golden eagle.
Below: Left, wedge-tailed eagle; right, harpy.*

coastal regions and the shores of lakes and streams, and live mainly on fish. One of these is the bald eagle, *Heliaeetus leucocephalus,* also known as the American eagle; by an act of the Second Continental Congress in 1782 it became the official emblem of the United States. The subspecies *H. leucocephalus leucocephalus,* or southern bald eagle, has a range extending from southern Canada into central Mexico. This bird is about the size of the golden eagle; the female, slightly larger than the male, attains a wingspread of seven and one-half feet. The northern bald eagle, *H. leucocephalus alascanus,* is a larger subspecies widely distributted in Alaska and Canada. Winter migrations bring it into the northern part of the United States, sometimes as far south as Connecticut. The bald eagle migrates only from the coldest sections of its range. The bird is not bald, but when three years old develops white feathers on the head and neck, and also a white tail, contrasting with the rest of its plumage, which is blackish brown. The young are entirely dark. Unlike the golden eagle, the bald eagle has no feathers on the lower legs. Compared to other eagles, the bald eagle is clumsy and inexpert in hunting and fishing. It depends heavily on injured or dead fish cast up by whirlpools or tides. It also steals from the osprey when the smaller bird has caught a live fish; the eagle attacks the osprey in the air, tormenting it until the osprey drops the fish, which the eagle catches in the air. The bald eagle's nest often is built in the top of a tall, dead tree. A pair of birds may use the same nest year after year.

A larger species is the white-tailed or gray sea eagle, *H. albicilla,* of Iceland, Greenland, northern Europe, and northern Asia; its plumage is a dark, grayish color with white on the tail. *H. pelagicus,* a brown species with white shoulders, rump, and tail, inhabits northeastern Asia. Steller's sea eagle, *Thalassoaëtus pelagicus,* also called the Kamchatkan sea eagle, grows to a length of forty-four inches or more. It inhabits northeastern Asia and the north Pacific islands, including islands off the coast of Alaska. It is marked with white on the forehead, breast, and wing coverts, and on the flanks, rump, and tail. *Polioateus ichthyaetus,* the fishing eagle of India, belongs in this group. Africa has several sea eagles.

Crested and Other Eagles. One of the largest and most powerful eagles, though relatively slow in flight, is the harpy or harpy eagle, *Thrasaëtus harpyia,* of Mexico, Central America, and northern South America. It is gray, with white on the head and lower parts. The upper parts are marked with black bands, and a dark band crosses the chest. The head has a double crest. Another large, crested bird is the monkey-eating eagle, *Pithecophaga jefferyi,* of the Philippines; it too is sometimes called the harpy eagle.

The spotted crested eagles of the genus *Spilornis,* of India and southeast Asia, feed on reptiles and are called serpent eagles. This latter name is given also to the harrier eagles of the genus *Bastatur,* and to the secretary bird. Several species of *Bastatur* and of *Circaëtus,* another genus of reptile-eaters, are found in Africa and southern Asia; *C. gallicus* appears in areas bordering the Mediterranean, and in Central Europe.

EAGLE OWL. See OWL.

EAGLE RAY. See STING RAY.

EAGLEWOOD. See ALOES WOOD.

EAGRE. See BORE.

EAKER, IRA CLARENCE (1896–   ), American aviator and army officer, born in Llano Co., Texas, and educated at South Eastern Normal College, Oklahoma, and the University of Southern California. Commissioned a 2nd lieutenant in the infantry in 1917, he was transferred to the air force and rated a pilot in 1918. He became a captain in 1920 and advanced through grades to temporary lieutenant general in 1943 and permanent major general in 1945. In 1929 he was the chief pilot of the army plane *Question Mark,* which set a world endurance flight record, and in 1936 he made the first transcontinental blind flight. He was commanding officer of the 20th Pursuit Group in 1941, and commanding general of the 8th Bomber Command in 1942, in which capacity he led the first attack by United States heavy bombers in Europe. He was commanding general of the U.S. 8th Air Force in the United Kingdom in 1943, and in 1944 he became commander in chief of the Mediterranean Allied Air Forces. He participated in the first shuttle bombing mission to Russia in June, 1944. In 1945 he became deputy commander of the Army Air Forces and chief of the Air Staff, a position he held until his retirement in June, 1947.

EAKINS, THOMAS (1844–1916), American painter and sculptor, born in Philadelphia. He studied painting at the Pennsylvania Academy of Fine Arts, Philadelphia, and at the École des Beaux-Arts, Paris, under Jean Léon Gérôme; in Paris he also studied sculpture, with Augustin Alexandre Dumont. Eakins was one of the foremost American painters of the realistic school of the late 19th and early 20th centuries. His paintings are notable not only for his exact rendering of the physical aspects of his subjects, but for his esthetically satisfying composition. He is especially noted for his portraits and genre paintings. Among his paintings are "The Surgical Clinic of Professor Gross" (Jefferson Medical College, Philadelphia), "The Cello Player" (Pennsylvania Academy of Fine Arts), and "The Chess Players" and "Max Schmitt in a Single Scull" (both in the Metropolitan Museum of Art, New York City). Among his sculptures are reliefs on the monument (Trenton, N.J.) to the Battle of Trenton, and the horses on the Soldiers and Sailors Monument (Brooklyn, N.Y.).

EALDRED. See ALDRED.

EALING, a municipal and parliamentary borough of Middlesex County, England, about 9 miles w. of the center of London. The manor of Ealing was once a part of the see of London. Ealing maintains a park system of about 980 acres, and contains technical and art schools. Pop. (1953 est.) 186,100.

EAR, the organ of hearing. In man and other mammals it is composed of three parts: the external ear, the middle ear or tympanum, and the internal ear or labyrinth.

The *external* ear consists of two portions, the *auricle* or *pinna* (the external flap of the ear), and the *auditory canal* or *external meatus.*

The *middle ear,* or cavity of the *tympanum,* is a space filled with air which is received from the pharynx through the Eustachian tube. The middle ear, separated from the external ear by the membrane of the tympanum (commonly called the eardrum), is traversed by a chain of three small movable bones (the *ossicles* of the tympanum). The ossicles connect the membrane of the tympanum acoustically with the internal ear. The tension of the membrane of the tympanum is maintained by a muscle, the *tensor tympani*, which is attached to the ossicles.

The Eustachian tube, into which the tympanic cavity opens anteriorly, is about 1½ inches in length, and passes downward, forward, and inward to its opening in the pharynx. It is partly osseous, but chiefly cartilaginous, and allows the free passage of air into and out of the tympanum.

The *internal ear* or *labyrinth* is the essential part of the organ of hearing, being the portion to which the ultimate filaments of the auditory nerve (see NERVOUS SYSTEM) are distributed. It is separated from the middle ear by the *fenestra ovalis* (oval window). The internal ear consists of convoluted canals in an exceptionally hard and dense portion of the temporal bone, and is divided by anatomists into the *cochlea* (Gr., "snail shell"), the *vestibule,* and the *semicircular canals.* All these canals communicate with one another. Sound waves are carried by the auditory canal to the membrane of the tympanum which then vibrates. Its vibrations are communicated to the chain of bones in the middle ear, through which sensations are conveyed to the tiny endings of the auditory nerve in the internal ear, and thence to the auditory center in the brain (see AUDITION).

The ear is simpler in animals lower than mammals. The pinna is usually absent and there is a simplified system of ossicles. Classes below the Amphibia possess only the internal ear.

The range of hearing, like that of vision, varies remarkably in different persons. Some people are insensitive to sounds which others can hear readily. The maximum range of human hearing includes sound frequencies from about 16 to 20,000 cycles per second (see SOUND). The least noticeable change in tone that can be picked up by the ear varies with pitch and loudness. A change of vibration frequency (pitch) corresponding to about 0.03% of the original frequency (or about 1/30 of a note) can be detected by the most sensitive human ears in the range between 500 and 8000 vibrations per second. The ear is less sensitive to frequency changes for sounds of low frequency or low intensity. See SOUND.

The sensitivity of the ear to sound intensity (loudness) also varies with vibration frequency. Sensitivity to change in loudness is greatest in the range from 1000 to 3000 cycles, where a change of one decibel can be detected, and becomes less when sound intensity levels are lowered.

The variation in the sensitivity of the ear to loud sounds causes several important phenomena. Very loud tones produce in the ear entirely different notes (such as sum and difference tones and harmonics) which are not present in the original tone. These *subjective tones* are probably caused by imperfections in the natural function of the middle ear. The harshness in tonality caused by greatly increasing sound intensities (as when a radio volume control is adjusted to produce excessively loud sounds), results from subjective tones produced in the ear. The loud-

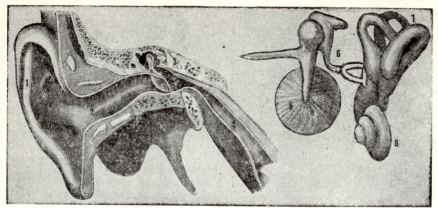

HUMAN EAR. *1, auricle; 2, auditory canal; 3, middle ear; 4, Eustachian tube; 5, the membrane of the tympanum; 6, middle-ear bones; 7, semicircular canals; 8, cochlea.*

ness of a pure tone also affects its pitch. High tones may increase as much as a whole musical-scale note; low tones tend to become lower as sound intensity increases. This effect is noticeable only for pure tones. Since most musical tones are complex, hearing is usually not affected to an appreciable degree by this phenomenon. Another phenomenon is known as *masking*. The production in the ear of harmonics of lower-pitched sounds may deafen the ear to the perception of higher-pitched sounds. Masking is the phenomenon which makes necessary the raising of one's voice in order to be heard in a noisy place. See also DEAFNESS; HEARING AIDS.

Equilibrium. Whereas the cochlea of the internal ear contains the essential mechanism of hearing, the semicircular canals are concerned with the sense of equilibrium; the centrally located vestibule probably has both functions. All three parts of the labyrinth contain, within a membranous lining, a gelatinous fluid called *endolymph.* Any motion of the endolymph agitates hairs extending from sensory cells in the membrane; hairs in the coils of the cochlea respond to vibrations of sound, while hairs in the vestibule and the semicircular canals respond to changes in the position of the head.

The three semicircular canals extend from the vestibule approximately at right angles to each other, providing hairs to record movements of the head in each of the three planes of space: up and down, forward and backward, to the left or right. Lying over the hairs in the vestibule are crystals of calcium carbonate, called *otoliths,* or "ear sand". When the head is tilted, the otoliths shift, and the hairs beneath respond to the change in pressure.

When the nerves connecting with these sensory hairs transmit to the brain impulses recording changes in the position of the head, contraction of various muscles is initiated. The body then endeavors by reflex movements to maintain its equilibrium in all positions. The eyes and certain sensory cells in the skin and in internal tissues also help to maintain equilibrium, but when the labyrinth of the ear is removed in animals, or diseased in man, disturbances of equilibrium invariably follow. With his eyes closed, a person with a serious disease of the internal ear may be unable to stand or even to sit up without swaying or falling.

EARACHE. See EAR, DISEASES OF.

EAR, DISEASES OF, diseases of the external, middle, or internal ear. Any ear disease may cause partial or total deafness (q.v.), and most diseases of the internal ear are associated with disturbances of the sense of equilibrium; see EAR. Diseases of the external ear include congenital and acquired malformations; inflammation caused by such factors as burns, frostbite, or skin diseases; and presence of foreign bodies in the external auditory canal. Diseases of the middle ear include perforation of the eardrum, and otitis media. Diseases of the internal ear include disturbances caused by anemia, hyperemia, and Ménière's disease.

In congenital malformations of the outer ear, the pinna and even the opening into the middle ear may be lacking. If the organs of the middle and inner ear are present, an opening into the middle ear can be made by

Harcourt, Brace & Co.

Amelia Earhart

surgery, and hearing can thus be restored. Acquired malformations include such conditions as cuts and wounds. Cauliflower ear, *hematoma auris*, of pugilists is a common result of injury to the ear cartilage followed by excessive production of reparative tissue.

Inflammation of the external ear may result from any condition which causes inflammation of the skin, such as dermatitis resulting from injury, burns, and frostbite. Diseases of the skin, such as erysipelas, impetigo, and eczema commonly affect the ear. Anthrax, skin tuberculosis, and all stages of syphilis are among more serious diseases which also affect the external ear. Foreign bodies such as insects and earwax commonly lodge in the external auditory canal causing ear disturbances, and must then be removed mechanically.

Perforation of the eardrum may be caused through accidental injury by some object able to penetrate the cavity of the middle ear, or by a blow on the ear, especially when the ear canal is full of liquid, as when one is swimming.

Otitis media is divided into suppurative and nonsuppurative otitis media, either of which may be acute or chronic. Acute suppurative otitis media includes all acute infections of the middle ear caused by pus-forming bacteria, which usually reach the middle ear by way of the Eustachian tube. The most common causative agents are staphylococci, streptococci, and pneumococci. Mastoid (q.v.) involvement may result as a complication of

the disease and impairment of hearing often follows, especially when pneumococci are present, because of the formation of adhesions and granulation tissue which affect the mobility of the eardrum and the ossicles. Suppurative otitis media often follows measles and scarlet fever. Diseased tonsils and adenoids are especially prone to result in suppurative infection of the middle ear. Penicillin and sulfa drugs usually bring about cures, although surgery may also be required when painful distention of the eardrum necessitates its perforation. Chronic suppurative otitis media often results from improper drainage of pus in the acute form. The chronic type of the disease is more likely to occur when the patient has lowered vitality, especially as a result of diabetes or tuberculosis. Penicillin and sulfa drugs have been used with some success. Basic iron sulfate, silver nitrate solutions, and zinc ionization have also been used. In the last method, zinc ions are driven into the tissues of the mucous membranes of the middle ear by a direct electric current.

Acute and chronic catarrhal or nonsuppurative otitis media are caused by occlusion of the Eustachian tube as a result of such conditions as a head cold, diseased tonsils and adenoids, or hay fever. A serous effusion from the blood vessels of the middle ear fills the cavity and exerts pressure on the eardrum, causing pain and impairment of hearing. Glycerin, which extracts fluid osmotically through the membrane, is used in treatment to reduce the pressure. Restoration of the occluded Eustachian tube to its normal function of supplying air to the inner ear is essential for a cure.

Diseases of the inner ear usually affect the sense of balance and induce symptoms similar to those of seasickness. Anemia (deficiency of blood or red blood cells) or hyperemia (excessive amount of blood in body tissue) can cause the symptoms. Ménière's disease results from lesions of the semicircular canals, and produces nausea, deafness, and lack of equilibrium. Surgical section of the eighth nerve (the auditory nerve) is often used to cure this disease.

Otalgia, earache not associated directly with an ear disease, is usually caused by impacted teeth, diseased tonsils, or inflamed neck glands. Treatment depends on finding and relieving the basic cause.

EARHART, AMELIA (1898–1937), American aviatrix, born in Atchison, Kansas, and educated at Columbia University and Harvard Summer School. In 1928 she accepted the invitation of Wilbur Stutz and Louis Gordon to join them on a transatlantic flight, and thus became the first woman to make the crossing by air. In 1932 she became the first woman to fly the Atlantic alone, and at the same time established a new record for the crossing: 13 hours, 30 minutes. For this feat she was awarded honors by the United States and French governments. In 1935 she became the first woman to fly the Pacific Ocean, crossing from Hawaii to California. Later the same year she set a new speed record by flying nonstop from Mexico City to New York City in 14 hours, 19 minutes. In June, 1937, she began a flight around the world, flying eastward from Miami, Fla., accompanied by Fred Noonan, a navigator. Their plane disappeared on July 3, while en route from Lae, New Guinea, to Howland Island. An extensive search by planes and ships of the U.S. Navy failed to discover any trace of the lost flyers, and their fate remains an unsolved mystery. Amelia Earhart described her first transatlantic flight in the book *20 Hrs. 40 Min.* (1928), and also wrote *The Fun Of It* (1931). Shortly after her disappearance, her husband, the book publisher George Palmer Putnam, edited and published *Last Flight* (1937), a book consisting largely of her diary of the last ill-fated journey, transmitted from the various stopping-places on the way.

EARLE, JOHN (1601?–65), English prelate, born in York, and educated at Christ Church and Merton colleges of Oxford University. In 1631 he was appointed proctor and chaplain to Philip, Earl of Pembroke, then chancellor of Oxford. In 1641, he became the tutor and chaplain of Prince Charles, later Charles II of England. After Oliver Cromwell's victory in the battle of Worcester in 1651, Earle, who was a partisan of the Stuarts, went to France, where he was named chaplain and clerk of the closet to the exiled Charles II. After the restoration of the Stuarts in 1660, Earle was appointed dean of Westminster. From 1662 to 1663, he officiated as bishop of Worcester and, in 1663, he was appointed bishop of Salisbury. He was the author of *Microcosmographie, or a Peece of the World Discovered, in Essayes and Characters* (1628), a collection of witty sketches.

EARLY, JUBAL ANDERSON (1816–94), Confederate army general, born in Franklin County, Va., and educated at the U.S. Military Academy, West Point. He resigned from the army to practice law, but interrupted his practice to serve in the army during the Mexican War. He entered the Confederate Army as a colonel in 1861 and rose to the rank of lieutenant general in 1864. Because of his defeats at the hands of Union generals Sheridan (1864) and Custer (1865) in Pennsylvania, he was relieved of his command in 1865. Early lived in Mexico and Canada until 1869, when he returned to Lynchburg, Va., and resumed his law practice.

EARLY ENGLISH, in architecture, term first used in the 19th century to designate a style of Gothic architecture which succeeded the Norman in Britain near the end of the 12th century, when the pointed arch, the pinnacle, and the buttress were introduced into British architecture. This style is often called *lancet-arched* because lancets, or high narrow openings, culminating in a pointed arch, were often used in groups of threes, fives, and sevens. The dog-tooth ornament is also characteristic of Early English architecture. Prominent examples of the style are the Salisbury cathedral (begun 1220) and parts of the transepts in the York cathedral (1230–60). As tracery and floral decoration became more profuse at the end of the 13th century,

British Information Services
Salisbury cathedral, an outstanding example of Early English architecture

Early English merged into the Decorated style. See GOTHIC ARCHITECTURE.

EARRING, an ornament for the ear, attached to the lobe, and usually worn one in each ear. Originally it was a ring, with or without pendants, which was passed through a hole pierced in the ear. Sometimes the pendants were suspended from a hook instead of a ring. The wearing of earrings dates from remote times and is mentioned in the Bible, in Genesis. Earrings made of various materials, particularly gold and other precious metals, and often decorated with gems, were worn by almost all ancient peoples. The Egyptians excelled at fine filigree work on their golden earrings; the jeweled earrings of the Greeks were of magnificent workmanship. Roman earrings were simple in form and decorated with precious stones. Among many of the Oriental peoples earrings have been worn by both men and women, but in the western world, as among the Greeks and Romans, their use has generally been confined to women. The wearing of earrings has been periodically fashionable in Europe and America during the 20th century, the use of inexpensive common metals, ceramics, and plastics making them available to the majority of women. Most modern earrings are in button form and are so constructed as to clamp on the ear lobe by means of a screw or a spring device.

EAR SHELL. See ABALONE.

EARTH, the third planet in the solar system in point of proximity to the sun, and the fifth in point of size and mass. Its mean distance from the sun is 92,897,000 miles. It is the only planet known to be capable of supporting life of any kind.

Shape and Size. The shape of the earth is not a perfect sphere but takes the approximate form of an oblate spheroid, a sphere slightly flattened at the poles. This flattening is presumably caused by centrifugal force resulting from the rotation of the earth about its polar axis. The extent of the flattening is such that the circumference of the earth at the equator is 24,902 m., whereas the circumference around the poles is 42.2 m. less. The diameter of the planet at the equator is 7926.6 m., and at the poles 7899.6, producing a difference of 27 m. in the diameters. The total area of the earth's surface is 196,940,000 sq.m. and its volume 259,880,000,000 cu.m. Since the average density of the planet is about 5.5, the total mass of the earth is approximately 6,595,000,-000,000,000,000,000 (6595×10^{18}) tons.

Motion. In common with the entire solar system, the earth is moving through space at the rate of approximately 12.5 miles per second, or 45,000 miles per hour, toward the constellation of Hercules. The earth and its satellite the moon also move together in an elliptical orbit about the sun. The eccentricity of the orbit is very slight, so that the orbit is virtually a circle. The approximate length of the earth's orbit is 583,400,000 miles and the earth travels along it at a velocity of about 66,000 m.p.h. The earth rotates on its axis once every 23 hrs., 56 min., 4.1 sec. (based on the solar year). A point on the equator therefore moves at a rate of a little over 1000 m.p.h. because of rotation, and a point on the earth at the latitude of Portland, Ore. (45°N.) at about 667 m.p.h.

In addition to these primary motions, three other components of the earth's total motion exist: the precession of the equinoxes (q.v.), nutation, and variation of latitude (q.v.)

Composition. From the scientific point of view, the entire earth is considered to consist of four parts: the atmosphere, the lithosphere, the hydrosphere, and the barysphere. The atmosphere (q.v.) is the gaseous envelope which surrounds the solid body of the planet, to a thickness of at least 700 miles. The lithosphere is the solid, rocky crust of the earth, extending to a depth of perhaps 60 miles. The hydrosphere is the layer of water which, in the form of the oceans, covers approximately 73.7 percent of the surface of the earth. The barysphere, sometimes called the centrosphere, is the heavy core of the earth, comprising more than 99.6 percent of the earth's mass.

The rocks of the lithosphere have an average density of 2.7, and are almost entirely made up of eleven elements, which together account for 99.5 percent of its mass. The most abundant is oxygen (about 47 percent of the total), followed by silicon (about 28 percent), aluminum (nearly 8 percent), iron (about 5 percent), calcium (3.6 percent), sodium (2.75 percent), potassium (2.6 percent), magnesium (2 percent), and titanium, hydrogen, and phosphorous (totaling less than 1 percent). In addition, eleven other elements are present in trace amounts of from one tenth to two hundredths of one percent. These elements, in order of abundance, are: carbon, manganese, sulfur, barium, chlorine, chromium, fluorine, zirconium, nickel, strontium, and vanadium. The elements are present in the lithosphere almost entirely in the form of compounds rather than in their free state. The most common compounds of the earth's crust are silicates and aluminosilicates of various metals. The prevalent modern geological view of the lithosphere regards it as divided into three shells the density of which increases with depth. The innermost shell contains such rock types as basalt and gabbro; above these is a shell of diorite; and the upper shell is made up of rocks of the granite type. The earth's surface is largely covered with sedimentary rocks and soil.

Beneath the lithosphere is a layer of rock, more than 500 miles thick, with a density of about 4; and beneath this in turn is a layer, approximately 1200 miles in depth, of metallic oxides and sulfides with a density of approximately 5.6. There are probably no clear divisions between the layers postulated by modern theory, but their general position and composition is in accordance with the evidence of the transmission of earthquake vibrations.

The hydrosphere consists chiefly of the oceans, but technically includes all water surfaces in the world, including inland seas, lakes, and rivers. The average depth of the oceans is 11,480 ft., five times the average height of the continents. The mass of the oceans is about 1,490,000,000,000,000,000 (1.49 x 10^{18}) short tons, or 1/4400 of the earth's total mass. Seismological research has shown that the density of the earth increases with increasing depth. At a depth of approximately 1800 m. below the earth's surface, however, such experiments show that the density increases very sharply and is substantially constant thereafter. Furthermore, the characteristics of the transmission indicate that the material below this depth is not solid, as are rocks of the lithosphere, but is in the liquid state. From this and other evidence, geologists believe that the core of the earth, the barysphere, is a mass of highly compressed molten material, about 90 percent iron, with a few percent each of nickel, cobalt, and copper, having a density of about 8. The temperature of the center of the earth, according to this hypothesis, is in the neighborhood of 1500° C. (2432° F.).

Age of the Earth. A number of methods have been suggested for estimating the age of the earth. One such method involves comparing the thickness of sedimentary deposits with the known rate of the deposition of silt at the mouths of modern rivers. Another method is to assume that the seas were originally composed of fresh water and have become salty as a result of the salts carried to them by the rivers of the continents, and to calculate the planet's age from the amount of salt that modern rivers carry annually. Both these methods are subject to large errors because of the assumption that silt deposition and salt

content have been constant throughout geologic history. Modern knowledge of radioactivity makes possible the dating of certain rocks with some accuracy. One part of lead by weight is known to be produced each year by the breaking down of 7400 million parts of uranium. By comparing the amounts of radium and lead present in a rock, its age can be determined. The oldest rocks so far studied are about 3500 million years old. The maximum time required for the formation of all the elements in the earth's crust was determined (1953) to be about 5500 million years. The age of the earth, therefore, is probably between 3500 and 5500 million years. See Cosmogony; Earthquake; Geophysics; Planets; Seismology.

EARTH, in chemistry. See Rare Earths.

EARTHENWARE. See Pottery.

EARTH HOG, or Earth Pig. See Aardvark.

EARTH LODGE, the type of house formerly used by the Mandan, Hidatsa, Arikara, Pawnee, Ponca, Omaha, and perhaps other Indian tribes of the Mississippi valley. A circular, pointed framework of logs was set up, covered with fine brush or grass and the whole given a heavy coating of mud. The lodge was in a sense an underground house, although surface soil within was removed to a depth of two or three feet to secure a firm earth floor, and to give added protection from the climate. True subterranean houses were used by natives of Alaska and parts of British Columbia, Washington, and California.

EARTHNUT, name applied to certain tubers, roots, or underground pods which are used as human or animal food. The peanut is sometimes called an earthnut, as is the tuber of *Conopodium denudatum* of the Carrot family. The small edible tubers or earthnuts of the European sedge *Cyperus esculentus,* also known as chufa, or earth almonds, are edible and eagerly sought by hogs. The root of the heath pea, a European legume, bears small edible tubers or earthnuts which are used in Scotland to flavor whiskey.

EARTH PILLAR, a natural tall cone of earth or soft rock with a large stone or boulder on the apex. Earth pillars usually range from 30 to 100 feet in height. Unlike dikes, which consist of igneous rock and are of volcanic origin (see Dike), earth pillars are formed by erosion of glacial drift and moraine deposits. The earth and clay everywhere except under huge rocks are slowly eroded by wind and rain, leaving columns and finally cones of earth under the boulders. These formations occur in

"Balancing Rock," earth pillar in Arizona

regions of recent glaciation and where the rainfall is sparse and concentrated in a short time. The "bad lands" of the western part of North America contain many earth pillars. They are also common in Colorado, and in the Tirol and other parts of the Alps. See BAD LANDS.

EARTHQUAKE, a vibration of the earth's crustal layer caused by sudden motions which relieve stresses in the crust. It was formerly believed that earthquakes were generally the result of volcanic action, but modern research in geology indicates that such action is a comparatively unimportant cause of earthquakes. The lack of uniformity in the composition of the crust of the earth, plus the action of gravity and other forces such as centrifugal force, set up tremendous stresses both on and below the surface of the earth. When such stresses become sufficiently large the crust breaks. The line of such a break is called a *fault* (q.v.), and may extend in any direction. The force released by such a break sets up a series of vibrations, or waves, in the body of the earth which travel outward from the fault. These waves may be so small that they are no more dan-

gerous than the tremors caused by passing traffic or a waterfall, or they may be so large, particularly in the immediate vicinity of the fault, that they have sufficient force to overthrow buildings.

The waves formed by an earthquake are of two kinds: *primary waves,* a series of rapid compressions and expansions that travel directly outward from the source of the quake; and *secondary waves,* slower vibrations, perpendicular to the direction of travel. The secondary waves rather than the primary cause earthquake damage. Although the waves are usually only a few inches in magnitude, their force is extremely great, and they can be observed and recorded many thousands of miles from their source.

The fault where an earthquake begins is known as the earthquake's *centrum.* The centrum is frequently below the surface of the earth. The point on the earth's surface directly above the centrum, the point from which the waves apparently radiate, is called the *epicenter.* In most cases an earthquake has the form of a line rather than a point, and the waves radiate out from the epicenter elliptically rather than in perfect circles.

More than 100,000 earthquakes occur annually in all parts of the world, but most of the more serious quakes are confined to two broad belts. One of these runs along the coastline of the Pacific Ocean from Chile in South America, northward along the w. coast of the U.S. and Alaska, westward along the Aleutian Islands, and south through Japan and the Philippine Islands to the East Indies. The other belt runs eastward from Spain through the Mediterranean basin, Turkey, the Caucasus Mountains, and the Himalayas to Malaya and the East Indies, where it intersects the first. These regions are also the area of greatest volcanic activity. The earthquake belts, which are characterized by ranges of recently formed mountains, are believed to be regions in which the earth's crust is comparatively weak.

Many of the tens of thousands of earthquakes which are recorded each year occur beneath the surface of the sea. A large undersea quake produces a series of huge water waves which travel across the surface of the ocean much as the secondary earthquake waves travel through the earth. These waves are usually called tidal waves, although they have no relation to the tides. They are more correctly known as seismic sea waves or by the Japanese name *tsunami* (q.v.).

Seismology (q.v.), the study of earthquakes,

is a comparatively new science which has yielded much information about the interior structure of the earth. The chief instrument of seismological research is the seismograph (q.v.), a device for recording earthquake tremors. By timing the arrival of the primary and secondary waves at a seismograph station it is possible to determine the distance of an earthquake's epicenter from the station, and if the distances from three widely separated stations are known, the position of the epicenter can be accurately located.

EARTHQUAKES, MEMORABLE. Historical records of earthquakes prior to the middle of the 18th century are either lacking or largely unreliable. These disasters were known in ancient times, but in most instances the reports available on them in the writings of such authors as Aristotle and Seneca are accompanied by irrational and unscientific explanations of the phenomena. Among the earthquakes of antiquity of which reasonably trust-

worthy records exist are that which occurred off the coast of Greece in 425 B.C., making Eubœa an island; that which destroyed the city of Ephesus, Asia Minor, in the year 17 A.D.; that which levelled much of Pompeii in 63; and those which destroyed Rome in 476 and Constantinople in 557 and 936. During the later Middle Ages severe earthquakes were recorded in England in 1318, Naples in 1456, and Lisbon in 1531; in the last two, great numbers of people were killed.

The most notable earthquake of the 17th century is that which took an estimated 60,000 lives on the island of Sicily in 1693. Early in the 18th century the Japanese city of Edo, the present Tokyo, was destroyed with the loss of some 200,000 lives. In 1755 the city of Lisbon, Portugal, was devastated: about 60,000 persons died; the shock was felt in Southern France and North Africa; and inland waters of Great Britain and Scandinavia were agitated. Quito, now the capital city of Ecuador,

Ewing Galloway

SAN FRANCISCO EARTHQUAKE AND FIRE. *The tremor occurred on the morning of April 18, 1906. In the resulting three-day fire an area of four square miles was destroyed.*

Buffalo Museum of Science

Museum model of the triple earthstar

was visited by earthquake in 1797, and more than 40,000 people lost their lives. As a result of an earthquake which ravaged the state of Cutch, India, in 1819, an area of 2000 square miles sank below the level of the surrounding terrain, and became the bed of an inland sea. The violent eruption of Krakatoa in Sonda Strait in 1883 was accompanied by major earthquakes which wreaked havoc in Java and other nearby islands of the East Indies, and killed 36,000 people. Three years later the first serious earthquake disaster to occur in the United States seriously damaged the city of Charleston, S.C., with some loss of life. An earthquake in Japan took 26,000 lives in 1896.

The United States suffered its second severe earthquake in 1906, when the city of San Francisco, and neighboring towns and villages, were severely damaged; this disaster caused a great conflagration and, by breaking water mains, prevented its control. As a result, more than 500 persons perished and property valued at $350,000,000 was destroyed. Two years later a large area of southern Italy was ravaged, with the number of deaths amounting to about 100,000. Italy was again stricken in 1915, when almost 30,000 persons living in its central regions were killed. In the earthquake which visited Kansu, China, in 1920, the number of residents who lost their lives cannot be determined precisely, but it has been estimated at between 100,000 and 200,000. One of the severest earthquakes ever recorded struck Tokyo, Japan, and its surrounding area in 1923, killing more than 150,000 persons and destroying property valued at $4,500,000,000. Kansu, China, suffered again in 1932, the death

toll amounting to 70,000. In 1933 a large area of southern California was affected; 130 persons died and $50,000,000 worth of property was destroyed. Early in 1939 six provinces of central Chile were ravaged, 50,000 Chileans perished, 700,000 were left homeless, and property worth $30,000,000 was demolished. Near the end of the same year an area of approximately 15,000 square miles in Anatolia, Turkey, was stricken by several consecutive earthquakes which, combined with the floods and heavy snowstorms which followed them, resulted in the death of approximately 45,000 persons.

About 2000 persons were killed in Turkey by an earthquake in 1943. On Dec. 21, 1946, a severe shock hit the Japanese islands of Honshu, Shikoku, and Kyushu, causing disastrous tidal waves. More than 1000 persons were killed. An earthquake devastated the city of Fukui, Honshu Island, Japan, late in June, 1948. Casualties totaled over 10,500, including 3254 dead. About 8000 persons were killed by an earthquake in central Ecuador in August, 1949. Property damage, estimated at $86 million, included total destruction of four towns and partial destruction of over forty others. Later the same month an earthquake destroyed forty-five villages and killed almost 500 persons in Erzurum Il, Turkey. A severe tremor badly damaged Cuzco, Peru, in May, 1950, leaving 30,000 persons homeless and killing nearly 100. The town of El Tocuyo, Venezuela, was practically demolished by an earthquake on the following Aug. 3. Deaths numbered about 100.

The second-heaviest earthquake on record occurred in Assam State, Union of India, on August 15, 1950. Casualties included 574 killed and property damage, extending over an area of 30,000 sq.m., was virtually incalculable. An estimated 100,000 buildings were destroyed. On May 6–7, 1951, earthquakes killed 375 persons and left 25,000 homeless in El Salvador. Turud, Iran, and a number of nearby villages were struck by an earthquake on Feb. 12, 1953, with a loss of 531 lives. On the following March 18 more than 1200 persons were killed by an earthquake in N.W. Turkey. A protracted series of earthquakes devastated the Ionian islands of Cephalonia, Zante, and Ithaca in August, 1953. Among the casualties were an estimated 1000 dead. Almost the entire population (118,000) of the islands was left homeless. Between Sept. 9 and 12, 1954, earthquakes killed more than 1650 persons and left an estimated 10,000 homeless in N. Algeria.

EARTHS. See RARE EARTHS.

EARTHSTAR, common name for any fungus of the genus *Geaster* in the class Basidiomycetes. Earthstars are found in nearly all parts of the world, and in America are common in pastures and open woodlands. They are characterized by a double peridium (spore sack or puffball). The outer layer of the peridium splits radially from the center apex into triangular segments which spread into a starlike arrangement. The inner layer of the peridium encloses the powdery spores.

EARTH WOLF. See AARDWOLF.

EARTHWORM, name given to certain worms in the order Oligochaeta. They have cylindrically shaped, segmented bodies, tapering at both ends, and covered by minute bristles called *setae*. Although there is a difference in shading between the upper and under surfaces, and between different parts of the body, earthworms are in general of a uniform color, usually flesh red, but varying from dull pink to dirty brown. Many species grow to a length of only a few inches, but some tropical species attain a length of several feet. Large specimens of the common American species are 8 to 12 in. long. In such specimens as many as 180 segments may be present, but 130 is the usual number.

Earthworms are mostly subterranean, and in order to survive must live in moist soil containing organic matter. They are never encountered in deserts or in pure sands. They usually live in the upper layers of the soil, but during the winter they penetrate more deeply into the soil to escape frost. During unusually hot weather they also penetrate downward, in order to avoid desiccation. They shun daylight, but frequently come to the surface of the soil during the night to feed and to throw off their castings. During the daytime they appear upon the surface of the soil only under unusual conditions, such as the flooding of their burrows by excessive rainfall. Earthworms are capable of burrowing with considerable speed, especially in loose soil, by thrusting their bluntly pointed heads between particles of earth and forcing them apart, or by actually swallowing much of the opposing material and excreting it after passage through their bodies. In all their movements, the short but stiff bristles along the sides of the body are of great assistance.

In burrowing, earthworms swallow large quantities of earth that often contains considerable amounts of vegetable remains. They are able to digest the nutritive matter of the soil, depositing or casting out the remains on the surface of the earth or in their burrows.

The muscular system of the earthworm is well developed. It consists of an outer series of circular or transverse muscle fibers which girdle the body, and an inner series of longitudinal muscle fibers forming five principal bands and several smaller ones. The latter are employed in moving the setae. The circulatory system is likewise well developed, and consists of a prominent dorsal blood vessel and at least four ventral blood vessels, running longitudinally in the body, and connected with each other by a regularly arranged series of transverse vessels. These transverse vessels form a network of capillaries in the wall of the intestine and in the muscles. In several of the anterior segments, some transverse vessels are much larger than elsewhere, and form prominent arches, often called "hearts"; however, most of the pumping of blood is performed by general muscular movements. The nervous system consists of a large ganglion, above the esophagus, which is often called the brain, and a ventral cord which lies beneath the alimentary canal, bearing ganglia in every segment. Although earthworms can detect the presence of light, it is believed that they have no sense organs other than those of touch. The digestive system consists of a muscular pharynx, a slender esophagus, a muscular gizzard used for

Common American Earthworm

Spanish State Tour. Dept.

EASTER CUSTOMS

Above, left: The crucifixion and resurrection of Christ is commemorated in all parts of the world at Easter time. A crucifix in Seville, Spain, is shown here.

Above: In Malaga, Spain, the members of a church society, wearing traditional hoods, conduct a procession for purpose of transporting a figure of Christ from their own church to the cathedral of the city.

Left: A sunrise service being conducted on Easter Sunday, on the shore of Mirror Lake, Yosemite Valley, California.

grinding ingested earth, and a long, straight intestine.

Earthworms are hermaphrodites; both male and female reproductive organs occur in every individual. Mutual cross-fertilization probably always takes place. After the eggs, containing considerable yolk, have been laid, they are buried in the earth in capsules which serve to protect the young until they are well developed. These capsules are probably formed from the secretion of the clitellum, a thickened portion of the body wall between the 29th and 35th segments. When the young emerge, they are small, fully developed earthworms.

Earthworms have been divided into five families: Lumbricidae, inhabiting North America, Europe, and northern Asia; Moniligastridae, inhabiting India, Ceylon, Malaya, and the eastern part of Africa; Megascolecidae, inhabiting India, Australasia, Africa, and South America; Eudrilidae, inhabiting central parts of Africa; and Glossoscolecidae, inhabiting South and Central America, Africa, and southern Europe. Over 1000 species of earthworms are known. Especially well known are *Lumbricus terrestris* and *Allobophora foetida*, widely distributed in temperate and tropical lands; *Megascolides australis*, inhabiting Australia, and attaining the enormous length of 6 to 7 feet; and *Glossoscolex giganteus*, inhabiting South America.

Charles Darwin (q.v.) was the first to recognize the important role played by earthworms in the subsoil. By being continually loosened, stirred up, and aerated by the action of earthworms, soil is made more fertile. Earthworms also form a source of food for many animals, constituting the principal food of moles and shrews. They are the most frequently used bait for fishing in the United States, where they are commonly known as "angleworms". See ANNELIDA; CHAETOPODA.

EARWIG, common name for the various nocturnal insects comprising the order Dermaptera. They are of world-wide distribution, and in the U.S. are frequently found in the southern States. They live under the decayed bark of trees, under stones, and in old straw, and feed chiefly upon flowers and ripe fruit. They resemble the rove beetles (q.v.) in appearance, but are distinguished from them by pincerlike processes at the posterior ends of their abdomens. The earwig, a completely harmless insect, was so named because of the belief that it sometimes creeps into human ears. The name earwig is also applied in the United States to several small centipedes in the genus *Geophilus*.

EAR WORM. See BOLLWORM.

EAST AFRICA COMPANY, BRITISH, a commercial association founded to develop African trade following upon the International Congress on the partitioning and colonial administration of Africa held at Berlin in 1884–85. The company received its charter in 1888. Its main activity was the construction of the Kenya and Uganda Railway. The sovereign rights of the company within present-day Kenya Colony and Protectorate and the Uganda Protectorate (qq.v.) were acquired by the British crown in 1895.

EAST ANGLIA. See ANGLIA, EAST.

EASTBOURNE, a county borough and seaside resort of East Sussex, England, situated on the English Channel, between Hastings and Brighton, and 66 m. by rail s.s.e. of London. It is noted for its esplanade, and is the site of Eastbourne College, founded in 1867. Eastbourne was incorporated as a town in 1883, as a county borough in 1911, and became a Parliamentary division in 1918. Much of the land in Eastbourne is owned by the duke of Devonshire. The town suffered heavily from German air raids in World War II. Pop. (1953 est.) 57,190.

EAST CAPE, the name of two peninsulas, one of which forms the northeastern extremity of Asia (see CAPE DEZHNEV), and

the other, the eastern point of North Island, New Zealand.

EAST CHICAGO, a city of Lake Co., Ind., situated on Lake Michigan, in the industrially important Calumet region. It is 17 miles s.e. of the center of Chicago, Ill., and is served by five major railroads. The city comprises three sections, East Chicago (the original town), Calumet, and Indiana Harbor. The last-named is the port, and is connected with the Grand Calumet R. by the Indiana Harbor Canal. East Chicago is an important manufacturing center. Large quantities of coal, iron ore, limestone, and other raw materials are unloaded at its docks. The city contains vast steel mills and foundries, metal and oil refineries, and chemical plants. In addition, East Chicago has meat-packing plants, railroad shops, and factories manufacturing machinery, cement, gypsum, and wooden boxes. The park system includes a zoological garden. East Chicago was settled and incorporated as a village in 1885 and was chartered as a city in 1890. The city grew rapidly, its population increasing from 3411 in 1900 to 35,967 in 1920. Pop. (1950) 54,263.

EAST CLEVELAND, a city of Cuyahoga Co., Ohio, situated 7 m. by rail e. of Cleveland, of which it forms a residential suburb. The city contains electrical-research laboratories and plants producing electrical appliances. East Cleveland is the site of the Case School of Applied Science, and the former summer estate of the late John D. Rockefeller, Sr., which is now a part of the municipal park system and is called Forest Hills Park. It was settled in 1799, incorporated as a village in 1895, and chartered as a city in 1911. Pop. (1950) 40,047.

EASTER, annual Christian festival commemorating the resurrection of Jesus Christ, the principal feast of the Christian year. It is celebrated on a Sunday on varying dates between March 22 and April 25, and hence is called a movable feast. The dates of several other ecclesiastical festivals, extending over a period between Septuagesima Sunday and the first Sunday of Advent, are fixed in relation to the date of Easter.

Connected with the observance of Easter are the forty-day fast of Lent, beginning on Ash Wednesday and concluding at noon on Holy Saturday, the day before Easter Sunday; Holy Week, commencing on Palm Sunday, including Good Friday, the day of the crucifixion, and terminating two days later with Holy Saturday; and the Octave of Easter, extending from Easter Sunday through the following Sunday. During the Octave of Easter in early Christian times, the newly baptized wore white garments, white being the liturgical color of Easter and signifying light, purity, and joy.

Although Easter is a Christian festival, it embodies traditions of an ancient time antedating the rise of Christianity. The origin of its name is lost in the dim past; some scholars believe it probably is derived from *Ēastre*, Anglo-Saxon name of a Teutonic goddess of spring and fertility, to whom was dedicated *Ēastre mōnath*, corresponding to April. Her festival was celebrated on the day of the vernal equinox, and traditions associated with the festival survive in the familiar Easter bunny, symbol of the fertile rabbit, and in the equally familiar colored Easter eggs originally painted with gay hues to represent the sunlight of spring.

Such festivals, and the myths and legends which explain their origin, abounded in ancient religions. The Greek myth of the return of the earth-goddess Demeter from the underworld to the light of day, symbolizing the resurrection of life in the spring after the long hibernation of winter, had its counterpart, among many others, in the Latin legend of Ceres and Persephone. The Phrygians believed that their all-powerful deity went to sleep at the time of the winter solstice, and they performed ceremonies at the spring equinox to awaken him with music and dancing. The universality of such festivals and myths among ancient peoples has led some scholars to interpret the resurrection of Christ as a mystical and exalted variant of fertility myths.

Other scholars agree that the Easter festival of Christianity embodies a number of converging traditions; they concede some measure of truth in the above interpretation, but consider it too narrow, and emphasize the original relation of Easter to the Jewish festival of Passover (q.v.), or Pesach, whence is derived Pasach, another name for Easter. It was on the eve of the festival of Passover that Christ was crucified; the central belief of the Christian religion is that He shortly afterward rose from the dead. The early Christians, many of whom were of Jewish origin, were brought up in Hebrew tradition, and thought of Easter as a new feature of the Passover festival, as a commemoration of the advent of the Messiah, foretold by the prophets.

In time, a serious difference over the date of the Easter festival arose among Christians. Those of Jewish origin celebrated the resurrection immediately following the Passover festival, which, according to their ancient lunar calendar borrowed from the Babylonians, fell on the evening of the full moon, i.e., on the fourteenth day in the month of Nisan, the first month of the year; by their reckoning, Easter, from year to year, fell on different days of the week.

Christians of gentile origin, however, wished to commemorate the resurrection on the first day of the week, Sunday; by their method, Easter always occurred on the same day of the week, but, from year to year, it fell on different days of the month, i.e., on different dates.

An important historic result of the difference was that the Christian churches in the East, which were closer to the birthplace of the new religion, and in which old traditions were strong, observed Easter according to the date of the Passover festival, while the churches of the West, whose communicants were descendants of Græco-Roman civilization, celebrated Easter on a Sunday.

Settlement of this difference was one of the objects of the Roman emperor Constantine in convoking, in 325 A.D., the Council of Nicæa (see NICÆA, COUNCIL OF). The Council ruled unanimously that the Easter festival should be celebrated throughout the Christian world on the first Sunday after the full moon following the vernal equinox; and that should the full moon occur on a Sunday and thereby coincide with the Passover festival of the Jews, Easter should be commemorated on the Sunday following. Coincidence of the feasts of Easter and Passover was thus forever to be avoided.

The Council of Nicæa also decided that the calendar date of Easter was to be calculated at Alexandria, then the principal astronomical center of the world. The accurate determination of the date, however, proved to be an impossible task, in the imperfect state of knowledge of the time. The principal astronomical problem involved was the discrepancy between the solar year and the lunar year, called the epact (q.v.). The chief calendric problem was a gradually increasing discrepancy between the true astronomical year and the Julian Calendar, then in vogue.

Various methods of calculating the date, tried by the Church, proved unsatisfactory, and Easter was celebrated on different dates in different parts of the world. In 387, the dates of Easter in France and Egypt, for example, were 35 days apart. About 465, the Church adopted a system of calculation pro-

Stone carvings found on Easter Island, descriptive of an ancient Polynesian culture

posed by the astronomer Victorinus, who had been commissioned by Pope Hilarius to reform the calendar and fix the date of Easter. Elements of his method are still in use (see GOLDEN NUMBER). Refusal of the British and Celtic Christian churches to adopt Victorinus' method led to a bitter dispute between them and Rome in the 7th century.

Reform of the Julian Calendar in 1582, by Pope Gregory XIII, through adoption of the Gregorian, or New Style, Calendar, eliminated much of the difficulty in fixing the date of Easter and in arranging the ecclesiastical year; and since 1752, when the Gregorian Calendar was also adopted in Great Britain and Ireland, Easter has been celebrated on the same day in the western part of the Christian world. The Eastern churches, however, which did not adopt the Gregorian Calendar, commemorate Easter on a Sunday which either precedes or follows the date observed by the Western Church. Occasionally the dates coincide; the most recent time was in 1865.

As the Easter holiday seriously affects a varied number of secular affairs in many countries, it has long been urged as a matter of convenience that the movable dates of the festival be either narrowed in range, or replaced by a fixed date in the manner of Christmas. Since 1900, national and international conferences of chambers of commerce and international interdenominational conclaves have urged a fixed date. In 1923 the problem was referred to the Holy See, which has stated that there is no canonical objection to the proposed reform. Some time after 1923, the question was discussed by the League of Nations. The British Parliament, in 1928, enacted a measure allowing the Anglican Church to commemorate Easter on the first Sunday after the second Saturday in April. Notwithstanding these and other pressures, Easter continues to be a movable feast. See CALENDAR.

EASTER ISLAND (Sp. *Isla de Pascua;* Polynesian, *Rapa Nui*), an island belonging to Chile, situated in the South Pacific Ocean about 2000 miles w. of the Chilean coast. Spanish geographers credit Mendaña de Neyrá, a Spanish mariner and explorer, with the discovery of Easter Island in 1566. However, the island received its name from the Dutch navigator, Admiral Jacob Roggeveen, who landed there on Easter Sunday, 1772. The island, triangular in shape, is a volcanic formation, with extinct craters at each apex of the triangle. It is about 45 sq.m. in area. The greater part is owned by a Chilean agency for the development of Easter Island, and is used as grazing land for sheep and cattle. Timber is scanty and water almost absent. An area on the w. coast of about 5000 acres is reserved for the native inhabitants by the Chilean government, which annexed the island in 1888. The natives are the easternmost of the Polynesian group. In 1772, they numbered about 3000, but disease, raids by slave traders, and emigration have reduced the native population to less than 200.

Easter Island is of considerable importance archeologically as the richest site of the megaliths (see MEGALITHIC MONUMENTS) of the Pacific island groups, and as the only source of evidence of a form of writing in Polynesia. The latter was discovered carved on wooden tablets.

Very little is known about the people who made the megaliths and carved the wooden tablets. The general belief is that settlement of Easter Island took place more than ten centuries ago, although some scholars contend it occurred more recently. Linguistic and anthropological studies indicate that the original inhabitants were predominantly of the Polynesian racial stock, with an admixture of Melanesian.

The megaliths of Easter Island are found in three forms, all cyclopean. Largest of the stone monuments are the great burial platforms, called *ahu*, situated upon the bluffs and in other positions commanding a view of the sea. They number about 260, and are constructed of neatly fitted stone blocks set without mortar. A survey disclosed one such platform, known as Tongariki, to measure 150 ft. in length, 9 ft. in width, and 8 ft. in height. Other *ahu* measure up to 300 ft. in length and 15 ft. in height. A stone weighing six tons was used in the construction of the platform known as Ohau.

Equally impressive are some 550 statues, varying from 3 ft. to 36 ft. in height, which are found throughout the island. They are carved from compressed volcanic ash, and are all of similar design, representing only heads (with elongated ears) and shoulders. The statues were quarried from the volcano called Rano-Raraku, and stand around it in large numbers. An immense statue, almost 70 ft. long, was found lying unfinished in the quarry. Many of the statues surmounted the burial platforms at one time, and bore cylindrical, brimmed crowns of red volcanic tuff, the largest being 12 ft., 6 inches in diameter. It is believed that the statues on the *ahu* were erected in honor of ancestors and were sacred objects.

In the s.w. corner of the island is a village, unique in Polynesia because its 48 houses are constructed entirely of stone. The interior of many of the houses, as well as those of several caves, are decorated with colored pictographs.

The wooden tablets which have been collected on Easter Island are covered with finely carved and stylized figures, constituting a form of picture writing. Each tablet must be inverted upon the reading of a line, for in each alternate line the characters have been cut upside down. Although a few of the stories recorded on the tablets have been translated by living natives, chiefly from memory, the figures cannot be translated word for word, and no satisfactory method of interpreting the symbols has been found to date.

EASTERN CHURCH. See ORTHODOX CHURCH.

EASTERN EMPIRE. See BYZANTINE EMPIRE.

EASTERN QUESTION. See EUROPE: *History.*

EASTERN RITE, CHURCHES OF THE, term designating several bodies of Eastern Christians, or Uniates, now considered part of the Roman Catholic Church. These bodies, including Greeks, Copts, Armenians, Maronites, and Syrians, originally espoused but have now renounced the heretical teachings of Eutyches and of the Nestorians (q.v.). Although they accept the authority of the Pope at Rome and agree with the Roman Catholic Church on matters of faith, they differ on various points of discipline, such as the procedure during the Communion service, the marriage of priests, and the choice of liturgical language. Leavened bread is permitted in the consecration; both bread and wine instead of merely bread may be distributed by the Uniates in Communion. Before becoming deacons, priests are allowed to marry. Rather than Latin, the liturgical languages of the churches of the Eastern Rite are those spoken by the original missionary founders.

EASTERN STAR, ORDER OF THE, international fraternal and benevolent society, composed of Masons and their close female relatives. The society was probably introduced in New York City by French officers, about 1778, but its present organization was not established until 1868 with the founding of Alpha Chapter No. 1 in New York City. The order has chapters throughout the U.S. and in several foreign countries; the total membership in 1954 was over 3,000,000.

EASTER REBELLION, an armed uprising of Irish patriots against British overlordship in

Ireland, launched on Easter Monday, April 24, 1916, and centered mainly in Dublin. The chief objectives of the revolutionaries were the attainment of political freedom and the establishment of an Irish republic. Centuries of discontent, marked by numerous rebellions, preceded the uprising. The new crisis began to develop when, in September, 1914, following the outbreak of World War I, the British government suspended execution of the recently enacted Home Rule Bill, which guaranteed a measure of political autonomy to the Irish. Suspension of the Bill stimulated the growth of the Citizen Army, an illegal force of Dublin citizens organized by James Larkin and James Connolly; the Irish Volunteers, a national defense body; and the extremist Sinn Fein (q.v.) party. The uprising was planned by the leaders of these organizations, among whom were Padhraic Pearse, Sir Roger David Casement, and Thomas MacDonagh (qq.v.).

Hostilities began about midday on April 24, when about 2000 men commanded by Pearse seized control of the Dublin post office and other strategic points within the city. Shortly after winning these initial successes, the leaders of the rebellion proclaimed the independence of Ireland and announced the establishment of a provisional government of the Irish Republic. Additional positions were occupied by the rebels during the night and, by the morning of April 25, they controlled a considerable part of Dublin. With the arrival of reinforcements on Tuesday, the British counteroffensive began. Martial law was proclaimed throughout Ireland. Bitter street fighting developed in Dublin, with the strengthened British forces steadily driving the Irish from their positions. By the morning of April 29, the post-office building, site of rebel headquarters, was under violent attack. Recognizing the futility of further resistance, Pearse surrendered unconditionally in the afternoon of April 29. The British immediately brought the leaders of the uprising to trial before a field court-martial. Fifteen of the group, including Pearse, Connolly, and MacDonagh, were sentenced to death and executed by shooting. Four others, Eamon de Valera (q.v.) among them, received death sentences which were later commuted to life imprisonment. Sir Roger Casement was convicted of treason and hanged. Many others prominently connected with the rebellion were sentenced to long prison terms. Casualties in the uprising, the first of a series of events that culminated in the establishment

of Eire, totaled about 440 British troops and an undetermined number of Irish. Property damage included the destruction of about 200 buildings in Dublin.

EAST FLANDERS. See FLANDERS, EAST.

EAST HAM, municipal, county, and parliamentary borough of Essex County, England. It is situated 6 m. by rail N.E. of London, and is separated from that city by the Lea R., an affluent of the Thames. East Ham extends from Wanstead Flats on the N. to the Royal Albert Docks and the Thames on the S. Before the Norman conquest in 1066, East Ham was a part of the ancient market town of Waltham Abbey. In 1904 East Ham was incorporated, and in 1915 was made a county borough. Since 1918 it has returned two members to Parliament. The principal products manufactured in East Ham are iron castings, chemicals, and foodstuffs. The shipyards and docks provide the bulk of employment for East Ham residents in the southern district. Pop. (1953 est.) 119,000.

EAST HARTFORD, a town of Hartford Co., Conn., situated on the Connecticut R., 2 miles E. of Hartford. It is served by a railroad and has an airport. In the surrounding area, tobacco and general farm crops are grown. The chief products of the town are airplane motors and propellers, power boats, fertilizers, preserves, pickles, tobacco leaf, furniture, paper and sanitary tissues, ladders, automatic marking machines, tools, gears, and cold-drawn steel. East Hartford was founded in 1633 and incorporated in 1783. Government is by a town council. Pop. (1950) 29,933.

EAST INDIA COMPANY, any of a number of commercial companies formed in Europe during the 17th and 18th centuries to acquire trade in the East Indies. The companies, which had varying degrees of governmental support, grew out of the associations of merchant adventurers who voyaged to the East Indies following Vasco da Gama's discovery of the Cape of Good Hope route in 1498. The most important of the companies were given charters by their respective governments, authorizing them to acquire territory wherever they were able and to exercise in the acquired territory various functions of government, including legislation, the issuance of currency, the negotiation of treaties, the waging of war, and the administration of justice. Historically, the most notable companies were the following.

DANISH EAST INDIA COMPANY, chartered in 1729 by King Frederick IV, after unsuccessful attempts by Denmark to gain a share of the East India trade in 1616 and 1634. It enjoyed great prosperity in India until the advance of British power there in the late 18th century. As a consequence of the destruction of Danish naval power in the war between Great Britain and Denmark in 1801, the power of the Danish company was broken. Its principal Indian possessions, Tranquebar in Madras, and Serampore in Bengal, were purchased by Great Britain in 1845.

DUTCH EAST INDIA COMPANY, incorporated from a number of smaller companies by the States-General of the Netherlands in 1602. Its monopoly extended from the Cape of Good Hope eastward to the Straits of Magellan, with sovereign rights in whatever territory it might acquire. In 1619 Jan Pieterszoon Coen, regarded as the founder of the Dutch colonial empire in the East Indies, established the city of Batavia, in Java, as the headquarters of the company. From Batavia, Dutch influence and activity spread throughout the Malay Archipelago, and to China, Japan, India, Persia, and the Cape of Good Hope. During the course of the sixty-year war between Spain and the Netherlands (1605–65), the Dutch company despoiled Portugal, which was then united to Spain, of all its East Indian possessions. It supplanted the Portuguese in the Sunda and Molucca (Spice) Islands, the Malay peninsula, Ceylon, the Malabar coast of India, Malacca, and Japan. During this period it was also successful in driving English rivals from the Malay Archipelago and the Molucca Islands. In 1632 the Dutch killed the English factors at Amboina, capital of the Dutch Moluccas, an act for which the English government later exacted compensation. In 1652 the company established on the Cape of Good Hope the first European settlement in South Africa. At the peak of its power, in 1669, the Dutch company had 40 warships, 150 merchantmen, and 10,000 soldiers. Between 1602 and 1696 the annual dividends that the company paid were never less than 12% and sometimes as high as 63%. The charter of the company was renewed every twenty years, in return for financial concessions to the Dutch government. In the 18th century, internal disorders, the growth of English and French power, and the consequences of a harsh native policy caused the decline of the Dutch company. It was unable to pay a dividend after 1724, and continued in existence only by exacting levies from native populations. It was powerless to resist a British attack on its possessions in

1780. In 1795 the company's effective existence ended with the proclamation of the Batavian Republic, which succeeded the States-General of the Netherlands. Three years later, in 1798, the company was dissolved and the republic assumed the company's possessions and debts.

ENGLISH EAST INDIA COMPANY, the most important of the various East India companies, and a major factor in the history of India for over 200 years. Its original charter was granted by Queen Elizabeth on December 31, 1600, under the title of "The Governor and Company of Merchants of London trading into the East Indies". It was granted a monopoly of trade in Asia, Africa, and America, with the sole restriction that it might not contest the prior trading rights of "any Christian prince". The company was managed by a governor and twenty-four directors chosen from its stockholders. Its early voyages penetrated as far as Japan, and in 1610 and 1611 its first factories or trading posts were established in India in the provinces of Madras and Bombay. Under a perpetual charter granted in 1609 by James I, the company began to compete with the Dutch trading monopoly in the East Indian Archipelago, but after the massacre of Amboina (see *Dutch East India Company,* above) the company conceded to the Dutch the area that became known as the Netherlands East Indies. However, its armed merchantmen continued sea warfare with Dutch, French, and Portuguese competitors. In 1650 and 1655 the company absorbed rival companies which had been incorporated under the Commonwealth and Protectorate by Oliver Cromwell. In 1657 Oliver Cromwell ordered it reorganized as the sole joint stock company with rights to the Indian trade. During the reign of Charles II, it acquired sovereign rights in addition to its trading privileges. In 1689, with the establishment of presidencies in the Indian provinces of Bengal, Madras, and Bombay, the company began its long rule in India. It was continually harassed by interlopers, traders who were not members of the company and were not licensed by the crown to trade. In 1698, under a Parliamentary ruling in favor of free trade, these private newcomers were able to set up a new company, called the New, or English, Company. The East India Company, however, bought control of this new company and the two were amalgamated (as The United Company of Merchants of England Trading to the East Indies) in 1702 by act of Parliament. The company's charter

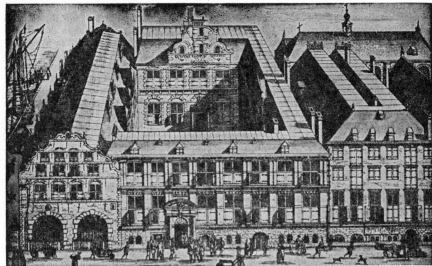

Netherlands Information Bureau
Above: The East India House in Amsterdam, headquarters of the Dutch East India Company in the 17th century. Right: Merchant ships used by the company (old engravings).

was renewed a number of times in the 18th century, upon the making of financial concessions to the crown. The victories of Robert Clive (q.v.), a company official, over the French at Arcot in 1751 and at Plassey in 1757, made the company the dominant power in India. All European rivalry vanished with the defeat of the French at Pondichéry in 1761. In 1773 the British government established a governor-generalship in India, greatly decreasing the company's control of Indian administration. The company's governor of Bengal, Warren Hastings (q.v.), became the first governor-general of India. In 1784 the India Act created a department of the British government to exercise political, military, and financial control over the company's Indian affairs. In 1813 its monopoly of the Indian trade was abolished and in 1833 it lost its China trade monopoly. Its annual dividends of 10 guineas per £100 were made a fixed charge on Indian revenues. The company continued its administrative functions until the Indian Mutiny of 1857–58. In 1858 the crown assumed all the company's governmental responsibilities by the Act for the Better Government of India. The company's military force of 24,000 men was made part of the Queen's army. The company was dissolved in 1873, as of January 1, 1874, when

the East India Stock Dividend Redemption Act went into force.

FRENCH EAST INDIA COMPANY (*La Compagnie des Indes Orientales*), established in 1664 by Jean-Baptiste Colbert, financial minister of Louis XIV. In 1675 the company established its first factory, or trading post, at Surat in Bombay, India, and in 1676 it set up its principal Indian base at Pondichéry, on the Coromandel Coast. The company prospered and extended its operations to China and Persia. In 1719 the company was reorganized with the American and African French colonial companies as the Compagnie des Indes. This company, headed by John Law (q.v.), suffered severely with the collapse of the Mississippi Scheme. In 1730 it lost its slave trade with Africa, in 1731 its general trade with Louisiana, and in 1736 its coffee trade with the Americas. However, the company prospered in India under its governors, Dumas (1735–41) and Joseph François Dupleix (1742–54), who directed the unsuccessful French struggles against the British control of India. Robert Clive's capture of Arcot in 1751 limited French control to s. India, where it remained supreme until 1761, when the British captured the French base of Pondichéry. The operations of the company were finally suspended by royal decree in 1769, and in the following year it turned over its capital of more than 500,000,000 livres to the crown. In 1785 a new company was established with commercial privileges, but it was abolished in 1794 during the French Revolution.

EAST INDIES, the name formerly applied to the southeastern part of Asia, embracing the entire area of geographic India, Indochina, and the Malay Archipelago. The name "East Indies" is now applied to the Malay Archipelago alone. See NETHERLANDS INDIES; REPUBLIC OF INDONESIA.

EASTLAKE, SIR CHARLES LOCK (1793–1865), English painter and authority on art, born in Plymouth. He studied with the English historical painter Benjamin Robert Haydon, and later at the Royal Academy, London. Eastlake first attracted wide public attention by his two full-length portraits (1816) of Napoleon; he executed these from sketches of Napoleon which he drew in a small boat while the British ship *Bellerophon*, on which the French emperor was a prisoner, was in Plymouth harbor. Eastlake became a member of the Royal Academy in 1830; in 1850 he was elected its president and also was knighted. He was noted for his paintings of Italian bandits and for his historical and religious pictures. Among his paintings are "The Raising of Jairus's Daughter" (1810), "Pilgrims in Sight of Rome" (1828), and "Christ Weeping Over Jerusalem" (1841). Among his writings on art are *Materials for a History of Oil Painting* (1847) and *Contributions to the Literature of the Fine Arts* (1848); and the translations (1840 and 1851, respectively) of *Theory of Colours* by Johann Wolfgang von Goethe and *History of the Italian School of Painting* by Franz Kugler.

EAST LIVERPOOL, a city of Columbiana Co., Ohio, situated on the Ohio R., 44 miles N.W. of Pittsburgh, Pa. Bridges connect the city with Chester and Newell, in West Virginia. East Liverpool is one of the leading pottery centers of the U.S., and contains plants producing semivitreous porcelain ware, electrical porcelain, pottery supplies, floor tile, and clay novelties. Other industries are the manufacture of sewer pipe, drawn steel, building brick, firebrick, knob and tube work, and barrels. The pottery industry is an outgrowth of a kiln established in 1839 by James Bennett, a potter from England. At that time, only yellowware was produced. Whiteware production commenced in 1872, and semivitreous china was first manufactured around 1890. With the exception of the yellow clay, which is dug in the vicinity, the raw materials are imported from England, and from Florida, North Carolina, and Kentucky. Pop. (1950) 24,217.

EAST LONDON, a seaport and resort town at the mouth of the Buffalo R., on the E. coast of Cape of Good Hope Province, Union of South Africa. The town was established as Port Rex in 1846 to serve as a base port during the wars of 1846–47 between the British and the natives of the area. Most of the wool and mohair exported by the Union is shipped from East London. Population (1951 prelim.) 90,978.

EAST LOTHIAN or HADDINGTONSHIRE, maritime county of S.E. Scotland, bounded on the N. by the Firth of Forth and on the N.E. by the North Sea. In the s. part of East Lothian are the Lammermuir Hills (q.v.). The chief river of the county is the Tyne. Celts were early inhabitants of the region, and many ancient Celtic relics have been discovered. Roman relics also have been unearthed in East Lothian, notable among which are 770 ounces of 4th-century Roman silver plate. East Lothian was part of the Saxon kingdom of Northumbria (q.v.) until 1018, when the Scottish King Malcolm II incorporated it into Scotland. Agriculture is widespread. Oats, barley, wheat, potatoes, and turnips are the chief crops. Numerous sheep are raised in the vicinity of the Lammermuirs, and fish are caught off the North Sea coast. Coal and iron ore are mined and fire clay is quarried in the region. The principal industrial establishments are factories producing agricultural implements, textiles, and pottery; brick kilns; saltworks; and breweries and distilleries. Haddington is the county town of East Lothian. Other important towns are

North Berwick (q.v.), Dunbar, Prestopans, and Tranent. Area, 267 sq.m.; pop. (1953 est.) 52,200.

EASTMAN, GEORGE (1854–1932), American inventor, and philanthropist, born in Waterville, N.Y. During his lifetime he played a leading role in transforming photography from an expensive hobby of a few devotees into a relatively inexpensive and immensely widespread popular pastime. In 1884 he patented a roll film, the first film in roll form to prove practicable; in 1888 he perfected the "Kodak" camera, the first ever designed specifically for roll film. In 1892 he established the Eastman Kodak Company, at Rochester, N.Y., one of the first firms to manufacture standardized photograph equipment on a mass-production basis. This company also manufactured the flexible transparent film, devised by Eastman in 1889, which proved vital to the subsequent development of the motion-picture industry. Eastman was associated with this company in an administrative and executive capacity until his death, and contributed much to the development of its notable research facilities. He was also one of the outstanding philanthropists of his time; he donated a total of more than $75,000,000 to various projects. Notable among his contributions are a gift of $19,500,000 to the Massachusetts Institute of Technology, the endowment of $4,500,000 with which the Eastman School of Music was established in 1918 as a department of the University of Rochester, and the endowment of $4,000,000 with which a school of medicine and dentistry was founded at the same institution in 1921.

EASTMAN, MAX (FORRESTER) (1883–), American writer, born in Canandaigua, N.Y., and educated at Williams College and Columbia University. In 1913, in association with a group of writers and artists, including the poet John Reed (q.v.), he founded the revolutionary periodical *The Masses,* which he edited for five years. After its suppression by the government for its opposition to the entry of the United States into World War I, he founded a similar publication, *The Liberator,* in 1918. He edited *The Liberator* until 1922, when he went to the Soviet Union, where he became a close associate of the Bolshevik leaders. Eastman later broke with Bolshevism (q.v.), and became an opponent of the Soviet regime. After 1941 he was an editor of the monthly magazine *The Reader's Digest.* His poetical and critical works include *Enjoyment of Poetry* (1913), *Colors of Life* (1918), *The Literary Mind, Its Place in an Age of Science*

Harper & Bros.
Max Eastman

(1931), *Enjoyment of Laughter* (1936), and *Lot's Wife* (1942). Notable among his books on political themes is *Since Lenin Died* (1925), making public for the first time the suppressed "Last Will and Testament" of the Bolshevik leader Nicolai Lenin, which urged the removal of Joseph Stalin from the leadership of the Bolshevik party. Other political works include *Marx and Lenin, the Science of Revolution* (1926), *Artists in Uniform* (1934), and *The End of Socialism in Russia* (1937). He edited *Capital and Other Writings* (1932) by the German revolutionist Karl Marx. His autobiography *The Enjoyment of Living* appeared in 1948.

EASTON, county seat of Northampton Co., Pa., situated at the fork of the Delaware and Lehigh rivers, 79 miles w. of New York City, and opposite Phillipsburg, N.J., with which it is connected by a bridge. It is served by five railroads and is a railroad division point. Easton lies in a rich agricultural, mining, and quarrying region. It is an important manufacturing center of the cement and slate industries, and it contains large iron, steel, hosiery, silk, and feed mills; crayon, chemical, and printing plants; and factories manufacturing mining, quarrying, hydraulic, bookbinding, and sugar-refining machinery, and power-plant equipment, paper cups, railroad cars, textiles, awnings, and clothing.

Easton is the site of Lafayette College (q.v.). Notable buildings in the city include a church, dating from 1776, which was the site, in 1777, of a treaty between the Americans and the Five Nations of the Iroquois Indians, whereby the latter agreed to remain neutral during the American Revolution. An old stone house, dating from 1757, was the home of George Taylor, one of the signers of the Declaration of Independence. A monument marks the site where the first courthouse in Northampton County was constructed in 1765 on a tract presented by the family of William Penn for an annual rental of one red rose. In the belfry of the present courthouse hangs a bell which was rung on July 8, 1776, in celebration of the Declaration of Independence. The public library in Easton contains the flag which was unfurled on that occasion.

The site of Easton was first settled in 1739, but the town was not founded until 1752, when the land was acquired from the Indians by Thomas and John Penn, brothers of William Penn. The town was incorporated as a borough in 1789, and as a city in 1887. Pop. (1950) 35,632.

EAST ORANGE, a city of Essex Co., N.J., situated 3 miles w.n.w. of Newark and 11 miles w. of New York City. It is a part of a large suburban residential community known as "the Oranges", comprising Orange, South Orange, West Orange, and East Orange. The chief industries, concentrated in the Ampere section of the city, are the manufacture of dynamos, electric motors, sewer pipe, and pipe fittings. East Orange is the site of Upsala College (Lutheran), founded in 1893. East Orange was established separately from Orange in 1863, and was chartered as a city in 1899. It is governed by a mayor and council. Pop. (1950) 79,340.

EAST PROVIDENCE, a town of Providence Co., R.I., situated on Providence Bay and the estuary of the Seekonk R., opposite the city of Providence. The town consists of four sections: Watchemoket, Riverside, the manufacturing center Phillipsdale, and Rumford, the site of a chemical works said to be the oldest producer of baking powder in the U.S. Other leading industries are the manufacture of lacquer, printers' equipment, wire, and lubricants. In addition, East Providence is a shipping point for oysters. With Seekonk, Mass., East Providence was once a part of the old town of Rehoboth. It was set off from Seekonk when the Massachusetts-Rhode Island boundary question was settled in 1862, and incorporated as a separate town. Pop. (1950) 35,871.

EAST PRUSSIA, easternmost province of the former state of Prussia, Germany. Its capital was the Baltic port of Königsberg (q.v.), renamed Kaliningrad by the Russians in 1946. East Prussia was part of the state of the Teutonic Order from the 13th century until 1525, when it became a secular duchy. In 1618 it was united to Brandenburg (q.v.), which later joined with other territories to form Prussia (q.v.). Following World War I, East Prussia was separated geographically from the state of Prussia by the terms of the Treaty of Versailles, which ceded West Prussia and Posen (Polish, *Poznan*) to Poland, as a corridor to the Baltic Sea. In the course of the German-Polish War of 1939, Germany regained West Prussia and Posen, thus reestablishing East Prussia as a contiguous part of Prussia. At the end of World War II, the Potsdam Agreement (q.v.) granted the northeastern part of East Prussia to the Soviet Union; the southern and northwestern portions, including the port of Danzig (Polish, *Gdansk*), were given to Poland.

During World War I, East Prussia was the site of a series of battles between the Germans and Russians, which finally resulted in a complete rout of the Russian forces. During World War II, East Prussia was again an area of battle between German and Russian forces, this time resulting in the military defeat of the Germans.

East Prussia was long a region of large feudal estates, owned by the Prussian aristocracy (the Junkers). Since 1945 much of the land has been distributed to the peasants. Flax, potatoes, oats, and rye are the principal crops, and large numbers of horses and cattle are raised. Industry in East Prussia is of minor importance, limited mainly to the quarrying of amber. Area of former East Prussia, about 14,300 sq.m.; pop., about 2,500,000.

EAST RIDING. See YORKSHIRE.

EAST RIVER, a strait connecting Long Island Sound and upper New York Bay, and separating Manhattan Island from Long Island. It is connected by the Harlem R. and Spuyten Duyvil Creek with the Hudson R. On its w. bank are the boroughs of Manhattan and Bronx, and on its E. bank are those of Brooklyn and Queens. The East R. is 15 m. long and varies from ½ to 3½ m. in width. Its principal islands are Welfare, Ward's, Randall's, Riker's, and North Brother, all containing city institutions. The dangerous rapids, Hell Gate, between Ward's Island and Long Island, have been made navigable by blasting out the rock shoals. The Brooklyn, Manhat-

Port of N.Y. Authority

The East River, seen from lower Manhattan. Brooklyn is on the opposite shore.

tan, Williamsburg, Queensboro, Triborough, Hell Gate, and Bronx-Whitestone bridges span the river. Under the river are the Queens-Midtown automobile tunnel, several rapid-transit tunnels, a railroad tunnel, and several private-utility tunnels.

EAST ST. LOUIS, a city of St. Clair Co., Ill., in a coal-mining region, and on the Mississippi R., opposite St. Louis, Missouri, with which it is connected by three bridges. East St. Louis is an important railway, manufacturing, and meat-packing center. Twenty-one railroads serve the city, and the East St. Louis stockyards are among the most important in the U.S. In addition to meat-packing plants, the city contains iron and steel foundries, smelteries, machine shops, oil refineries, chemical and rubber-reclaiming plants, railroad-equipment shops, and factories manufacturing zinc and aluminum products, bottles, paint pigments, pipe-line valves, roofing, brick, and building tile. East St. Louis is the site of Park College of Aeronautical Technology of St. Louis University. In the vicinity of the city is Cahokia Mounds State Park, which contains many prehistoric Indian mounds, one of which, the Cahokia, or Monk's Mound, is the largest aboriginal earthen structure in the country, measuring 1000 ft. in length, 720 ft. in width, and 100 ft. in height. East St. Louis was settled around 1808. and was chartered as

a city in 1865. It grew rapidly, the population increasing from 5644 in 1870 to 29,655 in 1900. Pop. (1950) 82,295.

EAU CLAIRE (Fr., "Clear Water"), county seat of Eau Claire Co., Wis., situated at the confluence of the Chippewa and Eau Claire rivers, 85 miles E. of St. Paul, Minnesota. The surrounding area is noted for dairying and lumbering. Eau Claire is the commercial center of N.W. Wisconsin. It is served by three railroads, and is at the head of navigation on the Chippewa R. The city contains creameries, machine shops, packing houses, pickling works, paper mills, and factories manufacturing refrigerators, railroad equipment, aluminum ware, harness, and tires and inner tubes. A State fish hatchery is located in the vicinity. Eau Claire is the site of a State teachers college and of two county hospitals. The city was settled about 1848 and grew rapidly between 1870 and 1880 with the development of the Chippewa lumber industry. It was chartered as a city in 1872. Pop. (1950) 36,058.

EBBW VALE, town of Monmouthshire, England, on the N. edge of the South Wales coal field, and 21 m. by rail N.W. of Newport. It is an important coal-mining and iron-smelting center. Pop. (1951 est.) 29,205.

EBENACEAE, or EBONY FAMILY, a family of dicotyledonous trees and shrubs belonging to the order Ebenales. About 250 species are known, most of them tropical. Many, such as the ebony (q.v.) tree, furnish hard and durable timber. The persimmon (q.v.) tree is another commercially important member of this family.

EBENEZER (Heb., "the stone of help"), in the Old Testament, the name of a place marked by a monumental stone set up by Samuel in recognition of the divine assistance received in a battle with the Philistines (1 Sam. 7:10–12). Two earlier battles were fought at Ebenezer between the Israelites and the Philistines. In both battles the Israelites were beaten, and in the second the Ark of the Covenant was captured (1 Sam. 4:1–11). Although the exact site of Ebenezer is unknown, it is thought to be in the immediate vicinity of Jerusalem.

EBER. See HEBREWS.

EBERHARD, surnamed IM BART. See WÜRTTEMBURG, EBERHARD I, DUKE OF.

EBERLE, ABASTENIA ST. LEGER (1878–1942), American sculptor, born at Webster City, La. She studied at the Art Students' League, New York City, under Kenyon Cox and George Grey Barnard. She drew many of her subjects from life on New York's East Side. Among her works are "The Girl on Roller Skates", "Mowgli", and "Victory" (Metropolitan Museum of Art, New York City); and "Little Mother" (Art Institute of Chicago).

EBERS, GEORG MORITZ (1837–98), German Egyptologist and novelist, born in Berlin, and educated at the University of Göttingen. In 1865 he became a lecturer on Egyptology at the University of Jena, and from 1870 to 1889 he was professor at the University of Leipzig. Between 1869 and 1873 he traveled twice to Egypt, and on the second journey found the famous hieratic medical papyrus which bears his name. It is now in the library of the University of Leipzig. His first important scientific work was *Egypt and the Books of Moses* (1867–68). In addition to scientific works on Egyptology he wrote historical novels with an Egyptian setting, the most successful of which was *An Egyptian Princess* (3 vols., 1864).

EBERT, FRIEDRICH (1871–1925), German socialist and first president of the Weimar Republic of Germany, born at Heidelberg. He learned the saddler's trade and joined the Social Democratic Party, becoming a member of its central committee in 1905. He was elected to the Reichstag in 1912 and a year later became the recognized leader of his party. During World War I he led the majority wing of the Social Democratic Party in the Reichstag in supporting a policy of national defense. He favored a negotiated peace and opposed the creation of a republic in Germany, supporting instead a liberalized monarchy. In Oct., 1918, he induced his party to support and participate in the new government formed by Prince Max of Baden as chancellor. However, the desire of the people for an end to the war and the abolition of the monarchy manifested itself by mutiny in the armed forces and by strikes led by the radical Spartacists, headed by Karl Liebknecht and Rosa Luxemburg (qq.v.). Ebert and his party then pressed for the immediate abdication of Kaiser Wilhelm II. On Nov. 9, 1918, Prince Max turned the government over to Ebert, and on the following day Wilhelm II fled to Holland. As chancellor, Ebert was successful in putting down the revolts led by the Spartacists. He was elected president of the new republic by the parliament assembled at Weimar in Feb., 1919. In 1920 Ebert faced an insurrection headed by Wolfgang Kapp (q.v.). The Kapp Putsch was suppressed with the aid of the workers, called out on a general strike; but a new crisis arose when many of the workers refused to return to their jobs, demanding various governmental reforms and more severe punishment of the Kappists than had been meted out by Ebert's government. The attempt to maintain the general strike was put down by force, in the course of which a number of workers were killed. In 1922 the Reichstag extended Ebert's term as president to 1925. In 1923 he suppressed an attempt by Adolf Hitler and Gen. Erich Ludendorff (qq.v.) to establish a dictatorship in Bavaria.

EBIONITES (Heb. *ebyōn,* "poor"), name applied in the 2nd and 3rd centuries to a group of Jewish Christians who retained much of Judaism in their beliefs. The sect is supposed to have originated when the old church of Jerusalem was dispersed by an edict of the Roman emperor Hadrian in 135 A.D. and some of the Jewish Christians migrated beyond the Jordan into Peraea, cutting themselves off from the main body of the Christian Church. They adopted a conservative Pharisaic creed at first, but after the 2nd century, some of these Judaistic Christians espoused a mixture of Essenism (see ESSENES), Gnosticism (q.v.), and Christianity. According to Irenaeus (q.v.), they differed from orthodox Christians in denying the divinity of Christ and in considering Paul an apostate for having declared the supremacy of Christian teaching over the Mosaic law. Origen (q.v.) classified the Ebionites in two groups: those who believed in the Virgin Birth and those who rejected it. Both the Sabbath and the Christian Lord's Day were holy to them, and they expected the establishment of a Messianic kingdom in Jerusalem. Until the 5th century, remnants of the sect were known to have existed in Palestine and Syria.

EBONY, the hard, heavy, and dark-colored heartwood of various species of the genus *Diospyros* (q.v.). The wood is highly prized for cabinet making and other types of woodwork. The best quality is black, takes a high polish, and is obtained from *D. ebenum,* a large tree of India, Ceylon, and other tropical countries. Logs of this species of ebony are often found in which the heartwood is 2 feet in diameter and 10 to 15 feet in length. Cadoobergia wood, which has a striped appearance, also comes from *D. ebenum.* Ebony of good quality (Coromandel ebony) is obtained in the East Indies from *D. melanoxylon.* The heartwood of *D. tomentosa,* which grows in N. Bengal also yields qood-quality ebony. Calamander wood comes from *D. hirsuta.* The American species, *D. virginiana* and *D. texana,* supply a fairly good quality of ebony which is chiefly used as a veneer.

Many imitations of ebony are current. Green ebony, also called Jamaica or American ebony, comes from a leguminous tree *Byra ebenus.* Its hard, dark-brown heartwood takes a high polish. Several other leguminous trees also share the name ebony, notably *Ebenus cretica,* which yields the red or brown ebony of Crete. German ebony is simply stained yew wood. Bastard ebony is produced by the tropical tree *Jacaranda ovalifolia,* of the family Bignoniaceae, and is exported from Brazil.

EBORACUM. See YORK.

EBRO (anc. *Iberus* or *Hiberus*), a river of N.E. Spain, rising in the Cantabrian Mts. in Santander Province, and emptying into the Mediterranean Sea after a southeasterly course of about 465 miles. The Ebro is the only major river of Spain which flows into the Mediterranean. Its principal tributaries are the Ega, Aragon, Arba, Gallego, and Segre, from the N., and the Jalon, Huerva, Aguas, Martin, Guadalope, and Matarraña, from the S. The Ebro is important for irrigation purposes, and drains an area of almost 32,000 sq.m. Ocean vessels are able to ascend the river only to the city of Tortosa, a distance of about 20 miles. During the Spanish Civil War, 1936–39, the Ebro was of tactical importance to the Republican government. Late in July, 1938, Spanish Loyalists started an offensive alongside the river which halted the progress of the insurgent army of Gen. Francisco Franco for the rest of the year.

ECA DE QUEIROZ, JOSÉ MARIA (1843–1900), Portuguese novelist, born at Póvoa-de-Varzim, and educated at Coimbra University. He entered the consular service in 1872, and after serving successively in Havana, Newcastle, and Bristol, he was appointed in 1888 to a post in Paris, where he remained until his death. His early work showed the influence of French naturalism, but he later developed an individual style that was a mixture of fantasy and reality. He instituted a revolutionary development in Portuguese prose and was the founder of the Realist Naturalist school of Portuguese writers. His works include *The Mystery of the Cintra Road* (with Ramalho Ortigão, 1870), *The Crime of Father Amaro* (1875), *Cousin Basil* (1878), *The Maias* (1880), *The City and the Mountains* (1901), and *Contos* (1902).

ECARTÉ, a card game, originating in France in the 19th century, played by two players with a deck from which all cards from the deuce to the six have been removed. The cards rank, in descending order, K, Q, J, A, 10, 9, 8, 7. Five cards are dealt to each player, three at a time and two at a time, and the eleventh card is turned up for trumps. If it is a king, the dealer scores one; if the king of trumps is in either hand, the holder scores one, providing he announces it before playing his first card. If the nondealer is not satisfied with his hand, he may propose to discard. The dealer may either accept or refuse. If he accepts, each player discards as many cards as he pleases, an equivalent number of cards being dealt from the stock. After taking cards, the nondealer may propose again, and the dealer may again accept or refuse. On refusal of the dealer, or on completion of the discard and redeal, the hand is played. The nondealer leads the first card. The highest card of the suit led wins the trick, except that trumps win over other suits. The second player must follow suit and is required to take the trick if he can, and with a trump card, if he is out of the suit led. The trick-winner leads after each succeeding trick. In scoring, three tricks count one; five tricks count two. If the nondealer plays without proposing, and fails to make three tricks, or if the dealer refuses the first proposal and fails to make three tricks, the opponent scores two points. The game is five points.

ECCE HOMO (Lat., "Behold the man!"), the words spoken by Pontius Pilate (John 19:5) when presenting Christ, dressed in a purple robe and crowned with thorns, to the multitude, prior to condemning Him to crucifixion. Representations of the occasion on which the words were uttered, or of details from the scene, especially the head of Christ crowned with thorns, are generally known by the title "Ecce Homo". The scene has been painted under this and other titles by many eminent artists. Among the most celebrated of such pictures are those by Il Sodoma (Pitti Palace, Florence, and Sienna Academy), by Correggio (National Gallery, London), by Titian (Scuola di San Rocco, Venice, the Madrid Museum, and the Vienna Museum), by Tintoretto (Munich Gallery and the Scuola di San Rocco), by Guido Reni (Dresden Gallery, the Louvre, Paris, and The National Gallery, London), and by Murillo (Cadiz Museum and the Prado, Madrid).

ECCLES, municipal and parliamentary borough, Lancashire, N.W. England, 4 miles W. of Manchester, on the Irwell R., a tributary of the Mersey. Eccles is practically a suburb of Manchester, and is connected with that city by railway and the Manchester Ship Canal. Of its many churches, foremost is that of St. Mary's, believed to date from the 12th century. The principal industry is the manufacture of textiles. Pop. (1951 est.) 43,927.

ECCLESIASTES (Greek paraphrase of the Hebrew *Koheleth,* meaning one who addresses an assembly, i.e., "a preacher"), the Septuagint title of a book of the Old Testament, the twelve chapters of which contain discourses on the vanity of life. The author of the book describes himself as *Koheleth,* "a son of David, king in Jerusalem", which is thought to refer to Solomon. However, "son of David" could have been merely an interpolation equivalent to "anonymous". The wide application of the thesis of "the vanity of earthly things" gave Ecclesiastes a skeptical tone, and, much to the alarm of the rabbis, the book became popular. Conversely, the implication that Solomon was the author of Ecclesiastes obscured the character of the book, and gave rise to a method of interpretation that overlooked its skepticism. Some religionists assert that in order to give the book a pious rather than a skeptical conclusion, its chapters were interspersed with material giving indications of the author's piety; and contend that only as a result of the orthodoxy such material imparted was Ecclesiastes able to withstand the close scrutiny to which the rabbis subjected it, and thus allowed to remain in the synagogue as sacred matter.

ECCLESIASTICAL COURTS, tribunals exercising jurisdiction in religious affairs. In its broadest sense, the term ecclesiastical court is applied to any former or existing tribunal established by religious authority. In a more restricted sense, it is applied only to the tribunals of the Christian Church, which are also sometimes called Courts Christian and are found now in the Roman Catholic Church and in many Protestant churches, particularly in the established Church of England. Included are the bodies established by some U.S. Protestant denominations to legislate with respect to church policy and administration, and to exercise church discipline.

The Courts Christian originated among the Christian brethren, under the Romans, prior to the adoption of Christianity by the emperor Constantine in the 4th century A.D. The Christians, as a persecuted sect, had no access to the Roman courts; these courts, moreover, were pagan and were proscribed by Christian leaders on religious and moral grounds. Early Christian courts were simple tribunals whose chief function was the arbitration of disputes among the brethren; bishops acted as the arbitrators.

After the conversion of the emperor Constantine, Christianity became the state religion of Rome, and the ecclesiastical courts were incorporated in the Roman judicial system. As the Christian Church developed on a pontifical and hierarchical basis and as its power grew, the simple courts of primitive Christianity underwent a corresponding development. In time they comprised a complex system exercising jurisdiction delegated by the pope in his capacity as the supreme judicial power in the Christian Church. Then, as Rome declined and its institutions decayed, the ecclesiastical courts began to assume jurisdiction in secular affairs.

In the Middle Ages, the Roman Catholic Church reached the zenith of its power and greatness: it became a world state, the popes became powerful temporal potentates, and canon law (q.v.) and the jurisdiction of the ecclesiastical courts were extended to embrace virtually the entire range of human relationships. Extension of the jurisdiction of the ecclesiastical courts was facilitated by the dual character of the princes of the Church, as functioning ecclesiastics—bishops, archbishops, cardinals, and popes—and as powerful landowners and temporal rulers. When courts established by secular authority resisted the incursions of the ecclesiastical courts into their jurisdictions, the ecclesiastical courts fought persistently for supremacy, engaging in a protracted struggle which shaped much of the legal history of the later Middle Ages. From the 13th century, the great judicial power of the Church was manifested especially through the tribunal commonly called the Holy Office, created to ferret out and punish heresy; see INQUISITION.

The Reformation was a basic cause of tne subsequent decline of the ecclesiastical courts. Other causes included the rise of representative government, the separation of judicial from executive and legislative powers of government, and the separation of church and state, all of which combined to reduce gradually the power and jurisdiction of the ecclesiastical courts to their present limited form and scope.

A remnant of the former extensive jurisdiction of the ecclesiastical courts survives in the three papal tribunals, the Sacred Penitentiaria, Sacred Roman Rota, and Apostolic Signatura, which comprise the judicial branch of the Roman Curia; see ROMAN CATHOLIC CHURCH: *Curia Romana.* In England, which has an established church, the ecclesiastical courts derive their authority nominally from the crown; the principal tribunals are called Archdeacon's Court, Bishop's or Consistory Court, Chancery Court of York, Court of Arches, and Final Appeal Court, the latter comprising the Judicial Committee of the Privy Council. In the Protestant parts of Germany, and in Holland, Switzerland, and other countries where Protestantism is nonepiscopal, ecclesiastical courts have virtually ceased to exist.

ECCLESIASTICAL HISTORY. See CHURCH HISTORY.

ECCLESIASTICAL LAW. See CANON LAW; ANGLICAN CHURCH; SCOTLAND, CHURCH OF; ROMAN CATHOLIC CHURCH.

ECCLESIASTICAL YEAR. See CALENDAR; CHRONOLOGY; EASTER; YEAR.

ECCLESIASTICUS, apocryphal or deuterocanonical book of the Old Testament, consisting, for the most part, of a series of maxims concerning practical and moral aspects of life. It was known to scholars through a Greek translation, by Jesus, son of Sirach Eleazar of Jerusalem, from the original Hebrew text. Fragments of a Hebrew text dating from about the 11th century were discovered and published between 1896 and 1900, and in this text the author's name is given as Simeon, the son of Jeshua, the son of Eleazar, the son of Sira. Ecclesiasticus is of uncertain date, its translator into Greek indicating that he did his work after 132 B.C., when he came into Egypt, and that his grandfather wrote the original. It is possible, therefore, that the author of Ecclesiasticus lived and wrote about 190–170 B.C. The theological views of the book are

The echidna of Australia

similar to those of the later Sadducees (q.v.). Ecclesiasticus does not recognize the existence of angels, devils, or demons, and gives rationalistic interpretations of angels mentioned in Biblical passages. It gives no hope of a Messiah, and ignores the question of the immortality of the soul. Its moral philosophy, utilitarian and individualistic, is based on the personal happiness to be gained in following its precepts, which are in the form of rules for behavior on specific occasions, rather than of general principles.

ECHEGARAY Y EIZAGUIRRE, JOSÉ (1832–1916), Spanish playwright and statesman, born in Madrid. He was a professor of mathematics and physics at the Madrid engineering school from 1854 to 1868. He became minister of public instruction in 1873, and of finance in 1874 and 1905. He first began writing plays in 1874, and is the author of over 70 dramas in prose and verse. He was corecipient, with Frédéric Mistral, of the Nobel Prize in literature in 1904. His plays include *La Esposa del Vengador* (1874), *O Locura o Santidad* (1876; English trans., *Madman or Saint*), *El Gran Galeoto* (1881; produced in U.S. as *The World and His Wife*), *Mariana* (1892), *El Estigma* (1895), *La Duda* (1898), *El Loco Diós* (1900), *La Desequilibrada* (1903), and *A Fuerza de Arrastrarse* (1905).

ECHIDNA, SPINY ANTEATER, or PORCUPINE ANTEATER, one of the two existing species of the order Monotremata (egg-laying mammals), *Tachyglossus aculeatus.* It is found only in Tasmania, Australia, and New Guinea. The echidna is about 12 to 18 inches in length, and has a broad, depressed body mounted upon short, strong legs. The legs have powerful claws, adapting the animal for rapid digging into hard ground. The back is covered with stiff, hedgehoglike spines, mixed with long, coarse hairs. The echidna has a small head, and its nose is prolonged into a slender snout. Its toothless mouth has an extensible, glutinous

THE ECHINODERMATA
Above, left: Sea urchin (Echinus acutis).
Above: Starfish (Astropecten irregularis).
Left: Sea cucumber (Cucumaria normani).

tongue suitable for catching ants and other small insects. The female lays one or two eggs after a period of gestation of 27 to 28 days. The eggs are placed in the mother's pouch, where they hatch after about two weeks. The offspring are carried in the mother's pouch until they are able to walk. The echidna is often kept as a pet, for it is gentle in disposition, very active, and endures confinement well. See MONOTREMATA.

ECHINOCOCCUS. See TAPEWORMS.

ECHINODERMATA, a phylum of marine animals having a symmetrical calcareous exoskeleton. Most adult echinoderms have an apparent radial symmetry, being divided into five equal rays or arms. Even within the limits of the same family, some species have soft, leathery body walls, and others have firm, almost immovable "shells". This diversity is due mainly to variation in the amount of mineral matter deposited in the body wall. The body walls are often covered with knobs, tubercles, or spines. Echinoderms have well-developed alimentary canals, suspended in, and distinct from, the general body cavity, and provided with both mouth and anus. A combined respiratory and locomotory system of complicated structure, called the water-vascular system, occurs only in the members of this phylum. It consists of a ring vessel about the mouth, from which a number of tubes radiate to the ambulacral areas, of which

there is one in each ray. The tubes connect with the tube feet, which are extensible, saclike tentacles or suckers that project from the surface of the body through pores in the plates. In some cases the tube feet assist in conveying food to the mouth. The nervous systems, blood-vascular systems, and reproductive systems of echinoderms are well developed. The sexes are separate. The eggs, when hatched, produce bilaterally symmetrical, free-swimming larvae, which differ somewhat in form in the different classes. Three types of larvae have been distinguished among the various species, and have been given the names auricularia, bipinnaria, and pluteus.

About 3000 living species of echinoderms are known. They are found in all the seas on the globe, and at all depths, but are most abundant in the warm seas of the tropics. Echinodermata comprises the classes Asteroidea (starfish), Blastoidea (pentremite), Crinoidea (sea lily), Echinoidea (sea urchin), Holothurioidea (sea cucumber), Ophiuroidea (brittle star), and Cystoidea. See BRITTLE STAR; CRINOIDEA; ECHINOIDEA; HOLOTHURIOIDEA; STARFISH.

ECHINOIDEA, a class of marine animals in the phylum Echinodermata, consisting of the sea urchins and their allies. They have unattached, disk-shaped shells and movable spines. Sea urchins have, scattered over their surfaces, microscopic, buttonlike bodies called sphaeridia, which are thought to be organs of balance. They have a complicated masticatory apparatus called *Aristotle's lantern*, consisting of five converging jaws and accessory ossicles. Echinoids feed on various types of organic matter, including plants, small animals, and waste material. Some species are occasionally used as food. The class Echinoidea comprises the orders Cidaroida, Centrechinoida, and Exocycloida. The Cidaroida are sea urchins without gills about the mouth; Centrechinoida are sea urchins having gills around the mouth; and Exocycloida are sand dollars, many of which are flattened, and show both radial and bilateral symmetry. See ECHINODERMATA.

ECIJA, city of Sevilla Province, Spain, on the Genil R., 48 miles E.N.E. of Seville. Its known history dates back to Roman times, when it was called *Astigi*. According to tradition, the Apostle Paul visited the city, and converted to Christianity his hostess, Santa Xantippa. The city, which was called *Estadja* by the Arabs, is noted architecturally for its Moorish gateways and glazed-tile church towers. Because of the intense heat of its climate, Ecija is known as the "Frying Pan of Andalusia". Olives, wine grapes, cereals, cotton, beet sugar, and tobacco are grown in the surrounding fertile area. In the city, olive oil, wine, starch, soap, candles, shoes, textiles, straw hats, and pottery are manufactured. Pop., about 30,000.

ECK, JOHANN, original surname MAYER (1486–1543), German Roman Catholic theologian and outstanding opponent of the Reformation, born in Eck, Swabia, and educated at the universities of Heidelberg, Tübingen, and Cologne. In 1510 he became professor of theology at Ingolstadt, where he remained for thirty years. He had already acquired recognition as the defender of the established order when Martin Luther sent him copies of the 95 theses in 1517, and in the following year Eck circulated his *Obelesci* attacking Luther. These were answered by Karlstadt, who challenged him to a public disputation which took place at Leipzig in June and July, 1519. Eck first disputed with Karlstadt about grace and free will, defending the Roman viewpoint with great ability. He then contended with Luther about the primacy of the Pope, penance, indulgences, and purgatory, and pressed the charge of Hussite heresy against the reformer. Although the arbitrators gave no verdict, public opinion gave the victory to Eck. In 1520, he went to Rome and returned as papal legate to enforce the papal bull of June 15, which condemned Luther as a heretic. The bull was unpopular and Eck continued the struggle against the Reformation and defended Catholicism at the Augs-burg Diet (1530) and the religious conferences at Worms (1540) and Ratisbon (1541). His most important work was *De Primatu Petri* (1519). His polemics against Luther are collected in *Operum Johannis Eckii contra Lutherum* (5 vols., 1530–35).

ECKENER, HUGO (1868–1954), German airship designer and navigator, born in Flensburg. After studying economics, he took up the study of the construction and navigation of Zeppelins in 1908. He became an instructor in naval aviation during World War I, and in 1920 a director of the Zeppelin Company. He later became part owner and president of the company. He made two dirigible flights to the United States from Germany, in October, 1923, as commander of the *ZR 3*, and again in 1928 as commander of the *Graf Zeppelin*, which he had built. He repeated his trips to this country several times and in 1929 arranged for a round-the-world cruise which was successfully completed. Eckener worked actively for the development of air transportation by dirigible. He was awarded the British Gold Medal for Aeronautics, 1936, and the Guggenheim Gold Medal, 1937.

ECLECTICISM (Gr. *eklegein*, "to pick out"), in philosophy, the formulation of a system of thought by choosing from the doctrines of other, already developed systems. The eclectic philosopher combines what he regards as the most plausible doctrines, but often the doctrines selected do not combine to make an integral unity.

Eclecticism manifested itself to a great extent among the Greeks, beginning about the 2nd century B.C. This period was marked by a loss of the vigor of the spirit of intellectual inquiry which had motivated the great Greek philosophers, such as Plato and Aristotle, to develop unified cosmologies in their search for truth. The later Greek philosophers, such as Antiochus of Ascalon (1st century B.C.), who combined Stoicism and Skepticism, and Panætius (2nd century B.C.), who based his thought on Stoicism and Platonism, adopted the doctrines which pleased them most. Roman thinkers, who never developed an independent philosophic system, were notably eclectic; Marcus Tullius Cicero, for example, combined elements of Stoicism, Peripateticism, and Skepticism in his philosophical works, without regard for their essential disunity.

Among the early Christian philosophers, Clement of Alexandria and Origen developed their works by selecting elements of Greek metaphysics and combining them with He-

American Museum of Natural History

Solar eclipse as seen in Middletown, Connecticut, 1925 (painting by Howard R. Butler)

brew thought expressed in the Old and New Testaments. Later, Johannes Eckhart (1260?–1327?), the German theologian and mystic, formulated a system of Christian philosophy based on Aristotle, Neoplatonism, and Arabic and Hebrew doctrine.

The modern school of eclectic philosophy arose in France during the 19th century; its most distinguished figure was Victor Cousin (q.v.), who tried to unite the idealism of Immanuel Kant with the philosophy of Common Sense and the doctrines of René Descartes.

ECLIPSE, the obscuring of one celestial body by another, particularly the obscuring of the sun or a planetary satellite. Two kinds of eclipses involve the earth: eclipses of the moon, or lunar eclipses; and eclipses of the sun, or solar eclipses. A lunar eclipse occurs when the earth is between the sun and the moon, and its shadow darkens the moon. A solar eclipse occurs when the moon is between the sun and the earth, and its shadow sweeps across the face of the earth. Transits (q.v.) and occultations are similar astronomical phenomena, involving either planets or stars, but are not as spectacular as eclipses because of the small size of these bodies as seen from the earth.

Lunar Eclipses. The earth, lit by the sun, casts a long conical shadow in space. At any point within the cone the light of the sun is wholly obscured. Surrounding the shadow cone, also called the *umbra*, is an area of partial shadow called the *penumbra*. The approximate mean length of the umbra is 857,-000 m.; at a distance of 239,000 m., the mean distance of the moon from the earth, it has a diameter of about 5700 m.

A total lunar eclipse occurs when the moon passes completely into the umbra. If the moon passes directly through the center of the umbra, it is obscured for a total of about two hours. If it does not pass through the center, the period of totality is less and may last for only an instant in the case where the moon passes through the very edge of the umbra.

A partial lunar eclipse occurs when only a part of the moon enters the umbra and is obscured. Such eclipses range from virtual totality, where only a small portion of the moon's surface is not obscured, to eclipses where only a small portion of the earth's shadow is seen on the moon's face.

Before the moon actually enters the umbra in either total or partial eclipse, it is within the penumbra and its surface becomes visibly darker. The portion that enters the umbra seems almost black. During a total eclipse, the moon's disk is not completely dark, however, but is orange colored because it is faintly illuminated with light refracted by the earth's atmosphere, which filters out the blue rays of light. Occasionally an eclipse occurs when the earth is covered with a heavy layer of clouds. In such a case no light is refracted and the moon's surface is invisible during totality. All lunar eclipses are visible over an entire hemisphere of the earth.

Solar Eclipses. The length of the moon's umbra varies from 228,000 to 236,000 m., and the distance between the earth and the moon varies from 222,000, to 253,000 m. Total solar eclipses occur when the moon's umbra reaches the earth. The diameter of the umbra is never greater than 167 m. where it touches the earth's surface, so that the area in which a total solar eclipse is visible never exceeds 167 m. in width and is usually considerably narrower. At certain times when the moon passes between the earth and the sun its shadow will not reach the earth. On such occasions a form of eclipse called an *annular eclipse* occurs in which an annulus or bright ring of the sun's disk appears surrounding the black disk of the moon.

The shadow of the moon moves across the surface of the earth in an easterly direction and, because the earth is also rotating eastward, its speed is equal to the speed of the moon's travel along its orbit minus the speed of the earth's rotation. The speed of the shadow at the equator is about 1060 m. per hour; near the poles, where the speed of rotation is virtually zero, it is about 2100 m. per hour. The path of totality of an eclipse and the time of totality can be calculated from the size of the moon's shadow and from its speed. The maximum duration of a total eclipse of the sun is about 7.5 min., but such eclipses are rare, occurring only once in several thousand years. On the average a total eclipse is visible for about 3 min. from a point in the center of the path of totality.

In areas outside the band swept by the moon's umbra but within the penumbra, the sun is only partly obscured and a partial eclipse occurs.

At the approach of a total eclipse, the moon begins to move across the sun's disk about an hour before totality. The sun's illumination gradually decreases, and during totality falls off to the intensity of bright moonlight. This residual light is due largely to the sun's corona. As the surface of the sun narrows to a thin crescent, the corona becomes visible. At the moment before the eclipse becomes total, brilliant points of light, called *Baily's beads*, flash out in a crescent shape. These points are caused by the sun shining through valleys and irregularities on the moon's surface. They are observed also at the instant when totality is ending, called *emersion*. Just before, just after, and sometimes during totality, narrow bands of moving shadows can be seen. These shadow bands are not fully understood but are apparently caused by irregular refraction of light in the atmosphere of the earth. Both before and after totality an observer located on a hill or in an airplane can see the moon's shadow moving eastward across the earth's surface like a swiftly moving cloud shadow.

Frequency of Eclipses. If the earth's orbit, the ecliptic (q.v.), were in the same plane as the moon's orbit, two total eclipses would occur each lunar month, a lunar eclipse at the time of each full moon, and a solar eclipse at the time of each new moon. The two orbits, however, are inclined, and, as a result, eclipses occur only when the moon or the sun is within a few degrees of either of the two points (called the *nodes*) where the orbits intersect.

Periodically both the sun and the moon return to the same position relative to one of the nodes, with the result that eclipses repeat themselves at regular intervals. The time of the interval, called the *saros*, is a little over 6585.3 days or about 18 years, 9 to 11 days (depending on the number of intervening leap years), and 8 hours. The saros corresponds almost exactly to 19 returns of the sun to the same node, 242 returns of the moon to the same node, and 223 lunar months. The difference between the number of returns of the moon and the number of lunar months is accounted for by the fact that the nodes

Diagram showing areas of shadow thrown upon the earth when the sun is in eclipse

move westward at the rate of 19.5° per year. An eclipse that recurs after the saros will be a duplicate of the earlier eclipse, but will be visible 120° farther west on the earth's surface, because of the rotation of the earth during the third of a day included in the interval. Lunar eclipses recur 48 or 49 times and solar eclipses from 68 to 75 times before slight differences in the motions of the sun and moon eliminate the eclipse. The saros has been known since the time of ancient Babylon.

During one saros approximately 70 eclipses take place, usually 29 lunar and 41 solar, of which 10 are total, 17 are annular and 14 are partial. The minimum number of eclipses which can occur in a given year is two, and the maximum seven. On the average, four eclipses take place each year.

During the 20th century 375 eclipses have taken, or will take place: 228 solar and 147 lunar. Total eclipses of the sun visible in the U.S. will occur on Oct. 2, 1959, March 7, 1970; Feb. 26, 1979; and May 30, 1984.

Observation of Eclipses. A number of astronomical problems could formerly be studied only during a total eclipse of the sun. Among these problems were the size and composition of the sun's corona and the bending of light rays passing close to the sun because of the sun's gravitational field; see CORONA; RELATIVITY. The brilliance of the sun's disk makes observations of the corona and nearby stars impossible with ordinary telescopes, except during an eclipse. However, the coronagraph, a photographic telescope, permits direct observation of the corona at all times. In present day astronomy solar-eclipse observations are valuable, particularly when the path of the eclipse traverses large land areas, as a means of making precise determinations of intercontinental distances. Such an eclipse occurred on June 30, 1954, and an elaborate network of special observatories was set up in North America, Europe, and Asia, to obtain the distance data required for modern guided-missile warfare.

ECLIPTIC, in astronomy, the apparent great-circle path of the sun in the celestial sphere, as seen from the earth. It is so named because eclipses happen only when the moon is on or near this path. The plane of this path, called the plane of the ecliptic, intersects the celestial equator (the projection of the earth's equator on the celestial sphere) at an angle of about 23° 27'. This angle is known as the obliquity of the ecliptic, and is approximately constant over a period of millions of years, although at present it is

decreasing at the rate of 48 seconds of arc per century, and will decrease for several millenniums until it reaches a minimum of 22° 54', after which it will again increase.

The two points at which the ecliptic intersects the celestial equator are called nodes or equinoxes. The sun is at the vernal equinox about March 21st, and at the autumnal equinox about September 23rd. Halfway on the ecliptic between the equinoxes are the summer and winter solstices. The sun is at these points of its path about June 21st and December 22nd respectively. The names of the four points correspond to the seasons beginning in the northern hemisphere on these dates. The equinoxes do not occur at the same points of the ecliptic every year, for the plane of the ecliptic and the plane of the equator revolve in opposite directions. The two planes make a complete revolution with respect to each other once every 25,868 years. The movement of the equinoxes along the ecliptic is called the precession of the equinoxes. A correction for precession has to applied to celestial charts in order to find the true position of the stars at any particular time; see ARIES, FIRST POINT OF.

The ecliptic is also used in astronomy as the fundamental circle for a system of coordinates called the ecliptic system. Celestial latitude is measured north and south of the ecliptic; celestial longitude is measured east and west of the vernal equinox.

In astrology (q.v.), the ecliptic is divided into twelve arcs of thirty degrees each, called the signs of the Zodiac. These signs or "houses of heaven" have been named after the constellations through which the ecliptic passes; see ZODIAC.

ÉCOLE DES BEAUX-ARTS. See BEAUX-ARTS, ÉCOLE DES.

ÉCOLE POLYTECHNIQUE. See TECHNICAL EDUCATION.

ECOLOGY or **BIONOMICS,** the branch of biology dealing with the interrelations of organisms and their environment. This science includes in its field the adaptation of species to physical conditions such as temperature, pressure, and the presence (in air) or absence (as in water) of free oxygen. It deals with physical modifications which enable a species to prosper in the same habitat with other organisms. Animals with protective coloring (q.v.) and plants equipped to attract insects which assist in pollination illustrate adaptation to biological factors in the habitat. Ecology is concerned also with the effects of both physical and biological environmental

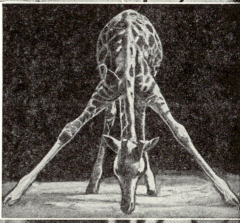

ANIMALS AND THEIR ENVIRONMENT

Above: Horny scales of the pangolin, an African mammal, protect it from natural enemies. Above, right: Walking-stick insects resemble the twigs of trees. The camouflage may help them to survive. Right: Although giraffe's stance is awkward when it eats from ground, its long neck is well adapted for reaching leaves of tall trees. Below: Prairie dog can survive in dry places, deriving moisture from plant food. Below, right: Crocodile's powerful jaws enable it to seize large prey.

Left: Pitcher of the nepenthes plant. To provide a type of food matter lacking in the soil, the plant captures insects by means of slippery hairs inside pitchers. Right: A crossbill. Mandibles of this bird are well fitted for opening pine cones to get seeds.

factors on the number and distribution of members of a species.

Inevitably ecology overlaps the fields of many sciences, including geography, geology, and meteorology, and in large measure requires the organization of existing knowledge. It is a relatively new science, still largely undeveloped. Since the German biologist Ernst Haeckel introduced the term "oecology" in 1869, considerable work in this field has been done by botanists; less has been done by zoologists and anthropologists.

In the past, most ecological investigations were quests for evidence to support the Darwinian theory of natural selection. Today ecological studies are usually directed toward the solution of immediate practical problems. In Hawaii, ecological methods were applied in the control of an unwelcome immigrant, the Australian sugar-cane leaf hopper. In the absence of its natural enemies and with an abundant food supply, this insect flourished in its new environment, doing enormous damage to crops, until insects which prey on the leaf hopper were sought out in Australia and imported to Hawaii. (See also ENTOMOLOGY, ECONOMIC.)

Ecology of Man. The ecology of man is concerned with such physical environmental factors as climate and the geographic distribution of natural resources. As a branch of sociology, it is the study of the effect of such physical factors on the distribution of populations, with an added factor, social environment, created by man himself. Studies yielding more direct benefits have been made in the economic and medical fields. In economics, enormous benefits have resulted from man's efforts to develop plant strains with high resistance to climatic variations, fungus diseases, and insect pests. In medicine the control of malaria, for example, requires the study not only of man, but also of the malarial parasite and of its vectors, the anopheline mosquitoes; and further of mosquito-eating birds and reptiles, and of local factors of climate, vegetation, and topography, which may help or hinder extermination of the mosquitoes or their enemies.

Inevitably, the ecology of man interlocks with that of plants and animals. While comparatively little work has been done in the ecology of man, clues to the complex ecological interrelationships of man with plants and animals are given in the following sections.

Ecology of Animals. The habitats of animals are classifiable according to various physical and chemical factors which affect animals directly. The earth may conveniently be divided into temperature zones from the equator to the poles; temperature zones may be determined by altitude as well as latitude. Aqueous habitats may be classified according to their salt content, lowest in Alpine lakes and high in the oceans, and bodies of water may also be zoned vertically according to light, aeration, and pressure. In each type of habitat, animal populations are adapted to that particular environment. The various types of mammalian fur illustrate adaptation to temperature; the blindfish (q.v.) found in caves is adapted to lack of light. The freshwater crayfish illustrates selective influence by a chemical factor; because this crustacean needs water with a high content of calcium carbonate, it flourishes in country where limestone is abundant, but is not found where granite is the predominant rock.

For many animals the direct effect of physical and chemical factors in the environment may be less important than the indirect effect through plants. Plants provide the food supply of the herbivores, which in turn support the carnivores. For some species, grass, shrubs, or trees are necessary as protective cover. Plants may affect animals also by modifying the local climate, that is, by increasing humidity or decreasing light. Animals living at ground level in a pine forest, for example, must be adapted to perpetual twilight.

Because animals profoundly affect each other, any given type of habitat has a characteristic community of species bound together by a web of interrelations including relations of co-operation, dependency, competition, and predatism. Animals of the same species may be in competition for a limited food supply, with the effect that their numbers in a particular area tend to be self-limiting; a single pair of eagles, for example, may pre-empt an extensive territory. Similarly, members of different species may be in competition. Animals of one species may co-operate, as when a few individuals in a herd of antelope serve as sentries; co-operation may even take the form of a complicated division of labor, as among ants and bees. Generally co-operation makes it possible for a larger number of individuals to live in a given area. Among members of different species, relationships of varying degrees of dependency occur. One native of the deserts of Arizona and California is the elf owl, *Micropallas whitneyi*, which lives only in holes made in cacti by woodpeckers; woodpeckers are an essential factor in this owl's environment. More extreme forms

of dependency are commensalism and symbiosis (qq.v.) and parasitism (see PARASITE).

The outstanding pattern of relationship in an animal community is that linking chain of eaters and eaten. As the links in a chain progress from larger to smaller species, their relative numbers increase; a waterside community includes far more fish than fish-eating birds, and far more insects than fish, and one insect may be the host of a vast number of parasites.

Each species in a community has an optimum density for that type of habitat. If its members are too few, the species risks extinction in that locality in the event of severe weather or an increase of enemies. On the other hand, excessive numbers soon exhaust the food supply. Each species apparently tends to increase without limit, but animal populations usually are held in check by starvation and by disease, if not by predators. Predators, though they may destroy many individual members of a species, are not necessarily dangerous to the survival of the species. In Norway a decrease in the number of hawks was followed by an increase in willow grouse, but epidemics soon occurred among the grouse nearly every year instead of about once in four years. Whereas formerly the hawks had weeded out many of the weaker specimens, diseased birds now survived long enough to spread infection through a grouse population which had reached a dangerous density; and eventually the grouse were permanently reduced in numbers.

An animal community seems to struggle toward a stable pattern of numerical relations among species, but actually this so-called natural balance rarely is achieved; variations from the hypothetical norm are the rule rather than the exception. The variations may be extreme; a not uncommon phenomenon is the so-called plague of small herbivorous animals. Unusually favorable conditions, especially a superabundant food supply, may make possible a sudden increase in a particular species. Predators are inadequate to check such spurts of population growth, for the predator has a lower rate of reproduction than its prey; the fox produces fewer young in a year than the field mouse, for example. Parasites, however, can accomplish what predators cannot. Viruses, bacteria, protozoans, and helminths multiply more rapidly than their hosts, and the conditions for an epidemic are created when the host species reaches a certain density. It is noteworthy that plagues of herbivores are checked more often by disease than

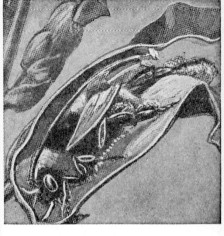

COMMUNITY OF SPECIES

Above, left: Young mason bees emerging from a snail shell, which has provided necessary shelter for them during their larval stage. Above: Bumblebee in snapdragon flower. Bee gets nectar while cross-pollinating flower. Left: A foster-parent pipit (right) feeding fledgling cuckoo. Mother cuckoos invariably lay their eggs in the nests of other birds.

they are by failure of the food supply. See also GEOGRAPHICAL DISTRIBUTION OF ANIMALS.

Ecology of Plants. Climatic factors exert a strong selective influence on plant life. The effect is illustrated in the tropical, temperate, and north temperate forest areas: in the first, broad-leaved evergreens predominate; in the second, deciduous trees; and in the third, evergreen conifers. The mean annual temperature determines the northern limit of cultivation of such crops as wheat and corn. Although most plants are adaptable to a wide range of temperatures, each species has its optimum temperature for growth and reproduction.

Within temperature zones the amount of available moisture may determine the type of vegetation. Because plants take water from the soil and lose it to the air by evaporation, the seasonal distribution of rainfall and its ratio to evaporation are more important than total annual precipitation. Although in desert areas the annual precipitation may be as high as 15 inches, it occurs within a short season, and most of the water is quickly evaporated from the soil. The lack of adequate year-round moisture in the soil is the factor that accounts for the absence of trees in the prairies of the United States.

The intensity and duration of light also affect plant distribution. Some species reach their maximum rates of growth only in direct sunlight, whereas others are adapted to shade. If the days are too brief, a plant cannot photosynthesize sufficient carbohydrates for its needs. The duration of daylight also affects reproduction, each plant making what is known as the photoperiodic response; a species adapted to long days flowers in summer; one adapted to short days flowers in spring or autumn. The photoperiodic response also determines the seasons for pollination and dissemination.

Climatic influences determine the general character of the great plant communities called climatic formations, of which the principal types are forest, grassland, and desert; see also GEOGRAPHIC DISTRIBUTION OF PLANTS. Locally, climatic formations are modified by edaphic influences, that is, by the physical and chemical character of the soil. The structure and texture of the soil determine its capacity for holding water, and the amount of atmosphere contained in the pores between soil particles. Sandy soil holds less water than does soil containing a large proportion of clay or organic matter. In fine-textured, hard-packed soil, plant roots can get little oxygen. The chemical character of the soil affect its fertility. Thus within climatic formations are found edaphic formations such as communities of marsh plants or rock plants.

In relations between plants, competition is conspicuous, both among members of the same species and among different species with similar needs. In the competition for light and water and for nourishment from the soil, only one of several thousand seedlings may survive to become a tree. In the processes of pollination and dissemination, many plants are in competition for the services of insects and other animals.

Co-operation among members of one species does not occur, but members of one species may assist those of another. Nitrogen-fixing bacteria, such as *Clostridium pasteurianum,* in the soil help to restore its fertility. Legumes are able to survive in exhausted soil when assisted by nitrogen-fixing bacteria such as *Rhizobium radicicola,* which live symbiotically in tubercles on the roots of the plants; see NITROGEN FIXATION. Forest trees make their locality habitable for plants adapted to shade. Relations of parasitism among plants are common.

Aside from losses through consumption by herbivores and through other forms of use or destruction by animals, plant life is affected by animals, including man, in various ways. Earthworms play an important role in aerating soil; insects in pollination. The seeds borne within burs are spread by the clinging of the bur to animal fur, and various berry seeds are distributed in animal droppings; see also ELAIOSOMES. Grazing herbivores discourage seed-bearing plants in favor of those which spread by means of rhizomes. The selective influence of man on plant communities is seen in farms and gardens.

Agriculture and animal husbandry have greatly altered the type of vegetation found over wide areas, as have climatic changes such as those which accompanied the passing of the great glaciers. Any plant association (community) is subject to continual change, however, for its environment is continually being modified by erosion (q.v.) or by the deposition of new soil. Plants themselves modify their environment, as successive generations contribute humus to the soil. So-called pioneer plants on sand dunes or on a rocky surface eventually are succeeded by prairie or forest vegetation adapted to the changed conditions which the pioneer plants helped to bring about. Successive plant associations, beginning with an association of microscopic seaweeds, in time convert a salt marsh to grassland. Plant successions culminate in what is called climax vegetation, which is characteristic of the local climate. In much of the western United States, the climax is prairie vegetation; in the East it is deciduous forest.

ECONOMIC AND SOCIAL COUNCIL, one of the six principal organs of the United Nations. It consists of the representatives of eighteen UN member states, elected for three-year terms by a two-thirds vote of the members of the General Assembly. It meets thrice annually under the presidency of one of its members; its decisions are made by a simple majority vote of those present and voting.

The Council is charged with the execution of UN functions in connection with economic, social, cultural, educational, health, and related problems. It has established the following commissions: Commission for Human Rights, Commission on Narcotic Drugs, Commission on the Status of Women, Economic and Employment Commission, Fiscal Commission, Population Commission, Social Commission, Statistical Commission, and Transport and Communications Commission. Two regional commissions were established in 1946 to give aid to war-devastated European and Asiatic countries; these are the Economic Commission for Europe, and the Economic Commission for Asia and the Far East.

Two standing committees have also been created by the Council, one to negotiate agreements establishing relations between the UN and such specialized agencies as the International Labor Organization (q.v.); and the other to consult nongovernmental organizations in various countries after prior consultation with the governments of those countries.

In 1946, the Economic and Social Council established the World Health Organization and the International Refugee Organization (qq.v.), which were created as specialized subsidiary agencies to cope with problems in the fields designated by their titles. The Council also sponsored the organization of the International Children's Emergency Fund which, in 1948, opened a global drive to raise funds to feed as many as possible of the world's underfed children, estimated at 400,-000,000; the U.S. Congress authorized a contribution of $60,000,000 to this fund. Two years later the Council recommended that the

A meeting of the Economic and Social Council of the United Nations, July 19, 1948

work of this important agency be continued by a United Nations International Children's Endowment Fund, with an emphasis on long-term rather than immediate objectives. See UNITED NATIONS.

ECONOMICS, a social science concerned with the production, distribution, exchange, and consumption of economic goods; i.e., goods which exist in quantities less than sufficient to satisfy all wants for them. The older term for the science is *political economy*.

The development of economics as a social science has been responsive to social conditions of which it is itself a part. Thus the agricultural economy of the 18th and preceding centuries resulted in the formulation of one group of economic theories and practices, whereas the period of the Industrial Revolution (q.v.) and after resulted in the formulation of another set of theories and practices. The first modern exposition of economics as a social science is to be found in Adam Smith's *Inquiry into the Nature and Causes of the Wealth of Nations* (1776). The development of economic thought since the time of Adam Smith has paralleled the growth in economic institutions and the increasing complexity of the problems of modern economic life. The advance in theory has comprised more and more extensive investigation of the laws of production, distribution, exchange, and consumption of wealth, while the advance in practice has concerned itself with the application of those laws to the understanding and solution of social problems.

History. Long before economics achieved the status of a science, economic problems occupied men's minds. The principal Greek writers, Plato, Aristotle, and Xenophon, subordinated economic to ethical and moral considerations. They viewed the primary object of life to be self-knowledge, not the acquisition of riches, and they did not regard wealth as of fundamental importance to the individual or the state. Plato in his *Republic* wrote of an ideal society in which the ills of society would be corrected by a communistic state. Aristotle in his *Politics* defended the institution of private property and formulated ideas about the functions of money, but condemned the taking of interest because money was "barren". Both Plato and Aristotle were prejudiced against trade and commerce, feeling that to live by trade was despicable.

The economic ideas of the Romans were borrowed from the Greeks and showed the same contempt for trade and commerce and the same condemnation of interest. Cicero, Cato, and Varro wrote on agricultural problems, which field they deemed worthy of consideration.

During the Middle Ages the economic ideas of the Church found expression in the *corpus juris canonici* or the canon law (q.v.). The canonists condemned usury, which signified any loan interest, and regarded trade and commerce as inferior to agriculture. With the development of commerce the canonists formulated the doctrine of *justum pretium*, that every commodity had a just price or value which it was sinful for the seller to exceed.

The development of modern nationalism during the 16th century shifted attention to the problem of increasing the wealth and power of the various national states. The economic policy of the statesmen of that time, known as *Mercantilism* (see MERCANTILE SYSTEM), sought to encourage national self-sufficiency. Exports were encouraged and imports discouraged in order to secure the maximum amount of bullion or specie to the state on the basis of a favorable balance of trade. Thomas Mun, Sir William Petty, David Hume, and Sir James Stuart-Wortley-Mackenzie were the principal British writers who explained or extolled mercantilism.

In the 18th century a reaction developed in England and France against the narrow and restrictive policies of mercantilism. In France the reaction found its expression in the writings of the physiocrats, principally François Quesnay, Jean Claude de Gournay, Anne Robert Jacques Turgot, and Richard Cantillon. The physiocrats taught the doctrine of natural laws, proclaimed the maxim of *laissez faire,* claimed that agriculture alone yielded a net surplus, over the expenses of production, maintained that the state's revenue should be raised by a single direct tax levied upon land, and extolled free trade. In England the reaction against mercantilism developed toward the end of the 18th century and took the form of a movement in favor of agriculture and against government restrictions on business.

The publication in 1776 of Adam Smith's *Wealth of Nations* marked the first serious attempt made to study economics apart from the sister sciences of politics, ethics, and jurisprudence. Smith gave great weight to the causal nature of economic phenomena. Through his emphasis on consumption, rather than on production, the scope of economics was considerably broadened. He was the first to present a well-rounded treatment of value and distributive shares. He called attention to the importance of permitting each individual to follow his own self-interest as a means of promoting national prosperity. His discussion of the division of labor and his support of free trade policies were significant contributions to the development of economic thought.

The writings of the classical or orthodox school of economists, during the first half of the 19th century, began the formulation of a body of economic principles based on the study of the economic process as a whole. David Ricardo was the first economist to emphasize the problem of the distribution of wealth. Ricardo adopted as the basis of his theory of distribution the law of population developed by Thomas Robert Malthus in his book, *An Essay on the Principles of Population* (1798). Malthus believed, as a result of historical and statistical investigation, that population continually outstrips the means of subsistence and that this condition would always tend to keep wages low. Ricardo believed that, as population increased, society would be forced to resort to poorer and poorer soils in order to obtain food, with the result that an increasing share of the product of industry would go to the landlord in the shape of economic rent. Ricardo's theory of distribution held that with an increasing share of the product of industry going to rent, wages would receive a constant or slowly increasing amount, and profits would dwindle both absolutely and relatively. Ricardo also made contributions to the knowledge of monetary phenomena and international trade. He was outstanding in his use of the deductive method of economic analysis, namely, singling out a few main facts of the external physical world and human nature, and showing how men must act under the guidance of these laws. Other classical economists were James Mill and John Ramsay McCulloch.

Probably the leading exponent of classical economics was John Stuart Mill, who started as a follower of Ricardo, adopting his theories of value, rent, wages, and profits. However in his *Principles of Political Economy* he emphasized that, while the laws and conditions of the production of wealth partake of the nature of physical truths, the distribution of wealth is not arbitrary but depends upon the laws and customs of society. The materialistic and pessimistic doctrines of the classical economists earned for economics the epithet of "the dismal science".

Opposition to the classical theory of distribution came from the socialist writers and others. The classical doctrine had supported *laissez faire* and the system of private capitalist enterprise, and against both of these concepts socialism protested. The early academic and utopian socialism of Claude Henri de Saint-Simon and Louis Blanc in France, and William Thompson and Robert Owen in England was subordinated in importance to the "scientific" socialism of Karl Marx. Marx built his theories on a materialistic interpretation of history, directing his theory against those fundamental institutions of the social order which the classical economists took for granted.

Other writers who attacked the classical doctrines were the Sociologists, the most famous of whom was Auguste Comte. He maintained that it was impossible to develop a helpful science of economics distinct from history, ethics, and politics. The Historical school of writers, which developed in Germany in the middle of the 19th century, denied that economic science could discover laws which held true for all times and all places. They emphasized the importance of inductive methods (see INDUCTION) and the study of legal institutions, custom, and ethics in their relation to economic life. Gustav Schmoller was the outstanding exponent of the Historical school.

The Austrian school of economists, among whom the leader was Eugen Böhm-Bawerk, directed their criticism against the classical economist's theory of value, and developed the concept of the marginal utility theory of value (see VALUE).

The early American economists also reacted against the classical theories. Daniel Raymond and Henry C. Carey were the most influential of the early American economists. They were outstanding exponents of the doctrine of protection (q.v.) as opposed to the classical laissez faire doctrine.

The economic writings of the early 20th century both in England and America employed both the deductive and the historical methods of economic analysis. Economic writers maintained, with respect to the theory of value, that supply and demand, cost of production, and marginal utility (q.v.) exert an influence in the determination of values. The leading writers in this period in England and America were Alfred Marshall, Frank Taussig, John Bates Clark, and Edwin R. A. Seligman.

Following World War I, and later with the breakdown in domestic and international economic conditions, emphasis in economic writing was directed away from disputes in economic theory to the solution of the problems of current economic life. John Maynard Keynes was the outstanding economist of this era.

In recent years, with the rise in economic power of the Soviet Union, economists have given considerable attention to the problems and structures of the spreading economic systems of socialism and communism, as against the private capitalistic system in America. The study of all economic systems, however, whether capitalism, socialism, or communism, begins with the analysis of the principles of production and distribution when there exists scarcity in the means of production (land, labor, capital, and management) in relation to the limited amount of goods available to satisfy human desires.

Specific economic concepts and problems are treated under the topics CAPITAL; COLLECTIVISM; COMMUNISM; COMPETITION; CONSUMPTION; CURRENCY; DIVISION OF LABOR; FINANCE; FREE TRADE; INTEREST; INTERNATIONAL TRADE; LAND; MANAGEMENT; MONEY; NATIONAL INCOME; PROTECTION; PUBLIC DEBT; RENT; VALUE; WEALTH. See also articles on many of the economists mentioned.

ECTODERM. See EMBRYOLOGY: *Germ Layers.*

ECUADOR, a republic of South America, situated in the N.W. part of the continent, bordering the Pacific Ocean and extending inland between Colombia on the N. and Peru on the S. Including the Colón Archipelago, consisting of the fifteen Galápagos Islands (q.v.), the area has been variously estimated at 276,008 sq.m. and 175,851 sq.m.; pop. (1953 est.) 3,406,550.

The capital is Quito (q.v.). Other important cities are Guayaquil, the chief port, and Cuenca, Riobamba, Loja (qq.v.), and Ambato. Ecuador contains eighteen provinces. The provinces are Esmeraldas, Manabí, Los Ríos, Guayas, El Oro, Carchi, Imbabura, Pichincha, Cotaxapi, Tungurahua, Chimborazo, Bolívar, Cañar, Azuay, Loja, the Galapagos Islands (officially Colón), Napo Pastaza, and Zamora. The last two provinces constitute the "Region Oriental" of Ecuador, and are the most sparsely inhabited, having a population density of less than one per sq.m.

Physical Features and Climate. Ecuador is an Andean nation situated directly on the equator. The low Pacific coastal strip, w. of the Andes mountain ranges, averages about 80 m. in width. Most of it is deep in jungleland and largely unexplored. At the s. end of the coast, the Gulf of Guayaquil extends inland to the Andes. Rio Guayas, which flows across the strip, reaching the gulf through a long estuary, is the largest navigable river emptying into the Pacific from the continent of South America. Many of the other rivers and streams flowing across the coastal strip are tributaries of the Guayas. Beyond the Andes, on the E., is the Amazon region, or Oriente, a rainy, forested, tropical plain, largely uninhabited and still in the process of

Pan American World Airways

ECUADOR. *Left: Rooftops of a village in the Andes Mountains seen from the bell tower of a small church. Right: Entrance to Campania Church in Quito, capital of the republic.*

exploration. It is crossed by numerous rivers, most of which rise in the Andes. The largest of these, Rio Napo, a tributary of the Amazon R., becomes navigable at 850 ft. above sea level.

The parallel Andean ranges in Ecuador are narrow but high, and contain various volcanic peaks, a few of which are active. Chimborazo, in central Ecuador, rises 20,702 ft. above sea level. A few peaks higher than Chimborazo are situated in Bolivia, Argentina, and Chile, but in Ecuador are more lofty Andean peaks than in any other South American country. Altogether there are nineteen mountains rising more than 15,000 ft. above sea level. Between the Andean ranges is the inter-Andean plateau, with an average altitude of 8000 ft. above sea level. Fertile and temperate in climate, the plateau contains the bulk of the population of the country.

Though Ecuador lies on the equator (as its name implies), the climate varies according to the altitude, ranging from torrid, tropical, and temperate to arctic, on the peaks of the major mountains. The rainy season, or winter, extends from December through April or May. Little rain falls, and sometimes no rain outside the Oriente, from June through November.

People, Religion, and Education. The larg-est of the population groups in Ecuador are the pure Indian and the mestizo (Indian and European descent). Persons of pure European descent comprise about 10% of the population. A sprinkling of Negroes and mulattoes is found, chiefly in the coastal region. The language is Spanish. However, the great majority of the Indians reside in rural areas and speak Quechua, the original language of the Incas. (Jivaro is spoken by the little-known tribes of the Oriente.)

Most Ecuadorian Indians were converted to the Roman Catholic religion during the years that followed the conquest of Peru and Ecuador by the Spanish. Shortly after the naming of Hernando de Luque as bishop of Peru, on July 26, 1529, large numbers of priests were sent to the area from Spain. By the end of the 17th century Ecuador supported a total of forty-two convents belonging to the Jesuits (q.v.) and other orders. It has been estimated that at that time about 1000 priests were in the city of Quito. Charges of "lack of virtue and good manners" were made against the priests, while in their defense it was said that "the convents were the cradle of culture". In 1767 the Jesuits, the most powerful of the religious orders and the most prominent in the establishment of Indian missions, were banished by the Spanish

Indians of Ecuador sailing a dugout canoe

king Charles III from all Spanish-held territories in the Americas. An opposition to an official religion developed in Ecuador, and by 1889 a liberal movement resulted in a partial severance of church from state. In 1902 civil marriage was introduced, and in 1904 a ukase placed the church under state control. Properties of religious orders were confiscated and the friars were put on a state pension. As a result, absolute freedom of religion was introduced into Ecuador.

Divorce is permitted. The people are obliged by law to register births, deaths, and marriages, but among the Indians these obligations are often ignored. In 1945 the state declared that illegitimate children have all the rights of rearing, education, and inheritance accorded legitimate children.

All educational institutions in Ecuador are under the supervision of the ministry of public instruction. There are five universities, including Central of Quito, Cuenca of Guayaquil, and Junta of Loja; four normal schools for the training of teachers, two in Quito and the others in Guayaquil and Cuenca, and limited normal courses in seven other cities. Primary education is free and compulsory, but school enrollment is low. In 1952 about 384,-800 students attended 3706 primary and 182 secondary schools; university enrollment was 4562. Three music schools and one law school

(at Loja) are maintained by the national government.

Government. Ecuador is governed under the provisions of the constitution of 1946. By the terms of this document executive authority is vested in a president elected by direct popular vote for a four-year term. The president may not succeed himself. Legislative authority is vested in a bicameral legislature consisting of a chamber of deputies and a senate. Deputies are elected by the provinces in the proportion of one for every 50,000 inhabitants. Two senators are elected from each of the provinces, and in addition there are functional senators representing cultural, professional, labor, and business groups. Justices of the supreme and other high courts are appointed by the national legislature.

Industry and Commerce. Although most of Ecuador is covered by forest, and less than 12,000,000 acres of land are cultivated, agriculture is the basis of Ecuador's economy. The country is one of the world's largest producers of cacao (cocoa), and the chief source of balsa wood. Cacao, coffee, bananas, sugar cane, rice, tobacco, and cotton are cultivated in the coast regions and low river valleys. Cereal grains, potatoes, and temperate fruits and vegetables are grown in the mountain valleys and the inter-Andean plateau, and

Keystone

Native hut on stilts in the interior of Ecuador

dairy and beef cattle, horses, sheep, goats, and pigs are raised. Forest products include (besides balsa) kapok, mangrove bark, tagua nuts (vegetable ivory), and rubber.

Gold, silver, lead, and salt are mined in Ecuador, the last-named under government monopoly; and the country contains deposits of copper, iron, coal, and sulfur. Petroleum resources were uncovered in the early 1920's and have since formed a major industry. The deposits are the property of the state. Large petroleum concessions have been made to foreign concerns, the state taxing all production. Petroleum production has increased in recent years, but most of the output is consumed domestically, leaving little for export.

The principal manufactured product of Ecuador is the toquilla hat, better known as the Panama hat. The processing of tobacco, a government monopoly, is becoming increasingly important.

Ecuador's trade, chiefly with the United States, is nearly balanced. In 1952 the United States took about 53 percent of the exports and supplied about 65 percent of the imports. The leading exports are bananas, coffee, cacao, and rice. As a group, these constitute 93 percent of all exports by value. The balance of the export trade is in tagua nuts, balsa, Panama hats, mangrove bark, kapok, alligator skins, and wild animals sought mainly by zoos and private collectors. Machinery, iron and steel products, foodstuffs, chemicals, pharmaceuticals, and cotton textiles are the principal imports.

Communications. Guayaquil is Ecuador's main port of entry by air or sea, and is connected with Quito and other major cities by spur air lines and railroads. There are nine other seaports besides Guayaquil. Nine railroads transport freight and passengers over approximately 600 m. of rail, all nationalized. In recent years extensive road improvements have been made. The highway system comprises (1950) about 5800 m. of roads, of which about 2700 are main roads. In the rural sections few roads are paved, most of them no wider than the width of an automobile. The Pan-American Highway is currently under construction and when completed will extend from Rumichaca on the Colombian border to Macará in the south, a distance of 672 m.

River communications have been greatly improved by dredging throughout the agricultural areas of the lowlands. Rivers recently made navigable by improvements are the Guayas, Daule, and Vinces. Some of the tributaries of these rivers can be used during the rainy season. A highway under construction from Latacunga to the river port of Napo will provide Ecuador with an outlet to the Atlantic Ocean by way of the Napo and Amazon rivers.

History. Architectural remains have been discovered in Ecuador of ancient civilizations dating back thousands of years. These civilizations, probably related to the Maya civilization of Central America, were followed by that of the Incas. Neither the Incas nor the pre-Incas left written records of their cultures. The Incas of Ecuador were an overflow from the center of Inca civilization in and around Cuzco and the Lake Titicaca area, Peru. The Incas dominated the Indian tribes of Ecuador and provided the early Spanish with their major military obstacles.

The first Spanish to land on the shores of what is now the coast of Ecuador were led by Bartolomé Ruiz, in 1526. However, it was not until 1532 that Spanish conquistadores invaded the country. They were led by Francisco Pizarro (q.v.), who landed 183 men and 37 horses from three small vessels on the banks of the Bay of San Mateo in northern Ecuador. Two years later Pizarro's forces were in control of the area.

Discord among the conquistadores followed Pizarro's successes. One of the conquerors of Mexico, Pedro de Alvarado, sailing from Guatemala, sought to conquer Ecuador. Defeated by Pizarro, he was obliged to retire from the country on Aug. 26, 1534. Pizarro, acting in the name of the Spanish crown, appointed his brother, Gonzalo, governor of Quito on Dec. 1, 1540. A short time later Francisco Pizarro was assassinated, and Gonzalo Pizarro led a rebellion against Spain. His independent rule lasted until April 9, 1548, when crown forces under the leadership of Pedro de la Gasca defeated Pizarro's army at Jaquijaguana. Pizarro was promptly executed.

Colonial Ecuador was at first a territory directly under the rule of the viceroyalty of Peru, one of the two major administrative divisions of 16th-century Spanish America. In 1563 Ecuador became a presidency, or a judicial district of the viceroyalty, with its own court, or *audiencia*, presided over by a president. Theoretically the presidency of Quito, as Ecuador was then called, had only judicial authority, but to this was soon added administrative authority. In 1717 the Quito presidency was placed under the authority of the newly created viceroyalty of Nueva Granada in Bogotá. Six years later the Nueva Granada viceroyalty was abolished and the presidency

Pan American World Airways

Mestizo workman of Ecuador at a hand loom on which he is weaving a woolen rug

of Quito was returned to the authority of the viceroy of Peru, at Lima.

The first revolt of the colonists against Spain took place in 1809, but not until 1822 did the Spanish royalists, in the Battle of Pichincha, lose their power to republican forces led by General Antonio José de Sucre (q.v.), chief lieutenant of Simón Bolívar (q.v.). With Sucre's victory, Ecuador became the Department of the South, part of the confederacy known as the Republic of Colombia, or Great Colombia, which included Venezuela and Colombia.

In 1830 Bolivar's confederacy fell apart and Ecuador became an independent state under its present name. The first president was General Juan José Flores, born in Venezuela and a hero of the independence wars. Flores represented the arch conservatives of Quito, including the Roman Catholic Church. In 1833 he was confronted by a civil war. The war, between the liberal elements of Guayaquil and the conservatives of Quito, was the first of a long series of revolutions. Most of Ecuador's revolutions have led to dictatorships. There have been three outstanding dictators in Ecuadorean history: Flores, Gabriel García Moreno, and Eloy Alfaro. The revolutionary struggles have invariably been between conservatives centered in Quito, the highland capital, and liberals centered in Guayaquil,

the lowland port. Throughout Ecuador's history and up to the present day, Guayaquil has been known as a hotbed of revolutionaries. The sectional rivalry spearheaded by the two principal cities of Ecuador has been intense. The conservatives of Ecuador have invariably been associated with the church and have advocated church-sponsored religious education for all Ecuadoreans and rigid controls on labor; the liberals oppose church intervention in political affairs and advocate less state control of economic activities.

In the years 1907–11, during the second period of rule by President Eloy Alfaro, a new constitution following the tenets of the liberals was introduced to the country. Numerous liberal reforms were promulgated.

The constitution promulgated under Alfaro lasted twenty-two years. During that period there were various revolutions and regimes, and a declaration of war against Germany during World War I.

Ecuador entered World War II against the Axis Powers upon the entrance, into the war, of the United States. A revolution, starting in Guayaquil, in May, 1944, brought Dr. José Maria Velasco Ibarra, deposed by the military as president in 1935, back to Ecuador from exile. In August the constituent assembly named Velasco Ibarra president. Border warfare between Ecuador and Peru had been intermittent since the early days of the republic. In 1941, on a resumption of hostilities, the long-standing dispute over the boundary between the two countries was submitted to mediation by Argentina, Brazil, and the United States. The arbitration decision, made final in 1944, awarded most of the disputed territory to Peru.

The constituent assembly promulgated a new constitution, the nation's thirteenth, on March 6, 1945. Conservative forces opposed to this document, which contained many liberal features, secured the election of a new constituent assembly in June, 1946. The assembly, a predominantly conservative body, completed its labors on Dec. 31. In August, 1947, Velasco was again deposed, by a pro-Argentina military group of revolutionists led by the minister of defense, Col. Carlos Mancheno Cajas. Mancheno, however, was swept out of office almost immediately by counter-revolutionaries, who announced that new elections would be held on June 5, 1948. On that date the choice of the electorate to succeed Velasco was Galo Plaza Lasso, a former ambassador to the United States. Ecuador had participated meanwhile in the 9th Inter-American Conference, held (April-May) at Bogotá, Colombia, and become a signatory of the charter of the Organization of American States. In August the government concluded a pact (called the Quito Charter) with Panama, Venezuela, and Colombia providing for the gradual creation of a customs union. President Plaz Lasso was inaugurated on Sept. 1.

During 1949 the government developed plans for increases in national productivity, particularly in agriculture. Soil conservation, redistribution of land, improvement of seed strains, and agricultural mechanization were among major objectives of the program. Central Ecuador was devastated by an earthquake on August 5. About 6000 persons lost their lives and fifty cities and towns were almost totally destroyed.

In July, 1950, Guayaquil was the scene of an abortive uprising, led by members of the Liberal Party. The government became involved (October) in another dispute with Peru over border territory. Tension increased during the ensuing months. On Aug. 14, 1951, the issue was submitted to the United States, Chile, Argentina, and Brazil for arbitration. The frontier clashes ceased soon thereafter, and the arbitration conference, which convened on Aug. 29, took no action.

Ecuador and the United States concluded a military-assistance pact in February, 1952.

The U.S. Export-Import Bank granted the country an $800,000 loan in April to finance reconstruction in the communities damaged by the 1949 earthquake. On June 1 former president Velasco Ibarra, the candidate of a coalition of leftist and right-wing extremist groups, was elected president by a large plurality. Aside from an abortive uprising in Guayaquil on Dec. 11, 1952, and government suppression (April, 1953) of two newspapers on charges of "incitement to revolution", the domestic scene was relatively tranquil during the new regime's first year in office. Provincial and municipal elections were held in November. Candidates opposed to the Ibarra regime won a large majority of the contested posts. On June 28, 1954, Ecuador became a signatory of the International Tin Agreement, which provides for the stabilization of world prices of tin.

ECUMENICAL COUNCILS. See COUNCIL.

ECZEMA, also called *tetter* or *salt rheum*, an inflammatory, chronic, vascular, noncontagious dermatitis caused by allergy and hypersensitivity. The term is loosely used to include many skin conditions more properly included under dermatitis (q.v.). Eczema is characterized by a number of cutaneous lesions, such as macules, papules, pustules, vesicles, scales, and crusts. Macules are nonelevated skin spots, but papules are hard, circular, and elevated. Pustules are papular-like lesions which contain pus, and vesicles are small skin blisters which contain fluid. Eczematous lesions are usually accompanied by an exudation of serous fluid and by intense itching. Diseases classified as eczemas represent from one third to one half of all cutaneous affections. See DERMATITIS.

EDAM, town of North Holland Province, Netherlands, situated about 15 m. by rail N.E. of Amsterdam, and on the IJsselmeer (formerly known as the Zuider Zee). In 1357, William V of Bavaria, Count of Holland, granted the town civil rights. In the 17th century, Edam was a shipping and shipbuilding center. However, large silt deposits formed in the harbor, and commercial traffic moved to other ports, with a consequent decline in shipbuilding. Edam's Great Church, or Church of St. Nicholas, completed in the 14th century, is particularly noted for its stained glass and carved woodwork. Cheese making is the principal industry in Edam, and the town gives its name to all of the sweet-milk cheese processed throughout North Holland. Leather, cordage, and sails are also manufactured. Pop. (1947) 3741.

Netherlands Information Bureau

Picturesque scene in Edam, the Netherlands. The Great Church is in background.

EDDA, the name given to two famous collections of Old Icelandic literature. The origin of the word is doubtful; scholars have variously derived it from the Old Norse word *edda*, "great-grandmother", because the stories told are similar to folk tales recounted by old women; from Oddi, the native locality of Sæmund (1056–1133), an Icelandic historian once thought to have been author of one of the *Eddas*; and from the Old Norse word *ōthr*, "poetry". The term is properly given only to the *Prose Edda*, or *Younger Edda*, a work which was written by Snorri Sturluson (see SNORRI) in the 13th century. The first historical use of the term *Edda* in describing Snorri's writings occurred in the *Uppsala Codex*, transcribed about 1300 and considered the most important manuscript of the work. The *Poetic Edda* or *Elder Edda*

was discovered in 1643 by an Icelandic bishop, Brynjolf Sveinsson, who erroneously ascribed it to Sæmund and named it the *Edda of Sæmund the Wise*.

The *Prose Edda* is primarily a guide to the poetry of the scalds (see SCALD), the early Scandinavian poets. It is divided into five sections: *Formáli* (Prologue), *Gylfaginning* (The Deception of Gylfi), *Bragaroethur* (The Sayings of Bragi), *Skaldskaparmál* (The Art of Poetry), and *Háttatal* (List of Meters). The prologue is an account of the Biblical story of the Creation and the Flood. The next two sections narrate ancient Scandinavian myths (q.v.), and are the most important source for modern knowledge of that subject. The fourth section consists of instructions and rules for writing scaldic poetry, and the fifth is a technical commentary on poetry

Christian Science Committee on Publication

Mary Baker Eddy

written by Snorri in honor of King Haakon IV (q.v.) of Norway.

The *Poetic Edda* is a collection of more than thirty poems, composed between the 9th and 12th centuries, concerning ancient Scandinavian myths and heroes. None of the poets are known by name, and the poems may have been written in the British Isles, Norway, Denmark, or Iceland. Many of the poems are incomplete; they were apparently written down in the 12th century after having been handed down by word of mouth. The work is approximately divisible into two sections, one concerning the gods and the other concerning human heroes. The most remarkable of the lays of the Gods is the *Völuspá* (The Prophecy of the Völva, or Sibyl), which narrates the Creation and prophesies the end of the world. The second section is, for the most part, the story of Sigurd, the German Siegfried. See RING OF THE NIBELUNGEN; ICELANDIC LANGUAGE AND LITERATURE.

EDDINGTON, SIR ARTHUR STANLEY (1882–1944), English astronomer and physicist, born at Kendal, and educated at Owens College (now Manchester University), and Trinity College, Cambridge University. He was chief assistant at the Royal Observatory at Greenwich from 1906 to 1913, when he became professor of astronomy at Cambridge. From 1921 to 1923 he was president of the Royal Astronomical Society. He was knighted in 1930. Eddington helped clarify Einstein's theory of relativity, but his most important

scientific work was on the evolution, constitution, and motion of stars. His book *The Internal Constitution of the Stars* (1926) was a classic on this subject. The following year he wrote *Stars and Atoms,* a popular condensation of the same material. Thereafter he was best known as a popularizer of science, and his work *The Nature of The Physical World* (1928) was one of the most widely read books on abstract science ever published. His later works, although also widely read, were regarded by some scientists as being too metaphysical to be of great value. Among his other books were *Space, Time, and Gravitation* (1920), *The Mathematical Theory of Relativity* (1923), *and New Pathways in Science* (1939).

EDDOES. See TARO.

EDDY, MARY BAKER (1821–1910), founder of the Christian Science Church, born in Bow, N.H., and educated privately. She married first at the age of twenty-two and twice thereafter; from the birth of her only child in 1844 until 1862 she suffered from nervous illness from which she constantly sought relief. In 1862 she met Dr. Phineas P. Quimby, a magnetic healer, who restored her health temporarily after a brief course of treatment. Impressed by Quimby's method, after 1862 she essayed to practice it. However, she abandoned it before she discovered Christian Science in 1866, at which time she recovered instantly from the serious effects of a bad fall. She attributed her recovery to spiritual illumination of a passage on Christian healing in the Bible (Matt. 9:2), and dated her discovery of Christian Science from this experience. *The Science of Man* (1870) was the first of her many works on Christian Science; from its date of publication to 1880 she taught her system in Lynn, Mass. In 1875 she completed her book *Science and Health with Key to the Scriptures,* which remains the basic text on Christian Science. She organized the Christian Scientist Association in 1875–76 and three years later obtained a charter for the Church of Christ, Scientist. The Massachusetts Metaphysical College, which she organized in Boston in 1881, trained "healers" whom she sent to many cities throughout the United States. When conflicts occurred among the students in 1889 she closed the college, and in 1892 reorganized the Church in Boston, centralizing control of the new Mother Church, The First Church of Christ, Scientist, in her own hands. She later retired, leaving the actual management to a board of directors, but she retained control of church affairs until shortly before she died. She was the founder of The Christian Science Publishing Society, established in 1883 and organized under a Deed of Trust in 1898, and the various publications connected with the Church. Among her works are *Christian Healing* (1886), *Retrospection and Introspection* (an autobiography, 1891), *Church Manual* (1895–1908), and *The First Church of Christ, Scientist, and Miscellany* (1913). See CHRISTIAN SCIENCE.

EDDYSTONE ROCKS, a group of gneiss, or granitelike, rocks in the English Channel, 9 m. off the coast of Cornwall and Devon counties, and 14 miles s.w. of the Plymouth breakwaters. The Eddystone rocks, submerged daily by the tide, have been the cause of many shipwrecks. Four lighthouses have been constructed on or near the rocks. The first, erected by Henry Winstanley in 1698, was destroyed by storm in 1699, and its occupants, including the builder, were drowned. The second, Rudyerd's Tower, built of bolted oak timbers, was finished in 1709, but was destroyed by fire in 1755. Between 1756 and 1759, John Smeaton, one of the great engineers of the 18th century, erected the third Eddystone Lighthouse (Smeaton's Tower). Smeaton was the first engineer to use a system of dovetailing, or of interlocking stonework, a revolutionary advance in lighthouse construction. In addition, he set the stones in a mortar composed of quicklime, clay, sand, and crushed iron slag. This was possibly the first use of concrete after Roman times. Smeaton's lighthouse was conical, broad at the foundation and narrowing at the base of the lantern housing. It was 72 ft. high from the foundation to the focal plane of the lantern; but was not tall enough to keep the waves from obscuring and damaging the lantern. The rocks upon which Smeaton's structure rested, however, finally began to split and crumble, and in 1877 work was begun on a new lighthouse, 120 ft. s.s.e. of the site of the former structure, and known as the J. N. Douglass Tower. It was cylindrical to a point 2½ ft. above the highest tides. Above this level, the tower extended 132 ft. to the focal plane of the lantern. The new Eddystone Lighthouse, completed in 1882, was constructed of interlocking stone, reinforced with bronze bolts. In previous lighthouses, the stones forming the gallery cornices were at times lifted from their beds by the shock of the heavy seas. Douglass departed from Smeaton's procedure in that he constructed corbelled (set-into-the-wall) stone floors. This

feature was first employed by R. Stevenson in 1807–11 in erecting the Bell Rock Lighthouse, 12 m. off the coast of Angus.

EDELWEISS, common name for *Leontopodium alpinum,* a perennial herb of the Thistle family. It is found at high altitudes in central Asia and in the Swiss Alps and other parts of Europe. Its inconspicuous blossoms are borne in heads surrounded by flowerlike leaves arranged in stellate clusters. It is readily cultivated in gardens in the United States and Europe and grows best on coarse, sandy loam. Its flower is Switzerland's floral emblem.

EDEMA. See DROPSY.

EDEN (Heb., "delight"), in the Bible, the first residence of man (see ADAM AND EVE). Endless controversy has revolved around the question of the geographic location of Eden, also called the Garden of Eden or Garden of Paradise. According to the Ethiopic Enoch 32:3, it was situated in the northeast, far beyond the Erythræan (Red) Sea. Some religious scholars favor s. Babylonia, near the Persian Gulf, while others are in favor of Armenia, near the sources of the Tigris and Euphrates rivers. The identification of Eden with Edinn (Sumerian for the plain of Babylon), although admissible, is considered highly conjectural. Of the vast amount of literature available on the subject of Eden, little is of value in the search for its exact location.

EDEN, SIR ANTHONY, in full SIR ROBERT ANTHONY EDEN (1897–   ), English statesman, born in Bishop Auckland, Durham, and educated at Eton and at Christ Church Col-

Anthony Eden

lege, Oxford University. He served as a captain, brigade major, and general-staff officer successively, during World War I, and was awarded the Military Cross. His political career began in 1923, when as a Conservative Party candidate he was elected to the House of Commons; from 1926 to 1929 he was Parliamentary secretary to Sir Austen Chamberlain, then secretary of state for foreign affairs. Eden became Parliamentary undersecretary of the British foreign office in 1931; three years later, he was appointed lord privy seal and privy councilor. In 1935 he was appointed minister without portfolio for League of Nations affairs and, in the same year, became secretary of state for foreign affairs. Eden resigned his office in 1938 because of his disagreement with the government's policy after the Munich conference (see MUNICH). He was appointed secretary of state for war in 1940, and again served as secretary of state for foreign affairs from 1940 to 1945. During the years 1942 to 1945, he was also leader of the House of Commons. In 1945 he became chancellor of Birmingham University. After the Labor Party victory in the election of 1945 Eden was a leading member of the opposition in the House of Commons; following victory by the Conservatives in the election of 1951 he again became foreign secretary in the cabinet of Winston Churchill. Eden is the author of *Days for Decision* (1950). He was knighted in 1954.

EDENTATA, or BRUTA, an order of primitive placental mammals, including the sloths, anteaters, armadillos, and certain extinct related species. Many animals of this order have skins covered with horny plates or scales. Some edentates have no teeth; teeth are present in other species, but they are undifferentiated, and without roots or enamel. Remains of edentates have been discovered in the Pleistocene and Pliocene formations in North and South America. The pangolins and the aardvarks, formerly included in this order, are now classified in the orders Pholidota and Tubulidentata respectively.

EDERLE, GERTRUDE CAROLINE (1907 ?–), American swimmer, first woman to swim across the English Channel. On Aug. 6, 1926, at nineteen years of age, she set a new record of 14 hours, 31 minutes, using the American crawl stroke. The Channel had at that time been crossed by swimmers only five times, the best time being 16 hours, 23 minutes. After returning to America, she devoted herself to the training of swimmers. See ENGᵀISH CHANNEL SWIMMERS.

EDGAR, or EADGER, known as THE PEACEFUL (944–75), Saxon king of the English, and younger son of King Edmund II. In 957, during the rule of his brother, King Edwy, Edgar was chosen by the Mercians and Northumbrians to be their sovereign. Two years later he succeeded to the entire English kingdom. One of his first acts was to recall Saint Dunstan, whom Edwy had exiled. Edgar made Dunstan bishop of Worcester and of London and archbishop of Canterbury. His reign was notable for the establishment of national consolidation, the reformation of the clergy, the improvement of the judiciary system, and the formation of a fleet to defend the coast against the Norsemen.

EDGE HILL, BATTLE OF, the first battle of the Great Rebellion (q.v.) in England. It was fought on Sunday, Oct. 23, 1642, on Edge Hill, an elevated ridge in Warwick County, near the Warwick-Oxfordshire border. The forces involved were the Royalists led by Charles I (q.v.), and the Parliamentarians led by the Earl of Essex (q.v.), each with approximately 14,000 infantry and cavalry troops. The outcome of the battle was indecisive militarily, exhausting equally the strength of both armies. Essex finally retired from Edge Hill on the 24th, forfeiting the victory to Charles. Oliver Cromwell (q.v.) fought in the battle as a captain in the Parliamentarian forces.

EDGEWORTH, MARIA (1767–1849), Irish novelist, daughter of Richard Lovell Edgeworth, born in Oxfordshire, England. She spent the greater part of her life in Edgeworthtown, Ireland, and, while acting as her father's assistant in managing his estate, she acquired a knowledge of the Irish peasantry which was of importance in her writing. She was greatly influenced by her father's ideas on education, especially evident in her books for children and her works of nonfiction. Her first work, *Letters to Literary Ladies* (1795) dealt with the importance of education for women; *The Parent's Assistant* (1796) is a collection of children's stories, each with a clearly drawn moral. *Practical Education* (1798) was written in collaboration with her father.

Maria Edgeworth is most noted, however for her novels of Irish life, which were the first works of fiction to present a careful study of Irish provincial and peasant life and manners. Her first novel, *Castle Rackrent,* published anonymously in 1800, was an immediate success. *The Absentee* (1812), one of her best works, depicts the evils of the system of absentee landlord. Her novels of English life, like her other works, are distinguished by humor, sprightly dialogue, and a clear style. The heroine of her *Belinda* (1801) was one of the first women in the English novel to abandon the simper and smelling salts which characterized women in Gothic novels, and this book is considered by some to have had an influence on Jane Austen. After her father's death in 1817, Maria completed his *Memoirs* and traveled abroad. Her last novel, *Helen,* appeared in 1834. Among her other works are *Early Lessons* (1801), *Essay on Irish Bulls* (with her father, 1802), *Popular Tales* (1804), *Leonora* (1806), *Patronage* (1814), *Ennui* (1809), and *Ormond* (1817).

EDICT OF NANTES, a decree giving partial religious freedom to the Huguenots (q.v.), proclaimed by Henry IV (q.v.) of France in 1598 and revoked by Louis XIV in 1685.

The Edict of Nantes ended the series of religious wars between Catholics and Protestants which ravaged France from 1562 to 1598; see FRANCE: *History.* During these wars, several ineffective treaties were concluded, embodying privileges for the Huguenots. The Edict of Nantes included the religious provisions of these treaties and added a number of others.

By the terms of the edict, the Huguenots were granted liberty of conscience throughout France. They were allowed to build churches and hold religious services in specified villages and the suburbs of any city except episcopal and archiepiscopal cities, royal residences, and within a five-mile radius of Paris; Huguenot nobles were permitted to hold services in their homes. Followers of the faith were granted civil rights and the right to hold official positions. Four universities or schools (at Montauban, Montpellier, Sedan, and Saumur) were permitted to be Huguenot. A special court, composed of one Huguenot and fifteen Catholics and called the *Chambre de l'Édit* ("the Chamber of the Edict") was established for Huguenot protection in the parlement (q.v.) of Paris; subsidiary chambers were established in the provincial parlements. Huguenot pastors were paid by the government, as were Catholic priests. As a guarantee of protection, 100 fortified cities were given to the Huguenots for eight years.

The provisions of the Edict of Nantes were never fully carried out, even during the reign of Henry IV. Catholic persecution of the Huguenots persisted, and in 1681 broke out into open brutality. The edict was revoked by Louis XIV in 1685; as his reason for revoca-

tion of the decree, he said that there were no more Huguenots in France.

EDINBURGH, city and royal burgh, capital of Scotland, and county seat of Midlothian County (Edinburghshire), situated 2 miles s. of the Firth of Forth and about 40 miles E. of Glasgow. After Glasgow, Edinburgh is the largest city in Scotland.

The former bed of the Nor' Loch separates the old and new portions of the city. Old Town, or West Edinburgh, lies amid a group of hills and valleys. On a rocky summit in the center is Edinburgh Castle, containing the royal palace, St. Margaret's Chapel, and other historical edifices. To the east is New Town, which began to take shape near the end of the 18th century, and was merged with the ancient burgh in 1856.

Portobello and parts of several parishes were incorporated into Edinburgh in 1896; parts of South Leith, Duddingston, and a few other areas were included in 1900; and Leith, four parishes, and many villages to the s. and w. became a part of the present city of Edinburgh in 1920.

The site on which Edinburgh now stands was occupied by the Romans for more than 300 years, after which control of the area reverted to the British tribes. The southern Picts, however, vanquished the Britons, and made the castle their seat of power until they were overthrown in the early 7th century by the Saxons under Edwin, king of Northumbria. For a long period possession of the territory was questionable, and tenure shortlived. In the 11th century the region, known as Lothian, was conquered by Malcolm II, first king of Scotland. It was subsequently resettled by Anglo-Saxons and Normans under Malcolm Canmore (Malcolm III). Robert I (Bruce) granted Edinburgh a charter in 1329, and the city became the national capital in 1436, following the assassination of James I at Perth, the former capital. In 1482 James III issued the Golden Charter which gave the city the right to impose and collect taxes. A general charter was granted Edinburgh in 1603 by James VI. However, in 1603 Edinburgh lost much of its national stature when James VI became James I of Great Britain and departed for London.

Although the early Scottish kings did much to improve and expand the city, basic improvements were not made until the 19th century. The Nor' Loch, main obstacle to the city's integration, and an unsanitary area, was drained completely and a road was built across it, connecting Old and New Town.

British Information Services

View of Edinburgh showing Edinburgh Castle (left background), Princess Street Gardens (middle), Sir Walter Scott monument (right foreground), and Princess Street (right).

The principal building in Edinburgh is Parliament House (1640), which became the seat of the supreme courts when the Scottish parliament was dissolved by the Act of Union in 1707. Parliament House contains the Signet Library of 110,000 volumes, and the Advocates' Library of some 550,000 volumes. The latter is the largest library in Great Britain and one of the five entitled to a copy of every book published in Great Britain. Other buildings are the General Register House (1774), archive for all national records; the Royal Institution, renamed in 1910 the Royal Scottish Academy of Painting, Sculpture, and Architecture; and the National Gallery (1850). Chief among the ecclesiastical buildings are the parish church of St. Giles (1100), the Cathedral of St. Giles, the two Greyfriars' churches (occupying separate halves of the same building), Tron church, St. Cuthbert's church, St. Andrew's church, and St. George's church.

Among the many monuments in Edinburgh are those commemorating Robert Burns, Robert Louis Stevenson, Sir Walter Scott, Lord Nelson, and the Duke of Wellington. A life-sized statue of Abraham Lincoln and a freed slave honor Scotsmen who died in the American Civil War. There is also a memorial marking the spot where the Solemn League and Covenant of 1643 was signed.

Edinburgh has many parks, commons, and points of interest, including the Princess Street Gardens, the house of the Protestant reformer John Knox, the Robert Louis Stevenson Memorial House, and King Arthur's seat, a hill 822 ft. high from which Arthur is supposed to have watched his forces defeat the Picts. Facing Salisbury Crags are the scenic spots described by Sir Walter Scott in *The Heart of Midlothian*.

The Royal College of Surgeons (1505), the Royal College of Physicians (1681), and three observatories best represent scientific institutions in Edinburgh. Educational institutions are varied, numerous, and of high repute. Because of its schools, and scientific and literary associations, Edinburgh is often referred to as "the modern Athens". However, local inhabitants refer to the city more intimately as "Auld Reekie", because of the heavy smoke, from the burning of low-grade coal, that hangs over the low areas. Edinburgh University (1583), the youngest of Scottish universities, was one of the first in Great Britain to admit women. Other important institutions of higher education are the Royal High School, Edinburgh Academy, Heriot-Watt College, Fettes

College, and Merchiston Academy, the last two modeled after Eton and Harrow in England. Various institutions for theological training are maintained by the United Free Church, the Church of Scotland, and the Roman Catholic Church.

Edinburgh is more a residential than a commercial or manufacturing city, but since the early 16th century the printing trades have enjoyed prosperity there. Publishing, however, is limited to a few houses. The principal industrial establishments in Edinburgh are paper mills, tanneries, iron and brass foundries, breweries and distilleries, and factories manufacturing rubber products, electric fittings, cordage, hosiery, soap, machine tools, paper, food products, and chemicals. The city is also a market center for agricultural produce, and contains a number of cattle and grain markets and slaughterhouses. Pop. (1953 est.) 470,800.

EDINBURGHSHIRE. See MIDLOTHIAN.

EDINBURGH UNIVERSITY, the youngest of the four Scottish universities (see ABERDEEN, GLASGOW, and ST. ANDREWS). It was established in 1583 by the town council of Edinburgh under a royal charter granted the year before by James VI (later James I of England). The institution began operating as a college of arts; a chair of theology was added in 1642, and one in medicine in 1685. After a reorganization in the 18th century, the school was given the status of a university and, in addition to the three courses of study already provided, offered courses in law, science, and music.

By acts of Parliament, in 1858 and 1889, the university was made independent of the authority of the Edinburgh town council, and became a self-governing corporation composed of the registered graduates, the student body, the professors, the principal, the Lord Rector (elected triennially by the matriculated students), the vice-chancellor, and the chancellor. (For description of the administrative offices, see UNIVERSITIES: *Great Britain*). The Universities Act of 1858 also instituted the university court, a governing body consisting of the Lord Rector (who presides), the principal, the Lord Provost of the city of Edinburgh, and eleven assessors representing both the university and the city. The university court administers the university's property and finances, and appoints examiners, lecturers, and certain professors. The curricula and discipline of the university are supervised by the Senatus Academicus, which includes the principal, the professors, and certain lecturers:

the decisions of the Senatus are subject to approval by the university court. There is finally, the general council, composed of all the persons listed above; it is an advisory body except for one function, the election of the chancellor. Under the Representation of the People Act of 1918, the general councils of the four Scottish universities act as one constituency and elect three representatives to Parliament.

The older buildings of the present university which date from 1789, were erected on the site of the church of St. Mary in the Field, the "Kirk O'Field" where Henry Stewart, Lord Darnley, was murdered in 1567. M'Ewan Hall, a famous structure in the early Italian Renaissance style, built between 1888 and 1897, is used for all public and academic functions. Other buildings include the School of Music, 1858; the medical school, built between 1878 and 1888; the John Usher Institute of Public Health, for training in bacteriology and chemistry, 1902; and the King's Buildings, for scientific studies and engineering, opened in 1924. The collection of the university library was begun in 1580 with 300 books given to the town council of Edinburgh by Clement Little, an advocate; in 1649, a notable addition was made to the collection with the books of William Drummond of Hawthornden, who had studied at the university. The library, in a recent year, contained more than 300,000 volumes and approximately 8,000 manuscripts, some of great value. The Royal Scottish Museum is part of the university structure, and the Royal Infirmary is associated with the medical school.

The income of the University is derived from legacies and endowments, parliamentary grants, and student fees. In 1901, Andrew Carnegie established a £2,000,000 fund for the four Scottish universities; half the income from the fund was allocated as tuition fees for Scottish students.

A three-year residence is required for the attainment of the "Ordinary" M.A., which, in Scotland, is the equivalent of the B.A. degree. Edinburgh was one of the first universities in Great Britain to admit women to its undergraduate colleges, and three dormitories for women were built in 1916. In 1953–54 the student enrollment was 5218, and the faculty numbered 677.

EDIRNE, formerly ADRIANOPLE (anc. *Hadrianopolis* or *Adrianopolis*), capital of the il of the same name, in w. European Turkey. The city is situated on both banks of the Tunja R., at its confluence with the Maritsa,

Edison Electric Institute

Thomas Edison in his later years

and is 137 m. by rail N.W. of Istanbul. Edirne lies in the center of the fertile Thracian coastal plain, and is a marketplace for fruit, wine grapes, and other agricultural produce. The principal products manufactured in the city are silk, cotton, linen, and woolen goods, leather articles, and tapestries. Raw silk, rose water, attar of roses, opium, wax, and "Turkey-red" dye are among the commodities exported from the city and il.

Originally known as Uskadama or Uskodama when it was part of E. Thrace, the city was rebuilt and renamed by the Roman emperor Hadrian about 125 A.D. It was the focal point of the battle of Adrianople (378 A.D.), in which the Romans under the emperor Valens were defeated by the Goths. Edirne was successively conquered by the Avars, the Bulgarians, and the Crusaders. In 1361 the Turks gained control of the city, and it was the residence of the Turkish sultans until 1453. During the Russo-Turkish wars of 1828-29 and 1877–78, and the Balkan Wars of 1912–13, Edirne constantly changed hands.

The il of Edirne, also formerly known as Adrianople, is located in that part of E. Thrace which is separated from Turkey proper by the Sea of Marmara and the Bosporus and Dardanelle straits. The il is bounded on the N. by Bulgaria and on the W. by Greece. Area

of il, 2241 sq.m.; pop. (1950) 221,125. Pop. of city (1950) 30,245.

EDISON, THOMAS ALVA (1847–1931), American inventor, born at Milan, Ohio. He attended school for only three months, in Port Huron, Mich. When he was twelve years old he began work as a newsboy on the Grand Trunk Railway, devoting his spare time mainly to experimentation with printing presses, and with electrical and mechanical apparatus. In 1862 he published a weekly, known as the *Grand Trunk Herald,* printing it in a freight car that also served as his laboratory. For saving the life of a station-master's child, he was rewarded by being taught telegraphy. Although he became an excellent telegraphic operator, he was too erratic and fond of experimentation to remain at one job for any length of time. However, while working as a telegraph operator, he made his first important invention, a telegraphic repeating instrument that enabled messages to be transmitted automatically over a second line without the presence of an operator.

Edison next secured employment in Boston, and devoted all his spare time there to research. He invented a vote recorder, which, although possessing many merits, was not sufficiently practical to warrant its adoption. He also devised and partly completed a stock-quotation printer. Later, while employed by the Gold and Stock Telegraph Company of New York, he greatly improved their apparatus and service. By the sale of telegraphic appliances, Edison earned $40,000, and with this money he established his own laboratory in 1876. Afterward, he devised an automatic telegraph system by means of which increased speed of transmission and range of action were obtained. Edison's crowning achievement in telegraphy was his invention of machines for quadruplex and sextuplex telegraphic transmission, which followed a duplex system he had previously devised. These inventions made possible simultaneous transmission of several messages on one line, and thus greatly increased the usefulness of existing telegraph lines. Important in the development of the telephone, then recently invented by the American physicist Alexander Graham Bell (q.v.), was Edison's invention of the carbon telephone transmitter.

In 1877 Edison announced his invention of a phonograph by which sound could be recorded mechanically on a tin-foil cylinder. Two years later he exhibited publicly his incandescent electric light bulb, his most important invention, and the one requiring the

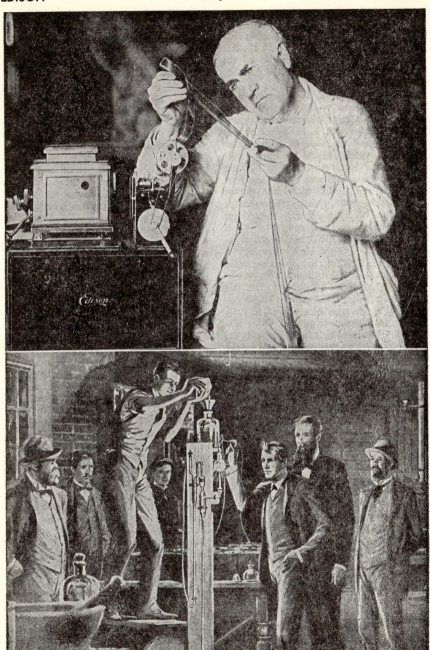

Thomas Alva Edison Foundation

Top: Thomas Edison looking at film for his kinetoscope, or motion-picture projector.
Bottom: Edison's laboratory on the eve of the invention of the electric light bulb.

most careful research and experimentation to secure its perfection (see ELECTRIC LIGHTING). This new light was a remarkable success; Edison promptly occupied himself with the improvement of the bulbs, and also of the dynamos for generating the necessary electric current.

In 1887 Edison moved his laboratory from Menlo Park, N.J., to West Orange, N.J., where he constructed a large laboratory for experimentation and research. In the following year he invented the kinetoscope, the first machine to produce motion pictures by a rapid succession of individual views. Among his later noteworthy inventions was the Edison storage battery (an alkaline nickel-iron storage battery), the result of many thousands of experiments. The Edison storage battery was extremely rugged, was practically incapable of electrical injury, and had a high electrical capacity per unit of weight. He also developed a phonograph in which the sound was impressed on a disk instead of a cylinder. This phonograph had a diamond needle and other improved features. By synchronizing his phonograph and kinetoscope, he produced, in 1913, the first talking moving pictures. Other discoveries by Edison include the electric pen, the mimeograph, the microtasimeter (used for the detection of minute changes in temperature), and a wireless telegraphic method for communicating with moving trains. At the outbreak of World War I, Edison designed, built, and operated plants for the manufacture of benzene, carbolic acid, and aniline derivatives. In 1915 he was appointed president of the Naval Consulting Board, and in that capacity made many valuable discoveries. His later work consisted mainly of improving and perfecting previous inventions. Altogether, Edison patented over 1000 inventions. Few, if any, great scientific discoveries can be credited to him, but by his skill and ingenuity, he was able to surpass in practical achievements many scientists with broad academic backgrounds.

In 1878 Edison was appointed Chevalier of the Legion of Honor of France, and in 1889 Commander of the Legion of Honor. In 1892 he was awarded the Albert medal of the Society of Arts of Great Britain, and in 1928 the Congressional gold medal "for development and application of inventions that have revolutionized civilization in the last century". In 1929 he was universally honored on the occasion of the celebration of the fiftieth anniversary of the invention of the incandescent lamp.

EDMONTON, capital of the province of Alberta, Canada, situated on the North Saskatchewan R., 192 miles N. of Calgary and about 300 miles N. of the U.S. boundary. Edmonton is a distribution point for the agricultural and mineral products of the surrounding area. Coal, precious metals, and uranium ore are mined, and the bituminous sand deposits at Ft. McMurray, adjacent to the city, constitute one of the largest reservoirs of oil in the British Empire. In the vicinity are also fields of natural gas, which supply the city with fuel. Edmonton is an important rail and air-transport center. It is strategically situated on the great circle route of aviation to the Orient, and was the first Canadian city to construct a municipal airport. Edmonton contains meat-packing plants, the output of which is the largest in Canada, and lumber mills, stockyards, and factories manufacturing furniture and bedding, cereal foods, biscuits, powdered eggs, clothing, brick, and soap. The city is the site of a teachers college, and of the University of Alberta, organized in 1907, which has faculties in arts, medicine, agriculture, and mining.

Edmonton derives its name from Fort Edmonton, a trading post of the Hudson's Bay Company, which was built in 1807 on the present site of the city, and served as a supply center for the fur trade of the Northwest. The rapid growth of the city commenced with the advent of communication by rail with Calgary in 1905. Pop. (1951) 159,631.

EDMONTON, a municipal and Parliamentary borough of Middlesex County, England, situated in the Lea R. valley, about 7 miles N. of London. It was the home of John Keats, William Cowper, and Charles Lamb, 19th-century English poets. William Cowper's humorous poem, *John Gilpin*, mentions Bell Inn, one of the local inns. Charles Lamb and his sister, Mary, are buried in the yard of The Church of All Saints, the oldest and finest restored church of the borough. Present-day Edmonton is an industrial city, noted for the manufacture of gas stoves and gas meters. Pop. (1951 prelim.) 104,244.

EDMUND, or EADMUND, SAINT (841?–870), King of the East Anglians from 855 to 870, known as "the Martyr". He was, according to tradition, born in Nurenberg, the son of the Saxon king Alkmund, and was adopted by the East Anglian king Offa, when the latter was journeying to the Holy Land. Nothing is recorded of Edmund's reign until the invasion made in the years 866 to 870 by the Danes, against whom he led the East Anglians in the battle of Hoxne (870). His forces were defeated by the Danes and he was slain. It is said that Edmund was martyred for his refusal to deny Christianity and to rule his kingdom in vassalage to the Danish overlords. The remains of the king, who was canonized, lie at Bury St. Edmunds.

EDMUND I, or EADMUND I, known as THE DEED-DOER or THE MAGNIFICENT (922?–46). Saxon king of England, and son of King Edward the Elder. He participated in the Battle of Brunanburh in 937, and succeeded his half brother Athelstan (q.v.) as king in 940. In that year Olaf Sitricson, a Dane who ruled part of Ireland, became king of Northumbria, a territory bordering on that of the English kingdom. In 944, on the breaking of a treaty by Olaf, Edmund drove the Northman king from Northumbria. In 945 Edmund occupied the kingdom of Strathclyde, w. of Northumbria, and turned it over to his ally King Malcolm I of Scotland. The following year Edmund was stabbed to death by a robber. He was succeeded by his brother Edred.

EDMUND II, or EADMUND II, known as IRONSIDE (980?–1016), Saxon king of the English, and son of King Ethelred II. When Ethelred died (1016), Edmund was chosen king by the people of London, but the Danish king, Canute, who was leading an invasion of England, secured the support of the council (*witan*) at Southampton and of Edric, Ethelred's son-in-law. Edmund met the Danes in battle, winning several engagements and relieving Canute's siege of London, but he was defeated at Assandun (now Ashington) through the treachery of Edric, who had appeared to desert Canute. A truce was arranged between Canute and Edmund, and the latter was permitted to rule the south of England until his death, when it reverted to Canute.

EDMUND RICH, SAINT (1175?–1240), English archbishop, born at Abingdon, Berkshire, England. He was educated at Oxford University, where he later taught logic (1219–26). Having acquired fame as a preacher in Paris as well as in England, he was commissioned by the Pope, about 1227, to preach the sixth Crusade throughout England. Six years later, at the instance of Pope Gregory IX, he was appointed Archbishop of Canterbury. As archbishop, he instituted reforms in courts, monasteries, and among the clergy. When Rich disputed with King Henry III over the attempt of the latter to acquire Church revenues, the king worked through the papal legate to nullify the power of the archbishop.

Fearing that his powerlessness to cope with the difficulty might appear to be sanction, the prelate retired to the abbey of Pontigny, in France (1240). He was canonized about 1249.

EDMUNDS, GEORGE FRANKLIN (1828–1919), American lawyer and senator, born at Richmond, Vt. He was a member of the Vermont legislature from 1854 to 1859 and of the State senate from 1861 to 1862. He was elected to the United States Senate in 1866 and served continuously until his resignation in 1891. Edmunds was instrumental in securing passage in 1877 of the act which provided for a Federal Electoral Commission (q.v.), and he served on the commission that year. An act which bears his name, passed in 1882, provided for the suppression of polygamy in the territories, and was aimed specifically at Utah, where Mormons were in control. Edmunds was the author of the greater part of the Sherman Antitrust Law passed in 1890 and was president protempore of the Senate during the term of President Chester A. Arthur. After his retirement from the Senate Edmunds became noted as an expert on constitutional law.

EDOM (Heb., "red"), the surname of Esau (q.v.), who, according to Gen. 25:29–34, was so named because of the "red" pottage sold him by his brother Jacob. When Esau left his father's house he went to the Mount Seir region, which he called Edom. The country originally inhabited by the cave-dwelling Horites, is situated between s. Palestine and the Gulf of Aqaba, and is 100 m. long from N. to s., and about 40 m. at its widest point. The mountainous terrain of Edom is broken by numerous glens and natural terraces, and is bounded by desert on the w., N., and N.E. At various times Edom has been called Seir, Udumu (in the Egyptian Tell el-Amarna Tablets, written about 1400 B.C.), and Idumæa by the Greeks. The chief cities of Edom were the seaports of Elath and Ezion-Geber on the Gulf of Aqaba, and in later periods Bozrah (now Buseirah) in the N. Despite the close kinship between the Edomites and the Hebrews (according to Gen. 25:23–26), their relationships were strained and hostile. This hostility seems to date from the time when the Hebrews were refused permission to pass through Edom on their way to Canaan (Num. 20:14–21). The Edomites were subjugated by the Israelites during the reigns of the Hebrew kings David and Solomon. Despite many uprisings, they remained subject to Israel until their liberation by Rezin, king of

EDUCATION: EARLY SCHOOLS
Above, left: School in ancient Greece (vase painting). Above: Monk teaching students in medieval Europe (woodcut). Left: An American schoolroom, about 1855.

Syria. Afterward they lost their freedom, and did not regain it until the defeat of the kingdom of Judah by the Medes and Chaldeans in the 8th century B.C. Little is known of the Edomites for the next several hundred years, until 312 B.C., when the Nabatæans defeated them and seized the E. part of Edom. The Edomites subsequently extended their territory to the S. portion of Palestine, and their kingdom became known as Idumæa. They were driven from Palestine in the 2nd century B.C. by Judas Maccabæus, and in 109 B.C. John Hyrcanus, Maccabæan leader, extended the kingdom of Judah to include the W. part of Edomitic lands. In the 1st century B.C. Roman expansion swept away the last vestige of Edomitic independence, and the country was placed, along with Judæa, Samaria, and Galilee, under the administration of Antipater, father of Herod the Great. After the destruction of Jerusalem by the Romans in 70 A.D., the country was merged with Arabia Petræa, and the name Idumæa disappeared from history.

EDUCATION (Lat. *educatio,* "bringing up, training"), in a general sense, the development of the whole nature of man, physical, intellectual, and moral, through interaction with every phase of his environment. More specifically, education denotes the deliberate methods of training and direction used by a society to inculcate its ideals of life and culture in its maturing individual members, and thus to perpetuate itself. Two distinct phases are involved in the educational process: first, the physical and mental development of the individual; second, the adjustment of the individual to his social environment and to the interests of his society as a whole. These individual and social phases are not separated in the actual educational process. However, with regard to their conception and realized purpose, they are quite distinct and may conflict; the history of education, therefore, presents a record of the varying emphasis which different societies have placed upon these phases.

History. The education of primitive children consisted essentially of training in the customs and folkways of the tribe. This training was first centered in the family group and was largely concerned with self-protection and methods of obtaining food, clothing, and shelter. As knowledge increased and social institutions became more complex, certain members of the tribe began to specialize in occupational skills, such as toolmaking and tattooing, which they taught to selected young people. One of the most important and powerful of these specialized groups was that including the medicine men and priests. Primitive fear of the supernatural caused every activity to have its associated religious ceremony, which became the province of the priesthood; the priests, moreover, took charge of the religious and moral training of all the young of the tribe, in addition to the systematic training of future priests. Although secular education later grew out of the invention of writing and its application to commerce about the fourth millenium B.C., the priesthood, having already established a tradition of teaching and youth training, maintained a great measure of control over education. In addition, because priests had leisure and were free of many of the immediate cares of life, they were able to devote themselves to reflection and study; from their training and thought grew the higher types of intellectual endeavor, such as science, philosophy, and literature.

The oldest systems of education in history had two characteristics in common: first, their intimate relation with religion, and second, their rigid traditional curricula. In ancient Egypt, this religious, traditional character was effected by the use as schoolbooks of priestly literature, notably the *Book of the Dead* and collections of proverbs (see EGYPTIAN LANGUAGE AND LITERATURE); the greatest emphasis was placed on writing, which was taught by having students copy religious literature with rigid exactitude. The extraordinary Chinese system, which developed an aristocracy of scholars, was an outstanding example of strict conformity to tradition. From its establishment under the Han dynasties (202 B.C.–220 A.D.) until the end of the 19th century, the Chinese system persisted almost unchanged. It was a complicated structure of higher and lower schools available to all males, and state-conducted examinations were the basis of selection for every public office. The texts used were the sacred Five Classics and Four Books (see CHINESE LANGUAGE AND LITERATURE); students were required to memorize their contents and imitate their form, avoiding all deviation from the original.

The same conformity characterized the education of the Jews. Their identity as a separate people was almost obliterated during the Babylonish Captivity (q.v.). After their return to Palestine, therefore, they established synagogues to preserve the Jewish religion, and the synagogues became centers of worship and education. The subjects of study were the religious law and scriptures (see TALMUD; TORAH), which students memorized and interpreted. The Jews, moreover, introduced an advanced view of education into the western world. Every other ancient civilization limited opportunities for education to the privileged classes, but in 70 B.C. the Jews established schools for orphans and, a century later, made education compulsory for all boys as soon as they reached the age of six. The distinctive advance of Jewish education was, however, cut short by the ascendancy of Greece and Rome.

The Greek, and particularly the Athenian, contribution to education was one of the greatest in history. The ideal of a liberal education was formulated by the Greeks, who tried to co-ordinate the moral, intellectual, and esthetic phases of life. For the first time, the individual was considered more important than the group. In the Greek conception of life, the culmination of an individual's development was his activity as a citizen of the state; education, therefore, was a preparation for the duties of citizenship. In Sparta, a state dedicated to war, the ideal citizen was an excellent soldier, and the training of boys was based on that ideal. From the time he was seven, a boy lived in the state barracks at public expense. His studies were chiefly gymnastics, sports, choral dancing, and military drill; only minor emphasis was placed on reading and writing. At eighteen, he began to study military science and weapons; at twenty, he became a soldier in the Spartan army; at thirty, after ten years of service, he was granted citizenship.

The Athenian state conceived as its ideal citizen one whose personality and character were developed harmoniously; intellectual and esthetic as well as physical development were regarded as educational necessities. A boy's primary education began at age seven and continued, if his family could afford it, until the age of fifteen or sixteen. Boys attended concurrently two types of private school: the music school, for general studies including reading, writing, and history; and the palæstra, for gymnastics and sports. When they were sixteen, boys began to attend public gymnasiums, where they mingled with their elders and, by listening to their discussions and imitating them, were prepared for adulthood. At eighteen, they began a two-year period of compulsory military service, and at twenty, after passing various tests, young men were given full citizenship.

In the 5th century B.C., as a result of the decline of democracy in Athens, the democratic ideal of education as harmonious development of the individual was replaced by the ideal of education as the fullest development of intellectual capacities. The stress on almost wholly intellectual education was strengthened by professional, itinerant teachers called Sophists (q.v.), who became extremely popular. In this period flourished Socrates (q.v.), who believed that education should concern itself with developing the power of thought, and created the so-called Socratic method of discussion: conversation, question, and answer. Elementary education became almost entirely literary, and the discussion groups in the Athenian gymnasiums gradually evolved into philosophical and rhetorical schools established outside the gymnasium. Of these institutions of higher learning, the most important were Plato's Academy and Aristotle's Lyceum, the names of which are still preserved in modern educational institutions (see ACADEMY; LYCEUM). Plato set down his educational theories in the *Republic* (q.v.). The most important function of his ideal state was education, a selective process designed to determine and train the rulers of the state. According to his theory, rulers should be trained until they reach the age of fifty, and their most important study is philosophy (metaphysics and dialectics). Plato emphasized intellectual discipline, but Aristotle, while agreeing with this principle, regarded the study of science, learning derived from direct experience, as an important part of the curriculum, and he believed that education should follow the growth pattern of the child. See INDUCTION.

During the 2nd and 3rd centuries B.C., Greek education began to be organized on three age levels, laying the foundation for the modern educational system. The school of the teacher of letters, the *grammatist,* became the primary school; a secondary school, taught by the *grammaticus,* was attended by boys from about the age of thirteen to about eighteen; and higher education was taught in the philosophical and rhetorical schools which were known collectively as the University of Athens. This pattern for education, together with the Greek emphasis on intellectual studies, was later the determining influence on Roman education.

Early Roman education, until about 250 B.C., consisted largely of character formation and training for the practical affairs of life; boys were taught at home, and the Twelve Tables (q.v.), which had to be memorized, comprised the subject matter. Under the influence of Greece, however, the educational system was almost completely Hellenized. The Roman elementary school, the *ludus,* was established to teach writing, reading, and counting. Secondary, or rhetorical, schools taught Greek grammar and literature; when a Latin literature began to develop, an additional secondary school which taught Latin became popular. For higher education, Romans went to Greece or to other centers of Hellenistic learning such as Alexandria. Their interest in Greek education led to a codification of the Greek liberal arts by Latin scholars; these arts were eventually fixed at seven by Martianus Capella (q.v.; see also SEVEN LIBERAL ARTS). Increasing support was given to schools by municipal authorities and many emperors; the Emperor Hadrian was particularly interested in learning, and about 135 A.D. he founded the Athenæum, which subsequently became the University of Rome. The foremost educational theorist of the Roman Empire was Quintilian (q.v.). In his *Institutio Oratoria,* he emphasized the individual differences of children which should be considered by teachers; he urged public rather than private education so that children would learn to adapt themselves to the group as a whole. Quintilian's educational theories were among the greatest influences on education during the later Roman Empire.

As personal liberty decreased under the absolute monarchy of the emperors, the Roman educational system lost its vitality and became formalized. The early Christian fathers (see FATHERS OF THE CHURCH), many of whom had been trained in Greek philosophical schools and Roman rhetorical schools, first approved this formal intellectual spirit; such training, moreover, fitted students for the philosophical elaboration of Christian doctrine. In the 3rd and 4th centuries A.D. the Christian teachers turned against Greek learning; the Christian ascetic spirit, characterized by strict mental and physical discipline, was opposed to certain aspects of learning and culture, which, involving sensory experience, were regarded as evil. Asceticism was the foundation of the monasticism (q.v.) which played such an important part in education during the Middle Ages.

The most important schools of the early medieval period were those founded by the monastic orders to train their novices. A second type of medieval school was the cathedral or episcopal school which each bishop maintained to train his clergy and boys preparing for the priesthood. These cathedral schools were a development of the catechetical schools and, with the monastery schools, were the principal educational institutions to survive in the period following conquest of the West by the barbarians. The curricula, aside from religious content, consisted of reading and writing Latin, which students learned by memorizing whatever textbook the teacher owned. Children of aristocrats were given training in chivalry (q.v.), which did not necessarily include the ability to read and write.

The first great intellectual revival, Scholasticism (q.v.), began about the 12th century. Its most important impact on education was the establishment of universities (see UNIVERSITY). The spread of Scholasticism and particularly the use of Latin as the common tongue in the universities as well as in the church resulted in the growth of Latin schools, designed to prepare boys for the universities or the Church. These schools were established by guilds, by private endowments, or as adjuncts to charity institutions. Most cities and towns in the western world had such Latin grammar schools by the end of the 16th century, and they eventually developed into the secondary-school system which dominated European education until the 19th century.

For nearly a thousand years, the duration of the Middle Ages, intellectual endeavor concentrated on religion. With the coming of the Renaissance (q.v.), however, scholars began once more to give secular knowledge a status equal to that of religion. One of the most important contributing factors to the literary aspect of the Renaissance, known as the Revival of Learning, was the rediscovery of the literature of the ancient world. This literature had been, to a large extent, preserved by the Saracens (q.v.), who had adopted and furthered the study of Greek philosophy, and had made notable contributions to mathematics, medicine, and science. Universities, libraries, and schools for children had been established by the Saracens in such centers as Baghdad, Basra, and Cordova. As the West re-established contact with the East, through the Crusades and the growth of commerce, Europe repossessed the classics of Greece and Rome (see HUMANISM). By the beginning of the 17th century, classical learning had replaced Latin grammar as the principal subject of study, and mental discipline had become the widely accepted object of education.

The Reformation (q.v.) resulted in warfare and conflict over fundamental differences of religion, but all the opposing religious groups agreed that a classical education was the mark of a truly educated man and the best preparation for leadership in church or state; in every country, the classics were established as the basis of secondary education and as preparation for university study. The Gymnasium (q.v.), which originated in the Lutheran Teutonic countries, was highly developed by Johannes Sturm (q.v.). In Catholic France, the Jesuits (q.v.) set up colleges, in which the standard course consisted of Latin, Greek, religion, and religious history. In England the great public schools, such as Eton College, Winchester College, and Rugby School (qq.v.), were founded; the English schools, however, stressed sports and athletics in addition to the classics. In spite of their classical curricula, however, these schools were still dominated by a formalistic, religious spirit, which was decried by such thinkers as Desiderius Erasmus, Michel Montaigne, and François Rabelais (qq.v.).

The Protestants advocated literacy as a corollary to their doctrines, for all Protestants were, in theory, required to read the Bible; elementary education in the vernacular derived from this concept. Such education became an actuality because of the unity of church and state in Protestant countries; Switzerland, the Netherlands, Scotland, and many German states established elementary schools by law, and in 1642 the German state of Saxe-Gotha issued a code which included compulsory attendance at its schools. The Catholic Church adopted the methods of Protestant religious education. The various teaching orders, notably the Jesuits and the Fathers of the Oratory, established elementary vernacular schools on the Protestant model in Catholic countries such as France, Spain, and Italy.

The schools of the period were, however, still characterized by medieval methods. The curriculum included reading, writing, arithmetic, and religion. Students were required to memorize from the textbook and recite what they had learned. In secondary schools, classical learning was so revered that students were required to imitate classical styles, particularly that of Cicero. Prominent educators, particularly Ratichius and John Amos Comenius (qq.v.), opposed such Ciceronian humanism. Comenius, the foremost Reformation educator, proposed a comprehensive school system which would educate children from birth to maturity; the curricula of these schools would be carefully graded to follow the child's natural development.

As strong national states began to develop, the power of the Church in temporal matters, including education, lessened. The Enlightenment (q.v.), with its protests against political and religious authoritarianism, resulted in educational theories based on experimental reality. John Locke (q.v.), one of the founders of modern empiricism (q.v.), extended his theories to education. He stressed environment and experience as the major elements in learning, and emphasized the physical and moral aspects of education. However, the man whose theories were in sharpest conflict with rationalistic education (i.e., that based on the theory that knowledge is independent of sensory experience; see RATIONALISM), was Jean Jacques Rousseau (q.v.). In his book *Émile*, Rousseau revolted against the strict and formal classical and religious education, and advocated naturalism. He believed in discarding all restrictions and letting the child learn that which interests him most.

Rousseau's theories greatly influenced educators of the late 18th and early 19th centuries. Though their interests and work were widely divergent, these educators agreed on the fundamental principle that the nature of the child should be the controlling factor in education. In elementary education, Johann Heinrich Pestalozzi (q.v.) applied Locke's empiricism and Rousseau's naturalism by insisting that teachers watch each individual child and educate him according to the child's particular mental traits. He advocated using the child's senses of sound, touch, and sight to acquaint him with the ideas of number, form, or language. For preschool education, Friedrich Froebel (q.v.) established the first kindergarten, using play activities to develop the whole nature of the child. Johann Friedrich Herbart (q.v.) exercised his greatest influence on secondary schools. Herbart stressed the moral and social character of education, and initiated a systematic method of learning and teaching; the "five formal steps" of the Herbartian method were preparation (of the child's mind to receive new ideas), presentation (of new ideas), association (between new ideas and those already learned), generalization (statement of general principles in new ideas), and application (to specific cases). This method was widely disseminated in 19th-century teacher training (see TEACHER TRAINING).

The political events of the late 18th and early 19th centuries necessarily affected education; of these events, the most important were the spread of nationalism and the development of democracy. The first country to institute a national system of compulsory education was the kingdom of Prussia, which, in 1787, took education out of the hands of the clergy and established a state ministry of education. The French Revolution established the right of every child to equality of opportunity in education. The Marquis de Condorcet drew up detailed plans for a complete system of national, democratic education which, though it was not put into effect, provided many ideas which were later incorporated in the French national school system (see EDUCATION, NATIONAL SYSTEMS OF), and was the first crystallization of a truly democratic ideal in European education.

As the 19th century matured, new political and philosophical concepts influenced education. The extension of democracy and the right of suffrage made a minimum of knowledge and literacy a requirement for the citizens of a state; thus, compulsory education became general for children between the ages of about six and about fourteen. The Industrial Revolution and the development of technology resulted in the revision of curricula to include scientific and technical subjects. Changes in social theories, amounting almost to social revolution, affected education by the general demand for broader, more human education that would reduce class distinctions, include the study of man as a social being, and give equal opportunity for education. The increasing surge of nationalism brought with it a concept of cultural nationality, for patriotism could be strengthened by making cultural unity, through education, identical with political unity. Modern education, therefore, eventually became a series of national systems, differently administered and differently organized, according to the social and political concepts most important to the society of each particular country.

During the first half of the 20th century, however, the combination of cultural and political nationalism was proved injurious as well as advantageous; educational systems devoted to promoting extreme nationalism were used by aggressor nations to indoctrinate their peoples for their intense prosecution of World War II. Therefore, in November, 1945, the charter of the United Nations Educational, Scientific, and Cultural Organization (q.v.) was approved by delegates of the United Nations. The principal objective of this organization was the promotion of international peace through education by reducing illiteracy, equalizing educational opportunities in the various nations, and combating doctrines of race superiority.

Modern Education: Theory and Science. During the 19th and early 20th centuries, education became one of the most important functions of every western state. Every movement and change, political, intellectual, social, or scientific, influenced the structure or curricula of educational systems. The fundamental factors which have determined the nature of modern education have been of two kinds: political and sociological, and individual. The first of these factors is the sum of the circumstances which determined the organization and basic purpose of the educational structures set up by different countries. Thus, generally, the intense nationalism of European countries resulted in the centralization of their school systems; in the United States, on the other hand, no national control was authorized, and each of the 48 States controls the schools within its borders. Furthermore, in most European countries, one legacy of history was the persistence of dual educational systems consisting, in the main, of one kind of schooling (usually elementary) for the lower classes and another kind (including secondary and higher) for the upper classes. In England, as late as 1944, only one out of ten children was given the opportunity for secondary education and even fewer for higher education. In France, fees for secondary education were not entirely abolished until 1939. American education, however, has reflected the democratic development of the United States and has achieved a complete public-school system which is organized to provide equality of opportunity for all at public expense. See EDUCATION, NATIONAL SYSTEMS OF.

The second determining factor deals with the needs of the maturing individual, both in themselves and in relation to the society of which he is a part. This individual factor has been an educational consideration since the rise of Greece, but it was of negligible importance until the late 18th century. Pestalozzi, Froebel, and Herbart gave the study of the individual child a paramount place in their educational theories; Herbart, in particular, prepared the way for the modern development of so-called progressive education with his investigations into the nature of interest and his psychological analysis of the teaching method. The mind, however, was still regarded as entirely separate from the body. In the middle of the 19th century, Herbert

Spencer (q.v.) became the first great figure to put forth the theory that the mind was an integral part of the total animal organism and, therefore, reacts with it to environmental influences. This theory, called the biological view of psychology, was the foundation of behaviorism (q.v.), which, in turn, gave way to the *gestalt* psychology (q.v.), which rests on the basic principle that a concept is understood as a whole and not as a mere summation of its parts.

These new theories became the foundation of what is termed the science of education, or the use of exact and systematic methods for organized study of the educative process. As psychology became more intensively studied and eventually developed its branches, psychiatry and psychoanalysis, educators turned their attention to the great importance of the early childhood years on personality development, increasingly a concern of the schools. The investigation of psychology in its application to education resulted in the specific science of educational psychology, which deals with the formulation of theories relative to the development of taste and character, methods of instruction, the ability of the individual to acquire knowledge, and the nature of the learning process. Education since the late 19th century has been profoundly affected by these theories and, in most cases, has been based on them.

At the beginning of the 20th century, the work of three men, all of whom were influenced by Spencer's view of the mind as a part of the biological organism, began to have a determining effect on American education. All three believed that education must involve the simultaneous development of mind and body as an organic unit, and, thus, that anything which rested on one would react on the other. Granville Stanley Hall (q.v.) turned the attention of educators to the need for careful study of child development in all its aspects. Hall founded the child-study movement, which concerned itself with the physical, mental, and social growth of children and, for their betterment, attacked such problems as juvenile delinquency, school hygiene, and child labor; this movement also gave rise to the child-welfare movement, an integral part of the American school system. (See CHILD PSYCHOLOGY; MATERNAL AND CHILD WELFARE.) A greater influence on American education was the work of John Dewey (q.v.), who rebelled against the moral and religious aim and strict discipline which had characterized education from the 17th to the 19th century. He believed that the school was primarily a social institution with a duty to give the child, rapidly and effectively, a share in the accumulated skills and knowledge of humanity. The teacher, in Dewey's view, must investigate the interests of the individual child and then direct his activities into social channels, not by enforced and arbitrary discipline, but by choosing the specific influences that will affect him. Dewey advised an educational method in which the child learns by experience and, hence, should be given the chance to test ideas and prove their validity before he applies them as facts; this theory was called the "learn by doing" theory. A third influence was the work of Edward Lee Thorndike, who stirred the educational world with his work *Educational Psychology* (3 vols., 1913). On the basis of carefully controlled experiments, Thorndike developed scientific theories concerning the nature of the learning process. He refuted the ancient concept that the study of intellectual subjects such as mathematics and languages disciplined the mind; thus, Thorndike helped to bring about the inclusion of such informational subjects as the physical and social sciences in the curricula of elementary and secondary schools.

A significant result of the growth of education as a science was the development of testing. The work of Alfred Binet and Theodore Simon in the devising of intelligence tests was adopted and so greatly amplified by American educational psychologists that the testing movement became an outstanding characteristic of American education in the 1920's and 1930's; tests for intelligence, achievement, and aptitude became elements of educational technique. See article on MENTAL TESTS.

These developments and movements found their most fruitful application in the U.S. for two reasons: first, because in the U.S. the educational system was developing simultaneously with educational psychology and science and could, therefore, be continually modified; and second, because the local control of State school systems permitted and encouraged experimentation in order to increase relative efficiency. Educational experiments in the U.S. included a great many private, so-called progressive schools, most of which have been influenced by Dewey's theories. Methods which proved successful in these private schools were gradually incorporated into the more conservative public schools. Thus, many public-school systems in the U.S. came to include special courses or, in some cases, special schools for subnormal, gifted, and physically-handicapped children, and for the development of specific talents. The American system of education, once profoundly influenced by European education, became, in turn, a great influence on European educational systems; after World War II, France, for example, and England, to a lesser extent, began to revise their educational systems on the basis of American methods.

EDUCATION, ADULT. Formal educational opportunities have been provided for adults since about the middle of the 18th century. The first efforts were almost exclusively American, and not until the 20th century did organized adult-education programs acquire any degree of importance in European countries.

Attempts were made early in the history of the American colonies to disseminate knowledge and information. Social scientists trace the beginnings of adult education to the New England town meeting (see TOWN), which was a center for open and free debate and discussion of public issues, and served as a clearinghouse for information. Many public libraries were founded, as were societies for spreading knowledge, notably the American Philosophical Society founded in 1769. By the time the United States was well established, a great number of philanthropic and humanitarian organizations had begun to reach all classes of American society with organized discussions, lectures, and debates. Libraries for working people, and agricultural and mechanical institutes (see INSTITUTE) became popular with the spread of the concept of bettering oneself through education. Employers and wealthy philanthropists began to endow such institutions for adult education as Cooper Union (q.v.) in New York City and Peabody Institute in Baltimore, Md. The lyceum (q.v.) movement became important in rural as well as urban areas, and by the late 1830's more than 3000 communities had lyceums of their own. Even larger audiences were attracted to the Chautauqua movement, founded in 1874 (see CHAUTAUQUA INSTITUTION). Evening schools and college extension courses for adults were established in the period following 1880, and spread rapidly.

The three countries which led in organized adult-education facilities during the first half of the 20th century were England, the U.S.S.R., and the U.S. In the first two countries, however, adult education concerned itself mainly with the education of working

James W. Welgos; N.Y.C. Board of Education

ADULT EDUCATION IN THE U.S.

Above: A group of New York City residents meeting in a public library to hear a lecture and exchange ideas on current events. Right: Middle-aged women sit in class with younger students during a high-school session held in the evening.

people. The Workers' Educational Associational Association, founded in 1903, established branches all over England where literature, lectures, and later, motion pictures on public issues and educational matters were provided. The Education Act of 1944 prescribed facilities for education for adults as well as for children. Trade unions, political parties, and religious groups organized programs for adult education. In the U.S.S.R., the Communist government, faced with the tremendous task of education in a country where more than 60% of the population was illiterate, established a great many institutes and extension classes for adults. The greatest organized adult-education movement, however, took place in the U.S. See EDUCATION, NATIONAL SYSTEMS OF.

The education of workers was as great a concern in the U.S. as it was in other countries. Federal aid was given to agricultural extension courses in 1914, and was extended to cover vocational courses in 1917. Various labor organizations established educational services and labor colleges for their members.

During the 1920's, as a result of an increase in immigration to the U.S. following the end of World War I, a concerted effort was made to "Americanize" the foreign-born in public evening classes held in elementary and high-school buildings. Other groups, such as men's and women's clubs and social and religious agencies, organized educational programs. All these activities were unrelated until 1926, when the American Association for Adult Education was established.

During the years between 1930, the beginning of the great depression, and 1941, the year in which the U.S. entered World War II, adult enrollment in educational activities became almost double what it had been in

Standard Oil Co. (N.J.)

Children leaving school at the end of the day's classes, in Lancaster, New Hampshire

the previous decade. This increase in enrollment was due to such factors as the desire for self-improvement in order to increase employment possibility, and added leisure time because of unemployment. A further reason was the establishment of adult-education projects by the Federal government as part of its relief program. The Works Project Administration (q.v.) was notably engaged in education. This WPA program concerned itself with both elementary education, designed for the more than 4% of the population which

was still illiterate in 1930, and higher education, giving university and advanced vocational courses. Such institutions as the New School for Social Research (q.v.) and the People's Institute of Cooper Union in New York City devoted themselves almost entirely to adult education. Public libraries instituted readers' advisory services, compiling special reading lists as guides to education which could be acquired entirely through reading; the so-called "Reading with a Purpose" series became a major concern of the

American Library Association. Adult classes were organized by municipal museums. The most prominent type of adult education however, became the public evening classes originally established fifty years previously. These classes offered both vocational and nonvocational courses and, during the 1930's more than 2,000,000 persons were enrolled in them. One of the most recent developments in evening schools has been the utilization of the public schools by citizen committees not under the control of school authorities. The first of such schools was established in 1935 in the Maplewood-South Orange school district in New Jersey; this adult school supported itself by charging low fees. The Maplewood-South Orange plan was copied by many other cities, particularly those near universities, which supplied teaching staffs. The movement also influenced the building of new schools designed for the use of children during the day and for separate adult schools in the evening. So strong has the adult-education movement become in the United States that, in 1954, an estimated 49,500,000 adults were engaged in formal or informal educational activities conducted by diverse schools, agencies, and organizations. See AGRICUL-TURAL EXTENSION SERVICE; CORRESPONDENCE SCHOOL.

EDUCATION, ELEMENTARY. Mass education, as a conception engendered by the Reformation (see EDUCATION: *History*; EDUCATION, NATIONAL SYSTEMS OF), meant, originally, mass literacy; religious instruction was also included in the elementary-school curriculum because schools were usually adjuncts of churches. Until the 19th century, therefore, the curriculum in elementary schools generally consisted of reading, writing, arithmetic, and religion. The political developments of the 18th and 19th centuries, especially the rise of nationalism and the growth of democratic states, gave a new basis to the curriculum: education for citizenship. In some countries, such as the U.S., religion was dropped from the curriculum; in others, such as the Scandinavian countries where education was a function of the state church, religious instruction retained its important role. In most countries, however, elementary schools began to teach social studies, such as history and civics, emphasizing the development of national pride and patriotism. Cultural subjects, such as music and drawing, were added; physical education, either as play or calisthenics, came

Students and teacher discuss problems of publishing the school newspaper.

to be included. At the same time, educators devoted increasing attention to child study, because of the pioneer work of such men as Johann Friedrich Pestalozzi and Friedrich Froebel (qq.v.), who influenced the teaching method; see also EDUCATION: *Modern Education: Theory and Science*. By the end of the 19th century, two distinct approaches to education became obvious, one in Europe and the other in the U.S.

In the European countries, where class distinctions continued to be important, elementary education was considered a complete education in itself, because it was all that most of the population received. Thorough knowledge of subject matter was the method stressed in the schools. French education put its emphasis on such subjects as reading, writing, arithmetic, morals, civics, French history and geography, drawing, and the manual and household arts. English education required, by law, only that children be taught reading, writing, and arithmetic, but, because of local administrative autonomy, a great variety of subjects entered the school curricula, according to the views held by each different school. In Europe, generally, elementary education was conceived as a training for life, and part of the school's duty, aside from giving practical knowledge and information, was to build character and instill a feeling of patriotism.

In the U.S., however, elementary education came to be profoundly influenced by the theories of such men as Granville Stanley Hall, Edward Thorndike, and, particularly, John Dewey (qq.v.). Moreover, elementary education was considered part of an educative process which extended from kindergarten to university. Thus, at the beginning of the 20th century, American schools began to place their emphasis on the development of the individual child rather than on a general imparting of information. One of the most popular teaching methods became the *project method*, notably developed in the Dalton plan, originated by the American educator Helen Parkhurst. In this method, a selected unit of study was assigned to each grade, and pupils could then proceed at their individual learning rate and in accordance with their individual aptitudes in mastering the material covered in the unit. Another method, extensively used in the 1920's, was the *ability plan*, by which classes were constituted of students separated according to their aptitude, measured by intelligence and aptitude tests (see MENTAL MEASUREMENT). In the 1930's, American educators began to argue against any strict curriculum or subject matter and instituted the *activity program*. In this program, classroom drill, recitation, and prescribed textbooks were abandoned, and pupils learned as they participated in activities growing out of a broad subject, such as "travel", "farms", or "poets". Later, in the 1940's, came the social concept of education, which viewed the elementary school as a vital part of the community; social problems, such as race discrimination, were considered important subjects for study, and were incorporated into the teaching programs. Toward the middle of the 20th century many American educators criticized these methods as being too progressive, and argued for a limited return to a stricter curriculum including drill directed toward the acquisition of specific skills and information. See VISUAL EDUCATION.